THE FUTURE OF FAMILY PROPERTY IN EUROPE

THE FUTURE OF FAMILY PROPERTY IN EUROPE

Edited by

Katharina Boele-Woelki
Jo Miles
Jens M. Scherpe

intersentia
Cambridge – Antwerp – Portland

Intersentia Ltd
Trinity House | Cambridge Business Park | Cowley Road
Cambridge CB4 0WZ | United Kingdom
mail@intersentia.co.uk

Distribution for the UK:
Hart Publishing Ltd.
16C Worcester Place
Oxford OX1 2JW
UK
Tel.: +44 1865 51 75 30
Email: mail@hartpub.co.uk

Distribution for the USA and Canada:
International Specialized Book Services
920 NE 58th Ave Suite 300
Portland, OR 97213
USA
Tel.: +1 800 944 6190 (toll free)
Tel.: +1 503 287 3093
Email: info@isbs.com

Distribution for Switzerland and Germany:
Stämpfli Verlag AG
Wölflistrasse 1
CH-3001 Bern
Switzerland
Tel.: +41 (0)31 300 66 66
Email: verlag@staempfli.com

Distribution for other countries:
Intersentia Publishers
Groenstraat 31
2640 Mortsel
Belgium
Tel.: +32 3 680 15 50
Email: mail@intersentia.be

The Future of Family Property in Europe
Edited by Katharina Boele-Woelki, Jo Miles and Jens M. Scherpe

ISBN 978-94-000-0054-4
D/2011/7849/50
NUR 822

PREFACE

The law relating to family property in Europe is at a key stage in its development. Unified conflict of law rules were adopted in December 2010 implementing enhanced cooperation for 14 Member States in relation to divorce, further proposals for the unification of private international law relating to matrimonial property and succession are being developed, and interest is growing in harmonisation of the substantive law itself.

The fourth conference of the Commission on European Family Law (CEFL) held in Cambridge in early April 2010 brought together around 180 participants from 32 jurisdictions in Europe and beyond to address a wide range of issues relating to the future of family property in Europe. This large and diverse group generated a stimulating discussion across the three days of the conference, prompted by the contributions of our conference speakers, most of which are produced in this volume.

The volume consists of eight parts. *Part 1* contains the keynote address which began the conference proceedings given by Lord Justice Thorpe, Head of International Family Justice for England & Wales. As was fitting for a European conference taking place in the UK, Sir Mathew Thorpe's address provoked important debate about the challenges inherent in common law and civil law jurisdictions co-operating in this sphere, a theme taken up again in *Part 8*, the closing remarks from the local conference organisers Jo Miles and Jens M. Scherpe. *Part 2* of the book examines in greater depth the issue of matrimonial property law in Europe, Professor Pintens' chapter providing an examination of the variety of regimes currently operating in Europe, while Professors Boele-Woelki and Jänterä-Jareborg preview the Commission on European Family Law's own attempts to develop Principles on which the harmonisation of domestic laws in this field might be based. *Part 3* takes us on to the question of party autonomy, both within and without marriage, in the marital context examining the extent to which parties are free by agreement to contract out of the default regime or remedies. Professor Dethloff's paper surveys the treatment of marital agreements across Europe, while Professor Cooke discusses the issues from the perspective of a law reformer in England & Wales. Professor Garrison brings an American and non-marital perspective to family property, addressing the regulation of cohabiting relationships and the significance of party autonomy in that sphere. *Parts 4 to 6* of the volume contain several of the papers from the conference workshops, in which early career researchers presented their work on three themes: the protection of older person in the law; freedom of testation and the protection of family members; and child maintenance. *Part 7* collects together all of the conference papers, both from plenary sessions and workshops, from the world of private international family and succession law, including Professor González-Beifuss's survey of European unification of private international law and Dr Dutta's examination of the draft Succession Regulation.

The conference organisers and editors of this book are immensely grateful to a number of individuals and organisations. The conference was generously supported by funding from the British Academy, and by sponsorship from Intersentia Publishing, the International Family Law Group, Charles Russell, Mills and Reeve, and Mohr Siebeck. The editorial team were greatly assisted by the work of Emily McGregor and Peter Morris. Thanks also to the staff of the Law Faculty at the University of Cambridge, the University Centre catering team, Destination Cambridge, the host colleges, and our conference assistants, without whom the conference would not have run so smoothly.

Katharina Boele-Woelki, Jo Miles and Jens M. Scherpe
Utrecht and Cambridge, January 2011

CONTENTS

PART THREE – FAMILY CONTRACTS – ISSUES OF AUTONOMY

PART FIVE – FREEDOM OF TESTATION AND PROTECTION OF FAMILY MEMBERS

PART SIX – CHILD MAINTENANCE

PART SEVEN – UNIFICATION OF PRIVATE INTERNATIONAL FAMILY LAW

PART EIGHT – CLOSING REMARKS

LIST OF AUTHORS

Dr John Asland
Associate Professor, Department of Private Law, University of Oslo, Norway

Professor Katharina Boele-Woelki
Professor of Private International Law, Comparative Law and Family Law at the Molengraaff Institute for Private Law, Utrecht University, The Netherlands and Extraordinary Professor at the University of the Western Cape, South-Africa

Philip Bremner
Postgraduate Research Student, School of Law, University of Aberdeen, Scotland

Professor Elizabeth Cooke
Law Commissioner for England and Wales, Professor of Law, University of Reading, England & Wales

Professor Nina Dethloff
Professor of Private Law, Private International Law, Comparative Law and European Private Law and Director of the Institute for German, European and International Family Law, University of Bonn, Germany

Dr Anatol Dutta
Senior Research Fellow at the Max Planck Institute for Comparative and International Private Law, Hamburg

Professor Marsha Garrison
Suzanne J. & Norman Miles Professor, Brooklyn Law School, New York

Professor Cristina González Beilfuss
Professor of Private International Law, University of Barcelona, Spain

Professor Maarit Jänterä-Jareborg
Professor of Private International Law and International Civil Procedure, Former Dean of the Faculty of Law, Uppsala University

Martin Kornel
PhD student, Department of Civil Law, Faculty of Law Masaryk University, Czech Republic

Pia Lokin
PhD researcher in International Succession Law, University of Utrecht, the Netherlands

Dr Joëlle Long
Lecturer in Family Law, University of Turin, Italy

Dr Irena Majstorović
Assistant Professor, Department of Family Law, Faculty of Law, University of Zagreb, Croatia

Alexandra Maschwitz
Academic Assistant (Wissenschaftliche Mitarbeiterin) to Professor Dethloff, Institute for German, European and International Family Law, University of Bonn, Germany

Jo Miles
University Lecturer and Fellow of Trinity College, University of Cambridge, England & Wales

Professor Walter Pintens
Professor Ordinarius, University of Leuven, Belgium and Honorary Professor, Saarland University, Germany

Dr Branka Rešetar
Assistant Professor, JJ Strossmayer University, Croatia

Dr Gediminas Sagatys
Associate Professor, Mykolas Romeris University, Lithuania

Dr Jens M. Scherpe
Senior University Lecturer and Fellow of Gonville & Caius College, University of Cambridge, England & Wales

Dr Brian Sloan
Bob Alexander College Lecturer in Law, King's College, University of Cambridge, England & Wales

The Rt. Hon. Lord Justice Mathew Thorpe
Lord Justice of Appeal and Head of International Family Justice for England and Wales

Anna Wysocka
PhD student at the Chair of Private International Law, Faculty of Law & Administration, Jagiellonian University, Poland

Dr Eleni Zervogianni
Lecturer in Civil Law, Law School of the Aristotle University of Thessaloniki, Greece

PART ONE
KEYNOTE LECTURE

FINANCIAL CONSEQUENCES OF DIVORCE: ENGLAND VERSUS THE REST OF EUROPE

The Rt. Hon. Lord Justice Mathew Thorpe*

* This paper was written before the Supreme Court decision in *Radmacher v Granatino* [2010] UKSC 42.

1. INTRODUCTION

In the common law world England & Wales is the powerful jurisdiction. What we do in London is followed in a number of other jurisdictions, both legislatively and by precedent.

We apply only the lex fori in family proceedings, we do not apply the law of another jurisdiction. Under our law there are no property consequences of marriage. However, there are profound property consequences of divorce. In that event the parties submit all relevant assets to a process of redistribution in the discretion of the trial judge, conducted now under Part II of the Matrimonial Causes Act 1973. Parliament has put few bounds on the exercise of that judicial discretion. There is only a checklist specifying first child welfare and then all the circumstances having particular regard to assets, needs, age, duration of marriage, health, contribution and conduct.[1] Rather more the exercise of the discretion is guided by precedent, that is to say previous reported decisions, particularly of the appellate courts.

2. HISTORY

It is worth sketching the background to see how statutory provisions not fundamentally reformed since their introduction in 1971 have been construed and to trace the steps by which we have walked from where we were then to where we are now.

The first powers to order capital payments had been introduced in 1963 but the judges had chosen to exercise them with great caution. At the outset the extensive powers introduced by the Matrimonial Proceedings Act 1970[2] were also hardly applied innovatively but as a component in a financial scheme at the heart of which lay periodical payment orders.

Economic growth, prosperity, the erosion of hallowed distinctions between capital and income, the decline of the aristocratic and landed classes, the emergence of huge fortunes very rapidly amassed: all contributed to a fresh approach. The clean break and the capitalisation of future liabilities in a single present payment became the norm when affluent people divorced. For this there was statutory foundation in the reforms introduced by the Matrimonial and Family Proceedings Act 1984.[3] However, there remained a distaste in the senior judiciary, still exclusively male,

1 Matrimonial Causes Act 1973, s 25.
2 Subsequently consolidated in the 1973 Act.
3 See in particular the insertion of s 25A of the 1973 Act.

for the megabucks publicised in Los Angeles settlements and a determination not to introduce standards that might encourage the gold-digger or spread cynical disregard for the marriage vows. This judicial attitude is well illustrated in the judgments in the appeal in *Preston v Preston*.[4]

The introduction of the yardstick of reasonable requirements steadied the evolutionary progress for some twenty years. It emerged in appellate decisions through the 1970's. The dominant architect of this approach was Ormerod LJ. It was perpetuated by judges who had developed skills in the use of this yardstick in their practice at the bar and who believed in its utility and essential fairness: after all it was a flexible rule.

In the end it fell victim to another aspect of fairness. Did it not discriminate against the wife and mother (the home-maker) in favour of the bread-winning husband? He might have generated the golden heap but it was not fair if it was treated as his rather than theirs.

Therefore the power to modernise the law in this field to match social and other change was exercised by the judges. In a process commencing in 2000 with the decision of the House of Lords in *White v White*[5] the judges have rejected the measure of the applicant's reasonable requirements, consistently applied throughout the previous twenty years, in favour of more liberal principles of need, equal sharing and compensation for an earning capacity sacrificed for the sake of the marriage and the family.

Although the judges' overarching objective is to impose a fair solution, and it might be thought that the search for fairness is common to judges from all jurisdictions, this is a highly specialist field of adjudication. The practitioners who do this work are highly specialised, as are the judges. Even within the Family Division of the High Court there are family judges who decline to do complex ancillary relief cases. Thus it is self evident that a judge from another European jurisdiction, especially without the assistance of specialist practitioners, would face a huge challenge in trying to apply legal principles that are derived not from legislation but from a corpus of complex case law.

3. THE PROBLEM

The fundamental difference of approach between civil law and common law jurisdictions leads to very different outcomes. This is not just the product of recent

4 [1982] Fam17.
5 [2001] AC 596.

developments in our respective jurisdictions. Even in the twentieth century the generous measure of reasonable requirements ensured that the applicant wife might receive a substantially greater award in London than in Paris. However, there can be no doubt that this gulf has widened in the twenty-first century with the introduction of the principles of equal sharing and compensation.

In the twentieth century we had a mechanism to avoid unfairness, the doctrine of forum conveniens. A statutory provision enabled the judge to stay divorce proceedings issued in London if, on the balance of fairness and convenience, another jurisdiction was better placed to do justice to the parties.[6] However, the Regulation Brussels II[7] removed our discretion to stay a divorce application on the grounds that another European jurisdiction would be more appropriate. Note that the widening of the gulf resulting from the shift from reasonable requirements to equality and compensation coincides fortuitously with the loss of the discretion to stay the divorce proceedings.

These observations are well illustrated by two cases. In 1988 the London divorce proceedings of the *Comtesse de Dampierre*[8] were stayed (on the application of her husband) on the grounds that the parties had much closer connections to the courts of France, their homeland. In 2009 in the case of *Granatino v Radmacher*,[9] a London judge was obliged to order very substantial payments from wife to husband despite the terms of the German marital property regime, simply because London was the court first seized. Only on the wife's appeal did our court, in the exercise of the broad discretion, give the wife some of the protection that the marital contract had intended.

4. SOLUTIONS

Let me begin by establishing the point from which we start the search for solutions:

(a) Rules governing jurisdiction and enforcement of maintenance orders are provided by Regulation Brussels I.[10]
(b) Neither Brussels I nor Brussels II bis apply to the property consequences of divorce.
(c) Brussels II bis provides jurisdictional rules for divorce. The jurisdictional grounds are widely drawn and the simple rule of lis alibi pendens determines which, of what may be the several states holding jurisdiction, prevails. The

6 Domicile and Matrimonial Proceedings Act 1973, Sch 1, para 9.
7 Now Council Reg (EC) No 2201/2003.
8 *De Dampierre v de Dampierre* [1988] AC 92.
9 [2009] EWCA Civ 649.
10 Council Reg (EC) No 44/2001.

power to transfer to a more appropriate jurisdiction is limited to cases of parental responsibility.

(d) The preferred European mechanism for providing justice in State A to parties who have a closer connection with State B is to apply in State A the law of State B. Applicable law provisions were incorporated in draft regulations such as Rome III,[11] the new Maintenance Regulation[12] and Rome IV, the Succession & Wills Regulation.[13] The inclusion of these provisions has always been seen in London as a minefield to be avoided. Thus we have consistently opted out of the negotiation of such regulations, in part to avoid the risk of having to apply foreign law.

(e) It is perfectly predictable that Rome V, the draft Regulation on the property consequences of divorce, will contain applicable law provisions. I say that not only because that is the European norm but also because:

   (i) The UK experienced some difficulties in framing a response to the Green Paper. Initially specialists in London comforted themselves by saying "well, none of this applies to us since we don't have a marital property regime." Nevertheless, there was a dawning appreciation that such optimism was misplaced. A brief response was submitted raising the concerns of English lawyers, but no detailed response was written.

   (ii) Nor has the voice of the family specialist been heard in the expert group convened by the European Commission to shape the draft in light of the response to the Green Paper. The two distinguished property lawyers who had served on the Succession & Wills expert group stayed on to deal with marital property regimes. Many of those who worked on the expert group spoke at the public meeting convened by the Commission in Brussels last September. The views of the family law experts from London clearly received an unsympathetic hearing. That is hardly surprising since we are indeed the oddity within the community. We can hardly expect the majority to abandon its traditions to adopt what may be seen as a curious if not eccentric minority position. In some senses it is we who have created a problem of a magnitude that cannot be ignored. The responsibility to propose a solution to the problem thus may be said to lie with us.

---

11 Proposed Council Regulation amending Regulation (EC) No 2201/2003 as regards jurisdiction and introducing rules concerning applicable law in matrimonial matters.

12 Council Reg (EC) No 4/2009.

13 Proposal for a Regulation on jurisdiction, applicable law, recognition and enforcement of decisions and authentic instruments in matters of succession, COM (2009) 154 final.

5. DOMESTIC LAW REFORM

What are the prospects of wholesale reform of our internal law, one aim of which might be to bring us more into line with other Member States of Europe?

In 1998 the Government announced its intention to reform our law of ancillary relief as a matter of high priority. Public consultation revealed no major opposition to general proposals accompanied by a specific proposal to introduce statutory rules that would regulate pre-nuptial contracting.[14]

However, despite the apparent encouragement to proceed, the Government quietly buried the whole exercise.

Thereafter I have consistently articulated the case for reform: see most recently *Charman v Charman*.[15]

At the same time the governmental advisory committee on Money and Property issues urged the Law Commission to include reform of the 1973 statutory provisions within its work programme. The Law Commission decided to focus on the narrower question of pre-nuptial contracts,[16] which may be indicative of a judgment that the larger task would be labour in vain. However my own opinion is that legislation may well result from the Law Commission's review and recommendations regarding pre-nuptial contracts.

Meanwhile modest judicial encouragement has come from the judges. Historically we have generally upheld contracts that do not oust the jurisdiction of the courts but anticipate its exercise: see *Edgar v Edgar*.[17] The House of Lords have recently upheld a post nuptial contract providing for the property consequences of divorce: see *McLeod v McLeod*.[18] The decision of the Court of Appeal in *Granatino v Radmacher*[19] was widely interpreted by general and specialist commentators as a significant shift towards the advent of pre-nuptial contracting. Our decision was well received. How long it will survive is questionable since the Supreme Court has granted permission, the appeal has been argued and judgment from no less than nine judges is awaited.[20] Whatever may be in those judgments, it is Parliament, guided by the Law Commission, that must ultimately determine the shape of pre-nuptial contracting, assuming that that will be the chosen path.

---

14 Home Office, *Supporting Families: a consultation document*, London: TSO (1998); *Supporting Families: summary of responses to the consultation document*, London: TSO (1999).
15 [2007] EWCA Civ 503.
16 Tenth Programme of Law Reform, Law Com No 311 (2008), para 2.17 and 5.4.
17 [1980] 1 W.L.R. 1410.
18 [2008] UKPC 64.
19 [2009] EWCA Civ 649.
20 At the time of writing, judgment was expected in October 2010.

I believe that the anticipated benefits of pre-nuptial contracting have been exaggerated. The option to contract pre-nuptially for the financial consequences of future divorce is not to be equated with a notarised marital property regime. The ability to contract pre-nuptially is most welcome to those who desire to protect an inherited or earned fortune, or even a fortune to be earned, against a judicial assessment of the claims of the wife on divorce. These are the cases that attract attention, whether in the press or even when specialists debate reforms. However, the vast majority of cases are determined by the needs of the parties and often their separate needs exceed what is available for division. No contract would permit escape from meeting needs. Thus the impact of introducing some degree of autonomy, whether domestically or for international families, would be restricted to the significantly rich, who hardly merit a general reform of law.

Of course there will be situations in which the arrival of the power to contract would be obviously useful: a couple embarking on a second marriage in middle life may legitimately wish to provide for a more predictable future and perhaps to protect the interests of children of an earlier marriage.

In summary a liberal power to contract pre-nuptially would take us a step, but only a small step, nearer to Europe. Indeed if the historic distaste for the right to contract before marriage for the consequences of its dissolution is overcome there would be a case for the introduction of marital property regimes which would bring us into step with the civil jurisdictions of Europe.

6. TRANSFER

As already demonstrated, the statutory power to transfer the divorce proceedings to the more convenient forum no longer operates between Member States of the European Union. But what about transferring financial claims ancillary to divorce to a more convenient European jurisdiction?

In the absence of a statutory power there are instances of judges claiming and exercising an inherent jurisdiction to effectively transfer by staying the financial claim in this jurisdiction in favour of competing proceedings in another jurisdiction.

The first reported instance is *W v W* (financial relief: appropriate forum).[21] In that case Holman J. found and exercised the inherent jurisdiction to stay proceedings in London to enable financial issues to be decided by the court in Alberta, Canada. The arguments for and against such a power were fully deployed and the judges'

21 [1997] 1 FLR 257.

reasons for rejecting the argument that a London decree necessarily anchored the financial claims in London are not extensive. All that the judge essentially said was:

> "In reality, issues of the divorce decree per se and of finance are in separate and discreet compartments".

Connell J. took the same path in the case of *D v P* (forum conveniens).[22] In that case he held that Italy was the more convenient forum for the exercise of ancillary relief jurisdiction despite the English divorce decree. He rested his judgment on the inherent jurisdiction and (the case arising before the Brussels II Regulation) also on the Brussels Convention of 1968. As in the case of *W v W* the outcome was heavily fact dependent and the source of the power was not independently investigated. The judge simply cited the reasoning of Holman J. with approval.

Nor does the third reported case extend our appreciation. *Krenge v Krenge*[23] was again listed before Holman J. In deciding the case as he did he cited and followed his earlier decision in *W v W* and the decision of Connell J. in *D v P.*

In these cases the application for stay and effective transfer had not been mounted prior to the London divorce. In the last of these three decisions Holman J was at pains to point out that stay applications should be made immediately on service of the petition for divorce and that only exceptionally would they succeed when directed subsequently to the ancillary relief claims, no application having been made for a statutory stay of the suit. That admonition no longer applies where two Member States of Europe are engaged.

What we see therefore is a cluster of 3 authorities decided in 1997, 1998 and 1999. None was tested in the Court of Appeal. I do not know to what extent they have been followed and applied since in the High Court. The authorities pre-date the development of judicial collaboration where parallel proceedings are under way concurrently in two jurisdictions. The availability of direct judicial communication should certainly facilitate such transfers.

A review of these authorities is to be found in the current edition of Rayden & Divorce[24] as follows:

> **Severance of suit and ancillary relief: bifurcation**
> **12.29** It has been held at first instance that as the decree of divorce and the application for ancillary relief are in separate and discrete compartments,

22 [1998] 3 FLR 403.

23 [1999] 1 FLR 696.

24 Everall, Waller, Dyer Bailey-Harris and Trowell, *Rayden and Jackson on Divorce and Family Matters,* Butterworths Law, 18th edition, 2005.

notwithstanding the grant of the decree absolute, in an appropriate case a pending ancillary relief application can be stayed under the inherent jurisdiction. It is submitted that the bifurcation approach may need to be tested on appeal as it is contrary to the purpose of obtaining a stay at the outset of the proceedings, namely, to stay the entire divorce proceedings, including the claim for ancillary relief. It can also be argued that the DMPA 1973 expressly provides for the stay of the matrimonial proceedings, as opposed to any part of those proceedings and relying on the inherent jurisdiction to bifurcate the proceedings is inconsistent with the intention of the statute. The approach taken by the Court of Appeal in *Charalambous v Charalambous* in refusing to allow a party in the course of ancillary relief proceedings to apply to vary a deed of trust in the Jersey court, and the dicta of Thorpe LJ in that case where he stated:

> "[31] … Once the wife has established the jurisdiction of the Family Division, the proposition that the husband has a right to the application of the law of Jersey in the determination of her s 24 application is completely misconceived. It is trite that a petition may only be defeated by a challenge to jurisdiction or stayed on a plea of forum non conveniens. Once a decree has been pronounced on the petition all ancillary issues must be determined in accordance with the relevant provisions of the 1973 Act."

might also add some weight to the argument that bifurcation is not a proper exercise of the inherent jurisdiction.

The editors of Rayden rightly question the strength of the authority supporting the discretionary power to bifurcate. However the citation from my judgment in the case of *Charalambous v Charalambous*[25] should not be taken as a contrary proposition. Although my words are capable of that construction I certainly did not have the bifurcation authorities in mind when dismissing a submission that the wife's ancillary relief claim in this jurisdiction should be determined by Jersey law. My essential point was that the wife was entitled to lex fori determination.

Some encouragement for the existence and exercise of the inherent jurisdiction to bifurcate is to be found indirectly in two cases to which I will come: *Moore v Moore*[26] in the Court of Appeal in 2007 and *Agbaje v Agbaje*[27] in the Supreme Court this year.

---

25 [2004] 2 FCR 721.
26 [2007] 2 FLR 339.
27 [2010] UKSC 13.

How then do other European jurisdictions categorise a claim for capital adjustment on or after divorce? Is it discrete and free standing or is it incapable of severance from the proceedings for dissolution to which it must undoubtedly trace its origins?

7. *MOORE V MOORE*

The case of *Moore v Moore*[28] sheds some light on the Spanish approach. The case called for the construction of provisions in Regulation Brussels I. The case was complex on its facts. However, it seems to demonstrate that Spain requires ancillary relief claims to be pleaded in the divorce suit before dissolution. Absent such claims Spain appears content for the issue to be determined in another Member State claiming jurisdiction despite it having had no hand in the dissolution of the marriage. Spain accepted the role of the London court which founded its jurisdiction on Part III of the Matrimonial and Family Proceedings Act 1984.

The origins of the Part III jurisdiction can be traced to a Law Commission report[29] and beyond that to decided cases in which the London court had been obliged to recognise a divorce pronounced in a jurisdiction in which the respondent wife had no, or no effective, claim for ancillary relief. Of course in the context of the Anglo/Spanish proceedings in *Moore* the wife had had every opportunity to advance an ancillary relief claim in the Spanish divorce proceedings but had plainly elected not to do so in order to seek the award of a London judge. But the case is instructive in that it demonstrates that the Spanish court readily accepted the London jurisdiction, steadfastly refusing to entertain an ancillary relief application by the husband, an application which he had failed to advance in his divorce proceedings. Equally London accepted the wife's application notwithstanding her tactical disinclination to apply in the court of the divorce.

The case has many curiosities including the fact that the husband sought to establish the Spanish jurisdiction but accepted that in exercising it the judge would apply English law. The only sane inference is that the husband anticipated that the Spanish judge would instinctively end up well below the bracket within which a London judge would operate.

The refusal of the Spanish court to entertain an ancillary relief claim not raised in the divorce proceeding is readily understandable. In our jurisdiction the right to seek financial provision under the Matrimonial Causes Act 1973 jurisdiction

[28] [2007] 2 FLR 339.

[29] Financial Relief After a Foreign Divorce, Law Com 117 (1982).

depends upon the necessary prayer in either the petition or the answer. Mrs Moore's ability to litigate money here depended entirely on the availability of the Part III statutory jurisdiction, only available to those divorced in some other jurisdiction.

For present purposes the real significance of the decision in *Moore* is that the husband's counsel asserted the inherent jurisdiction to bifurcate (citing *D v P* and *Krenge*) and the wife's counsel conceded that the inherent jurisdiction operated. Although the jurisdictional issue was thus not before the court, the submission and concession attracted no critical comment.

8. *AGBAJE V AGBAJE*

The recent judgment of the Supreme Court in *Agbaje*[30] gives helpful guidance on the use of Part III of the 1984 Act as well as guiding the judicial determination of such claims. Furthermore in his judgment Lord Collins offers some indirect support for the proponents of bifurcation when in paragraph 49 he writes:

> "The whole basis of Part III is that it may be appropriate for two jurisdictions to be involved, one for the divorce and one for ancillary relief."

Then again in paragraph 52:

> "There is nothing internationally objectionable in legislation which gives a court power to order financial provision notwithstanding a foreign decree of divorce, whether or not the foreign court has ordered financial provision, provided that the forum has an appropriate connection with the parties or their property."

That rationalisation of the statutory power applies equally to the inherent jurisdiction. Later in his judgment Lord Collins flags up likely future debate as to the inter-relationship of the Regulation Brussels I and Part III of the 1984 Act.

This brief review of the limited authority demonstrates that where London has dissolved the marriage it may nevertheless defer to a more convenient jurisdiction for the judgement on financial provision by exercising an inherent jurisdiction to stay proceedings.

Equally where the marriage has been dissolved in another European jurisdiction London may nonetheless rule on financial provision by exercising its discretionary powers under Part III of the 1984 Act.

---

30 [2010] UKSC 13.

9. APPLICABLE LAW *VERSUS* TRANSFER

Leaving aside questions of jurisdiction and principle, surely as a matter of convenience and practicality transferring the responsibility to the more appropriate forum is much to be preferred to obliging the less appropriate forum to apply the law of the more appropriate forum?

There are a number of points that can be made in support of that proposition. In our jurisdiction foreign law must be proved by expert evidence. Experts in foreign law are expensive, hired guns are often available and the process of trial is unnecessarily extended as practitioners, and ultimately the judge, wrestle with the complexities.

In continental systems the obligation is on the judge to educate himself as to the foreign law that he is obliged to apply. Judges in European jurisdictions are operating under very large case loads and should not be burdened by what would no doubt be a conscientious endeavour to master the almost incomprehensible jungle of the leading cases in our Appellate Courts.

Thus the European distaste for the doctrine of forum conveniens seems surprising. It is certainly not evident amongst the judges. At the practical level of judicial collaboration I know that there are many European judges who resolve their need to ascertain the basic English law or practice that their system requires them to apply by asking my office for the answer that they seek. But we cannot undertake an extensive or sophisticated service. We cannot offer to guide them through the leading cases of the last decade. Thus the advantages of transfer seem to me so overwhelming that I struggle to understand the contrary argument.

10. CONCLUSION

Transfer provisions, alien to Civil law traditions, have already been introduced into European Union instruments as a concession to common-law negotiators. As already noted, in Brussels II bis we find the innovative Article 15. Transfer provisions are also to be found in the draft Rome IV Regulation. The experience I have of Article 15, gleaned through the case load of my office, is that it is functional rather than ornamental. Cases are being transferred to as well as from this jurisdiction.

I would hope that the draft of the Rome V Regulation will place greatest reliance on autonomy, allowing the parties to a forthcoming marriage to stipulate the law of the contract and the jurisdiction to which any dispute must be submitted. I would favour the right to insert an enforceable provision that there must be a submission to binding arbitration or to the wide range of ADR mechanisms before the issue of legal proceedings.

In default of an autonomous stipulation, an applicable law provision (probably identified by the habitual residence of the parties at some date) seems inevitable. However, again as a concession to the common law jurisdictions, there should also be the power to transfer to a more appropriate jurisdiction in the exercise of a judicial discretion not much confined in the search for the balance of fairness and convenience.

Of course bridging the chasm requires a hefty contribution from the United Kingdom. The Privy Council in *McLeod v McLeod*[31] concluded that the introduction of pre-nuptial contracting was beyond judicial powers and must be an issue for Parliament. The legal advisers to the Government will have a considerable responsibility, since the issues are complex and the temptation not to opt in to negotiations will be strong. Our successful record of not opting in to the Rome III, the REMO and the Rome IV Regulations encourages that approach. However, in my judgment we now need to be vigorous in the formative process of Rome IV even if we risk an unpalatable outcome. We must never forget the families who provide the case law and illustrate the options that we debate. A couple who are enmeshed in a bitter litigation battle deserve a measure of compassion, even if their psychological disturbance may have been the only obstacle to compromise. It is important that parties accept the judicially imposed outcome as, if not fair, then at least as not grossly unfair. How could the respondent accept as fair a London order that he transfer or pay over a substantial proportion of his hard earned fortune knowing that in his homeland his liability would have been minimal?

The possible solutions that I propose are both partial and imperfect. There is no magic answer.

Pre-nuptial contracting must await a Law Commission report and then the will of our coalition government to legislate.

The great deficiency of bifurcation is that maintenance orders are governed as to jurisdiction and enforcement by the Regulation Brussels I. While that Regulation does allow whichever court has jurisdiction over the divorce suit also to deal with maintenance, it does not permit transfer. In substantial cases the boundary between maintenance and the property consequences of divorce was drawn by the decision of the ECJ in *Van der Boogaard v Laumen*.[32] The consequence is that the transferring court would have to retain and decide maintenance. Having half

31 [2008] UKPC 64.
32 [1997] QB 759.

a cake baked in one court and the other half in another hardly seems a practical proposal.

The only clear solution therefore would require transfer provisions in a revised Brussels I Regulation and in Rome V. That hardly seems negotiable.

Of course the clearest solution would be to return to the old order when statutory powers were exercised to ensure that the suit was swiftly located in the most appropriate European jurisdiction. That could be achieved by inserting into Brussels II revised a transfer provision for divorce proceedings akin to the Article 5 provision for the transfer of children proceedings. Again such a solution hardly seems negotiable.

I seem to end on a note of pessimism but in collaboration with the Bar Council we have re-activated what government officials call the Stakeholder Group to submit a UK proposal before the publication of the draft Regulation which is expected to emerge by the end of the year. The group consists of judges, practitioners, academics and government officials. The Group has now met twice and agreed a work programme to complete the proposal by the end of June. We are very reliant on the industry and ingenuity of Deepak Nagpal, Tim Amos and Jo Miles of Trinity Cambridge for the first draft which simply and comprehensively explained the common law position on property consequences of marriage and divorce. A second draft containing the group's proposals for bridging the gulf has recently been dispatched to the Commission.

PART TWO

MATRIMONIAL PROPERTY LAW IN EUROPE

MATRIMONIAL PROPERTY LAW IN EUROPE

Walter Pintens

1. PROPERTY RELATIONS BETWEEN SPOUSES: A DIFFERENCE IN APPROACH BETWEEN CIVIL AND COMMON LAW

Continental European legal systems generally regulate the proprietary consequences of marriage through a specific body of matrimonial property law,[1] rather than leaving them to be governed by general property law rules. While most continental legal systems contain some provisions relating to property in the general law on marriage (*régime primaire, allgemeine Ehewirkungen*), for example rules governing the family home and household assets,[2] which are binding independently of the matrimonial property regime (*régime sécondaire*), it is the matrimonial property regime which lies at their core. Spouses enjoy a large degree of autonomy and can choose their preferred matrimonial property regime in a pre-nuptial agreement, the statutory matrimonial property regime serving just as a default rule.

The common law does not have matrimonial property law as understood in the civil law systems, and therefore also does not have a default matrimonial property regime. Since the Married Women's Property Act 1882, marriage has no effect upon the proprietary rights of the parties in England and Wales. As a result, the spouses' assets remain separate. In contrast to continental law, marital agreements,

1 For a general overview of matrimonial property law in Europe see A. Bergmann, M Ferid and D. Henrich (ed.), *Internationales Ehe- und Kindschaftsrecht*, 20 vol., Frankfurt, 1983 ff.; K. Boele-Woelki et al., 'Huwelijksvermogensrecht in rechtsvergelijkend perspectief', in *Ars notarius*, CIII, Deventer, 2000; K. Boele-Woelki, B. Braat and I. Curry-Sumner (ed.), 'European Family Law in Action, IV, Property Relations between Spouses', in EFL Series, n°24, Antwerp, 2009; A. Bonomi and M. Steiner (ed.), *Les régimes matrimoniaux en droit comparé et en droit international privé*, Geneva, 2006; B. Braat, 'Indépendance et interdépendance patrimoniales des époux dans le régime matrimonial légal des droits français, néerlandais et suisse', in EFL Series, n° 6, Bern, 2004; A. Fusaro, 'I rapporti patrimoniali tra coniugi in prospettiva comparatistica', in G. Alpa and G. Capilli (ed.), *Diritto private europeo*, Padova 2006, 53 ff.; D. Henrich, 'Zur Zukunft des Ehegüterrecht in Europa', *FamRZ* 2002, 1521 ff.; D. Henrich and D. Schwab (ed.), *Eheliche Gemeinschaft, Partnerschaft und Vermögen im europäischen Vergleich*, Bielefeld, 1999; S. Hofer, D. Schwab and D. Henrich (ed.), *From Status to Contract? Die Bedeutung des Vertrags im europäischen Familienrecht*, Bielefeld, 2005; V. Lipp, E. Schumann and B. Veit (ed.), 'Die Zugewinngemeinschaft: ein europäisches Modell?', in *Göttinger Juristische Reihe*, Göttingen, 2009; A. Lüderitz and N. Dethloff, *Familienrecht*, 28th ed., Munich, 2007, 145 ff.; S. Patti, 'I regimi patrimoniali tra legge e contratto', in S. Patti and M. Cubeddu (ed.), *Introduzione al diritto delle famiglia in Europa*, Milan, 2008, 191 ff.; W. Pintens (ed.), 'Family and Succession Law', in *Encyclopaedia of laws*, 6 vol., The Hague, 1997 ff.; W. Pintens, *Ehegüterstände in Europa*, ZEuP 2009, 23 ff.; W. Pintens, 'Statutory matrimonial property regimes in Europe', *Pravni zivot (Legal life)* 2009/10, 909 ff.; R. Süß and G. Ring (ed.), *Eherecht in Europa*, Angelbachtal, 2006; A. Verbeke, *Goederenverdeling bij echtscheiding*, Antwerp, 1991. Articles or paragraphs without furter reference refer to the respective civil code.

2 See K. Boele-Woelki et al. (n 1), Question 10 and 11; M. Cubeddu, *La casa familiare*, Milan, 2005, 35 ff. See also Recommendation No. R (81) 15 of the Committee of Ministers of the Council of Europe of 16 October 1981 on the rights of spouses relating to the occupation of the family home and the use of the household contents.

which in England and Wales could more appropriately be termed separation or divorce agreements, traditionally are not binding. This is comparable to the legal situation in Ireland.

Most continental legal systems draw a clear distinction between matrimonial property and maintenance, whereas common law systems in principle deal with both issues simultaneously.

The function of maintenance will be of lesser importance in systems where the courts have the power to reallocate property. Reallocation of family assets is a particularly important mechanism in common law systems to guarantee the standard of living and equality between the spouses. Maintenance, in the form of financial provision, is mainly granted when property redistribution cannot guarantee the required standard of living. In continental systems reallocation is extremely rare, although a few examples can be found. In some Nordic legal systems the courts have the power of reallocation. The French *prestation compensatoire* and the Spanish *pensión compensatoria* are not totally comparable with the common law system of reallocation but combine elements of maintenance and matrimonial property. However, most continental legal systems do not have special provisions regulating the distribution of marital property and where a community system applies, the community is simply divided into equal parts. In those systems maintenance is considered as a separate issue and the interrelationship between maintenance and marital property is limited, the only interface being that the income obtained out of the marital property will reduce need and thus maintenance.

This paper focuses on matrimonial property law and takes maintenance into account only insofar as both are strongly interrelated. It deals first with the default regime and concentrates on the composition of the property masses and the distribution of the assets in case of divorce (2.). Then marital agreements and their binding or non-binding character are looked at (3.). A short comparative evaluation concludes this paper.

2. DEFAULT REGIME

A division runs through the various European default matrimonial property regimes. Legal systems in the Romanic legal family and the Middle and Eastern European legal traditions are more familiar with the community of acquests whereas the Nordic and Germanic legal families have a separation of property in connection with a deferred community or a compensation clause. A few Spanish *fueros*, ie the law of certain autonomous provinces, even prescribe separation of property as the default matrimonial property regime. Finally, the common law systems take an alternative approach, whereby judicial discretion leads to a form of deferred community in practice, rather than any formal matrimonial property law.

The Netherlands have a universal community as its default regime (Article 93).[3] Plans for reform to replace this system with a community of acquests have failed and what remains is a slightly modernised universal community.[4]

2.1. COMMUNITY OF ACQUESTS IN THE ROMANIC LEGAL FAMILY AND IN EASTERN EUROPEAN LEGAL SYSTEMS

The Romanic legal family systems remain faithful to the Napoleonic model and have a limited community, which can be qualified as a community of acquests, as their default matrimonial property regime. The fundamental characteristic of the community of acquests is the creation of a community, which encompasses all property acquired non-gratuitously throughout the duration of the marriage.

The community of acquests is the default matrimonial property regime in Belgium, France, Luxembourg and Portugal. Italian law, which departed from the *Code Napoléon* in 1942 by adopting separation of property as its default regime, also later adopted, through the *comunione dei beni* in 1975, a community of acquests as its default matrimonial property regime. In practice however, separation of property remains highly popular and is almost considered to be a second default matrimonial property regime. A pre-nuptial agreement is not required in order to agree upon such a separation of assets; it is sufficient to make a declaration before the civil status registrar during the marriage ceremony (Article 162, Abs. 1).[5] Spain also has a community of acquests regime in the form of the *sociedad de gananciales* (Article 1344) although the *Código Civil* is only applicable in so far as the *fueros* and the law of the autonomous communities do not make alternative provisions, which, by virtue of the constitution, take priority (Article 13.2 in conjunction with Article 149.1.8 Constitución Española). If this is the case, Spanish law is deemed to be *derecho supletorio*, applicable only where there are gaps in the *fueros* and in the law of the autonomous communities.

3 See B. Breederveld, *De huwelijksgemeenschap bij echtscheiding*, Amsterdam, 2008.

4 Hereto B. Breederveld, 'De aanpassing van de algehele gemeenschap van goederen', FJR 2009, 66 ff.; H. Schoordijk, 'Modernisering van ons huwelijksvermogensrecht', *NJB 2003*, 218. The Second Chamber of Parliament already confirmed the universal community. The First Chamber is deliberating since December 2008. See Parl. Doc. First Chamber 2008–09, Nr. 28867. For the composition of the masses see Article 94 (draft).

5 If during marriage the spouses want to agree upon separation of property, a marital agreement is necessary.

Aragon, the Basque region, Galicia and Navarre have a community of acquests which diverges from Spanish law in only a few areas.

The community of acquests model also constitutes the default matrimonial regime in most Middle and Eastern European legal systems, including those systems in Bosnia-Herzegovina, Bulgaria, Croatia, the Czech Republic, Latvia, Lithuania, Poland, Russia, Slovakia, Slovenia, Hungary and the Ukraine.[6] An attempt to introduce the German model of the community of accrued gains in Estonia failed. The new Family Act of 18 November 2009 which introduced marital agreements, kept the community of acquests as the default regime.[7]

2.1.1. Composition of the categories of property

The same principles governing the composition of the three property categories (the personal property of each spouse and the community) are applicable in all of the aforementioned legal systems, albeit with some subtle variation.

In the Belgian, French, Portuguese and Spanish legal systems the personal property of each spouse comprises assets acquired prior to marriage and those acquired gratuitously during marriage (for example through gift inheritance or legacy), as well as assets and rights which are closely connected to the person – such as clothing, personal effects, compensation for personal injury and immaterial damage, assets acquired through subrogation or reinvestment and professional assets.[8] The community encompasses all income, including income from employment, pensions, social welfare payments and insurance payments replacing income, as well as from personal property and all assets acquired with this income.[9] Personal and community property is composed along the same lines in most Middle and Eastern European legal systems.[10]

Some legal systems make further distinctions and differentiate between income derived from employment and income derived from personal property. Croatian, Serbian and Slovenian law provide that only professional income forms part of the

6 See K. Boele-Woelki et al. (n 1), Question 16.

7 § 24 para. 2 Family Act. This act will enter into force on 1 July 2010.

8 Belgium: Articles 1399–1404; W. Pintens, Ch. Declerck, J. Du Mongh and K. Vanwinckelen, *Familiaal vermogensrecht*, 2nd ed., Antwerp, 2010, 124 ff.; France: Articles 1403–1408; A. Colomer, *Régimes matrimoniaux*, 12th ed. Paris, 2004, 271 ff.; F. Terré and P. Simler, *Les régimes matrimoniaux*, 4th ed., Paris, 2005, 213 ff.; Portugal: Articles 1722–1728, 1733; G. de Oliveira, R. Martins and P. Vítor, 'Portuguese Report', in K. Boele-Woelki et al. (n 2), Question 22; Spain: Article 1346; E. Arroyo i Amayelas, 'Les régimes matrimoniaux en droit espagnol', in A. Bonomi and M. Steiner (n 1), 156 ff.

9 Belgium: Article 1405; France: Article 1401; Portugal: Article 1728; Spain: Article 1347.

10 Eg Czech Republic: § 144; Poland: Article 31 § 2 Family and Guardianship Code.

community whereas income arising from personal property remains personal.[11] Italian law distinguishes between the personal property of each spouse, the community and the community *de residuo* (Articles 177–179). Income from employment and from personal property do not become part of the community, but remain personal property. Whatever remains upon termination of the community of acquests, is part of the community *de residuo*. Assets acquired with income received in the course of employment belong to the community.[12]

Also, all community systems draw a distinction between the nature of the debt as between the spouses inter se and the liability for debts against creditors.[13]

As to the first issue, the characterisation of the debt as between the spouses *inter se*, in most community jurisdictions personal debts are those which came into existence before the marriage or are in consequence of donations, inheritances and bequests to one spouse during the marriage, as well as those debts which where contracted in the sole interest of the personal property of one of the spouses.[14] Debts resulting from a security a spouse did not perform in the interest of the community property, debts contracted in disregard of the marital duties as well as debts resulting from a criminal conviction or tort are also mostly personal.[15]

Community debts are liabilities that spouses entered into both jointly and severally or as co-debtors. Debts incurred for the interest of the household, children's education or the community are also common debts. Since professional earnings are part of the community, professional debts are community debts.[16]

With regard to the second issue, that is liability for debts against creditors, several solutions exist. Under Belgian law, personal property and earnings are liable for personal debts (Article 1409). All three property masses, the personal property of each spouse and the community, are liable for community debts (Article 1414 para. 1). Important exceptions are made to these two basic rules. Personal debts may be recovered against the community in so far as personal assets have fallen into the community (Article 1410). In the case of debts resulting from tortious conduct, not only personal property, but also the community up to half of its net-value is liable (Article 1414). For professional debts, only the debtor spouse's personal property and the community are liable, rather than all three property

11 Croatia: Article 248 Family Code; Slovenia: M. Geč-Korošec and V.Rijavec, 'Slovenia', in W. Pintens (ed.), *Family and succession law*, 130; Serbia: Article 138 Family Code; O. Antic, 'Serbia and Montenegro', in W. Pintens (n 1), 134.

12 Article 177; Cass. 23.9.1997, Foro. it. 1999, 46; F. Padovini, 'Les régimes matrimoniaux en droit italien', in A. Bononi and M. Steiner (n 1), 46.

13 K. Boele-Woelki et al. (n 1), Question 30 ff.

14 See eg Belgium: Article 1407; France: Articles 1410, 1416.

15 See eg Belgium: Article 1407; France: Articles 1415 and 1417.

16 See eg Belgium: Article 1408; France: Articles 1409 and 1416.

categories. French law does not make a clear distinction between personal debts and community debts.[17] In principle all debts may be recovered against the personal property of the debtor spouse and the community property, except in case of fraud by the debtor spouse and bad faith by the creditor (Article 1413). But further exceptions exist. Personal debts incurred before the marriage and debts from successions and gifts received during the marriage can only be recovered against the personal property of the debtor spouse, on his income and on the community property in so far as personal assets have been merged with community assets (Articles 1410–1411). In cases where only one spouse entered into a debt, the other spouse does not vouch with his earnings, although the latter is part of the community property (Article 1414). Some debts such as a loan or a security contracted by one spouse can only be recovered against personal property and income (Article 1415). Maintenance debts and debts for the household and the education of the children may be recovered against the personal property of both spouses and the community property (Articles 220 and 1414).

2.1.2. Administration of assets

Personal property is subject to personal administration.[18] However, most legal systems provide for exceptions to this rule, mainly with regard to the family home and household assets.

The community is subject to the principle of concurrent administration by both spouses.[19] On the basis of this rule, each spouse may autonomously administer the community and must tolerate legal acts performed by the other spouse. Administration comprises all capacities relating to the actual administration *sensu stricto*, disposal and utilisation. The property must however be administered in the family's interest.

The principle of concurrent administration is subject to exceptions. For a certain number of important dispositive legal acts the consent of both spouses is required.[20] Joint administration is applied for example to the sale of immovable community assets or to the gifting of community assets.

---

17 W. Pintens et al., in K. Boele-Woelki et al. (n 1), Question 32 and 33; Fr. Ferrand and B. Braat, in K. Boele-Woelki et al (n 1) Question 32 and 33.

18 Belgium: Article 1425; France: Article 1429.

19 K. Boele-Woelki et al. (n 1), Question 35.

20 See eg Belgium: Arts 1418–1419; France: Arts 1422–1425.

2.1.3. Liquidation and distribution

In the community of acquests, a division and distribution of assets is only possible upon dissolution of the community. Before distribution the community must be liquidated.

Liquidation requires a balance to be drawn up, in which the issue of compensation between the categories of assets will be of great significance.[21] Wherever the personal property of one spouse has gained an advantage from the community, or vice versa, the latter property mass is entitled to compensation by the former in order to avoid unjust enrichment.[22] Where, for example, the community has invested in a house belonging to the personal property of the wife, the personal property of the wife must reimburse the community. The same rule applies, where the community was used to discharge a personal debt of the husband. Compensation will usually be nominal, although many legal systems make an exception for investments made in order to acquire, improve or maintain an asset. In this latter situation the property entitled to compensation obtains a share in the increase in value of the asset in question.[23]

After compensation the balance will list all assets, claims and debts at the moment of dissolution.

The community of acquests distributes the community in two equal parts. Each spouse is entitled to half of the community assets.[24] Personal property remains personal. An increase in the value of personal assets accrues to the personal assets alone.

A judge generally has neither discretion to diverge from the division of assets into two equal parts, nor discretion to redistribute personal property of one of the spouses, albeit that some legal systems, such as those in Poland and Serbia, differ in this area and allow the court to deviate from equal division, taking into account the contribution of each spouse.[25] However, in practice the courts rarely make use of these powers.

---

21 See eg France: J.-M. De Carmo Silva and A. Fouquet, *Liquidations de régimes matrimoniaux et de successions*, 2nd ed., Paris, 2005; A. Pene, *Méthodologie des liquidations-partages en droit patrimonial de la famille*, Paris, 2005. For Spain: J. Montero Aroca, *Disolución y liquidación de la sociedad de gananciales*, Valencia, 2003.

22 Belgium: Articles 1432–1438; France: Articles 1468–1473; Spain: Article 1358.

23 Belgium: Article 1435; France: Article 1469.

24 K. Boele-Woelki et al. (n 1), Question 49.

25 Poland: Article 43 Family and Guardianship Code; Serbia: Article 180 Family Act. See O. Antic, 'Serbia and Montenegro', in W. Pintens (n 1), 180.

In many legal systems, the possibility exists to accord one of the spouses preferential treatment in the allocation of particular community assets, in particular the family home.[26] This preferred spouse must in turn allow that asset to be set off against his or her portion of the assets and, if necessary, make a payment to the other spouse where the value of the asset exceeds the value of his portion of the community.[27]

Distribution of community assets and maintenance are two separate issues. Distribution can however affect the maintenance quantum when the income of the creditor spouse increases as a result of community asset distribution. This income increase will decrease his needs. Maintenance is usually paid by way of monthly instalments, although many jurisdictions provide for alternative payment by way of a capital sum. In some jurisdictions, such as in France, payment by way of a capital sum, the *prestation compensatoire*, is the norm.[28] This lump sum can consist of community assets. In practice however there are often insufficient community assets or other means available for the payment of a lump sum. In this case maintenance will still be paid in periodical instalments.

2.2. PARTICIPATION SYSTEMS IN THE NORDIC AND GERMANIC LEGAL SYSTEMS

Matrimonial property regimes in Nordic and Germanic systems are based upon a participation system. Spousal assets remain separate during the marriage. However, upon marital dissolution, each spouse partakes in the assets of the other. It is necessary at this stage to distinguish between two models; under the first model, the spouses partake by way of a deferred community whereas under the second model they partake by way of a statutory compensation clause.

2.2.1. Deferred community

2.2.1.1. Nordic legal systems

The deferred community model can be found in the Nordic legal systems, where a distinction is drawn between reserved property and common property. Gifts and legacies, received upon the condition that they pass into the reserved property, as well as a number of personal assets and rights, belong to the reserved property.[29] All other assets are part of the common assets. During the marriage, the

[26] Italy: Article155, para. 2. See K. Boele-Woelki et al. (n 1), Question 51.

[27] Belgium: Article 1467; France: Article 1476 with reference to Article 832–832-4.

[28] Article 270. See also for Spain: the *pension compensatoria* (Article 95).

[29] Denmark: § 21 Marriage Act; Sweden: Ch. 7, s. 2 Marriage Act. All Nordic systems have the possibility to enlarge the reserved property.

distinction between these two categories of assets is of no significance and only becomes relevant upon marital dissolution, at which point a deferred community is created.

In principle, all debts are attributed to the personal assets of the spouses, except where the spouses incurred them jointly or severally on the basis of the general law of obligations. Debts for the education of children or for the household are incurred severally in Denmark,[30] Finland[31] and Norway[32] but mostly restricted to day-to-day needs.[33] In Sweden there are no special rules for household debts.[34] Each spouse administers his own property although legal acts involving the family home and chattels are subject to restrictions.[35]

A deferred community materialises upon dissolution of the marriage. This deferred community comprises the net assets of the community property of each spouse. If the liabilities are higher than the assets, then the property is evaluated as breaking even. Given that the definition of the composition of reserved property is rather restrictive, these deferred communities effectively are universal communities. This community should, in principle, be divided into equal shares, which means that each spouse not only partakes in assets acquired by the other spouse's income, but also in those assets he owned prior to the marriage or those acquired during the marriage by way of gift or inheritance.

All Nordic legal systems, except that of Norway which exhibits distinct particularities, recognise the possibility that the judge may refrain from an equal split for equitable reasons.[36] This may be relevant, when the marriage was of a short duration. Conversely, the judge also has the possibility to award the economically weaker spouse a part of the reserved property of the other spouse for equitable reasons.[37]

Since 1991 Norway has operated under a different system. Each spouse has the opportunity to exclude assets acquired prior to the marriage, or those accumulated through gifts or inheritance during the marriage from the division of assets. In

30 § 11 Act on the legal effects of marriage.
31 § 52 Marriage Act.
32 § 41 Marriage Act.
33 See K. Boele-Woelki et al. (n 1), Question 9.
34 M. Jänterä-Jareborg and M. Brattström, 'Swedish report', in K Boele-Woelki et al. (n 1), Question 9.
35 K. Boele-Woelki et al. (n 1), Question 10.
36 Denmark: § 69a Law on Liquidation 1986; Finland: § 103b Marriage Act; Island: § 104 Marriage Act; Sweden: Kap. 12 § 1 (1) Marriage Act. See I. Dübeck, Gütertrennungsreform in Dänemark und skandinavisches Güterstandsrecht, ZEuP 1995, 827; J. Scherpe, 'Privatautonomie im Familienrecht der nordischen Länder', in S. Hofer, D. Schwab and D. Henrich (ed.) (n 1), 214 ff.
37 Denmark: Article 56 Marriage Act.

order to do this, it is sufficient that the spouse provides evidence that the asset in question belonged to him previously or that it came into his property by way of gift or inheritance. The judge may however depart from this general rule where there is obvious inequity.[38]

However, it is important to note that despite the Nordic systems formally being described as a deferred community, in practice the property is kept separate even upon the creation of the deferred community. Each spouse then in principle has a right *in rem*, but the debtor spouse has the choice between satisfaction of the claim in kind or in money.[39]

2.2.1.2. Austria

The default matrimonial property regime in Austria also consists of a separation of property in combination with a deferred community of property upon dissolution of the marriage. However, if a spouse participates in the business of the other spouse, the former spouse has a claim for profits arising out of that business activity even during the marriage and does not have to wait until dissolution for that right to accrue (§ 98 ABGB).

The deferred community is composed of the matrimonial home and contents and the matrimonial savings (§ 81 Law on Marriage),[40] which amounts to the acquests. Personal property of the spouses is not taken into consideration (§ 82, para. 1 Marriage Act), although the matrimonial home and its household assets, which belong to the personal property of a spouse, are taken into account where the other spouse or a joint child is dependent upon it. In practice, the majority of divisions are in equal shares, although the law does prescribes an equitable division such that the interests of the child are to be taken into consideration (§ 83, para. 1 Marriage Act). Employment, responsibility for household duties and child-rearing are regarded as equal.[41] Distribution is effected in kind.

2.2.2. Statutory compensation clause

Under the second model, a deferred community is not created but rather a statutory monetary compensation clause is used. This model is found in the German and Greek community of accrued gains (*Zugewinngemeinschaft*) and the Swiss participation in acquests (*Errungenschaftsbeteiligung*).[42]

---

[38] § 59 Marriage Act.
[39] Finland: § 103b Marriage Act.
[40] See S. Ferrari and M. Koch-Hipp, 'Eherecht in Österreich', in R. Süß and G. Ring (n 1), 922 ff.
[41] S. Ferrari and M. Koch-Hipp, in R Süβ and G Ring (n 1) 923–924.
[42] 2002 the Swiss system was introduced as default regime in Turkey.

There are important differences between these three systems concerning the composition of the categories of assets. Neither German nor Greek law distinguishes between personal property and acquests, whereas the Swiss system does draw this distinction.

In all of the aforementioned legal systems, debts are principally calculated as part of the property of each spouse, unless the spouses have indebted themselves jointly or severally on the basis of the generally applicable law of obligations. Debts incurred in raising children or maintaining the household are to be regarded as severally incurred debts.[43]

2.2.2.1. Germany

German law is only familiar with the concept of the initial and final property.[44] The difference between initial and final property is only of significance once the property regime is terminated and it is time for the compensatory settlement.

The initial property is comprised of personal assets belonging to the spouse upon entering into the marriage, as well as assets accumulated by way of gift or inheritance during the marriage (§ 1374 BGB). Initial assets are net assets. Premarital debts are to be deducted and may exceed the assets of the initial property (§ 1374 para. 1).

The final property of each spouse comprises all his or her assets, after subtraction of liabilities and debts, upon dissolution of the matrimonial property regime (§ 1375 para. 1). Disproportionate gratuitous contributions and dissipation, as well as diminutions in value of the assets due to acts intended to harm the spouse are to be added to the assets (§ 1375 para. 2).

Dissolution of the marriage by divorce necessitates compensation for the accrued gains. Where the gains of one spouse exceed those of the other, the latter has a claim for half the excess (§ 1378, para. 1). The final property cannot be negative, so that one spouse is not burdened by the negative property of the other. The assessment of the initial and final property is based upon the market value of the assets (§ 1376). In order to prevent an increase in value, as a consequence of inflation, the value of the initial property is indexed.[45]

---

43 Eg Germany: § 1357; Switzerland: Article 166, para. 3 (only for day-to-day needs).

44 A. Lüderitz and N. Dethloff (n 1) 114 ff.; R Schröder and L. Bergschneider (ed.), 'Familienvermögensrecht', 2nd ed., Bielefeld 2007, 145 ff. For recent reform plans see R. Hoppenz, 'Reformbedarf und Reformbestrebungen im Zugewinnausgleich', *FamRZ* 2008, 1889 ff.; E. Koch, 'Die geplanten Neuregelungen des Zugewinnausgleichs', *FamRZ* 2008, 1124ff.

45 BGH 14.11.1973, *FamRZ* 1974, 83; BGH 14.3.1990, *FamRZ* 1990, 603. Hereto R. Schröder, *Bewertungen im Zugewinnausgleich,* 4th ed., Bielefeld, 2007.

As the gains are calculated for the entirety of a spouse's property, this not only leads to a partaking in the assets acquired during the marriage, but also a partaking in the gain of assets accrued prior to the marriage. This is an expression of a rather extreme understanding of matrimonial solidarity.

2.2.2.2. Switzerland

Swiss law distinguishes between personal property and acquests of each spouse so that the matrimonial property regime is comprised of, essentially, four different groups of assets (Article 196).[46] The personal property encompasses personal assets, assets acquired prior to the marriage, assets acquired gratuitously during the marriage, personal damages (for example damages for personal injury and immaterial damage)[47] and assets accumulated by investments (Article 198). All other assets are acquests.

Debts are allocated to the personal property or to the acquests in accordance with the character of the debt (Article 209).

The Swiss participation in acquests provides that each spouse retains his or her property after divorce. They both have a claim on the half of the acquests of the other (Article 215).[48] Proprietary dispositions which infringe the rights of the other are added. Debts are subtracted, but subtraction is limited to the extent of the assets' value (Articles 208–210). The claims of the spouses are balanced against each other and the difference paid off monetarily. Unlike the German system, indexing of the initial property is avoided by dividing the property of each spouse into two categories of assets, but compensation is due between the personal property and the acquests of a spouse, eg when personal assets have been invested in the acquests (Article 209).

Matrimonial solidarity is less extreme than under German law because only gains must be accounted for and the increase in value of personal assets is disregarded.[49]

---

46 See P. Tuor, B. Schnyder and A. Rumo-Jungo, *Das schweizerische Zivilgesetzbuch*, 13th ed., Zurich 2009, 362 ff.

47 Contrary to German law, where the case law of the Supreme Court ununderstandably denies to open the closed character of the initial property and counts damages for corporal or immaterial damage to the final property (BGH 27.5.1981, BGHZ 80, 384, NJW 1981, 1836; BGH 29.10.1981, BGHZ 82, 145). See the criticism by R. Schröder, in R. Schröder and L. Bergschneider (n 44), no. 4.203.

48 See P. Tuor, B. Schnyder and A. Rumo-Jungo (n 47), 368 ff.

49 Hereto S. Sandoz, 'Les régimes matrimoniaux en droit suisse', in A. Bonomi and M. Steiner (n. 1), 22 ff.; F. Sturm, 'La Zugewinngemeinschaft et les régimes conventionnels du droit allemand', in A. Bonomi and M. Steiner (n 1), 83.

2.2.2.3. Greece

Greek law does not define the initial and final assets but it does exclude certain assets from the compensatory settlement.[50]

Each spouse only participates in the acquests of the other spouse. Assets acquired before the marriage are excluded. The same applies to gifts and inheritance to one of the spouses during the marriage, as well as to income generated by these assets. Debts are offset in the same way as under German law and inflation is also taken into consideration.

Participation is restricted to those acquests acquired with participation of the creditor spouse, eg for the education of the children or the contribution to the professional activities of the debtor spouse (Article 1400 para. 1). This means that unlike German or Swiss law, participation in the accrued gains is not equal, but rather is proportional to each spouse's contribution. Since this contribution is not easy to prove, there is a presumption that each spouse contributed to the accrued property of the other partner by one third, but this presumption is rebuttable.[51] The entitled spouse may therefore prove that his or her contribution was higher and likewise the liable spouse may show that the contribution of the other was lower or indeed never occurred.

2.3. SEPARATION OF PROPERTY

Separation of property is the default regime in the Balearic Islands, Catalonia and Valencia. After divorce, neither a deferred community is created, nor a general compensation claim settlement applies.

In Catalonia, specific compensation may be awarded to the housekeeping spouse, or to the spouse who worked in the business of the other.[52]

Valencian law has comparable provisions which are not enshrined in matrimonial property law, but in the general laws on marriage.[53]

---

50 Article 1400, para. 3.

51 Article 1400, para. 1. See D. ANDRIOTIS, 'Les régimes matrimoniaux en droit grec', in A. BONOMI and M. STEINER (n 1), 213 ff.; D. STAMATIADIS and SP. TSANTINIS, 'Eherecht in Griechenland', in R. Süβ and G.RING (n 1), 575.

52 Article 41 Codi de família. Hereto J. FERRER I RIBA, 'Eherecht in Katalonien', in R. Süß and G. RING (n 1), 710 ff.; P. ORTUÑO MUÑOZ, in J. EGEA I FERNÁNDEZ and J. FERRER I RIBA (ed.), *Comentaris al Code de família, a la llei d'unions estables de parella i a llei de situacions convivencials d'ajuda mutual*, Madrid 2000, 231 ff.

53 Article 13 Act of 20.3.2007. Hereto J. FERRER I RIBA, 'Neueste Entwicklungen im spanischen Personen- und Familienrecht in den Jahren 2006–2007', *FamRZ* 2007, 1517.

2.4. ON THE WAY TO MATRIMONIAL PROPERTY LAW AND A DEFAULT REGIME IN THE COMMON LAW?

The common law does not have a real matrimonial property regime and therefore has no default matrimonial property regime either. Since the Married Women's Property Act 1882, marriage in England and Wales has no effect upon the property of the spouses, at least for the duration of the marriage.[54] This means that under common law, the property of the spouses remains separate. All debts are personal debts.

The legal situation in Ireland[55] and Scotland[56] is comparable, despite the latter not being a common law system.

As a reaction to previous restrictive case law of the House of Lords concerning the family home the Matrimonial Causes Act 1973 gave English judges wide powers to reallocate spousal assets by means of property adjustment orders in divorce cases.[57] Comparable legislation exists in Ireland and Scotland.[58]

It must be noted that in common law systems, a substantive distinction between division of assets and maintenance is, to a large extent, unknown. In accordance with the clean break principle (s. 25A MCA), the common law operates by way of global package solutions, which merge and combine division of assets and maintenance payments.[59]

When applying proprietary reallocation the court must have regard to all the circumstances of the case. First consideration should be given to the welfare of any children (s. 25(1) MCA). Further, the court shall have particular regard to (a) the income, earning capacity, property and other financial resources which each spouse has or is likely to have in the foreseeable future, including in the case of earning capacity any increase in that capacity which it would in the opinion of the court be reasonable to expect a spouse to take steps to acquire, (b) the financial needs, obligations and responsibilities which each spouse has or is likely

---

54 See N. Lowe and G. Douglas, *Bromley's Family Law*, 10th ed., Oxford, 2007, 129 ff.

55 G. Shannon, in K. Boele-Woelki et al. (n 1), Question 1; P. Ward, Ireland, in W. Pintens (n 1), 113 ff.

56 See J. Mair, 'Scottish report', in Boele-Woelki et al. (n 1), Question 1; J. Thomson, *Family Law in Scotland*, 4th. ed., Edinburgh, 2002, 135 ff.

57 S. 24 Matrimonial Causes Act 1973 (MCA). Hereto G. Douglas, 'Fairness and Equality: the English Courts' Struggles with Property Division on Divorce', in *Festschrift Frank*, Frankfurt, 2008, 171 ff.; J Eekelaar, *Financial and Property adjustment on divorce*, Oxford, 1998; K. Gray, *Reallocation of Property on Divorce*, Abingdon, 1977.

58 Ireland: s. 14 Family Law (Divorce) Act 1996. Hereto G. Shannon, 'Ireland', in K. Boele-Woelki et al. (n 1), Question 181; Scotland: s. 8 Family law Act. Hereto J. Mair, 'Scottish report', in K Boele-Woelki et al. (n 1), Question 181.

59 See J Miles and S. Harris-Short, *Family Law. Text, Cases and Materials*, Oxford, 2007, 544 ff.

to have in the foreseeable future, (c) the standard of living enjoyed by the family before the breakdown of the marriage, (d) the age of each spouse and the duration of the marriage, (e) any physical or mental disability of each spouse, (f) the contributions which each spouse has made or is likely in the foreseeable future to make to the welfare of the family, including any contribution by looking after the home or caring for the family, (g) the conduct of each spouse, if that conduct is such that it would in the opinion of the court be inequitable to disregard it; (h) the value to each spouse of any benefit which, by reason of the divorce, that spouse will lose the chance of acquiring (s. 25(2) MCA).[60] From this recital it can be deduced that reallocation of property focuses first of all on needs[61] and that the standard of living the spouses enjoyed before the breakdown of the marriage has to be taken into account. The second important factor is compensation for a relationship-generated economic disadvantage and covers cases where the wife gave up her job to take care of the children.[62] The issue of compensation is not considered very often, since available resources in many cases do not suffice to cover needs.[63]

The basic principles of the English system, extensive judicial discretion and the focus on need, were aptly described by Lord Denning in *Hanlon v. The Law Society*: "The Family Court takes the rights and obligations of the parties all together and puts the pieces into a mixed bag. Such pieces are the right to occupy the matrimonial home or have a share in it, the obligation to maintain the wife and children, and so forth. The court then takes out the pieces and hands them to the two parties – some to one party and some to the other – so that each can provide for the future with the pieces allotted to him or to her. The court hands them out without paying any too nice a regard to their legal or equitable rights but simply according to what is the fairest provision for the future – for mother and father and the children."[64]

In the past, the application of the Matrimonial Causes Act resulted in guaranteeing reasonable requirements to the claimant. This meant that the more affluent spouse was not under a duty to share his or her entire fortune with the needy spouse. The redistribution was only conducted to the extent that the spouse in need of maintenance was put in a position which enabled him or her to continue his or her matrimonial standard of living.[65] The result of the redistribution was, depending on the circumstances, very variable. Where one spouse took responsibility for

60 S. 25a (2) MCA. The Family Law (Scotland) Act 1985 has a comparable solution, but the instructions are more detailed (s. 8–14), so that the result is more predictable.

61 J. Miles and S. Harris-Short (n 59), 513.

62 See eg *SRj v DWJ (financial provision)* [1999] 3 FCR 153, 160 (CA).

63 J. Miles and S. Harris-Short (n 59), 515.

64 [1981] A.C. 124, [1980] 2 All E.R. 199, [1980] 2 W.L.R. 756.

65 Dart v. Dart [1966] 2 FLR 286.

the care of the children and only had modest means to dispose of, reallocation often led to the situation where the debtor spouse lost the matrimonial home, which in turn often meant a loss of his entire assets. If one spouse had a large fortune at his disposal this was not distributed in equal parts, but only to the extent required to maintain the matrimonial standard of living. In cases of large and medium fortunes, the courts usually applied the so called one-third rule, whereby the party entitled to maintenance received a third of the family assets and the remaining two thirds remained with the debtor spouse.[66]

This line of case law was changed by the famous *White v. White* decision,[67] dealing with a big money case, where the property clearly exceeded need. In his main speech, Lord Nicholls of Birkenhead placed great emphasis upon fairness, which is the overarching aim of the Matrimonial Causes Act and should therefore be the underlying consideration in every property adjustment order whatever division of labour is chosen by the husband and wife, or forced upon them by circumstance. If, in their different spheres, each spouse contributed equally to the family, then in principle it matters not which of them earned the money and built up the assets. There should be no bias in favour of the money-earner and against the home-maker and child-carer.[68]

By the *White* decision, the House of Lords rejected the restriction of reasonable requirements which was previously placed upon proprietary reallocation. This means that in cases where assets exceed need, not only need and compensation must be taken into account but also a third factor; equal sharing. Lord Nicholls did not go so far as to create a starting point of reallocation into equal halves and in fact left this question to the legislator. However a judge is now required to compare the final fair solution to the yardstick of equality, which amounts to the same solution.[69] The guideline is no longer a guarantee of equivalent matrimonial standard of living, but rather a guarantee of equal treatment of the spouses. If both have contributed to the family's wellbeing in equal shares, it is of no significance that one particular spouse built up the family's wealth and an equal division is still therefore appropriate. The House of Lords did however leave open the possibility of diverging from an equal division where there are good reasons to do so and subsequent case law continued to use this possibility to allow an uneven division. In most cases greater weight was given to monetary contribution than contributions through housekeeping, so that 60/40 divisions occurred with increasing frequency. In *Lambert v. Lambert* the Court

66 Wachtel v. Wachtel [1973] 2 W.L.R. 366.

67 [2000] 1 AC 596, [2000] 2 FLR 981, [2000] W.L.R. 1571. Hereto D. Hodson, 'White: Equality on divorce?', *Fam Law* 2000, 870 ff.; N. Lowe and G. Douglas (n 54), 1018 ff.; 'Fr. Ronchese, Regno Unito: una nuova regola sulla divisione dei beni dopo il divorzio', Familia 2001, 843 ff.

68 *White v White,* at para. 24.

69 G. Douglas, in *Festschrift Frank* (n 57) 109.

of Appeal severely limited the possibility of uneven distribution by confining it to exceptional cases.[70] The Court of Appeal emphasised that it was unacceptable to give greater weight to the contributions of the working spouse than those of the housekeeping spouse. The latter contribution was not in principle of lesser worth, and there was therefore no justification to distribute the fruits of the working partner's labours unevenly; only an extraordinary contribution could justify an uneven distribution. A bright idea, entrepreneurial skill or greater physical exertion is not sufficient. What might be deemed a special contribution is only vaguely touched upon by the Court of Appeal, although in academic discussion, pre-marital wealth or an inheritance are given as examples,[71] which were already mentioned in *White v. White.*[72] In *Miller v. Miller; McFarlane v. McFarlane* the House of Lords followed this line of reasoning and considered that the origin of the asset component was relevant with a distinction being drawn between matrimonial and non-matrimonial property (Lord Nicholls) or alternatively family assets and other assets (Baroness Hale).[73] The judgment of the House of Lords is not entirely clear on this point, but the decision seems to indicate that an uneven distribution is permissible where the origin of wealth lies outside of the marriage, for example in cases of gifts or inheritance. On the other hand however, any assets which can be regarded as income from employment are to be distributed equally as a matter of principle (except where an extraordinary contribution, as described above, exists).[74] What is remarkable is that the judge retains ultimate discretion, although he has to exercise this discretion within the framework developed in potentially contradictory legislation and case law. This ultimate discretion is underlined in *Miller v Miller; McFarlane v McFarlane*, where Lord Nicholls emphasised that fairness requires in principle an equal share of the assets of the partnership, unless there is good reason to the contrary. The yardstick of equality is to be applied as an aid, not as a rule.[75]

---

70 [2003] 1 FLR 139. Hereto G Douglas, in *Festschrift Frank* (n 57) 108 ff.; D. Hodson, M. Green and N. de Souza, 'Lambert – Shutting Pandora's Box', *Fam Law* 2003, 37 ff.

71 D. Hodson et al., *Fam Law* 2003, 45.

72 [2001] 1 AC 605, [2000] 2 FLR 994.

73 [2006] UKHL 24, [2006] 2 AC 618. Hereto J. Scherpe, 'Miller und McFarlane – Das House of Lords entscheidet erneut über Güteraufteilung nach Ehescheidung', *FamRZ* 2006, 1314; M. Welstead, 'Judicial Reform or an Increase in Discretion – the Decision in Miller v Miller; McFarlane v McFarlane, The International Survey of Family Law', Bristol 2008, 61 ff.

74 G. Douglas, in *Festschrift Frank* (n 57), 114.

75 No. 16. See also *Sharman v Charman* [2006] EWHC 1879 (Fam), [2007] 1 FCR 33, at para. 128.

3. MARITAL AGREEMENTS

3.1. PRIVATE AUTONOMY

In almost all civil law systems spouses can make a marital agreement and choose their matrimonial property regime.[76] But in most of these systems the spouses can only fully agree on their property relations upon and during marriage. They can also agree on the consequences of dissolution but they have to guarantee the stability of their matrimonial property regime. They can include *avantages matrimoniaux* (matrimonial benefits) that only have effect in the case of dissolution by death and not by dissolution by divorce, but they cannot vary their matrimonial property regime according to the ground of dissolution and agree on a community of acquests in case of dissolution by death and on a separation of property in case of dissolution by divorce.

Clauses on maintenance and especially clauses waiving spousal maintenance are considered to be against public policy and good morals and cannot be included in pre- and post-nuptial agreements. In most civil law systems they can only be included in divorce agreements concluded during divorce proceedings or in contemplation of a divorce. Agreements before marriage are excluded. Exceptions can however be found eg in Austria and Germany where marital agreements can contain clauses on maintenance.[77] Maintenance agreements are also possible in Switzerland, but in practice they will be agreed in a separate document.

Socialist legal systems rejected party autonomy and applied the community of property to all spouses without any possibility of deviating from it. After the fall of the communist regimes this rule was abolished and marital agreements were introduced.[78]

Under common law it is possible but not at all common to make an agreement to regulate the property consequences upon and during marriage.[79] Marital agreements therefore have to be understood as agreements providing for the event of divorce, made pre-nuptially, during the marriage or on separation. Such marital agreements regulating the consequences of separation and divorce are

---

76 See K. Boele-Woelki, Fr. Ferrand, Chr. González Beilfuss, M. Jänterä-Jareborg, N. Lowe, D. Martiny and W. Pintens, 'Principles of European Divorce and Maintenance Between Former Spouses', in EFL Series, n° 16, Antwerp, 2005, 125 ff.

77 See K. Boele-Woelki et al. (n 76) 126 ff.

78 See recently eg in Romania where the rule was abolished by the new civil code of 17 July 2009 (Article 329 ff.).

79 See N. Lowe and R. Kay, 'The Status of Prenuptial Agreements in English law – Eccentricity or sensible pragmatism?', in B. Verschraegen (ed.), *Family Finances*, Vienna, 2009, 395 ff.

more common but also not very usual.[80] In practice they are very often restricted to big money cases.

Spouses mostly enjoy a very broad freedom to choose their regime, for example as in Austria, Belgium (Article 1387), and France (Article 1387). They can choose an optional regime provided by their matrimonial property law, but they can also select a foreign regime or create their own. In many cases the spouses choose the default regime with some modifications.

In other legal systems as Denmark (§ 8 Act on the consequences of marriage), Finland (§ 41 Marriage Act), Italy,[81] Greece,[82] Slovakia (§ 143) and Switzerland (Article 182 para. 2) the spouses can only opt for one of the regimes offered in their codes. In Portugal spouses with children from a former relationship cannot enter into the universal community of property or bring certain listed assets into the community. Persons of more than sixty years of age have no choice: they have to marry under the separation of property (Article 1270 para. 1 and 2).[83]

The common law systems allow a broad freedom to regulate the property relations during the marriage but in practice agreements focus upon the consequences of separation.

In some legal systems there is a restriction on post-nuptial agreements. In Portugal they are impermissible (Article 1714). In France they are only possible after two years of marriage (Article 1397 para 1).

3.2. FORM AND PROCEDURE

In most legal systems such as those of Austria, Belgium, France, Germany, Italy and Switzerland, a marital agreement requires a notarial deed or, in the case of Denmark and Finland, a written agreement that has to be registered. In legal systems where spouses may agree on maintenance, a private document suffices for maintenance agreements which are not part of a marital agreement.

Common law jurisdictions traditionally attach enormous importance to independent legal advice. Each spouse must separately seek independent legal

80 The difference between an ante-nuptial settlement and an ante- or pre-nuptial agreement was explained by Wall in *N v N (divorce: ante nuptial agreement)* [1999] 2 FCR 583, 591 (Fam Div).
81 Cf. S. Patti, in S. Patti and M. Cubeddu (n 1), 209.
82 A. Koutsouradis, 'Greek report', in K. Boele-Woelki et al. (n 1), Question 198.
83 See G. de Oliveira, R. Martins and P. Vítor, 'Portuguese Report', in K. Boele-Woelki et al. (n 1), Question 198.

advice to guarantee spousal protection since the parties are considering giving up the protection provided for by the law.[84]

Most legal systems do not draw a distinction between form and procedure of an ante-nuptial or post-nuptial agreement. Homologation procedures have been abolished although a few systems still impose restrictions. In France judicial homologation is prescribed when the spouses have minor children or when major children or creditors oppose the modification (Article 1397 para. 5).

3.3. BINDING FORCE

In most civil law jurisdictions marital agreements are binding and cannot be set aside by the court. They can only be nullified in the case of vitiated consent or when they contain clauses contrary to public policy or good morals.[85]

In the Nordic jurisdictions marital agreements are binding in principle but can be set aside by the courts in cases of inequity. In those cases the courts can reallocate reserved property as in Finland or Sweden.[86]

The German Constitutional court has also stated that the courts can, in principle, scrutinise marital agreements, although the Constitutional Court left the issue of the scope of that scrutiny up to the Supreme Court, the Bundesgerichtshof.[87] In a landmark judgment the Supreme Court gave a narrow interpretation to the Constitutional Court's judgment.[88] Marital agreements may only be scrutinised in relation to the most important divorce consequences. The Supreme Court rejected marital agreements which deny any form of maintenance after divorce or exclude any compensation of pension rights. In principle an exclusion of compensation for accrued gains is acceptable, since marriage is a community of life but not necessarily a community of property. The Supreme Court admits scrutiny only in exceptional circumstances. This narrow interpretation was criticised by some legal scholars.[89]

---

84 But see *Radmacher v Granatino* [2010] UKSC 42 For Ireland: see G. Shannon, 'Irish report', in K. Boele-Woelki et al. (n 1), Question 193.

85 See K. Boele-Woelki et al. (n 1), Question 191.

86 Finland: § 103b Marriage Act; Sweden: s. 12 Marriage Act.

87 BVerfG 6 February 2001, *FamRz* 2001, 343, note Schwab, *NJW* 2001, 957; BVerfG 29 March 2001, *FamRZ* 2001, 985, *NJW* 2001, 2248.

88 BGH 11 February 2004, FamRZ 2004, 601, note Borth, *NJW* 2004, 930. See L. Bergschneider, *Richterliche Inhaltskontrolle von Eheverträgen und Scheidungsvereinbarungen*, Munich, 2008.

89 See eg B. Dauner-Lieb and A Sanders, 'Abdingbare Teilhabe – unabdingbare Verantwortung? Grenzen güterrechtlicher Vereinbarungen im Lichte der Rechtsprechung des BVerfG und des BGH', *FuR* 2005, 141 ff.

In Switzerland the court must scrutinise maintenance agreements (Article 140). The court verifies that the spouses have fully reflected upon the content of the agreement and that they came to an agreement without any pressure. The agreement has to be clear and complete and may not be evidently inequitable (Article 140 para. 2). The court has no power to scrutinise the matrimonial property regime.[90]

English law traditionally differentiates between pre-nuptial agreements, post-nuptial agreements and separation agreements.

It is helpful to start with separation agreements because their position is clear whereas pre- and post-nuptial agreements have undergone some developments.[91]

Separation agreements are legally binding and can be enforced as any other contract. There is no public policy argument against them since they are not agreed before the marriage with the possibility of pressure but rather are concluded in view of a divorce. Following the *Hyman* rule they cannot oust the jurisdiction of the court.[92] Each spouse can seek alternative provision from the court, when he or she thinks that the court will decide on a better provision.

Post-nuptial agreements reached before separation were long regarded as contrary to public policy since spouses had a duty to live together. It was therefore impermissible to contractually bargain on this matter.[93] But in the Privy Council case of *MacLeod* post-nuptial agreements were treated in the same way as separation agreements. Since the duty to cohabit no longer exists, the legal foundation for the public policy objection is very weak. Therefore spouses at any moment during the marriage can make legally binding agreements on a separation, but always subject to the *Hyman* rule.[94]

Pre-nuptial agreements are traditionally perceived as being contrary to public policy because they undermine the concept of marriage as a life-long union and therefore not binding.[95] However, s. 25 MCA allows the court to consider a marital agreement, since all the circumstances of the case must be taken into account. In practice the judge will respect the marital agreement when the terms of the

90 Tribunal federal 4 December 2003, JT 2004, I, 407.

91 See the recent Supreme Court decision in *Radmacher v Granatino* [2010] UKSC 42. For a comprehensive analysis of the preceding Court of Appeal decision see J. Miles, *Radmacher v Granatino* [2009] EWCA Civ 209: Upping the ante-nuptial agreement, CFLQ 2009, 515.

92 *Hyman v Hyman* [1925] AC 601. See also J. Miles, *CFLQ* 2009, 515 ff.

93 *Duchess of Marlborough v Duke of Marlborough* [1901] Ch165, at 171.

94 Baroness Hale, in *Macleod* [2008] UKPC 64, [2009] 1 FLR 641, at para. 171. See J. Miles, *CFLQ* 2009, 516.

95 Wall in *N v N (divorce: ante nuptial agreement)* [1999] 2 FCR 583, 591 (Fam Div). Also Thorpe in *F v F (Ancilary Relief: Substantial assets)* [1995] 2 FCR 397, 419.

agreement are relevant for the case and equitable.[96] In *Crossley v Crossley* the pre-nuptial agreement was even considered to be a factor of magnetic importance.[97] In recent case law there is a tendency to turn this reasoning on his head and accept binding force. In *Radmacher v. Granatino*, a case on a German marital agreement, the *Supreme Court, confirming the Court of Appeal's decision*, held that in principle marital agreements will be given effect "unless in the circumstances prevailing it would not be fair to hold the parties to their agreement".[98] Since in most legal systems marital agreements are binding and the parties when concluding such an agreement abroad have relied on its binding force, the *Supreme Court* saw it as a matter of fairness to give the agreement binding force to the greatest possible extent.[99] Although the case concerned a foreign marital agreement, the judgment is formulated in general terms, so that the ratio could also be applied to English marital agreements.[100]

In Ireland a marital agreement can be considered as part of the circumstances of the case.[101] In Scotland a marital agreement has binding force but it can be set aside if it was not fair and reasonable at the time it was entered into.[102]

4. COMPARATIVE PERSPECTIVES

4.1. DEFAULT REGIMES

In continental law there is a large identifiable division between the Romanic legal systems, which, together with the Middle and Eastern European legal systems favour a community of acquests, and the Germanic and Nordic legal systems which are more familiar with a participation system, consisting of a separation of property in combination with a deferred community or statutory compensation clause.

It is readily apparent, upon making a functional comparison between common law and continental law, that there are great similarities between English law

---

96 *K v K* (ancillary relief: pre-nuptial agreement [2003] 1 FLR 120; *Crosley v Crosley* [2007] EWCA Civ 1941, 1 FLR 1467; MacLeod v. MacLeod [2008] UKPC 64. See M. Harper and L. Alhadeff, Crosley v. Crosley: Are Pre-nuptial agreements now binding in England?, *Fam Law* 2008, 334.

97 [2007] EWCA Civ 1941, at para. 15.

98 *Radmacher v Granatino* [2010] UKSC 42, para 75.

99 Cf. J. Scherpe, 'Foreign Marital Agreements: the Approach of the English Courts', [2010] *Private Client Business* 190.

100 See also J. Scherpe, 'Eheverträge im Recht von England und Wales', *FamRZ* 2009, 1538.

101 See G. Shannon, 'Irish report', in Boele-K. Woelki et al. (n 1), Question 191.

102 S. 16 Family Law Act 1985. See J. Mair, 'Scottish report', in Boele-Woelki et al. (n 1), Question 191 and 201.

and the continental participation systems.[103] There are several indications that in practice, English law, even without a formal matrimonial property regime, is increasingly tending towards a type of deferred community, where judges retain wide judicial discretion.[104]

The judicial discretion is wider in common law than in civil law systems and much wider than in those having a community of acquests. The comparison between civil and common law reveals the tension between systems with detailed rules and systems with a wide judicial discretion.[105] Rules offer certainty, judicial discretion has the advantage of producing an individual solution based upon fairness. On the other hand, discretion also implies uncertainty and unpredictability, since the outcome depends to a certain extent on the approach of the judge.[106]

Both the community and participation systems emphasise the importance of spousal autonomy during the marriage, which is evident, not only in the composition of the assets, but also in the rules governing their administration. However, while they express it in different forms, both systems also attach great importance to the solidarity of spouses towards each other. Matrimonial solidarity in community systems is realised during the marriage by the creation of a community, which is administered by both spouses. Thus a spouse already has access to the other's wealth during the marriage and this differs greatly from the participation systems.[107] In this sense a community system creates equality from the very start of the marriage.[108] Given that participation systems are based upon separation of property, there of course is no participation during marriage, and only limited matrimonial solidarity which in most cases is given effect to via the general law of marriage.

Solidarity upon marital dissolution is also expressed differently in each system. In the community systems solidarity finds its expression through the equal division of the community, although this is of course limited to the acquests. Each spouse

[103] Cf. J. Scherpe, 'Matrimonial Causes for Concern? – A Comparative Analysis of Miller v Miller; McFarlane v McFarlane', (2007) 18 *King's Law Journal* 348, esp.. 356 ff.

[104] St. Cretney, 'Community of Property Imposed by Judicial Decision', *LQR* 2003, 349; W. Pintens, 'Europeanisation of Family Law', in K. Boele-Woelki (ed.), 'Perspectives for the Unification and Harmonisation of Family Law in Europe', in EFL Series, n° 4, Antwerp, 2003, 12; comp. J Scherpe, (2007) 18 *King's Law Journal* 356 ff. In Miller v. Miller; McFarlane v. McFarlane Baroness Hale stated that England and Wales "do not yet have a system of community of property, whether full or deferred" ([2006] UKHL 151). The 'yet' lets presume, that in the future such a development seems to be possible. A keen interest for matrimonial property regimes grows more and more. See E. Cooke, A. Barlow and T. Callus, *Community of Property. A Regime for England and Wales?*, London, 2006.

[105] J. Miles and S. Harris-Short (n 59), 569.

[106] J. Miles and S. Harris-Short (n 59), 570.

[107] A. Lüderitz and N. Dethloff (n 1), 146 f.

[108] A. Röthel, 'Die Zugewinngemeinschaft als europäisches Modell?', in V. Lipp et al. (n 1), 66.

has a right *in rem* to half of the community. Although the personal property of each spouse is not taken into account, there is some solidarity in this respect because income from personal property is often a component of the community. With the exception of the possibility for preferential assignments, most judges enjoy no discretion and can therefore not effect a reallocation. Participation systems lead to deferred communities or to compensation. The extent of the property to be distributed or compensated varies according to the legal system at issue. Most legal systems which have a broad definition of this property grant the courts discretion to delimit the assets to be distributed on equitable grounds.

In light of the rules on the composition of the categories of property, it is apparent that community systems afford spouses less autonomy than participation systems. However, they do enable the spouse who has limited or no income to exercise a certain amount of autonomy as he directly acquires common property and partakes in the administration of that asset. Participation systems grant the spouses a greater degree of autonomy, which is usually curtailed only by the law on marriage. The spouse who has no wealth of his own, nor accumulates any, cannot enjoy this autonomy as he does not acquire rights to the assets during the marriage and is therefore also not party to its administration. He or she may only make everyday dispositions with money which the other spouse has put at his disposal by virtue of his duty to contribute to the costs of the marriage. Although participation systems are a good compromise between community systems and pure separation systems, they better suit spouses who are financially independent, whereas community systems better suit spouses who are not so independent. The major differences in composition and administration of the assets impair the creation of a European default regime based on a *ius commune*.

The legal systems have a greater number of unifying features in relation to participation upon marital dissolution such that it is possible to ascertain a common core. Through their equal distribution, community systems ensure that each spouse can participate in the wealth that the other spouse acquired during marriage. The same goal is accomplished in participation systems, either by division of the deferred community, by reallocation or by compensation. In most legal systems, judicial discretion and exceptions to the general rules lead to a participation which is also limited to assets acquired during marriage by the spouses in ways other than by gift or inheritance. The basic principle in both systems is that each spouse should be able to partake in the wealth acquired by the other during marriage, independently of the distribution of duties between the spouses as these gains are in fact products of both spouses' labour.[109]

[109] Comp. A. Lüderitz and N. Dethloff (n 1), 146.

The differences between both leading systems will not be easily overcome. Those who support a community system as a default regime, emphasise the balance between independence and solidarity as well as the participation of both spouses in the community and its administration, including that of the spouse who has no income of his own. In addition, they criticise the complexity of certain participation systems, especially those with a statutory compensation clause. German law provides an extreme example as it admits the complexity of its system by only applying a mathematical settlement of surplus values on divorce, where, upon death, settlement is replaced with a fixed increase of the inheritance rights of the surviving spouse (§ 1371 BGB).[110] Those who support a separation of property in combination with a deferred community or a compensation clause mainly emphasise the great independence that each spouse enjoys during marriage. They fear the danger of deadlock when both spouses administer the community, which they consider to be an obstruction to the free market, and they fear shared liability for debts.[111]

Some of these views and concerns are however based upon misunderstandings and extreme examples. A comparison between the community systems and the German participation system is perhaps not the most ideal. According to the German *Zugewinnausgleich*, the spouse participates not only in the increased value[112] of the other spouse's acquisitions during the marriage but also in the property before marriage, which leads to extreme solidarity. Swiss law undoubtedly provides a better system. The accrued property consists only of acquisitions and personal property is not affected such that an equal and justified solidarity is accomplished. The danger of deadlock in the administration of the community is exaggerated because the consent of both spouses is only needed for important acts.[113] This consent is also necessary in a system of separation of property in transactions concerning joint property. Concerns regarding liability for debts should not be overstated because joint liability is restricted by the distinction which is drawn between personal and common debts.

4.2. FREEDOM OF CONTRACT

Although there is some evolution in common law broadening the autonomy of the spouses, it is not feasible to compare marital agreements under common and civil law since their content is completely different. In civil law marital agreements focus upon both the functioning of the matrimonial property regime during the

110 See also D. Schwab, 'Der Zugewinnausgleich in der Krise', in *Festschrift Söllner*, Munich 2000, 1079 ff.

111 D. Henrich, *FamRZ* 2002, 1525.

112 Except those that are the result of inflation.

113 See also A. Röthel, in V. Lipp et al. (n 1), 64 ff.

marriage and the consequences of any form of dissolution of the regime, whereas in common law the emphasis is placed upon the consequences of separation. Common law marital agreements are therefore not comparable with civil law marital agreements. They should be compared with civil law divorce agreements, which are still subject to restrictions in many civil law jurisdictions.

Now that almost all Middle and Eastern European jurisdictions have abolished the obligatory matrimonial property regime and allow some choice of optional regime, a certain harmonisation has been achieved between the civil law systems. The remaining difference is that while most systems allow a broad choice of regime, some systems restrict the choice to only those optional regimes provided for in their codes.

4.3. THE QUEST FOR HARMONISATION

Initiatives of harmonisation have been extremely rare. Reasons are the variety among the legal systems and their high degree of technicality. Around 1920 the Nordic family law co-operation lead to the adoption of a similar model of matrimonial property law in all the Nordic jurisdictions. Even if later legislation resulted in the re-emergence of many differences especially in Norway and Sweden, there is still a Nordic model based upon the same approach and the same concept of solidarity.[114]

A German-French Commission elaborated a bilateral convention on a common optional regime on the basis of the German community of accrued gains (*Zugewinngemeinschaft*) and the French participation in acquests (*participation aux acquêts*).[115] This proposal is to be integrated into the civil law codes of both states and should be available to persons regardless of their nationality or habitual residence. The project is concerned exclusively with substantive norms and is neutral in international private law. On 4 February 2004 the convention was signed by France and Germany, but ratification remains pending. All Member States of the European Union have the possibility of adhering to the convention.

The European Commission is preparing a regulation on conflict of laws in matters concerning matrimonial property regimes, including the question of jurisdiction

---

114 See J. Jänterä-Jareborg and M. Brattström, 'Swedish report', in K. Boele-Woelki et al. (n 1), Question 2.

115 See M. Cubeddu, 'Modelli uniformi di regime patrimoniale convenzionale', in S. Patti and M. Cubeddu, *Introduzione al diritto della famiglia in Europa*, Milan 2008, 260 ff.; T. Klippstein, 'Der deutsch-französische Wahlgüterstand der Wahl-Zugewinngemeinschaft', *FPR* 2010, 510 ff.; T. Meyer, 'Der neue deutsch-französische Wahlgüterstand', *FamRZ* 2010, 612 ff.

and mutual recognition.[116] Although the regulation is restricted to private international law since the European Union has no competence for the unification of the substantive family law of the Member States, the last tender published by the Commission included the elaboration of an optional matrimonial property regime. Article 81 TFEU (replacing Article 65 EC) prescribes that the Union shall develop judicial cooperation in civil matters having cross-border implications, based upon the principle of mutual recognition of judgments and of decisions in extra-judicial cases. Such cooperation may include the adoption of measures for the approximation of the laws and regulations of the Member States. Article 81 TFEU offers a basis for unification of substantive law in cross-border cases.[117]

The Commission on European Family Law currently is drafting principles of European family law regarding property relations between spouses based, where possible, on the common core of the European legal systems and, where necessary, improved with a better law approach.[118]

All those initiatives are not only a stimulus for comparative research in a field that comparative law has for so long neglected. These initiatives and this research will also lead to a better understanding and a rapprochement of the European legal systems. They will provoke spontaneous harmonisation and perhaps even unification. There is no reason to fear this evolution. The advantages will clearly supersede the disadvantages because harmonisation will lead to more certainty in cross-border cases and will contribute to a truly European area of law and justice. The beneficiaries of this will be the European citizens. This is surely what Europe should be all about.

116 See the Green paper of 20.7. 2006, COM (2006) 400 final.

117 W. Pintens, 'Harmonisierung im europäischen Familien- und Erbrecht', *FamRZ* 2005, 1599. Cf. E. Jayme and Chr. Kohler, 'Europäisches Kollisionsrecht' 2003, *IPrax* 2003, 486 on Article III-170 of a preparatory version of the European Constitution. The content of this article is identical with Article 81 TFEU.

118 See K. Boele- Woelki and M. Jänterä-Jareborg, Initial results of the work of the CEFL in the field of property relations between spouses, in this publication. See also D. Martiny, 'Europäisches Güterrecht? Die Arbeit der CEFL', in V. Lipp et al. (n 1), 37 ff.

INITIAL RESULTS OF THE WORK OF THE CEFL IN THE FIELD OF PROPERTY RELATIONS BETWEEN SPOUSES

Katharina Boele-Woelki and Maarit Jänterä-Jareborg

INTRODUCTORY REMARKS

Since its establishment in 2001, the Commission on European Family Law (CEFL) has drafted common European Principles which address core issues of family law. In doing so, the CEFL aims to contribute to the harmonization process of private law in Europe. In carrying out comparative research and proposing Principles of European Family Law, the CEFL is independent of any organisation or institution.[1] To date, 26 European jurisdictions[2] are represented by academics, judges and practising lawyers in the work of the CEFL. These experts have been working together pursuant to a self-established method[3] which has proven to be workable. The comparison of solutions which are presented in national reports compiled in response to an extensive list of questions constitutes the fundaments on which the CEFL Principles are built. If a national legislature takes this comparative material into account and – more importantly – finally decides to use the Principles as a source of inspiration when adopting new rules in family law, the ultimate goal of the CEFL has been achieved. It goes without saying that all legislatures are free "to take it or leave it". Given their lack of any enforceability, the Principles must convince on their own, as they are formulated (*imperio rationis* instead of *ratione imperii*). In 2008, the Portuguese legislature for example, in modernizing the law of divorce and parental authority took advantage of the work of the CEFL. As a result, some of the new Portuguese rules are identical to the CEFL Principles.[4] This example is not alone in illustrating that the final results are considered to be in accordance with the scientific standard for reliable and comprehensive comparative research.[5] Moreover, CEFL Principles are not black letter rules, but guidelines to be "filtered" into national – or European – legislation.[6]

After having completed the Principles of European Family Law regarding Divorce and Maintenance between Former Spouses (2004) and the Principles of European Family Law regarding Parental Responsibilities (2007), the CEFL is currently in the process of drafting Principles regarding Property Relations between Spouses. Due to the complexity of this area of law, it is to be expected that the work will be finalized no earlier than 2013.

---

1 K. Boele-Woelki, 'The Principles of European Family Law: Its Aims and Prospects', *Utrecht Law Review* 2005, pp. 160–168.

2 Most European Union Member States are represented with the involvement of experts from Norway, Russia and Switzerland.

3 See for an explanation: K. Boele-Woelki, 'The Working Method of the Commission on European Family Law', in: K. Boele-Woelki, (ed), *Common Core and Better Law in European Family Law*, European Family Law series No. 10, 2005, pp. 14–38.

4 Vgl. G. de Oliveira, 'Changes Going on in Portuguese Family Law', *FamRZ* 2008, pp. 1712–1714.

5 E. Örücü, 'Viewing the Work in Progress of the Commission on European Family Law', *International Law FORUM de droit international*, 2005 pp. 219–227.

6 See, eg, M. Jänterä-Jareborg, 'Europeanization of Law: Harmonization of Fragmentation – A Family Law Approach', *Tidskrift utgiven av Juridiska Föreningen i Finland*, 2010, p. 511.

This contribution aims to provide some information about the project as it currently stands. Some basic ideas regarding the possible structure of the new set of Principles as well as their content will be presented. It is meant to be a work-in-progress report.[7]

1. PREPARATORY RESULTS

The CEFL commenced its work in the field of matrimonial property in 2007; 26 national reports on this topic are available both in Volume 24[8] of the European Family Law Series[9] and on CEFL's homepage.[10] The Organising Committee has met several times since the publication of the national reports.[11] To date, however, a first overall draft has not yet been finalized. The collected material is overwhelming; the subject matter is complicated and diverse. As a result, no draft of the Principles has yet been discussed with the experts who wrote the national reports. The first meeting with the experts is planned to take place in September 2011. Just as during the drafting of the previous sets of Principles, these discussions are important to the final version of the Principles.

2. THE EXISTING EUROPEAN AND INTERNATIONAL LEGAL FRAMEWORK

For obvious reasons, the drafting of common Principles of European Family Law regarding the property relations between spouses should take the existing European and international legal framework into account.

To begin with, equality between men and women is established directly or indirectly in all European constitutions or legislation. Furthermore, this basic principle, extended to the law of family and marriage, finds support in several multilateral conventions. The most important of these, from a general European perspective, is the European Convention on Human Rights and Fundamental Freedoms of 1950, forbidding all forms of discrimination in the exercise of rights guaranteed by the Convention or as regards rights guaranteed by the

7 D. Martiny, 'Europäisches Güterrecht? Die Arbeit der CEFL', in: V. Lipp/E. Schumann/B. Veit (eds), *Die Zugewinngemeinschaft – ein europäisches Modell?*, Göttingen, 2009, pp. 39–55.

8 K. Boele-Woelki/B. Braat/I. Curry-Sumner (eds), *European Family Law, Volume IV: Property Relations between Spouses*, European Family Law series No. 24, 2009.

9 Since 2003, when the first title appeared in this series, published by the Organising Committee of the CEFL, more than 27 titles, all dealing with various aspects of family and succession law from a comparative point of view, have been published within this series.

10 Www.ceflonline.net.

11 3-5 Oct 2008 Barcelona; 12–14 Dec 2008 Frankfurt/Oder; 28–31 May 2009 Saarbrücken; 15–18 Oct 2009 Lyon; 4–7 March 2010 Barcelona; 2–4 Sept 2010 Uppsala; 9–12 Dec 2010 Utrecht.

additional Protocols supplementing the Convention. Article 5 of the Protocol No. 7 prescribes that spouses shall enjoy equality of rights and responsibilities of a private law character between them, and in their relations with their children, as to marriage, during marriage and in the event of its dissolution. However, this Article, which includes property rights, specifically provides that it shall not prevent States from taking such measures as are necessary in the interests of the children.[12] Furthermore, according to Article 1 of the first Protocol, every person is entitled to the peaceful enjoyment of his or her possessions. No one shall be deprived of his or her possessions except in the public interest and subject to the conditions provided for by law and by the general principles of international law.[13]

The European Charter of 1996, which the Lisbon Treaty "upgraded" to become a part of binding EU Treaty law, is even more explicit as regards equality between men and women, to be safeguarded within all areas.[14] European States[15] are, furthermore, parties to the United Nations Convention on the Elimination of all Forms of Discrimination against Women of 1979 which is also of immediate relevance for our topic. A special Committee on the Elimination of Discrimination against Women is at present working on a General recommendation on Economic Consequences of Marriage and Its Dissolution. The various recommendations made by the Council of Europe, dealing with different aspects of property rights betweens spouses, are naturally also of particular interest for the drafting of European Principles on the topic.[16] Recommendations of the Council of Europe are, however, not binding on Member States, and decades may have passed since they were launched, which might limit their adequacy in modern society.

3. GUIDING PRINCIPLES

As regards the *substance* of the forthcoming Principles on marital property relations, *equality* between the spouses is by no means the only principle that is to be taken into account. Principles of *sharing* and *fairness* and the promotion

12 Protocol No. 7 to the Convention for the Protection of Human Rights and Fundamental Freedoms, as amended by Protocol No. 11.

13 Protocol to the Convention for the Protection of Human Rights and Fundamental Freedoms, as amended by Protocol No. 11.

14 See Article 23 of the Charter.

15 See www.un.org.

16 Of relevance are, for example, Resolution on Equality of Spouses in Civil Law, adopted by the Committee of Ministers in September 1978; Recommendation on the Rights of the Spouses relating to the Occupation of the Family Home and the Use of the Household Contents, adopted by the Committee of Ministers in October 1981; Recommendation on Contributions following Divorce, adopted by the Committee of Ministers in January 1989; Recommendation on Gender Equality Standards and Mechanisms adopted by the Committee of Ministers in November 2007 and the Declaration on Making Gender Equality a Reality adopted by the Committee of Ministers in May 2009.

of *party-autonomy* are likewise of fundamental importance in this area of law. The *drafting* of the Principles, on the other hand, should be guided by concerns of *simplicity*, meaning that the proposed system should be relatively easy to understand even by people who are not lawyers and that the proposed solutions should be such as to enable spouses to settle their conflicts on their own without needing to engage lawyers and courts in the dispute. According to Swedish research, for example, 80% of divorced couples divide their assets by themselves without the help of, or 'interference' by, lawyers.[17] Inquiries show that couples who managed to share their assets without legal assistance are clearly more satisfied with the outcome than those who 'trusted' a lawyer.[18] Hence, if a system is too complicated or contains too many details, couples will have difficulties in comprehending what the rules prescribe which, in turn, can be a seedbed for legal disputes.

The crucial question is how to strike a balance between the different goals. Equal sharing might turn out to be unfair and in conflict with the aim of promoting party autonomy. Too much emphasis on the freedom of the spouses to determine their property relations might, on the other hand, lead to unfair results. Striving for simplicity in the proposed set of Principles brings the danger that the inevitable complexity of the division of property is not properly taken into account. Nor can one disregard the differences in the "legal milieu" in which divorce proceedings take place in the various European jurisdictions.[19]

4. CROSS-BORDER RELATIONSHIPS

During the last decades, all over Europe, marriages between persons of different nationalities and domicile/habitual residence have become more and more common.[20] In fact, this is also a global trend in large parts of the world. For more

---

17 During the Conference, Dr. Margareta Brattström focused participants' attention on her ongoing research in Sweden. An explanation of these Swedish experiences may be the "simplicity" of Swedish divorce proceedings, which are normally carried out without any assistance by lawyers. Moreover, the grant of divorce in Sweden is not dependent on the legal consequences of a divorce having been settled by the spouses. On the contrary, it is common in Sweden that spouses first divorce, and then settle the ancillary questions, such as property division. See K. Boele-Woelki/B. Braat/I. Curry-Sumner (eds), *European Family Law in Action, Volume I: Grounds for Divorce*, European Family Law series No. 2, 2003.

18 Again, we refer to Margareta Brattström's comments, ibid. An explanation is, most likely, that couples who manage on their own avoid the often considerable costs that a legal dispute would give rise to. When rules are clear and simple, there is not too much that is worth quarrelling about.

19 A crucial difference is that in many European jurisdictions the granting of a divorce requires that all relevant ancillary matters have been settled between the spouses. To our knowledge there are no empirical studies on how such differences affect the outcome of property division.

20 For example, according to recent EU statistics, of the 2.4 million marriages concluded within the EU in 2007, 300.000 were estimated to be "transnational". Of the 1.040.000 divorces

than thirty years, the issue of conflict of laws has been addressed in one of the Conventions adopted at The Hague Conference on Private International Law. This Convention on the Law Applicable to Matrimonial Property Regimes[21] has not turned out to be very successful in terms of ratifications; only France, Luxemburg and The Netherlands have ratified it. Yet this Convention has served as a source of inspiration in the drafting of choice of law rules in States which have abstained from ratifying it: for example in Finland and Sweden, in both cases years after the Convention's adoption.[22] Above all, the 1978 Hague Convention has paved the way for international acceptance of party autonomy in many jurisdictions, in the form of spouses' and future spouses' freedom to choose the law applicable to their matrimonial property regime.

In 2006, the choice of law rules concerning matrimonial property relations were revised in the Convention between Denmark, Finland, Iceland, Norway and Sweden on Issues of Private International Law concerning Marriage, Adoption and Guardianship,[23] originally from 1931. The new rules, endorsing spouses' and future spouses' right to choose the law applicable, came into force in all the Nordic countries on 1 December 2008. The focus on party autonomy was chosen to reflect the increasing differences between the Nordic States in respect of substantive matrimonial property law.[24] The Convention applies only to spouses who at the date of their marriage are citizens in a Nordic State, upon marriage take their habitual residence in a Nordic State, and maintain their habitual residence and citizenship in the Nordic States. In this way, it aims at facilitating free movement between the Nordic countries which have had a joint labour market for their citizens since 1955.

granted that year within the EU, 13% were estimated to be transnational. See COM(2010) 104 final, 2010/0066 (APP) Brussels, 24 March 2010.

21 Concluded in The Hague on 14 March 1978.

22 The Finnish rules were enacted in 2002. The Swedish rules were enacted in 1990. The preparatory works to both enactments specially refer to the Hague Convention as a source of inspiration. The adopted rules differ from the Hague Convention in some respects.

23 The Swedish Governmental Bill concerning this reform, Prop. 2006/07:60, explains the reasons behind the reform and the chosen solutions. This reform is commented by E. Meurling, 'Less Surprise for Spouses Moving Between the Nordic Countries? Amendments to the 1931 Nordic Convention on Marriage', *Yearbook of Private International Law* 2009, pp. 385–394.

24 Another novelty, corresponding to the increasing differences in substantive law, concerns the change of the law applicable in those cases where the spouses have not chosen the applicable law. In such cases, the law of the Nordic spouses' new habitual residence becomes applicable once it has lasted for two years, and covers all the spouses' property, ie, even property acquired before the change of habitual residence within the Nordic countries. Before this reform, the applicable law changed automatically and immediately upon change of habitual residence, and no party autonomy existed.

Brand new in this field is the bilateral Franco-German Agreement of February 2010[25] (not yet in force) which provides couples whose matrimonial property relations – according to German or French conflict of law rules – are governed by either German or French law with the possibility to choose the special, optional matrimonial property regime which has been established in this Convention (hereafter COMPR). The Agreement is not limited to German or French couples or to mixed German-French couples, but covers all spouses who, according to the applicable choice of law in a concerned State, are free to choose French or German law as applicable to their matrimonial property relations, given the spouses' or one of the spouse's connection to France or Germany.[26] As ANDREAS FÖTSCHL points out, "[E]very PIL-system that allows a couple to choose French or German law for their matrimonial regime also opens itself to the possibility of applying the COMPR".[27] In other words, even if the Convention primarily establishes a new matrimonial property regime (consisting of substantive family law rules) to be implemented in the national laws of both France and Germany, it also has a private international law dimension. Interestingly enough, the Convention does not exclude other European Union Member States from becoming parties to it, once it has been ratified by France and Germany.[28]

This bilateral Convention may surprise many, considering that the Member States of the EU are at present awaiting uniform private international law rules on matrimonial property relations (jurisdiction, applicable law and recognition and enforcement). The proposal for such a Regulation, to be presented by the Commission, is expected during 2011, following the earlier Green Paper[29] in which the EU indicated its interest in taking action in this area of law. Do Germany and France have the competence to enter into a bilateral treaty in an area where the EU plans to take legislative measures? Those aspects of their treaty that have a clear private international law dimension are, in other words, problematic from

25 Accord entre la République fédérale d'Allemagne et la République française instituant un régime matrimonial optionnel de la participation aux acquêts. For the background to this Agreement and the incentives, see A. FÖTSCHL, 'The Common Optional Matrimonial Property Regime of Germany and France – Epoch-Making in the Unification of Law', *Yearbook of Private International Law* 2009, pp. 395–404, also published in the *European Review of Private Law* 2010 pp. 881–889. See also M. BRAEUER, 'Der neue deutsch-französische Wahlgüterstand', *Forum Familienrecht* 2010, pp. 113–115.

26 See Article 1 concerning the scope of application of the Convention.

27 Ibid., (note 25) p. 402. An example of the private international law scope of the COMPR is the following: According to Swedish conflict of law rules, contained in an Act of 1990, when the wife is a German national and the husband a Swedish national, the spouses may choose German law as the law applicable to their matrimonial property relations and through the choice of German law, the regime established by the COMPR.

28 FÖTSCHL indicates as an explanation that France and Germany view themselves as the "motors of integration" in Europe, ibid, (note 25) p. 403. Indeed, with this self-image, it may appear natural to expect that other Member States of the EU will follow.

29 Green Paper on conflict of laws in matters concerning matrimonial property regimes, including the question of jurisdiction and mutual recognition, COM 2006/400, 17 July 2006.

the point of view of legislative competence at this stage of development in EU law. What about the duty of loyalty of these two Members States towards the EU in this respect? It is difficult to deny that the bilateral Convention will have an impact on the future operation of the coming EU-rules.[30]

Whatever the answer to these issues of competence and loyalty, we find it tempting to make a comparison with another long-planned and well-prepared treaty project, namely the revision of the Convention between Denmark, Finland, Iceland, Norway and Sweden on Rules of Private International Law concerning Inheritance, originally from 1934. The inter-Nordic working party had almost finalized its draft for the revision of this Convention when the Commission presented its proposal for an EU Regulation on the private international law aspects of inheritance law.[31] Although the Nordic draft was finalized shortly afterwards,[32] it was also concluded that the interest demonstrated by the EU to take legislative measures prevented, at least at this stage, the Nordic EU Member States from proceeding further with the inter-Nordic reform. If the Franco-German cooperation can be carried out as established in the bilateral Convention, it will constitute a most interesting and important precedent for future models of cooperation between European States. Indeed, the forthcoming CEFL Principles may then provide a true European model.[33]

No doubt, all the instruments on matrimonial property relations discussed above will need to be carefully analysed and taken into account in the forthcoming CEFL Principles. These Principles will – as in the previous sets of Principles – consist of the black letter text of each Principle together with: an overview of the International instruments on the issues dealt with by that Principle; a comparative overview of the issue addressed in the Principle; and, finally, an explanation of *why* the Principle has been drafted as proposed, provided in the comments to the Principle. The comparative information compiled in one volume of Principles is drafted with the aim of covering all relevant aspects of the regulation of property relations between spouses, at least as far as European systems[34] are concerned.

[30] Fötschl holds another opinion. According to him, competence is shared between the Union and the Member States of the EU. Furthermore, the COMPR is intended as a substantive law European regime. Fötschl, ibid. (note 25), pp. 398–399.

[31] Proposal for a Regulation of the European Parliament and of the Council on jurisdiction, applicable law, recognition and enforcement of decisions and authentic instruments in matters of succession and on the introduction of a European Certificate on Inheritance, COM(2009) 154 final, of 14 October 2009.

[32] Revidering av de internordiska reglerna om arv, testamente och boutredning, Den Nordiska Expertgruppen för Familjerätt, Januari 2010.

[33] See also Fötschl, ibid. (note 25), p. 401.

[34] It should be emphasized that the CEFL Principles are not only aimed for EU Member States but for all jurisdictions in Europe, as is reflected in the range of comparative surveys in the preparatory work of the forthcoming CEFL Principles.

For national legislatures considering reform in this area, a blueprint for reform is handed to them on a silver platter!

5. OTHER PROPOSALS AND THE CEFL

We are, naturally, fully aware of the fact that discussion about the introduction of one particular European matrimonial property regime is ongoing. In this respect, the recently launched Franco-German optional regime is just the latest of several proposals. Previously, in 1995, ANDERS AGELL[35] and, later in 2001, ALAIN VERBEKE[36] had proposed the drafting of a Treaty presenting a uniform law, available for spouses to choose, in the form of an optional international marital property agreement. The idea was, primarily, that on entering into a marriage, the spouses should be allowed to choose a treaty-based substantive matrimonial property law regime aimed at international marriages, just as they may choose any other regime, if alternative regimes are available under national law. However, the European Commission's Green Paper on Conflicts of Laws in Matters Concerning Matrimonial Property Regimes, Including the Question of Jurisdiction and Mutual Recognition of 17 July 2006 did not deal with this specific idea. This is to be regretted since it would have been interesting to know how an optional European matrimonial property regime would have been received in the Member States. Unexpectedly, however, in 2009, the European Commission requested an impact assessment (of community instruments on the rights of property arising out of matrimonial property regimes and property of unmarried couples[37]) which mainly focuses on the possibility of drafting an optional uniform European matrimonial property regime.[38] A draft of such a regime has recently been submitted by a group of European notaries.[39]

---

35 This initiative of Anders Agell was originally launched in a meeting of the Council of Europe in Cadíz, Spain in 1995. See further, A. AGELL, 'The Division of Property upon Divorce from a European Perspective', in: *Liber amicorum Marie-Thérèse Meulders-Klein: Droit comparé des personnes et de la famille,* 1998, pp. 1–20 (18–20).

36 A. VERBEKE, 'Perspectives for an International Marital Contract', *Maastricht Journal of European and Comparative Law,* 2001, pp. 189–200.

37 Task specifications for the assignment were issued by Direction E: Justice.

38 The institution undertaking the impact assessment is asked to: (1) assess the feasibility of such a uniform European optional regime; (2) analyse the added value, advantages and problems of such European optional regime and its certification; (3) assess the likely impacts – positive and negative – of such measures for citizens, stakeholders and Member States; (4) assess the main difficulties of this proposal; and (5) assess – if possible – whether there might be any relevant impact on the activity of stakeholders and on taxation.

39 F. SALERNO CARDILLO, (rapporteur), Propositions pour un contrat de mariage "Européen". The proposal contains the essential elements (*choix du régime matrimonial, loi applicable au régimes matrimonial, propriété des biens, pouvoirs des époux, inventaire – preuves et présomptions, dettes des époux, modification du régime, effets, publicité, opposabilité aux tiers, clauses particulaires*) of a marriage contract in which the spouses have designated the applicable (national) law governing their matrimonial property or in which it is stated which law (objectively) is to be applied.

All in all, when comparing these initiatives with the mission of the CEFL, we have to keep in mind that harmonisation of the different national matrimonial property regimes is not the primary aim of an optional European matrimonial property regime. Rather the aim there is to provide a tailor-made optional regime for spouses with cross-border links. The application of such a regime therefore depends on three conditions: first, that the property relationship of the spouses crosses borders, because of the different nationalities or habitual residences of the spouses; second, that the spouses explicitly choose this special European regime; and third, that the relevant conflict of law rules allow the application of this kind of supra-national matrimonial property law. By contrast, the work of the CEFL strives primarily towards harmonization of national law.

6. CRUCIAL CHOICES AND CONSIDERATIONS

In drafting European Principles for matrimonial property relations, the most crucial question for the CEFL is whether the Principles should focus on only one European matrimonial property regime or whether we should also offer draft Principles on an alternative matrimonial property regime. This issue has not yet been decided in favour of the one or the other. From the outset, it has been extensively discussed. Several issues must be taken into account:

First, six different systems can be distinguished within Europe. Roughly speaking, it is possible to divide these systems into two main systems: *A community system* on the one side and a *separation system* on the other side. In order to establish a model for a community system – which will most likely entail a community of acquisitions – we will derive our ideas from both systems of community of property and community of accrued gains. The other system which will probably be developed – the separation system – will be based upon systems such as participation in acquisitions, deferred community, separation of property and separation of property with distribution by the competent authority. The national reports contain extensive information on all these systems.

Second, it is self-evident that elements of all systems cannot be merged into one single matrimonial property regime. Indeed, the basic starting points may be diametrically opposed. In some systems, a community of property between the spouses automatically takes effect at the moment of concluding the marriage, whereas in other systems no community of property will ever arise by operation of law (*ex lege*): the property of each spouse is treated as the owner spouse's personal/separate property. Elsewhere, community of property may only come into existence later: deferred to the moment of dissolution of the marriage or the property regime.

Third, reducing the number of systems to only two might show that harmonisation of the law is possible within these two systems. Such a result – and the resulting simplicity compared to present law – might be regarded as a major achievement.

At this moment, we have almost finished drafting a proposal concerning Principles on a community of acquisition system, whereas we have just started drafting the second system. As a working title, we still describe this second system as "the separation of property regime". However, this might change, depending on the choices to be made as to whether we might introduce a new term such as "post-marital sharing" system or something along these lines. This is under discussion.

Once a draft exists on Principles for both systems, we will test them by asking "how are specific cases solved?" Subsequently, the results will be compared with the aim of identifying commonalities between both systems. When trying to do this, our focus will be on the dissolution of marriage, and in particular on situations of potential disagreement. This is the most critical and highly contentious part of the property relationship between spouses. In addition, the focus on divorce is in line with our first three sets of principles (divorce, spousal maintenance after divorce and parental responsibilities).

Finally, we are very much looking forward to the discussion with our experts. The discussions will be open and instructive. Still, we find it unlikely that our experts will advocate a totally different route having regard to the collected comparative material. At this stage, we think it inappropriate for us to choose only one of the two main systems mentioned above. The variety of existing systems hugely complicates the choice and we do not expect that circumstances will substantially change in a way which would make such a choice much easier.

7. STRUCTURE

The CEFL Principles on matrimonial property relations will most likely consist of three parts. However, the discussion about the precise order of these three parts is still to be finalized. At this stage of work, our plan is that the Principles should start by stating the existence of certain basic rights and duties of the spouses which would apply irrespective of the applicable matrimonial property regime(s). The rights and duties addressed in this part concern issues of spousal responsibility for family expenses, and protection of the family home and household goods, in the interests of both spouses and their children. A second part is planned to provide the structure and contents of the proposed matrimonial property regime. It has just been explained how difficult the decision will be: should we propose Principles for one system or two systems? To provide for more than two regimes would seem to be out of the question for various reasons. Finally, a third part should contain Principles relating to marital property agreements.

The basic question is whether we should take a more traditional view by structuring these three parts as follows:

I General rights and duties	**II Matrimonial Property Regimes**	**III Marital Property Agreements**
Fundamental rights and duties	Community of acquisitions	Pre-nuptial
Family home Household goods	Participation in acquisitions	Post-nuptial

Another possibility is to re-order parts II and III.

I General rights and duties	**III Marital Property Agreements**	**II Matrimonial Property Regimes**
Fundamental rights and duties	Pre-nuptial	Community of acquisitions
Family home Household goods	Post-nuptial	Participation in acquisitions

Under this alternative structure, marital property agreements would be addressed before presenting the Principles for the 'default' regimes. The latter Principles would then apply if the spouses had not stipulated the rules of their marital property relationship. Which structure is to be preferred? The answer requires careful thought, since both structures contain a message. Moreover, it depends for instance on to what extent – for example, independently of the applicable default system – we should emphasize party-autonomy. In any event, both issues are interlinked.

8. CONCEPTS

8.1. RIGHTS AND DUTIES

A draft of the Principles of the first part – concerning the generally applicable rights and duties – has almost been finalized. The idea is that rules of this kind should apply irrespective of the matrimonial property regime and any agreements between the spouses. As a result, the proposed solutions should be mandatorily applicable, which means that spouses should not be able to set them aside by agreement. In this part, two different types of Principles can be distinguished. First, the spouses' rights entailing full equality and, evidently also, full legal capacity, which means that they are free to enter into legal transactions with each other and with third persons. Second, the spouses' duties in respect of the family expenses and the household. To the extent that they are able to do so, both spouses should contribute to the expenses of the household, the personal needs of each other, and the maintenance, upbringing and education of the children. The common core of the jurisdictions surveyed reveals that taking care of the children and the family home is regarded as a contribution to family expenses, and it is suggested that this outlook should be followed.

Whether the spouses should be jointly and severally liable for the debts incurred by one of them to meet appropriate family expenses has not yet been decided. It will not come as a surprise that we consider it to be of paramount importance that the family home and the household goods should be protected through special provisions. This can be achieved through making any legally valid act disposing of rights in the home or household goods dependent on the spouses' joint consent. Retrospective consent by one of the spouses to a disposal effected by the other should also suffice. Finally, one spouse may authorise the other to represent him or her in legal transactions; and, if a spouse is unable to express his or her intentions, a decision of the competent authority should be requested. Furthermore, there may be reason to have a Principle in this part providing the spouses with a duty to inform each other about the administration of "community" property or about important acts of administration of one's own "personal" property. This will be included in the first part on the spouses' rights and duties.

8.2. COMMUNITY OF ACQUISITIONS

A draft proposal on Principles establishing a community of acquisitions has almost been completed. If Principles based on this regime are approved, this regime will be applied if the spouses have not stipulated by contract how they want to regulate their property relationship. In other words, it is aimed to apply as a default regime. All relevant situations which might arise at the beginning, during and end of the marriage should be taken into account; this concern was reflected in the questionnaire completed by national experts.

To begin with, we should know what the concept of the community of acquisitions entails. We have thought along the following lines. Three different kinds of property exist: the community property, the personal property of the wife and the personal property of the husband. The first Principle of the community of acquisitions regime might, in consequence, be formulated as follows:

1. The community of acquisitions is a matrimonial property regime comprising community property and personal property.

2. Community property is property acquired during the community of acquisitions which is not personal property.
3. Personal property is each spouse's own property.

More importantly, the composition of the community property and the personal property is to be defined. Substitution, investment and reinvestment are to be addressed, since it is essential to know which of the three kinds of property have been used to that end and, as a result, which one will be affected. Whether pension rights, insurance rights, gifts and bequests should be specifically covered by their own Principles is not yet decided. A Principle stating that assets that are not personal property are reputably presumed to be community property is deemed to be necessary. Furthermore, we need to decide which debts are community debts and which are personal debts, and from which property the different debts may be recovered. In addition, administration of the community and the personal property requires attention. When it comes to dissolution of the community of acquisitions – remember, we focus on divorce – the exact time of the dissolution must be determined, since this date is relevant for the determination and the valuation of the community property. At this stage, compensation for financial contributions made from the community property to the personal property, and vice versa, would also take place, and so must be addressed. At the very end of the whole process, the community of property would be dissolved and distributed. In the absence of a spousal agreement, the division should be in equal shares, and it might be proposed that the competent authority should have the power to allocate the family home to one of the spouses In cases of exceptional hardship, the competent authority should be able to deviate from the 50/50% division of the community property.

8.3. PARTICIPATION IN ACQUISITIONS

In contrast to the Principles on community of acquisitions, Principles establishing a participation in acquisitions would only comprise the personal property of each spouse. Principles concerning this regime will most likely cover the same issues that have just been discussed under the community of acquisitions regime. We have to deal with the composition of personal property; we have to draft a presumption of joint property which should not be mixed up with the term community of property; and we have to address debts, administration and the dissolution of the regime. At this stage, the information we can give you about the content of this part of our draft is very limited since we have just started to work on this second "default" regime. The first Principle of this regime might be formulated as follows:

1. The Participation in acquisitions is a matrimonial property regime in which each spouse's property is the owner spouse's personal property.
2. Upon dissolution of the regime, the spouses participate in the acquisitions made during the regime.

8.4. MARITAL PROPERTY AGREEMENTS

Marital agreements have not yet been discussed at all. Some general ideas have been ventured. The starting point should be that spouses should have the freedom and the responsibility to determine their property relationship according to their individual needs. The key is enhancing party autonomy. Undoubtedly, agreements should have to be in writing. A more complicated issue to address is whether some form of independent legal advice should be required preceding the conclusion of the agreement, and even whether some form/extent of disclosure should be required from both parties. It should be noted that in many countries, the spouses draft the agreement on their own and that most European jurisdictions do not require disclosure. The English preference for the inclusion of such formal requirements lacks counterparts elsewhere. But also, for example, Nordic lawyers find continental notaries' involvement in drafting foreign, having no counterpart in the Nordic states' laws. Furthermore, what limits, if any, should there be on the spouses' autonomy? Most importantly, how far does the adage *pacta sunt servanda* reach? In what circumstances should the competent authority intervene, if requested, to determine a dispute between spouses who are not in agreement anymore? So far, these appear to be among the most relevant issues which we have to deal with. In this context, we will naturally take into consideration the UK Supreme Court's reasoning in its judgment in the case of *Radmacher* v. *Granatino*.[40]

CONCLUDING REMARKS

A lot of work still needs to be carried out. However, we see some light at the end of the tunnel, and we have high hopes that the first meeting with our experts, which is planned to take place in September 2011, will enlighten us even more. At that time, the Proposal for the EU Regulation on matrimonial property will have been published. It would be a good moment to provide Europeans with common Principles as to how the national legislatures can draft their substantive law when the Regulation enters into force. If national legislatures feel inspired by our solutions and legislate accordingly, more harmonization in Europe will be

[40] Judgment of 20 October 2010, [2010] UKSC 42.

achieved. This aim cannot be attained by the EU Regulation, which only unifies private international law rules.

PART THREE

FAMILY CONTRACTS – ISSUES OF AUTONOMY

CONTRACTING IN FAMILY LAW: A EUROPEAN PERSPECTIVE

NINA DETHLOFF*

* The author wishes to thank Alexandra Maschwitz and Gianna Velte for their valuable assistance in the preparation of this publication.

1. INTRODUCTION

Honoré de Balzac proclaimed that to enter into a marriage contract was one of the holiest duties of a couple about to get married.[1] In his novel *Le contrat de mariage* he describes the long and intricate negotiations that traditionally took place in France before marriage, not only in aristocratic but also in bourgeois families. Contracts with regard to matrimonial property are to date an integral part of most Continental European legal systems, as is the ensuing freedom of contract. In English common law, on the contrary, pre- or post-nuptial contracts were for a long time considered to violate public policy, and only recently have courts begun to accord them a role in the granting of financial relief upon divorce.

This controversy about party autonomy and its boundaries goes to the heart of marriage and family law: in family law, contracting can affect either the parent-child relationship, as do agreements on the exercise of parental responsibility, or affect affiliation or surrogacy agreements.[2] Such contracts involve children as third parties, who are in particular need of the state's protection. Different questions generally arise when adults enter into agreements concerning their relationship: why and to what extent should they be free to determine the rights and obligations during the existence or upon the dissolution of their relationship? The degree to which couples may regulate their partnership by contract raises fundamental questions as to the role of marriage law in pluralistic societies. What is the state's role vis-à-vis increasingly diverse forms of partnerships and in view of a growing acceptance of different life styles and religious or ideological views? The answers to these questions vary: on the one hand, according to a postmodern view, we can dispense with marriage law completely and the regulation of intimate relationships should be left to private ordering.[3] On the other hand, there is a marked tendency to create new types of partnerships in response to the increasing diversity of family life.[4] In many Western countries, registered partnerships or civil unions provide new options for couples. In some parts of the US, state-sponsored alternative forms of marital agreement such as covenant

---

1 H. De Balzac, *Le contrat de mariage*, 1835, p 37.

2 For agreements on parental responsibility see K. Boele-Woelki, B. Braat and I. Curry-Sumner (eds), *European Family Law in Action, Volume III: Parental Responsibilities*, Intersentia, Antwerp, 2005, questions 17, 56 et seq and the discussion in K. Boele-Woelki et al (eds), *Principles of European Family Law Regarding Parental Responsibilities*, Intersentia, Antwerp, 2007, concerning principle 3:13.

3 B. Stark, 'Marriage Proposals: From One-Size-Fits-All to Postmodern Marriage Law', 89 *Cal. L. Rev. (California Law Review)* (2001), pp 1479–1548; C. Jones, 'A Marriage Proposal: Privatize It', *The Independent Review* v. XI, n. 1, (2006), 115–119.

4 For an overview N. Dethloff, 'New Models of Partnerships – Financial Consequences of Separation', in B. Verschraegen (ed), *Family Finances*, Jan Sramek Verlag, Vienna, 2009, pp 491–498; K. Boele-Woelki, 'Legal Recognition of Same-Sex Relationships within the European Union', *82 Tul. L. Rev. (Tulane Law Review)* 1949 (2007–2008).

marriages have been introduced.[5] State regulation of de facto relationships or cohabitation has also increased, especially with regard to the provision of certain financial adjustments upon the dissolution of the partnership.[6]

Whether we thus move from status to contract, back from contract to status or perhaps also towards a growing recognition of de facto relationships, is an old and ongoing controversy.[7] From a comparative perspective, the answer may well be that all of the above is true: the more varied family life has become, the more varied the legal responses will probably have to be. But whether traditional marriage alone is recognised, new forms of partnership created, or even the regulation of the partnership at least generally left to private ordering, the question remains how a balance can be struck between private autonomy and the ensuring of fundamental fairness for the economically vulnerable spouse upon the partners' separation.

The aim is to explore this increasingly intricate balancing process from a comparative perspective. Analysing party autonomy and its limits regarding the economic consequences of divorce with a view to the divergence and convergence in the treatment of pre- and post-nuptial contracts in Europe will serve a dual purpose: when considering law reforms or the future development of case-law, comparative law can serve as a fountain of inspiration in the debate on future

5 Cf. the statutory options of a covenant marriage in Louisiana (Covenant Marriage Act, 1997 La. Acts 1380 codified at LA. REV. STAT. 9:224, 9:272 et seq) and Arizona (SB 1133, 43d Leg., 2d Reg. Sess. Ariz. 1998 codified at ARIZ. REV. STAT. 25-901 et seq and 25-125 et seq); for details see B. Stark, 'Marriage Proposals: From One-Size-Fits-All to Postmodern Marriage Law', 89 *Cal. L. Rev.* (2001), 1479 at 1487 et seq with further references.

6 N. Dethloff, 'Vermögensausgleich bei Auflösung nichtehelicher Lebensgemeinschaften', in T. Helms and J.M. Zeppernick (eds), *Festschrift Rainer Frank – Lebendiges Familienrecht*, Verlag für Standesamtswesen, Frankfurt (Main), 2008, pp 81–99; for a comparative overview see also J. M. Scherpe and N. Yassari (eds), *Die Rechtsstellung nichtehelicher Lebensgemeinschaften – The Legal Status of Cohabitants*, Mohr Siebeck, Tübingen, 2005; a detailed analysis of the situation in the US can be found in M. Garrison, 'Nonmarital Cohabitation: Social Revolution and Legal Regulation', 42 *Fam. L. Q. (Family Law Quarterly)* (2008–2009), 309 et seq.

7 H. Maine, *Ancient Law – Its Connection With the Early History of Society, and Its Relation to Modern Ideas*, John Murray, London, 1861, ch. 5; I. Schwenzer, 'The Evolution of Family Law: From Status to Contract and Relation', *EJLR (European Journal of Law Reform)* (2001), 199–202; I. Schwenzer, *Vom Status zur Realbeziehung – Familienrecht im Wandel*, Nomos, Baden-Baden, 1987; S. Hofer, D. Schwab and D. Henrich (eds), *From Status to Contract? – Die Bedeutung des Vertrages im europäischen Familienrecht*, Gieseking, Bielefeld, 2005; A. Röthel, V. Lipp and P.A. Windel (eds), *Familienrechtlicher Status und Solidarität*, Mohr Siebeck, Tübingen, 2008; H.D. Krause and D.D. Meyer, 'What Family for the 21st Century?', *AJCL (The American Journal of Comparative Law)*, Vol. 50, Supplement: American Law in a Time of Global Interdependence: U. S. National Reports to the 16th International Congress of Comparative Law (autumn 2002), 101–120.

policy.[8] Moreover, growing mobility is leading to an increase in cross-border cases where divergences are particularly problematic – as has been illustrated by the recent English judgment in *Radmacher* v *Granatino*.[9] Several initiatives aim to alleviate the harsh effects resulting from the clash of diverging national answers. Some are based on the principle of mutual recognition, as is the Commission's draft proposal for a Regulation on matrimonial property regimes, which will likely include a provision on the recognition of authentic acts.[10] Mutual recognition is also at the heart of the European Parliament's initiatives for a European Authentic Act which will also embrace the area of family law.[11] A more bottom-up approach is constituted by the idea of generating a set of precedent marital agreements for use around the world.[12] Other initiatives embark upon the creation of optional law. Thus a European matrimonial property regime was proposed some time ago.[13] The recently signed Franco-German Treaty on the common contractual matrimonial property regime of equalisation of accrued gains could also amount to the first step in the creation of a uniform property regime since the Treaty is accessible to other Member States as well.[14] The proposal for a European Marriage

8 See the comparative study chaired by J. M. SCHERPE on 'Marital Agreements and Private Autonomy in a Comparative Perspective', aiding the Law Commission's Project 'Pre-nuptial and Post-nuptial Agreements' which commenced in 2009.

9 *Radmacher v Granatino* [2010] UKSC 42; see also the previous judgment of the England and Wales Court of Appeal [2009] EWCA Civ 649 (ann. J. MONTAGUE, *Cov.L.J. (Coventry Law Journal)* (2009), 14 (1) 44–46; G. DOUGLAS, *Fam Law (Family Law)* (September 2009). For a more detailed analysis see A. MEEHAN, 'Analyse This: Radmacher v Granatino', *Fam Law* (September 2009); J. MILES, 'Radmacher v Granatino [2009] EWCA Civ 649: 'Upping the ante-nuptial agreement', (2009) 21 (4) *CFLQ (Child and Family Law Quarterly)*; for difficulties in cross-border cases see N. DETHLOFF, 'Arguments for the Unification and Harmonisation of Family Law in Europe', in K. BOELE-WOELKI (ed), *Perspectives for the Unification and Harmonisation of Family Law in Europe*, Intersentia, Antwerp, 2003, pp 37–64.

10 See European Commission, *Report of the public hearing of 28 September 2009 – Preparation of a Community instrument on matrimonial property regimes and the patrimonial consequences of separation of couples in a cross-border context*, JLS E.2/FT/D/2009/17541.

11 *European Parliament, Resolution of 18 December 2008 with recommendations to the Commission on the European Authentic Act* (2008/2124(INI)) at para F and M; see also Council of the Notariats of the European Union (CNUE), *Comparative Study on Authentic Instruments – National Provisions of Private Law, Circulation, Mutual Recognition and Enforcement, Possible Legislative Initiative by the European Union – England, France, Germany, Poland, Romania, Sweden – Study for the European Parliament*, No IP/C/JURI/IC/2008-019, at p vii and continual references to family law.

12 See D. HODSON, 'International trends in Marital agreements: a Progress Report', *IFL (International Family Law)* 2009, 245 at 245 et seq.

13 A. AGELL, 'The Division of Property upon Divorce from a European Perspective', in J. POUSSON-PETIT (ed), *Liber Amivorum Marie-Thérèse Meulders-Klein – Droit comparé des personnes et de la famille*, Bruylant, Brussels, 1998, pp 18 et seq; D. HENRICH, 'Zur Zukunft des Güterrechts in Europa', *FamRZ (Zeitschrift für das gesamte Familienrecht)* (2002), 1521 et seq; D. MARTINY, 'Ein zusätzlicher Güterstand für Europa?, in S. HOFER, D. KIPPEL and U. WALTER (eds), *Perspektiven des Familienrechts – Festschrift für Dieter Schwab*, Gieseking, Bielefeld, 2005, pp 1189 et seq.

14 Cf. Article 21 Abkommen zwischen der Bundesrepublik Deutschland und der Französischen Republik über den Güterstand der Wahl-Zugewinngemeinschaft (Treaty between the Federal Republic of Germany and the French Republic on an optional property regime of accrued gains).

as an optional model takes this idea a step further, as transnational couples when getting married could opt for a comprehensive regime governing the overall financial consequences of divorce.[15] The success of all these endeavours depends upon finding some common ground with regard to the scope of contractual freedom as far as the consequences of divorce are concerned. The discussion of pre- and post-nuptial or marital agreements below will cover contracts between all partners in a status relationship, whether marriage or registered partnership, and regardless of the partners' sex since the underlying questions are the same.[16] Separation agreements, which pose both similar and also uniquely different problems, will not be dealt with.[17]

2. PARTY AUTONOMY AND THE CONSEQUENCES OF DIVORCE – DIVERGENCE AND CONVERGENCE

2.1. ROLE OF PARTY AUTONOMY IN VIEW OF THE DIFFERENT STATUTORY RULES – THE TRADITIONAL GAP

The role of party autonomy in any legal system depends on the respective statutory or default rules and must therefore be seen against their background. Here, the starting points in England and Wales and the Republic of Ireland[18] are diametrically opposed to those found in Continental Europe. In jurisdictions – such as England and Wales – where marriage has no influence on the spouses' property and the court is consequently vested with wide distributive powers upon divorce to achieve a fair and equitable result,[19] contractual freedom could easily be seen as ousting the court's jurisdiction and thus interfering with public policy – as has been the case for a long time.[20] In contrast, marital agreements

15 See for the concept of a European Marriage, which is subject of the ongoing DFG (German Research Foundation) research project, N. Dethloff, 'Europäische Vereinheitlichung des Familienrechts', *AcP (Archiv für die civilistische Praxis)* 204 (2004), 544–568 and N. Dethloff, 'Die Europäische Ehe', *StAZ* (Das Standesamt) (2006), 253–260; cf. also D. Coester-Waltjen, 'Überlegungen zu einem europäischen Familienrecht', in C. Müller-Magdeburg (ed), *Unsere Aufgaben im 21. Jahrhundert. Festschrift für Lore Maria Peschel-Gutzeit,* Nomos, Baden-Baden, 2002, p 35 at 36.

16 For different names such as *prenuptial agreement (pre-nups)* or *pre-civil partnership agreements (pre-reggies or pre-cips)* see N. Lowe and R. Kay, 'The Status of Pre-nuptial Agreements in English Law – Eccentricity or Sensible Pragmatism?', in B. Verschraegen (ed), *Family Finances,* Jan Sramek Verlag, Vienna, 2009, pp 393 at 394 et seq.

17 One of the relevant differences between marital contracts and separation agreements is that at the time of divorce in particular the needs and abilities of the spouses are known.

18 B. Barry, 'Modernising the Law on Pre-nuptial Agreements in Ireland', 12 *Trinity C.L.Rev. (Trinity College Law Review)* (2009), 80–96.

19 Cf. *White v White,* [2001] AC 596.

20 Cf. *Hyman v Hyman* [1929] FLR Rep 342.

play a totally different role in Continental Europe where they generally permit couples to choose a matrimonial property regime other than the default regime or to modify the respective statutory regime.[21] Where the default property regime is that of a community of property, as is the case in the majority of Europe,[22] a principal function of marital agreements is to allow spouses to opt for separation of property *during* the marriage, particularly as they may wish to avoid the other partner's creditors taking hold of community property.[23]

However, contractual freedom can also be seen as having been granted with a view to the rigidity of the default rules applying in case of divorce: both in community property systems and in community of accrued gains or participation of acquisition systems there is very little room for judges to deviate from the 50% division of the default rule. Thus, some countries, for example Portugal and Switzerland, do not allow any deviation.[24] The majority merely permits departure from the rule of equal shares in extreme situations: while in Belgium[25] and France[26] a deviation is only possible where one spouse misappropriated or concealed joint property, other countries have hardship clauses that leave the court with a certain margin of discretion;[27] in practice though, such deviations seem to be applied with extreme caution.[28] Only the Nordic countries take a different approach and explicitly allow a deviation from the general rule of equal shares.[29] However,

21 Only in Romania is the stipulated property regime, the community of property, mandatory, cf. Article 30 para 2 Romanian Family Code; other jurisdictions allow to opt for another statutory regime and/or modify the categories of assets in the community of property regime, cf. for instance Article 1403 Greek Civil Code, Article 47 para 1 Polish Family and Custody Act as well as sec 143a Slovakian Civil Code.

22 For a comparative overview see W. Pintens, 'Ehegüterstände in Europa', in V. Lipp, E. Schumann and B. Veit, *Die Zugewinngemeinschaft – ein europäisches Modell?*, Universitätsverlag, Göttingen, 2009, pp 24–28.

23 See M. Ryznar and A. Stępień-Sporek, 'To Have and to Hold, for Richer or Richer: Premarital Agreements in the Comparative Context', *13 Chapman Law Review (2009)*, 27 at 44 et seq also pointing out this difference in the significance of marital agreements in United States and in Continental European systems.

24 For Portugal explicitly Article 1730 para 1 Portuguese Civil Code; for Switzerland see the explanations for the waiver of a hardship clause in: Botschaft über die Änderung des Schweizerischen Zivilgesetzbuches (Wirkungen der Ehe im allgemeinen, Ehegüterrecht und Erbrecht) vom 11. Juli 1979, Bundesblatt 1979 II 1191 at 1321; in extreme cases an abuse of right according to Article 2 para 2 Swiss Civil Code might, however, be possible.

25 Article 1448 Belgian Civil Code.

26 Article 1477 para 1 French Civil Code; cf. Article 1477 para 2 French Civil Code for the concealment of a joint debt.

27 Eg Article 28 para 1 Bulgarian Family Code; sec 1381 German Civil Code; Article 3.123 para 1 Lithuanian Civil Code; Article 43 sec 2 and sec 3 Polish Family and Guardianship Code; Article 39 para 2 Russian Family Code.

28 Cf. K. Boele-Woelki, B. Braat and I. Curry-Sumner (eds), *European Family Law in Action, Volume IV: Property Relations Between Spouses*, Intersentia, Antwerp, 2009, questions 49, 55, 80 and 89.

29 For details see A. Agell, *Nordisk äktenskapsrätt: en jämförande studie av dansk, finsk, isländsk, norsk och svensk rätt med diskussion av reformbehov och harmoniseringsmöjligheter*, Nordiska Ministerrådet, Copenhagen, 2003, ch. 15.

where the statutory rules provide for equal sharing, as is the case in most other countries, the courts cannot take into consideration the kind of partnership the couple has lived and the different degrees of economic interdependency which exist particularly in the case of dual career couples without children, on the one hand, and a traditional homemaking marriage, on the other. One size does not fit all[30] and marital agreements allow couples to make the rules fit their partnership. This is considerably less necessary where the statutory regime applicable upon divorce is tailored to accommodate different types of partnership and already aims at arriving at a fair and equitable result in each and every case.

2.2. MARITAL AGREEMENTS IN RECENT ENGLISH CASE LAW – NARROWING OF THE GAP

The traditional gap between the English and the Continental European approach has narrowed considerably. Recent English case law, in particular *Crossley* v *Crossley*,[31] *MacLeod* v *MacLeod*[32] and lately *Radmacher* v *Granatino*,[33] has led to substantial changes in the treatment of marital agreements.[34] With regard to post-nuptial agreements, these are now generally binding and enforceable,[35] but parties cannot oust the jurisdiction of the court in matters of ancillary relief and hence cannot prevent each other from coming to court in a subsequent application for financial relief.[36] Until recently the treatment of pre-nuptials was much more restrained. However, in October 2010, the UK Supreme Court adjusted the treatment of post- and pre-nuptial agreements: Whereas already after recent judgments of the England and Wales Court of Appeal, eg *Crossley* v *Crossley* and *Radmacher* v *Granatino*, the treatment of pre- and post-nuptial agreements did not seem to differ that much anymore,[37] the UK Supreme Court now clearly stated obiter, that it does not consider pre- and post-nuptial agreements to be fundamentally different.[38] In the introduction of its judgment it outlined basic

[30] Cf. B. Stark, 'Marriage Proposals: From One-Size-Fits-All to Postmodern Marriage Law', 89 *Cal. L. Rev.* (2001), 1479–1548.

[31] *Crossley v Crossley* [2007] EWCA Civ 1491, [2008] 1 FLR 1467.

[32] *MacLeod v MacLeod* [2008] UKPC 64, [2009] 1 FLR 641.

[33] *Radmacher v Granatino* [2010] UKSC 42, [2009] EWCA Civ 649, 2 FLR 1181.

[34] For the status of pre-nuptial agreements in England see P. Duckworth, *Duckworth's Matrimonial Property and Finance*, Jordan Publishing, loose-leaf Issue 20 (Nov 2009), D1 (3); N. Lowe and R. Kay, 'The Status of Pre-nuptial-Agreements in English Law – Eccentricity or Sensible Pragmatism?', in B. Verschraegen (ed), *Family Finances*, Jan Sramek Verlag, Vienna, 2009, pp 393–411; J. Miles, 'Radmacher v Granatino [2009] EWCA Civ 649: Upping the ante-nuptial agreement', (2009) 21 *CFLQ*.

[35] *MacLeod v MacLeod* [2008] UKPC 64, [2009] 1 FLR 641 at para 39.

[36] This general principle was laid down in *Hyman v Hyman* [1929] AC 601, [1929] FLR Rep 342; cf. also sec 34 Matrimonial Property Act 1973 (England and Wales).

[37] Cf. J. Miles, 'Radmacher v Granatino [2009] EWCA Civ 649: 'Upping the ante-nuptial agreement', (2009) 21 *CFLQ*.

[38] *Radmacher v Granatino* [2010] UKSC 42 at para 66.

principles following the approach of post-nuptial agreements taken in *MacLeod* v *MacLeod* and applying it to pre-nuptial agreements accordingly: when a court is considering granting ancillary relief it is not obliged to give effect to nuptial agreements – whether they are ante-nuptial or post-nuptial. The parties cannot, by agreement, oust the jurisdiction of the court. However, the court must give appropriate weight to such an agreement.[39]

With regard to the weight, that should be accorded to a pre-nuptial agreement, the Supreme Court advanced to follow the proposition by the Board in *MacLeod* v *MacLeod* and stated that the court should give effect to a nuptial agreement which is freely entered into by both parties with a full appreciation of its implications unless in the circumstances prevailing it would not be fair to hold the parties to this agreement.[40] The weight given to a pre-nuptial agreement may thus be compelling or even decisive.[41] As guidance for *fairness* the Supreme Court stated that a nuptial agreement cannot be allowed to prejudice the reasonable requirements of any children of the family,[42] however, respect should be given to individual autonomy and the reasonable desire to make a provision for existing property.[43] Additionally circumstances that could not or were not envisaged at the time of the making of the agreement should be considered, rendering nuptial agreements of long marriages more likely to be unfair.[44] With regard to procedural safeguards the Supreme Court stressed that the parties must enter into it of their own free will, without undue influence or pressure, and informed of its implications, the question being in particular whether there has been any material lack of disclosure, information or advice.[45] Although this approach allows for a considerable degree of flexibility in the individual case and it seems clear from this judgment, that couples can expect, that their recent or future nuptial agreement will take effect,[46] it leaves a substantial degree of uncertainty, with regard to the content of the agreement and whether this will pass under the court's fairness assessment.[47]

39 *Radmacher v Granatino* [2010] UKSC 42 at para 2.
40 *Radmacher v Granatino* [2010] UKSC 42 at para 75.
41 *Radmacher v Granatino* [2010] UKSC 42 at para 83.
42 *Radmacher v Granatino* [2010] UKSC 42 at para 77, cf. for post-nuptials already *MacLeod v MacLeod* [2008] UKPC 64, [2009] 1 FLR 641, at para 4 in analogy to the rules on validity of maintenance agreements.
43 *Radmacher v Granatino* [2010] UKSC 42 at para 78 and 79.
44 *Radmacher v Granatino* [2010] UKSC 42 at para 80.
45 *Radmacher v Granatino* [2010] UKSC 42 at para 68 and 69.
46 *Radmacher v Granatino* [2010] UKSC 42 at para 74.
47 For attempts to counteract these problems cf. the paper of the solicitor organisation RESOLUTION, 'A More Certain Future – Recognition of Pre-marital Agreements in England and Wales', 2005, available at: www.resolution.org.uk/site_content_files/files/a_more_certain_future___resolution.pdf as well as the LAW COMMISSION'S Project on 'Pre- and Post-nuptial Agreements', for more information see www.lawcom.gov.uk/marital_property.htm.

2.3. CONTRACTUAL FREEDOM IN CONTINENTAL EUROPEAN MATRIMONIAL PROPERTY LAW – PRECONDITIONS AND LIMITS

2.3.1. *Formal requirements*

An assessment of the scope of contractual freedom in Continental European matrimonial property law requires that we consider its preconditions as well as its limits. First of all, almost universally there are formal requirements which have to be met: most legal systems require the marriage contract to be signed by both spouses.[48] Furthermore, in many countries marital agreements must be entered into before a notary. This holds true not only for the legal systems of Roman[49] or Germanic[50] descent, including that in the Netherlands,[51] but is also the case in many central European countries[52] including Russia.[53] Though the role and responsibility of notaries as well as their training, expertise and supervision vary in detail in the notary systems of Latin origin in civil law countries, as a basic principle according to the terms of their professional codes, European notaries are appointed as impartial advisors.[54] When performing a notarisation they are generally obliged to provide independent advice to both parties.[55] Thus the requirement of notarial authentication aims to ensure the protection of the weaker and less well-informed or prepared spouse.

Moreover, a marital agreement can usually only be entered into if both parties are present at the same time.[56] However, where representation is possible they need

48 See expressly eg sec 66 Finnish Marriage Act; sec 54 Norwegian Marriage Act; ch. 7 sec 3 para 2–3 Swedish Marriage Act; Article 184 Swiss Civil Code.

49 Sec 1 para 1a) Austrian Notarial Deed Act; Article 1392 Belgian Civil Code; Article 1394 French Civil Code; Article 1327 and 1280 Spanish Civil Code.

50 Sec 1410 German Civil Code; Article 184 Swiss Civil Code.

51 Sec 1:115 Dutch Civil Code.

52 Sec 143a Czech Civil Code; Article 1403 et seq Greek Civil Code; sec 27 para 3 Hungarian Family Act (however, instead of a notarial deed, the counter-signature of a legal representative can be sufficient according to sec 27 para 3 Hungarian Family Act); Article 47 sec 1 Polish Law on Families and Legal Custody, sec 143a para 1 Slovakian Civil Code.

53 Article 41 para 2 Russian Family Code.

54 S. Matyk, 'The European Union – A driving force for a European Notarial Profile', in: CENTER OF THE LEGAL COMPETENCE ET AL (eds), *Notaries in Europe – Growing Fields of Competence*, Intersentia, Vienna – Graz, 2007, p 22; see also Council of the Notariats of the European Union (CNUE) (eds), *European Notarial Code of Conduct,* available at: www.cnue.be (last accessed on 24.3.2010).

55 Compare: study for the European Parliament – No. IP/C/JURI/IC/2008–019, Council of the Notariats of the European Union (eds), *Comparative Study on authentic instruments*, p 40, available at: http://www.cnue-nouvelles.be/en/000/actualites/aae-etude-acte-authentique-final-25-11-2008-en.pdf (last accessed on 10.3.2010); S. Matyk, 'The European Union – A driving force for a European Notarial Profile', in: Center of Legal Competence et al (eds), *Notaries in Europe – Growing Fields of Competence*, Intersentia, Vienna – Graz, 2007, p 22.

56 Article 1392 Belgian Civil Code; Article 1394 French Civil Code.

not appear in person.[57] In order to maintain a certain level of protection and to avoid rash acts, some legal systems do, however, stipulate formal requirements for powers of representation to be granted; for example, in France the authorisation needs to be in the form of an authentic act.[58] By contrast, other countries, like Switzerland[59] or Latvia,[60] require that the spouses be present in person. In addition to the notarial deed some countries call for registration as a supplementary protection for third parties. Thus contractual agreements can only be held against *third parties* who acted in good faith after registration has been completed.[61] In order to provide further protection for third parties, countries that have not set up such public registers often demand the other party's positive knowledge of the marriage contract and its legal contents in addition to notarisation of the contract.[62]

Instead of a notarial act for a marital agreement to be valid, the Nordic countries require that the contract, or settlement as it is called, be in writing, signed by both spouses and either countersigned by two witnesses as used to be the case in Sweden[63] and still is in Norwegian law,[64] or registered in a public register or with a court, like in Denmark,[65] Finland[66] and now also in Sweden.[67]

---

57 Agency is for example allowed in France, cf. LexisNexis JurisClasseur, Fasc. unique: Contrat de mariage. – Forme. Publicité. Antériorité, Article 1394 and 1395 Mn 7; Cour de Cassation, Judgment dated 5.02.1957; and also in Germany, see G. Brudermüller, in P. Bassenge et al (eds), *Palandt Bürgerliches Gesetzbuch*, C.H. Beck, Munich, 2010, sec 1410 BGB, Mn 5.

58 Article 1394 French Civil Code; J. Carbonnier,, 'Droit Civil, Tome 2, La famille, l'enfant, le couple', Paris, 2002, p 405, p 514; J.-F. Pillebout, 'La participation aux acquêts – Pratique notariale', Paris, 2005, pp 11–12; also, in Austria the Supreme Court has clarified that the authority needs to be issued in the form of a notarial deed; compare Judgment dated 23.2.1949, case 2 Ob 247/48 and Judgment dated 26.6.1984, case 4Ob144/62.

59 H. Hausheer, T. Geiser and R. E. Aebi-Müller, *Das Familienrecht des Schweizerischen Zivilgesetzbuches*, Stämpfli Verlag, Bern, 2007, Mn 11.20; C. Hegenauer and P. Breitschmid, *Grundriss des Eherechts*, Stämpfli, Bern, 1993, Mn 23.04; M. Näf-Hofmann and H. Näf-Hofman, *Das neue Ehe- und Erbrecht im Zivilgesetzbuch*, Schulthess Polygraphischer Verlag, Zurich, 1986, Mn 1228 et seq.

60 Article 115 Latvian Civil Code.

61 Sec 36 Austrian Business Enterprise Code; Article 1:116 Dutch Civil Code for cases in which agreements on the property relationship form part of the contract; sec 1412 German Civil Code; Article 1246 Maltese Civil Code; Article 1711 para 1 Portuguese Civil Code and Article 191 para 1 Portuguese Act on Civil Procedure.

62 Sec 143a para 4 Czech Civil Code; sec 143a para 3 Slovakian Civil Code; Article 47 Polish Act on Family and Legal Custody.

63 A. Agell, *Nordisk äktenskapsrätt*, Nordiska ministerrådet, Copenhagen, 2003, p 190.

64 Sec 54 Norwegian Marriage Act.

65 Sec 35 and 37 Act on the Celebration and Termination of Marriage.

66 Cf. K.-F. v. Knorre, 'Eherecht in Finnland', in J. Süß and G. Ring (eds), *Eherecht in Europa*, Zerb Verlag, Angelbachtal, 2006, p 468 et seq.

67 Ch. 7 sec 3 para 3 Swedish Marriage Code.

2.3.2. *Pre- and post-nuptial agreements*

Although in general pre- and post-nuptial contracts are treated alike, some systems limit contractual freedom before marriage. In Slovakia, agreements made upon or after the marriage alone are valid.[68] In the Ukraine, a pre-nuptial marriage contract cannot be signed before the couple has filed for marriage at the civil registry office.[69] By contrast, in other countries there are specific restrictions on post-nuptial agreements. For example, in France spouses are not allowed to modify their matrimonial property regime freely once they are married. They may only make modifications once the property regime has been in force for two years and provided the amendment is in the interest of the family.[70] Since a reform in 2006, judicial approval, ie homologation, is no longer required as a norm but solely if there are under-aged children or in case of a third parties' opposition.[71] In Belgium, the requirement of the court's approval, which was previously essential for post-nuptial agreements, was abolished in 2008 in accordance with the general trend of allowing both pre- and post-nuptial agreements. Although there appears to be a tendency to reduce such requirements, in a few jurisdictions judicial approval may still be necessary: in the Netherlands, Article 1:119 para 1 Civil Code demands the approbation of the regional court for the conclusion or amendment of a marriage contract *after* the wedding. The same holds true in Malta.[72] In Portugal, the traditional principle of immutability of property regimes in Roman-derived systems still applies;[73] no post-nuptial marriage contract can be concluded, nor can an existing contract be amended after the wedding. Post-nuptial agreements are hence not part of the law at all.

2.3.3. *General rules of contract law*

As concerns the substantive requirements in general, the rules of contract law apply to marital agreements. Regardless of the many differences in detail which exist in European contract law there is at least some general consensus regarding the conditions for the validity of the consent: the contract may not be the result

68 M. Hatapka, in K. Boele-Woelki, B. Braat and I. Curry-Sumner (eds), *European Family Law in Action, Volume IV: Property relations between spouses*, Intersentia, Antwerp – Oxford – Portland, 2009, p 1139.

69 Article 92 para 1 Ukrainian Act on Family Law.

70 Article 1396 para 3; Article 1397 French Civil Code; B. Beignier, J. Combret, E. Frèmont, 'Le changement de régime matrimonial depuis le 1er janvier 2007 Questions diverses. Éléments de réponses', in *Droit de la famille* no°4, April 2007, étude 11.

71 Article 1397 para 3 and 5 French Civil Code.

72 Article 1244 Maltese Civil Code.

73 Article 1714 Portuguese Civil Code.

of a mistake,[74] fraud,[75] threat[76] or coercion.[77] Moreover, it must not be contrary to morality[78] or public policy.[79] Many systems refuse to uphold contracts under various concepts where an obviously gross disparity in the values exchanged is the result of unfair exploitation, excessive taking of advantage or abuse of circumstances.[80] Hence in English law unconscionability may be raised as a defence to a manifestly unfair contract where one party consciously took advantage of the other's weakness.[81] In France, jurisprudence treats the exploitation of a party's special circumstances as a form of violence.[82] Whereas some systems require *deliberate* exploitation of the other party's plight,[83] others let it suffice that the gaining party *ought* to have known of the conditions that result in the other party's weaker position.[84] Moreover, courts will often infer that one party has deliberately taken advantage of the other from the existence of gross disparity.[85]

In the absence of such circumstances that constitute a taking of advantage, however, it is only in a few countries that contracts may be avoided simply because they are grossly unfair in substance. For example, in the Nordic legal systems a contract that is manifestly and grossly unfair can be terminated or adjusted simply on the grounds of unfairness, without the need to prove that the other party's situation has been deliberately taken advantage of.[86] Slovenian law allows the avoidance of a contract within one year of its conclusion if the performances of the parties were grossly disproportionate.[87] In the Czech Republic, contracts that

74 Cf. Article 7:201 DCFR, C. von Bar and E. Clive (eds), *Principles, Definitions and Model Rules of European Private Law – Volume 1*, Sellier European law publishers, Munich, 2009, p 457; Article 4:103 PECL, O. Lando and H. Beale (eds), *Principles of European Contract law*, Kluwer Law international, The Hague – London – Boston, 2000, pp 229–239.

75 Cf. Article 7:205 DCFR, (n 74 above), p 492 et seq; Article 4:107 PECL, (n 74 above), p 264 et seq.

76 Cf. Article 7:206 DCFR, (n 74 above), p 500 et seq; Article 4:108 PECL, (n 74 above), p 257 et seq.

77 Cf. Article 7:206 DCFR, (n 74 above), p 500; Article 4:108 PECL, (n 74 above), p 257 et seq.

78 Cf. Article 7:301 DCFR, (n 74 above), p 536 et seq.

79 Cf. Article 7:301, Article 7:302 DCFR, (n 74 above), see p 536 et seq.

80 Cf. Article 3:44 (para 1 and 4) Dutch Civil Code; sec 138 para 2 German Civil Code; Article 1448 Italian Civil Code; Article 282, 283 Portuguese Civil Code; sec 31 Swedish Contracts Act.

81 *Hart v O'Connor* [1985] AC 1000.

82 Cass. soc., 5 juillet 1965: Bull. civ. IV, N° 545; cass. civ. 1ère, 3 avril 2002: Bull. civ. I, N° 108.

83 Eg in English law, relief upon mental incapacity or unconscionability can only be granted if the other side consciously took advantage of the resulting weakness, O. Lando and H. Beale (eds), *Principles of European Contract law*, Kluwer Law international, The Hague – London – Boston, 2000, p 264.

84 Eg Article 3:44 Dutch Civil Code.

85 For further details, see C. von Bar and E. Clive (eds), *Principles, Definitions and Model Rules of European Private Law – Volume 1*, Sellier European law publishers, Munich, 2009, p 513.

86 Eg sec 36 Danish Contracts Act; sec 36 Finnish Contracts Act; sec 36 Norwegian Contracts Act; sec 36 Swedish Contracts Act.

87 Sec 118 LOA (Law of Obligations Act), see C. von Bar and E. Clive (eds), *Principles, Definitions and Model Rules of European Private Law – Volume 1*, Sellier European law publishers, Munich, 2009, p 513; this does not apply where the price was higher because of personal circumstances (pretium affectionis); see also the concept of lesion in Austrian law which allows the avoidance

were agreed on under obviously and excessively unfair terms, can be contrary to good morals and hence be void as of right.[88]

There is even less common ground in contract law as to whether and under what conditions a contract may be *modified* on account of a *change in circumstances*. A fair number of legal systems acknowledge the possibility of modifying or terminating a contract due to a change of circumstances.[89] Where this is not stipulated by law, courts may have established this option through case law.[90] However, where there are such instruments that allow for an adjustment of the contract, they are usually limited to events that could not reasonably have been foreseen or controlled by the parties and that make the completion of the contract extremely onerous.[91] Some countries reject the idea of modification of contracts due to a change of circumstances altogether.[92] In any event, there seems to be hardly any discussion about the application of such instruments to marital agreements.

How the rest of the well-developed, albeit somewhat diverging general rules on the validity of contracts are applied to marital agreements is a question which is debated in some jurisdictions, whereas in others it is merely stated that being contracts, marriage agreements have to comply with the legal limitations of contractual freedom.[93] In addition, where courts have scrutinised marital agreements, they have for the most part been found unobjectionable. Although according to the German Federal Supreme Court contractual freedom must not result in an unacceptable and clearly one-sided distribution of burdens between the spouses, according to the ranking which the court has established to determine the importance of the respective statutory provisions in the system of

or adaptation of a synallagmatic contract where a party has received less than 50% of the value of the other party's performance, see sec 934, 935 Austrian Civil Code.

88 Cf. Article 7:207 DCFR, (n 74 above), p 513.

89 Sec 936, 1170a Austrian Civil Code ; sec 313 German Civil Code; Article 1467 Italian Civil Code; sec 437 Portuguese Civil Code; Article 451 Russian Civil Code.

90 Eg in Spain, case law permits reviewing the contract, or in the Nordic countries, courts do generally not accept a change of circumstances as a ground for the revision of an agreement, but have modified under certain conditions contracts by applying the Contract Act (sec 36 of the respective Contract Act), see O. Lando and H. Beale (eds), *Principles of European Contract law*, Kluwer Law international, The Hague – London – Boston, 2000, p 328.

91 Article 1467 Italian Civil Code; Spanish courts require 'extraordinary' or 'radically unforeseeable' changes in circumstances, leading to an 'exorbitant' disproportion, see B. Fauvarque-Cosson and D. Mazeaud (eds), *European Contract law*, Sellier European law publishers, Munich, 2008, p 468.

92 Belgium and France (except for administrative contracts), see B. Fauvarque-Cosson and D. Mazeaud (eds), *European Contract law*, Sellier European law publishers, Munich, 2008, p 469; England (unless changed circumstances result in impossibility), O. Lando and H. Beale (eds), *Principles of European Contract law*, Kluwer Law international, The Hague – London – Boston, 2000, p 328.

93 See for example Article 1335 Spanish Civil Code; for Austria cf. E. Gitschthaler and J. Höllwerth, *EheG Kommentar*, Springer-Verlag, Vienna, 2008, before sec 1217 Mn 5.

the law on the consequences of divorce, the equalisation of accrued gains ranks last, behind various kinds of maintenance claims and the adjustment of pension rights.[94] What this means for the matrimonial property regime and, in particular, for the equalisation of accrued gains, is that the spouses are able to conclude very far-reaching agreements. Excluding the matrimonial property regime of the community of accrued gains and thereby opting for the matrimonial property regime of separation of property, will regularly pass judicial scrutiny and be both valid and enforceable.[95] All in all, case law is rare, evidencing that there is only very limited judicial control of marital agreements.

2.3.4. Special provisions in matrimonial law

In addition to the general rules of contract law, quite a few legal systems include special and explicit regulations for marital agreements. Frequently such provisions merely specify that marital contracts, or clauses in such contracts, may not be contrary to public order or morality. They either explicitly state that such agreements or clauses are void, as is the case for example in Spain,[96] Malta[97] or Lithuania,[98] or, as in Greece, that the court can declare them invalid.[99] In the Nordic countries, obligations law is only subsidiary. Thus Danish marriage law provides that a marriage contract can be terminated by a court, if one of the conditions for contractual invalidity (fraud, duress, lack of capacity etc.) applies.[100] Furthermore, all Nordic legal systems have established special rules concerning the adjustment of unfair marriage contracts.[101] Although the term of fairness used in these provisions gives the courts a much wider discretionary power,[102] in practice even here the courts seem to take the principle of *pacta sunt servanda* rather seriously and, in spite of some criticism in legal literature, are very restrictive in modifying a matrimonial agreement.[103] The same holds true

---

94 BGH (Federal Court of justice), 11.2.2004, *NJW (Neue Juristische Wochenschrift)* (2004), 934–937; BGH, 17.5.2006, *FamRZ* (2006), 1097–1098; BGH, 17.10.2007, *FamRZ* (2008), 386–390.

95 BGH, 28.3.2007, *FamRZ* (2007), 1311–1313.

96 Article 1328 Spanish Civil Code.

97 Article 1237 para 1; Article 1244 para 3 Maltese Civil Code.

98 Article 3:105 para 1 Lithuanian Civil Code.

99 Article 178–187 Greek Civil Code, A. G. Koutsouradis et al, in K. Boele-Woelki, B. Braat and I. Curry-Sumner (eds), *European Family Law in Action, Volume IV: Property relations between spouses*, Intersentia, Antwerp - Oxford - Portland, 2009, p 1232.

100 I. Lund-Andersen and I. Magnussen, in K. Boele-Woelki, B. Braat and I. Curry-Sumner (eds), *European Family Law in Action, Volume IV: Property relations between spouses*, Intersentia, Antwerp - Oxford - Portland, 2009, p 1229.

101 Sec 58 Danish Marriage Act, sec 103b Finnish Marriage Act; sec 46 Norwegian Marriage Act; ch. 12 sec 3 Swedish Marriage Act.

102 For an overview of the law in the Nordic countries see A. AGELL, *Nordisk äktenskapsrätt: en jämförande studie av dansk, finsk, isländsk, norsk och svensk rätt med diskussion av reformbehov och harmoniseringsmöjligheter*, Nordiska Ministerrådet, Copenhagen, 2003, ch. 15.

103 For Sweden and Norway cf. K. Boele-Woelki, B. Braat and I. Curry-Sumner (eds), *European Family Law in Action, Volume IV: Property relations between spouses*, Intersentia, Antwerp - Oxford - Portland, 2009, question 201.

for Russia where Article 43 para 2 Family Code refers to the general provisions of the Civil Code concerning the amendment and termination of contracts.[104] According to these provisions, Russian courts may inter alia amend or terminate contracts due to a change of circumstances according to Article 451 Russian Civil Code. However, in the Russian literature it is highly disputed if these general provisions of the Civil Code, which actually deal with commercial contracts, may be applied to marriage agreements.[105]

Moreover, quite a few countries like Poland,[106] Lithuania,[107] Russia,[108] or Spain[109] require that the contract must not infringe the principle of legal equality of the spouses. The extent of scrutiny remains hard to predict. For instance, Lithuania requires a serious violation of this principle or that the agreement is especially unfavourable to one of the spouses.[110] In the case of a breach of this principle, a marriage contract can be amended or terminated by a judgment following the requirements of the 6th book of the Lithuanian Civil Code (Article 6.204 Lithuanian Civil Code).[111] The Hungarian Family Act provides that equity has to be taken into account by the courts when deciding upon property issues between spouses; it is debated, however, whether *spouses* can refer to this principle when challenging existing marital agreements.[112] In Italy, spouses may enter into a marital agreement choosing among, or modifying one of, the statutory regimes; however a pre- or post-nuptial contract on the financial consequences of divorce

---

104 Namely to Part I, Section III, Subsection 2, chapter 29 Russian Civil Code.

105 See M. Antokolskaia, in K. Boele-Woelki, B. Braat and I. Curry-Sumner (eds), *European Family Law in Action, Volume IV: Property relations between spouses*, Intersentia, Antwerp – Oxford – Portland, 2009, p 1235; L. Pčelinceva, *Kommentarij k Semejnomu kodeksu Rossijskoj Federazii*, 5th edition, Moscow 2009, p 202 et seq; M. Antokolskaia, *Semejnoe pravo: učebnik*, 3rd edition, Moscow 2010, p 215; A. Nečaeva, *Kommentarij k Semejnomu kodeksu Rossijskoj Federazii*, 2nd edition, Moscow 2010, p 159.

106 A. Mączyński, in K. Boele-Woelki, B. Braat and I. Curry-Sumner (eds), *European Family Law in Action, Volume IV: Property relations between spouses*, Intersentia, Antwerp – Oxford – Portland, 2009, p 1235.

107 Article 3.108 para 2 Lithuanian Civil Code.

108 Article 42 para 3, 1 para 3 Russian Family Code.

109 Article 1328 Spanish Civil Code.

110 V. Mikelenas, in K. Boele-Woelki, B. Braat and I. Curry-Sumner (eds), *European Family Law in Action, Volume IV: Property relations between spouses*, Intersentia, Antwerp – Oxford – Portland, 2009, p 1233.

111 V. Mikelenas, in K. Boele-Woelki, B. Braat and I. Curry-Sumner (eds), *European Family Law in Action, Volume IV: Property relations between spouses*, Intersentia, Antwerp – Oxford – Portland, 2009, p 1146.

112 O. Szeibert Erdös, 'The Role of Self-determination in Hungarian Family Law', in: M. Martín-Casals and J. Ribot (eds), *The Role of Self-determination in the Modernisation of Family Law in Europe*, Documenta Universitaria, Girona, 2006, pp 140–141; see also E. Weiss, 'Die Bedeutung des Vertrages im ungarischen Familienrecht', in S. Hofer, D. Schwab and D. Henrich (eds), *From Status to Contract? – Die Bedeutung des Vertrages im europäischen Familienrecht*, Gieseking, Bielefeld, 2005, p 194 et seq.

which is entered into in order to prevent later conflict is void.[113] In Switzerland the general, albeit not undisputed, view is that marital agreements do not have to pass the same scrutiny as separation agreements.[114] Consequently, even where there are special provisions, in practice there appears to be a lot of uncertainty and some reluctance to void or modify marital agreements.

2.4. CONTRACTUAL FREEDOM REGARDING MAINTENANCE AND OTHER FINANCIAL CONSEQUENCES OF DIVORCE

However, one cannot take the full measure of the extent of private autonomy on the other side of the Channel if matrimonial property issues alone are considered. Since in England a wide variety of measures can be granted as ancillary relief, such as financial provision orders, eg as a lump sum payment or in form of periodical payments, as well as property adjustment and pension orders, the weight given to a pre- or post-nuptial agreement concerns the spouses' overall post-divorce economic situation.[115] Although in Continental systems matrimonial property, maintenance and, where available, the sharing of pension rights, are generally separate instruments, here too the overall financial consequences of divorce have to be taken into consideration: the degree of autonomy with regard to maintenance is traditionally a lot more restricted. Whereas agreements on maintenance in contemplation of divorce, during or even after divorce are generally accepted, pre- or post-nuptial agreements on maintenance are treated with much more reservation.[116]

---

113 Cf. S. Patti, in K. Boele-Woelki, B. Braat and I. Curry-Sumner (eds), *European Family Law in Action, Volume IV: Property relations between spouses*, Intersentia, Antwerp – Oxford – Portland, 2009, p 1145 et seq; G. Ferrando, *Manuale di diritto di famiglia*, Gius. Laterza & Figli, Roma – Bari, 2005, pp 200–201.

114 Article 140 para 2 Swiss Civil Code, which governs the judicial control of divorce agreements, is not applicable, see Bundesgericht (Federal Court), 4.12.2003, *FamPra.ch (Die Praxis des Familienrechts)* (2004), 345 at 348 et seq; for criticism of this judgment see I. Schwander, 'Eheverträge? zwischen "ewigen" Verträgen und Inhaltskontrolle', *AJP (Aktuelle Juristische Praxis)* (2003), 572 et seq; I. Schwenzer, ‚Grenzen der Vertragsfreiheit in Scheidungskonventionen und Eheverträgen', *FamPra.ch* (2005), 7 et seq; H. Stöckli, 'Die Ehevertragsfreiheit und ihre Schranken', in A. Rumo-Jungo and P. Pichonnaz (eds), *Symposium zum Familienrecht 2007, Scheidungsrecht – Aktuelle Probleme und Reformbedarf*, Universität Freiburg, Zurich – Basel – Geneva, 2008, p 88 et seq.

115 According to sec 25 para 1 Matrimonial Causes Act (1987) "all the circumstances" of the case have to be considered. For the consideration of matrimonial contracts see LJ Thorpe in *Radmacher v. Granatino* [2009] EWCA Civ 649 at para. 19 and previously Baron J as quoted in para 34.

116 Cf. K. Boele-Woelki, F. Ferrand, C. González Beilfuss, M. Jänterä-Jareborg, N. Lowe, D. Martiny and W. Pintens (eds), *Principles of European Family Law Regarding Divorce and Maintenance Between Former Spouses*, Intersentia, Antwerp, 2004, p 127 et seq; D. Martiny, 'Ehescheidung und nachehlicher Unterhalt in Europa', *EJCL (Electronic Journal of Comparative*

In some systems, maintenance is strictly off-limits. For instance, in Poland[117] or in Norway[118] an agreement is not allowed during the marriage, but only in view of actual divorce proceedings; in the Netherlands the agreement must have been concluded during, but not before the marriage.[119] In Italy the right to maintenance is protected through Article 160 Italian Civil Code, according to which agreements which are entered into before or during marriage with the purpose of regulating future divorce are invalid as they violate the principle of indisponibility of the legal effects of marriage;[120] however, maintenance may be agreed upon in a joint petition for divorce.[121] Other countries merely limit the scope of maintenance agreements and prohibit one (or both) spouses from renouncing his or her future right to maintenance.[122]

However, even where maintenance agreements before or during the marriage are allowed, the agreement might still be scrutinised and rejected by a competent authority: either in subsequent divorce proceedings[123] or in a decision on the enforceability of the maintenance agreement.[124] Although the threshold differs, the standard is basically one of fairness and reasonableness.[125] The agreement may not violate good faith,[126] be manifestly unjust, preposterous[127] or highly detrimental to one spouse.[128] What constitutes manifest unfairness to the spouse

Law), Vol. 8.3 (2004), at C II 6 and J.M. Scherpe, 'A Comparative View of Pre-Nuptial Agreements', 2007 *IFLJ (International Family Law Journal)* 18 et seq.

117 A. Mączyński and T. Sokołowski, in K. Boele-Woelki, B. Braat and I. Curry-Sumner (eds), *European Family Law in Action. Volume II: Maintenance Between Former Spouses,* Intersentia, Antwerp, 2003, p 468 et seq.

118 Sec 83 Norwegian Marriage Act.

119 Article 1:158 Dutch Civil Code.

120 G. Ferrando, *Manuale di diritto di famiglia,* Gius. Laterza & Figli, Roma – Bari, 2005, pp 200–201; C. Rimini and G. Vigano, *Diritto di famiglia, Repertorio sistematico di Giurisprudenza,* Wolters Kluwer Italia Srl, Padua, 2009, p 393 et seq with references to relevant case law. However, the contractual choice of a statutory property regime is permitted, cf. Article 190 Italian Civil Code.

121 S. Patti et al, in K. Boele-Woelki, B. Braat and I. Curry-Sumner (eds), *European Family Law in Action. Volume II: Maintenance Between Former Spouses,* Intersentia, Antwerp, 2003, question 102 (see country report http://www.ceflonline.net/Reports/pdf/Italy02.pdf).

122 In Belgium (Article 301 para 9 (1) Civil Code); the Czech Republic, Denmark, England and Wales, Ireland, Poland, Portugal; cf. K. Boele-Woelki, B. Braat and I. Curry-Sumner (eds), *European Family Law in Action. Volume II: Maintenance Between Former Spouses,* Intersentia, Antwerp, 2003, question 103.

123 Article 278 French Civil Code, Article 4 para 13 Italian Divorce Law (Law 1.12.1970 no. 898) and Article 140 Swiss Civil Code.

124 For example, Finland (competency of the local social board, cf. sec 50 Finnish Marriage Code).

125 Cf. K. Boele-Woelki, F. Ferrand, C. González Beilfuss, M. Jänterä-Jareborg, N. Lowe, D. Martiny and W. Pintens (eds), *Principles of European Family Law Regarding Divorce and Maintenance Between Former Spouses,* Intersentia, Antwerp, 2004, p 131.

126 According to general rules of contract law eg in Belgium (Article 1134 Belgian Civil Code) and in Germany (sec 242 German Civil Code).

127 In Denmark, sec 58 Danish Marriage Act.

128 Article 232 para 2 French Civil Code; Article 90 para 2 Spanish Civil Code; Article 140 para 2 Swiss Civil Code.

though is, in the absence of more specific criteria, hard to foresee. A maintenance agreement may also not be contrary to the children's interests.[129] Thus to waive maintenance where the ongoing care for children precludes gainful employment may not be compatible with their interests.[130]

Contractual freedom is even more limited with respect to other financial consequences of divorce. Instead of or in addition to periodical payments of maintenance – and apart from the regulation of matrimonial property – some jurisdictions provide for compensatory payments after divorce. For instance, in France the *prestation compensatoire*, which aims at an adjustment of the economic disparities between the spouses and – in line with the clean break principle – generally consists of a lump sum payment, cannot be waived.[131] It is not quite as clear whether and if so, under what circumstances, the right to compensation for domestic work or work in the other spouse's business, which Catalonian and Spanish law provide for, can be contractually excluded or limited.[132]

Where there exists a mechanism for the adjustment of pensions, as is the case in Switzerland or Germany, autonomy with regard to the splitting of pensions is usually also a lot more restricted. In Germany, according to the Federal Supreme Court the pension rights adjustment, the *Versorgungsausgleich*, ranks between maintenance and the adjustment of accrued gains and consequently only limited

[129] Article 232 para 2 French Civil Code; Article 90 para 2 Spanish Civil Code; Article 4 para 13 Italian Divorce Law (Law 1.12.1970 no. 898) – concerning agreements by parties in a joint petition see for Italy also Cass., 11.06.1997, No 5244, Giur.it., 1998, I, 1, c.218.

[130] For Germany see BGH, 24.4.1985, *NJW* (1985), 1835 and more differentiated BGH, 28.3.2007, *NJW* (2007), 2851; similarly demanded for Switzerland by I. Schwenzer, 'Betreuungsunterhalt – Gretchenfrage des Unterhaltsrechts', *Fampra.ch* (2010), 18 at 31.

[131] Cass. civ. 2e, 21 fév. 1988, N° 86-16.598; P. Courbe, *Droit de la famille,* Dalloz, 5th edition, Paris, 2008, p 209.

[132] See for Article 41 Catalonian Family Code, cf. J. Egea Fernández and J. Ferrer i Riba (dir), A. Lamarca i Marqués and C. Ruisánchez Capelastegui (eds*), Comentaris al codi de familia, a la Llei d'unions estables de parella i a la Llei de situacions convivencials d'ajuda mutual*, Tecnos, Madrid, 2002, pp 158, 246–247; for a more liberal approach Article 232-7, 231-20 para. 5 Projecte de llei; for Spanish Law cf. B. Ribera Blanes, in J. Rams Albesa and J.A. Moreno Martínez, *El régimen económico del matrimonio. Comentarios al Código civil: especial consideración de la doctrina jurisprudencial,* Dykinson, Madrid 2006, p 905; diff. M. P. García Rubio, 'Acuerdos prematrimoniales. De nuevo la libertad y sus límites en el Derecho de Familia', in *University of Girona, Nous reptes del Dret de Família, Materials de les Tretzenes Jornades de Dret Català a Tossa*, Documenta Universitaria, Girona 2005, p 112 et seq ; for a comparative overview J. Seevogel, *Der Wahlgüterstand der Gütertrennung für die Europäische Ehe* (to be published).

freedom is granted.[133] In Switzerland, pension adjustments can be made in divorce agreements only.[134]

That contracting is often much more limited with respect to maintenance and pension sharing, offsets to a certain extent the harsh results of a more or less unbounded contractual freedom in matrimonial property law. With maintenance in particular the well-being of children who need continuing care comes into play. But restricting party autonomy here also seeks to prevent undue hardship to the other spouse as well as detrimental consequences to the welfare system and thus the public in general. Yet this safety valve fails in those systems where no or only very limited maintenance is granted. The degree to which maintenance after divorce can be claimed varies substantially.[135] In some countries it may only be granted for a rather limited time and/or amount, either because of a relatively high level of employment of women, in particular of those with children, or as a matter of policy with regard to a clean break, whereas in others maintenance is paid to a much larger extent. Everything considered, however, having widened the view to include other financial consequences has led to a further narrowing of the gap between the Continental European and English legal systems.

3. AUTONOMY AND ITS BOUNDARIES – PERSPECTIVES

3.1. THE PRINCIPLE OF SELF-DETERMINATION

In view of the still considerable differences in the overall systems, we will now explore whether some common ground can be found regarding the extent

---

133 Sec 1408 para 2 German Civil Code refers to sec 6 and 8 Pension Adjustment Act which narrows the possibilities for marital agreements; for the restricted freedom concerning pension rights adjustment see also BVerfG, 6.2.2001, *NJW* (2001), 957; BGH, 11.2.2004, *FamRZ* (2004), 601; BGH, 6.10.2004, *FamRZ* (2005), 26, 27; for details see G. Brambring, 'Vereinbarungen über den Versorgungsausgleich und Familiengericht', *FGPrax (Praxis der freiwilligen Gerichtsbarkeit)* (2010), 7 et seq and J. Bredthauer, 'Vereinbarungen über den Versorgungsausgleich', *FPR (Familie Partnerschaft Recht)* (2009), 500 et seq.

134 Cf. H. Hausheer, 'Vertragsfreiheit im Familienrecht in der Schweiz', in S. Hofer, D. Schwab, D. Henrich (eds), *From Status to Contract? – Die Bedeutung des Vertrages im europäischen Familienrecht,* Gieseking, Bielefeld, 2005, p 76; see also M. Courvoisier, *Voreheliche und eheliche Scheidungsfolgenvereinbarungen – Zulässigkeit und Gültigkeitsvoraussetzungen,* Helbing & Lichtenhahn, Basel – Geneva – Munich, 2002, p 225; unlike the Netherlands, where Article 2 para 1 Pension Rights Adjustments Act allows deviation through marital or divorce agreements.

135 For an overview see D. Martiny, 'Ehescheidung und nachehlicher Unterhalt in Europa', *EJCL*, Vol. 8.3 (2004); cf. also the comparative examination in K. Boele-Woelki, F. Ferrand, C. González Beilfuss, M. Jänterä-Jareborg, N. Lowe, D. Martiny and W. Pintens (eds), *Principles of European Family Law Regarding Divorce and Maintenance Between Former Spouses,* Intersentia, Antwerp, 2004, p 79 et seq.

to which couples should be able to contract on the consequences of divorce. Contractual freedom constitutes an expression of the fundamental principle of self-determination, which is not only recognised by Article 8 ECHR guaranteeing the right to respect for private and family life,[136] but is universally accepted and sometimes even constitutionally protected.[137] Questions of family law may not be excluded since they often touch upon very personal issues where self-determination is of the utmost importance.[138] Encouraging couples to consider the consequences of a potential divorce before or after getting married does not encourage divorce, but might on the contrary even promote stability.[139] Mutual expectations are expressed and the likelihood of a hidden dissent concerning the future of the relationship, the sharing of tasks and the required contributions is thus diminished. As private-ordering of the economic consequences of divorce should therefore generally be promoted, contracts may not be disregarded or lightly set aside later. However, the recognition of marital contracts does not necessarily imply boundless freedom.

3.2. THE BOUNDARIES OF CONTRACTUAL FREEDOM

3.2.1. *Their justification*

Why should there be limits to private ordering? Marital agreements cannot be treated just like any commercial contract. There are fundamental differences between contracts in general and those between spouses with regard to their relationship.[140] In a marital relationship there is no immediate exchange of goods or services: it is founded on reciprocity over the time. It constitutes a relationship

136 Cf. ECHR, 16.12.1992, Case 13710/88, *Niemitz v Germany*, Mn 29 'Respect for private life must also comprise to a certain degree the right to establish and develop relationships with other human beings'; for contractual relations see D.J. Harris, M. O'Boyle, C. Warbrick, E. Bates and C. Buckley, *Law of the European Convention on Human Rights*, Oxford University Press, 2nd ed, Oxford, 2009, p 364 et seq and C. Grabenwarter, *Europäische Menschenrechtskonvention*, C.H. Beck, 4th ed, Munich, 2009, para 22, Mn 13.

137 Cf. also Article 7 of the European Charter of Fundamental Rights (2007/C 303/01); rather explicitly Article 2 para 1 German Basic Law; for the interaction of self-determination and marital contracts see also B. Dauner-Lieb, 'Gütertrennung zwischen Privatautonomie und Inhaltskontrolle', *AcP* 210 (2010), 580–609 as well as A. Sanders, *Statischer Vertrag und dynamische Vertragsbeziehung*, Gieseking, Bielefeld, 2008, pp 106–107.

138 For the role of self-determination in family law see the collection of essays by various authors in M. Martín Casals and J. Ribot (eds), *The Role of Self-determination in the Modernisation of Family Law in Europe*, Documenta Universitaria, Girona, 2006.

139 B. Stark, 'Marriage Proposals: From One-Size-Fits-All to Postmodern Marriage Law', 89 *Cal. L. Rev.* (2001), 1479 at 1523; for "contract marriages" see also A. Tsaoussis, 'Less Status, More Contract: an Economic Analysis of "Contract Marriage"', Sept. 2006, pp 6, 9 and 10, available at SSRN: http://ssrn.com/abstract=1119664.

140 B. Bix, 'The ALI Principles and Agreements: Seeking a Balance between Status and Contract', in R.F. Wilson (ed), *Reconceiving the Family. Critique on the American Law Institute's Principles of the Law of Family Dissolution*, Cambridge University Press, New York, 2006, p 375; see also

of indefinite duration; it is all-encompassing so as to involve emotional as well as economic aspects and is usually based on fundamental principles of love and trust. Marriage is a dynamic relationship in the sense that over time significant changes may occur to which spouses continually adapt, generally by mutual agreement.[141] Such processes can concern external circumstances, such as illness, unemployment, a new job or birth of children, but may also pertain to the partners' preferences and the development of their individual personalities as well as their relationship. It is often difficult or impossible to foresee such circumstances as well as how spouses will adjust to the changes themselves.

In view of these characteristics of marital relationships it is not surprising that the formation of a contract is frequently not preceded by bargaining at arm's length as is typically or at least ideally the case with commercial contracts, thereby resulting in a fair contract.[142] Bargaining leverage depends on a number of external as well as internal factors, such as the statutory regime for married and cohabitating partners, the respective emotional involvement of the partners, the existence of children in the partnership or the investments which have already been made. There may therefore be a considerable disparity in the value attached to getting married. The costs involved in foregoing the conclusion of the marital agreement also depend on the likelihood of separation in case an agreement fails. Depending on the point in the partners' lives at which the contract was concluded the potential for renegotiation might be reduced. Besides the wish for a contract often arises where there are significant differences in the bargaining power because one party is particularly wealthy. Moreover, typically couples at the time of marriage do not really consider divorce to be a serious risk.[143] Even if

M. Ryznar and A. Stępień-Sporek, 'To Have and to Hold, for Richer or Richer: Premarital Agreements in the Comparative Context', *13 Chapman Law Review* (2009), 27 at 38.

141 On the dynamic of spousal relationships see especially A. Sanders, *Statischer Vertrag und dynamische Vertragsbeziehung*, Gieseking, Bielefeld, 2008, p 109 et seq as well as 'Private Autonomy and Marital Property Agreements', 59 *ICLQ* (2010), 571 at 596.

142 For the warranty of fairness of contracts in general see W. Schmidt-Rimpler, 'Grundfragen einer Erneuerung des Privatrechts', *AcP* 147 (1941), 130 at 149 et seq; W. Schmidt-Rimpler, 'Zum Vertragsproblem', in F. Baur, J. Esser, F. Kübler and E. Steindorff (eds), *Funktionswandel der Privatrechtsinstitutionen – Festschrift für Ludwig Raiser zum 70. Geburtstag*, Mohr, Tübingen, 1974, p 8 et seq; D. Coester-Waltjen, 'Die Inhaltskontrolle von Verträgen außerhalb des AGBG', *AcP* 190 (1990), 1 at 14 et seq on marital agreements especially 22–23; for substantial inferiority of the wife's position, I. Schwenzer, 'Vertragsfreiheit im Ehevermögens- und Scheidungsfolgenrecht', *AcP* 196 (1996), 88–113 at 104 et seq; for examples of possible imbalances of the spouses bargaining positions, see B. Dauner-Lieb, 'Reichweite und Grenzen der Privatautonomie im Ehevertragsrecht', *AcP* 201 (2001), 294–332 at 299, 300 and for an unequal bargaining position cf. *ibidem* p 321 et seq.

143 For striking evidence see the survey of H. Mahar, according to which people succeeded in estimating the general divorce risk of 50% in the US but saw their own risk at 11% (including a fairly large number of people who estimated their own risk at 0%), H. Mahar, 'Why Are There So Few Pre-nuptial Agreements?', *(2003) John M. Olin Ctr. for Law, Econ., & Bus., Harvard Law School, Discussion Paper No. 436*, pp 4 and 11.

they enter into a marital agreement they are generally myopic or overoptimistic.[144] Their rationality can be characterised as bounded.[145] Consequently, the risk posed by disadvantageous terms is underestimated and the need to provide in detail for future changes disregarded. A spouse may also fear that to bargain is interpreted as a lack of trust.[146] Due to such signalling, notably the cost of negotiating clauses which provide for potential changes may be considered too high.

3.2.2. *The requirement of special provisions*

Although of course there are contracts in other areas which also show some of the above characteristics, such as employment contracts, partnership agreements[147] or other long-term relational contracts,[148] taken together the particular features of a marital or any comparable intimate relationship result in special risks which require at least an adaptation of the general rules or even a different set of rules.[149] They must effectively counter potential imperfections at the formation stage as well as protect against the consequences of subsequent changes in the circumstances.

3.2.2.1. Procedural safeguards

Procedural safeguards may *ex ante* diminish the risk of cognitive defects or counteract the danger of substantial imbalance. This reduces the need for

144 Cf. for this "unrealistic optimism" American Law Institute, *Principles of the Law of Family Dissolution: Analysis and Recommendation*, Lexis Nexis, San Francisco, 2002, pp 986–987.

145 B. Bix, 'The ALI Principles and Agreements: Seeking a Balance between Status and Contract', in R.F. Wilson (ed), *Reconceiving the Family. Critique on the American Law Institute's Principles of the Law of Family Dissolution*, Cambridge University Press, New York, 2006, p 375. In depth A. Sanders, *Statischer Vertrag und dynamische Vertragsbeziehung*, Gieseking, Bielefeld, 2008, p 115 et seq; see also E. Wiemer, *Inhaltskontrolle von Eheverträgen*, Gieseking, Bielefeld, 2008, p 35 et seq; for the concept of bounded rationality see H.A. Simons, 'Bounded Rationality in Social Science: Today and Tomorrow', *Mind & Society* 1 (2000), 25–39.

146 Cf. the survey in H. Mahar, 'Why Are There So Few Pre-nuptial Agreements?', *(2003) John M. Olin Ctr. for Law, Econ., & Bus., Harvard Law Sch., Discussion Paper No. 436*, p 16; see also A. Nicolo and P. Tedeschi, 'Missing Contracts: On the Rationality of not Signing a Pre-nuptial Agreement', University of Padua Economics Discussion Paper No. 39-2003, available at SSRN: http://ssrn.com/abstract=555261.

147 For this comparison see most notably B. Dauner-Lieb, 'Gütertrennung zwischen Privatautonomie und Inhaltskontrolle', *AcP* 210 (2010), 580 at 585 et seq as well as A. Sanders, *Statischer Vertrag und dynamische Vertragsbeziehung*, Gieseking, Bielefeld, 2008; for analogies between various business models and different intimate affiliations M. ERTMANN, 'Marriage as a Trade: Bridging the Private/Private Distinction', 36 *Harvard Civil Rights-Civil Liberties Law Review* (2001), 79–132.

148 On long-term relational contracts see only C.J. Goetz and R.E. Scott, 'Principles of Relational Contracts', 67 *Va. L. Rev. (Virginia Law Review)* 1089 (1981); I. Macneil and D. Campbell, *The Relational Theory of Contracts: Selected Works of Ian Macneil*, Sweet & Maxwell, London, 2001.

149 See for the application of the general rules as well as specific provisions in various European legal systems above II.3.

subsequent judicial control and thus increases predictability.[150] Requiring compliance with certain formalities is thus also preferable to the need for judicial approval following the conclusion of the agreement, which in some systems serves to prevent contracts that are manifestly unfair at the moment of formation.[151] In particular, formalities such as the notarial form which provides for information and independent counselling, help to prevent rash acts or overreaching.[152] They also ensure that the importance of the agreement as well as the meaning of its terms is fully understood. This is especially important where a spouse does not possess any legal or business experience or is not sufficiently fluent in the language of negotiation. Interpreting during the negotiations as well as the translation of the respective documents may be indispensable. Requiring the notarisation of marital agreements may also increase the likelihood that the partners are aware of the risks which potential changes of material circumstances in a life-long relationship pose and that they provide for these in advance as far as possible. Effective counselling should include the suggestion that the partners plan ahead for a change of circumstances. Requiring the spouses' physical presence appears vital in order to ensure the purpose of this formal requirement. Where the notarial form calls for the agreement to be signed in the presence of both partners, separate counselling and ascertaining the validity of the consent may additionally be preferable.

In countries which do not have the notarial system, the requirement of a written and signed agreement in addition to guaranteeing independent counselling by two solicitors may well serve the same purpose and thus constitutes a functional equivalent.[153] In any event, requiring a written and signed document serves evidentiary purposes. In helping to avoid ambiguous terms it also improves clarity and legal certainty and thus reduces litigation.

Yet too little importance has so far been attached to the timing:[154] in case of a pre-nuptial agreement a sufficient period of time must pass before the wedding takes

[150] Another way to prevent contracts that are manifestly unfair at the moment of the formation may be requiring a judicial homologation after the conclusion of the agreement.

[151] See above II.3.

[152] On the advantages of the notary form see G. Brambring, 'Die Ehevertragsfreiheit und ihre Grenzen', in S. Hofer, D. Schwab and D. Henrich (eds), *From Status to Contract - Die Bedeutung des Vertrages im europäischen Familienrecht*, Gieseking, Bielefeld, 2005, pp 24–27.

[153] In English case law increasing value is placed on independent legal advice, importance attributed to a pre-nuptial depending on information, informed consent, cf. P. Duckworth, *Duckworth's Matrimonial Property and Finance*, Jordan Publishing, Looseleaf Issue 20 (Nov 2009), D1 (3D) as well as *Radmacher v Granatino* [2010] UKSC 42 at para 69, however, reducing negative consequences for the weight attributed to an agreement to *material* lacks of disclosure, information and advice only.

[154] In England the Home Office advises to sign a pre-nuptial agreements at least 21 days before the wedding, cf. Home Office, *Supporting Families – A Consultation Paper*, 1998, *4.23* – however, the courts seem to apply no specific time limit, cf. *K v K (Ancillary Relief: Pre-nuptial Agreement) [2003] 1 FLR 120* as well as Thorpe LJ in *Radmacher v Granatino*

place. Where the contract is entered into on the eve of the wedding day this would suggest that the decision was taken hastily and not enough warning was given. Thus, for instance, the American Law Institute's Principles of the Law of Family Dissolution require that the agreement was entered into at least 30 days before the conclusion of the marriage in order to consult counsel or otherwise consider properly the implications of the marital contract.[155] The agreement would then benefit from the presumption "that the other party's consent to it was informed and free of duress".[156]

Whether information regarding the financial circumstances should be required depends upon two aspects: with post-nuptial agreements disclosure is generally essential, as the significance of the contract can only be assessed in light of the rights that would otherwise exist in the event of divorce.[157] With pre-nuptial agreements the answer hinges on whether the statutory regime provides for a sharing of premarital assets and the extent to which such sharing should be susceptible to contractual exclusion.[158]

3.2.2.2. Judicial control

However, safeguards at the formation stage are not enough: judicial control is especially called for in order to counter the danger resulting from a substantial change in circumstances after the conclusion of the agreement. This is particularly crucial if such changes have not been foreseen and have led to significantly unjust conditions. But it may also be necessary if the agreement – despite the procedural safeguards – contains manifestly unfair provisions.

[2009] EWCA Civ 649, [2009] 2 FLR 1181 at para 33, the Supreme Court did not mention the timing explicitly, for the circumstances attending the making of the agreement in general cf. *Radmacher v Granatina* [2010] UKSC 42 at para 68 et seq; while in the US the Uniform Premarital Agreement Act did not set a time period, some states amended that act and included the requirement of a lapse of a certain time period between the signing of the pre-nuptial agreement and the wedding, eg Californian Family Code para 1615 (c) (2) (seven days). In other states the fact that the agreement was signed several weeks before the wedding will be considered in establishing the voluntariness, cf. P. A. Katz and A. Clayman, 'When Your Elderly Clients Marry: Pre-nuptial Agreements and Other Considerations', 16. *J. Am. Acad. Matrimonial Law (Journal of the American Academy of Matrimonial Lawyers)* (1999–2000), 445 at 447.

155 American Law Institute, *Principles of the Law of Family Dissolution: Analysis and Recommendation*, Lexis Nexis, San Francisco, 2002, sec 7.04 para 3 (a) (p 960).

156 American Law Institute, *Principles of the Law of Family Dissolution: Analysis and Recommendation*, Lexis Nexis, San Francisco, 2002, pp 966–967.

157 For the duty of the spouses to provide information on assets during marriage see K. Boele-Woelki, B. Braat and I. Curry-Sumner (eds), *European Family Law in Action. Volume IV: Property Relations Between Spouses*, Intersentia, Antwerp, 2009, questions 39, 74, 110, 144, 176.

158 See for the general possibility to opt out of such sharing as well as its limits below 3.2.2.3.2.2; cf. also the meaning of disclosure for pre-nuptial agreements in England, *Radmacher v Granatino* [2009] EWCA Civ 649, [2009] 2 FLR 1181 at para 141, confirmed in *Radmacher v Granatino* [2010] UKSC 42 at 115 and 117.

3.2.2.3. Criteria for fairness – fundamental principles of statutory rules as yardstick

3.2.2.3.1. Compensation for marriage-related economic disparities

In order to foresee the extent of judicial control it is essential to provide more detailed criteria instead of merely referring to an unspecified fairness test. The yardstick for fairness should be determined in view of the underlying principles of the statutory or default rules on the financial consequences of divorce so as to ensure that their primary goals are achieved. Although there are obviously many differences in detail, comparative research reveals some fundamental principles: as has been shown in previous works and can only briefly be recounted here, most systems in one way or another aim to provide compensation where marriage has led to an imbalance in the spouses' economic situation.[159] Such disparities occur particularly where, due to a division of labour, one partner has been able to pursue his or her career to an extent he or she could not have done otherwise and has thereby increased his or her assets and furthered his or her earning capacity, whereas the other partner has taken on more of the domestic work or foregone career opportunities.[160] Consequently these disparities can regard property or assets as well as pension rights accumulated during the marriage or affect the post-divorce earning capacity. In Continental Europe, where they are counterbalanced by separate systems, the sharing of property acquired during the marriage – as is provided for in practically all Continental matrimonial property regimes, either at divorce, as in systems based on a separation of property, or even during the marriage, as is the case in community property systems – finds its justification not only in the fact that both spouses contribute to the accumulation of assets: it can also constitute compensation for detriments which one spouse has suffered as a result of the marriage.[161] Now that the fault principle has been abandoned, maintenance law in most European systems also focuses

[159] N. Dethloff, 'Unterhalt, Zugewinn, Versorgungsausgleich – Sind unsere familienrechtlichen Ausgleichssysteme noch zeitgemäß?', in Ständige Deputation des deutschen Juristentages (ed), *Gutachten zum 67. Deutschen Juristentag Erfurt 2008,* C.H. Beck, Munich, 2008, A 28 et seq; for a similar approach see American Law Institute, *Principles of the Law of Family Dissolution: Analysis and Recommendation,* Lexis Nexis, San Francisco, 2002, ch. 5 (compensatory spousal payments) as well as I. Schwenzer, *Model Family Code,* Intersentia, Antwerp – Oxford, 2006, ch. 2 (Partnership-Related Benefits and Detriments) and 3 sec 1 (Equitable Adjustment – Compensation Principle).

[160] See for a more detailed analysis of such marriage-related disparities N. Dethloff, 'Unterhalt, Zugewinn, Versorgungsausgleich – Sind unsere familienrechtlichen Ausgleichssysteme noch zeitgemäß?', in Ständige Deputation des deutschen Juristentages (ed), *Gutachten zum 67. Deutschen Juristentag Erfurt 2008,* C.H. Beck, Munich, 2008, A 16–19, 29, 46–50, 87–92.

[161] For the justification in German family law see N. Dethloff, 'Unterhalt, Zugewinn, Versorgungsausgleich – Sind unsere familienrechtlichen Ausgleichssysteme noch zeitgemäß?', in Ständige Deputation des deutschen Juristentages (ed), *Gutachten zum 67. Deutschen Juristentag Erfurt 2008,* C.H. Beck, Munich, 2008, A 87–92; for a comparative overview see N. Dethloff, *Familienrecht,* C.H. Beck, 29th ed, Munich, 2009, pp 166–168.

on compensating marriage-related detriments.[162] Some systems even provide for specific compensatory payments, like France[163] or Catalonia.[164] When considering the many criteria which in English law Article 25 Matrimonial Causes Act requires to be taken into account in granting ancillary relief, countering disparities in financial resources and earning capacities, especially in the light of the spouses' contributions, is a central aspect.[165]

3.2.2.3.2. Consequences for party autonomy

3.2.2.3.2.1. Limits on waiving compensation for marriage-related detriments

Determining the extent of judicial control in view of this goal implies that where no such marriage-related imbalances exist, couples should generally be free to exclude any sharing of assets, of provisions for old age or maintenance – a result that could be reached both in Continental European systems as well as in English law. In such cases there should only be very limited restrictions on freedom. Thus one might consider whether restrictions should be imposed on partners leaving a sick spouse after a long-term marriage without any provision, even though his or her earning capacity has definitely not been affected by the marriage.

In contrast, if such imbalances exist, autonomy should be more restricted.[166] Again whether the starting point is contractual freedom in Continental Europe or the English system with a set of criteria according to which ancillary relief is granted, the extent of judicial control or the boundaries of autonomy can and should be the same. Thus where default or statutory rules – as in most cases in Continental

---

162 D. Martiny, 'Ehescheidung und nachehelicher Unterhalt in Europa', *EJCL*, vol. 8.3 (2004), 13, http://www.ejcl.org/; K. Boele-Woelki, F. Ferrand, C. González Beilfuss, M. Jänterä-Jareborg, N. Lowe, D. Martiny and W. Pintens, *Principles of European Family Law Regarding Divorce and Maintenance Between Former Spouses,* Intersentia, Anwerp – Oxford, 2004, pp 73–76.

163 See above at II. 4. for the *prestation compensatoire* which more specifically aims at the compensation of divorce-related disparities in the standard of living, A. Batteur, 'Droit des Personnes, de la Famille et des Incapacités', L.G.D.J., Paris, 2007, Mn 725; J. Carbonnier, 'Droit Civil, Tome 2, La famille, l'enfant, le couple', Presses Univ. de France, Paris, 2002, p 611.

164 See above 2.4.

165 Sec 25 para 2 (a) Matrimonial Causes Act 1973 requires to take into account 'the income, earning capacity, property and other financial resources which each of the parties to the marriage has or is likely to have in the foreseeable future, including in the case of earning capacity any increase in that capacity which it would in the opinion of the court be reasonable to expect a party to the marriage to take steps to acquire'; see for compensation as one of the key themes besides needs and sharing *Miller v Miller* and *McFarlane v McFarlane* [2006] UKHL 24 para 13 (Lord Nichols) and 140 (Baroness Hale).

166 Similarly E. Wiemer, *Inhaltskontrolle von Eheverträgen,* Gieseking, Bielefeld, 2008, p 53 et seq; cf. also B. Dauner-Lieb, 'Reichweite und Grenzen der Privatautonomie im Ehevertragsrecht', *AcP* 201 (2001), 295–332, at 316 et seq as well as 'Gütertrennung zwischen Privatautonomie und Inhaltskontrolle', *AcP* 210 (2010), 580–609, at 607.

Europe, but in the wake of the *White* v *White*[167] ruling increasingly also in England – provide for equal sharing this could be contractually reduced if a sharing to this extent is not required to compensate for the marriage-related detriments; that is, where the other spouse's profits are clearly a result of his or her individual skills, particularly skills he or she already possessed prior to marriage. Where statutory regimes provide for a sharing of premarital assets, as is the case in the deferred community of property in the Nordic countries with the exception of Norway,[168] the general community property regimes in the Netherlands[169] or the English system of ancillary relief,[170] partners should in general be free to contractually exclude this – with an exception which will be set out below.[171] Apart from that, judicial control must ensure that there are strict limits for waiving compensation for partnership-related detriments.

One cannot object that everybody should have the freedom to waive all compensation for any detriments. Most legal systems acknowledge that there are limits to binding oneself for the future: agreeing, for example, to waive the right to divorce or to make divorce more difficult would not be possible;[172] after a long-term marriage the waiving of any compensation for marriage-related detriments might leave a spouse with no or dramatically reduced exit-options. This is especially true if there are children in the family, whose existence substantially changes the exit-options. Moreover, not doing so would typically result in women bearing the burden as they still more often take on the role of homemaker, reduce their gainful employment at least for some time or forego a more promising career in order to care for the children.[173]

Moreover, a waiver of compensation for marriage-related detriments evidently results from a substantial imbalance in bargaining power if the contract already proved to be clearly disadvantageous to one spouse at the outset. And where the contract only later turned out to be exceedingly detrimental to him or her due to a subsequent change of the circumstances, eg the unplanned for birth of a child,

167 *White v White* [2001] 1 A.C. 596, [2000] 2 FLR 981.

168 A. Agell, *Nordisk äktenskapsrätt: en jämförande studie av dansk, finsk, isländsk, norsk och svensk rätt med diskussion av reformbehov och harmoniseringsmöjligheter*, Nordiska Ministerrådet, Copenhagen, 2003, pp 167–169.

169 Article 1:94 para 1 Dutch Civil Code.

170 For an overview see M. R. Probert, *Cretney's Family Law*, Sweet & Maxwell, London, 2006, 8–001, 8–008 et seq and M. Welstead and S. Edwards, *Family Law*, Oxford University Press, New York, 2008, 7.38 et seq.

171 See below bb).

172 For the possibilities of a covenant marriage in some states of the U.S. see the overview in P. Hay, 'The American "Covenant Marriage" in the Conflict of Laws', in J. Witte Jr. and E. Ellison (eds), *Covenant Marriage in Comparative Perspective*, William B. Erdmans Publishing Company, Grand Rapids, Michigan – Cambridge UK, 2006, pp 294–299.

173 In depth data on the employment of women with children is provided in EUROSTAT, *Gender gaps in the reconciliation between work and family life*, Statistics in Focus, Theme 3, Population and Social conditions, 4/2005.

the failure to provide adequately for such changes is usually also brought about by a bounded rationality when entering into a marital agreement.

It may not always be easy to determine the extent of the financial detriments which a spouse has suffered as a result of the marriage. The longer a marriage has lasted and the younger the couple were when their relationship began and they started to invest in the partnership in a way that would leave one of them worse off in the case of divorce, the more difficult it will be to establish the spouse's hypothetical professional development.

3.2.2.3.2.2. Consideration of the overall financial consequences

An assessment of whether economic disadvantages resulting from marriage are sufficiently offset requires that the overall financial consequences of divorce be taken into account. A greater share in the property or payment of compensation can make up for the other partner's reduced earning capacity and obviate the need for periodical payments or maintenance. Although the English system contains better mechanisms to do so, the Continental differentiation between property, maintenance and pension sharing does not preclude this: when reviewing a marital agreement, judges simply must consider the overall consequences. At this point other goals come into play as well, namely the principle of a clean break, which an increasing number of countries now make their aim.[174] Ending the economic ties once and for all is clearly a desirable objective, given that it is not understood as simply leaving one spouse to bear alone the detrimental financial consequences of the partnership.[175] To achieve both a clean break and an adequate compensation for marriage-related detriments, it may sometimes also be necessary to share premarital assets. This would in particular be the case if during the marriage one spouse has significantly improved his professional skills and thus his earning capacity at the expense of the other, but had not had time to amass a lot of assets before the divorce. Consequently, there may even be limits to the spouses' contractual freedom to exclude all sharing of premarital assets.

[174] Cf. K. Boele-Woelki, F. Ferrand, C. GonzáLez Beilfuss, M. Jänterä-jareborg, N. Lowe, D. Martiny and W. Pintens, *Principles of European Family Law Regarding Divorce and Maintenance Between Former Spouses,* Intersentia, Anwerp – Oxford, 2004, pp 77–78 (principle of self-sufficiency after divorce); for an overview on the clean break principle in common law countries see I. Schwenzer, 'Die Scheidung – clean break auch für die nacheheliche Versorgung', in Stiftung Gesellschaft für Rechtspoliltik (Trier) and Institut für Rechtspolitik der Universität Trier (ed), *Bitburger Gespräche, Jahrbuch 2001*, C.H. Beck, Munich, 2001, pp 39–55.

[175] For the clean break principle in English law see R. Probert, *Cretney's Family Law,* Sweet & Maxwell, London, 2006, 8-035 to 8-039 and M. Welstead and S. Edwards, *Family Law,* Oxford University Press, New York, 2008, 7.73–7.74. For a different approach towards the clean break principle in Canadian law see C. Rogerson, 'The Canadian Law of Spousal Support', 38 *Fam. L. Q.* 69 at 76 (2004).

Yet another goal which might affect the extent of contractual freedom is the well-being of children who need continuing care. Spouses should not be able to waive financial burdens resulting from parental responsibilities, as divorce does not end their obligations arising from parentage. Thus, to the extent that maintenance or periodical payments are necessary to care for children, they cannot be renounced – just as, mostly, child support cannot.

4. CONCLUSION

Whether national law reforms are discussed or the mutual recognition of marital agreements and the creation of optional instruments in transnational cases considered, contractual freedom regarding the financial consequences of divorce should be recognised as a fundamental principle. However, its boundaries must be determined with a view to the specifics of marital relationships. The general rules of contract law are not sufficient to safeguard against agreements that are substantially detrimental to one of the spouses. Procedural safeguards are called for in order to counter cognitive defects and thus reduce the necessity of subsequent control. Judicial review is nevertheless still required, especially in view of any potential changes of circumstances. Contracts which waive all compensation for marriage-related detriments when taking the overall financial consequences into consideration are deemed manifestly unfair. Thus self-determination as well as fundamental fairness for the economically disadvantaged spouse is ensured while at the same time legal certainty is improved. As in life, in law – and notably in family law – there is no certainty. But where certainty and predictability can at least be increased a little, a lot can be gained.

MARITAL PROPERTY AGREEMENTS AND THE WORK OF THE LAW COMMISSION FOR ENGLAND AND WALES

ELIZABETH COOKE*

* Professor of Law, University of Reading, and currently serving as a Law Commissioner for England and Wales with responsibility for family law and property law. I write here in my personal capacity, but of course much of what I say draws on the Law Commission project. I gratefully acknowledge the work of the Law Commission team, Matthew Jolley and Catherine Vine. This chapter was written before the decision of the Supreme Court in *Radmacher v Granatino* [2010] UKSC 42.

1. INTRODUCTION

I was very grateful for the opportunity to speak at the Cambridge conference of the Commission for European Family Law in April 2010. The CEFL conferences are always a wonderful opportunity to share ideas and culture; on this occasion we discussed some peculiarly English problems, with the benefit of the insights and inspiration of a wide range of European colleagues.

My own remit was to discuss one of the current projects of the Law Commission for England and Wales. The Law Commission is an independent, non-political statutory body, set up by the Law Commissions Act 1965;[1] our task is to keep the law under review and to recommend reform to Government. Like the CEFL, therefore, we have no power to make legislation happen. But we are accountable for our use of public funds; we proceed by the widest possible consultation and take into account research that provides us with statistically significant measures of public opinion where that is available. One of our highest priorities is to assess the impact of our proposals and to produce solutions that combine practicability with acceptability.

We pursue projects on individual areas of the law that seem to us – following consultation – to be ripe for reform, and to be suitable for the Law Commission's work in terms of our resources and expertise. While we do not take on highly political issues (such as immigration or the death penalty), we have worked in some very high profile areas of the law. In family law, our work led to the Children Act 1989 (which remains the primary statute on child law) and the Family Law Act 1996 (domestic violence and divorce reform). Our working method generally is to research the law relevant to a particular project and to publish a consultation paper, in which we seek views on provisional proposals. We then assess the responses of consultees, and finally produce a Report with recommendations, and usually also a draft Bill which can then be adopted by Government if our recommendations are accepted. We work closely with Government departments during the passage through Parliament of any of our Bills; overall, since our foundation, around 75% of our projects have led to acceptance of our recommendations and thence to legislation.

1 "Law Commissions" in the plural because the Act also established the Scottish Law Commission.

2. THE LAW COMMISSION'S PROJECT ON MARITAL PROPERTY AGREEMENTS

Our project on marital property agreements was announced in 2008 when we published our Tenth Programme of Law Reform,[2] as follows:

> This project will examine the status and enforceability of agreements made between spouses and civil partners (or those contemplating marriage or civil partnership) concerning their property and finances. Such agreements might regulate the couple's financial affairs during the course of their relationship; equally they might seek to determine how the parties would divide their property in the event of divorce, dissolution or separation. They might be made before marriage (often called "pre-nups") or during the course of marriage or civil partnership. They need not be made in anticipation of impending separation; but they might constitute separation agreements reached at the point of relationship breakdown.
>
> Unlike in many other jurisdictions, marital property agreements are not currently enforceable in the event of the spouses' divorce or the dissolution of the civil partnership. The court may, however, have regard to them in determining what ancillary relief is appropriate.

This cannot be understood without an appreciation of our background law of matrimonial property and ancillary relief. In what follows I go through both of these and seek to set the context for the reform of marital property agreements. I then discuss very briefly the options for reform, but the reader is referred to the Law Commission's consultation paper for the detail of those options. At the time of writing, that paper is not yet published; although our initial intention was to publish in the early summer, we took the decision during the spring of 2010 not to publish our paper until the decision of the Supreme Court in *Radmacher v Granatino*[3] has been handed down. By the time of the publication of this book, that decision will have been reported and the Law Commission's consultation paper will almost certainly have been published.[4]

---

2 Tenth Programme of Law Reform (2008) Law Com No 311, paras 2.17 to 2.20.

3 See *Radmacher v Granatino* [2009] EWCA Civ 649 for the Court of Appeal decision.

4 For details see http://www.lawcom.gov.uk/marital_property.htm.

3. THE CURRENT LAW

3.1. SEPARATION OF PROPERTY DURING MARRIAGE

In England and Wales, the law of matrimonial property has travelled a strange journey.

The nascent feminist movement in the nineteenth century gave rise to the Married Women's Property Acts, with the result that since 1882 marriage has had no effect upon the property rights of spouses. The same, of course, can be said for civil partnership since its introduction in 2004. So at a time when most continental European jurisdictions operated a regime of community of property during marriage, so as to provide some level of protection for the non-earning spouse (as well as the ability to obtain credit), English law opted for a rigid separation of property that benefited the rich, but gave no protection to the financially weaker party in the event of the termination of the marriage by death or divorce. The Married Women's Property Acts did establish the married woman as an owner of property in her own right, but that gave no assistance to the non-earning spouse, who might have nothing of her own.

In 1938 family provision legislation was enacted so as to ensure that widows and widowers were not left with insufficient provision as a result of the operation of the rules of intestacy.[5] But it took considerably longer for the law to devise adequate financial protection for a non-earning spouse on divorce.

3.2. THE LAW OF ANCILLARY RELIEF

Until 1970, the courts had power to order the payment of maintenance for an "innocent" spouse in the event of divorce; their powers of property adjustment (ie to change the ownership of property, rather than to award income provision) were very limited indeed. The regime of separation of property was, for the most part, operated in its full rigour.

The 1970s saw agitation for change because of the unfair results that this produced. As Sir Jocelyn Simon put it:

5 That of course begs a question, and a full discussion of what is sufficient provision on death is outside the scope of this paper. For a summary of the recent position under the Inheritance (Provision for Family and Dependants) Act 1975 see *Intestacy and Family Provision Claims on Death* Law Commission Consultation Paper 191, 2009.

> ... the cock bird can feather the nest precisely because he does not have to spend most of his time sitting on it.[6]

Reform was in the air, and the Divorce Reform Act 1969 ushered in new law on the grounds for divorce. In the period leading up to reform there was considerable pressure for the introduction of a community of property regime.[7]

No regime was introduced. The Matrimonial Proceedings and Property Act 1970 introduced new law in relation to the financial consequences of divorce. The reforming statutes were consolidated in the Matrimonial Causes Act 1973, which remains the current statute.

The 1973 Act provides that the financial consequences of divorce or of dissolution of a civil partnership[8] may be determined by the court, and it gives the court a very wide discretion to determine those consequences. Orders may be made for periodical payments, property adjustment, pension sharing and so on having regard to a list of factors set out in section 25 of the 1973 Act:

> (a) the income, earning capacity, property and other financial resources which each of the parties to the marriage has or is likely to have in the foreseeable future, including in the case of earning capacity any increase in that capacity which it would in the opinion of the court be reasonable to expect a party to the marriage to take steps to acquire;
> (b) the financial needs, obligations and responsibilities which each of the parties to the marriage has or is likely to have in the foreseeable future;
> (c) the standard of living enjoyed by the family before the breakdown of the marriage;
> (d) the age of each party to the marriage and the duration of the marriage;
> (e) any physical or mental disability of either of the parties to the marriage;
> (f) the contributions which each of the parties has made or is likely in the foreseeable future to make to the welfare of the family, including any contribution by looking after the home or caring for the family;
> (g) the conduct of each of the parties, if that conduct is such that it would in the opinion of the court be inequitable to disregard it;
> (h) in the case of proceedings for divorce or nullity of marriage, the value to each of the parties to the marriage of any benefit (for example, a pension) which, by

6 Sir J Simon, *With all my Worldly Goods...* (1965) p 14 (reproducing an address to the Holdsworth Club at the University of Birmingham on 20 March 1964). See the discussion by E Cooke, in M Dixon and G Griffiths (eds), *Contemporary Perspectives on Property, Equity and Trust Law*, Oxford, OUP, 2007, chapter 3.

7 S Cretney, *Family Law in the Twentieth century*, OUP, Oxford, 2003, 133 ff.

8 As to which see similar provisions in the Civil Partnership Act 2004, Schedule 5.

> reason of the dissolution or annulment of the marriage, that party will lose the chance of acquiring.

Faced with such a breadth of discretion, the courts have evolved some principles. Those principles changed dramatically in 2000.

Before 2000, the courts' approach was to ensure that the "needs"[9] of each party were met, as generously as possible; the rest of the couple's property was untouched. That meant, generally, that it remained with the husband.[10] That was the logical consequence of the separation of property regime. However, in the vast majority of cases that consequence was not visible, because in the vast majority of cases the couples' assets did not exceed – and very often fell short of – their joint needs. And as a result of the requirement in section 25(1) of the 1973 Act to give priority to the needs of the couple's children during their minority, in many cases the result of the operation of the statutory discretion[11] gave most of the assets to the wife who had the day-to-day care of the children.[12] However, in the "big money" cases the effect was dramatic; the divorced wife of a wealthy man would not receive more than £12 million – £15 million no matter what her husband's wealth.[13] This would be in stark contrast to what such a wife might have expected under a continental community of property regime where the norm, in the absence of a contract, is to share equally.

It is worth noting that the concept of "needs", in England and Wales, is rather broader than its counterpart concepts, however labelled (generally known as maintenance) throughout Europe. "Needs" is likely to include, where resources are sufficient to do so, long term provision to ensure that the parties are able to be owner-occupiers of a home. There are a number of reasons for this. For one, it may be that the courts' decision not to require the parties to share the assets beyond what was required for needs may have impelled them to take a very generous view of needs, particularly in order to ensure that the very rich divorcée did not suffer a drop in her standard of living. But for another, there are socio-economic factors to take into account. England and Wales has a limited rental housing market; that, combined with a culture that inclines us to regard renting as undesirable, means that needs inevitably comprises, where it is available, capital provision for

---

9 See section 25(b) quoted above.

10 The pre-*White* position can be seen in R Bird, "Ancillary relief outcomes" (2000) *Family Law* 831.

11 Or of the parties "bargaining in the shadow of the law" (see RH Mnookin and L Kornhauser, 'Bargaining in the Shadow of the Law: The case of Divorce' (1979) 88 *YLR (Yale Law Review)* 950).

12 Despite that, it is well-established that in general women fare less well, economically after divorce than do men: see Institute for Social and Economic Research, S Jenkins, *Marital splits and income changes over the long term* (2008), No 2008–07.

13 See for example *A v A (Financial provision)* [1998] 3 FCR 421; *Dart v Dart* [1996] 2 FLR 286.

housing. Moreover, the courts have been very conscious of the difficulties faced by those seeking to return to employment, perhaps in their 40s and 50s, after many years spent looking after children at home; as a result, they have tended to be very reluctant to restrict those who care for children, in particular, to only a defined term of maintenance payments, and have preferred to make open-ended awards that can subsequently be varied on the application of either party.

Following the House of Lords' decision in *White v White*[14] in 2000, the courts' approach has changed. Once the needs of the parties have been met out of their joint resources, generally the courts will divide the rest of the property of the couple equally. This may sound to continental ears very much like a regime of deferred community of property, but there are the following significant differences:

- There is no conceptual or practical separation between property and maintenance as there is for the most part throughout Europe. The court looks at income and capital together.
- The courts have not evolved clear rules as to whether or not pre-acquired or inherited property is to be shared. Nor is the status of individual business property clear. All property *may* be shared; and it is more likely to be shared the longer the marriage.[15] Insofar as pre-acquired property is not shared then the system looks rather like a deferred community of acquests, but with far too much inherent uncertainty to be so labelled.

Is this a regime at all? English lawyers say no.[16] We can highlight a number of reasons why: the level of discretion within the system; the lack of distinction between property and income; the inability to state clearly what property is matrimonial and what is not; and – crucially to the Law Commission's concerns – the lack of any reliable ability to contract out of the system of ancillary relief and into an alternative.

The Law Commission's project is related to that final point. We are not examining the law of ancillary relief; but we are looking at the law relating to a couple's ability, or lack of ability, to contract out of it.

---

[14] [2000] UKHL 54; [2001] 1 AC 596.

[15] See for example the dicta of Lord Nicholls in *Miller v Miller; McFarlane v McFarlane* [2006] UKHL 24, [2006] 2 AC 618 at [25].

[16] Despite the fact that the change resulting from *White v White* [2000] UKHL 54; [2001] 1 AC 596 brought us far nearer to a community regime: see S Cretney, 'Community of property imposed by judicial decision' [2003] 119 *LQR (Law Quarterly Review)* 349.

4. MARITAL PROPERTY AGREEMENTS: THE CURRENT LAW IN ENGLAND AND WALES

As the text quoted from our Tenth Programme indicates, we are looking at three types of agreement:

- Pre-nuptial agreements, made before marriage or civil partnership;
- Post-nuptial agreements, made after marriage or civil partnership and at a time when the couple does not intend to separate;
- Separation agreements, made when separation is imminent or has already taken place.

The first two types of agreement may, of course, make arrangements for the financial relationship of the couple during marriage. Such terms will be enforceable, under the current law, if they conform to the requirements of the law of contract and, in particular, if they were made with the intention of creating legal relationships. They are not problematic, although so far as we are aware they are rarely made. They may also set out non-financial terms, which probably have no legal effect and with which we are not concerned.

Our project engages, by contrast, with the terms in such agreements – that is, pre-nuptial or post-nuptial agreements – insofar as they make provision for a future separation that has not yet happened and is not at that stage intended to happen. Such terms in a pre-nuptial agreement are contrary to public policy and therefore void.[17] In a post-nuptial agreement they are not contrary to public policy,[18] but they cannot exclude the court's discretion to grant whatever financial relief it considers fair in the event of divorce.

As a result, neither pre-nuptial agreements nor post-nuptial agreements can be enforced as contracts; neither party can prevent the other making an application for ancillary relief and asking the court to make an order inconsistent with the terms of the agreement. However, increasingly in recent years the courts have been willing to follow the terms of agreements[19] reached properly and without undue pressure,[20] provided that both parties' needs are met and that there is no manifest injustice.[21]

---

17 The authorities for this date back to the nineteenth century; the status of pre-nuptial agreements was confirmed recently in the Privy Council's decision in *Macleod v MacLeod* [2008] UKPC 64.

18 *Macleod v MacLeod* [2008] UKPC 64.

19 See in particular *Crossley v Crossley* [2007] EWCA Civ 1491, [2008] 1 FCR 323.

20 See in particular *NA v MA* [2006] EWHC 2900 (Fam), [2007] 1 FLR 1760.

21 *Macleod v MacLeod* [2008] UKPC 64, [2010] 1 AC 298.

Separation agreements have not been regarded as contrary to public policy, because they provide for an actual separation (and so cannot be said to be providing for, and potentially encouraging, a future separation that might not happen). They cannot exclude the jurisdiction of the court to grant financial relief and so cannot be enforced as contracts; they are usually therefore given legal force by a consent order.[22] A party can ask the court to make an order that subverts the agreement; but it is well-established that if the agreement was fairly made the courts will normally be very willing to make orders confirming the terms of the agreement.[23]

We hear very little concern about the operation of the law in relation to separation agreements. But there is considerable dissatisfaction with the law relating to pre- and post-nuptial agreements. It is simply not possible to be certain what their effect will be. Spouses and fiancés may conclude them with the benefit of expensive legal advice; they and their advisers are equally frustrated by the uncertainty about their effect. The frustration is the more potent because the intention in making such agreements is very often to try to contract out of the uncertainty within the law of ancillary relief; the courts have not made clear rules as to what is to happen to, say, pre-acquired property, and it may seem very hard to a couple that they cannot, in effect, contract out of future litigation by making that decision contractually.

So there is a demand for enforceable marital property agreements. It is hard to state the extent of that demand. Certainly it can come from couples where one or both of the spouses comes from another jurisdiction where marital property agreements are enforceable; but we think that it also comes from people with special property to preserve – perhaps the home or savings salvaged from an earlier divorce – or with prospects of future wealth that they do not want to share.

5. MARITAL PROPERTY AGREEMENTS: THE OPTIONS FOR REFORM

So there is dissatisfaction with the current law. There are a number of options for change. I discuss first a very small step that could be taken to rationalise the current law, without making any real changes to current practice. In particular, it would not take the parties to a marital property agreement outside the discretion of the court, and therefore would not enable the predictability that some desire. So we then have to discuss whether or not it is right to go further and create truly

22 In other words, the parties apply for ancillary relief and ask the court to make an order that mirrors the terms of their agreement. The court is not obliged to do so.

23 *Edgar v Edgar* [1980] 1 WLR 1410.

enforceable agreements that could take effect as contracts and would leave no, or very little, scope for discretionary adjustment by the courts.

5.1. A SMALL STEP

Whether or not major reform is to take place, I suggest that there is a small and relatively uncontroversial step that might be taken to rationalise the current law. It is the reversal of the rule that pre-nuptial contracts are contrary to public policy, and therefore void, on the basis that they provide for a future separation.

This rule has already been abrogated, by judicial decision so far as post-nuptial contracts are concerned.[24] The Privy Council declined to cast doubt upon the rule for pre-nuptial contracts; one of the reasons for their refusal to do so was the vulnerability of people during their engagement, especially if signature of a pre-nuptial contract may be the price of the wedding.[25]

Whether people who sign pre-nuptial contracts are more vulnerable than those who sign post-nuptial contracts is an interesting question; it is almost certainly untestable. What we can say is that since we are not discussing, here, the question whether or not a pre-nuptial contract should exclude the court's discretion in ancillary relief, there will always be a safeguard for the spouse who claims that she had no realistic choice but to enter the contract. Just as the courts have shown themselves well able to protect those who are pressurised in a post-nuptial situation,[26] that protection can be extended to those who signed contracts before marriage.[27]

In *N v N*[28] it was said that

> An agreement made prior to marriage which contemplates the steps the parties will take in the event of divorce or separation is perceived as being contrary to public policy because it undermines the concept of marriage as a life-long union.

Whilst this was an accurate statement of the law, it is now an out-dated view of marital property agreements and should be reversed.

---

24 *MacLeod v MacLeod* [2008] UKPC 64.

25 *MacLeod v MacLeod* [2008] UKPC 64 at paragraph [31].

26 *NA v MA* [2006] EWHC 2900 (Fam).

27 The Privy Council's other argument (at [2008] UKPC 64 paragraph [35]) was the absence of a statutory jurisdiction to vary pre-nuptial contracts. With every respect, I suggest that the jurisdiction of the court in ancillary relief is adequate to manage variation where a spouse applies for provision in terms different from that of the contract.

28 [1999] 2 FLR 745, 752, by Wilson J.

5.2. GOING FURTHER: THE ARGUMENTS FOR AND AGAINST ENFORCEABLE CONTRACTS

The big question is whether or not there should be reform of marital property agreements so as to enable them to oust the jurisdiction of the court.

That is the way that English lawyers generally pose the question. What would that reform entail?

I suggest that it would mean that marital property agreements – pre-nuptial, post-nuptial and separation agreements – could be enforced as contracts. Currently, an attempt to sue on a marital property agreement in the civil courts would fail, and the claimant would be required to apply instead for ancillary relief. Reform would mean that the agreement would take effect as an ordinary contract.

However, there would be likely to be two qualifications to that position:

- First, it is likely that such agreements, as well as having to be contractually valid (and therefore neither void for mistake nor voidable for undue influence, for example) would also be required to comply with further requirements. At the very least, the law would be likely to require them to be in writing. It might also require disclosure of assets at the time of the making of the agreement, and/or the taking of legal advice, or at least proof that a party now opposing enforcement had the opportunity to take legal advice.
- Second, it is likely that in some circumstances an application for ancillary relief will be appropriate despite of the terms of the agreement. All the law reform proposals currently in the public domain in England and Wales envisage leaving open the door for the court to vary or set aside the agreement in some form of extreme circumstances – if the agreement caused "substantial hardship", for example.[29]

So what are the pros and cons of such reform?

This is a question to be explored at some length in our Consultation Paper and readers are referred to what I hope will be a comprehensive review of the arguments. To this book's audience I make just three points.

The first is the need to remember that in England and Wales, marital property agreements are not entered into in order to change from one regime to another, as they are throughout Europe. We have no legal regime. The current law can be

[29] See the proposals put forward by Resolution, at http://www.resolution.org.uk/editorial.asp?page_id=309.

said to be a regime of separate property during marriage, followed by a system of ancillary relief on divorce or dissolution that can be compared to a regime of deferred community but cannot be equated with such a regime, because of its discretionary content. So to allow marital property agreements to have binding effect as contracts is to allow the parties to contract out of discretion and therefore out of protection.

The second is that the discourse regarding marital property agreements in England and Wales involves both property and what European colleagues would call maintenance, while we would refer to it as provision for needs. The law of ancillary relief, as already remarked, does not make a rigid distinction between property and income, and has a broad concept of needs that includes capital provision. So in discussing the question of the validity of marital property contracts in this jurisdiction, we have to take considerable care not to make assumptions about their scope. Envious comments are often made to the effect that couples in continental Europe can make binding marital property agreements, while we cannot; but that is only half the truth, because by and large marital property agreements in continental Europe involve only the ownership of property and not a maintenance obligation.[30] So freedom of contract in this context does not have to mean freedom to walk away and leave one's partner with nothing; depending upon motivation, that may be an argument for or against reform here.

The third point to make is that a number of arguments advanced in favour of reform may equally be construed as arguments against it. An obvious example is the support of marriage. Some say that it is inappropriate for parties to a marriage or civil partnership to make advance provision for what is to happen on divorce or dissolution; commitment should mean that that possibility is not considered. Others observe that it is clear that the current law is deterring some people from marrying or forming civil partnerships. We have heard considerable anecdotal evidence from solicitors whose clients are from overseas and are shocked to hear that if they marry here they cannot safeguard their inherited or pre-acquired property from sharing on divorce. Some do not marry as a result. Lawyers have also told us that, in advising clients who want to marry but want a guarantee that they can keep that property, they are often obliged to say that the only way to guarantee continued ownership is not to marry.

Another argument that goes either way is autonomy. It is said that there should be freedom of contract, and that couples should be entitled to determine for themselves the financial consequences of the ending of their relationship.

30 In some European jurisdictions it is possible to regulate the provision of maintenance by contract; but there is only limited freedom to contract out of the maintenance obligation. See further K Boele-Woelki, B Braat, I Sumner (eds), *European Family Law in Action vol II: maintenance between former spouses*, Intersentia, Antwerp, 2003, p 461 ff.

One answer to that is that of course they can; they are perfectly free to make an agreement and stick to it. But the autonomy that is being argued for here is potentially the freedom to force one's partner to abide by an agreement that may have been made some time ago and that may now have disastrous consequences. Add to that the obvious potential for pressure in the making of the agreement, and the argument for autonomy loses some strength.

It cannot be stressed too often that these points are important in the context of England and Wales, however strange they may seem to continental ears, because the choice being made in this jurisdiction is not between a range of reasonably well-tried regimes that are agreed to be appropriate in certain circumstances, often for the protection of both parties.[31] In this context, it is a contracting out of a system that has been developed for the protection of the financially weaker spouse. One of the pressing questions for the law reformer is whether it is possible to deliver freedom of contract without incurring the social costs of allowing people to contract out of protection that they need – as they surely will do if they can. People are notoriously inaccurate in their view of risk when they marry or celebrate a civil partnership; relationship breakdown is something that happens to other people.

There are clear pros and cons to reform; there is no knock-down argument either way. We can confidently say two things. First, that there is demand for reform. Second, that reform has to be approached with caution, and with ingenuity, because of the potential for parties to contract out of protection.

5.3. ENFORCEABLE CONTRACTS: THE PRE-CONDITIONS FOR VALIDITY

The observations just made point to considerable caution in devising reform, and the Law Commission's consultation paper will be begging no questions. In particular, it will not be positively proposing that reform should take place. Instead it will rehearse the arguments either way and ask an open question of consultees.

Having asked that question, the consultation paper will then go on to ask some further hypothetical questions: *if* binding marital property agreements were to be introduced, what should be

[31] I have in mind the fact that in a jurisdiction where the default regime is immediate community, a couple will contract out of the default regime and into separation of property if one of them owns his or her own business, not to keep the business profits away from the other spouse, but to protect the other spouse from the business debts.

(a) the preconditions for their validity; and
(b) the circumstances in which, despite the existence of a binding agreement, the court should nevertheless have discretion, to a greater or lesser extent, to set aside the agreement.

Looking first at the pre-conditions, this is rather well-trodden ground but benefits from some analysis. Again, the reader is referred to the consultation paper for the full story. But it is worth noting that all the jurisdictions we are aware of impose some preconditions upon marital property agreements, beyond those that are involved in simple contractual validity. Perhaps the most interesting development recently has been in Australia, where statutory reform introduced in 2000 has been the subject of several legislative amendments as a result of what turned out to be unworkable provisions in the original legislation. What we can draw from that experience is the necessity to impose pre-conditions that are rigid enough to provide protection but not so inflexible that they invalidate agreements that ought to be upheld, nor so demanding of the lawyers involved that those lawyers are deterred from acting.[32]

It should be noted that although we have notaries in this country, they have a very specialised role and are not involved in private family law; nor is there any tradition of using one lawyer to advise both parties to an agreement. So the whole business of legal advice is rather difficult. Under the current law a pre- or post-nuptial agreement has more chance of being upheld if it can be shown that both parties had legal advice at the time it was made; we have been made aware of a number of instances where one party has paid for the other to have legal advice but at a very restricted level. For one party to have unlimited assistance in drafting and negotiation, while the other has merely a half-hour interview, does not provide anything like an adequate safeguard for the financially weaker party. Yet to require that both parties take comparable and comprehensive legal advice is obviously expensive; what are the chances of anyone supporting a reform that seems to provide money for lawyers? We have endeavoured in the consultation paper to come up with some compromise solutions here that will not be inordinately expensive for the parties or risky for the lawyers, but will ensure, at least, that each party will have enough information on which to make a decision, as well as having the opportunity to speak, alone, to a lawyer as an impartial third party.

It should also be noted that some thought will have to be given to the common law of contract, which developed without reference to marital property agreements. The law relating to undue influence and misrepresentation has, however, been put to use recently in the analysis of arrangements reached between husband and wife

[32] Family Law Act 1975, as amended.

in cases where one has in effect stood surety for the other's debts – for example by allowing the family home to be charged with the husband's business liabilities. What constitutes undue influence in such a context? The courts have developed a healthy suspicion of contracts entered into by parties in an intimate relationship that, in the words of the courts, "call for explanation" because they do not benefit both parties.[33] One recent case found that a husband's persuading a wife to enter into an agreement without, in effect, making full and frank disclosure not only of his financial position but also about his personal life constituted undue influence.[34] The fact that the courts exercise that level of surveillance in that context makes it clear that marital property agreements are by no means the only type of agreement that cannot be entered into without legal safeguards, as some have claimed; pressure does happen, and that people in a loving relationship are vulnerable to it.[35]

So the preconditions for the validity of a binding marital property agreement will have to be very carefully crafted to provide as much protection as can realistically be provided, without making the requirements so onerous that they negate the usefulness of reform.

5.4. ENFORCEABLE CONTRACTS: THE REMAINING SCOPE FOR DISCRETION

A further area explored in the Law Commission's consultation concerns the other end of the lifespan of an agreement. Suppose that all the preconditions have been met and an apparently binding agreement has been formed. The intention will be that this can be enforced as a contract and that there will simply be no possibility of an application for ancillary relief. Will there nevertheless be circumstances in which an application for ancillary relief might be entertained by the courts?

In order to analyse this issue we have to go back to the rather peculiar way in which the discourse about marital property agreements has been developed in this jurisdiction. These contracts are assumed, generally, to relate to all aspects of a couple's future financial position: they are in effect a divorce settlement.

It is not surprising therefore that some of the provisos placed upon enforceability by some organisations have focused on the holistic effect of the agreement. The Centre for Social Justice recommends that agreements be enforceable unless they cause "significant injustice".[36] Resolution want agreements to be enforceable

33 *Royal Bank of Scotland v Etridge (No 2)* [2001] UKHL 44, [2002] 2 AC 773.
34 *Jayne Hewett v First Plus Financial Group Plc* [2010] EWCA Civ 312.
35 *NA v MA* [2006] EWHC 2900 (Fam), [2007] 1 FLR 1760.
36 The Centre for Social Justice, *Breakthrough Britain: Every Family Matters* (2009).

unless they cause "significant hardship" to either of the parties or to a child of the family.[37]

The difficulty with these suggestions is their use of terms that cannot be defined. We have heard judges say that significant injustice is something that they recognise when they see. But there are fundamental questions to be asked about the use of such a term. Unjust by whose standards? Unjust by comparison with the results that would be obtained on an application for ancillary relief? If not, by what standard(s)? These difficulties are not insoluble.

But it may be rather easier to analyse the effect that binding marital property agreements are to have if we break them down somewhat and look at the different aspects of a couple's financial position that they may cover. It is not suggested that we adopt a rigid distinction between capital and income; that would be unrealistic in the legal and social context of England and Wales. But it would make sense to look at the responsibilities that are involved in ancillary relief, and to work out which ones we might say cannot be contracted out of.

Two easy rules spring to mind.

The first is that it cannot be possible to contract out of ancillary relief if the result of that is that one party is left reliant on state benefits, when they otherwise would not have been. In other words, one cannot contract out of a responsibility by leaving it to the state. There is of course no *a priori* reason why that should be so. It is not logically necessary that one should ensure that, at least for the foreseeable future, a spouse is not left reliant on social security after divorce. But political and practical reality makes this a necessary qualification to the enforceability of marital property agreements; it is difficult to imagine any government agreeing to implement reform that did not make this point clear.

Another easy ground rule must surely be that it is not possible to contract out of one's responsibilities to one's children. That is not to say that the parents cannot decide, and fix by contract, how those responsibilities are to be met. But the children have no part in the contract; it makes no sense to allow the parties to agree that responsibilities to children are not to be met, let alone that they should be caused hardship as a result of the agreement. I am not aware of any jurisdiction that allows this, and cannot see why any should.

Perhaps the most crucial question for this topic, however, is whether or not it should be possible to contract out of making provision for the other party's needs. That is a large question, because meeting needs is a serious, long-term and heavy

---

[37] Http://www.resolution.org.uk/editorial.asp?page_id=309.

commitment. We have no arbitrary limits to the time during which periodical payments may have to be made, subject to the fact that they will cease when the payee re-marries. Although the court is directed to consider the possibility of a clean break, there is no obligation to achieve one, and maintenance may have to be paid for many years if a spouse cannot go back into employment for a good reason.

So at first sight, to provide that it is not possible to contract out of needs-based provision sounds like a significant restriction upon autonomy. But that is only because we have for so long discussed marital property agreements as if they must cover every aspect of ancillary relief. It is the norm throughout Europe that it is possible to regulate one's property regime by contract, but not, in most jurisdictions, to contract out of maintenance obligations; and the fact that those obligations may appear more restrictive than the concept of needs in England and Wales is, by itself, misleading, because it does not take into account a host of social factors, including tax, social security levels, the availability of jobs, the acceptability of rented accommodation, etc.

The advantage of regarding needs as an area of responsibility out of which it is not possible to contract would be that the possibility of hardship as a result of the agreement (not "significant hardship", but hardship) is pretty much eliminated. And the concern about justice/significant injustice and the like is largely, I suggest, motivated by concern about hardship. If agreements cannot touch responsibility for needs, a great deal of heat is taken out of the debate about a suitable limitation to the enforceability of binding marital property agreements. It is unlikely to result in a great deal of litigation about needs, because provided the enforceability of the agreement was guaranteed so far as concerned property not required to meet needs, there would be a considerable incentive upon the parties to provide generously for needs rather than risk litigation. The main prize would be secure.

If needs were off limits, there would be considerable scope to develop a model of marital property agreement that was not about depriving one's partner of what he or she needs, but about preserving special property. It might be inherited; it might be a precious purchase; it might be a gift; it might be the proceeds of one's business. It might be the property recovered after a previous divorce; and we all know people who will not re-marry because they are frightened of losing the property they salvaged from the shipwreck the first time round. Provided needs were met, a marital property agreement would be a reliable way to plan for the future, and indeed to construct – if the parties so wished – something very like a deferred community of acquests.[38]

The Law Commission has made no formal proposal that needs should be a base-line responsibility out of which one cannot contract. I have dwelt on the possibility here because it is the model of marital property agreement that seems to me to resonate most with the models seen in continental Europe, although that fact is as yet, I think, not properly understood by the public here nor even by some professionals who regard continental Europe as rather more of a haven of contractual freedom than perhaps it is.

6. CONCLUSION

For the detail of the models discussed by the Law Commission, again readers are referred to our consultation paper where a great deal more detail is set out; and readers are urged to respond with their suggestions and preferences.

This conference featured a lot of discussion of problems of international law, and the issues arising from the Green Paper on Marital Property Regimes.[39] The Law Commission project is not directly concerned with these, although of course we watch developments with interest. But our project has a significant international aspect, because much of the demand for enforceable marital property agreements comes from those who have lived abroad and expect, on marrying here, to be able to contract into a regime of choice. Their expectations are disappointed, not so much by the absence of a regime as by the impossibility of choice; and if a form of enforceable agreement were introduced, this group would find marriage, and the management of their property, considerably more practicable.

However, the introduction of a new form of binding agreement in England and Wales would not assist a different group: those who have married elsewhere and expect their marital property regime – whether applicable by law or adopted by contract – to be valid here. It would therefore be of no assistance in the context of private international law, where the English court will not decide the financial consequences of the ending of marriage on the basis of anything other than the *lex fori*. Yet even in that context, the law is moving on. The agreement in *Radmacher v Granatino* was not ignored; it cannot even be said to have been merely a factor in the decision. This is not the place for a commentary on that case, because what

---

38 A model that allowed the safeguarding of property, without jeopardising provision for needs, can hardly be said to be in any sense an attack on marriage, since it would reflect the financial consequences of marriage as they stood for decades until the decision in *White v White*.

39 Commission of the European Communities, *green paper: On conflict of laws in matters concerning matrimonial property regimes*, COM (2006) 400.

I write now will be superseded by the time this book is published. But I note with interest that the effect of the agreement as to the wife's capital assets has for the most part not been in dispute; the issue is only about needs and the extent to which provision must be made for them in despite of the terms of the agreement. Sharing of capital beyond that is off the table; and in that sense the parties, the first instance judge and the Court of Appeal observed and enforced the overseas agreement. So the *lex fori* is by no means so insular as once it was.

It is difficult to be wholly insular in the environment of a CEFL conference. A unified European family law is hard to imagine, but a Europe in which family lawyers understand each other and can work together is becoming a reality. Long may the CEFL's deliberations continue.

COHABITANT OBLIGATIONS: CONTRACT VERSUS STATUS

Marsha Garrison

Family property law governs the property rights and obligations that flow from family relationships. It defines the relationships that may produce property interests; it determines when, and how, such interests arise.

This chapter considers how family property law should treat non-marital cohabitation, a relational status that has increased dramatically over the past half century. Indeed, within a single decade, the number of unmarried-cohabitant households in the UK increased by 67%, and the number with minor children doubled.[1] Similar developments have occurred in most developed nations, and there is no sign that the trend in favor of premarital cohabitation has yet abated.

Are the relationships of non-marital cohabitants familial? If yes, should cohabitation give rise to status-based property entitlements some or all of the time? This chapter addresses these important questions.

1. COHABITATION AND FAMILY PROPERTY LAW: TRADITION AND CHANGE

Traditional family property law did not view cohabitants as family members, and no rights or obligations flowed from such a relationship. Some legal regimes did recognize customary or "common-law" marriage, but the rights and obligations attached to common-law marriage were identical to those attached to formal, ceremonial marriage. This does not mean that jurisdictions which recognized common-law marriage saw cohabitation as the equivalent of marriage. Quite to the contrary, the cohabitant who wished to claim common-law marital status was required to prove not only cohabitation, but also an agreement to be married and a reputation, or "holding-out," as a married couple. "Far from equating cohabitation and marriage", the common-law marriage doctrine and other related customary-marriage laws "in fact depended on there being a sharp distinction between the two."[2] Participants in a common-law marriage were seen as a married couple, not as non-marital cohabitants. Cohabitation *per se* created no status-based rights or obligations; indeed, cohabitants could not contract to create such rights or obligations based on their private relationship.[3]

---

1. *See* LAW COMMISSION FOR ENGLAND AND WALES, 'Cohabitation: The Financial Consequences of Relationship Breakdown – Executive Summary,' Law Com No 307, 31 July 2007, at 4–5.
2. R. PROBERT, 'Cohabitation: Current Legal Solutions,' (2009) 62 *Current Legal Problems* 316, at 320.
3. *See, eg,* Hill v. Estate of Westbrook, 39 Cal.2d 458, 247 P.2d 19 (Cal. 1952); Otis v. Freeman, 85 N.E. 168 (Mass. 1908). *See generally* J.M. DRAPER, Annot., 'Recovery for Services Rendered by Persons Living in Apparent Relation of Husband and Wife Without Express Agreement for Compensation' (1980) 94 *A.L.R.3d* 552.

Cohabitants could typically enter into business contracts, or even service contracts if the services specified were typically compensated.[4] In some legal systems, courts of equity also provided relief to cohabitants who had relied on the promises of a non-marital partner to his or her detriment. The purchase money resulting trust sometimes protected the cohabitant who had paid money toward the purchase of property when title was taken in the name of his or her partner.[5] Quantum meruit claims provided a means of obtaining payment for services that would generally be compensated when the expected payment had not been made.[6] And constructive trust provided "a flexible remedy imposed in a wide variety of situations to prevent unjust enrichment."[7] Throughout the twentieth century, these various forms of equitable relief ensured that, in many cases, one cohabitant who had been cheated by the other could obtain recovery for some or all of his losses.

Family property law did not provide cohabitants with more than equitable or contractual relief for two reasons. First, compensation for non-marital cohabitation was widely viewed as a thinly veiled form of prostitution. Courts and legislators thus viewed non-marital cohabitation as socially undesirable and wanted to discourage such arrangements. Second, open cohabitation was rare, and those who engaged in the practice were generally very poor, very bohemian, or both;[8] existing equitable and contractual remedies seemed adequate to handle the legal problems such cohabitants brought to court.[9]

---

4 *See, eg,* Fernandez v. Zorrilla, 8 Ariz. 214, 354 P.2d 260 (1960); Henderson v. Spratlen, 44 Colo. 278, 98 P. 14 (1908); Kurtz v. Frank, 76 Ind. 594, 40 Am. Rep. 275 (1881); Zytka v. Dmochowski, 302 Mass. 63, 18 N.E.2d 332 (1938); Emmerson v. Botkin, 26 Okla. 218; 109 P. 531 (1910); Stewart v. Waterman, 98 Vt. 408, 123 A. 524 (1924). *See also* Restatement of Contracts § 589 (1932); 6 Williston on Contracts (rev. ed.) §1745 n. 5 ("The fact that past cohabitation is the motive for a promise will not invalidate it.").

5 *See Restatement (Third) of Trusts* §§ 7–9; Suggs v. Morris, 392 P.2d 313 (Ala. 1964); Hall v. Hall, 98 Cal. App. 209, 219 P.2d 808 (1950).

6 *See* J.M. Draper, Annot., 'Recovery for Services Rendered by Persons Living in Apparent Relation of Husband and Wife Without Express Agreement for Compensation' (1980) 94 A.L.R.3d 552.

7 *See* J. Dukeminier & S. M. Johanson, *Wills, Trusts, and Estates,* 6th ed, Aspen Publishing, New York, NY 2000, at 585 ("[t]he usual requirements for imposition of a constructive trust are: 1) a confidential or fiduciary relationship; 2) a promise, express or implied, by the transferee; 3) a transfer of property in reliance on the promise; and 4) unjust enrichment of the transferee. But the constructive trust remedy is not limited to these circumstances... [and] may be imposed in situations where ... the court is moved simply by the desire to prevent unjust enrichment.").

8 *See* W. Ehrmann, 'Premarital Sexual Behavior and Sex Codes of Conduct with Acquaintances, Friends, and Lovers,' (1959) 38 *SF (Social Forces)* 158; M.Z. Ferrell et al.,' Maturational and Societal Changes in the Sexual Double-Standard: A Panel Analysis (1967–1971; 1970–1974),' (1977) 39 *JMF (Journal of Marriage & Family)* 255 (1977).

9 *See* J.T. Oldham & D.S. Caudill, 'A Reconnaissance of Public Policy Restrictions upon Enforcement of Contracts Between Cohabitants,' (1984) 18 *FLQ (Family Law Quarterly)* 93; *Restatement of Contracts* § 512 (1932).

During the 1960s, technology and social change combined to dramatically change sexual behavior among the young. The new birth control pill offered young women, for the first time, near certain protection from pregnancy that was entirely within their own control. The social upheaval of the 1960s produced a more permissive society which sanctioned premarital sex and even open, premarital cohabitation.[10]

With widespread premarital cohabitation has come a decline in marriage and a dramatic increase in non-marital births. Everywhere, young adults are marrying later.[11] In many nations, significant numbers may not marry at all.[12] With the notable exceptions of Asia and southern Europe, the proportion of children born outside of marriage has skyrocketed.[13] Indeed, in some of the Scandinavian nations, non-marital births now outweigh marital.[14]

These new behavioral norms, originally associated with youthful rebellion against traditional social mores, have also spread rapidly into older, more settled age cohorts; by 1990, the parents of young cohabitants were often choosing to cohabit themselves.[15] Some of these more mature cohabitants have already been divorced and thus feel hesitant about a new marital commitment; some, making use of cohabitation's new respectability, have chosen cohabitation over marriage for more pragmatic reasons.

The net result is that cohabitation is now common, socially acceptable, multi-generational, and multi-purpose. Cohabitation appeals not just to the poor and bohemian, but also to individuals with substantial assets. It includes young men and women who are sharing living space with a dating partner in order to save money, more committed couples who are testing the strength of their relationship, engaged couples who are planning to marry, committed couples who view their relationship as marital but have chosen to avoid marriage for practical reasons such as the potential loss of alimony or a surviving-spouse entitlement, and

10 *See* G. Akerlof et al., 'An Analysis of Out-of-Wedlock Childbearing in the United States,' (1996) 111 *Quarterly Journal Economics* 279; D. Besharov & K. Gardiner, 'Trends in Teen Sexual Behavior,' (1997) 19 *Child & Youth Services Review* 328; A. Thornton, 'Changing Attitudes Toward Family Issues in the United States,' (1989) 51 *JMF* 873, at 884 tbl. 4.

11 *See* K. Kiernan, 'European Perspectives on Union Formation,' in L.Waite (ed.), *The Ties That Bind*, Aldine de Gruyter, New York, 2000, at 41 tbl. 3.1.

12 *See Marriages and Divorces in the EU (1960–95)*, http://www.eurohealth.ie/newrep/socio.htm; US Bureau of the Census, *Statistical Abstract of the United States 2001* at 59 tbl. 68.

13 *See* S.J. Ventura & C. Bachrach, 'Nonmarital Childbearing in the United States 1940–99,' (2003) 48 *Nat. Vital Statistics Reports No. 16*, http://www.cdc.gov/nchs/data/nvsr/nvsr48/nvs48_16.pdf; T.M. Smeeding et al., 'The Challenge of Family System Changes for Research and Policy,' in D.M. Moynihan et al.(eds.), *The Future of the Family* (2004), Russell Sage Foundation, New York, NY, at 1, 8 fig. 1.3.

14 *See id.*

15 *See* S.L. Brown et al., 'Cohabitation Among Older Adults: A National Portrait,' (2006) 61 *Journal Gerontology Series B: Psychology, Science & Social Science S71* (2006).

many couples whose motives are mixed or who disagree about the nature of their relationship.[16]

2. NEW REGULATORY REGIMES: HOW SHOULD WE CHOOSE?

2.1. GOALS AND QUESTIONS

As cohabitation has moved from the fringes to the center of society, courts and legislatures have responded with new regulatory regimes. These regimes vary quite dramatically in their operation and effect; no consensus has as yet evolved on what, if any, rights and obligations should attach to cohabitation. Some nations have preserved the traditional approach which bars all status-based relief, even if based on an explicit agreement between the cohabitants. Others, notably the United States, have adopted a contractual regime under which cohabitants may enter into agreements to create relational rights and responsibilities. Yet others, notably France, have established registration schemes under which cohabitants may elect to enter into a status that confers some, but not all, marital rights and responsibilities. And finally, some countries, notably Canada and New Zealand, have established conscriptive regimes that impose some or all marital rights and responsibilities on cohabitants based either on a wide-ranging factual inquiry or on a legislatively specified variable such as the duration of cohabitation.

Which of these various approaches is best? Certainly, existing approaches offer wildly different pros and cons. Contractual schemes offer individually determined and tailored results, if cohabitants can agree and if they undertake the effort to enter into relational contracts. Registration schemes also offer choice; although the choices are typically standardized, potentially stressful and expensive negotiation over terms and litigation to resolve contractual disagreements are both unnecessary. Registration and contract can, of course, be combined to give cohabitants a standard "package" plus individualized fine-tuning, if desired. Conscriptive models offer choice only to the extent that they permit cohabitants to opt out of whatever entitlements they would otherwise obtain under the scheme. Their potential advantage is the possibility of ensuring fair and consistent treatment of cohabitants without affirmative steps on their part, but this possibility depends on our capacity to craft criteria with the capacity to achieve workable, appropriate classifications that meet the expectations of cohabitants. In evaluating this wide array of possibilities, policy makers must assess the capacity of various regimes to achieve several different public policy goals.

16 *See* sources cited in notes 20–31.

One important goal is administrative efficiency. To the extent possible, all legal systems prefer rules that require fewer resources to administer. Efficiency thus strongly prefers legal regimes that offer prospective status determination to those that require retrospective, fact-intensive inquiry. Efficiency tends to disfavor regimes that are heavily reliant on individual negotiation; it typically favors bright-line rules over discretionary standards.

A second important goal is individual equity. The legal regime must ensure that cohabitants do not rely on a relationship to their detriment and that their reasonable expectations are met. The rules employed should also comport with public understandings of justice and fair play.

A third goal – one that I would argue should be paramount – is child protection. A primary goal of family law in all its aspects is ensuring that children receive adequate care and support. Parents' rights invariably give way to children's interests, and parental agreements are invariably voidable if they do not protect their child's interests. Reflecting the overriding importance of child protection, rules governing cohabitants must ensure that the children of cohabitants suffer no discrimination because of their parents' legal status. To the extent possible, these rules should also foster parental responsibility both with respect to children's support and care.

Comparing the various legal regimes we might apply to cohabitation in light of efficiency, equity, and child protection goals, several factual issues become apparent. One obvious question is whether cohabitation, or a readily ascertainable type of cohabitation, is like marriage. A scheme that grants cohabitants some or all marital rights and obligations makes sense only if the policy justifications for marital rights and obligations apply to cohabitants. Another question is whether affirmative schemes like contract and registration have the capacity to ensure fair outcomes; if equity requires that cohabitants obtain property rights, and cohabitants rarely contract or register to obtain such rights, then affirmative schemes alone cannot provide adequate protection against unjust enrichment. A third factual issue is the impact of cohabitation on children.

2.2. COHABITATION AND MARRIAGE: THE SAME OR DIFFERENT?

Marriage triggers property rights and obligations because, with the couple's marriage vows, each spouse voluntarily makes a commitment to the relationship and "agrees to be subject to a complex set of behavioral expectations defining the roles of spouse and parent, expectations that will restrict their freedom and guide their behavior in the relationship."[17] Marriage vows signal acceptance of these expectations both to one's partner and to the world at large.

The most important behavioral expectation of marriage is sharing. When average citizens, married or single, talk about marriage, they typically focus on sharing, and married couples "speak of sharing – thoughts, feelings, tasks, values, or life goals – as the greatest virtue in a relationship."[18] Reflecting this sharing ethic, married couples overwhelmingly report that they share economic resources and that such sharing is a product of love, trust, and commitment.[19]

The entitlements that marital property law grants to spouses reflect, and reinforce, the marital sharing ethic. Divorce and succession law protect marriage partners who have relied on the sharing norm. They also encourage sharing by assuring spouses that a partner cannot unilaterally end the marital partnership without taking account of the legitimate expectations of the spouse left behind.

Cohabitation is unlike marriage in that there is no event that signals mutual understanding of behavioral expectations. Put somewhat differently, while marriage vows represent a short-form sharing contract, the decision to live together does not. Clearly, some cohabitating couples do have sharing expectations like those of a married couple. But certainly not all do. Surveying the data, demographers have enumerated six or seven different cohabitation "types," ranging from a substitute for being single, to a stage in the marriage process, to informal, "common-law" marriage.[20] Cohabitation thus differs dramatically from

---

17 E.S. Scott, 'Social Norms and the Legal Regulation of Marriage,' (2000) 86 *VLR (Virginia Law Review)* 1901, at 1907. *See also* E.A. Posner, 'Family Law and Social Norms', in F.H. Buckley (ed), *The Fall and Rise of Freedom of Contract* 256, at 259–62 (1999); E.S. Scott & R.E. Scott, 'Marriage as Relational Contract,' (1998) 84 *VLR* 1225, at 1288–92.

18 *See* R.N. Bellah et al., *Habits of the Heart: Individualism and Commitment in American Life*, Harper & Row, New York, NY, 1985, at 90, 91 (96% of survey group valued "the ideal of two people sharing a life and a home together").

19 *See* P. Blumstein & P. Schwartz, *American Couples*, Wm. Morrow & Co., New York, NY, 1993, at 101, 110 (only 12% of surveyed wives and 8% of surveyed husbands strongly disagreed that couples should pool everything); J.Pahl, *Money and Marriage*, St. Martin's Press, New York, NY, 1989, at 78, 83, 126–27 (in a study of UK married couples, spouses saw income-sharing as the norm and widely shared income; within research sample, couples forgoing pooling were too infrequent to include in analysis); J. Stocks et al. (eds), *Modern Couples Sharing Money, Sharing Life*, Palgrave Macmillon, Houndsmill Basingstoke, UK, 2007, at 11, 16–17, 49 (a majority of surveyed couples, from Spain, Sweden, and the US, viewed sharing resources as natural; the majority had a jointly managed asset pool, and independent-management system was used by a only small portion of couples); J. Treas, 'Money in the Bank: Transaction Costs and the Economic Organization of Marriage',(1993) 58 *ASR (American Sociological Review)* 723 (95% of married couples pooled assets, although sometimes not all assets).

20 *See* P. Heuveline & J. M. Timberlake, 'The Role of Cohabitation in Family Formation: The United States in Comparative Perspective,' (2004) 66 *JMF* 1214; K. Kiernan, 'The Rise of Cohabitation and Childbearing Outside Marriage in Western Europe,' (2001) 15 *Int'l Journal of Law, Policy, & Family* 1. *See also* A. Barlow & G. James, 'Regulating Marriage

marriage in its capacity to reveal a couple's understanding about their relationship; both the lack of any clear status-change marker and the array of cohabitation types ensures that we cannot simply assume that any particular cohabiting couple have adopted marital sharing expectations or behaviors.

As I have reported in more detail elsewhere,[21] the available evidence also strongly suggests that cohabitants do not *typically* embrace the marital sharing norm. Researchers consistently report that cohabitants are less likely than married couples to support their partners and more likely to split expenses instead of pooling their resources.[22] Compared to married couples, cohabitants are less likely to value commitment or express commitment toward their partners.[23] These patterns persist even in Scandinavia, where there are few economic incentives to marry and cohabitation is "widely accepted as a way of living together, even when there are children."[24]

Reflecting the divide between marriage and cohabitation, surveyed cohabitants in the UK tended to describe the advantages of cohabitation as a function of non-commitment. In one survey, almost 30% of cohabitants cited lack of legal ties and greater freedom as advantages of cohabitation.[25] In another, among

and Cohabitation in 21st Century Britain' (2004) 67 MLR (*Modern Law Review)* 143, 157–61 (quoting British cohabitants describing range of reasons for cohabitation).

21 *See* M. Garrison, 'Is Consent Necessary? An Evaluation of the Emerging Law of Cohabitant Obligations,' (2005) 52 *UCLA Law Review* 815, at 840; M. Garrison, 'Marriage Matters: What's Wrong with the ALI's Domestic Partnership Proposal,' in R.H. Wilson (ed), *Reconceiving the Family: Perspectives on the American Law Institute's Principles of Family Dissolution*, Cambridge Univ. Press, Cambridge, 2006, at 305–330; M. Garrison, 'Nonmarital Cohabitation: Social Revolution and Legal Regulation,' (2008) 42 *FLQ* 309.

22 *See* P. Blumstein & P. Schwartz, *American Couples*, Wm. Morrow & Co., New York, NY, 1993, at 94–100 figs. 8–9; M. Clarksberg et al., 'Attitudes, Values, and Entrance into Cohabitational versus Marital Unions,' (1995) 74 *SF* 609; H. Glezer & E. Mills, 'Controlling the Purse Strings,' (1991) 29 *Family Matters* 35 at tbl. 2; R.S. Oropesa et al., 'Income Allocation in Marital and Cohabiting Unions: The Case of Mainland Puerto Ricans,' (2003) 65 *JMF* 910; C. Vogler, 'Managing Money: Similarities and Differences Betweeen Cohabiting and Married Couples,' in J. Miles & R. Probert, *Sharing Lives, Dividing Assets: An Interdisciplinary Study,* Oxford Univ. Press, Oxford, 2009; A.E. Winkler, 'Economic Decision-Making by Cohabitors: Findings Regarding Income Pooling,' (1997) 29 *AE (Applied. Economics)* 1079.

23 *See, eg*, P. Blumstein & P. Schwartz, *American Couples*, Wm. Morrow & Co., New York, 1993, at 184 fig. 26; W.G. Axinn & A. Thornton, 'The Relationship Between Cohabitation and Divorce: Selectivity or Causal Influence?,' (1992) 29 *Demography* 357, at 358-59; S.L. Nock, 'A Comparison of Marriages and Cohabiting Relationships,' (1995) 16 *JFI* (*Journal Family Issues)* 53, 65–67 tbl. 1, 73; S.M. Stanley, 'Interpersonal Commitment and Premarital or Nonmarital Cohabitation,' (2004) 25 *JFI* 496; Cohabitants with the lowest level of commitment are also the most likely to split up. *See* L.M. Casper & S.M. Bianchi, *Continuity and Change in the American Family,* Sage Publications, Thousand Oaks, CA, 2002, at 59 tbl. 2.5.

24 K.A. Wik et al., 'A Study of Commitment and Relationship Quality in Sweden and Norway,' (2009) 72 *JMF* 465, at 466. *See also* K.R. Heimdal & S.. Houseknecht, 'Cohabiting and Married Couples' Income Organization: Approaches in Sweden and the United States,' (2003) 65 *JMF* 525, at 533 tbl. 2.

25 *See* S. MacRae, *Cohabiting Mothers*, Policy Studies Institute, London, 1993.

the first-cited advantages of cohabitation, three of the four most frequently mentioned – no legal ties (24.5%), a chance to trial marriage (23.6%), personal independence (10.7%) – also rest on the assumption that cohabitation does not entail the same commitments as marriage.[26] Indeed, in a US survey, literally *none* of the cohabitants interviewed indicated that the decision to cohabit represented a commitment to their relationship. As one cohabitant put it, the decision to cohabit instead meant that:

> I wasn't ready . . . to get like, I mean, that close to somebody and I mean I lived with her but we still had our freedom we still let each other do what we wanted to do so I had my space and she had her space.[27]

Highlighting the distinction between cohabitation and marriage, the vast majority of cohabitants report that they plan to get married. And, even in Sweden and Norway, where cohabitation is a widely accepted alternative to marriage, most cohabitants do go on to marry a current or future partner.[28]

The diversity of cohabiting relationships also ensures that many cohabiting couples have different understandings about their relationships. Researchers have found that, in 20–40% of cohabiting relationships, partners express different views on whether they plan to marry each other.[29] Moreover, in one survey, about a third of the time, only one partner felt that the couple spent a lot of time together; in 40% of the cases, one partner but not the other reported a high degree of happiness with the relationship.[30] And in the UK survey I just described, 35% of surveyed

[26] *See* E. Coast, 'Currently Cohabiting: Relationship Attitudes and Intentions,' in J. Stillwell et al. (eds), *Fertility, Living Arrangements, Care and Mobility*, Springer, Dordrecht, NL, 2009. This was also true of cited disadvantages. Three of four first-cited disadvantages of cohabitation as compared to marriage – no legal status (32.5%), financial insecurity (30.1%), and lack of commitment (9.6%) – also reflect the fact that cohabitation does not necessitate formal commitment.

[27] W. Manning & P.J. Smock, 'Measuring and Modeling Cohabitation: New Perspectives from Qualitative Data,' (2005) 67 *JMF* 989 at 999.

[28] *See* K.A. Wik et al., 'A Study of Commitment and Relationship Quality in Sweden and Norway,' (2009) 72 *JMF* 465, at 466 (based on census data, 63% (Swedish) and 73% (Norwegian) of cohabiting men and 72% (Swedish) and 81% (Norwegian) cohabiting women will marry.

[29] *See* S.L. Brown, 'Union Transitions Among Cohabiters: The Significance of Relationship Assessment and Expectations,' (2000) 62 *JMF* 833, 838 (about 20% of cohabitants disagreed about strength of their relationship); L.L. Bumpass et al., 'The Role of Cohabitation in Declining Rates of Marriage,' (1991) 53 *JMF* 913, 923 (same); S. Sassler & J. McNally, 'Cohabiting Couples Economic Circumstances and Union Transitions: A Re-Examination Using Multiple Imputation Techniques', (2004) 32 *Social Science Research*.553 (2004) (42% of surveyed cohabiting couples disagreed about the future of their relationship).

[30] *See* S.L. Brown, 'Union Transitions Among Cohabiters: The Significance of Relationship Assessment and Expectations,' (2000) 62 *JMF* 833.

couples disagreed about the advantages of cohabitation, and 25% disagreed about the disadvantages.[31]

The range of relationship types encompassed by cohabitation, the failure of most cohabitants to adhere to the marital sharing norms that justify marital property entitlements, and the large risk that a particular pair of cohabitants will not even agree about the type of relationship they have, all provide very strong arguments against a family-property regime that assimilates cohabitation to marriage. If cohabitation does not typically entail the same commitments and sharing behaviors that accompany marriage, there is no obvious reason to grant cohabitants marital property entitlements based on the fact of cohabitation.

Of course, no legal regime *simply* assimilates cohabitation to marriage. All of the existing conscriptive regimes require something more than cohabitation to produce a claim to some or all marital property entitlements. Some schemes rely on highly fact-intensive, wide-ranging inquiries into the specific couple's relationship, while others rely on more limited criteria, such as cohabitation plus joint parenthood or cohabitation for a stated period.[32] Both of these approaches entail serious disadvantages, however. Schemes relying on wide-ranging, fact-intensive criteria offer the possibility of fully assessing relationship type, but they do so at the cost of unpredictability. Retrospective litigation will almost always be necessary to determine a given couple's status; cohabiting couples have no notice of their rights and obligations before such litigation is concluded. Such an approach is inefficient. It may also produce results that are inconsistent and unfair.

The American experience with common law marriage provides an instructive example of the difficulties inherent in such an approach. At one time, nearly two-thirds of the states recognized common law marriage; by 2007, only ten did so,[33] and two of the ten had adopted strict limitations on its establishment.[34] Common law marriage is based on a public "holding out" as a married couple and a private agreement to be married; a formal, written agreement is not required. But once a couple have decided to separate, they are quite unlikely to have the same view of their prior understanding and, even on the holding out requirement, the evidence will often be inconclusive; one party may have represented the relationship as

31 *See* E. Coast, 'Currently Cohabiting: Relationship Attitudes and Intentions,' in J. Stillwell et al. (eds.), *Fertility, Living Arrangements, Care and Mobility*, Springer, Dordrecht, NL, 2009.
32 *See* M. Garrison, 'Is Consent Necessary? An Evaluation of the Emerging Law of Cohabitant Obligations,' (2005) 52 *UCLA Law Review* 815, at 818–19.
33 *See* H.L. Krause et al., *Family Law: Cases, Comments, and Questions*, Thomson-West, St, Paul, MN, 2007, at 129.
34 *See* Tex. Fam. Code '2.402 (requiring affirmation of the marriage in a state declaration form); Utah Code Ann.' 30-1-4.5(2) (requiring establishment of common law marriage within one year of its dissolution).

marital when the other did not, or their representations may be equivocal or contradictory. American courts and legislatures have thus come to agree with the family law expert who opined that the common law marriage doctrine should be abolished because it leads to "fraud and uncertainty in the most important of human relationships".[35] And if two facts – public holding out as a married couple and an agreement to be married – are so hard to determine that the potential for fraud and uncertainty outweigh the benefit of the doctrine, then one must assume that the wide-ranging inquiry contemplated by multi-factor conscriptive schemes would produce even more fraud and uncertainty, with even less off-setting benefit.

Conscriptive schemes that employ simple criteria face the opposite problem: The criteria employed must strongly predict marital commitment and sharing or their use will lead to misclassification. However, while the research evidence is still, unfortunately, sparse, that which is available does not show that either of the variables currently in use – relationship duration or having a common child – is predictive of either sharing or commitment.

Lengthier periods of cohabitation do not seem to induce marital norms or relationship quality. Although one economist who employed a labor-supply model to infer cohabitant behavior, did find evidence of some income-pooling in long-term cohabitation,[36] surveys of cohabitants themselves do not show that lengthier periods of cohabitation are associated with more sharing or higher expectations of sharing. In an American survey, couples who had cohabited for a period between two and ten years were no more likely to pool funds than those whose relationships had endured less than two years;[37] and in a cross-national survey, Swedish cohabitants, whose relationships are typically longer than the American and European norm, were not more likely to pool resources than their American counterparts.[38] Second, the available evidence does not show that lengthier periods of cohabitation are significantly associated with relationship quality or stability. For example, in a recent Scandinavian study, "the probability of being satisfied [with the relationship] was highest for respondents living in partnerships of shorter duration."[39] Researchers also report that the duration of a

35 H.H. Clark, *The Law of Domestic Relations in the United States,* West Publishing Co., St. Paul, MN, 2d ed., 1988, at 59.

36 *See* A.E. Winkler, 'Economic Decision-Making by Cohabitors: Findings Regarding Income Pooling,' (1997) 29 *AE,* at 1079 (drawing inferences from a generalized model of labour supply applied to survey data and reporting that [t]hese data sets provide evidence that cohabitors, taken as a group, do not pool all income. However, income pooling is not rejected for cohabitors in longer-term relationships and for those who have a biological child together.).

37 *See* P. Blumstein & P. Schwartz, *American Couples,* Wm. Morrow & Co., New York, 1993, at 95 fig. 8.

38 *See* K.R. Heimdal & S.. Houseknecht, 'Cohabiting and Married Couples' Income Organization: Approaches in Sweden and the United States,' (2003) 65 *JMF* 525.

39 *See* K.A. Wik et al., 'A Study of Commitment and Relationship Quality in Sweden and Norway,' (2009) 72 *JMF* 465, at 472–73 tbl. 2.

cohabiting relationship is significantly – and negatively – correlated with several variables related to relationship quality.[40]

The evidence on having a common child is even more limited, but it again fails to demonstrate a link with marital norms or relationship satisfaction. The US Fragile Family Study, which sponsored in-depth interviews of a nationally representative group of unmarried parents, found that "most of these cohabiting pairs espouse a strong *individualistic ethic* . . . in which personal happiness and fulfillment hold the highest value."[41] Childbearing during cohabitation is far more likely to be unplanned than it is during marriage,[42] and cohabiting couples with children report lower levels of psychological well-being than couples without children.[43] Although a Canadian researcher found that childbearing significantly enhanced the stability of cohabitants' relationships,[44] US researchers have generally failed to find such an effect.[45] And Scandinavian researchers have reported that having a common child was not significantly related to cohabitants' relationship seriousness; it was significantly – and negatively – related to their relationship satisfaction.[46]

Although some conscriptive schemes give cohabitants the right to "opt out" of obligations imposed on cohabiting couples, there are many reasons to doubt that this will solve the classification difficulties inherent in the conscriptive model. First, few cohabiting couples currently enter into relationship contracts even where they are legally empowered to do so.[47] Second, because cohabitation often

---

40 S.L. Brown & A. Booth, 'Cohabitation Versus Marriage: A Comparison of Relationship Quality,' (1996) 58 *JMF* 668, at 674. *See also* L. Bumpass et al., 'The Role of Cohabitation in Declining Rates of Marriage,' (1991) 53 *JMF* 913, at 922 tbl. 10 (a higher proportion of cohabitants whose relationships had lasted at least three years said that, during the past year, they had thought that [their]. . . relationship might be in trouble than cohabitants whose relationships had lasted less than one year).

41 K. Edin et al., 'A Peek Inside the Black Box: What Marriage Means for Poor Unmarried Parents,' (2004) 66 *JMF* 1007, at 1011 (emphasis in original).

42 *See* S.S. Brown & L. Eisenberg (eds), *The Best Intentions: Unintended Pregnancy and the Well-Being of Children and Families* 31–32 tbl. 2.2; W.D. Manning, 'Childbearing in Cohabiting Unions: Racial and Ethnic Differences,' (2001) 33 *FPP (Family Planning Perspectives)* 217, at tbl. 5.

43 *See* S.L. Brown, 'Union Transitions Among Cohabiters: The Role of Relationship Assessments and Expectations,' (2000) 62 *JMF* 833.

44 *See* Z. Wu, 'The Stability of Cohabitation Relationships: The Role of Children,' (1995) 57 *JMF* 231.

45 *See* W.D. Manning, 'Children and the Stability of Cohabiting Couples,' (2004) 66 *JMF* 674 (summarizing research).

46 *See* K.A. Wik et al., 'A Study of Commitment and Relationship Quality in Sweden and Norway,' (2009) 72 *JMF* 465, at 472–73 tbl. 2. *See also* W.D. Manning, 'Children and the Stability of Cohabiting Couples,' (2004) 66 *JMF* 674 (the conception of a child during cohabitation was associated with greater stability in the parents' relationship, but only if the couple married before the child was born).

47 "Real data on the frequency of contracting are scarce, but the basic claim is not in serious dispute. Certainly written agreements are rare among the reported cases … [and an

develops over time, there is no obvious event that signals the need to contract out. Third, many couples will not perceive the need to contract out; some will be unrealistically optimistic about the relationship, some will be uncomfortable discussing dissolution, and some will simply not understand the law.[48] Finally, even those who do perceive the desirability of opting out may be inhibited by the time and cost of entering into an agreement. And even if all cohabitants who should opt out did so, the associated discomfort, expense, and inconvenience weigh heavily against the conscriptive approach.

Marriage partners have publicly assumed binding obligations to each other that restrict other marital opportunities, inhibit participation in other sexual and sharing relationships, structure public and private expectations about their relationship, and burden exit from it. Cohabitants have not. This fundamental difference distinguishes marital relationships, for all their variability, from non-marital relationships. This difference explains why marriage continues to foster "shared expectations for appropriate behavior within the partnership" while cohabitation remains an "incomplete institution" offering "no widely recognized social blueprint . . . for the appropriate behavior of cohabitors, or for the behavior of the friends, families, and other individuals and institutions with whom they interact."[49] Because cohabitation typically does not entail the adoption of marital norms or commitments, there is no obvious reason to assign marital entitlements to cohabitants without some affirmative action – a contract, registration – that signals mutual agreement to a package of rights and responsibilities.

2.3. CONTRACT AND REGISTRATION: CAN CHOICE ENSURE FAIRNESS?

Contract and registration schemes cure the classification problems inherent in the conscriptive approach by leaving it to cohabiting couples to assume

experienced attorney] whose practice focuses on unmarried couples ... told the author ... that in his experience the proportion of such couples who enter written agreements is 'miniscule'." I.M. Ellman, 'Contract Thinking Was Marvins Fatal Flaw,' (2001) 76 *Notre Dame Law Review* 1365, at 1367 n. 17. *See also* K.S. Bull, 'Non-marital Cohabitation in Norway,' (1986) 30 *Scandinavian Studies Law* 31 (5% of surveyed Danish and Norwegian cohabitants had entered into contracts).

48 *See* N. Bala, 'Controversy Over Couples in Canada: The Evolution of Marriage and Other Adult Interdependent Relationships,' (2003) 29 *Queen's Law Journal* 41, at 54–55 ("People are generally not psychologically prepared to make contracts about their personal relationships, and the evolving roles and expectations of the partners in non-marital relationships ... tend to make contracts problematic....").

49 L.M. Casper & S.M. Bianchi, *Continuity and Change in the American Family*, Sage Publications, Thousand Oaks, CA, 2002, at 40. *See also* S.L. Nock, 'A Comparison of Marriages and Cohabiting Relationships, (1995) 16 *JFI* 53, at 74 ("Cohabitation is an incomplete institution. No matter how widespread the practice, non-marital unions are not yet governed by strong consensual norms. . . ").

rights and obligations. The evidence showing that cohabitation is not typically associated with marital sharing supports the contract/registration approach; so does evidence showing that committed couples are more likely than the general group of cohabitants to enter into relational contracts; while the limited evidence suggests that only "miniscule" numbers of cohabitants enter into written agreements, a survey of "committed" cohabitants found that 29% of this group had entered into formal contracts.[50] The cost, time, and relational stress associated with negotiating an individualized agreement can also be eliminated through a registration option that establishes a set package of rights and obligations.

A registration option coupled with the possibility of individualized contracts thus solves the classification problems inherent in the conscriptive model, and it does so in a way that meets the parties' expectations – they have chosen the option that suits them best – and provides prospective notice of status, with virtually no administrative costs. This approach also fosters individual autonomy and avoids paternalism, an approach that is consistent with the norms of liberal democracy, while the conscriptive scheme paternalistically coerces cohabitants into rights and obligations they have not affirmatively chosen. In sum, the merits of the registration/contract approach are so large and so obvious that, at first blush, it is not obvious where the disadvantages might lie.

The risk that opponents of contract and registration typically cite is the possibility of unjust enrichment. As the Law Commission for England and Wales put it, "current law can produce unfair outcomes for cohabitants, in particular for the primary carer of children who may experience significant economic disadvantage following separation":

> … [A]n opt-in scheme is likely to leave too many economically vulnerable people facing unjustified hardship on separation. The factors that led to their economic vulnerability are all too likely to be the same factors that led them to agree with an economically stronger partner not to opt in, meant that they failed to convince their partner to opt in, or led them to be understandably ignorant of the law, in the first place. A scheme of general application would better address that problem.[51]

Similar claims have been made in other nations during debates over conscriptive cohabitation laws. For example, the Ontario Attorney General, responding to concerns about proposed legislation extending support obligations to cohabitants, argued that the legislation was necessary to protect "exploited" cohabitants who

---

[50] *See* J.K. Robbennolt & M. K. Johnson, 'Legal Planning for Unmarried Committed Partners: Empirical Lessons for a Preventative and Therapeutic Approach,' (1999) 42 *Arizona Law Review* 417, at 436.

[51] Law Commission for England and Wales, *Cohabitation: The Financial Consequences of Relationship Breakdown*, Law Com. No. 307, 2007, at 42–43.

had been "induced to enter relationships and to stay at home and rear children".[52] Although both the Law Commission for England and Wales and the Ontario Attorney General put their arguments in gender-neutral terms, it seems clear that both viewed women as the "vulnerable" and "exploited" group. Thus, in New Zealand, "[t]he focus of debate on the property provisions of the [New Zealand] Property Relationships Bill was essentially on the situation of women in existing relationships."[53]

But are women actually induced by men to enter relationships and stay at home to rear children? Do cohabiting women have less bargaining leverage than men? And is cohabitation a state in which men prosper while women do not? These are complex questions on which we have incomplete data. But momentarily putting aside the case of women who have children with a cohabitant, it is not obvious why cohabitation would systematically exploit either women or men.

First, cohabitation produces economies of scale and labor sharing that will almost invariably benefit both individuals who make a home together. Admittedly, because cohabitants are less inclined to pool resources than married couples,[54] they will accrue smaller income advantages. But if they engage in any form of expense-sharing, their overall expenditure on shared goods like rent and household utilities should decline. Women do more housework than men in both cohabiting and marital relationships.[55] But even if cohabiting men do *no* housework, it is not obvious that the women with whom they are living would expend significantly more time on household chores than they would have spent living alone.

Second, the evidence does not suggest that cohabiting women have bargaining disadvantages. Indeed, sociologist Andrew Cherlin has argued that the rising tide of cohabitation is in part due to improvements in women's bargaining position:

> The bargaining position of women has improved in part because of their greater earning potential, compared to men. . . The bargaining position of women also has improved because of better birth control technology. . . and the availability of abortion. These technological advances have allowed women to have intimate

52 Ontario Legislative Assembly, Debates, 9 June 1994, at 4973, *quoted in* W. Holland, 'Intimate Relationships in the New Millenium: The Assimilation of Marriage and Cohabitation?', (2000) 17 *Canadian Journal Family Law* 114, at 128.

53 S. Birks, *LEANZ Seminar on the Property Relationships Act*, Wellington, NZ, 6 Aug. 2001, http://www.massey.ac.nz/~kbirks/gender/econ/pra.htm.

54 *See* sources cited in note.

55 *See* J.A. Batalova & P.N. Cohen, 'Premarital Cohabitation and Housework: Couples in Cross-National Perspective, (2002) 64 *JMF* 743; B.A. Shelton, 'Understanding the Distribution of Housework Between Husbands and Wives,' in L J. Waite (ed), *The Ties that Bind: Perspectives on Marriage and Cohabitation*, Aldine de Gruyter, New York, NY, 2000, at 343.

> relationships and residential partnerships with men without fear of pregnancy. They can therefore extend their search process to include trial relationships and partnerships prior to marriage.[56]

Cherlin concludes that women are "incorporating premarital cohabitation into the search and bargaining processes because cohabitation provides a better opportunity to observe men's skills and preferences for home production."[57]

Finally, because cohabitation does not typically produce marital sharing or commitment, it should only rarely induce dependency. If a cohabiting woman pursues her usual occupation, it is hard to see how or why she would be economically disadvantaged by cohabitation. Cohabiting women do, on average, earn less than cohabiting men.[58] As a result of this discrepancy, they may be comparatively disadvantaged to the extent that there has been resource pooling, when their relationship ends. But a woman would suffer the same kind of financial disadvantage if she lost a room-mate with whom she split the rent.

While the claim that cohabiting women *generally* suffer from exploitation does not appear to be supported by any evidence whatsoever, child-bearing does clearly burdens women, who provide a disproportionate share of child care and sometimes forgo labor-market opportunities because of child-care responsibilities.[59] It is this type of case that the Law Commission for England and Wales seems to have in mind in urging that a former cohabitant (C) whose partner (D) has borne a child during their relationship and remained at home to care for the child should "be required to share the economic disadvantage caused by D's contributions." The Law Commission urges that the disadvantages inherent in D's situation justify rules that would permit courts to "make a capital award, if necessary payable by instalments, to meet D's claim."[60]

In evaluating the Law Commission's claim, we should keep in mind that the fact of cohabitation is largely irrelevant to the economic disadvantage suffered by a stay-at-home parent like D. Any woman – married, cohabiting, or dating – who gives birth expecting a continued relationship with her child's father is disadvantaged if that relationship ends, whether or not she has stayed out of the

---

56 A.J. Cherlin, 'Toward a New Home Socioeconomics of Union Formation,' in L J. Waite (ed), *The Ties that Bind: Perspectives on Marriage and Cohabitation*, Aldine de Gruyter, New York, NY, 2000, at 131–32.

57 *Id.* at 131.

58 *See* L.M. Casper & S.M. Bianchi, *Continuity and Change in the American Family*, Sage Publications, Thousand Oaks, CA, 2002, at at 53 tbl. 2.3.

59 *See* M.J. Budig & P. England, 'The Wage Penalty for Motherhood,' (2001) 66 *AS R* 204; J. Waldfogel, 'The Effect of Children on Women=s Wages,' (1997) 62 *ASR* 209.

60 Law Commission for England and Wales, *Cohabitation: The Financial Consequences of Relationship Breakdown, Executive Summary*, Law Com No 307, 2007, at 6.

work force for some period. A scheme, applicable to cohabitants alone, that bases an entitlement on child-bearing is thus both under- and over-inclusive: non-residential dating partners might rely on continuation of their relationship just like a cohabitant; married women will almost always rely on the continuation of their relationships. But divorce laws do not provide entitlements based solely on the fact of having been disadvantaged by child-bearing and rearing: A marital property award depends on the accrual of marital assets during the marriage; spousal support, where it exists, typically depends on a multifactor assessment of contribution, marital duration, and need; the evidence suggests that it is rarely awarded in a short relationship like that of D and her partner.[61]

Schemes that create *marital* support and/or property entitlements based on the fact of childbearing avoid the inconsistency inherent in the Law Commission approach, but they lack any clear policy basis: The marital sharing norm cannot justify the extension of support and property entitlements to cohabitants who bear children during a period of co-residence because childbirth does not entail a commitment to share. For those cohabitants who have detrimentally relied with an understanding with a partner, there is no obvious reason why equitable remedies that have protected cohabitants in the past are not adequate to prevent unjust enrichment or, to the extent that there are inadequacies, it is unclear why the focus should not be on altering the remedies to cure the problem.

It also bears mentioning that legal regimes based on the supposition that cohabiting women need protection are highly paternalistic. Such schemes rely on classic female stereotypes – weakness, dependence, vulnerability, irrationality – that long justified laws which disadvantaged women. In an era when family policy

---

[61] Data on overall alimony rates are sparse. See J. Behrens & B. Smyth, 'Spousal Support in Australia: A Study of Incidence and Attitudes' (1999) Working Paper 16, Australian Inst. Family Studies, at 10 (reporting that 7% of Australian divorce sample had received or paid spousal support); M.F. Brinig, 'Unhappy Contracts: The Case of Divorce,' (2005) 1 *Review of Law & Economics* 241 (reporting 7.9% alimony rate in Iowa divorce sample and finding that all alimony awards were short-term). In the U.K., one survey found that only 31% of divorced women with children received any form of maintenance – child support or alimony -- from a former husband. *See* S.P. Jenkins, 'Marital Splits and Income Changes Over the Longer Term,' (2008) Institute of Social & Economic Research, Univ. of Essex, at 13 tbl. 3. At least in the United States, the low incidence of alimony awards has been fairly constant over the long term. 15–17% of surveyed divorced women reported to the U.S. Census Bureau that they had been awarded alimony from the late 1970s through 1989, the last year the Census Bureau collected alimony data. U.S. Bureau of the Census, 'Child Support and Alimony, 1989' (1990) Current Pop. Rpts., Series P–60, No. 173. U.S. census data from the turn of the century indicate that 9.3% of divorces included alimony awards. See P.H. Jacobson, *American Marriage and Divorce* 127–28 (1959) Rhinehart & Co., New York, NY. The typical alimony recipient is long-married and has a very low income in relation to that of her spouse. See Behrens & Smyth, (all alimony recipients had been in relatively long marriages); M. Garrison, 'How Do Judges Decide Divorce Cases? An Empirical Analysis of Discretionary Decision Making,' (1996) 74 *N.C. L. Rev.* 401, 468–69, tbls. 14–16; M. Garrison, 'Good Intentions Gone Awry: The Impact of New York's Equitable Distribution Law on Divorce Outcomes' (1991) 57 *Brooklyn L. Rev.* 621, 711, tbl. 48.

is firmly committed to gender equality, policy makers should surely think twice before relying on such outmoded and negative stereotypes as a basis for legal policy.

2.4. PROTECTING CHILDREN: WHAT APPROACH BEST SERVES CHILDREN'S INTERESTS?

A registration plus contract regime seems fully capable of meeting the reasonable expectations of cohabitants, at least if coupled with a robust set of equitable remedies. Such an approach also has the merits of predictability and administrative efficiency. But in selecting a regime to govern cohabitants, policy makers must also consider children's interests.

Any scheme to govern cohabitants should ensure that children born to cohabiting parents have the same entitlements as those born to married parents. Modern child support guidelines do some of the work here, in that they ensure that the same support schedule applies to unmarried and married support obligors. Rules which require married support obligors to pay a portion of child-care, educational, and health care costs should also, of course, apply equally to non-marital as well as marital children. So should rules governing allocation of the family home during the period when the children are minors.

Policymakers should make sure that their statute books contain such provisions. They should also look closely at child support standards to ensure that the support payments they mandate are adequate to meet children's needs, to ensure that children share in both parents' standard of living, and that children are protected against parental death or disability through insurance and inheritance entitlements.

But do children's interests require that *adult* former cohabitants obtain property or support entitlements? It is not obvious how such entitlements could be justified given that married parents cannot claim support or property based on child-rearing obligations. There is also real risk that the extension of marital obligations to cohabitants might ultimately conflict with children's interests by signaling that non-marital child-bearing is the same as marital childbearing. This is undesirable for two reasons.

First, marital birth continues to be associated with significant advantages to children. Children born to cohabiting parents are two to four times more likely to experience their parents' separation than are children born to married parents.[62] Because of the greater stability that marriage provides, marital children are exposed to many fewer financial,[63] physical,[64] and educational risks;[65] these lower risks are associated with higher levels of well-being.[66] There is also evidence that the advantages conferred by marital childbearing and rearing transcend the specific benefits associated with residential and economic stability. For example, married fathers appear to be more involved and spend more time with their children than unmarried fathers; if parental separation occurs, they see their children more often and pay child support more regularly.[67] The advantages of marriage appear to extend into a child's adulthood and even to his or her children. Researchers

62 *See, eg,* J. Ermisch & M. Francesconi, 'Patterns of Household and Family Formation,' in R. Berthoud & G. Gershuny (eds), *Seven Years in the Lies of British Families*, Bristol, 2000; K. Kiernan, 'Unmarried Cohabitation and Parenthood in Britain and Europe,' (2004), 26 *Law & Policy* 33; W. Manning et al., 'The Relative Stability of Cohabiting and Marital Unions for Children,' (2004) 23 *PRPR (Population Research & Policy Review)* 135.

63 *See* L.M. Casper & S.M. Bianchi, *Continuity and Change in the American Family*, Sage Publications, Thousand Oaks, CA, 2002, at 111–12 fig.4.3. Noncustodial divorced and never-married parents are also less likely to pass wealth to their adult children. *See* F.F. Furstenberg, Jr. et al., 'The Effect of Divorce on Intergenerational Transfers: New Evidence,' (1995) 32 *Demography* 319; N.F. Marks, 'Midlife Marital Status Differences in Social Support Relationships with Adult Children and Psychological Well-Being,' (1995) 16 *JFI* 5.

64 *See* M.N. Stiffman et al., 'Household Composition and Risk of Fatal Child Maltreatment,' 109 *Pediatrics* 615 (2002) (children residing in households with an unrelated adult were eight times more likely to die of maltreatment than children in households with two biological parents); R.F. Wilson, 'Undeserved Trust: Reflections on the ALI's Treatment of De Facto Parents,' in R.F. Wilson (ed), *Reconceiving the Family:* Cambridge University Press, Cambridge, UK, 2007, at 90–120 (reviewing evidence).

65 *See* S. McLanahan & G. Sandefur, *Growing Up with a Single Parent: What Hurts, What Helps*, Harvard University Press, Cambridge, MA, 1994, at 39–63 (reviewing evidence); W. Sigle-Rushton & S. McLanahan, 'Father Absence and Child Well-Being: A Critical Review,' in D.M. Moynihan et al.(eds), *The Future of the Family*, Russell Sage Foundation, New York, NY, 2004, at 116, 120–22 (same).

66 *See* P.R. Amato, 'The Impact of Family Formation Change on the Cognitive, Social, and Emotional Well-Being of the Next Generation,' (2005) 15 *Future of Children* 75 (summarizing studies); W. Sigle-Rushton & S. McLanahan, 'Father Absence and Child Well-Being: A Critical Review,' in D.M. Moynihan et al.(eds), *The Future of the Family*, Russell Sage Foundation, New York, NY, 2004, at 116, 122–25 (same). In the United States, living with married parents is also significantly linked to age of sexual initiation, likelihood of having a teen birth, and high school graduation, even after family instability is taken into account. *See* W.E. Manning & R.D. Bulanda, 'Parental Cohabitation Experiences and Adolescent Behavioral Outcomes,' (2008) 5 *PRPR* 593.

67 *See* L.M. Casper & S.M. Bianchi, *Continuity and Change in the American Family*, Sage Publications, Thousand Oaks, CA, 2002, at 46; M. Carlson et al., *Unmarried But Not Absent: Fathers' Involvement With Children After a Nonmarital Birth* (CRCW Working Paper 2005-07); L. Hao, 'Family Structure, Private Transfers, and the Economic Well-Being of Families with Children,' (1996) 75 *SF* 269; S.L. Hofferth & K.G. Anderson, 'Are All Dads Equal? Biology Versus Marriage as a Basis for Paternal Investment,' (2003) 65 *JMF* 213, 223–24. The evidence suggests that, even after controlling for observable characteristics like education, academic test scores, and premarital pregnancy, marriage contributes significantly to living standards, "not only relative to single parents living alone but also compared to parents in cohabiting relationships and single parents living with other adult relatives." R.I. Lerman, *Married and Unmarried Parenthood and Economic Well-Being: A Dynamic Analysis of a Recent Cohort* , Urban Institute, 2002, at 32, http://www.urban.org/UploadedPDF/410540_Parenthood.pdf.

have documented a strong link between growing up in a single-parent household and adult income, health, and emotional stability.[68] A number of studies have also found that both men and women who experience a single-parent household as children are more likely, as adults, to experience marital discord and to divorce or separate.[69]

The benefits of marriage are not, of course, invariable. So-called "selection effects" explain away a significant portion of the marital advantage; remarriage does not confer the same advantages as a first marriage.[70] Moreover, for both adults and children, the marital advantage is concentrated in low-conflict relationships. Researchers have found that the continuation of a high-conflict marriage is *negatively* associated with the health and happiness; indeed, longitudinal surveys show that "parents' marital unhappiness and discord have a broad negative impact on virtually every dimension of offspring well-being."[71]

However, despite these important caveats, the evidence strongly suggests that the marital advantage is real, and that it persists across national, cultural, and socioeconomic boundaries.[72] Much of the research on marriage does come from the United States, which may not be typical. But even in Scandinavia, which has the longest experience with cohabitation as a mainstream family form, demographers continue to find that marital childbearing is associated with much

---

See also A. Thomas & I. Sawhill, 'For Love and Money? The Impact of Family Structure on Family Income,' 15 *Future of Children* 57, Fall, 2005.

68 *See* W. Sigle-Rushton & S. McLanahan, 'Father Absence and Child Well-Being: A Critical Review,' in D.M. Moynihan et al.(eds), *The Future of the Family*, Russell Sage Foundation, New York, NY, 2004, at 116, 124–26; P.R. Amato, 'The Impact of Family Formation Change on the Cognitive, Social, and Emotional Well-Being of the Next Generation,' (2005) 15 *Future of Children* 75.

69 *See* Paul R. Amato & Alan Booth, *'A Generation at Risk: Growing Up in an Era of Family Upheaval' 106*–17, Harvard University Press, Cambridge, MA, 1997 (summarizing studies); P.R. Amato & J. Cheadle, 'The Long Reach of Divorce: Divorce and Child Well-Being Across Three Generations,' (2005) 67 JMF 191, at 192–93 (same); D.M. Fergusson et al., 'Exposure to Single Parenthood in Childhood and Later Mental Health, Educational, Economic, and Criminal Behavior Outcomes,' (2007) 64 *Archives General Psychiatry* 1089.

70 *See* M. Garrison, 'The Decline of Formal Marriage: Inevitable or Reversible?,' (2007) 41 *FLQ* 491, at 498–99 (reviewing research).

71 Paul R. Amato & Alan Booth, *'A Generation at Risk: Growing Up in an Era of Family Upheaval'* Harvard University Press, Cambridge, MA, 1997, at 219. *See also* D. Umberson et al., 'You Make Me Sick: Marital Quality and Health Over the Life Course,' PRC Working Paper No. 03–04–05, 2005), http://www.prc.utexas.edu/working_papers/wp_pdf/03-04-05.pdf (reviewing evidence); J.K. Kiecolt-Glaser & T.L. Newton, 'Marriage and Health: His and Hers,' (2001) 127 *Psychological Bulletin* 472.

72 *See, eg,* P.J. Smock et al., 'The Effect of Marriage and Divorce on Women's Economic Well-Being,' (1999) 64 *ASR* 794; H.K. Kim & P.C. McHenry, 'The Relationship Between Marriage and Psychological Well-Being – A Longitudinal Analysis,' (2002) 23 *JFI* 885; W. Sigle-Rushton & S. McLanahan, 'Father Absence and Child Well-Being: A Critical Review,' in D.M. Moynihan et al.(eds), *The Future of the Family*, Russell Sage Foundation, New York, NY, 2004, at 126–30, 130.

greater childhood stability,[73] smaller risks to youthful and adult well-being,[74] and lower rates of divorce and non-marital childbearing.[75]

As family sociologist Paul Amato has put it, "the evidence consistently indicates that children with two happily and securely married parents have a statistical advantage over children raised in other family groups." And "because we all have an interest in the well-being of children, it is reasonable for social institutions (such as the state) to attempt to increase the proportion of children raised by married parents with satisfying and stable marriages."[76]

The marital advantage justifies state policies which support marital childbearing, and laws that treat non-marital parenting as the equivalent of marital parenting conflict with such policies. Such laws may also encourage non-marital parenting by suggesting that public support for marriage is declining. This is undesirable because "bandwagon" effects often play an important role in determining public opinion, and public opinion, over time, plays an important role in determining private attitudes and behavior.[77]

Consider the rapid shift in attitudes toward premarital sex noted in Part I: In 1965, 69% of surveyed women and 65% of surveyed men under 30 said that premarital sex was "always" or "almost always" wrong; in 1972, only 24% of women and 21%

---

73 *See* A.-M. Jensen & S.-E. Clausen, 'Children and Family Dissolution in Norway: The Impact of Consensual Unions,' (2003) 10 *Childhood* 65 (2003) (children of Norwegian cohabiting parents run a much higher risk of dissolution compared to children in marital unions and "this risk is not diminishing as cohabitation becomes more widespread"); K. Kiernan, 'Unmarried Cohabitation and Parenthood: Here to Stay? European Perspectives', *in* D.M. Moynihan et al. (eds), *The Future of the Family*, Russell Sage Foundation, New York, NY, 2004, at 84 fig. 3.6 (6% of Swedish marital unions and 25% of non-marital unions dissolve within five years after birth of first child).

74 *See* K. Breivik & D. Olweus, 'Children of Divorce in a Scandinavian Welfare State: Are They Less Affected than US Children?,' (2006) 47 *SJP (Scandinavian Journal Psychiatry)* 61 (2006); H. Hansagi et al., 'Parental Divorce: Psychosocial Well-Being, Mental Health and Mortality During Youth and Young Adulthood: A Longitudinal Study of Swedish Conscripts,' (2000) 10 *European Journal Public Health* 335; I. Storksen et al., Marriages and Psychological Distress Among Adult Offspring of Divorce: A Norwegian Study,' (2007) 48 *SJP* 467; G.R. Weitoft et al., 'Mortality, Severe Morbidity, and Injury in Children Living with Single Parents in Sweden: A Population-Based Study,' (2003) 361 *Lancet* 289.

75 *See* K. Kiernan, 'Redrawing the Boundaries of Marriage,' (2004) 66 *JMF* 980, at 983.

76 P. Amato, 'Tension Between Institutional and Individual Views of Marriage,' (2004) 66 *JMF* 959, at 962–63.

77 The "bandwagon" phenomenon is the subject of a large literature. *See generally* T.C. Schelling, *Micromotives and Macrobehavior*, Norton & Co, New York, NY, 1978; S.R.G. Jones, *The Economics of Conformism*, Basil Blackwell, New York, NY, 1984; J.S. Coleman, *Foundations of Social Theory*, Harvard University Press, Cambridge, MA, 1990. *See also* T. Kuran, *Private Truths, Public Lies: The Social Consequences of Preference Falsification*, Harvard University Press, Cambridge, MA, 1995, at 69–82.

of men did so.[78] A similar, although somewhat less dramatic shift in attitudes toward marriage and divorce took place during the same time period: in the early 1960s, 80% of the public agreed that "a couple should stay together" for the sake of the children; by the 1980s agreement with this statement had dropped to 50%.[79] As these examples suggest, if individuals *believe* that public opinion about formal marriage is increasingly dismissive, individuals without strongly held views on the subject may well become more dismissive themselves. Indeed, there is evidence suggesting that the low marriage rate in Quebec – a rate that is about half that of the other Canadian provinces[80] – has been induced, in part, by such a bandwagon effect.[81]

Given the advantages to children associated with formal marriage, the variety of cohabiting relationships and attendant difficulty of drafting standards that separate relationships involving expectations of sharing from the majority that do not give rise to such expectations, and the risk of creating bandwagon effects that might reduce public support for formal marriage and marital childbearing, there is every reason for courts and legislatures to remain cautious in legislating standards to govern cohabiting relationships.

3. CONCLUSION

At this point, the evidence clearly supports several policy initiatives for cohabitants. First, it supports an overhaul of custody and support laws to ensure that children born to cohabitants suffer no discrimination or disadvantage. Second, it supports a public education campaign to ensure that cohabitants understand the legal disadvantages inherent in their failure to formalize their relationship as well as the social and economic disadvantages associated with non-marital childbearing. Third, it supports an examination of existing equitable remedies to ensure that cohabitants who have justifiably relied on a partner's promises to share resources or pay compensation for services can obtain relief. Finally, it supports the legalization of written relationship contracts between cohabitants and a registration option for those who want to formalize their status

---

78 *See* A. Thornton, 'Changing Attitudes Toward Family Issues in the United States,' (1989) 51 *JMF* 873, 884 tbl. 4.

79 *See* L. Bumpass, 'The Changing Context of Parenting in the United States,' http://parenthood.library.wisc.edu/Bumpass/Bumpass.html.

80 *See* Statistics Canada, *2003 Marriage Rates*, http://www.statcan.ca/Daily/English/070117/d070117a.htm. Correspondingly, the proportion of adults living in nonmarital relationships is double the proportion in the rest of Canada. *See* R. Lachapelle, 'The High Prevalence of Cohabitation Among Franco-phones: Some Implications for Exogamous Couples,' Annual Meeting Canadian Population Society, 2007); B. Laplante, 'The Rise of Cohabitation in Quebec: Power of Religion and Power over Religion,' (2006) 31 *Canadian Journal Sociology* 1.

81 *See* M. Garrison, 'The Decline of Formal Marriage: Inevitable or Reversible?,' (2007) 41 *FLQ* 491 at 512–16 (summarizing evidence).

and obtain family property rights and obligations. With respect to this latter option, policy makers must take care to ensure that registration options do not undermine the institution of marriage and that they comport with the goals and desires of typical cohabiting couples. Public education is essential here; so are public surveys of cohabitants.

Conscriptive laws that grant property or support rights to cohabitants without any affirmative action on their part appear to be unwarranted. Marital property and support laws rest on marital commitment and sharing. Cohabitants have not made binding commitments and the evidence shows that they do not typically adopt the marital sharing norm. Equity, efficiency, and child protection goals all support a legal regime that honors the choices and commitments that couples choose to make.

PART FOUR

PROTECTION OF OLDER PEOPLE IN LAW

'LIVING WILL' LAW UNDER THE GERMAN CIVIL CODE

Alexandra Maschwitz

1. INTRODUCTION

European legislators have come up with different legal regimes to provide for situations in which a person – due to old age and/or disease – is unable to make decisions for him- or herself. One of these instruments is the living will, also known as an "advance decision"[1] or an "advance directive"[2] concerning medical care. This legal instrument has been constructed to ensure that a person's will concerning medical treatment is adhered to even at a time when the patient is unable to make the required decisions. This does not apply to elderly people only, but also to people with terminal illnesses and people who, for religious reasons, object to special medical treatments.[3]

Providing health care directions for a future incapacity is a legal undertaking which stands at the threshold between many legal disciplines. The link to health law and the law dealing with incapacity is obvious. However, health care directions are also linked to criminal law when it comes to the question of differing between rightful medical treatment, to which the patient consented, and penalized treatment causing bodily harm or even homicide, where the patient did not consent. Here physicians need clear guidelines on the existence of a valid consent. Public law is also involved when it comes to the questions of how far the duty of a state with respect to the protection of life goes, and how far the self-determination of a patient reaches respectively.

This article will focus on the private law aspects of living wills as part of the law on incapacity. Before I go into the details of the German law on living wills, I would like to provide a short overview of the legal rights and interests concerned; followed by a detailed analysis of the preconditions and legal consequences of a living will as set out in the German Civil Code. I conclude with a short analysis of whether the German law succeeds in striking a balance between the rights and interests involved.

---

1 England and Wales.

2 Scotland; the terminology is further discussed in the Irish LAW REFORM COMMISSION'S *Report on Bioethics: Advance Care Directives* 2009, pp 2–3.

3 Cf. for Austria J. Inthorn and M. Kletecka-Pulker, in S. Brauer, N. Biller-Andorno and R. Andorno (eds), *Country Reports on Advance Directives*, University of Zurich 2008, p 9.

2. THE PROTECTION OF ELDERLY PERSONS ESP. CONCERNING MEDICAL CARE

2.1. RIGHTS AND INTERESTS

Low birth rates and a slow but steady increase in life expectancy characterise the age structure in the European Union.[4] In 2007, nearly 29% of the population were over 65 years old[5] and the number of persons over 80 is expected to increase leading up to an estimated 12% in 2060.[6] These demographic changes have drawn the attention of European academics as well as politicians to the concerns of the elderly population.[7]

The rights of the elderly regarding health care are protected in laws and conventions of differing intensity. A first category includes older international conventions and national constitutions which do not mention the rights of elderly persons explicitly. Instead these conventions offer protection through the general rights and freedoms as stated for example in the Council of Europe's Convention for the Protection of Human Rights and Fundamental Freedoms. Here, the right to self-determination as an aspect of the right to respect for private life (Article 8)[8] is especially relevant. Additionally, the right to life (Article 2) and even the protection from inhuman and degrading treatment (Article 3) can be of importance with regard to health care issues.[9]

More recent legal instruments which protect the rights of the elderly explicitly form a second category. Thus for instance the European Charter of Fundamental

4 EUROSTAT, *EUROPE IN FIGURES – Eurostat yearbook 2009*, Luxembourg 2009, p 133.
5 EUROSTAT, *EUROPE IN FIGURES – Eurostat yearbook 2009*, Luxembourg 2009, p 136.
6 EUROSTAT, *EUROPE IN FIGURES – Eurostat yearbook 2009*, Luxembourg 2009, p 136.
7 See especially E. Rynning, 'The Ageing Populations of Europe – Implications for Health Systems and Patents' Rights', (2008) 15 *EJHL (European Journal of Health Law)* 297–306; R. Andorno, N. Biller-Andorno and S. Brauer, 'Advance Health Care Directives: Towards a Coordinated European Policy', (2009) 16 *EJHL* 207–227.
8 "Private life" covers both the physical and the psychological integrity of a person, cf. ECHR 22 March 2003, Case 24209/94, *Y.F. v Turkey*, § 33; ECHR 26 March 1985, Case 8978/80, *X and Y v the Netherlands*, § 22. Furthermore, a deprivation of liberty within the meaning of art 5 para 1 is possible; however, the ECHR rejected a deprivation in that sense in a case where an adult was placed in a nursing home, ECHR 26 February 2002, Case *39187/98*, H.M. v Switzerland, para 44–48. As this interpretation narrows the scope of art 5 immensely, it seems more reasonable to assume a deprivation and further examine whether a violation of art 5 para 1 exists or whether the placement was justified according to art 5 para 1 a – f, cf. the concurring opinion of Judge G. Jörundsson, ECHR, 26 February 2002, Case *39187/98*, *H.M. v Switzerland*.
9 Cf. also the protection under the Charter of Fundamental Rights of the European Union (2010/C 83/02) in art 2 para 1 (right to life), art 3 para 2 (a) (principle of free and informed consent in medicine), art 4 (prohibition of inhumane or degrading treatment) and art 7 (protection of private life). Even art 10 para 2 with the right to conscientious objection might be of relevance where a patient refuses treatment on grounds of religion or beliefs.

Rights, which after the Lisbon Treaty has a binding character, ensures in its Article 25 the "rights of the elderly to lead a life of dignity and independence and to participate in social and cultural life". Regarding health care, a life of dignity and independence demands that a person's autonomy is ensured for as long as possible.[10]

The third and last category comprises individual conventions and declarations, that emerged in the last 20 years, and which deal with the rights of the elderly and/or health law in detail. In this manner the autonomy of a patient is the focal point of the Council of Europe's Convention on Human Rights and Biomedicine,[11] which in Article 5 enshrines the requirement of free and informed consent and thus the respect for patient autonomy.[12] With regard to the living will, Article 9 of the Council of Europe's Convention on Human Rights and Biomedicine deals explicitly with previously expressed wishes. It states: "*The previously expressed wishes relating to a medical intervention by a patient who is not, at the time of the intervention, in a state to express his or her wishes shall be taken into account*". While it is clear that these wishes cannot be completely ignored, this provision neither states to which extent or under which conditions a patient's wishes have to be considered nor which form they should take. Thus it merely indicates that a living will should at least have an advisory effect, but does not require that it has a legally binding status.[13]

A similar wide margin of discretion is left to the European legislators in the Council of Europe's Recommendation on Principles Concerning Continuing Powers of Attorney and Advance Directives for Incapacity of 2009.[14]

2.2. NATIONAL MEASURES

On a national level the aforementioned demographic changes have also drawn the attention of legislators to adult protection issues. The protection of vulnerable adults generally comprises two fields: on the one hand are all matters in relation

10 For the implications of human dignity for medical treatment cf. W. Härle, 'Patienten'autonomie' aus ethischer Sicht – Zur Aufhebung des Widerspruchs zwischen Selbstbestimmung und Fürsorge', *FPR (Familie Partnerschaft Recht)* 2007, 47 at 51.

11 Oviedo Convention, ETS No. 164, 1997. So far it has been ratified in 24 Member States of the Council of Europe. However, most central European Countries, such as France and Germany, have not ratified the Convention.

12 R. Andorno, N. Biller-Andorno and S. Brauer, 'Advance Health Care Directives: Towards a Coordinated European Policy', (2009) 16 *EJHL* 207 at 207.

13 R. Andorno, N. Biller-Andorno and S. Brauer, 'Advance Health Care Directives: Towards a Coordinated European Policy', (2009) 16 *EJHL* 207 at 211.

14 Recommendation CM/Rec(2009)11 of the Committee of Ministers to Member States on principles concerning continuing powers of attorney and advance directives for incapacity. Cf. also art 9 (b) iv Council of Europe's Recommendation 1418 (1999) on the Protection of the human rights and dignity of the terminally ill and the dying.

to property and finance, and on the other hand matters concerning the healthcare and personal welfare of adults. In contrast to earlier legislation, which tended to see the only solution for their protection in declarations of incapacity and placements under guardianship, nowadays legislators try to take a more varied approach towards the protection of the elderly.[15] Thus, some countries have enacted laws with several protection measures of varying impact. Others, for example Austria, opted for one single legal regime, which provides flexible solutions depending on the kind and scope of a person's need of assistance.[16]

With regard to healthcare, a movement from paternalism towards a more social model based on self-determination is taking place.[17] Several countries enacted specific laws on patient's rights, focussing on the principle of informed consent.[18] Thus, multiple new legal instruments have been created in European countries to ensure a person's autonomy for as long as possible. Examples are continuing powers of attorney[19] and advance directives regarding personal care.[20] Recent reforms in this area took place in England and Wales (Mental Capacity Act 2005), in Austria (Austrian Act on Living Wills 2006) as well as in Germany in 2009. Reforms are currently planned in Switzerland, Italy and Ireland.[21]

---

15 Cf. I. Doron, 'Elder Guardianship Kaleidoscope – A Comparative Perspective', *Int'l J L Pol Fam (International Journal of Law, Policy, & the Family)* 16 (2002) 368 et seq.

16 For an overview see N. Dethloff, *Familienrecht*, Verlag C.H. Beck, 29th ed Munich 2009, § 17 mn. 43 et seq.

17 Cf. H. NYS, 'Emerging legislation in Europe on the legal status of advance directives and medical decision-making with respect to an incompetent patient ('living wills')', (1997) 4 *EJHL* 61 at 63. For the difficulties to strike a balance between paternalism and patient autonomy see A. Bagheri, 'Regulating Medical Futility: Neither Excessive Patient's Autonomy Nor Physician's Paternalism', (2008) 15 *EJHL* 45 et seq and W. Härle, 'Patienten'autonomie' aus ethischer Sicht – Zur Aufhebung des Widerspruchs zwischen Selbstbestimmung und Fürsorge', *FPR* 2007, 47 at 47; for philosophical and ethical issues concerning advance directives see for instance C. Buford, 'Advancing an Advance Directive Debate', (2008) 22 *Bioethics* 423–430 with further references.

18 For an overview on national legislation on patient's rights see: http://europatientrights.eu/types/general_overview_of_types_of_legislation.html.

19 As for instance in Austria (sec 284f Austrian Civil Code), Belgium (art 14 Belgian Act on Patient's Rights), England and Wales (sec 9–14 Mental Capacity Act 2005), France (art 1111–6 French Public Health Code), and Hungary (art 22.2 Hungarian Health Care Act).

20 Eg Austria (Austrian Act on Living Wills), Belgium (art 8 para 4 Belgian Act on Patient's Rights), Denmark (sec 26 para 1 Danish Health Law), England and Wales (sec 24 et seq Mental Capacity Act 2005), Finland (art 8 Finish Act on the Status and Rights of Patients), France (art 1111–11 et seq French Public Health Code), Hungary (art 22.1 Hungarian Health Care Act), The Netherlands (art 450 para 3 Dutch Civil Code as well as Dutch Law on Euthanasia and Assisted Suicide) and Spain (art 11 Spanish Basic Law 41/2002 on Patient Autonomy and Rights and Obligations Regarding Medical Information and Documentation).

21 For Italy see F. Giardini, 'The Living Will in the Italian Legal System', in B. Atkin and F. Banda (eds), *The International Survey of Family Law*, Jordan Publishing, Bristol 2009, pp 241 et seq; in Switzerland proposed Art 370 et seq Swiss Civil Code deal with living wills, cf. in German http://www.parlament.ch/sites/doc/CuriaFolgeseite/2006/20060063/Schlussabstimmungstext%20NS%20D.pdf; the draft Mental Capacity (Advance Care Directives) Bill 2009 in Ireland is part of the LAW REFORM COMMISSION'S *Report on Bioethics: Advance Care Directives* (LRC 94 -2009). See also the lapsed initiative in Portugal (Projecto de Lei n.° 788/X – Direitos

3. THE "LIVING WILL" IN GERMANY

3.1. HISTORICAL DEVELOPMENT

Even though approximately 8.6 million people in Germany have made living wills,[22] until recently the living will had not been expressly regulated in German law. Hence, the legal practice was determined by uncertainty with regard to the binding nature of living wills.[23] Scholars as well as courts tried to establish rules as to when a living will had to be adhered to.[24] However, no clear guidelines emerged. Following two dissenting judgments of the Bundesgerichtshof (German Federal Court of Justice) concerning the valid scope of a living will,[25] political, ethical as well as legal committees intensely discussed the subject of living wills and several drafts of an act on living wills were created.[26] The German legislator finally reacted to this deficit, and since 1 September 2009 the German Civil Code includes a codification of the living will.[27]

The new rules in sec 1901a et seq. of the German Civil Code were introduced as part of the third reform of the law for the protection of adults. The main purpose of this law reform was to ensure the patient's autonomy – which is also safeguarded through Articles 1 and 2 para 2 of the Grundgesetz (German Basic Law, the German constitution) – and to create a legal framework that allows a person to anticipate certain situations and to decide in advance which measures should be taken and which persons should be entrusted with necessary decisions, if he or she becomes unable to act for him- or herself.

---

dos doentes à informação e ao consentimento informado, cf. in Portuguese http://www.parlamento.pt/ActividadeParlamentar/Paginas/DetalheIniciativa.aspx?BID=34574).

22 Deutsche Hospiz Stiftung, *Wie denken die Deutschen über Patientenverfügungen*, 2005, p 3, http://www.hospize.de/docs/stellungnahmen/32.pdf.

23 For an analysis of the views of judges of the former courts of guardianship (Vormundschaftsgerichte) before the codification of the living will, which shows the broad variety in preconditions and legal effects as applied in the courts, see W. Höfling, 'Patientenautonomie und Patientenverfügungen aus der Sicht der deutschen Vormundschaftsrichter/innen', *FPR* 2007, 67 – 69. Cf. also BT-Drs (Bundestags Drucksachen) 16/8442 p 2.

24 For an overview on the discussion among legal academics see W. Lange, *Inhalt und Auslegung von Patientenverfügungen*, Nomos, Baden-Baden 2009, pp 36 et seq.

25 Cf. the decision of the Federal Court of Justice, Criminal Panel, BGH 13 September 1994, *NJW (Neue Juristische Wochenschrift)* 1995, 204 and the misinterpretation thereof in the Federal Court of Justice, Civil Panel XII, BGH 17 March 2003, *NJW* 2003, 1588.

26 The living will was subject of the 63rd (2000) and 66th (2006) Conference of the Association of German Jurists (DJT- Deutscher Juristentag); cf. further the report of the Enquete-Kommission "Ethik und Recht der modernen Medizin" (Parliamentary Commission of the German Parliament on ethics and law of modern medicin), BT-Drs 15/3700 (2004) as well as the comment of the Nationaler Ethikrat (National Ethic Committee), *Patientenverfügung – ein Instrument der Selbstbestimmung*, 2005. For draft bills cf. so-called Bosbach-draft, BT-Drs 16/11360, so-called Zöller-draft, BT Drs 16/11493 as well as the later slightly modified enacted so-called Stünker-draft, BT-Drs 16/8442.

27 BGBl I 2009, 2286.

3.2. LEGAL DEFINITION

With regard to the living will, the German Civil Code now provides a legal definition. According to its sec 1901a para 1 sentence 1 a living will exists, if *"a person of full age who is able to consent has determined in writing, for the event of his becoming unable to consent, whether he consents to or prohibits specific tests of his state of health, treatment or medical interventions not yet directly immanent at the time of determination".*[28]

3.3. REQUIREMENTS FOR A BINDING LIVING WILL

The requirements for living wills are also set out in sec 1901a para 1 sentence 1 of the German Civil Code: in short, a living will requires the testator's capacity to consent, majority and has to be in writing. Furthermore, the living will must not have been revoked at the time of the implementation[29] and must not be made a condition for another contract.[30] In order to distinguish a living will from a traditional contemporary consent, the medical treatment concerned must not be directly imminent at the time of the determination. Thus, even if the patient consents in writing to a medical treatment – which due to the anaesthesia will commence when he or she is unable to continue consenting – this does not qualify as a living will and therefore does not need to comply with the requirements of sec 1901a of the German Civil Code, which will now be discussed in turn.[31]

3.3.1. Capacity to consent

First, just as in the case of consenting to a medical treatment, the testator has to be able to consent at the time of the writing of the living will. The capacity to consent must not be confused with the individual's legal capacity: it merely means the *natural* ability to consent and requires that the patient is able to comprehend the character, meaning, consequences as well as risks of a treatment and that he or she can form his will accordingly.[32]

---

28 Translation provided by the Langenscheidt Translation Service, regularly updated by Neil Mussett, available at http://www.gesetze-im-internet.de/englisch_bgb/englisch_bgb.html.

29 Sec 1901a para 1 sentence 3 German Civil Code.

30 Sec 1901a para 4 German Civil Code. For more detail see below 3.5.2.

31 M. Probst, ‚Patientenverfügung – gelöste und ungelöste Probleme nach der Neuregelung', *FF (forum familienrecht)* 2010, 144 at 146.

32 BGH 5 December 1958, *NJW* 1959, 811; BGH 2 December 1963, *NJW* 1964, 1177 at 1178. Clearly stated also in the Stünker-draft, BT-Drs 16/8442 p 9.

3.3.2. *Majority*

Secondly, only persons of full age can establish a living will. Similarly to almost all European countries, the age of majority in Germany is 18 years.[33]

It has been criticised that the legislator did not opt for a minimum age of 16 years,[34] adjusting it to the legal age required for testators.[35] As the consent to medical treatment is not based on legal capacity but on the capacity to encompass the nature and scope of a medical measure, majority is not necessarily the mandatory starting point.[36] Accordingly, living will laws in Europe differ on this requirement. While for instance England and Wales require majority,[37] it is not a precondition in Austria.[38] However, in Austria the ability of the minor to understand and judge the nature and scope of a medical measure is decisive.[39] As treatments of the minor that are usually linked to grave and lasting impairments of the physical or mental integrity require the additional consent of the person holding the personal custody,[40] this consent should be added in the living will document.[41]

However, bearing in mind the impact of most measures governed by a living will, the decision to choose an age limit of 18 years seems justifiable. The anticipation of future situations is difficult even for adults and requires a thorough examination of one's personal view on medical treatments and life in general. It should therefore

---

33 Sec 2 German Civil Code.

34 Critical W. LANGE, 'Das Patientenverfügungsgesetz – Überblick und kritische Würdigung', *ZEV (Zeitschrift für Erbrecht und Vermögensnachfolge)* 2009, 537 at 539 and A. SPICKHOFF, 'Rechtssicherheit kraft Gesetzes durch sog. Patientenverfügung', *FamRZ (Zeitschrift für das gesamte Familienrecht)* 2009, 1949 at 1950.

35 Cf. sec 2229 para 1 German Civil Code, however with more stringent formal requirements according to sec 2233 para 1 German Civil Code. For a criticism see W. LANGE, 'Das Patientenverfügungsgesetz – Überblick und kritische Würdigung', *ZEV* 2009, 537 at 539.

36 On the nature of the living will as a special form of consent and not as a "declaration of intent" see A. SPICKHOFF, 'Rechtssicherheit kraft Gesetzes durch sog. Patientenverfügung', *FamRZ* 2009, 1949 at 1950.

37 Sec 24 para 1 Mental Capacity Act 2005.

38 M. KLETEČKA-PULKER, 'Grundzüge und Zielsetzungen des Patientenverfügungs-Gesetzes', in U. KÖRTNER, C. KOPETZKI and M. KLETEČKA-PULKER (eds), *Das österreichische Patientenverfügungsgesetz – Ethische und rechtliche Aspekte,* Springer, Vienna – New York, 2007, p 85. Compare also art 370 para 1 of the Swiss Civil Code as proposed in the reform bill, which does not state majority as a requirement and thus allows minors to set up a living will; cf. B. SCHNYDER, 'Auf dem Weg zu einem umfassenden schweizerischen Erwachsenenschutzrecht', *FamRZ* 2006, 1569 at 1572.

39 Art. 146c Austrian Civil Code (Allgemeines Bürgerliches Gesetzbuch – ABGB).

40 Art. 146c para 2 Austrian Civil Code (Allgemeines Bürgerliches Gesetzbuch – ABGB).

41 Cf. for instance NÖ Patienten- und Pflegeanwaltschaft and Wiener Pflege-, Patientinnen- und Patientenanwaltschaft, *Ratgeber Patientenverfügung,* 2nd ed Vienna 2009, p 22.

be assumed that the age limit does neither violate the right to self-determination of minors nor the principle of equality.[42]

Due to the strictly personal character of the right to establish a living will[43] parents cannot make a living will for their child. The right to establish a living will cannot be transferred.[44] However, as parents are as a rule entrusted with the personal care of their children, their consent generally will be decisive, especially when the child is no longer able to articulate his or her own will.

3.3.3. *Written form*

Thirdly, the living will has to be in writing. According to sec 126 para 1 of the German Civil Code this means that the document must be signed by the issuer with his or her name in their own hand or by their notarially certified initials. In consequence, an oral advance directive is void due to the lack of form.[45] The requirement of a written living will is meant to ensure clarity and to prevent hasty or premature decisions.[46] Furthermore it simplifies the proof of the content of a living will. A rich variety of formulae, provided by public authorities, religious communities as well as organisations which represent patients' interests, is meant to help the testator with the wording.[47]

To me the requirement of at least a written living will seems adequate with regard to the protection of health and life of the testator.[48] More stringent formal requirements – as proposed in prior drafts and required in other countries – were

---

42 Critical A. Spickhoff, 'Rechtssicherheit kraft Gesetzes durch sog. Patientenverfügung', *FamRZ* 2009, 1949 at 1950 et seq, and G. Müller in H.G. Bamberger and H. ROTH (eds), Beck'scher Onlinekommentar, BGB, Verlag C.H. Beck, 16th ed Munich 2009, § 1901a mn. 15.

43 Cf. BGH 17 March 2003, *NJW* 2003, 1588 at 1590; E. ALBRECHT and A. ALBRECHT, 'Die Patientenverfügung – jetzt gesetzlich geregelt', *MittBayNot (Mitteilungen des Bayerischen Notarvereins, der Notarkasse und der Landesnotarkammer Bayern)* 2009, 426 at 431.

44 This seems to be the prevailing view in courts as well as in literature, see AG Lüdenhausen 24 November 2003 *FamRZ* 2004, 835 (ann. W. Bienwald), G. Müller, in H.G. Bamberger und H. Roth (eds), *Beck'scher Online-Kommentar*, Verlag C.H. Beck, 15th ed Munich 2009, § 1901a BGB mn. 15; A. Spickhoff, 'Rechtssicherheit kraft Gesetzes durch sog. Patientenverfügung', *FamRZ* 2009, 1949 at 1950.

45 For oral living wills made before the coming into force of the new codification see E. Albrecht and A. Albrecht, *Die Patientenverfügung*, Gieseking, Bielefeld 2009, p 66. For a different approach cf. sec 4 para 2 Irish Draft Mental Capacity (Advance Care Directive) Bill 2009, according to which even an oral living will would be enforceable.

46 BT-Drs 16/8442 p 13.

47 There are over 200 formulae, but many of them are outdated and probably do not meet the requirements set up in sec 1901a German Civil Code. An in-depth analysis has been made before the codification by W. Lange, *Inhalt und Auslegung von Patientenverfügungen*, Nomos, Baden-Baden 2009. See the updated version of the Federal Ministry of Justice available at http://www.bmj.bund.de/enid/Publikationen/Patientenverfuegung_oe.html.

48 W. Lange, 'Das Patientenverfügungsgesetz – Überblick und kritische Würdigung', *ZEV* 2009, 537 at 540. Bt-Drs 16/8442 p 13.

seen as placing an undue burden on individuals and thus preventing them from making a living will. In particular, neither the testimony of witnesses – as is the case in England and Wales for advance decisions concerning life-sustaining measures[49] – nor the participation of a notary, lawyer or other qualified person, as set out in sec 6 para 1 Austrian Act on Living Wills, is required. In practice, however, it might still be advisable to use a notary. Not only can the notary establish the testator's capacity to consent (which might be an issue particularly for elderly persons) and freedom of choice at the time of the formation of the living will, but also provide information about the binding nature of the living will and ensure a clear legal wording of the testator's wishes.[50] If the living will has been set up in combination with the establishment of a person with continuing powers of attorney or directives for the choice of a future custodian (Betreuer),[51] a registration at the Federal Association of Notaries (Bundesnotarkammer) is possible, too.[52] A registration helps to insure that the physician gets to know about the living will. In custody proceedings – initiated for instance by the physician – the court of custody can require a registration statement.[53] This is done not only to find out whether the patient has stated directives concerning the person who should become his or her custodian or whether he or she has appointed a person with continuing powers of attorney, but also whether a living will exists.[54] In case of the existence of a living will the court of custody will then inform the physician accordingly. Whereas the register does not contain the living will document as such, it will contain information about the whereabouts of the document.

3.4. SCOPE OF LIVING WILLS

The scope of medical treatments to which a living will can apply according to the new codification is rather broad: in contrast to many other countries that have

---

49 Sec 25 para 5 and 6 Mental Capacity Act 2005.

50 G. Müller, in H.G. Bamberger und H. Roth (eds), *Beck'scher Online-Kommentar*, Verlag C.H. Beck, 15th ed Munich 2009, § 1901a BGB mn.12.

51 Under German law the custodian is a person appointed by the court of custody either on the request of the incapable adult or *ex officio*, when a person of full age is unable (in whole or in part) to properly take care of his or her affairs, sec 1896 para 1 German Civil Code. Custodianship is limited to those affairs, in which a custodian is necessary, sec. 1896 para 2 German Civil Code. In cases where a person with continuing powers of attorney exists, a custodianship will not be necessary, provided this person can take care of the affairs in question in a similarly effective way.

52 See sec 78a para 1 Federal Notary Order; explicitely S. Görk, in H. Schippel and U. Bracker (eds), *Bundesnotarordnung*, Verlag Franz Vahlen, 8th ed Munich 2006, § 78a mn. 24 and S. Görk, 'Das zentrale Vorsorgeregister der Bundesnotarkammer – ein zentraler Baustein bei der Durchsetzung des Selbstbestimmungsrechts', *FPR 2007, 82–84.*

53 Cf. sec 6 Ordinance on the Central Register of the Federal Association of Notaries (Vorsorgeregister-Verordnung).

54 For the content of the register see sec 1 Ordinance on the Central Register of the Federal Association of Notaries (Vorsorgeregister-Verordnung).

enacted laws on living wills, German law does not limit itself to the refusal of life-prolonging or life-sustaining measures or the refusal of medical treatment in general.[55] Even though refusals tend to be the most likely directives made in a living will,[56] German law allows explicit consent to or prohibition of specific tests of the testator's state of health, treatment or medical interventions.

Furthermore, living wills are not limited to irreversibly fatal diseases; instead they apply regardless of nature and stage of any illness.[57] Consequently, an advance directive can have the same scope as a contemporary consent.[58] Hence, the testator can for instance also make directives for his or her suffering of Alzheimer disease or being in a persistent vegetative state.[59] With regard to the nature and stage of an illness, the unlimited scope of the living will in Germany shall ensure that the patient is not forced to undergo unwanted medical treatment at any time in his or her life.[60]

While in principle there is great freedom to draft a legal will in Germany, there are certain limitations. For instance, the scope of a living will is limited through the definition of the living will, which does not include basic medical care.[61] Thus, humane accommodation, personal hygiene, the alleviation of pain, shortness of breath and nausea as well as the natural alleviation of hunger and thirst cannot be refused through a living will.[62]

The scope of advance directives is further limited by the principle of clarity. Indeed, the precondition of instructions for specific treatment in likely situations as set out in sec 1901a para 1 sentence 1 of the German Civil Code is probably one of the most difficult requirements. To write detailed descriptions of treatment for a situation which has not yet arisen and whose circumstances therefore cannot

---

55 It should be noted, however, that the Biomedicine Convention (see supra fn. 10) encompasses consents, too.

56 See G. Müller, in H.G. Bamberger und H. Roth (eds), *Beck'scher Online-Kommentar*, Verlag C.H. Beck, 15th ed Munich 2009, § 1901a BGB mn. 2; W. Lange, 'Das Patientenverfügungsgesetz – Überblick und kritische Würdigung', *ZEV* 2009, 537 at 543.

57 Sec 1901a para 3 German Civil Code. By contrast, the so called *Bosbach-Draft* (BT-Drs 16/11360) would have limited the application of living wills to situations in which the underlying disease is irreversibly fatal.

58 W. Lange, 'Das Patientenverfügungsgesetz – Überblick und kritische Würdigung', *ZEV* 2009, 537 at 538.

59 With further examples E. Albrecht and A. Albrecht, *Die Patientenverfügung*, Gieseking, Bielefeld 2009, p 39.

60 BT-Drs 16/8442 p 3.

61 Cf. for Ireland LAW REFORM COMMISSION, 'Consultation Paper on Bioethics: Advance Care Directives' (LRC CP 51–2008) at para 1.48 and 'Report on Bioethics: Advance Care Directives' (LRC 94 – 2009) at para 3.07 and at para 3.10–3.13 et seq concerning the inclusion of palliative care (ie esp alleviation of pain).

62 BT-Drs 16/8442 p 13. On the problem of basic care for patients who refuse hospitalization see W. Lange, 'Das Patientenverfügungsgesetz – Überblick und kritische Würdigung', *ZEV* 2009, 537 at 538.

be foreseen in its entirety, stretches the imagination of every testator. Hence, the requirement should not be construed too narrowly as this might lead to a forfeiture of the binding effect of the living will.[63] While one ought not to require medical training to formulate a living will, mere wishes and general guidelines certainly do not qualify for a binding living will.[64] In practice it will be advisable to consult a physician and/or a specially trained notary to ensure that the wording is legally binding.[65]

3.5. LEGAL EFFECTS OF THE LIVING WILL

In principle, a living will as set out in sec 1901a para 1 sentence 1 of the German Civil Code is binding. The German approach to the legal status of living wills is thus in line with countries such as England and Wales, Austria, Spain, Hungary, Belgium, Finland and The Netherlands. Only when the requirements of the law are not met or certain limits are crossed, the living will is not enforced. However, in this case the living will has to be taken into account for the establishment of the "presumed intent" of the patient.[66]

3.5.1. General rule: Binding

If a living will fulfils the requirements of sec 1901a para 1 sentence 1 of the German Civil Code "*the custodian must see to it that the will of the person under custodianship is done*". This implies that a living will fulfilling these requirements contains binding consent to a medical treatment, or binding refusal. There is no need for an additional decision of the custodian or a person with lasting powers of attorney for medical care (health care proxy).[67]

As the physician is not obliged to enquire about the existence of a living will, the testator has to make sure that a trusted person or a health care proxy provides this information when the need arises.

If a document with directives for medical treatment exists, the physician and the health care proxy have to take several steps in order to examine whether this

---

63 G. Müller, in H.G. Bamberger und H. Roth (eds), *Beck'scher Online-Kommentar*, Beck Verlag, 15th ed Munich 2009, § 1901a BGB mn. 10.

64 BT-Drs 16/8442 p 13.

65 Cf. E. Albrecht and A. Albrecht, 'Die Patientenverfügung – jetzt gesetzlich geregelt', *MittBayNot (Mitteilungen des Bayerischen Notarvereins, der Notarkasse und der Landesnotarkammer Bayern)* 2009, 426 at 428.

66 Sec 1901a para 2 German Civil Code.

67 The term "health care proxy" encompasses in the following both the custodian and the person with lasting powers of attorney for medical care. Cf. furthermore in contrast the "Zöller-draft", which made the decision of the health care proxy paramount, cf. BT-Drs 16/11493 p 5.

document contains a living will and whether it is applicable under the current circumstances. Thus, to ensure that the living will really contains binding directives for the current situation, the law sets out a procedure according to which the applicability of the living will must be ascertained.

While the attending physician must determine which medical measure is indicated in the current circumstances,[68] the health care proxy has to verify whether a living will in terms of the German Civil Codes exists and whether the directions in the living will apply to the current life and treatment situation.[69] This implies that a living will always requires the existence of a health care proxy.[70] In practice, a person setting up a living will is thus well advised to appoint a person with continuing powers of attorney for medical care or at least determine a person, which the Court of Custody then – in the absence of a person with continuing powers of attorney for medical care – can appoint as a custodian.[71]

Subsequently, the physician and the health care proxy have to discuss the indicated medical treatment, considering the patient's will as set out in the living will. If it is possible without undue delay, close relatives and persons in the patient's trust should be afforded the opportunity to make a statement to help ascertaining the patient's will. This is meant to involve a "social control" of the decision of the physician and the health care proxy, and to lead to a thorough basis for the establishment of the patient's will.[72]

If the physician and the health care proxy agree that the indicated medical measure or the omission thereof is consistent with the patient's will the medical treatment can commence or be omitted, respectively.[73] Only where the physician and the health care proxy disagree on the patient's will, and the medical treatment or the lack thereof implies the risk of death or of grave and lasting injuries, the Court of Custody will have to establish the patient's will.[74] This could for instance be a situation in which an operation or the treatment of an arising additional illness is refused, or in which artificial nutrition, artificial hydration, dialysis or artificial

68 Sec 1901b German Civil Code.

69 Sec 1901a para 1 sentence 1 German Civil Code. Cf. E. Albrecht and A. Albrecht, 'Die Patientenverfügung – jetzt gesetzlich geregelt', *MittBayNot* 2009, 426 at 427.

70 So R. Beckmann, 'Patientenverfügungen: Entscheidungswege nach der gesetzlichen Regelung', *MedR* 2009, 582 at 583, exceptions may only be made where time is of the essence. A different position apparently is taken by W. Lange, 'Das Patientenverfügungsgesetz – Überblick und kritische Würdigung', *ZEV* 2009, 537 at 540. Undecided in a situation where no health care proxy has been appointed, A. Spickhoff, 'Rechtssicherheit kraft Gesetzes durch sog. Patientenverfügung', *FamRZ* 2009, 1949 at 1953.

71 Cf. sec 1904 para 5 and 1897 para 4 sentence 3 German Civil Code respectively.

72 R. Beckmann, 'Patientenverfügungen: Entscheidungswege nach der gesetzlichen Regelung', *MedR* 2009, 582 at 583.

73 Sec 1904 para 4 German Civil Code.

74 Sec 1904 para 1 and 2 German Civil Code.

respiration shall be withdrawn.[75] The Court of Custody will then apply the same yardstick as the physician and health care proxy: approval of a medical treatment "*must be given if the consent, non-consent or revocation of consent corresponds to the will of the patient*".[76] Here again relatives and/or persons in the patient's trust should be included in the process of determining the patient's will.[77]

Where the physician and the health care proxy dissent on the content of a living will, and where the planned treatment is not life threatening, there is no need to apply for a judgment of the Court of Custody. Even though the physician has no decision power, he or she would be entitled to treat the patient according to the directives in the living will, due to the fact that the living will contains the binding consent of the patient. However, if the health care proxy has a different view on the content of the living will, the physician would be better advised to apply for a decision of the Court of Custody. Otherwise he or she risks that their interpretation of the living will is not shared by the Court of Custody and that he or she is thus treating without consent and might even be prosecuted for inflicting bodily harm (assault/battery).

As an additional safeguard of the patient's will, everybody involved is entitled to seek the court's decision in order to ensure that the patient's will is adhered to.[78]

3.5.2. *Limits of the binding nature*

First and foremost, with regard to its content, a living will is only binding as long as the patient's will is not contrary to law.[79] For example: a living will requesting active euthanasia[80] would violate sec 216 of the German Criminal Code,[81] which penalizes killing on the express and earnest request of the victim and therefore would not be enforceable.

---

75 E. Albrecht and A. Albrecht, *Die Patientenverfügung*, Gieseking, Bielefeld 2009, p 23.

76 Cf. sec 1904 para 3 German Civil Code. Before the codification of the living will, the welfare of the patient was paramount to determine the patient's will, cf. D. Schwab, in K. Rebmann, F.J. Säcker and R. Rixecker (eds), MÜNCHENER *Kommentar zum Bürgerlichen Gesetzbuch, Verlag C.H. Beck*, 5th ed Munich 2008, § 1904 mn. 33.

77 Sec 298 para 2 and 3 German Family Procedure Code (Familienverfahrensgesetz).

78 Cf. draft law, BT-Drs 16/8442 p 11 and BT-Drs 16/13314 p 4. This could be either a relative or a person trusted by the patient, but also medical professionals involved in the treatment of the patient.

79 The living will would be void according to sec 134 of the German Civil Code in conjunction with the rules of the German Criminal Code. Supporting this as limit for all jurisdictions, cf. R. Andorno/N. Biller-Andorno/S. Brauer, 'Advance Health Care Directives: Towards a Coordinated European Policy', (2009) 16 *EJHL* 207 at 212.

80 The term active euthanasia here is used to denominate the active and intentional action on the express and earnest request of the patient through which the death of the patient is accelerated.

81 Strafgesetzbuch – StGB, translation available at http://www.gesetze-im-internet.de/englisch_stgb/index.html.

The enforcement of a living will is also precluded if it has been revoked. According to sec 1901a para 1 sentence 3 of the German Civil Code a living will may be revoked at any time without a specific form. Thus it is possible to revoke a living will orally or even through nonverbal communication.[82] It is currently debated whether a withdrawal requires also the capacity to consent.[83]

Even though the living will is not considered to be a "Willenserklärung" (declaration of intent), but rather a "rechtsgeschäftsähnliche Handlung" (akin to a legal act),[84] the rules of the general part of the German Civil Code apply by analogy. Thus, a living will for example is void if it was established through duress or fraud. The importance of the testator's freedom of choice at the time of the formation of the living will is further emphasized by sec 1901a para 4 of the German Civil Code. According to this provision the "conclusion of a contract may not be made contingent on the establishment or submission of a living will".[85] Its aim is to address concerns with regard to insurance companies and nursing homes, which could use living wills – especially those refusing life-sustaining and life-saving treatments – in order to reduce health care costs.

The interpretation of the living will is another threshold. While at least with regard to the existence of the living will no interpretation is needed, it has to be established whether the description in the living will mirrors the current life and treatment situation. As the wording of the law is unclear on the scope of the health care proxy's discretion in this matter, it seems self-evident that debates on the limits of the binding character of a living will and the discretion concerning the applicability in the given situation will arise.[86] Here, the long debated issue of binding living wills as opposed to the principle of *in dubio pro vita* (when in doubt, favour life) will probably be discussed again.[87] To me it seems rather clear that the legislator's option for a binding living will implicates that non-observance of a living will must remain an exception. To enhance legal certainty, clarification through court decisions or even through legislation itself is needed.

---

82 BT-Drs 16/8442 p 13.

83 The capacity to consent is needed for a withdrawal for instance in Belgium, see art 8 para 4 sentence 4 Belgian Act on Patients' Rights.

84 A "Willenserklärung" must be aimed at legal consequences, a fact that is lacking in the statements of a living will.

85 Translation provided by the Langenscheidt Translation Service, regularly updated by Neil Mussett, available at www.gesetze-im-internet.de/englisch_bgb/englisch_bgb.html.

86 The interpretation of the term "current life and treatment situation" seems to be in dispute, cf. A. Spickhoff, 'Rechtssicherheit kraft Gesetzes durch sog. Patientenverfügung', *FamRZ* 2009, 1949 at 1951 et seq.

87 See eg the Stünker-draft, BT-Drs 16/8442 p 16. Cf. A. Spickhoff, 'Rechtssicherheit kraft Gesetzes durch sog. Patientenverfügung', *FamRZ* 2009, 1949 at 1952.

The fact that the living will was written many years before its application, does not in itself hinder its enforcement.[88] If, however, the testator has changed his or her view on certain points in the meantime, this could be seen as an implied withdrawal. Furthermore, if significant advances in medical sciences relevant to the living will have taken place in the interim, the interpretation of whether the situation described in the living will mirrors the current life and treatment situation may be decisive. Thus for instance the enforcement of the living will would be limited if it could be reasonably assumed that the patient did not envision the possibilities of a successful medical treatment, but a successful treatment now is possible.[89]

3.6. LEGAL EFFECTS OF OTHER STATEMENTS

If the advance statement does not fulfil the criteria for a binding living will as set out in sec 1901a para 1 of the German Civil Code, the health care proxy has to decide on the basis of the presumed will of the patient whether he would have consented or refused a medical measure.[90] The presumed will must be ascertained on the basis of "konkrete Anhaltspunkte" (concrete indications). Consideration must be given in particular to previous oral or written statements, ethical or religious convictions and other personal values of the patient. These statements, lacking the preconditions for a valid living will, are termed *Behandlungswünsche,* ie wishes concerning medical treatment.[91]

Even though living wills established before the codification are enforceable as long as they fulfil the requirements as set out by the German Civil Code,[92] many of them are unlikely to comply with these requirements. Here, sec 1901a para 2 of the German Civil Code ensures that these advance statements will still be taken into account either as wishes or as the presumed will of the patient.[93]

---

88 BT-Drs 16/8442 p 14. This was, however, suggested in R. Andorno, N. Biller-Andorno and S. Brauer, 'Advance Health Care Directives: Towards a Coordinated European Policy', (2009) 16 *EJHL* 207 at 212.

89 Cf. the explicit ground for invalidity in sec 10 para 1 no. 3 Austrian Act on Living Wills; the Explanatory Report to the Convention on Human Rights and Biomedicine (ETS No. 164, 1997) requires that technical progress is at least taken into account, cf. at para 62; see also R. Andorno, N. Biller-Andorno and S. Brauer, 'Advance Health Care Directives: Towards a Coordinated European Policy', (2009) 16 *EJHL* 207 at 212.

90 Sec 1901a para 2 German Civil Code.

91 E. Albrecht and A. Albrecht, *Die Patientenverfügung*, Gieseking, Bielefeld 2009, p 16.

92 E. Albrecht and A. Albrecht, 'Die Patientenverfügung – jetzt gesetzlich geregelt', *MittBayNot* 2009, 426 at 427.

93 E. Albrecht and A. Albrecht, *Die Patientenverfügung*, Gieseking, Bielefeld 2009, p 66.

3.7. THE APPROACH OF THE GERMAN FEDERAL COURT OF JUSTICE

With the new law in force for less than a year, some time will pass until the German Federal Court of Justice deals with the first cases arising under it. However, in June 2010 the German Federal Court of Justice had to decide a criminal case concerning a lawyer who in 2007, ie before the codification of the living will law in 2009, advised a client to actively clip her mothers PEG tube to fulfil the mothers wishes.[94] The circumstances of the case were as follows: the patient had been in a persistent vegetative state with no hope of recovery and was fed through a PEG tube. In accordance with the earlier oral directives for a case like this, the patient's children who were also her custodians, tried to effectuate the cessation of the artificial nutrition of the patient. However, when the management of the nursing home contrary to an earlier decision demanded the resumption of the artificial nutrition, the lawyer advised the patient's children to actively clip the PEG tube in order to fulfil the patient's directives. The PEG tube was later restored in hospital and the patient died a natural death two weeks later. The lawyer was then charged with attempted manslaughter. The German Federal Court of Justice acknowledged in its judgment that at the time of the offence it was unclear what constituted a binding will in cases where the patient was no longer able to decide for him- or herself.[95] With regard to the new codification of the living will, the Court however saw itself no longer bound by its prior judgments. It thus stated that an advance directive applied regardless of nature and stage of any illness, adapting the same approach as the legislator in the new sec. 1901a para. 3 of the German Civil Code. Accordingly, the decision of the nursing home management conflicted with the patient's will; the advice to actively end the artificial nutrition therefore was justified by the patient's will and the lawyer was acquitted.

While the decision of the German Federal Court of Justice to value the patient's will highly was generally seen positively, criticism has been uttered in public debates concerning the "clouded" differentiation between active and passive action applied to end a person's life.[96] The withdrawal of nutrition is generally seen as an omission. That the court applied this view, even where the tube was actively clipped,[97] seemed to many as going too far – obviously fearing that the judgment could encourage people to unauthorized actions and defusing the line

[94] BGH, 27.6.2010, 2 Str 454/09.

[95] See above at 3.1.

[96] A collection of the different views can be found at www.aerzteblatt.de/nachrichten/41736/Freispruch_im_Sterbehilfe-Prozess.htm.

[97] The German Federal Court of Justice however, in the 1st guiding principle (BGH, 27 June 2010, 2 Str 454/09) defines a cessation of treatment (Behandlungsabbruch) as assisted dying through omission, limitation or cessation of an ongoing medical treatment. Whether the cessation of treatment is caused by active or passive treatment is irrelevant according to the 2nd guiding principle.

between criminalised killing on the express and earnest request of the patient and the non-criminalised assisted dying.

Summing up, one cannot help but notice that the people involved in this case, especially the nursing home management with its changing decisions upon the cessation of the artificial nutrition, seem to have been influenced by the former legal uncertainty regarding the binding character of a living will, especially with concern to the applicability of a directive in a situation without an irreversibly fatal disease. This matter now has been clarified through the new law.

4. STRIKING A BALANCE

Looking back at the rights and interests involved, does the German Civil Code succeed in striking a balance between ensuring patient autonomy and the state's duty for the protection of life?[98] While European conventions and declarations[99] demand the strengthening of patient autonomy and legislation on living wills, they remain vague in relation to the modalities of living wills.[100] Hence, even though the codification of living wills is progressing in European countries, one cannot help but realise a broad variety in formal requirements, preconditions and legal effects.

Arguably, German law is taking the patient's right to self-determination very far. Even though self-determination is limited with regard to active euthanasia, the otherwise virtually unlimited scope of living wills combined with very restricted requirements leaves patients with a broad freedom for their decisions. Especially the non-requirement of a mandatory prior consultation with a medical professional – as for instance required in Austria[101] – leaves the patient alone to struggle with the unpredictability of future situations as well as the possibilities of medical treatment. One has to ask whether a healthy patient is really able to make "binding" treatment directions for an unforeseeable future on his or her own.

Furthermore, it seems questionable whether a strict approach to the binding nature of the living will is compatible with the lack of a certain period for reconfirmation. While the stability of preferences for end-of-life treatment by elderly persons was recently confirmed by the John Hopkins Precursors Study

---

98 For the conflict between autonomy and heteronomy see A. Spickhoff, 'Autonomie und Heteronomie im Alter', (2008) 208 *AcP (Archiv für die civilistische Praxis)* 345 et seq.

99 See above 2.1.

100 See also H. NYS, 'Emerging legislation in Europe on the legal status of advance directives and medical decision-making with respect to an incompetent patient ('living wills')', (1997) 4 *EJHL* 61 at 68.

101 Sec 5 Austrian Act on Living Wills.

according to which 80 percent had stable preferences,[102] many European countries have set up certain time periods for a reconfirmation of the living will. With regard to the length of the period, the countries differ widely: while in Austria a living will is binding only when it has not been drafted more than five years before its implementation,[103] Hungarian law requires a renewal every two years.[104] In order to deal with the lapse of longer time periods, one could argue that German law in consequence must allow for a broader margin of interpretation when it comes to establishing the current life and treatment situation. It remains to be seen how the courts deal with this problem.

Additionally, the very limited necessity for an approval of the Court of Custody leaves physicians and health care proxies with strong decision-making powers. While this decreases the caseload of the courts and frees physicians and health care proxies from a general mistrust;[105] it generates a risk of collusion between the physician and health care proxy. Time will show how efficient – and with regard to the protection of the patient's will sufficient – the mutual control through physician and health care proxy is. Finally, it will be interesting to see to what extent the involvement of family and trusted persons of the patient will be effective as a social control in practice.[106]

5. CONCLUSION

To sum up, the balance between paternalism, the protection of life and self-determination is hard to strike. To put it simply, it can be said that the stricter the binding character of a living will is applied, the stronger the formal requirements and preconditions should be. Surely there are many different possibilities to regulate living wills. The codification of the living will in German law is in line with European trends for the provision of binding living wills. In contrast to the previous situation, the codification improves legal certainty. However, new problems and questions arise. Especially the limits of a binding living will and the margin of interpretation, specifically in determining whether the living will covers "the current life and treatment situation", will need to be clarified through

102 The percentages were even higher where the person in question had a living will and had opted for a less aggressive treatment (up to 95 percent) in a survey of 818 physicians, mean age at baseline 69 years. See M.N. Wittink, K.H. Morales, L.A. Meoni, D.E. Ford, N. Wang, M.J. Klag and J.J. Gallo,'Stability of Preferences for End-of-life Treatment After 3 Years of Follow-up', (2008) *Arch Intern Med (Archive of Internal Medicine)* 168 (19), 2125–2130.

103 Sec 7 para 1 sentence 1 Austrian Act on Living Wills.

104 Sec 22 para 3 sentence 2 Hungarian Health Care Act of 1997.

105 BT-Drs 16/8442 p 19.

106 For a rather pessimistic view on the practical involvement of relatives see M. Probst, Patientenverfügung – gelöste und ungelöste Probleme nach der Neuregelung', *FF* 2010, 144 at 146–147.

the courts or even in legislation itself. The practice will show how workable the German legislation on living wills actually is and how successful the law ensures patient autonomy.

ANNEX: GERMAN CIVIL CODE[107]

Section 1901a
Living will

(1) If a person of full age who is able to consent has determined in writing, for the event of his becoming unable to consent, whether he consents to or prohibits specific tests of his state of health, treatment or medical interventions not yet directly imminent at the time of determination (living will), the custodian must examine whether these determinations correspond to the current life and treatment situation. If this is the case, the custodian must see to it that the will of the person under custodianship is done. A living will may be revoked at any time without a specific form.
(2) If there is no living will, or if the determinations of a living will do not correspond to the current life and treatment situation, the custodian must determine the wishes with regard to treatment or the presumed will of the person under custodianship, and decide on this basis whether he consents to or prohibits a medical measure pursuant to subsection (1). The presumed will must be ascertained on the basis of concrete indications. Consideration must be given, in particular, to previous oral or written statements, ethical or religious convictions and other personal values of the person under custodianship.
(3) Subsections (1) and (2) apply regardless of the nature and stage of any illness of the person under custodianship.
(4) No one may be obliged to establish a living will. The conclusion of a contract may not be made contingent on the establishment or submission of a living will.
(5) Subsections (1) to (3) apply to authorised representatives with the necessary modifications.

Section 1901b
Discussion to ascertain the patient's will

(1) The physician in attendance must examine which medical measure is indicated with regard to the patient's overall condition and prognosis. He

[107] Translation provided by the Langenscheidt Translation Service, regularly updated by Neil Mussett, cf. www.gesetze-im-internet.de/englisch_bgb/englisch_bgb.html.

and the custodian must discuss this measure, considering the patient's will as a basis for the decision to be taken pursuant to section 1901a.

(2) When ascertaining the patient's will pursuant to § 1901a (1) or the wishes with regard to treatment or the presumed will pursuant to section 1901a (2), close relatives and other persons enjoying the confidence of the person under custodianship should be afforded the opportunity to make a statement insofar as this is possible without any considerable delay.

(3) Subsections (1) and (2) apply to authorised representatives with the necessary modifications.

Section 1901c
Wishes in writing with regard to custodianship, enduring power of attorney

A person who is in possession of a document in which a person, for the contingency that he is under custodianship, has communicated suggestions on the choice of the custodian or wishes for the conduct of the custodianship, must without undue delay deliver it to the custodianship court after he obtains knowledge that proceedings for the appointment of a custodian have been commenced. Similarly, the possessor must inform the custodianship court of documents in which the person concerned has authorised another person to take care of his affairs. The custodianship court may require a copy to be submitted.

Section 1904
Approval of the custodianship court in the case of medical measures

(1) The consent of the custodian to an examination of the state of health of the person under custodianship, to therapeutic treatment or to an operation is subject to the approval of the court of custody if the justified danger exists that the person under custodianship will die or will suffer serious injury to his health that lasts for a long period by reason of the measure. Without the approval, the measure may be carried out only if delay entails danger.

(2) The non-consent to or revocation of the consent of the custodian to a test of the state of health, treatment or medical intervention requires the approval of the court of custody if the measure is medically indicated and there is justified reason to fear that the person under custodianship will die or suffer serious, long-term detriment to health if the measure is not carried out or is discontinued.

(3) Approval pursuant to subsections (1) and (2) must be given if the consent, non-consent or revocation of consent corresponds to the will of the person under custodianship.

(4) Approval pursuant to subsections (1) and (2) is not required if agreement is reached between the custodian and the physician in attendance that the

granting, non-granting or revocation of consent corresponds to the will of the person under custodianship established pursuant to section 1901a.

(5) Subsections (1) to (4) also apply to an authorised representative. The latter may only consent to, not consent to or revoke consent to one of the measures designated in subsection (1) sentence 1 or subsection (2) if the power of attorney expressly includes these measures and is given in writing.

THE PROTECTION OF ELDERLY FAMILY MEMBERS AND THE ROLE OF THE STATE: A FAMILY LAW PERSPECTIVE

Irena Majstorović

The aim of this chapter is to achieve two complementary goals. The first is to define the most important issues related to the protection of elderly family members through a family law prism. In that regard, special attention is devoted to questions of guardianship, maintenance and family violence. The second goal is to define the role the state has, or, even more so, the role the state should have in relation to the family. It is my intention to prove that the role of the state is not only to provide help and care for elderly family members, but also to influence changes in the family, so that care within the family itself is re-established. I believe that only a strong family, which takes care of all its members, is able to resist all the temptations imposed upon it by modern society. If the process of losing its value continues, the family shall be deprived of its wholeness, which would in turn lead to destruction of basic human values, causing insufficient and inadequate protection of all its members, and elderly family members in particular.

1. CHANGES IN DEFINITION, THE ROLE AND THE FUNCTION OF A FAMILY

The definition of a family is a constantly changing one, both in its legal and its every-day notion. Hence, the legal definition of family is not often found in national family law sources.[1] The unwillingness of the legislator to define the notion of family is caused by awareness of the dynamics of family relations.[2] Namely, within these relationships, like in all other relationships in society, constant changes occur, which sooner or later deprive the legal definitions of their practical value.[3] If we analyse international documents, a similar definition of family is found in numerous sources, based on the concept that a family is the natural and fundamental group unit of society and is entitled to protection by society and the state.[4]

Furthermore, like the legal definition, the every-day notion of family is also vague. Until recently, it was not hard to define a family: a traditional structure made of

---

1 Certain national statutes include a definition of "family", but mostly with the limitation that it is formed for the purposes of that particular statute.

2 The definitions that are found are usually those restraining the notion of a family. Eg Croatian Social Welfare Act defines in Article 2 Paragraph 2 Point 2 that "Family consists of spouses, children and other relatives living together". Zakon o socijalnoj skrbi, Narodne novine (Official gazette), 73/1997, 27/2001, 59/2001, 82/2001, 103/2003, 44/2006, 79/2007.

3 M. Alinčić, Obitelj u obiteljskom zakonodavstvu (Family in the family legislature), *RSP* (*Revija za socijalnu politiku – Journal of social policy*), 1,1994, 3, p 226.

4 *Cf.* Article 16 Paragraph 3 of the Universal Declaration of Human Rights (1948) or Article 23 Paragraph 1 of the International Covenant on Civil and Political Rights (1966).

spouses and their children.[5] Today, the paradigm has changed.[6] Nevertheless, no matter which definition of family we should or should not accept, it is beyond doubt that members of family should be protected as much as possible at all times. This is the very *ratio* of the existence of family law itself.

Modern society is facing radical changes in the structure and models of family life. It can be said that the most important change, from the viewpoint of elderly people, was the transformation of the enlarged family to the nuclear family. In an enlarged family, as Kregar reminds, there was a respect for seniority and individuality and independence were sacrificed for the safety and warmth of the family community.[7] It can also be said that once care for elderly people was considered a "holy duty". Research conducted in Croatia[8] a decade ago, showed that family was highly appreciated in Croatian society and it dominated the list of the basic values of citizens.[9]

However, traditional family and social networks that provided safety for the older family members are almost completely ruined.[10] On the other hand, as Šućur underlines, particular formal support systems are in crisis due to ever growing costs and are therefore becoming increasingly unable to provide support and protection to elderly people.[11] As Schiratzki puts it, "if the public sector cannot provide basic protection, the individual is bound to build up formal and informal networks to secure his or her needs of survival. An example of such a network is the family in its various forms".[12] In order to compensate for the deficiencies of the support networks, it is necessary to develop and promote cooperation between

5 As Sörgjerd accentuates, this was the only acknowledged form of family. *Cf.* C. Sörgjerd: "Neutrality: the death or revival of the traditional family? Regulating informal partnerships in Sweden", in: Boele-Woelki, K. (*Ed.*): *Common core and better law in European family law*, Intersentia, Antwerp – New York, 2005, p 335.

6 Similar: D. Schwab: Familie und Staat, *FamRZ* (*Zeitschrift für das gesamte Familienrecht*), 54, 2007, 1, p 3.

7 J. Kregar: Promjene u strukturi obiteljskih zajednica (Changes in the family structure), *RSP*, 1, 1994, 3, p 220.

8 I have chosen to present the legal provisions of Croatian family law system, as well as to base my research on results of work of Croatian legal scientists. The reason for such an approach lays in my belief that it is necessary to know and understand the national legal system and only then to attempt to draw conclusions on a wider level.

9 On the list of basic values, family is defined as very important by 78.8% and as important by 19.4% of the respondents, which added together define family as an important value in the lives of 98.2% of Croatian citizens. These answers form part of a European research of values, conducted in 1999. *Cf.* T. Matulić: Obiteljske vrijednosti i neki aspekti socijalne zaštite obitelji (Family values and some aspects of the social protection of the family), *RSP*, 9, 2002, 2, especially pp 140–148.

10 *Cf.* Z. Šućur: 'Bračna i obiteljska situacija starih slijepih osoba u Hrvatskoj' (Marital and family situation of elderly blind persons in Croatia), *Društvena istraživanja*, 9, 2000, 4–5, p 664.

11 *Ibid.*

12 J. Schiratzki: 'Litigation in the shadow of mediation: supporting children in Sweden', in: *Family law and family values*, M. Maclean (Ed.), Hart publishing, Oxford and Portland, Oregon, 2005, p 123.

the family and the state in the care for elderly citizens. Some authors point out that this cooperation includes a whole range of socio-psychological, educational and economic forms of support, based on a flexible approach adjusted to the established needs of each individual and his/her family.[13] This is of particular importance in so-called "traditional" societies, especially those whose citizens are used to a high level of state protection and higher standards of living in general, such as Croatian society.

It is impossible to return to historically defined, already determined value patterns which have formed the development of the traditional family.[14] However, the changes and trends are not all that, if at all, positive. In this context, it should be said that the protection of weaker members of the family has always been considered a task of the family. It has, with more or less success and respect for dignity, been executed for centuries. Nowadays, it is believed that it is primarily the role of the state, and not the family, to take care of elderly people. This will, beyond any doubt, in coming years become a grave legal problem, since the elderly population is growing, unlike the financial support provided for them, causing their legal status to be inadequate. I argue here that this development is undesirable and that the state should undertake all efforts to reverse it, strengthening the family, for the family has the primary duty to take care of all its members, and its elderly members in particular.

2. CROATIAN LEGISLATION RELATED TO THE PROTECTION OF ELDERLY PEOPLE

Basic principles on which Croatian family law legislation lies are foremost defined in the Constitution and the Family Act. In this chapter I shall address the provisions which are most important in connection with the protection of elderly people. Besides the Constitution and the Family Act, also mentioned are the relevant anti-discrimination international documents, as well as national legislative solutions contained in two statutes, not necessarily closely linked to family law theory and practice, namely the Social Welfare Act and the Act on the Prevention of Discrimination.

---

13 D. Poredoš, G. Tošić, Z. Grgić: 'Nasilje u obitelji nad osobama starije životne dobi' (Violence in families affecting elderly), *Socijalna psihijatrija*, 33, 3005, 4, p 217.

14 *Cf.* T. Matulić: 'Obiteljske vrijednosti i neki aspekti socijalne zaštite obitelji' (Family values and some aspects of the social protection of the family), *RSP*, 9, 2002, 2, p 139.

2.1. THE CONSTITUTION

The Constitution of the Republic of Croatia[15] states in Article 61 that the family shall enjoy the special protection of the state.[16] Furthermore, in Paragraph 2 of the same Article it is said that marriage and legal relations in marriage, common-law marriage and families shall be regulated by law.

This constitutional norm is of a general nature and it obliges all relevant parts of society to be considerate of the various needs of members of the family community in all areas of life.[17] As Alinčić states, the notion of family in this regard reflects a commonly known feature of social reality, and it is up to the legislator to decide whether it shall define it more precisely and furthermore, which family relationships shall be legally regulated and on which value systems this regulation shall be based.[18]

Also, it is stated (Article 63 Para 4) that everyone shall have a duty to protect children and helpless persons.[19] Although this is a blanket norm, it is primarily addressed to members of the family, while family is the first structure supposed to take care of its helpless and elderly members.[20]

2.2. INTERNATIONAL AGREEMENTS

The Croatian Constitution determines in Article 140 that "international agreements concluded and ratified in accordance with the Constitution and made public, and which are in force, shall be part of the internal legal order of the Republic of Croatia and shall be above law in terms of legal effects." However, this *fons* of law is not particularly relevant for the topic of this contribution, since the international system of human rights protection does not have a special apparatus intended exclusively for the protection of elderly people.

---

15 The consolidated text published in Narodne novine (Official Gazette), 41/2001, together with its corrections published in Narodne novine, 55/2001.

16 This has been a constant characteristic of Croatian legal system for decades now. Indeed, it has been explicitly defined in the first (then Yugoslav) legal acts after the World War II. *Cf.* eg Article 58 of the Constitution of the Socialist Federative Republic of Yugoslavia of 1963 (Službeni list (Official gazette), 14/1963).

17 M. Alinčić: 'Obitelj u obiteljskom zakonodavstvu' (Family in the family legislature), *RSP*, 1, 1994, 3, p 225.

18 *Ibid.*

19 This is an extended version of the idea included in European civil codes, that children owe their parents honours and respect. *Cf.* eg § 371 of the French Code Civil (L'enfant, à tout âge, doit honneur et respect à ses père et mère).

20 H. Ujević-Buljeta: 'Kako zakonski urediti obiteljske odnose?' (How to legislate family relationships?), *RSP*, 2, 1995, 1, p 51.

Therefore, their protection derives from the protection of human rights in general, within the framework of which elderly people are more often explicitly mentioned as a particularly vulnerable part of society.[21] In that regard, it is important to mention Article 25 of the Universal Declaration of Human Rights of 1948,[22] Article 23 of the Revised European Social Charter of 1996,[23] Articles 21[24] and 25[25] of the Charter of Fundamental Rights of the European Union of 2000[26] or Article 28 of the Convention on the Rights of Persons with Disabilities of 2006.[27]

2.3. FAMILY ACT

The Croatian Family Act[28] defines three principles of legal regulation of family relationships,[29] which are completely in accordance with the constitutional provisions as well as provisions of most important international documents. The first principle is the equality of women and men and the mutual respect and help

---

21 *Cf.* I. Milas Klarić: *Pravni status skrbnika kao jamstvo zaštite ljudskih prava odraslih* (*Legal status of guardian as a guarantee of adults human rights protection*), Dissertation, Faculty of law, University of Zagreb, Zagreb, 2009, p 104.

22 1) Everyone has the right to a standard of living adequate for the health and well-being of himself and of his family, including food, clothing, housing and medical care and necessary social services, and the right to security in the event of unemployment, sickness, disability, widowhood, **old age** or other lack of livelihood in circumstances beyond his control.

23 With a view to ensuring the effective exercise of the right of elderly persons to social protection, the Parties undertake to adopt or encourage, either directly or in co-operation with public or private organisations, appropriate measures designed in particular:
– to enable elderly persons to remain full members of society for as long as possible, by means of: adequate resources enabling them to lead a decent life and play an active part in public, social and cultural life; provision of information about services and facilities available for elderly persons and their opportunities to make use of them;
– to enable elderly persons to choose their life-style freely and to lead independent lives in their familiar surroundings for as long as they wish and are able, by means of: provision of housing suited to their needs and their state of health or of adequate support for adapting their housing; the health care and the services necessitated by their state;
– to guarantee elderly persons living in institutions appropriate support, while respecting their privacy, and participation in decisions concerning living conditions in the institution.

24 1. Any discrimination based on any ground such as sex, race, colour, ethnic or social origin, genetic features, language, religion or belief, political or any other opinion, membership of a national minority, property, birth, disability, **age** or sexual orientation shall be prohibited.

25 **The rights of elderly people**: The Union recognises and respects the rights of elderly people to lead a life of dignity and independence and to participate in social and cultural life.

26 Croatia is not a Member State of the European Union, but since the Charter contains the high standards all states should accept, it is for its meaning important for the Croatian legal system.

27 2. States Parties recognize the right of persons with disabilities to social protection and to the enjoyment of that right without discrimination on the basis of disability, and shall take appropriate steps to safeguard and promote the realization of this right, including measures: ...
b) To ensure access by persons with disabilities, in particular women and girls with disabilities and **older persons** with disabilities, to social protection programmes and poverty reduction programmes.

28 Family Act (Obiteljski zakon), Narodne novine (Official gazette), 116/2003, 17/2004, 136/2004, 107/2007.

29 Article 2 of the Croatian Family Act.

between all family members. The second principle underlines the protection of the welfare and the rights of child, and the responsibility of both parents for the upbringing and raising a child. Finally, the third principle is one of adequate guardian protection of children without parental care and of adults suffering from mental difficulties. These principles are further elaborated in other provisions of the Croatian Family Act. Particularly important for the purpose of this chapter, are those concerning guardianship and maintenance, which shall be addressed later on.

2.4. SOCIAL WELFARE ACT

This Act identifies social welfare as a service of particular interest for the Republic of Croatia, through which assistance for the fulfilment of basic life needs is secured and accomplished, to the benefit of the following categories of citizens: socially endangered, incapable and other persons who, alone or with the assistance of other family members, cannot fulfil those needs due to adverse personal, economic, social and other circumstances.[30]

With regard to the topic of this chapter, two provisions of particular importance should be emphasised, which establish the principle of self-responsibility and responsibility for members of the family. They both request active behaviour from the citizen and define social assistance only as a secondary option. Namely, pursuant to Article 4 Paragraph 1 of the Croatian Social Welfare Act, everyone shall take care in fulfilling his/her own livelihood, as well as the needs of the persons they are obligated to maintain, in accordance with the law or on the basis of another legal ground. Also, pursuant to Paragraph 2 of the same Article, everyone shall, by means of work, earnings and property contribute to avoidance, mitigation or minimisation of his/her own social endangerment, as well as the social endangerment of the members of his/her family, in particular of children and other family members incapable of taking care of themselves.

If this provision is not respected, then the state does not accept responsibility for assistance. In accordance with Article 21 of the same Act, the right to assistance in maintenance is not granted, *inter alia*, to a member of the family who does not want to ask for maintenance from the persons obligated to maintain him/her on the basis of family law provision, unless the social welfare centre establishes that this latter person is unable to provide for the maintenance.

---

[30] Article 3 of the Croatian Social Welfare Act.

2.5. ACT ON THE PREVENTION OF DISCRIMINATION

The content of this Act regarding the issue of protection of elderly people, ie the fight against so-called ageism, leans on the basic non-discrimination provision of the Croatian Constitution. In Article 14, the Constitution does not explicitly mention age as a forbidden ground of discrimination, but it states that everyone in the Republic of Croatia shall enjoy rights and freedoms, regardless of (race, colour, gender, language, religion, political or other belief, national or social origin, property, birth, education, social status or) other characteristics, which notion beyond any doubt includes age, and that all shall be equal before the law.

This newer source of law, the Act on the Prevention of Discrimination,[31] which entered into force almost two decades later, includes an explicit prohibition of discrimination, taking into account the changes in modern societies and legal systems. In Article 1, it is said that the purpose of the Act is to secure protection and equality as the highest values of the constitutional order of the Republic of Croatia. In the same provision, age is explicitly mentioned as a forbidden discrimination ground. In Article 25, a monetary fine is prescribed as the punishment for the violation of the principle of non-discrimination.

3. ON GUARDIANSHIP, MAINTENANCE AND PROTECTION FROM FAMILY VIOLENCE AS PARTICULARLY IMPORTANT AREAS OF HUMAN RIGHTS PROTECTION OF ELDERLY PEOPLE

Analysis of the legal status of elderly people through a family law prism shows that there are three main areas which deserve particular attention: guardianship, maintenance and protection from family violence. Of course, it is quite possible that an elderly person may never come into contact with any of the institutions and phenomena mentioned. If they are in good physical and mental health, if they have enough financial means for their livelihood and property to support themselves and if they live in stable families, their life will eventually come to an end without have been burdened by these family law issues.

However, the strong inter-generational link and solidarity which existed in society is certainly weakening. Speaking generally, we could state that in most cases elderly people can rely on some kind of help and support that is to be provided voluntarily by their children. Research conducted in Croatia in 1995 showed that

31 Act on the Prevention of Discrimination (Zakon o suzbijanju diskriminacije), Narodne novine (Official gazette), 85/2008.

elderly people mostly had a positive attitude towards their families.[32] Nevertheless, they expressed their discontent with their own role in the family decision making processes. Furthermore, 80% of elderly people surveyed stated their conviction that in their youth the older people had been much more respected. Also, almost all of them believed that society should take better care of elderly people.

Unfortunately, the situation is changing and ever more elderly persons are facing several and sometimes all of the three situations. The reasons for such a development are numerous and varied, the most important being demographic changes. Dramatic changes are taking place to the demographic structure of a large number of societies. In the 1960's, in almost all European countries, a big shift in demographic trends occurred.[33] It was above all defined by a decrease in fertility rate, which resulted in disturbance of the entire demographic structure.[34] The population is growing older, the life expectancy rate has increased and the fertility rate has decreased.[35] It is only normal that the older the people get, the more assistance they need from others. Consequently, the more people need help, the more reluctant the state is to provide adequate assistance in numerous fields.[36] Therefore, it is once again the responsibility of the family to help its elderly members and consider state support only as a supplementary form of assistance to vulnerable family members.

---

32 Survey was conducted in 1995 on 174 examinees throughout Croatia. The main aim was to explore the basic features of marital and family situation of elderly blind people, as well as their perception of their own position in the family. Although the focus was on the blind, it can be concluded that the general results, namely their own view of the family situation was not altered due to their blindness, and that similar results would occur in general population. Cf.: Z. Šućur: 'Bračna i obiteljska situacija starih slijepih osoba u Hrvatskoj' (Marital and family situation of elderly blind persons in Croatia), *Društvena istraživanja*, 9, 2000, 4–5, pp 663–686.

33 V. Puljiz: 'Demografski procesi i struktura obitelji (europska iskustva)' (Demographic processes and family structure (European experiences), *RSP*, 2, 1995, 2, p 123. This can be said for the Western societies as a whole as well and Fukuyama justifiably calls this event "The great disruption" (according to: J. Eekelaar: 'Personal obligations', in: M. Maclean (Ed.), *Family law and family values,* Hart publishing, Oxford and Portland, Oregon, 2005, p 9.).

34 As Puljiz suggests, the main causes for this demographic recession were a changed relationship between young people and their family, the employment of women and birth control, as well as a difference in family forms in general. *Cf.* V. Puljiz: 'Demografski procesi i struktura obitelji (europska iskustva)' (Demographic processes and family structure (European experiences), *RSP*, 2, 1995, 2, pp 123–130, especially p 127.

35 The situation has been quite similar in Croatia, which is also facing the aforementioned trends. *Cf.* A. Akrap: 'Demografsko stanje i procesi u Hrvatskoj s osvrtom na privremeno okupirani prostor' (Demographic situation and processes in Croatia with respect to temporarily occupied territory), *RSP*, 2, 1995, 1, pp. 37–50.

36 According to a recent research, 12.4% of elderly people in Croatia do not receive pensions, out of which 95% are women. The survey was a part of wider European research on quality of life, conducted in Croatia by United nations development fund in 2006. *Cf.*: Z. Šućur: 'Socijalna sigurnost i kvaliteta života starijih osoba bez mirovinskih primanja u Republici Hrvatskoj' (Social security and quality of life of elderly persons without pensions in the Republic of Croatia), *RSP*, 15, 2008, 3, pp. 435–454, and in particular 452.

4. GUARDIANSHIP

4.1. GENERAL REMARKS

Guardianship as a phenomenon was created by the basic human need for help and protection. Roman writer Servius defined guardianship as a power and authority over a free person, construed for the protection of those who, due to their age, cannot protect themselves.[37] In Roman times, guardianship was focused mainly on taking care of children without parental care (*tutela*) and of adult family members who, as a result of illness or other causes, need help and assistance (*cura*).[38]

For centuries, this role and function was in the hands of the family, ie one of its members. As Alinčić and Bakarić-Mihanović accentuate, the institute of guardianship, seen in a developmental perspective, could not have remained at the level of family solidarity.[39] Guardianship has evolved as a result of the needs of intergenerational solidarity and it became a legal institution.

Hence, it is today a specific form of socially organised protection of all persons, who, due to different reasons, are incapable of taking care of themselves. Unlike in Roman times, contemporary guardianship systems are based on considerable powers of state bodies, mostly courts and social care institutions.

The guardian is not elected by the family, as it used to be,[40] but is named by the authorised state organ, which both limits his/her powers, and also oversees the quality of protection of personal and property interests of the persons under guardianship.

---

37 Est autem tutela vis ac potestas in capite libero ad tuendam eu, qui propter aetatem se defendere nequit. J, 13, I.

38 In the context of this chapter, special types of cura need to be mentioned: cura furiosi (person suffering from mental illness), cura minorum (persons between the age of 18 and 25), cura prodigi (persons who are prodigous) and cura debilium personarum (persons who are seriously ill or uncapable). *Cf.* M. Horvat: *Rimsko pravo* (Roman law), Školska knjiga Zagreb, Zagreb, 1980, p 92.

39 M. Alinčić, A. Bakarić-Abramović: *'Porodično pravo – Osnove starateljstva i usvojenja'* (*Family law – Foundations of guardianship and adoption*), Pravni fakultet Zagreb, Sveučilište u Zagrebu, Zagreb, 1976, p 5.

40 Primary guardians, or tutors, were persons designated as such in the will of the pater familias (tutela testamentaria); if there were no such provision in the will, then the tutors were relatives in accordance with the law (tutela legitima); and finally, if they were not alive or could not have taken the duty, then the guardianship judge could have appointed a tutor (tutela dativa). *Cf.* M. Alinčić, A. Bakarić-Mihanović: *Porodično pravo – Zakonodavstvo SR Hrvatske* (*Family law – Legislation of the Socialist Republic of Croatia*), Pravni fakultet Zagreb, Biblioteka Udžbenici i skripta, Zagreb, 1980, p 257 note 2.

The aims of guardianship as a contemporary family law institution are threefold.[41] First, the aim is to protect those person incapable of taking care of themselves. Secondly, the aim is to protect the rights and interests of those persons; and thirdly, the aim is to protect their property.

4.2. CROATIAN FAMILY LAW LEGISLATION

Although the family law institution of guardianship is not exclusively developed for the protection of elderly people, this part of the law will in coming years become one of the most important issues. Today, two basic principles of guardianship derive from the already mentioned Constitutional and introductory provisions of the Family Act. The first is the principle of adequate guardian protection of children without parental care and adults suffering from mental difficulties. The second, but only in sequence and not according to importance, is the principle of social care for persons incapable of taking care of their rights and interests. This principle is further elaborated in another important provision:[42] each and every person is obligated to inform the social welfare centre of the need of providing protection to adults who cannot take care of their rights and interests. Also, health institutions are obliged to deliver, upon request by the social welfare centre or *ex officio*, all information to the centre regarding the mental difficulties or other causes which make a person incapable of taking care of him/herself.

If their health status so requires, elderly persons are protected by this institution. The precondition for their being made subject to guardianship is the deprivation of business capacity. According to Article 159 of the Croatian Family Act, the court shall, acting in a non-contentious procedure, deprive of business capacity, in full or partly, an adult who, due to mental difficulties or other causes is incapable of taking care of his/her own needs, rights and interests or who endangers the rights and interest of others.

The two most frequent difficulties regarding the mental health of elderly people are depression and dementia. Dementia is not necessarily linked to old age, but it is closely linked to it. As Milas Klarić argues, dementia often represents a problem not only for the person suffering from it, but also for the members of his/her family who take care of the ill person.[43] Unlike depression, the state of dementia

41 Article 150 Paragraph 2 of the Croatian Family Act states that the institution of guardianship guarantees the adult protégés the protection of their personality, by means of care, medical treatment and making them capable for life and work, as well as the protection of property rights and interests.

42 Article 160 Paragraphs 1 and 2 of the Croatian Family Act.

43 I. Milas Klarić: *Pravni status skrbnika kao jamstvo zaštite ljudskih prava odraslih* (*Legal status of guardian as a guarantee of adults human rights protection*), Dissertation, Faculty of law, University of Zagreb, Zagreb, 2009, p 109.

is definitely an example of a situation where a person has to be protected, as is the case also with Alzheimer's disease and other mental difficulties which make a person incapable of taking care of him/herself.

The social welfare centre shall place a person deprived of business capacity, in full or partly, under guardianship and appoint a guardian within thirty days of the court decision becoming final.[44] The procedure for putting under guardianship, as well as the implementation of particular forms of protection, is that the social welfare centre shall commence on the basis of direct knowledge or upon information which should be provided, *inter alia*, by spouses, relatives and other household members of the person who is to be protected by means of guardianship.[45]

The Family Act does not require a guardian to live with his/her protégé (ie the person subject to guardianship), but research shows that adult protégés very often live with their guardians.[46] This is mostly the case when a protégé's close relative or spouse is appointed as guardian.[47]

The role of the family is emphasised in several further provisions of the Family Act. Namely, any complaints with regard to the guardian's work can be filed, *inter alia*, by the protégé him/herself, as well as his/her spouse and ascendants.[48] Also, the family with which the protégé lives is obligated to inform the guardian and the social welfare centre of all important circumstances relating to the protégé's person.[49]

---

44 Article 162 of the Croatian Family Act.

45 Article 198 Paragraph 2 of the Croatian Family Act.

46 According to the data of the Croatian Ministry of health and social welfare, on the day of 31.12.2008, there were 17,810 adult protégés, out of which 9,460 live in their own family and 1,865 in the family of a relative, which together makes up for almost 65% of all protégés. The other protégés live in foster homes (1,119) or are in institutions (4,866) or hospitals (500). *Cf.* http://www.mzss.hr/hr/zdravstvo_i_socijalna_skrb/socijalna_skrb/statisticka_izvjesca/godisnje_izvjesce_2008, 24.3.2010.

47 I. Milas Klarić researched the practice of two Croatian social welfare centres and analysed fifty files, during which analysis she encountered numerous interesting data. For instance, out of those 50 cases, in 24 of them, a guardian is a member of the close family of the protégé (spouse, parent, child, sibling); in one case a close relative did not express his unwillingness to become a guardian explicitly, but he stated he was not fit to be a guardian (due to his age (19)); in three cases close relatives (namely siblings) explicitly declined the invitation of the centre to become guardians; in one case a close relative asked to be relieved of such a duty.

48 Article 204 Paragraph 1 of the Croatian Family Act.

49 Article 201 Paragraph 2 of the Croatian Family Act.

4.3. THE ROLE OF THE STATE

Analysis of law and practice in this area as it concerns the role of the family reflects the erosion of family solidarity. It is obvious that relatives are becoming ever more reluctant to accept the role of a guardian, especially if they are supposed to take care of an adult deprived of business capacity, due to mental illness. It is quite understandable, since this duty is an extremely difficult one and the guardians undoubtedly suffer from great stress taking care of their protégés. Also, they are often facing the feeling of isolation and stigma which they sense through and because of the care of the protégés.[50]

Therefore, the role of the state[51] should consist of implementing various incentives for reversing such a process, both in connection to the family and to the public understanding of the institution and the protection of protégés in general.

In regard to relatives as possible guardians, the state is not making enough effort to encourage them to accept such a difficult task and duty. For instance, guardians who are according to the law obliged to maintain the protégé, do not receive any remuneration for their work.[52] Although close relatives are mostly those who are, in a way, expected to be guardians, notwithstanding all the aforementioned doubts, it is exactly they who do not receive any compensation. This may be regarded as unjust.

The principle of family solidarity would, of course, require that relatives undertake such a task without any thought about the financial consequences. However, since family cohesion is weakening, providing adequate remuneration is necessary. The amounts paid to other guardians are not high *per se*, hence this would not be an important financial burden for the state, and it would show the gratitude of the state to persons who are guardians, since they put in not only their time and skills, but regularly also their love and affection, which in any case cannot be financially compensated.

In regard to the wider family circle and society as a whole, numerous extra-legal actions should be undertaken as well. Most important are those concerning media coverage of the situation of protégés, awareness raising campaigns and the better organisation of the local community in assisting families to take care of their ill members.

---

50 I. Milas Klarić: *Pravni status skrbnika kao jamstvo zaštite ljudskih prava odraslih* (*Legal status of guardian as a guarantee of adults human rights protection*), Dissertation, Faculty of law, University of Zagreb, Zagreb, 2009, p 441.

51 In this sense, we refer to the desirable actions of the Republic of Croatia, but it can be said that similar measures could be adequately adopted in other countries as well.

52 Article 188 Paragraph 2 of the Croatian Family Act.

Reports in the media are regrettably quite often sensationalistic and depict persons who suffer from mental difficulties as ill-minded, completely incapable and dangerous members of society. Of course, there are cases when such a person really poses a threat to those around him; however, in the majority of cases they are a threat only to themselves. When so treated by the media, elderly persons develop serious further mental problems, since they accept the picture of themselves as being the burden of the family and society in general.

Also, awareness raising campaigns should be started with the aim of de-stigmatising persons under guardianship. It should be made clear by the state that their condition is a normal one and that they require all the help that can be provided. As already mentioned, the members of their families also suffer a large level of stress and often face the misunderstanding of, and even humiliation by, their colleagues, neighbours, etc who treat them in such a manner as indicated that they have not been educated about this special position.

Furthermore, the local community should be more active in assisting families to take care of their ill and/or elderly members. This should above all involve state-funded activities which would be completely free for elderly people. For those who are able to leave the home, it could include lectures about the challenges of the third life age, library membership or different courses (eg in foreign languages, pottery, dancing). For those at home this could include weekly conversations with a professional on daily topics or personalised courses intended to provide them with various skills, eg computing. Also, support groups for the families taking care of their ill and elderly members should be organised, in order not only to provide them with further knowledge of how to help a family member in need, but also to try to relieve them of the stress which is, due to their particular circumstances, undoubtedly present in their daily lives.

5. MAINTENANCE

5.1. GENERAL REMARKS

Maintenance between family members also reflects the need for solidarity between them.[53] If one of them finds him/herself in a difficult economic situation, ie if a family member is indigent and incapable of work, the fact of kinship generates both a strong moral and legal obligation on the others to assist him. Only where there are no relatives under a legal duty to help him should the larger social community be obliged to do it. The law regulates the mutual obligation and

[53] In regard to property relations, this could be said for the inheritance as well, but this is not the subject matter of this work.

right of maintenance between a rather large circle of persons. Nevertheless, recent development shows that this circle is narrowing, while this task of the family is increasingly taken by the state through the social security system.

This does not mean that moral or ethical obligations or expectations no longer exist. Society as a whole expects, or should expect, the fulfilment of various duties of children towards their parents. However, only a few jurisdictions regulate it. Croatian family legislation is almost an exception compared to other legal systems, since it explicitly mentions certain duties of children towards members of their families, and their parents in particular, on the basis that life in a family automatically entails adequate activities and co-operation.[54]

Therefore the Croatian Family Act imposes upon children an obligation to respect and help their parents, as well as to be considerate towards all family members.[55] The duty to assist the parents is of a moral nature, since the material assistance, namely the maintenance, analysed in subsequent paragraphs, is foreseen as an obligation of the adult (children) only.[56] All other duties or obligations are mostly of a moral nature and therefore unfit to be legally regulated and sanctioned.[57] However, they entail adequate means of physical help in all activities in the functioning of the family community.[58] Such regulation is necessary and educative, since it explicitly defines moral values that are losing their importance in modern society.

5.2. CROATIAN FAMILY LAW LEGISLATION

Croatian family law legislation in the field of maintenance is based upon four principles,[59] of which three are relevant to this chapter.[60] The first and the most important is the principle of mutual assistance between members of the family, ie the principle of family solidarity. The second is the principle that alimony be determined in accordance with the needs of the recipient and the possibilities of the provider of maintenance; and the third is the principle of fairness.

---

54 *Cf.* D. Hrabar, in: M. Alinčić, D. Hrabar, D. Jakovac-Lozić, A. Korać Graovac, *Obiteljsko pravo* (*Family law*), Narodne novine, Zagreb, 2007, p 254.

55 Article 90 of the Croatian Family Act.

56 Article 213 of the Croatian Family Act.

57 *Cf.* M. Alinčić, A. Bakarić-Mihanović: '*Porodično pravo - Zakonodavstvo SR Hrvatske*' (*Family law - Legislation of the Socialist Republic of Croatia*), Pravni fakultet Zagreb, Biblioteka Udžbenici i skripta, Zagreb, 1980, p 330.

58 *Cf.* D. Hrabar, in: M. Alinčić et al, '*Obiteljsko pravo*' (*Family law*), Narodne novine, Zagreb, 2007, p 254.

59 *Cf.* A. Korać Graovac, in: M. Alinčić et al., *Obiteljsko pravo* (*Family law*), Narodne novine, Zagreb, 2007, especially pp 440–442.

60 The fourth principle is the one of particular protection of right of a child to be maintained.

The principle of family solidarity asks all members of the family to assist each other before they ask for help from the state in the form of social assistance.[61] The ties which in this case define family members are kinship (notwithstanding marital status of the children and including the legal relationship based on adoption), marriage and relatives by marriage.[62] Due to affectionate relationships between these persons, the maintenance is usually voluntarily achieved, ie there is no need for enforcement of such a right before the court.

For present purposes, the most important maintenance obligation is that of parents by their adult children.[63] It should be stressed that parents are very often unwilling and mostly also too proud to ask for maintenance.[64] However, if they fail to commence a court procedure in order to achieve maintenance from their children, they lose various social rights. As already mentioned, pursuant to Article 21 of the Croatian Social Welfare Act, the right to assistance in maintenance is not granted to a family member who declines to ask for maintenance from the persons who are obligated to maintain him/her on the basis of family law provision, unless the social welfare centre establishes that this latter person is unable to provide for the maintenance.

It is an autonomous duty, and it does not represent the return of alimony given by parents to their children.[65] However, it is a subsidiary duty; a child shall be

61 This principle is explicitly defined, as already mentioned, in Article 4 of the Croatian Social Welfare Act.

62 According to Article 206 of the Croatian Family Act, maintenance is a duty and a right of parents and children, spouses and partners in extramarital unions, as well as relatives by blood and by marriage in the vertical line of kinship, when it is foreseen by the law. Pursuant to the Croatian Same-Sex Unions Act / Zakon o istospolnim zajednicama (Narodne novine (Official gazette, 116/2003), maintenance as an institute is relevant for same sex partners as well.

63 Although the cases are very rare, the ones brought before the courts depict the complexity of family relationships and the strong intention and persistence of children sued for alimony by their parents that the demand for maintenance is declined. For instance, in a case brought before the Croatian Constitutional Court, a son sued for alimony by his parents claimed that by the decisions of the lower courts (condemnating him to pay the alimony) his numerous rights were breached (equal rights, equality before the law, administering justice by the courts according to the Constitution and law, as well as the right to effective remedy). The Constitutional Court found all of his claims to be unjustified. *Cf.* The decision of the Constitutional Court of the Republic of Croatia, no. U-III / 3063 / 2003, published in Narodne novine (Official gazette), 21/2004.

64 As Van Houtte and Breda put it, "when demands for financial assistance from their children interfere with emotional ties, elderly people feel that those ties are more important. Thus many are reluctant to ask for assistance for fear that this would harm relationships with children and also damage their own independence." *Cf.* J. van Houtte, J. Breda: 'Maintenance of the aged by their adult children', in:, M. Maclean (Ed.), *Family law and family values,* Hart publishing, Oxford and Portland, Oregon, 2005, p 249.

65 *Cf.* A. Korać Graovac, in: M. Alinčić et al., *Obiteljsko pravo* (*Family law*), Narodne novine, Zagreb, 2007, p 453. The preconditions set by Croatian Family Act needed in order to achieve maintenance from an adult child on the part of the parent are:
- The parent is incapable for work and indigent, or cannot acquire them from his/her property (Article 213 Paragraph 1 of the Croatian Family Act),

obligated to maintain a parent only when there is no other means of assisting a parent in fulfilling their existential needs. It is prescribed only for adult children, and it is not intended either for minor children or grandchildren.[66] Minors enjoy the particular protection of the state, hence they are not obligated to participate in the maintenance of family members. Grandchildren are not obligated to maintain their grandparents even if the grandparents maintained them when they needed such assistance.

It is important to mention that the behaviour of the parents, unlike the behaviour of the children, could lead to loss of the right to maintenance. If a parent did not provide maintenance to the child when he should have provided it, without justification,[67] the court shall, acting upon a request by the child, decline their petition for maintenance.[68] Hence, the criterion of fairness is used as a corrective element in deciding on maintenance cases.

5.3. THE ROLE OF THE STATE

Care of elderly members of the family is ever more considered an unwanted burden. Adult children are quite often prepared to provide only minimal forms of care and protection. They are also reluctant to include their ascendants in their everyday lives. For instance, more and more parents are unwilling to assist or allow regular contact between their children and their parents, namely between grandchildren and grandparents. In order to allow the grandparents to overcome this (sometimes unnecessary) obstacle, modern family law legislation, such as that in Croatia, authorises grandparents apply to the court for their contact with the children be realised in full.[69]

- The parent cannot realise maintenance from his/her spouse or extra-marital partner, and the preconditions for maintenance by other persons are not fulfilled (*arg ex* Article 217 and Article 227 Paragraph 1 of the Croatian Family Act) and
- The child is of age (ie older than 18 years of age) and is capable of providing maintenance.

66 If a parent has more (biological) children, then the duty of maintenance is divided among them, in accordance with the capacity of each to provide maintenance (Article 228 of the Croatian Family Act). If a person has both biological children and step-children, the duty of maintenance shall as a rule be divided between them, if the preconditions for maintenance by the relatives by marriage are fulfilled (ie if the step-parents have maintained or taken care of the step-child for a longer period of time (Article 215 in relation to Article 213 and Article 212 a to Article 212 c of the Croatian Family Act)).

67 Reasons which could be found justifiable include illness of a parent, serving a prison sentence *etc. Cf.* A. Korać Graovac, in: M. Alinčić et al., *'Obiteljsko pravo'* (*Family law*), Narodne novine, Zagreb, 2007, p 454.

68 Article 213 Paragraph 2 of the Croatian Family Act.

69 *Cf.* Article 107 of the Croatian Family Act – The court shall, acting in a non-contentious procedure, upon request of grandmother or grandfather, or the child, decide upon the contact of a grandchild with its grandmother or grandfather, taking into consideration the welfare of the child. Of course, if that contact is found to be harmful for the child, the court shall forbid the grandparents to access the child (Article 116 of the Croatian Family Act).

Furthermore, although cases of parents applying to court for maintenance from their children are rare, regulation is necessary in the interests of legal security. In regard to the role of the state, the actions it should undertake should be directed towards children as maintenance providers, towards courts deciding upon the requests for maintenance, and towards the general public as an incentive to achieve voluntary maintenance.

With regard to the children, the state should not ignore the level of financial burdens on a person. It is legitimate to adjust one's life to one's own needs and wishes. However, this does not imply completely ignoring all others. It is beyond doubt that family members are becoming ever more unaware of each other. They are progressively acting selfishly and without respect for one another.[70] In general, irresponsible and selfish behaviour results in particularly negative and dangerous consequences to all family members. The consequences are particularly grave for helpless and weaker family members, such as elderly people quite often are.[71]

Whilst far from an absurd proposition, it would to my mind be undesirable to introduce a tax deduction in relation to maintenance paid by children to their parents as a means of incentivising such payments. While the whole concept of maintenance is based on family solidarity, personal motivations should have priority over financial ones. To introduce a tax deduction would seem simply to confirm that modern societies are founded more on financial than emotional values.

Regarding the legal procedure, the courts should be repeatedly advised to be very cautious and pass just decisions, reflecting the circumstances of particular families. In accordance with the principle *modum patrimonii spectare debet, cum alimenta decernuntur*,[72] they should diminish the alimony if a child at the same time has a new family which should be taken care of. Otherwise the obligation to take care of both families at the same time could well be seen as an important generator of stress.

Croatian psychologists Čudina-Obradović and Obradović define four groups of reasons that impede good intergenerational relationships and consequently lead to the endangerment of the care that adult children should provide for their parents: intergenerational ambivalence, circumstances of care giving, characteristics of

---

70 Similarly, Eekelaar states that "law seems to be walking in step with broad social changes which suggest a weakening of associative ties". *Cf.* J. Eekelaar: 'Personal obligations', in: M. Maclean (Ed.), *Family law and family values*, Hart publishing, Oxford and Portland, Oregon, 2005, p 10. I fully agree with Morgan's conclusion that this process encouraged increasing amorality (as mentioned in Eekellar's text, *ibid*, p 10).

71 H. Ujević-Buljeta: 'Kako zakonski urediti obiteljske odnose?' (How to legislate family relationships?), *RSP*, 2, 1995, 1, p 52.

72 Ulpianus, D. 27, 2, 3, 1.

the care receiver, and the characteristics and wellbeing of the care provider.[73] Although each of those is understandable, I do not find them sufficient to justify such a shift in family relationships. It is therefore the role of the state to endeavour to change behaviour patterns, such that none of the above-mentioned reasons would impede the necessary provision of help for elderly people. This issue shall further be addressed later in the chapter.

And finally, by taking regular action in raising awareness, targeted at strengthening family solidarity, children should be encouraged to take care of their parents in various ways, including financial assistance. It should be clearly said in all public debates, as it is for instance defined in the Croatian Constitution, that children are obliged to take care of their elderly and helpless parents. It is quite sad that the state should have to remind children of this, but, as has already been emphasised, it is exactly the role of the state to take an active approach and to do all in its power to re-strengthen family cohesion.

6. PROTECTION FROM FAMILY VIOLENCE

6.1. GENERAL REMARKS

Violence against elderly people is not a recent phenomenon. However, it was until recently a private matter, hidden from public view. During the last few decades it has become obvious that it happens more often than presumed. Today it is often described as "a single or repeated act, or lack of appropriate action, occurring within any relationship where there is a expectation of trust which causes harm or distress to an older person".[74]

Croatian scientists[75] for instance have done a research on the issue of violence, conducted in the area of the City of Zagreb on a sample of 303 persons (23.4% of men and 76.6% of women) aged between 65 and 97. The results showed that 61.1% of the respondents had experienced at least one form of family violence during the previous year.[76] The legal regulation of such a situation is not dealt with by family

73 *Cf.* M. Čudina-Obradović, J. Obradović: 'Psihosocijalne pretpostavke skrbi za stare ljude' (Psycho-social prerequisites for the care for elderly people), *RSP*, 11, 2004, 2, pp 179–186.

74 This definition is developed by Action on elder abuse in the United Kingdom and adopted by the International network for the prevention of elder abuse. Cited according to: E. G. Krug, L. L. Dahlberg, J. A. Mercy, A. B. Zwi, R. Lozano (Eds.): *World report on violence and health*, World health organisation, Geneva, 2002, pp 126, 127.

75 M. Ajduković, S. Rusac, J. Ogresta: 'Izloženost starijih osoba nasilju u obitelji' (Exposure of elderly persons to family violence), *RSP*, 15, 2008, 1, pp 3–22.

76 On average, they mostly experienced psychical violence (24.1%), then material abuse (6.4%), physical abuse (4.4%) and sexual abuse (2.1%). The most frequent perpetrators included husbands (30.15%), sons (16.4%) and daughters (14.01%).

law provisions, but it is so closely linked to the subject matter of this chapter, that it deserves particular attention, despite the fact that it is primarily a criminal and offence law issue.

6.2. CROATIAN LEGISLATION

The two main statutes regulating the problem of family violence are the Act on the Protection from Family Violence[77] and the Criminal Code.[78]

The Act on the Protection from Family Violence is intended to prevent, sanction and restrain all types of family violence, by implementing adequate measures against the perpetrator, as well as mitigating the consequences of past violence through providing protection to the victim.[79]

Unlike numerous other laws which do not define the family, this Act mentions the following persons as family members:[80] spouses, their common children and the children of each spouse; partners in an extra-marital relationship, their common children and the children of each partner; blood relatives in the vertical line without limitations; blood relatives in the lateral line including the third grade of relationship; relatives by marriage including the second grade in marriage and extra-marital union; persons who have common children; guardian and protégé; foster parent, beneficiary of accommodation with a foster family and members of their families while such a relationship lasts; a woman and a man who lived together in a marital or extra-marital union, children of each of them and their common children, if after the breakdown of a union the cause of conflict was previous marital or extra-marital relationships.

The circle of persons included is of course not a perfect one, but elderly persons can be identified in many family roles, which enables them to receive comprehensive protection. If a court finds the perpetrator guilty, he/she can be sanctioned by protective measures, imprisonment, financial fine, as well as other sanctions for the offence as defined in the Offences Act.[81]

The Croatian Criminal Code in its 16th Chapter – Criminal Acts against Marriage, Family and Youth, contains three provisions which are particularly

77 Act on the Protection from Family Violence (Zakon o zaštiti od nasilja u obitelji), Narodne novine (Official gazette), 137/2009, 14/2010.
78 Criminal Code (Kazneni zakon), Narodne novine (Official gazette), 110/1997, 27/1998, 50/2000, 129/2000, 51/2001, 111/2003, 190/2003, 105/2004, 84/2005, 71/2006, 110/2007, 152/2008.
79 Article 1 Paragraph 2 of the Croatian Act on the Protection from Family Violence.
80 Article 3 of the Croatian Act on the Protection from Family Violence.
81 Offences Act (Prekršajni zakon), Narodne novine (Official gazette), 107/2007.

relevant for the issue of elderly protection. Those are: breach of family obligations (Article 208), breach of maintenance duty (Article 209), and violent behaviour in a family (Article 215 a).

Breach of family obligations means non-fulfilment of legal family obligations, as a consequence of which a family member who cannot take care of him/herself, finds him/herself in grave position. This criminal act shall be considered as a grave form of the offence, if it results in the death of the family member left in a grave position, or the family member is severely physically hurt or his/her health is gravely harmed.

The provision of Article 215 a is a superstructure of the offence provisions of the Act on the Prevention of Family Violence. The Criminal Code sanctions situations when one family member puts another in a humiliating position, through violence, maltreatment or particularly impudent behaviour.

6.3. THE ROLE OF THE STATE

It is obvious from the previous discussion that the phenomenon of family violence is quite comprehensively regulated in the Croatian legal system. However, further improvements are always welcome. In that regard, I propose *de lege ferenda* that two additional provisions be incorporated in the Croatian Criminal Code. At present the Code regulates the neglecting and maltreatment of a child,[82] but the principle of special protection of vulnerable family members requires another provision, ie the introduction of a special criminal act of neglect and maltreatment of elderly members of a family. Also, the criminal act of breach of a maintenance obligation should be extended in its graver form, as is already the case regarding the maintenance of a child,[83] when it is committed against an elderly member of the family as well.

Furthermore, it is necessary to extend the fight against family violence against elderly people outside the legal arena. On the one hand, this implies continuation of general projects and activities against violence, but on the other, particular attention in awareness raising campaigns should be devoted to elderly family members specifically.

Also, as a further means of preventing family violence, it is necessary to provide concrete support for families taking care of their elderly members. As Ajduković *et al.* define it, they should be regularly informed of the existing services network

[82] Article 213 of the Croatian Criminal Code.
[83] Article 209 Paragraph 2 of the Croatian Criminal Code.

and help a family can receive within a local community or within wider social surroundings as a relief in the constant care of elderly family members.[84]

7. CONCLUDING NOTES

Some authors warn us that legalistic, moralistic and propagandistic pressures directed towards adult children to take care of their elderly parents in contemporary society can lead to enhanced ambivalence and deterioration of relationships, accepting the duty with lowered emotional quality of the relationship.[85] This argument is definitely a justified sign for necessary caution. Nevertheless, I would argue that the role of the state must be proactive in that regard and that quite to the contrary, legal and moral pressures have to be made. Namely, it is the role of the state to ensure that family members provide adequate support to their elderly members. The co-operation between the family and the state should be constant and effective, preventing the creation of a legal gap between state and individual responsibilities. Although it is not an easy task to achieve, one of the purposes, or goals, of the legal system is to define the path society should follow.

Law is usually considered to be an efficient instrument of social regulation. However, it is neither only, nor a perfect regulatory instrument.[86] It has to be adjusted to the particularities of a certain field and, as it was noticed long ago, it has to be in line with social changes, and above all, it has to be a reflection of a society.[87] Hence, regulation of elderly protection issues is definitely a sign of the humanity of a certain society. Alienation has been dominant for decades now; perhaps it would take a few decades more to influence family members with the aim of raising awareness that it is primarily role of the family to take care of its elderly members. This process is undoubtedly slow, costly and in phases almost invisible, but it should be commenced as soon as possible. Otherwise, family shall continue losing its characteristics and values. This would in turn lead to deterioration in the protection of human rights of family members, and its vulnerable members, such as elderly people, in particular.

---

84 M. Ajduković, S. Rusac, J. Ogresta: 'Izloženost starijih osoba nasilju u obitelji' (Exposure of elderly persons to family violence), *RSP*, 15, 2008, 1, p 20.

85 M. Čudina-Obradović, J. Obradović: 'Psihosocijalna prepostavke skrbi za stare ljude' (Psycho-social prerequisites for the care for the elderly), *RSP*, 11, 2004, 2, p 188.

86 *Cf.* J. Kregar: 'Promjene u strukturi obiteljskih zajednica' (Changes in the family structure), *RSP*, 1, 1994, 3, p 213.

87 *Cf.* W. Müller-Freienfels: 'The unification of family law', *The American journal of comparative law*, 16, The international unification of law: A symposium, (Winter-Spring, 1998), 1/2, p 177, p. 183. Similarly, Frank describes family law as a mirror of social reality. *Cf.* R. Frank: 'Entwicklung des Familienrechts', *FamRZ*, 51, 2004, 11, p 846.

NON-INSTITUTIONAL CARE FOR SENIORS FROM A CIVIL LAW PERSPECTIVE

A comparative study of housing with services and adult placement in France and Germany

Eleni Zervogianni

1. INTRODUCTION

Europe is getting older. Due to increased life expectancy but also to a decreased birth rate, the proportion of seniors in the overall population is constantly rising.[1] Seniors may no longer be seen as forming a homogeneous group. Distinctions have been proposed between the "young old", the "old", and the "oldest old" or between persons of the third and of the fourth age.[2] The definitions of the people who fall within these groups may vary.[3] In any case, there is little doubt that the seniors belonging in the last of these categories, meaning the "oldest old" or the "fourth age", constitute the fastest growing segment of the population.[4] This increase is coupled with a rise in the number of people with declining health, be it their physical, psychological and/or mental state.

Under these conditions, elder law is evolving as a new area of law. Apart from issues regarding inheritance, legal ability to enter contracts and legal representation in cases of incapability, health insurance and pension schemes, which have been discussed at length in the traditional legal literature, elder law also pertains to questions of everyday care of older people.[5] This last issue gains more relevance, the less the family are able to assume elder care responsibilities, as is nowadays the case.[6] Due to increased life expectancy, the children of older seniors are often seniors themselves. Moreover, because of the decreased birth rate, the responsibility of caring for older relatives rests upon the shoulders of fewer family members, while an increase in female employment has led to a further reduction of care resources within the family.[7] Finally, given the increased mobility of

---

1 See Study of the *Bundesverband freier Immobilien- und Wohnungsunternehmen* (BFW-Studie), 'Wohnen im Alter. Eine Zukunftsaufgabe der europäischen Wohnungs- und Immobilienwirtschaft', 2007, available at: www.uepc.org/documents/en/uepc-docs-15.pdf (last accessed: 11.07.2010), pp 5–7.

2 For a brief survey of this literature see J. Smith, 'The fourth age. A period of psychological mortality?' in Max-Planck-Gesellschaft (ed), *Biomolecular aspects of aging: The social and ethical implications*, Munich, 2002, pp 75–88, esp pp 76–77, with further references.

3 *Ibid.*

4 See N.R. Hooyman/H.A. Kiyak, *Social Gerontology. A multidisciplinary perspective*, Allyn & Bacon, Boston MA, 2008 (8th ed), p 16.

5 See L.A. Frolik, 'Later life planning', in I. Doron (ed), *Theories on law and ageing*, Springer, Berlin-Heidelberg, 2009, pp 11–30, esp p 14. For the scope of elder law in general see L. A. Frolik/R. L. Kaplan, *Elder Law in a nutshell*, West Publishing Co., St Paul Minn., 1995, § 2 esp pp 3–7.

6 For an overview of the changes in family structure and lifestyles see, among others, A. Schulz, *Traditionelle und alternative Wohnformen für Seniorinnen und Senioren. Zur Entscheidungsfindung zwischen Heimunterbringung und betreutem Wohnen*, GRIN Verlag, Munich, 2004, pp 35–38; E. Kyriakidou/S. Kotzabassaki/I. Christopoulou, 'Care of the elderly in Greece. A family centered approach', *ICUs and Nursing Web Journal* October 2001 (8th issue), at 3–6.

7 See C. Baudson, *L'accueil familial des personnes âgées: La réalité au quotidien* (mémoire), 2007, available at: www.famidac.fr/IMG/pdf/MemoireBaudson.pdf (last accessed: 11.07.2010), pp 11–12.

persons within a country, or even internationally, children often no longer live in the vicinity of their parents.

For many decades, the common response to the inability of an older person to live independently was his admission to a care or nursing home. Thus, the provision of care and services came together with a significant compromise of his autonomy. This unsatisfactory trade-off of independence for care,[8] on the one hand, and the realisation that the scarce supply of places in nursing homes could not cope with the expected increase in demand in the near future, on the other hand, made evident the need to seek other creative and cost-efficient solutions. Hence, over the years, a whole range of flexible long-term housing alternatives has developed, which combine both accommodation and support in a non-institutionalised setting, thus filling the gap between the two extremes of living at home or in a care or nursing home.[9]

The aim of the paper is to examine the advantages and weaknesses of the two main alternatives to institutionalised care, namely specialist housing with services and adult placement, and to identify areas where measures for the protection of older people are needed . The focus lies on civil law issues and are specific to these care arrangements. I thus do not consider the general discussion of legal representation of seniors who are unable to enter into legal transactions. Emphasis is given to cases where care is rendered by private providers. For the purpose of this study, issues of social policy which pertain purely to the financing of the schemes are immaterial. I approach the topic in the following way: in sections 2 and 3 I discuss specialist housing for seniors and adult placement schemes respectively, drawing on experience mainly in France and in Germany. In section 4, I evaluate the results of the analysis and proceed to some concluding remarks.

---

8 It is worth noting that, according to a number of surveys, the psychological status of elderly people who live in nursing homes deteriorates compared with persons who live in more independent settings. On this issue see among others J. Reinardy/R.A. Kane, 'Choosing an adult foster home or a nursing home. Residents' perception about decision making and control', *Social Work* 1999 (Vol 44), 571–585; S.M. Cummings, 'Predictors of psychological well-being among assisted living residents', *Health and Social Work* 2002 (Vol 27), 293–302.

9 For an overview of the most significant such options see, among others, U. Kremer-Preiss/H. Stolarz, 'Neue Wohnkonzepte für das Alter und praktische Erfahrungen bei der Umsetzung – eine Bestandsanalyse', intermediate report in the framework of the Project "*Leben und Wohnen im Alter*" of the *Bertelsmann Stiftung* and the *Kuratorium Deutsche Altershilfe*, Cologne, 2003, available at: www.kda.de/tl_files/kda/Projekte/Leben%20und%20 Wohnen%20im%20Alter/2003-LuW-Band1.pdf (last accessed: 11.07.2010), esp p 12–15; A. Schulz, *supra* note 6, pp 39–57.

2. SPECIALIST HOUSING FOR SENIORS COUPLED WITH SERVICES

2.1. GENERAL REMARKS

The generic and descriptive term "specialist housing for seniors coupled with services" is used in this paper to cover all forms of accommodation, usually in an individual apartment, where protective supervision and necessary assistance is provided to seniors with limiting conditions, who live either alone or as a couple. Typically, but not necessarily, the property is reserved for older people and has communal lounges, where social activities may be organised. These "senior friendly dwellings" can be bought or, more often, rented. Their conveniences may vary from simple comforts, like walk-in showers and the absence of stairs or steps, to sophisticated technological devices, like sensitive floors which activate an alarm in the event of a fall. The scope of the services which may be provided is also wide, ranging from the reassurance guaranteed by the mere presence of an in-house warden and the organisation of social events, to help with household tasks and errands, or even medical assistance. Depending on the intensity and nature of the support provided, different technical terms are used, such as "sheltered housing" or "retirement housing", when the services do not go much beyond supervision and emergency assistance, treating mainly the insecurity of the residents, or "very sheltered housing", "extra care housing" or "assisted living", when the services also include actual personal care of the older person.

Historically, notwithstanding sporadic small-scale initiatives in the past, sheltered housing for seniors has been expanding rapidly especially in the UK since the 1960s,[10] and in the Netherlands since the 1970s.[11] Gradually, together with the general spreading out of "de-institutionalisation" of care in the 1970s and 1980s,[12] the level of available services increased, and extra care housing evolved for frail seniors.[13] Experience of these developments has generally been positive as seniors, while feeling secure, also enjoy the freedom of having their own front door.[14]

---

10 See N. Appleton, 'Landbericht Großbritannien', in H. May (ed), *Betreutes Wohnen in Europa*, Loccumer Protokolle 76–92, 1993, pp 93–102, at 93; BFW-Studie, *supra* note 1, p 10.

11 See J.P.J. Singelenberg, 'Landbericht Niederlande', in H. May (ed), *supra* note 10, pp 55–69 at 55; BFW Studie, *supra* note 1, p 11; U. Kremer-Preiss/H. Stolarz, *supra* note 9, pp 96–97 with further references. See also www.lvgo.nl/ which is the site of the Dutch association on collective housing projects for the elderly (*Landelijke Vereniging Gemeenschappelijk Wonen van Ouderen*).

12 On this issue see, among others, D. Surtees, 'What can Elder Law learn from Disability Law', in I. Doron (ed), *supra* note 5, pp 93–105, at pp 95–96.

13 Cf J. Heinemann, '"Betreutes Wohnen" und notarieller Gestaltungsbedarf – zugleich eine kritische Betrachtung zur Neufassung des Heimgesetzes', *Mitteilungen des Bayerischen Notarvereins, der Notarkasse und des Landesnotarkammer Bayern* (*MittBayNot*) 2/2002, 69–77, at 69.

14 Cf also *supra* note 8.

Moreover, sheltered living is seen as a remedy against the isolation of older people. This model of intermediate accommodation has been promoted in many other European countries, like Germany, where it is known as "*betreutes Wohnen*" or "*Wohnen mit Service*",[15] and France where, depending on its configuration, it is named "*résidence services*" or "*logement-foyer pour personnes âgées*".[16]

While in the UK the vast majority of sheltered housing schemes are provided by local councils, non-profit housing organisations, and voluntary initiatives,[17] in France and Germany, the private sector is much more involved with the supply of specialist housing with services, thus giving rise to civil law issues. These issues pertain mainly to the protection of the senior as a consumer, during both the pre-contractual stage and the time after the conclusion of the contract. At the negotiation stage, problems arise due to the lack of transparency as to the bundle of services provided in each facility, as well as their cost. After the conclusion of the contract, problems arise in the case of breach of contract, revision of its terms or its termination, due to the uneven distribution of bargaining power between the provider of the housing and the seniors. In what follows, we take a closer look into the way these issues are dealt with in the German and French legal systems.

2.2. SPECIALIST HOUSING WITH SERVICES IN GERMANY

Specialist housing with services in Germany is a relatively new development, dating from the 1990s.[18] The term "*betreutes Wohnen*" is not defined in law and covers all types of specialist housing with services.[19] As to the legal provisions which govern this form of living arrangement for seniors, there is a crucial distinction between facilities which offer only "general support services"[20] (such as help with

---

15 See *infra*, section 2.2.

16 See *infra*, section 2.3.

17 See the information sheet provided by the charity organisation "Help the aged", available at: www.firststopcareadvice.org.uk/downloads/resources/sheltered-housing-6-2008_92.pdf (last accessed: 11.07.2010), pp 5 *et seq.*

18 See U. Kremer-Preiss/H. Stolarz, *supra* note 9, p 72. Cf BFW-Studie, *supra* note 1, p 12.

19 This is mentioned in the information provided by the Federal Consumer Protection Association (*Verbraucherzentrale Bundesverband*), in its text entitled *Betreutes Wohnen für Senioren* (December 2008), available at: www.verbraucherbildung.de/projekt01/media/Pflegetagung2009/Betreutes%20Wohnen/Service/Wohnen_mit_Service.pdf (last accessed: 11.07.2010), p 1. See also U. Kremer-Preiss/H. Stolarz, *supra* note 9, pp 75–76 and 90. Cf the information provided by the county of Coesfeld, available at: www.kreis-coesfeld.de/menschen-und-pflege/Bewo/leistung.htm (last accessed 11.07.2010), where there is a list of different types of "*betreutes Wohnen*", based on the number and type of the services offered, as well as information provided by the Lobby of elderly persons 'BAGSO' (*Bundesarbeitsgemeinschaft der Senioren-Organisationen*), in its document on *Betreutes Wohnen: Information und Checkliste*, available at: www.bagso.de/fileadmin/Themen/Wohnen/ChecklisteBetreutes_Wohnen.pdf (last accessed: 11.07.2010).

20 In German, "*allgemeine Unterstützungsleistungen*", in the sense of § 1 I 3 of the Law on the regulation of contracts on housing with services of care or assistance (*Gesetz zur*

housekeeping, procurement of care and assistance from external providers, as well as emergency services), and those providing "care and assistance in order to cover needs arising from old age, care dependency or disability",[21] which are in fact rather similar to care homes where seniors rent individual apartments.

2.2.1. *Housing with general support services*

There are no special legal provisions regarding "housing with general support services", which could be characterised "*betreutes Wohnen* in a narrow sense". This form of living arrangement for seniors is thus regulated contractually by two interconnected agreements: a lease or a sales contract, depending on whether the senior rents or buys the property, and a service contract. If the lessor and the provider of the services is the same person, the lease and the agreement for provision of services may be united in one mixed contract.[22]

More concretely, the object of the service contract is the supply of assistance and care to the senior. It lies on the parties to specify the content of this agreement. In practice, the supplier sets forth a "package of basic services", which is mandatory and usually comprises technical support for the household, emergency and counselling services as well as information and support for the organisation of social events.[23] Further services, such as help with housekeeping, care and paramedical treatment, may be provided upon request, at an additional price.[24] In the absence of a contrary agreement, the service contract is in principle regulated by §§ 611 *et seq.* of the German Civil Code (*bürgerliches Gesetzbuch – BGB*). According to these provisions, no form is required for the validity of the service contract. If the services in question are normally provided for remuneration, it is considered that it has been implicitly agreed that remuneration will be provided, and the amount due is assessed on the basis of the sum usually owed in such circumstances.[25] If the supply of services is faulty, the senior may demand the proper fulfilment of the services insofar as this is possible. If their fulfilment has

---

Regulierung von Verträgen über Wohnraum mit Pflege- oder Betreuungsleistungen (Wohn- und Betreuungsvertragsgesetz – WBVG).

21 These last cases fall within the scope of application of WBVG (See § 1 I 1 WBVG). See in more detail *infra*, section 2.2.2.

22 See § 311 I of the German Civil Code (*Bürgerliches Gesetzbuch – BGB*) on contractual freedom. On this issue see also in more detail H. PAULY, 'Betreutes Wohnen – notwendige Problembewältigung einer neuen Wohnform', *Zeitschrift für Miet- und Raumrecht* (*ZMR*) 2008, 864–865. Cf also M. HÄUBLEIN, *Münchener Kommentar zum BGB*, 2008 (5th ed), Vor § 535, nr 38. However, according to the rules of the German Regulatory Institute (*Deutsches Institut für Normung – DIN*) on "Quality requirements for providers of assisted living for the elderly", the lease contract and the service contract shall be separate (see DIN 77800, esp section 4.4.1.2).

23 Cf DIN 77800, under section 4.2.1.

24 Cf DIN 77800, under section 4.2.2.

25 See § 612 BGB.

become impossible, he is relieved from the obligation to pay for them.[26] Moreover, if the senior suffered any losses due to a culpable breach of contract by the service provider, he may claim compensation.[27] As to the termination of the contract, if it had been concluded for an indefinite time, each party may terminate it any time, by giving notice to the other party in advance.[28] The immediate termination of the contract is possible where there is a compelling reason, eg substantial breach of duty by one party.[29] Notice of termination of contract must be given in writing.[30]

If the senior rents the apartment, the lease agreement is mainly regulated by §§ 549 *et seq*. BGB on "leases for residential space".[31] According to these provisions, the agreement does not necessarily have to be in writing.[32] The parties are in principle free to set the due amount of rent. The law permits the lessor to demand an increase in rent or operating costs of the apartment under restrictive conditions.[33] In addition, the lessees are granted protection in the event of the contract being terminated: if the contract is concluded for indefinite time, as is the usual case in a housing with services plan,[34] the lessor may only terminate if he has justifiable cause to do so, for instance in the event of substantial breach of contract by the lessee or if the lessor needs the premises as a dwelling for himself or for members of his family.[35] It is forbidden for the lessor to terminate the contract merely because he wishes to rent the residential space to a third party at a higher price.[36] The contract is not terminated immediately, but only after the expiration of a notice period, set by law.[37] The lessor may however terminate the lease without notice for a compelling reason.[38] In any case, the lessee should be informed of the termination of the contract in writing.[39]

The interdependency of the lease and the services is evident in cases where both agreements are united in the same contract. Even if the contracts are separate,

---

26 See esp § 326 I BGB.

27 See §§ 280 I, 283 BGB.

28 See § 620 II BGB in combination with § 621 BGB. If the contract had been concluded for a definite period of time, it is terminated by the end of this period (§ 620 I BGB).

29 See § 626 BGB.

30 See § 623 BGB.

31 §§ 535 *et seq* BGB on the "general provision on leases" apply to leases for residential space, to the extent it is not otherwise stipulated by §§ 549–577a BGB.

32 This is derived by § 550 BGB according to which "a lease agreement for a period longer than one year is considered as a lease for an indefinite period of time, unless it is concluded in writing".

33 See §§ 558–560 BGB.

34 See also the restrictions as to the conclusion of a lease contract for definite time set by § 575 BGB.

35 In cases of "*betreutes Wohnen*" the parties usually rule out this possibility of termination of the contract.

36 See § 573 II nr 3 BGB.

37 See § 573c BGB.

38 See § 569 BGB.

39 See § 568 I BGB.

this interdependency may be achieved through a contractual clause according to which the continuation of one contract is conditional upon the continuation of the other. In practice problems arise in cases where the seniors, realising that they do not actually need the services, wish to terminate the service contract, while keeping the lease. If the other party agrees to this new arrangement, the issue is resolved. If, however, this is not the case, it has been disputed whether the other party may respond to the termination of the service contract by terminating the lease.[40] This issue has been, at least partially, resolved by the decision of the Federal Court of Justice (*Bundesgerichtshof – BGH*) of 23.2.2006.[41] In this case, the lessor and the provider of the services were the same person. The Court stated that the clause on the interconnection of the lease and the service agreement does not constitute a disproportionate disadvantage for the senior, and therefore it may not be considered void on the basis of either § 138 BGB or § 307 II BGB.[42] More concretely, according to the opinion of the Court, this contractual arrangement is meant to serve the interests of both parties to the contract; the possibility of each individual resident terminating the service contract while continuing to live in the apartment would endanger the whole concept of "*betreutes Wohnen*". The Court also added that in the case of breach of the service contract, the senior is sufficiently protected.[43] If, however, the lessor and the provider of services are different persons, it remains unclear whether § 309 nr 9a BGB on long term contracts shall apply. If so, the senior shall not be bound to a specific service provider for more than two years.[44]

If the senior decides to buy the apartment where the services will be provided, the sales contract is governed by the relevant provisions of the German Civil Code.[45] As to the rights and duties of the apartment owners, the Law on condominiums (*Wohneigentumsgesetz – WoEigG*) applies. According to § 15 I of this law, the co-owners may regulate by contract the use of individual apartments and of the common parts of the building. This agreement may be incorporated in the legal act by which the condominium is established.[46] In this framework, restrictions can be imposed on the use of apartments, which are also binding on future

[40] See H. Pauly, *supra* note 22, at 865.

[41] *Zeitschrift für Miet- und Raumrecht* (*ZMR*) 2006, 443.

[42] § 138 BGB refers to usury contracts, whereas § 307 II nr 1 BGB refers to standard form contractual terms which lead to the unreasonable disadvantage of one of the parties.

[43] See *supra* note 29.

[44] See the decision of the Court of first instance (*Landgericht – LG*) of Lüneburg of 18.7.2001, *Neue juristische Wochenschrift Rechtsprechungs-Report* (NJW-RR) 2001, 1637. See also the Note (*Praxishinweis*) on BGH 23.2.2006, *NJW Spezial* 2006, 290 and cf *infra* note 49.

[45] See §§ 433 *et seq* BGB.

[46] This act is called in German "*Teilungserklärung*". According to § 2 WoEigG, a condominium may be established either by means of a contractual arrangement between co-owners ("*Vertragliche Einräumung von Sondereigentum*" [§ 3]) or by the sole owner on his own ("*Teilung durch den Eigentümer*" [§ 8]). See H. Pauly, *supra* note 22, at 866.

owners.[47] In this context, these restrictions pertain to the use of apartments only by seniors, in the framework of a "housing with services" plan.[48] Hence, it is through this constellation that the interdependence of the sales and the service contract may be achieved: the owners of such apartments have an obligation to conclude contracts for the procurement of services. Nevertheless, according to the decision of the Federal Court of Justice of 13 October 2006,[49] the owners may not be bound to a specific service provider for a period longer than two years.[50]

2.2.2. Housing with major care and assistance services for dependent seniors

In housing with major care and assistance, although seniors rent their own apartment, the level of care provided is similar to that of a care or nursing home. Due to the great vulnerability of seniors who are in need of such enhanced care, the contracts concluded between those individuals and these facilities are subject to special legal provisions. More concretely, since October 2009, these contracts are governed by the new Law on the regulation of contracts of housing with services of care or assistance.[51]

The new law aims to protect the seniors as consumers.[52] It provides extensive pre-contractual information duties (§ 3). It stipulates, further, that the contracts between the seniors and the facilities shall be concluded in writing (§ 6) and, at least in principle, for an indefinite period of time (§ 4 I). In addition, it specifies the rights and duties of the parties (§ 7) as well as the consequences of breach of contract (§ 10), and regulates the amendment of terms in the event of a change in circumstances ie a change in the senior's needs (§ 8). An increase in the fee owed is only permitted under restrictive conditions (§ 9). Finally, special provisions are set regarding termination of the contract. The facility may terminate the contract with the senior-consumer only in the case of a compelling reason. Thus, the fact that a third party would be prepared to pay a higher rent for the same facility does not constitute a lawful reason for the termination of the contract (§ 12 I). If the

---

47 See esp § 10 III WoEigG; W. Niedenführ, 'Note to the decision of BGH of 13.10.2006' in *Lindenmaier-Möhring Kommentierte BGH-Rechtsprechung* (*LMK*), 12/2006, 97 (nr 204532). See also J. Heinemann, *supra* note 13, at 71.

48 See J. Heinemann, *supra* note 13, at 61; M. Drasdo, 'Betreutes Wohnen in der Immobilienverwaltung', *Neue juristische Wochenschrift (NJW)-Spezial* 2007, 193–194. Cf also H. Kahlen, '"Betreutes Wohnen" in der Eigentumswohnung', *Zeitschrift für Miet- und Raumrecht* (*ZMR*) 2007, 671–674, at 671–672.

49 *Neue juristische Wochenschrift (NJW)* 2007, 213.

50 See § 309 nr 9a BGB, which applies by analogy, in combination with § 242 BGB on good faith. See W. Niedenführ, *supra* note 47, at 98. Cf also note 44.

51 In German "*Gesetz zur Regulierung von Verträgen über Wohnraum mit Pflege- oder Betreuungsleistungen (Wohn- und Betreuungsvertragsgesetz - WBVG)*". Before the enactment of this law, the relevant provisions of the Law on the care and nursing homes applied (*Heimgesetz - HeimG*).

52 The provisions set the minimum protection of the elderly, so deviation from these rules is possible only to the advantage of the consumer (§ 16 WBVG).

reason of the termination is a result of the conduct of the facility, the latter may have to compensate the senior and cover his moving costs (§ 13).

2.3. SPECIALIST HOUSING WITH SERVICES IN FRANCE

Developments regarding specialist housing with services in France have been parallel to those in Germany. The first generation of housing with services, for rent or purchase, started expanding in the 1990s.[53] Initially, the services provided were limited. However, as the seniors who lived there grew older and had to move to care or nursing homes, a new concept of housing with services, with more assistance, developed. Nowadays two types of housing with services may be distinguished: the "*logements-foyers*" for older people and the "résidences services". There exist significant differences in the organisation of these facilities.

2.3.1. Logements-foyers

The term "*logement-foyer*" denotes a special type of social housing,[54] as the majority of these residences (around 70%) are still run by the state and local authorities.[55] The notion of "*logement-foyer*" is defined as a type of housing which consists of private apartments, furnished or not, and of common areas dedicated to collective activities.[56] The residents of "*logements-foyers*" may be provided with meals, if they wish, or enjoy, at an extra cost, other basic services, regarding mostly housekeeping and the organisation of social activities,[57] while some facilities also offer paramedical services.[58] "*Logements-foyers*" fall within the definition of social or socio-medical establishments, in the sense of Article L 312-1 I nr 6 of the Code

[53] See F. Walther, 'Investir dans une résidence où on serait prêt à vivre' (14.7.2009), available at: http://bieninvestir.blogs.nouvelobs.com (last accessed: 11.07.2010).

[54] More concretely, a "*habitation à loyer moderé* – HLM" (housing in a moderate rent). See Article R 351-55 of the Code of Construction and Housing (*Code de la construction et de l'habitation – CCH*). See also in more detail B. Herbert, 'La convergence des politiques publiques du vieillissement et des politiques de l'habitat. Réalités et perspectives', Study of the National Agency for information on housing (*Agence Nationale pour l'information sur le logement [Anil]*), April 2010, available at www.anil.org/fileadmin/ANIL/Etudes/2010/vieillissement.pdf (last accessed: 11.07.2010), p 98.

[55] This information is also mentioned in the positioning paper of UNCCAS (*Union Nationale des Centres Communaux d'Action Sociale*) of 25.5.2007, entitled 'Logements-foyers pour personnes âgées : enfin des perspectives claires pour les CCAS/CIAS gestionnaires !', available at www.unccas.org/positionnements/docs/070525-logements-foyers.pdf (last accessed: 11.07.2010).

[56] See Article L 633-1 of the Code of Construction and Housing (Code de la construction et de l'habitation – CCH), as amended by Law 2009-323 of 25.3.2009.

[57] See Article R 633-1 CCH.

[58] See Article R 633-1 CCH, according to which "*logements-foyers*" may provide care services.

of Social Action and Families (*Code de l'action sociale et des familles – CASF*), and are thus subject to the relevant quality and organisation provisions.[59]

The Code of Construction and Housing includes a whole chapter dedicated to the protection of persons residing in "*logements-foyers*".[60] As to the contract concluded between the residents and the scheme managers, the law stipulates that it should be in writing[61] and include all significant rights and duties of the parties, especially the amount due for rent and for services, which should be detailed.[62] Some of the services may be "obligatory", in the sense that the resident has to pay for them regardless of whether he uses them or not.[63] The senior shall also agree to the internal regulation of the housing plan, which is annexed to his contract.[64] Moreover, protection is granted to the senior as to the termination of the contract. The manager of the scheme may terminate the contract of the senior only in one of the following three situations:[65] a. if the senior does not comply with his contractual obligations or repeatedly violates the internal regulation of the plan; b. if the housing plan closes down; and c. if the senior no longer fulfils the conditions of admission in the specific housing plan. In any event, notice of termination shall be given to the resident in advance.[66] Finally, it is of particular interest that Article L 633-4 CCH grants rights to the residents to participate in the administration of the scheme.[67]

2.3.2. *Résidences services*

Like "*logements-foyers*", the "*résidences services*" also provide housing coupled with services. However, the "*résidences services*" are private establishments that lack the social character of the "*logements-foyers*". The apartments in "*résidences services*", which are often adapted to the special needs of seniors, may be rented or bought. Due to the increased cost of this type of housing, this living arrangement is currently confined to the middle and upper middle classes.[68] Nevertheless, in anticipation of future need for such facilities, the state is providing incentives for

---

59 See Articles L 313-1 to 313-9 CASF. It is worth noting that according to Article L 313-1 CASF these establishments are subject to licensing.

60 See Articles L 633-1 to L 633-5 CCH.

61 See Article L 633-2 par 1 CCH.

62 See Articles L 633-2 par 2 and R 633-2 CCH.

63 Cf Articles R 633-2 and R 633-4 CCH.

64 See Article L 633-2 par 3 CCH.

65 See Article L 633-2 par 4 CCH.

66 See Article R 633-3 par 2 CCH. This notice should be given (at least) one month in advance if the termination of the contract is due to the breach of duties by the resident and (at least) three months in advance in any other case.

67 See Articles L 633-4 par 2 and R 633-5 *et seq* CCH.

68 Cf B. Herbert, *supra* note 54, p 104–105.

the further development of this model, granting tax benefits to persons investing in such housing plans.[69]

The organisation of "*résidences services*" is subject to Law 65–557 of 10.7.1965 on the regulation of condominiums,[70] as amended by Law 2006–872 of 13.7.2006. According to Article 41–1 of that law, the "syndicate of co-owners"[71] may include in the contractual arrangement of the condominium[72] the provision that certain services will be offered to residents of the building, be they owners or tenants. The services pertain mainly to the preparation of meals, supervision and general support, such as laundry facilities, or entertainment. The provision of these services may also be assigned by contract to a third party. The costs of providing each service and its maintenance costs are borne by all co-owners, whether they make use of the service or not.[73] In addition, each resident bears the cost of any individualised service he receives.[74] In all other respects, the "*résidences services*" do not differ from other residences, where the owners or tenants live an independent life.

According to this law, the "*résidences services*" shall not provide additional services aimed at the care, assistance or attendance of a specific person.[75] In practice, however, such services are often provided.[76] As the Ministry of Health and Sports responded to a relevant parliamentary question, the law does not prohibit the operation of an office of nurses in the building, provided that the latter perform their services independently and not exclusively to the residents of the specific building.[77] If, however, the provision of medical or paramedical services goes further, the "*résidences services*" may be assimilated to socio-medical facilities, in the sense of Article L 312 I nr 6 of the Code of Social Action and Families (*Code de l'action sociale et des familles – CASF*) and so be subjected to the provisions regarding the operation of such facilities.[78]

---

69 See the "Scellier Law" ("*loi Scellier*"), that modified the General Code on Taxes (*Code general des impots*), esp Article 199-septvicies. For more information on this issue see: www.scellier.org/ or www.loiscellier-info.org (last accessed: 11.07.2010).

70 In French "*Loi fixant le statut de la copropriété des immeubles bâtis*".

71 In French "*syndicat des coproprietaires*", meaning a legal person in which all co-owners of an immovable property participate as members, and whose aim is to manage the building.

72 In the sense of Article 8 of Law 65–557.

73 See Article 41–3 in combination with Articles 10 and 14–1 of Law 65–557.

74 See Article 41–3 of Law 65–557.

75 See Article 41–1 of Law 65–557 *in fine*.

76 See B. Herbert, *supra* note 54, p 105.

77 The answer of the Ministry of Health and Sports, published in the Official Journal (*Journal Officiel-JO*) of 7.7.2009, p 6919 to the question nr 45666 posed by J. Didier, available at: http://questions.assemblee-nationale.fr/q13/13-45666QE.htm (last accessed: 11.07.2010).

78 Cf the decision 145008 of the Council of the State (*Conseil d'Etat-CE*) of 29.12.1995 (*Société civile immobilière [sci] "Résidence et services-Association 'Gere Home'"*) and CE 171017 of 16.10.1998 (*Société à responsabilité limitée [sarl] "Société rhodanienne d'intendance et de*

2.4. EVALUATION OF THE RESULTS

Given the increased vulnerability of older people for whom living at home is no longer an option, it becomes evident that there is a need for special consumer protection provisions. Emphasis should be given to the duty of the housing and services provider to inform the senior adequately of his rights and obligations before the conclusion of the contract. The conclusion of the contract in writing provides further guarantees that the decision is thought through, as well as a clear point of reference in case of future disputes. Special provisions as to termination of the contract would also be useful, although the guarantees provided by the general law could be seen as satisfactory. Both the German and the French legislators have to a certain degree taken into account these issues. However, it is only in the cases which fall within the new German law on housing with major care and assistance services that the older people are granted full protection.[79] As to the rest, the relevant legal framework both in Germany and in France is far from comprehensive.

The situation is aggravated by the lack of transparency as to the supply of housing alternatives. The market provides a variety of service packages under varying conditions.[80] No matter how extensive the duty to inform the senior may be, it is doubtful whether the individual will be able to assess this quantity of information. Under these circumstances, the role of standardisation of contracts and certification of services becomes evident. The German Institute for Standardisation (*deutsches Institut für Normung – DIN*) published in September 2006 the standard nr 77800 on "Quality requirements for providers of assisted living for the elderly". However, until now few providers of such accommodation for seniors seem to have gone through the DIN certification procedure.[81] Nevertheless, there are other certification procedures in Germany, at a regional level, which seem to be catching on.[82] The situation in France is similar, where the Association of Standardisation (*Association française de Normalisation – AFNor*) issued rules (NF X 50–058) on specialist accommodation for seniors

services"). On the provisions which apply in the case of socio-medical facilities see *supra* note 59.

79 See *supra*, section 2.2.2.

80 See U. Kremer-Preiss/H. Stolarz, *supra* note 9, p 90.

81 See *Verbraucherzentrale Bundesverband*, *supra* note 19, at p 10. See also 'Leben und Wohnen für alle Lebensalter' (25.9.2009), The Federal Ministry of Family, Senior Citizens, Women and Youth (*Bundesministerium für Familie, Senioren, Frauen und Jugend*), available at: www.bmfsfj.de/RedaktionBMFSFJ/Broschuerenstelle/Pdf-Anlagen/leben-und-wohnen-fuer-alle-lebensalter,property=pdf,bereich=bmfsfj,sprache=de,rwb=true.pdf (last accessed: 11.07.2010), p 50.

82 For an overview of these initiatives see *Verbraucherzentrale Bundesverband*, *supra* note 19, at 10–11.

in February 2003.[83] Realising the need to help clarify this area, the European Committee for Standardisation (CEN) is also working on such a project, which is expected to be completed by 2012.[84] Until standardisation and certification takes on, state authorities as well as private associations provide checklists in order to facilitate the older people in their decision-making process.[85]

3. ADULT PLACEMENT

3.1. GENERAL REMARKS

"Adult placement of seniors" as a long-term housing alternative is the equivalent to "foster care of minors": the person in charge assumes the daily care of the senior, who lives under the same roof in a family-like setting. Hence it falls within the general concept of living with services, with the special characteristic that both the housing space, usually a room, and the services are provided by the carer at the carer's home. This alternative is especially suitable for dependent seniors. Their dependence may be either physical, mental, or even psychological, due to the insecurity and loneliness they feel, especially after experiencing the death of a close family member or friend.

The roots of this institution can be traced back for centuries. In fact, adult placement can be seen as the precursor of modern care homes.[86] However, it was not until the 1990s that renewed interest was shown in it, as a remedy against the de-familisation of elder care and the resulting isolation of older people. Accordingly, provided that the match between the senior and the carer is a successful one, adult placement presents significant advantages for seniors: the obvious benefit of individualised care is coupled with the feeling of stability, as the people who provide services to the senior do not constantly change.[87] Furthermore, the senior may derive satisfaction from forming part of a family, participating in its everyday

---

83 This regulation is entitled '*Établissements d'hébergement pour personnes âgées – Cadre éthique et engagements de service*'.

84 The relevant draft has already been published (see Pr EN 16118:2010 Sheltered housing – Requirements for services for elderly people provided in a sheltered housing scheme).

85 See *eg* the check lists of BAGSO, *supra* note 19 and of U. Kremer-Preiss/H. Stolarz, *supra* note 81.

86 See J.S. Oktay/P.J. Volland, 'Foster home care for the frail elderly as an alternative to nursing home care: an experimental evaluation', *American Journal of Public Health (AJPH)* 1987 (Vol 77), 1505–1510, at 1505; A. Villez, 'L'accueil familial à titre honéreux. Suivance du passé ou pratique d'avenir', *Gérontologie et Société* nr 127 (décembre 2008), 181–198, at 181. Cf also H.H. Holmes/G.D. Rowles "Adult foster care homes" in R. Schulz/ L.S.Noelker/K Rockwood/R.L. Sprott, *The encyclopedia of aging* Vol. 1, Springer, New York 2006 (4th ed), p 25.

87 See A. Bertrand, *L'hébergement des* personnes âgées *en famille d'accueil* (mémoire) 1998, available at www.famidac.fr/article143.html (last accessed: 11.07.2010), section II E 1.

life and contributing to it, according to his capabilities.[88] From the perspective of the carer, there is no doubt that his occupation may be rewarding, even if his burden is heavy, given that responsibility for the senior is continuous.[89]

Nonetheless, the vulnerability of the older person and his dependence on the carer gives rise to problems in protecting the former's personality right, in all respects, such as his well-being and security, his privacy, his freedom to make choices etc. It is especially crucial to prevent mistreatment of every form, such as physical, psychological, as well as financial abuse, like the extraction of pecuniary benefits from the older person, other than the sums due for the services provided. Legal provisions on adult placement have gradually been adopted in a number of European countries, such as Greece[90] and Portugal.[91] As before, however, in the following sections we focus on the way German and French law have faced these challenges.

3.2. ADULT PLACEMENT IN GERMANY

Adult placement for seniors in Germany is still in a rather embryonic state. The relevant programs, usually entitled "*Gastfamilien für Senioren*", are run by local communities and non-profit organisations.[92] They were first developed for

88 See A. Bertrand, *supra* note 87; Cf C. Baudson, *supra* note 7, p 30.

89 See A. Bertrand, *supra* note 87, section II E 2. Cf C. Baudson, *supra* note 7, p 28.

90 See Article 9 par 3 of Law 2082/1992 as amended by Article 65 par 1 of Law 2447/1996. According to this provision adult placement is allowed. A presidential decree shall further regulate the specifics of this institution, but no such decree has yet been issued. Despite the absence of a precise legal framework, adult placement is practised in an informal way, often with the encouragement of local communities. See A. Amira, 'Anadochi kai triti ilikia' (Foster care and third age) in: T. Kallinikaki (ed) *Anadochi Frontida (Foster Care)*, Ellinika Grammata, Athens, 2001, pp 219–225; P. Stathopoulos, *Koinoniki Pronoia. Istoriki exelixi – Nees Katefthinseis (Social Welfare. Historical development – New directions)*, Papazisis, Athens 2005, esp pp 343 *et seq.*

91 See Decreto-Lei (Decree-Law) nr 391/1991 of 10.10.1991, with detailed provisions regulating adult placement, in combination with Despacho (ministerial order) nr 26 208/2007 of 12.9.2007.

92 See for instance the project "*Senioren leben in Gastfamilien*" in the county of Minden-Lübbecke, which is run by the associations "*Paritätischer Verein für freie Sozialarbeit*" and "*Diakonischen Werk – Innere Mission e.V*" (information on this project is available at: www.familie-mal-anders.de/Kurzkonzept-Gastfamilien.pdf); the project "*Gastfamilien für Senioren*" in the country of Gütersloh which is run by the association AWO of the Ost Westfallen-Lippe area, sponsored by *Stiftung Wohlfahrtspflege* (for information see www.pflege-gt.de/index.php?page_id=148 and http://www.awo-owl.de/pages/angebote/seniorinnenundsenioren/gastfamilienfuersenioren.html?res=1280); the new project of the association "*Arkade für Senioren*" with the support of the counties of Ravensburg and Bodensee (for information see www.schwaebische.de/lokales/ravensburg/rund-um-ravensburg_artikel,-Neues-Projekt-bietet-Gastfamilien-fuer-Senioren-_arid,2470402.html); the gerontopsychiatric pilot-project "*Pflegefamilien für Senioren*" for the whole of Bayern, which is run by the Hospital of Kaubeuren and is financed by the "*Zentrum Bayern Familie und Soziales*" (for information see www.pflegen-online.de/nachrichten/ambulante_pflege/betreutes-wohnen-in-gastfamilien-

persons with physical disabilities or mental and psychological conditions,[93] and it was not until recently that they started extending to seniors.[94]

The specific rules governing adult placement differ from programme to programme. In principle, the administrators of the adult placement scheme, ie the communities or the non-profit organisations, set the conditions under which a carer can be admitted.[95] The latter should fully understand the obligations deriving from adult placement and be considered able to deal with the pressure and responsibilities associated with taking care of the senior.[96] Moreover, the whole family should be stable, and should agree to the placement. An additional condition for the eligibility of a person as a carer in such a scheme is that he should be able to support himself and his family without relying on the additional income received for the support of the senior.[97] Each carer may be assigned the support of up to two seniors.[98]

Once these basic conditions are fulfilled, the carer and the senior or, in some cases the carer, the senior and the administrator of the adult placement scheme, conclude a contract, usually in writing.[99] The contract specifies the rights and duties of the parties and, among other issues, sets the remuneration of the carer. Social security may cover these costs to the extent that the senior, given his income, is entitled to social benefits.[100] The remuneration consists typically of a sum paid as rent for the provision of housing, an allowance for the maintenance of the senior and an amount for the support provided.[101] In total, it rarely exceeds

fuer-gerontopsychiatrisch-erkrankte-menschen.htm?PHPSESSID=a). [All these sites were last accessed on 11.07.2010.].

93 On the history of the institution of placement of adults with psychiatric problems in Germany see C. Hecht, *Psychiatrische Familienpflege – neues Konzept oder Auslaufmodell?*, 2006, available at www.bwf-info.de/bwf_e4/literatur/DA_08_C-Hecht_FH-Kiel.pdf, esp p 20 *et seq* (last accessed: 11.07.2010).

94 See. M. Seigel, 'Betreutes Wohnen für Senioren in Familien' (2.7.2009) available at: http://generation-50-plus.suite101.de/article.cfm/betreutes_wohnen_fuer_senioren_in_familien (last accessed: 11.07.2010). This is the case for all abovementioned projects (at note 92).

95 This is derived from the information provided for the projects referred *supra*, at note 92. Cf R. Eisenhut, 'Der Fachausschuss Familienpflege der DGSP. Ziele, Standards und Entwicklungen', *Soziale Psychiatrie* 3/2005, 37 *et seq*.

96 See M. Seigel, *supra* note 94 as well as the information on the project "*Senioren leben in Gastfamilien*" of the county of Minden-Lübbecke, *supra* note 92.

97 *Ibid*.

98 See M. Seigel, *supra* note 94 and the information on the project "*Gastfamilien für Senioren*" of the AWO association, *supra* note 92.

99 See M. Seigel, *supra* note 94; Cf R. Eisenhut, *supra* note 95 and the project "*Senioren leben in Gastfamilien*" of the county of Minden-Lübbecke, *supra* note 92.

100 More concretely, adult placement is considered to be a special form of assisted living in the sense of § 98 V of the Code of Social Security XII (*Sozialgesetzbuch- SGB XII*).

101 See the projects "*Senioren leben in Gastfamilien*" of the county of Minden-Lübbecke and "*Gastfamilien für Senioren*" of the AWO association, *supra* note 92.

800 euro per senior.[102] This remuneration is therefore mainly thought to cover the costs of the carer and does not turn the provision of care into a profit earning activity.[103] Moreover, it is not subject to tax.[104] The proper performance of the contract is constantly supervised by the administrator of the adult placement programme, who is entitled to pay regular visits to the family and carry out any further controls that are deemed necessary.[105]

Given these conditions, it seems that the occupation of carer is seen as a "vocation", where the carers are expected to act out of more or less selfless concerns.[106]

3.3. ADULT PLACEMENT IN FRANCE

Adult placement in France has a longer tradition than in Germany. The first law referring to "*placement familial*", or as it is more commonly known "*accueil familial*", dates back to 1905, while further relevant provisions were enacted in the 1950s and 1960s.[107] This legal framework approached the institution from a purely contract law perspective, without providing any supervision or other safeguards for the quality of the services. Hence many instances of abuse of the older people were recorded.[108] In response to this situation, Law 89-475 of 10.7.1989, as complemented by the decrees 90-504 of 22.6.1990 and 90-635 of 18.7.1990, comprehensively regulated the institution. In an effort to expand the use of adult placement, further laws and decrees have been enacted since then, gradually leading to the full professionalization of a caring occupation.[109] In this spirit, the most recent legal texts no longer refer to regulation of the institution of "*accueil familial*", but rather to the exercise of the profession of the carer ("*accueillant familial*").

102 This is so for the projects of the association "*Arkade für Senioren*" in Ravensburg and "*Senioren leben in Gastfamilien*" of the county of Minden-Lübbecke (see *supra* note 92), whereas in the gerontopsychiatric pilot-project "*Pflegefamilien für Senioren*" of the hospital of Kaufbeuren, the remuneration is set at 700 euros. Cf U. Hellmann, 'Fiskus lässt Betreuungsgeld für Gastfamilien ungetastet', *Lebenshilfe-Zeitung* 1/2009, where it is taken as granted that the remuneration of a carer is set at around 800 euros.

103 This conclusion may also be drawn from the fact that the remuneration of the carer is often referred to as "reimbursement of expenses" (in German: *Aufwandserschaedigung*). See esp M. Seigel, *supra* note 94.

104 See § 3 nr 10 of the Law on Income Tax (*Einkommensteuergesetz-EStG*), as amended by the Yearly Tax Law (*Jahressteuergesetz*) 2009 of 19.12.2008.

105 This is explicitly mentioned in the projects "*Senioren leben in Gastfamilien*" of the county of Minden-Lübbecke and "*Gastfamilien für Senioren*" of the AWO association, *supra* note 92 Cf R. Eisenhut, *supra* note 95.

106 Cf J.S. Oktay/P.J. Volland, *supra* note 86, at 1506.

107 See J.C. Cébula, *L'accueil familial des adultes*, éditions Dunod, Paris, 1999, p 10.

108 *Ibid.* See also A. Bertrand, *supra* note 87, section II B 1.

109 See esp Law 2002-73 of 17.1.2002 and the decrees 1538, 1541 and 1542 of 30.12.2004, as well as Law 2007-290 of 5.3.2007, while the issue of further decrees is expected in 2010.

More concretely, the legal provisions on adult placement have been codified in the Code of Social Action and Families (CASF).[110] The basic characteristics of the current legal framework for adult placement are the following: The occupation of the carer is subject to licensing.[111] The license is valid for 5 years, but may be renewed.[112] A carer may be licensed to care for up to three seniors.[113] In order to become licensed, the carer must provide guarantees for the well-being of the senior and ensure his continuous support, by appointing a substitute carer, in case (for whatever reason) he is not in a position, permanently or temporarily, to take care of the older person.[114] He must provide for him an individual room with heating and sanitary facilities.[115] The carers must declare themselves willing to participate in a special training.[116] Due to the lack of further provisions regulating the training, it is usually short and of varying quality among different regions of France.[117] The local authorities follow up on the senior and control the carer.[118] If they realise that the carer no longer fulfils the abovementioned conditions, they may deprive him of his licence. To act as a carer without a license constitutes a criminal offence.[119]

The carer and the senior, or his legal representative, conclude a contract in writing, the minimum contents of which are regulated by law.[120] The contract provides the rights and duties of the parties. Moreover, it should specify a trial period, and the conditions under which the parties may revise or terminate the contract. The contract should further spell out the material and financial conditions of the adult placement. The total remuneration of the carer has the following components: a sum for the rent of the room, a sum for the maintenance of the senior, and an amount of money for his services. This last component is treated like a normal salary, so it is taxed as a salary, is subject to social security contributions, and may

110 See Article L 441-1 *et seq* in combination with Article R 441-1 *et seq* CASF.

111 See Articles L 441-1 to L 441-3 as well as R 441-1 CASF.

112 See Articles R 441-5 and R 441-7 CASF.

113 See Article L 441-1 par 3 in combination with Article R 441-5 par 2 CASF. Due to the professionalization of the institution, these laws do not apply in cases where the person taken care of is a relative of the carer. (see L 441-1 par 1 CASF).

114 See Article L 441-1 par 4 CASF. However, the legal framework as to the way this replacement may be effectuated is not clear. V. Rosso-Debord addresses this problem in her report *Vers un nouvel accueil familial des personnes âgées et des personnes handicapées*, of 2008 (esp at p 10) and proceeds to the proposition of solutions (p 14–15, proposition nr 4), available at: http://lesrapports.ladocumentationfrancaise.fr/BRP/084000724/0000.pdf (last accessed: 11.07.2010).

115 See Article R 441-1 par 3 CASF in combination with Article R 831-13-1 of the Code of Social Security (Code de la sécurité sociale). On this issue see also A. Villez, *supra* note 86, p 187.

116 See Article L 441-1 par 4 CASF.

117 See A. Villez, *supra* note 86, p 188. See also the report of V. Rosso-Debord, *supra* note 114, p 8–9 and her propositions nr 7 and 8 (p 16–17).

118 See Article L 441-1 par 4 in combination with Article R 441-1 par 5 CASF.

119 See Article L 443-9 in combination with Article L 321-4 CASF.

120 See Article L 442-1 CASF.

not fall below the minimum wage.[121] Furthermore, the carer is entitled to holiday allowance.[122] An extra amount of money is due if the carer provides additional services owing to a serious disability of the senior. Thus in practice the total amount due to the carer ranges from 1100 to 1800 euro per month, depending on the needs of the particular senior.[123]

Further provisions organise the specific aspects of the relationship between the carer and the senior. It is particularly interesting to mention that neither the carer himself nor his family may benefit from transactions with the senior or be appointed as his heir.[124] This does not apply if the senior disposes of a specific asset to one of these persons in exchange for services they supplied to him.[125]

Finally, as to the legal position of the carer, it is worth noting that, since 2007, carers may work as employees of legal persons, whether public or private.[126] All aforementioned provisions apply in this case as well. Thus, this possibility has no real impact on the senior, but instead provides greater job security to the carer. Namely, if adult placement is suspended, eg because the senior spends some time with his natural family or because he has been admitted to the hospital, the carer is entitled to an allowance, paid by his employer.[127] Moreover, the employer is obliged to provide employment to the carer, according to the labour contract which has been concluded. Hence, if the employer has not assigned any senior to the carer for at least four consecutive months, the carer is entitled to demand either his full salary, meaning the remuneration he would get for the care of a

121 For more details on the calculation of the carer's remuneration, see also Article D 442-2 CASF. For a concrete calculation of the minimum remuneration of the carer, see the information provided by the French administration at http://vosdroits.service-public.fr/particuliers/F253.xhtml (last accessed: 11.07.2010). See also A. Villez, *supra* note 86, pp 191–192.

122 See *supra* notes 120 and 121.

123 See also *supra* note 121. The minimum sum provided for the services of the carer and the maintenance of the senior is around 950 euros, excluding both the rent for the room, which may vary, and additional amounts due owing to any serious disabilities of the senior. In practice, according to the information provided by the association of carers and their partners "*Famidac*" (at: www.famidac.fr/article10.html,) which was last updated on March 2010, remuneration starts from 1.340 euros per month. See also I. Palacin, 'Choisir devenir famille d'accueil' (3.9.2007) available at www.seniorplus.fr/maison/maison-de-retraite/choisir/devenir-famille-d-accueil, who refers to a salary between 1200 and 2000 euro per month and C. Baudson, *supra* note 7, p 18 referring to an amount between 1150 and 1700 euro.

124 See Article L 443-6 CASF.

125 See Article L 443-6 CASF in combination with Article 909 of the French Civil Code (CC). The second exception provided by Article 909 CC refers to the case where the recipient is a relative (see supra note 113). However, in these cases the provisions on adult placement do not apply. Cf also Article 911 CC.

126 See Article L 444-1 CASF. It is worth noting that this possibility had been already introduced by Law 2002-73. However, owing to the lack of further provisions, in practice it never applied. A. Villez, *supra* note 86, p 192.

127 See Article L 444-5 par 1 CASF.

senior, or his due redundancy pay.[128] This way, carers may enjoy a more stable financial situation.

3.4. EVALUATION OF THE RESULTS

Both in Germany and France the interest in adult placement is increasing. In view of the vulnerability and dependency of seniors, it is common understanding that purely contractual arrangements do not suffice for their protection.[129] Thus in all such schemes measures are adopted for the supervision of the carer, which focus mainly on the physical and psychological well-being of the senior. As to the financial abuse of seniors, given the difficulties of detecting it,[130] additional prevention measures are needed. Thus special provisions, such as those in French law which restrict the grant of gifts or succession rights to the carer, are required.

Regarding the specific organisation and implementation of adult placement schemes, Germany and France follow different patterns. The German approach, which is the more traditional one, is somehow idealistic, as it presupposes more or less selfless motives of the carer.[131] France on the other hand has clearly proceeded to the professionalization of the institution and makes further steps in this direction.[132] There can be little doubt that this last development favours the expansion of the institution. Moreover, although the incentives of the carer may be less noble, professionalization could be expected to lead to an improvement in the quality of the services provided as, knowing that his living depends on his activity, the carer has more incentive to invest in it.

4. COMPARATIVE CONCLUSIONS

Both specialist housing with services and adult placement constitute significant alternatives to institutionalised care of seniors, representing a more modern response to the increasing de-familisation of care. In the case of specialist housing with services, seniors are provided with a range of comforts, which enable them to keep their own household for as long as possible, while adult placement provides a substitute for the natural family of the senior in providing care.

---

128 See Article L 444-5 par 2 CASF.

129 See *supra* note 108.

130 See esp C.L. Dessin, 'Financial abuse of the elderly', *Idaho Law Review* 1999-2000 (Vol 36), 203-226 at 222.

131 See *supra* note 106.

132 See V. Rosso-Debord, *supra* note 114, proposition 1 (p 12).

A common element of both options is that the senior enjoys individualised care, while preserving, as much as possible, his autonomy. This development is in line with the new concept of human rights of disabled persons, as expressed in the United Nations Convention on the Dignity of Persons with Disabilities of 2006.[133] More concretely, according to this Convention persons with disabilities shall be enabled to develop their own capabilities to the full, rather than passively rely on the receipt of assistance, as the paternalistic approach of the past would suggest.[134] Moreover, both specialist housing with services and adult placement provide a remedy against the isolation of older people, though in different ways. Specialist housing with services allows for the socialisation of the tenants of the individual apartments among themselves, whereas in the case of adult placement, socialisation takes place within a multi-generational framework.

When a senior is called on to choose between these two alternatives, a first criterion is in fact the nature and extent of his own limiting conditions. For elders who are particularly frail, specialist housing with services may no longer be an option. As to the others, the choice would depend on personal preferences; a senior who values independence and privacy over reassurance would most probably opt for specialist housing with services, while a senior who places constant company over autonomy would be expected to opt for adult placement.[135]

Hence, despite the common characteristics of these non-institutional alternatives, both options need to be further developed, as they do not address the same needs. The source of the problem is on both occasions the same, namely the quasi-monopolistic position of the care-provider following the conclusion of the contract, given the high, often prohibitive, costs for the seniors to switch to another provider. However, due to the differences in the nature of the alternatives, the ways of confronting it differ. In the case of specialist housing with services, special consumer protection provisions together with increased transparency in this field, mainly through standardisation and certification procedures, would

[133] On the relation between Elder law and Disability law, see D. Surtees, supra note 12. Cf also Article 1 of the German Charta on the rights of persons who need help and care (*Charta der Rechte hilfe- und pflegebedürftiger Menschen*).

[134] The Convention marks a "paradigm shift" from the social welfare approach, according to which persons with disabilities are considered objects of charity, social protection and medical treatment, to the human rights approach, according to which these persons are subjects of human rights, able to make decisions about their life and future as well as to claim rights on their own behalf. On this issue see in more detail R. Kayess/P. French, 'Out of darkness into light? Introducing the Convention on the rights of persons with disabilities', *Human Rights Law Review* 2008 (Vol 8), 1–34. It is worth noting, that according to Article 1 of this Convention, "Persons with disabilities include those who have long-term physical, mental, intellectual or sensory impairments which, in interaction with various barriers, may hinder their full and effective participation in society on an equal basis with others". Hence seniors may fall within its scope of application.

[135] These observations could perhaps shed some light to the reasons why specialist housing with services is prevalent in Germany, whereas adult placement is more popular in France.

yield satisfactory results. In the case of adult placement, the dependence of the senior on his carer is more intense. Thus the assurance of quality of care demands the adoption of measures which go well beyond the field of private law, such as the monitoring of the carer by a public authority.

CARING BY CONTRACT: CARE ARRANGEMENTS FOR OLDER PEOPLE

Joëlle Long

1. INTRODUCTION

Recent years have seen a wide and increasing diffusion of care arrangements for older people. This development has arisen owing to the convergence of multiple factors related to the pan-European problem of an ageing population with increasing demands for care.[1] Although, of course, older people are not necessarily dependent on others for continuous non-medical care, the passing of the years does mean that many will eventually, in various ways, require assistance in performing daily tasks.[2] Not only is the population ageing, but fertility rates across Europe are dropping, leading to the elderly constituting a larger proportion of the overall population and charging the growing costs of elder care to a shrinking number of tax-payers.[3] Moreover, the rise of the nuclear family model, consisting of only two generations, parents and children, living together,[4] and the increasing number of people seeking and finding employment out of their birth town have been weakening the function of the family as primary support structure for older people.[5] The raising of retirement age and the growth of women's work outside the home further contribute to the diminution of informal caregivers available. In addition, the growing level of women's education and income from paid employment increases the economic resources of the family, making it economically more attractive for families to have women working outside their household and to hire caregivers for children and older dependent persons.[6]

Besides, the crisis of the modern Welfare State, worsened by the global economic crisis, has been causing a reduction of quality and quantity in social services.[7]

---

1 For an overview of data see K. Giannakouris, *Ageing characterises the demographic perspectives of the European societies*, Eurostat, 2008. On the effects of ageing on State social policy A. Razin, E. Sadka, P. Swagel, *The Aging Population and the Size of the Welfare State*, in *The Journal of Political Economy*, vol. 110, n. 4 (Aug., 2002), pp. 900–918.

2 I intend to address not only to basic activities of daily living (i.e. personal hygiene, dressing, eating, moving around and transferring from bed to chair, and back), but also to activities necessary for independent living, such as managing money and taking medication.

3 In Italy, in 2008, the old-age-dependency ratio, ie the percentage of the population that is generally economically inactive (aged 65 and over) per persons of working age (from 15 to 64), was 36.0%. In Europe it was 31.1%. Source: Eurostat, *Old-age-dependency ratio*, 2009.

4 In Italy only 4.9% of single people aged over 65 years live with relatives (ISTAT , *Famiglia e soggetti sociali. Anno 2003*, Roma, 2006).

5 A national Italian survey shows that 77% of married people aged between 18 and 64 years who do not live with their mother see her at least once a week (ISTAT, *Famiglie, abitazioni e sicurezza dei cittadini – Anno 1999*, Roma, 2001).

6 See A. Colombo, *Il mito del lavoro domestico: strutture e cambiamenti in Italia (1970–2003)*, in *Polis*, 2005, n.3, p 449.

7 Only 3.3% of Italian population aged over 65 years benefit from home care provided by the State (ISTAT, *Noi Italia: 100 statistiche per capire il Paese in cui viviamo*, cit. above, 88). Nearly 80% of families with a dependent person do not receive in home care (ISTAT, *Condizioni di salute, fattori di rischio e ricorso ai servizi sanitari* (year 2005), Roma, 2007, p10). Private expenditure for home care for dependent people is nearly double than the public investement on social

The introduction of the so-called welfare mix model, in which social services are supplied both by the municipalities themselves and by the private sector, has further stimulated the development of private care arrangements. [8] The moving of the hospital health system towards assistance only for severe acute condition increases the demand for palliative treatments and general care of the sort frequently required by older non-dependent persons.[9] Indeed, "care" encompasses not just diagnostic and therapeutic action, but all other aspects of preserving mental and physical well being.

The deficiencies in the social security system encourage individuals to move to private contracts to supplement their pensions with other financial resources which can be used, in the event of dependency, to pay a home health aide or a room in a retirement home. Following the path of the U.S., insurance companies have been offering in Europe long-term care insurance policies which pay for long-term care (ie home care, hospice care, nursing home) in the event that the stipulator loses his or her ability to perform the basic activities of daily living (such as dressing, bathing, eating, toileting, moving and out of a bed or chair, walking).

As a result of all these changes, private arrangements to provide material and/or moral assistance to an older person are therefore now a widespread phenomenon. Sometimes agreements are concluded directly by the senior, but on many occasions they are finalised by the dependent's family for his or her benefit.[10] Some arrangements are made between older people and other private individuals acting in a personal capacity (eg transfer of the family home to a family member or a friend in exchange for a promise of life time care); more often, the counterpart is a professional, as in the case of home health aide contracts, long-term continuing care contracts with a retirement home or long-term care insurances. Usually the reciprocal performances of the contracting parties are at least presumed to be equivalent in value, but at times the law requires, for the validity of the agreement itself, that the parties *do not* have a clear knowledge of the advantages and losses deriving from the care contract. This is the case, in civil law countries, with life annuities and life care agreements which the law classifies as "aleatory" or

home care (NNA-Network Non Autosufficienza, *L'assistenza agli anziani non autosufficienti in Italia. Rapporto 2009*, 2009, Maggioli, Santarcangelo di Romagna, p 27).

8 On this model see E. Jorio, *Il diritto dell'assistenza sociale*, Giuffré, Milano, 2006, particularly p 40 f. and 154ff.; S. Campi, *Sistemi di welfare mix e nuovi meccanismi di regolazione nel campo dei servizi alla persona. Un confronto tra Italia e Belgio*, in *Impresa e progetto*, 2006, n.1, particularly p 3 ff.

9 See for Italy the interesting data reported in Ministero del Lavoro e delle Politiche sociali, *Rapporto sulla non autosufficienza in Italia*, Roma, 2010, p 12 ff.

10 Occasionally contracts in favour of a third party postpone their effects until the death of the stipulator (eg in the case of a husband who wants to arrange care for his spouse affected by Alzheimer's disease transferring a lump sum to a caregiver in exchange for care which should be provided to the stipulator's wife only after his death).

"wagering" agreements (ie they are dependent on chance), and treats differently from other contracts (see below section 2).

There are many advantages in receiving care pursuant to a contract. Care obligations established by private agreements need not depend upon the assets of the dependent person.[11] In addition, the contracting parties can include specific care duties, according to the dependent person's needs, even for example daily phone calls and visits.

Owing to the difficulty involved in considering care agreements as a single genus, in the following paragraphs I will begin by focusing on agreements converting the home into long term care providing a comparison between civil law countries (namely Italy, France and Spain) and common law countries (namely the United Kingdom and the United States). I will then offer some general comments on common features and general issues related to these arrangements and conclude with some remarks aiming to overcome a number of prejudices about caring by contract.

2. CONVERTING THE FAMILY HOME INTO LONG TERM CARE

In this section I pay specific attention to contracts aimed at converting the family home into long term care, leaving the house at the seller's disposal until his or her death. As I will demonstrate, this does not imply a transfer of the family home from the older person to his or her contractual counterpart: in the reverse mortgage (on which, see below), for instance, the lender never acquires the ownership of the house, but only guarantees the loan.

The choice to examine this particular group of care arrangements is motivated by its practical importance for seniors. Indeed, older persons are very often "house rich, cash poor," ie the family home is the principal asset which can be exchanged for assistance.[12] Furthermore, they usually have a strong desire to prevent institutionalisation and to remain in their lifetime home.

---

11 The principle is expressly referred to in art. 1793 *Código civil* with reference to the *contrato de alimentos*. By contrast, legal obligations of support among members of the extended family are usually subject to the condition that the person to be supported is in need and unable to provide for his or her own maintenance (see for instance art. 438 para. 1 *Codice civile*).

12 In Italy, for example, in 2006 73.3% of the families and 74.7% of individuals were owners of their own family home and 9.1% of families and 8.7% of individuals live in the home as rent-free tenants: see ISTAT, *L'accesso alla casa d'abitazione in Italia: proprietà, mutui, affitti e spesa delle famiglie*, Rome, 17th July 2007 (in http://www.istat.it/istat/audizioni/170707/E-Dossier4.pdf).

Both in civil law and in common law countries, the first model which appeared to achieve the goal of converting the family home into long term care was the *do ut des* model. According to this model, the older person (or his or her family) exchanges the family home for a series of fixed regular payments which can be used, for instance, to pay a home health aide or a room in a retirement home.

In civil law countries, the first contractual tool regulated by the law to pursue these goals is the life annuity (in Italy *rendita vitalizia*, in Spain *renta vitalicia*, in France *rente viagère* or simply *viager*). Life annuity agreements transfer movable or immovable property,[13] or assign capital in exchange for fixed regular lifelong payments.[14] The present analysis will be limited to conveyances which transfer the family home, giving the seller the right to enjoy the use of the house for his or her lifetime. A French sociological analysis on life annuities performed in the early nineties by one of the biggest agencies in this field indicates that the average age of the annuitant is 72–75 and that in the majority of cases she is a widow.[15] Besides, nowadays the seller is increasingly a private licensed agency, eg a real estate agency, a financial group, or an insurance company. Increasingly, at least in Italy, city councils try to resolve social hardship issues by buying houses from institutionalised older persons in exchange for life annuities (to pay the fees of the nursing facility) and then granting the tenancy for free to families at risk (particularly those with children, disabled persons, etc).[16]

In continental Europe since the Middle Ages, ecclesiastical institutions and, latterly, cities and governments financed themselves through life annuities.[17] Between the VIIIth and the XIth centuries, it was relatively common for individuals to give their land and properties to the Church in return for the legal right to use and derive profit or benefit from the properties given (this right was often known as a "usufruct"): the profit for the life tenant was immediate but

13 In civil law, the expression "immovable property" refers to an immovable object that cannot be moved (in common law countries it is also known as "real estate"). By contrast, movable property is a residual category which contains any non immovable thing. See. U. Mattei, *Basic principles of property law: a comparative legal and economic introduction*, Greenwood Press, Westport, 2000, p 83 ff.

14 See art. 1872 *Codice civile*; art. 1968 *Code civil.*

15 F. Drosso, 'Le viager, essai d'une définition', in *Revue de sociologie francaise*, 1993, p 223.

16 For an example see *Comune di Ponte San Nicolò, Verbale di deliberazione del consiglio comunale n.21 del 12.07.2004*, in <http://www.comune.pontesannicolo.pd.it/upload/DCN_N_21_12-07-2004.pdf>.

17 R. Génestal, *Rôle des monastères comme établissements de crédit étudié en Normandie du XI' à la fin du XIII' siècle*, Paris, 1901; and more recently see Società internazionale di studi francescani, *L'economia dei conventi dei Frati Minori e Predicatori fino alla metà del Trecento. Atti del 31° Convegno internazionale (Assisi, 9–11 ottobre 2003)*, Spoleto, 2004 and N. Beriou et J. Chiffoleau (ed. by), *Economie et religion: l'expérience des ordres mendiants (13.-15. siècle)*, Lyon, Presses Universitaires de Lyon, 2009.

short term, whereas the Church would improve its assets in the long term.[18] These instruments varied in their names and legal natures: indeed, they were referred as "donations", "sales", "exchanges", "*precaria oblata*" or "*remuneratoria*" (as distinguished from the *precaria data*, where the Church was the owner of the land given in usufruct).[19] In some cases the seller directly retained the life estate; in others it was the Church which, after becoming the owner of the assets, turned it back to the seller as leasehold or granted real estates/properties.[20] In addition to this model, the direct ancestor of current life annuities developed: *the promise* of regular lifelong payments was sold in exchange for the assignment of capital or for the transfer of immovable property.[21] According to this second pattern, life annuities constitute *a personal obligation* of the seller and not a real right of limited duration on the property (as in the case of the usufruct).[22] Consequently, for example, the buyer continues to be personally bound to pay life annuities even if he sells the property.

Whether the right of the buyer was of a proprietary or personal nature, life annuities were often accused of usury.[23] To reject this charge, legal doctrine and case law explained that the profit of the seller was not seen as interest on a loan but as compensation for the risk deriving from the uncertain duration of the beneficiary's life and health.[24] This led to the current idea that life annuities should be classified among aleatory contracts, because one of their essential features is the uncertainty of the value of the buyer's performance (the so-called *alea*).[25]

---

18 L. Morelle, 'Les actes de précaire, instruments de transferts patrimoniaux (France du Nord et de l'Est, VIIIe-XIe siècle)', in *Mélanges de l'Ecole française de Rome. Moyen-Age*, Temps modernes T. 111, n. 2. 1999, p 632.

19 See P. Grossi, *Le situazioni reali nell'esperienza giuridica medioevale*, Cedam, Padova, 1968; L. Morelle, 'Les actes de précaire, instruments de transferts patimoniaux (France du Nord et de l'Est, VIIIe-XIe siècle)', in *Mélanges de l'Ecole française de Rome. Moyen-Age*, Temps modernes T. 111, n.2. 1999, pp. 607–647; B. H. Rosenwein, *Property transfers and the Church, eighth to eleventh centuries. An overview*, ivi, pp. 563–575 (in part 572) and J. Brissaud, *History of French Public Law*, Beard Books, in part p 144.

20 Although the *precaria* cannot be considered as a type of life annuity, it is an historical precedent of that phenomenon: F. Varaja, *Le origini della controversia teologica sul contratto di censo nel XIII secolo*, Edizioni di storia e letteratura, Roma, 1960, p 4 ff.

21 Against the widespread thesis that, during the Middle Ages, the nature of the right of the annuitant was only real, Soffietti demonstrated that at times it was undoubtedly personal: I. Soffietti, *La rendita vitalizia nel pensiero dei civilisti fino alla metà del XIII secolo*, in *Rivista di storia del diritto italiano*, 1969, p 69, p 75 ff.

22 In civil law "real rights", as opposed to personal or obligatory rights, are rights attached to a thing rather than a person. Real rights include ownership, use, pledge, usufruct, mortgage, and predial servitude.

23 On usury see B. Nelson, *The idea of usury from tribal brotherhood to universal otherhood*, 2nd ed., University of Chicago Press, Chicago, 1969; T. P. McLaughlin, *The Teaching of the Canonists on Usury*, in 2 *Mediaeval Studies* 1 (1940); S. Herman, *Medieval usury and the commercialization of feudal bonds*, Duncker & Humblot, Berlin, 1993.

24 An interesting historical prospective is offered by P. L. Bernstein, *Against the Gods. The Remarkable Story of Risk*, Wiley and Sons, New York, 1996.

25 L. Tartufari, *Dell'alea nella costituzione di rendita vitalizia*, in *Archivio giuridico*, 1889, p 424.

According to this view, for example, the French and Spanish Civil Codes state that a contract by which an annuity was created on the head of a person already dead or suffering from an illness from which he died within twenty days of the date of the contract does not produce any effect (art. 1794 e 1795 *Code Napoléon* and art. 1804 *Código civil*).

The advantages for older people who choose to enter into a life annuity agreement, keeping the right to live in their own houses, are clearly visible: they continue to stay in their family home, supplementing their pensions with other financial resources. Instead, the weaknesses of this instrument lie in the fact that the obligation of the buyer is merely to give (*dare*) something (nowadays chiefly a periodic amount of money) and not personally and practically to take care of the older person; moreover, the instalments are fixed and do not vary according to the changing needs of the older person (and even in the event of devaluation, except if expressly stated in the contract).

Because of these limits, since the XVIIIth century, civil law countries have been moving to a *do ut facias* model, developing from life annuities an *ad hoc* contract (in Italy *vitalizio assistenziale* or *vitalizio atipico*, in France *bail à nourriture*, in Spain *contrato de alimentos*) where the buyer's obligation is a promise of lifetime care and therefore not merely the delivery (*dare*) of something, but an action (*facere*): to take care of the transferor for all his or her life.[26] This act can be performed only by the original debtor[27] and is variable according to the assisted person's needs. Although these care contracts have long been considered a species in the genus of life annuities, they later acquired independence.[28] Spain and Switzerland are presently the only countries which regulate these contracts expressly by law: articles 1791–1797 *Código civil*, as amended by *ley 41/2003 de*

[26] A good example of this is now provided by art.1791 *Código civil* which defines the contents of the *contrato de alimentos* as obligations to *proporcionar vivienda, manutención y asistencia de todo tipo* (ensuring board, lodging and assistance). Legal doctrine emphasises that this expression must be interpreted as if at least one of these obligations is necessary for the existence of such a contract: E. Llamas Pombo, 'La tipificación del contrato de alimentos', in M. A. Pérez, E. M. Martínez Gallego and J. Reguero Celada (eds), *Protección jurídica de los mayors*, La Ley, Madrid, 2004, p 210. For an historical study of the origins of this contract to supply board and lodging in Spain, see E E. Llamas Pombo, 'La tipificación del contrato de alimentos', in M. A. Pérez, E. M. Martínez Gallego and J. Reguero Celada (eds), *Protección jurídica de los mayors*, La Ley, Madrid, 2004, p 198 f.

[27] The relationship between the contracting parties is *intuitu personae*, ie grounded on a special relation of trust. As a consequence of this, for instance, art. 1792 *Código civil* states the possibility to transform the life care contract into a life annuity in the event of the death of the debtor or if the "peaceful cohabitation" between the caregiver and the assisted person is no longer possible.

[28] In Spain, from judgment 23rd May 1965 of the *Tribunal Supremo*. In Italy, since *Corte di Cassazione*, 28th July 1975, n.2924, and most importantly *Corte di Cassazione* (United Sections), 18th August 1990, n.8432, in *Giurisprudenza italiana*, 1191, I, 1, at 30.

18 noviembre 2003 de protección patrimonial de las personas con discapacidad[29] and articles 521–529 of the *Codice delle obbligazioni*.

In the last decade, in the United States, life care agreements between seniors and friends or family members have started to develop because of Medicaid eligibility policies, according to which gifting of assets (eg gift of the family home to a younger family member subject to the implicit condition of lifetime care) disqualifies the applicant from receiving Medicaid until a penalty period (the length of which depends on the total value of the gift) expires.[30] In parallel to this, there are life care agreements stipulated directly between the older person and the retirement home: the lifelong (and therefore unknown) duration of the care provided by the seller distinguishes these care agreements from general contracts for admission to retirement homes.[31]

Actually, in common law countries, the most frequent model used by older people to supplement their pensions, keeping the right to stay at home until their death, remains the *do ut des* model. Indeed, the widespread tool is the reverse mortgage (or lifetime mortgage). A reverse mortgage is a loan specifically available to seniors and aimed at releasing the home equity in the property as multiple payments; the homeowner's obligation to repay the loan is deferred until his or her death, the sale of the property, or his or her leaving the house (eg to move into a retirement home).

In the United Kingdom, agreements similar to reverse mortgages (home-equity reversions) first appeared in the thirties and found their current structure in

---

[29] It is worth mentioning that some *comunidades autónomas* also have their own specific disciplines: see for *Galicia* the *Ley de Derecho Civil de Galicia, de 24 de mayo de 1995* (arts. 96–99) and for Cataluña the *pacto de acogida* regulated by *Ley 22/2000 de acogimiento de personas mayores* and Ley 11/2001 de 13 *de julio de acogimiento familiar entre personas mayores*. For an analysis of the two latter acts, stressing the lack of coordination between them, see E. Torrelles Torrea, 'La protección de las persona mayores en Cataluña: perspectiva civil', in M. A. Pérez, E. M. Martínez Gallego e J. Reguero Celada (eds) *Protección jurídica de los mayores*, La Ley, Madrid, 2004, p 223 ff.

[30] The insertion in the agreement of a clause whereby the receiver should grant the conveyor lifelong assistance qualifies it as a contract and therefore does not affect Medicaid requirements. On the development of these agreements see M. I. HALL, 'Care for Life: Private Care Agreements Between Older Adults and Friends or Family Members', (2003) 2 *Elder Law Review* 24.

[31] See R. A. Bretzner, *Validity and construction of contract under which applicant for admission to home for aged or infirm turns over his property to institution in return for lifetime care*, in 44 *A. L.R.3d* 11174; C. T. Drechsler, *Obligations as between applicant for admission to charitable home, and home, respecting compensation to home, and property rights of applicant*, in A. L. R.2d and L. Hunter Dietz, *Admission and life care contracts – Construction and operation of contracts*, in 5 *Am. Jur. Charities* § 182.

1965.[32] Presently, 90% of the reverse mortgage market is covered by financial institutions and more than 20,000 new reverse mortgages are entered into each year.

In the United States of America, by contrast, reverse mortgages have been developing on a mass scale only since 1989.[33] Another striking difference from the UK is that the majority of American reverse mortgages are stipulated in the framework of the Federal Program Home Equity Conversion Mortgage (HECM) and are therefore covered by the Federal Housing Administration (FHA), which is part of the Department of Housing and Urban Development (HUD). These public bodies determine the value of the instalments, the costs of the operation and monitor (at least in part) the fulfilment of the contracting parties' obligations.

From a civil law perspective, it is worth noticing that Italy, France and Spain have recently introduced seniors' reverse mortgages. In Italy, by Decree Law 30 September 2005 n.203 on tax evasion (!).[34] In France, by the *ordonnance* n. 2006–346 of 23rd March 2006 which modified the *Code de la consommation* introducing the *hypothèque viagère*.[35] In Spain, by *Ley 41/2007* of 7th December 2007 which open the *hipoteca inversa* not only to people aged more than 65 years, but to every "frail" adult.[36] However, at least in Italy, the use of this instrument has so far been limited, possibly because of the public's limited awareness of its existence and of the loans crisis which has discouraged financial institutions from embarking on new ventures.

Let us now consider the advantages and disadvantages of the above-mentioned civil law and common law models and tools for converting the family home into long term care.

---

32 See C. Huan, J. Mahoney, *Equity release mortgages*, in *Housing Finance International*, 2002, in particular p 32 ff. also in www.housingfinance.org/uploads/Publicationsmanager/0206_Equ.pdf.

33 On reverse mortgages in the United States see among many C. J. Mayer, K. V. Simons, 'Reverse mortgages and the liquidity of housing wealth', in 22 *Real Estate Economics* 235 (1994); S. R. Merrill, M. Finkel, N. K. Kutty, 'Potential Beneficiaries from Reverse Mortgage Products for Elderly Homeowners: An Analysis of American Housing Survey Data', in 22 *Real Estate Economics* 257 (1994); C. Huan, J. Mahoney, 'Equity release mortgages', in *Housing Finance International*, 2002, 29 also in < http://www.housingfinance.org/uploads/Publicationsmanager/0206_Equ.pdf>; H. Shan, *Reversing the Trend: The Recent Expansion of the Reverse Mortgage Market*, 2009, in www.federalreserve.gov/PUBS/feds/2009/200942/#screen_reader_explanation.

34 See art. 11-quaterdecies para 12° Decree Law 30 September 2005 n.203, as amended by Law 2 December 2005 n.248. On this topic: S. Milianta, *La rendita vitalizia ipotecaria. Un'opportunità per finanziare il long term care?*, 2006, Progetto Fuoriorario e Programma europeo Equal per la tutela e il sostegno alle politiche del lavoro, in www.equalfuoriorario.it; E. Fornero, M. C. Rossi, *Anziani, la casa è più di un tesoro*, in *Il Sole 24 ore*, 11th October 2007; M. Maggi, *Se il nonno si gioca la casa*, in www.finanzaonline.com, 20th January 2006).

35 See art. L. 314-1 *Code de la consommation.*

36 *Disposición adicional primera Ley* 41/2007.

As previously noticed, an important advantage of life care contracts over reverse mortgages and life annuities is that care obligations consist of the act (*facere*) of taking care of the older person by a specific caregiver chosen by the assisted person for his or her personal qualities and experience (often he or she is a friend or a family member). This suits the older person's personal and variable needs better than the duty to give a periodical amount of money, which is the compensation for the family home involved in both reverse mortgage and in life annuities.

From a civil law point of view, life care contracts and life annuities present, in my opinion, some important issues.

A first set of difficulties comes from the fact that in civil law countries life care contracts and life annuities are by law always aleatory, ie one of their distinguishing features is the uncertainty of the value of the care obligation because of the uncertainty of both the time of the death and the health of the assisted person. This feature could render void the agreements where the assisted person suffers from a terminal illness or is very old: indeed, according to Italian, Spanish and French case law, the contract is void for lack of *alea* when the risk is not mutual, for instance because the old age or the illness of the assisted person makes it certain that he or she will die within a predictable amount of time.[37] Moreover, the aleatory nature of life care contracts makes it impossible to terminate these contracts in the event of supervening unconscionability or hardship. It is, indeed, a principle deeply rooted in civil law countries that contracts which are aleatory by nature or by intention of the parties cannot be terminated on demand of the party for whom the performance has become excessively onerous because of an extraordinary and unforeseeable event (see art. 1469 *Codice civile*), for instance a severe supervening illness of the assisted person.

The growing importance of these difficulties rising from the aleatory nature of life care agreements arises from an interesting phenomenon occurring in all the civil law countries mentioned above, which causes many difficulties for the lawyers and notaries responsible for drafting these contracts. In open contrast with the tradition which considers life annuities and life care contracts aleatory, contracting parties are increasingly bypassing the uncertainty required by the law by seeking to establish a level of compensation which is fair for both parties. A significant example of this is that the amount of the life annuity to be paid is usually calculated through an algorithm that considers the value of the immovable property and the age and sex of the buyer (annuitant): this clearly demonstrates the decisive role of the annuitant's life expectancy in the quantification of the annuity. In addition, the increasing circulation of life annuities and life care agreements stipulated by very old and ill persons should be considered: in relation

[37] For Italy see *Corte di Cassazione*, judgement 9th April 1980, n.2283.

to these, Italian case law has been elaborating an *ad hoc* doctrine which considers a minimum contingency sufficient for the validity of the agreement, ie the near death of the assisted persons is not certain.[38] Furthermore, models of life care contracts, notwithstanding the formal statement of the aleatority nature of the agreement (to avoid a finding that it is void), contain clauses aimed to modify the condition of the contract equitably if the performance of one of the parties becomes excessively onerous. For example, it might allow the party for whom the obligation became too burdensome to ask for contract to be dissolved,[39] or specify that "if the assistance at home of the older person costs more than *n* euro, the caregiver has the choice to assist him or her at home or to put him or her in a care home, bearing the entire cost of that hospitality".[40] Consistent with this approach is the choice of the Catalan legislator to allow one contracting party to request that the contract be dissolved if the other party's behaviour makes cohabitation difficult, or to ask for modification of the contract if the assisted person marries or enters into a stable partnership.[41]

Lastly, life care contracts and life annuities could, in some civil law countries, infringe the rights of forced heirs and the legal prohibition of inheritance agreements.[42] This risk is particularly notable where the conveyor chooses to postpone *post mortem* the effects of the care arrangement, or where the life care agreement is simulated (for instance because the parties' true intent is to realise a gift of the family home and not a contract) or conceived partly as a gift because both parties are perfectly aware that the value of the assistance is much less then the value of the property conveyed.[43] According to Italian case law, the choice to postpone *post mortem* the effects of the contract does not infringe the prohibition of inheritance agreements.[44] It is however interesting to note that the French sociological analysis on life annuities cited above demonstrates that 50%

---

38 According to this doctrine, the minimum contingency (*alea*) necessary to consider the agreement valid exists even if the dependent person is so old and/or so ill that is likely he or she will die soon (see among many: *Tribunale di Cosenza*, 03rd April 2006, in *Foro italiano*, 2006, 10, 1, at 2937; *Cassazione civile*, 12th October 2005, n. 19673; *Tribunale di Verona*, 07th of June 2001, in *Giurisprudenza di merito*, 2002, p 1273; *Cassazione civile*, 24th August 1998, n. 8357).

39 According to some authors, the aside "unless otherwise agreed" included in art. 1879 par. 2 *Codice civile* should be interpreted as recognizing the contracting parties' right to introduce a clause which allows the dissolution of contracts in the event of supervening hardship, departing from the general principle that aleatory contracts cannot be dissolved in this way.

40 See for instance G. Petrelli, *Formulario notarile*, Giuffré, Milano, 2001.

41 Art. 5 parr. 1 and 3 *Ley 22/2000 de 29 de diciembre de acogida de personas mayores.*

42 In civil law systems, forced heirs are persons (usually spouses and children) whom the testator cannot deprive of the portion of his estate reserved for them by law. France, Italy, Spain, Portugal, Belgium and Luxemburg prohibit inheritance agreements, ie agreements under which a person makes arrangements for the time after their death.

43 It is interesting to note that art. 9.2 of the Spanish *Ley 22/2000 de acogimiento de personas mayores* allows forced heirs compensation if their inheritance rights are violated because of a disproportion between the value of the properties conveyed and the value of the assistance actually given.

44 *Corte di cassazione*, 11.11.1988, n.6083, in *Foro italiano*, 1989, I, at 1163.

of persons who convey their own home in exchange for a periodic payment have children and that, in 90% of these cases, the children agreed with their parent's decision because it prevented them from assuming direct financial responsibility for their senior parents in a phase of life which is often characterised by heavy economic burdens (usually to repay a mortgage loan and to raise their own children).[45]

3. CARE ARRANGEMENTS FOR OLDER PEOPLE AS A SINGLE GENUS

3.1. COMMON FEATURES

As previously explained, arrangements aimed at converting the family home into long term care are not the only type of "care agreements". Indeed, at times, the older person or his or her family buy temporary assistance services paying a periodic fee to the caregiver: in some cases, care is provided at home (eg contracts for home services with a home health aide or with a licensed home care agency); in others, in an institution, such as a retirement home, a care home or a "rest home". The analysis and comparison of the different types of arrangements used to provide elder care demonstrate the difficulty of treating "care agreements" as a single genus. Nonetheless, it is, in my opinion, possible to single out some common features.

First of all, care agreements are all aimed at pursuing a non-economic interest of one of the parties, ie the need of the dependent person to be cared for. The "care" provided can be either a payment (*dare*) or a set of clearly defined actions aimed at assisting the older person (*facere*), even, for instance, visiting the dependent person or phoning him or her on a daily basis. A notable example of the first group of arrangements is provided by the life annuities and reverse mortgages analysed above. To the second group, instead, belong life care agreements such as the French *bail à nourriture,* the Italian *vitalizio atipico,* and the Spanish *contrato de alimentos.*

Furthermore, care obligations are long-term: periodic in the case of obligations of *dare*; continuing in the case of obligations of *facere*. Indeed, the caregiver does not fulfil his or her obligation at a single moment, once and for all, but is obliged by the law to perform a number of tasks which may last anywhere from a couple of days to the remaining life span of the assisted person.

45 F. Drosso, 'Le viager, essai d'une définition', in *Revue de sociologie francaise*, 1993, p 223.

Lastly, care agreements are increasingly designed to establish a contractual relationship grounded in an equitable exchange (a fair trade) between the care services and the compensation paid by the assisted person or his or her family. Care contracts stipulated totally or partially as a gift (as in the case of the conveyance of an expensive home in exchange for care for an old and/or ill relative) are increasingly unusual. Besides, as has been previously demonstrated, even care contracts which are by law aleatory are nowadays in practice designed to preserve the reciprocity originally agreed between the contracting parties and intended to persist for the whole term of the contractual relationship.

3.2. GENERAL ISSUES

3.2.1. *The competence of the frail older people*

Although this topic has thus far been discussed mainly with regard to matters of patients' consent to medical treatments,[46] the assessment of the mental capacity (competence) of older people to enter into contracts is crucial. Different but equally important is the issue of whether a legally fully competent dependent person is ineligible to enter into care agreements because he or she cannot *de facto* afford to pay for care services. However, the present section will focus only on the legal notion of competence.

As is well known, contractual competence is excluded *ex ante* in the case of young people below the full age of eighteen (artt. 388 and 1124 *Code civil*; artt. 2 and 1425 *Codice civile*; artt. 315, 322 and 1263 *Código civil*) or of adults judicially declared incompetent (artt. 488 and 1124 *Code civil*; art. 404 ff. *Codice civile*; 1263 *Código civil*). A formal adjudication of incompetency usually deprives the older person of any contractual capacity, thus making any contract entered into void. At times, however, the person maintains competence for routine acts (eg artt.409, 427 *Codice civile*). The stipulation of care agreements, either conveying the property of the family home or agreeing on a periodic payment for care, appears to be outside these routine acts and therefore cannot be made by the dependent him or herself. It therefore requires, on some occasions, assistance for the older person and, on others, his substitution by a guardian. Sometimes, judicial authorisation is also needed. Contracts can be annulled regardless of

46 See P. S. Appelbaum, 'Assessment of Patients' Competence to Consent to Treatment', in 18 *The New England Journal of Medicine* 1834 (2007); M. B. Kapp, 'Informed, assisted, delegated consent for elderly patients', 52 *AORN (Association of Operative Registered Nurses) Journal* 857 (1990); A. Maclean, *Autonomy, informed consent and medical law: a relational challenge*, Cambridge University Press, New York, 2009; M. G. Rikkert, J. H. van den Bercken, H. A. ten Have, W. H. Hoefnagels, 'Experienced consent in geriatrics research: a new method to optimize the capacity to consent in frail elderly subjects', 23 *Journal of Medical Ethics* 271 (1997).

whether the other contracting party was aware of the incapacity at the time of the stipulation: indeed, the publicity ensured by the registration of the judgment declaring the person incompetent is deemed to be sufficient notice of the other party's legal status.

Courts can also exclude contractual competence *ex post*, annulling an agreement concluded by a person who was, at the time of entering into the contract, *de facto* incapable of understanding the nature, extent and scope of the transaction he was about to perform (see for Italy art. 428 *Codice civile*).[47] If a person has not been adjudicated legally incompetent there is usually a presumption of contractual competence and therefore the burden of proving lack of competence lies with the plaintiff claiming the judicial annulment (and often it is difficult for the plaintiff who is not legally incompetent but who *de facto* has significant barriers to understanding and consenting owing to his or her mental health to exercise his or her rights in court): if the presumption is rebutted, the contract entered into by the older person is voidable. It is self-evident that this interpretation places the greatest burden on the vulnerable party, often frustrating the intention to protect the weaker party. In order to avoid this, Canadian legislation and case law have moved towards a presumption of undue influence in relationships of dependence (particularly in the context of inter-generational family relationships). The law presumes that where one person benefits another in the context of these relationships, that gain is the result of undue influence. The presumption may be displaced where the one receiving a benefit is able to establish true consent on the part of the conferrer, *in primis* receiving competent and independent advice about the nature and effect of the transaction.[48] New Brunswick grants the court a power to set aside or vary private care agreements which "convey" or "transfer" a "property" in exchange for "maintenance" and "support".[49] As a rule, annulment is possible only if the other contracting party was aware of the mental status of their counterpart and took advantage of it. Artt. 428 and 1425 *Codice civile*, for

[47] In an Italian case, the plaintiff asked for the annulment of a life care contract entered into by his deceased mother claiming the latter was *de facto* incapable of understanding the implications of the contract (Trib. Cosenza, 3rd April 2006, in *Foro italiano*, 2006, 2937). On the assessment of contractual competence of the elderly see generally G. Ashton, *Elderly People and the Law*, Butterworths, London, 1996, p 6 ff. and 22 ff.

[48] M. I. Hall, 'Equitable Fraud: Material Exploitation in Domestic Settings', 4 *Elder Law Review* (2005); the author emphasises that the presumption of undue influence does not obviously arise if the older person is the dominant figure in the relationship by reason of personality and inter-personal dynamics.

[49] "The Court may, on such terms as appear just, set aside or vary at the instance of an interested party any conveyance or transfer of property, the consideration for which, in whole or in part, whether expressed in the instrument of conveyance or in a collateral agreement, is the maintenance and support of any person; but nothing done hereunder affects the title of a bona fide purchaser for value." (Section 24, Judicature Act, R.S.N.B. 1973, c.J-2). See British Columbia Law Institute, *Private Care Agreements Between Older Adults and Friends or Family Members*, BCLI Report No. 18, March 2002, in http://papers.ssrn.com/sol3/papers.cfm?abstract_id=1424151).

instance, state that a contract made by a person incapable of understanding or evaluating the consequences of his or her actions is voidable if the counterpart was aware of the mental status of the other and took advantage of it. In common law countries, courts have elaborated the doctrine of "equitable fraud", annulling agreements deemed inequitable because one contracting party exercised an excessively powerful influence ("undue influence") over the other or benefited from the deliberate exploitation of a power imbalance ("unconscionability").[50] The policy underlying this solution is to balance the general interest in protecting vulnerable persons (predominant in the traditional paternalistic view) with the right of older adults to make their own mistakes.

In all countries, the assessment of contractual competence, both in general (ie *ex ante* for every legal act) and by reference to a single agreement (ie *ex post*), is a matter for the courts. In Italy, for instance, it lies within the competence of the *Tribunali ordinari*. Notwithstanding this, in order to avoid judicial disputes, it is strongly advisable for lawyers and notaries to pay special attention to contractual competence when working with older clients.[51]

If the contracting party is legally incapable of entering into contracts, the care agreement can be stipulated in his or her name and interest by a legal representative. The legal representative may be appointed by the court or appointed directly by the assisted person before he or she becomes incapable.[52] In the case of persons *de facto* incompetent, care arrangements are usually made by family members: the senior acquires the rights deriving from the contract directly against the promisor as a result of the stipulation in favour of him or her (art. 1411 par. 2 *Codice civile*). However, owing to his or her mental condition and to the lack of a legal representative, the person will not be able, in practice, to exercise these rights. The self determination principle and the right to human dignity in general tend to place limits on substitution of the assisted person by either his or her legal representative or family members.

An assessment of contractual competence is obviously crucial in the case of institutionalisation of the elderly in retirement or care homes.[53] If the older person

50 See B. Atkin, 'The Elderly, The Law and Accommodation Arrangements: Some Reflections From New Zealand', (2003) 2 *Elder Law Review* 33; M. I. Hall, 'Equitable Fraud: Material Exploitation in Domestic Settings', 4 *Elder Law Review* (2005).

51 An interesting analysis of lawyers' techniques was performed in Australia: see E. Helmes, V. E. Lewis and A. Allan, 'Australian Lawyers' Views on Competency Issues in Older Adults', in 22 *Behavioral Sciences and the Law* 823 (2004).

52 On the differences between welfare guardian, property manager and attorney (under an enduring power of attorney) see B. Atkin, 'The Elderly, The Law and Accommodation Arrangements: Some Reflections From New Zealand', (2003) 2 *Elder Law Review* 33.

53 Cfr. J. A. Martín Pérez, 'El internamiento o ingreso de personas mayores en centros geriátricos', in M. A. Pérez, E. M. Martínez Gallego and J. Reguero Celada (eds), *Protección jurídica de los mayores*, La Ley, Madrid, 2004 p 167.

is legally incapable, the contract can be stipulated by the legal representative. General opinion favours the need for judicial scrutiny of the legal representative's decision and, moreover, for the involvement of the older person, even if not legally competent, in the decision-making process. Article 271 n. 1 *Código civil* states the need for judicial authorization for the institutionalisation of the assisted person (either a child or an adult judicially declared incompetent). In addition, the Catalan *ley 22/2000 de acogimiento de personas mayors* expressly affirms that, in the event of incapacity of the assisted person, the contract can be stipulated by his or her legal representative after judicial authorization, which can be granted only after the dependent person, capable of sufficient understanding, has been heard (art. 3). The Italian framework is quite complex: guardians can institutionalise children without any need for judicial scrutiny (art. 371 only requires that a child aged over ten is heard); vulnerable adults who are beneficiaries of an *amministrazione di sostegno* (administration of support) can be institutionalised by their guardian (*amministratore)* only if the judicial decree of appointment of the guardian so states, or if the guardian has been authorized by the court;[54] in the case of the *interdizione* (limited to adult persons of unsound mind *ex* art. 414 ff. *Codice civile*) the law requires judicial scrutiny only of patrimonial acts of major importance, leaving, therefore, all personal acts for which representation is possible to the guardian (exceptions to this include, for instance, marriage and the writing of a will).

If the older person is legally capable, he or she cannot be institutionalised against his or her own will.[55] Spanish case law, ruled that if the person stays silent, institutionalisation through a contract signed by third parties (eg family members), is possible and effective.[56] However, the decision to institutionalise a senior in a retirement or care home whose features could limit the personal freedom of the dependent person (for instance, through physical barriers which prevent free entrance and exit) requires judicial scrutiny, either if the person, although legally incompetent, is capable of sufficient understanding and openly states his or her refusal, or if he or she is legally capable but *de facto* incompetent.[57] Besides, judicial scrutiny is required in cases where the assisted person initially consented to institutionalisation but then lost the legal capacity, or anyhow changed his or

[54] The *amministrazione di sostegno* was introduced in the Italian legal system by Act 6/2004 with the aim "to protect, with the minimum possible limitation of the capacity to act, people who are wholly or partially deprived of autonomy in performing the functions of everyday life through interventions of temporary or permanent support" (art. 1).

[55] Legal systems permit institutionalisation only in the case of mental illnesses and with due guarantees, usually a judicial scrutiny: see for instance in Italy artt. 33 ff. Act 833/1978.

[56] See J. A. Martín Pérez, 'El internamiento o ingreso de personas mayores en centros geriátricos', in M. A. Pérez, E. M. Martínez Gallego and J. Reguero Celada (eds), *Protección jurídica de los mayores*, La Ley, Madrid, 2004, p 167 ff.

[57] J. A. Martín Pérez, 'El internamiento o ingreso de personas mayores en centros geriátricos', in M. A. Pérez, E. M. Martínez Gallego and J. Reguero Celada (eds), *Protección jurídica de los mayores*, La Ley, Madrid, 2004, p 180 ff.

her mind and rejected it.[58] Courts would authorize institutionalisation against the older person's will only if the person was not deemed capable of understanding the consequences of the lack of institutionalisation; if he or she is *de facto* capable, refusal should be respected.[59] The abovementioned principles were derived by Spanish case law from a broad interpretation of the legal disposition requiring judicial authorization for the institutionalisation of adults of unsound mind.[60]

3.2.2. The relationship with care obligations established by the law

The stipulation of a care agreement with a caregiver already bound by the law to provide support may, on some occasions, result in the voidness of the agreement itself.

Courts sometimes consider to be void care contracts concluded between spouses who are already bound by law to support each other.[61] This thesis is deeply rooted in the idea that marriage is grounded on gift and therefore incompatible with market logic, which is a distinguishing feature of contracts.[62] Hence, care arrangements between spouses duplicate the legal obligation of support (see art. 143 f. *Codice civile*), which already includes the right to be morally and financially assisted in order to maintain the level of material comfort, in terms of goods and services, available to the other spouse. On the other hand, care agreements between parents and an adult son or daughter or members of the extended family are generally considered valid because between these people the measure of support is by law restricted to what is "necessary for the life of the person supported, having regard to his social position" (art. 428 par. 2 *Codice civile*).[63]

---

[58] J. A. Martín Pérez, 'El internamiento o ingreso de personas mayores en centros geriátricos', in M. A. Pérez, E. M. Martínez Gallego and J. Reguero Celada (eds), *Protección jurídica de los mayores*, La Ley, Madrid, 2004, in part. p 177 ff. On the former system, see R. M. de Couto Gálvez, '*¿Se cumplen las normas jurídicas que regulan el internamiento de una persona mayor en un centro?*', in S. Adroher Biosca (ed), *Mayores y familia*, Universidad Pontificia Comillas de Madrid, 2000, p 191 ff.

[59] J. A. Martín Pérez, 'El internamiento o ingreso de personas mayores en centros geriátricos', in M. A. Pérez, E. M. Martínez Gallego and J. Reguero Celada (eds), *Protección jurídica de los mayores*, La Ley, Madrid, 2004, p 189.

[60] Art. 763 *Ley de Enjuiciamento civil* (*Ley* 1/2000). The provision is similar to artt. 33 ff. Italian Act 833/1978.

[61] Trib. Cagliari 9th April 1993, in *Rivista di giurisprudenza sarda*, 1994, p 583. American case law expresses itself in similar terms (see the numerous judgements cited by T. Bateman Farrell, *Husband and Wife*, in 41 *Am. Jur.* 2d *Husband and Wife* 118).

[62] For the same reason, both criminal and civil actions and gifts between spouses were traditionally prohibited.

[63] For some examples provided by Italian case law see *Cassazione civile* 9th April 1980, n. 2283, in *Rivista del notariato*, 1980, p 1261; Trib. Cagliari, 13th October 1997, in *Rivista di giurisprudenza sarda*, 1999, p 127.

Furthermore, according to various Italian authors, the State's duty to care for needy older people, and, more generally, for all people whose fundamental human rights and especially human dignity are at risk, should lead to the annulment of contracts stipulated between a dependent person or his or her family and the public institution providing care, for instance a public retirement home. Annulment of the contract arises because of the contract having an unlawful object (for the reason that the obligation is already imposed by the law)[64] or an essential mistake regarding the object of the obligation[65] or even duress or threat if, as sometimes happens, family members are forced to guarantee payments as a condition to a resident's admission to a nursing facility. So far, though, Italian case law has rejected this thesis.[66] The existence of a State's duty to care for needy people has however been used by various authors to criticize the vast majority of case law which grants municipalities (which have financial responsibility for social services) repayments from family members bound by law (and not by contract) to support each other for care fees, such as hospitality in a public retirement home or in a nursing facility.[67]

4. CONCLUSION

The previous sections of this study allow us now to challenge some myths about caring by contract.

First of all, it should be emphasized that "care arrangements for older people" *are not* something new, but have long been a common practice. During the Middle Ages it was quite common for ecclesiastical institutions and later on for cities and governments, to finance themselves through the selling of life annuities. Moreover, rich people used to donate their land and properties to the Church in exchange for care, albeit originally mainly limited to prayers in favour of the donor after his or her death (see above para.2). An old literary example of life

---

64 Such is the thesis of G. Ferrando, 'v. Alimenti. Aggiornamento', in *Digesto discipline privatistiche*, Utet, Torino, 2003 and of M. Dogliotti, *Doveri familiari e obbligazioni familiari*, cit., 214). The same interpretation is strongly supported by consumers' organisations, for instance ADUC (Association for the defence of users' and consumers' rights): <www.aduc.it>.

65 An author suggests that contracts should be considered void because families and dependent persons often do not know the State is already bounded by the law to provide assistance to dependent people: P. Rescigno, 'L'assistenza agli anziani non autosufficienti: notazioni civilistiche', in *Giurisprudenza italiana*, 1993, I, 2, at 690.

66 Trib. Torino 12 August 1994, in *Giustizia civile*, 1995, p 3145.

67 See M. Dogliotti, 'Ancora sul pagamento delle rette di ricovero a carico dei parenti: "errare humanum est, perseverare diabolicum', in *Prospettive assistenziali*, 2002, n.138; Idem, 'Esiste un diritto alla salute degli anziani non autosufficienti?', in *Giustizia civile*, 1995, p 3149; A. Figone, 'Diritto degli anziani non autosufficienti e pagamento delle rette di ricovero', in *Famiglia e diritto*, 2000, p 49; A. Ansaldo, 'Anziani non autosufficienti: obbligo alimentare e pagamento della retta degli istituti di assistenza', in *Famiglia e diritto*, 1997, p 56.

annuity can be found in Maupassant's "The Little Cask" where mother Magloire, a "woman of about seventy-two, very thin, shrivelled and wrinkled, almost dried up in fact and much bent but as active and untiring as a girl", signed a deed transferring her farmhouse over to a smart innkeeper in exchange for a life annuity; after some months, the man succeeded in driving her to death by turning her into an alcoholic.[68] Although their importance decreased with the advent of the welfare state, care arrangements for the elderly have continued to survive in areas not covered by state provision. At times this has been for political reasons,[69] or as a result of limited resources and deficiencies in the public welfare system. The introduction of the so-called welfare mix model, in which social services are supplied both by the municipalities themselves and by the private sector, has further stimulated the development of private care arrangements.

Moreover, the existence of a care arrangement *does not* necessarily imply that the caregiver is an economic operator who offers care services on the market. The vast majority of contracts transferring the family home to a caregiver in exchange for a promise of life time care (above para.2) are stipulated between the older person and family members or friends. Besides, non-profit organisations are usually compensated either by the assisted person or by the State (paying personnel or awarding vouchers, home care allowances, etc), but retain these earnings to help pursue their own goals and not to enrich shareholders.

Finally , the contractualisation of elder care *does not* mean that the State is giving up its duty to provide welfare support to needy people. Indeed, the wide and increasing diffusion of care arrangements must be contextualized within the principle of "horizontal subsidiarity", ie the allocation and exercise of competences preferably on private individuals or entities, with public bodies intervening only if and insofar as the objectives or the action cannot be sufficiently achieved by the private sector.[70] This principle, presently enshrined in many European laws, has

68 G. de Maupassant, *The Little Cask*, 1884 (trans. by Albert M.C. McMaster, A.E. Henderson, Mme. Quesada, & others, in <http://classiclit.about.com/library/bl-etexts/gdemaupassant/bl-gdemaup-littlecask.htm>).

69 I think, for example, of the diversity of national approaches in the area of social assistance to needy persons whose families are wealthy.

70 The general idea is that the public sector should not attempt to do anything that the private sector can do as well. On the principle of "horizontal subsidiarity" in Italy see A. Colombo, 'The 'Lombardy Model': Subsidiarity-informed Regional Governance', in *Social Policy & Administration*, vol. 42, n.2 (April 2008) p 177 ff.; Y. Kazepov, M. Arlotti, E. Barberis, B. da Roit, S. Sabatinelli, *Rescaling Social Welfare Policies in Italy*, Urbino, 2006, in www.euro.centre.org/rescalingDocuments/files/Italy.pdf.. In Italian see L. Antonini, 'Il principio della sussidiarietà orizzontale: dal welfare state al welfare society', in *Rivista di diritto finanziario*, 2000, p 99; R. Barbanera, 'La riforma dei servizi sociali in Italia: il ruolo del terzo settore', in *Contratto e Impresa*, 2008, n. 1, p 243; A. D'Atena, 'Costituzione e principio di sussidiarietà', in *Quaderni costituzionali*, 2001, p 19; ID., 'Il principio di sussidiarietà nella costituzione italiana', *in Riv. it. dir. pubbl. comp., 1997, 603; P.* Duret, 'La sussidiarietà "orizzontale": le radici e le suggestioni di un concetto', in *Jus*, 2000, p 95; S. Staiano, 'La sussidiarietà orizzontale: profili

frequently been used to justify the reduction of social services to the "neediest of the needy", to allow State bodies to sue the dependent person's family for reimbursement of care costs and to support the thesis of the voidness of contracts concluded with a caregiver (a family member, but – according to some Italian authors – even the State) already obliged by the law to provide care (see above para. 3.2.2). Still, a correct interpretation of the principle of horizontal subsidiarity imposes on States a duty to support and reinforce informal caregiving for older persons through both economic assistance and focused service support. Only if and when both public and private bodies, as well as the society itself, embrace this idea shall an equitable and affordable balance between social solidarity and private responsibility be possible.

---

teorici', in *federalismi.it*, 2006, n.5. On the relationship between social and private solidarity see among many others J. Ribot Igualada, *Alimentos entre parientes y subsidiariedad de la protección social*, Tirant Lo Blanch, Valencia, 1999.

PART FIVE

FREEDOM OF TESTATION AND PROTECTION OF FAMILY MEMBERS

BALANCING INTERESTS – HOW MUCH FREEDOM OF TESTATION?

John Asland

1. INTRODUCTION

In my view, the main purpose of succession law legislation is to strike a reasonable balance between the interests of (1) the surviving spouse (or cohabitant), (2) the interests of other family members and (3) the deceased's own preferences for the distribution of his property. The question of how to perform this balancing act has been answered in widely diverse ways throughout history and in different jurisdictions.[1] The purpose of this paper is to identify different ways of balancing these, often conflicting, interests. Within the rules of inheritance law, there are several concepts of legal protection of the surviving spouse or other surviving relatives. I will focus on four main concepts of legal protection within the law of succession and show how – and to what extent – these concepts are applied in Norwegian law.

There are of course alternatives that do not imply any balancing of interests. One unbalanced solution is to provide the lineal descendants with a legitimate portion or indefeasible share of the entire estate.[2] Another solution, unbalanced in favour of the surviving spouse, is to provide her with a legitimate portion which amounts to the entire estate.[3] A third alternative is to provide the deceased with unlimited freedom of testation.[4] My focus is to identify different ways of *balancing* the interests. Therefore, I will not pay much attention to unbalanced solutions.

---

1 See some illustrating examples in C. Castelein, R. Foque and A. Verbeke (eds.) *Imperative Inheritance Law in a Late Modern Society*, Intersentia, Antwerp – Oxford – Portland, 2009 and in A. Röthel (Hrsg.) *Reformfragen des Pflichtteilsrechts*, Carl Heymanns Verlag, Köln – Berlin – München, 2007.

2 The aim of law of succession in old Germanic law (including Norwegian law) before this law was influenced by canon law, was to protect the family and to make sure that the family property remained within the family. Thus, no freedom of testation was granted. Illustrating for this way of thinking is the old saying: "Gott, nicht der Mensch, macht den Erben". The concept of wills or *donationes mortis causae*, was unknown in Norwegian law until medieval time. It was introduced in Norway by the Catholic Church in 1152 when cardinal Nicolaus Breakspeare visited Norway. The extent of the freedom of testation became a controversy between the church and the king until the Lutheran reformation in 1536. See Utkast til lov om arv [The Inheritance Act Commission], Oslo 1962 p. 11–14; O. Platou, *Norsk Arveret*, 2. Udgave, A.W. Brøggers Bogtrykkeri, Christiania, 1910 and C. J. Arnholm, *Arveretten*, Johan Grundt Tanum forlag, Oslo 1974 p. 44–50.

3 There are also other – dramatic – ways of solving the problem of the surviving spouse. The religious funeral practice among some Hindu communities, Sati (widow burning), of course makes the distribution of the property among the relatives easier – one does not have to take into account the needs of the widow. However, there are some obviously worrying aspects of this tradition (it has been outlawed in India since 1829). Another solution is levirate marriage, a type of marriage in which the brother of a deceased man is obliged to marry his brother's widow, and the widow is obliged to marry her deceased husband's brother. Levirate marriage has been practiced by societies with a strong clan structure where it is of utmost importance to keep family fortune within the family. It is or was known in many societies around the world. The term is a derivate of the Latin word *levir*, meaning "husband's brother". Like widow burning, levirate marriages obviously raise some human rights issues.

4 Freedom of testation was an important part of Roman law of succession. However, the concept of reserving a part of the decedent's estate for the children or other close relatives – the *portio*

When discussing inheritance rights, especially the inheritance rights of the surviving spouse,[5] one should bear in mind that community property is the default family property regime in many civil law jurisdictions. Thus inheritance and legitimate portion[6] is a question of how much the widow or widower is entitled to of the deceased's assets in *addition to* his or her share of the community property. Upon one spouse's death, community property is usually split into halves. One half constitutes the survivor's share in the community property and thus belongs to him, whereas the estate of the predeceasing spouse consists of the other half of the community property, along with such assets as the predeceasing spouse may have owned in his own right (as separate assets). To some extent the surviving spouse receives double protection.[7]

Firstly, the surviving spouse, cohabitant, or other relatives or dependants may be given a right to inherit the whole or part of the assets of the deceased spouse, with the free right to dispose of the assets *inter vivos* and by will. As long as the deceased has not made a valid will, these rules of distribution are applicable – they constitute the default legal regulations. If there are other persons with a legitimate interest in inheriting some of the deceased's assets, the spouse's share of the assets is often limited to some extent; for example, in Norway, the spouse is entitled to one-quarter of the inheritance when the deceased has lineal descendants. If the deceased's closest heirs are his parents or first line collaterals (brothers and sisters, nephews and nieces), the spouse is entitled to one-half of the inheritance. If the deceased's closest blood relations are further removed, the spouse takes the entire inheritance.[8]

A second way of securing the surviving spouse, or other relatives or dependants, is to grant him or her a right to keep assets of a fixed value either in money or in chattels or real estate. This inheritance right may be a qualification of the

---

legitima – is also of Roman origin. See R. Zimmermann, 'Die Erbfolge gegen das Testament im Römischen Recht', in A. Röthel (Hrsg.) *Reformfragen des Pflichtteilsrechts*, Carl Heymanns Verlag, Köln – Berlin – München, 2007 p. 97–119. Freedom of testation is also a basic principle in Anglo-American law. However, there are mechanisms – at least in English and Welsh law – that secures the surviving spouse and other dependants of the deceased.

5 The terms 'marriage' and 'spouse' apply to same-sex couples as well where/when they are married, which is possible in several jurisdictions today (including Norway). The Norwegian Marriage Act was amended by a new law dated 27 June 2008, giving same-sex couples the opportunity to marry. The new law became effective as of 1 January 2009.

6 Legitimate portion or forced share is in Civil law the part of a testator's property that his or her children (and occasionally other heirs) are legally entitled to regardless of the will's terms.

7 C. Castelein, 'Introduction and objectives' in C. Castelein, R. Foqué and A. Verbeke (eds.) *Imperative Inheritance Law in a Late Modern Society*, Intersentia, Antwerp – Oxford – Portland, 2009 p. 12. For an overview of American law and the somewhat different American approach, see J.T. Oldham, 'You Can't Take It with You, and Maybe You Can' Even Give It Away: The Case of Elizabeth Baldwin Rice', (2010) *University of Memphis Law Review* with further references.

8 Inheritance Act s. 6.

concept mentioned above – especially if it is protected against dispositions in the deceased's will – so called forced or legitimate portion (or share). This share or sum can either be in the form of a supplement to the beneficiary's own assets, so that his or her own assets are subtracted when the share is calculated, which is the situation in Denmark and Sweden, or a claim towards the deceased's estate, which is the situation in Norway and in England and Wales.[9] To what extent life assurance policies and pensions are taken into account when calculating the claim varies. With a regulation such as is in force in the Scandinavian countries and in the United States through the Uniform Probate Code, the spouse may very well inherit the entire estate of the deceased.[10] However, the other heirs of the deceased may have secondary heirship to the assets after the death of the surviving spouse. This is the situation in Denmark and Sweden. This protection is in many countries of an imperative nature and may not be taken away by will. In the Scandinavian countries the surviving spouse's right to inherit a certain sum or certain assets is a right that applies not only in intestate situations but also where the deceased spouse has made a will. These rights cannot be restricted or taken away from the surviving spouse by will.[11] In England and Wales, however, such rules only apply to intestate situations. If the deceased spouse leaves a will,

---

9 In England, a surviving spouse or civil partner takes, if the deceased is survived by descendants, everything where the net estate is not more than £250,000.Where the net estate is over £250,000, the surviving spouse or civil partner takes the first £250,000 plus personal possessions. Half of the rest is shared equally amongst the children. The spouse or civil partner gets the income or interest on the other half during his or her lifetime, and when the spouse or civil partner dies, the capital goes to the deceased's children equally.
Where the deceased leaves a spouse or civil partner (but no children), and either parents, or brothers or sisters of the whole blood, everything goes to the surviving spouse or civil partner where the net estate is not more than £450,000. Where the net estate is over £450,000, the first £450,000 plus personal possessions plus half of the balance over and above £450,000 goes to the surviving spouse or civil partner. The other half of the balance over and above £450,000 goes to the deceased's parents equally; but if there are no parents, it will go to brothers and sisters of the whole blood and to any children or other issue of brothers and sisters of the whole blood who have predeceased the deceased in equal shares. The sums were increased to the present level from 1 February 2009 based on the Ministry of Justice's consultation paper: Administration of estates – review of the statutory legacy (CP 11/05) published in 2005. See: http://webarchive.nationalarchives.gov.uk/+/http://www.justice.gov.uk/publications/cp1105.htm. For further reading, see also the Law Commission, Consultation paper No 191, 'Intestacy and family provision claims on death': www.lawcom.gov.uk/intestacy.htm.

10 In the Uniform Probate Code of the United States, section 2–102, the intestate share of a surviving spouse who was married to the deceased for at least 15 years is: (1) The entire intestate estate if there is no surviving issue or parent of the decedent; (2) $200,000 and three-quarters of the remaining estate if there is no surviving issue but the decedent is survived by a parent or parents; (3) $150,000 and one-half of the remaining estate if there are surviving issue all of whom are also issue of the spouse and the spouse has issue from a prior marriage; (4) $100,000 and one-half of the remaining estate if there are surviving issue, one or more of whom are not issue of the surviving spouse. In cases where the surviving spouse was married to the decedent for less than 15 years, the spouse receives less than half of the remaining estate, the amount increasing by approximately 3.25 percent for every year of marriage under 15. (For states with community-property laws, an alternative provision for the intestate rights of the surviving spouse exists.)

11 See P. Lødrup, *Nordisk arverett*, Nordisk Ministerråd, København 2002 p. 138.

the surviving spouse will be dependant on the protection given in the Inheritance (Provision for Family and Dependants) Act 1975.[12]

Thirdly, the acquisition of the assets or a part of the assets by the legal heirs may be postponed for a period of time during which the spouse, cohabitant or other relative or dependant is in possession of the assets as owner. The possessor may be the primary heir, whereas the other relatives are secondary heirs who come into possession of the assets after the death of the possessor (the surviving spouse). This is a possibility in the Scandinavian countries: Denmark, Finland, Iceland, Norway and Sweden.[13] To secure the heirs a fair share of the assets after the death of the surviving spouse or other possessor, there may be limitations on the possessor's disposal of the assets. Such limitations are stated in the regulations of Denmark, Iceland and Norway regarding '*uskifte*'.[14]

Another possibility that in practice does not necessarily differ very much from the above method, is that the heirs become owners of the deceased's estate directly after the death of the deceased spouse, but that the surviving spouse, cohabitant, relative or other dependant acquires a right of use or a *usufruct* to the entire assets or a part of the assets. This is a common way of securing the surviving spouse in Central-European and Mediterranean countries. In France and Belgium, the surviving spouse has the right to a life-interest or a right of usufruct over the entire estate.[15] Finnish law also grants the surviving spouse a usufruct.[16] The surviving spouse has a right of use to the common residence (and household goods) or another residence within the estate suitable for the surviving

---

12 See below.

13 A comparative study is P. Lødrup, *Nordisk arverett*, Nordisk Ministerråd, København 2002 p. 157–209. For Norway, see also, J. Asland, *Uskifte*, Gyldendal akademisk, Oslo, 2008 and P. Hambro, *Arveplanlegging og avtalt uskifte*, Universitetsforlaget, Oslo, 2006. For Denmark, see I. Nørgaard, *Arveret*, 5. udgave, Jurist- og Økonomforbundets Forlag, København 2008 p. 81–118. For Sweden, see M. Brattström and A. Singer, *Rätt arv*, 3:a upplagan, Iustus förlag, Uppsala, 2011 p. 58–84 and 124–146. For Finland, see U. Kangas, *Introduktion till familjeförmögenhetsrätten*, Helsinki, Publikationer från juridiska fakulteten vid Helsingfors universitet, Helsinki, 2004 p. 114–116 and 140–145. For Iceland, see Ármann Snævarr, *Erfdarettur*, Námssjóþur Lögmannaflags, Reykjavík 1991.

14 More in detail about '*uskifte*', see 2.4. infra.

15 H. Casman, 'Comparative Law – Belgium' in C. Castelein, R. Foqué and A. Verbeke (eds.) *Imperative Inheritance Law in a Late Modern Society*, Antwerp – Oxford – Portland, Intersentia, 2009 p.156; S. Ferré-André, A. Gouttenoire-Cornut and H. Fulchiron, 'Work in Hand for the Reform of French Family Law' in A. Bainham (ed.) *The International Survey of Family Law 2003 Edition*, Bristol, Family Law, 2003 p. 163–174 and F. Ferrand, 'Comparative Law – France. Réserve héréditaire, ordre public et autonomie de la volonté en droit français des successions' in C. Castelein, R. Foqué and A. Verbeke (eds.) *Imperative Inheritance Law in a Late Modern Society*, Antwerp – Oxford – Portland, Intersentia, 2009 p. 189–202.

16 See the Finnish Inheritance Act [Ärvdabalk 5 February 1965 No. 40] chapter 3 section 1 a. See also M. Savolainen, 'Efterlevande makes rätt till bostad I', *Tidskrift utgiven av juridiska föreningen Finland*, 1989 p. 254–278; M. Savolainen, 'Efterlevande makes rätt till bostad II', *Tidskrift utgiven av juridiska föreningen Finland*, 1989 p. 349–366 and U. Kangas,

spouse. This usufruct has priority over the inheritance right of the deceased's children and beneficiaries in the deceased's will. The heirs or beneficiaries will have to wait until the death of the surviving spouse to make use of this part of their inheritance. The usufruct does not apply if the surviving spouse owns a suitable residence in his or her own capacity. One may say that the Finnish usufruct is needs-based.[17]

A variation of this concept of usufruct is to provide the heirs with a pecuniary claim against the surviving spouse, stipulated to his or her share of the estate, that will be payable after the death of the surviving spouse or on other occasions that bring the claim into force. This is the solution chosen in the Dutch Civil Code.[18] The postponement of the payment of the heirs' shares may be combined with a right to use the assets, eg real property, until the payment is due. Again, this is the situation in Dutch law. The distribution of property may be postponed until the children of the deceased have reached their majority or other occurrences set down by law where the heirs may claim distribution.

Fourthly, an independent third party, for instance the court, decides in each case how the assets shall be distributed among the heirs according to their needs. One can imagine a totally free discretion, or some more or less strict guidelines within such a system. English and Welsh law of succession has substantive elements of discretionary distribution by the court. The Inheritance (Provision for Family and Dependants) Act 1975 provides a surviving spouse, former spouses of the deceased who have not remarried, children and stepchildren of the deceased and other dependants of the deceased (eg cohabitants), with financial provisions from the deceased's estate. These dependants may apply to the court for an order under section 2 of this Act on the ground that the disposition of the deceased's estate effected by his will or the law relating to intestacy, or the combination of his will and the law, are not such as to make reasonable financial provision for the

Introduktion till familjeförmögenhetsrätten, Helsinki, Publikationer från juridiska fakulteten vid Helsingfors universitet, Helsinki 2004 p. 140–145.

17 About needs-based remedies, see J. Miles, 'Financial Relief between Cohabitants on Separation: Options for European Jurisdictions' in K. Boele-Woelki and T. Sverdrup (eds.) *European Challenges in Contemporary Family Law*, Intersentia, Antwerp – Oxford – Portland, 2008 p.269–287 on p. 285–286.

18 For further reading see M.J.A. van Mourik, 'Comparative Law – the Netherlands' in C. Castelein, R. Foqué and A. Verbeke (eds.) *Imperative Inheritance Law in a Late Modern Society*, Antwerp – Oxford – Portland, Intersentia, 2009 p. 107–122; A. J. M. Nuytinck, A short introduction to the new Dutch succession law, Rotterdam/Nijmegen, 2002 and I. Sumner and H. Warendorf, *Inheritance Legislation of the Netherlands – A Translation of Book 4 of the Dutch Civil Code, procedural provisions and private international law legislation*,Intersentia, Atwerp – Oxford, 2005.

applicant. The court may order periodical payments, a lump sum and the transfer of property from the estate.[19]

2. BALANCING OF INTERESTS UNDER NORWEGIAN INHERITANCE LAW

2.1. INTRODUCTION

Norwegian law has elements of all these concepts. The rights of the surviving spouse have gradually been improved over the last 150 years.[20] The protection of the surviving spouse is comparatively strong in contemporary Norwegian inheritance law.[21] An important development in recent Norwegian inheritance law was the introduction of inheritance rights for certain cohabitants in 2008.[22] Before I turn to the different concepts of protection in Norwegian law, I will give some introductionary comments to the amendments relating to cohabitants and identify to which cohabitants these new regulations apply.

2.2. INHERITANCE RIGHTS FOR COHABITANTS

The introduction of a right to inherit by law and '*uskifte*' (a right to keep whole or parts of the decedent's estate undivided)[23] for cohabitants in 2008 was a remarkable progress in the protection and recognition of cohabitants in Norwegian law.[24] Until this law, cohabitants have neither had the legal right to inherit or keep the estate in '*uskifte*'. Cohabitants have of course had the possibility to make each other beneficiaries in their wills, but if the cohabitants have children – either together or from a previous relationship – the children's legitimate portion has been an onerous limitation on the freedom of testation. Even though the surviving

19 See P. Matthews, 'Comparative Law – United Kingdom' in C. Castelein, R. Foqué and A. Verbeke (eds.) *Imperative Inheritance Law in a Late Modern Society*, Antwerp – Oxford – Portland, Intersentia, 2009 p. 137–150.

20 Historical overviews are given in Utkast til lov om arv [The Inheritance Act Commission], Oslo 1962 p. 14–24 and J. Asland, *Uskifte*, Gyldendal Akademisk, Oslo, 2008 p. 26–56.

21 A Comparative analysis of the situation for the surviving spouse in the Nordic countries is given in P. Lødrup, *Nordisk arverett*, Nordisk Ministerråd, København 2002 p. 122–256.

22 See 2.6 infra.

23 For the detail, see below in 2.5.

24 These changes were enacted by a law dated 19 December 2008. Most of the changes are contained in a new chapter III A (§§ 28 a–28 g) in the Inheritance Act. The new law became effective as of 1 July 2009. A brief introduction of the new legislation is given by J. Asland and P. Hambro, 'New Developments and Expansion of Relationships Covered by Norwegian Law' in B: Atkin (ed.) *The International Survey of Family Law 2009 Edition*, Family Law, Bristol, 2009 p. 375–384. For further reading, see T. Eeg, '*Samboeres arve- og uskifterettslige stilling*', Tidsskrift for familierett, arverett og barnevernrettslige spørsmål, 2009 p. 25–58 and T. Frantzen, '*Rett til arv og uskifte for samboere*', Lov og Rett, 2009 p. 387–405.

cohabitants' rights are limited compared to those of the surviving spouses, both concerning the size of the intestate share and the extent of the 'uskifte',[25] the new legislation is a quite progressive regulation of the inheritance rights of surviving cohabitants.

Inheritance rights for cohabitants have been – and still are – widely discussed in jurisdictions around the world.[26] Some jurisdictions have had inheritance rights for cohabitants for many years. The old doctrine of common law marriage still applies in eleven American states. This doctrine offers cohabitants the same legal protection as married couples are entitled to, provided that they are living together in a relationship that fulfils the criteria of a common law marriage.[27] In Slovenia and Kosovo, inheritance rights for surviving cohabitants were introduced as early as the 1970s.[28] New Zealand and the Australian states and territories introduced inheritance rights for cohabitants ('de facto relationships' or 'domestic partners') from the 1980s onwards.[29] Instead of developing an alternative set of rules for cohabitants' inheritance – like in Norway – the approach both in the doctrine

---

25 For the details see 2.4 and 2.5 below.

26 However, proposals or bills introducing such rights are often turned down by the legislators. In the recent years this has happened eg in Denmark and in Italy. For Denmark, see I. Nørgaard, *Arveret*, 5. udgave, Jurist- og Økonomforbundets Forlag, København 2008 p. 243. For Italy, see E. Urso, '*De Facto* Families and the Law: Dealing with Rules and Freedom of Choice' in A. Bainham (ed.) *The International Survey of Family Law 2001 Edition*, Family Law, Bristol, 2001 p. 187–222 and G. Lind, 'Legislation for the Surviving Cohabitant from a Comparative Perspective' in K. Boele-Woelki and T. Sverdrup (eds.) *European Challenges in Contemporary Family Law*, Intersentia, Antwerp – Oxford – Portland, 2008 p. 243–268.

27 See G. Lind, *Common Law Marriage*, Uppsala Universitet, Uppsala 2006 and G. Lind, 'Legislation for the Surviving Cohabitant from a Comparative Perspective' in K. Boele-Woelki and T. Sverdrup (eds.) *European Challenges in Contemporary Family Law*, Intersentia, Antwerp – Oxford – Portland, 2008 p. 243–268 .

28 See P. Sarcevic, 'Cohabitation without Formal Marriage in Yugoslav Law' J.M. Ekelaar and S. N. Katz (eds.) Marriage and Cohabitation in Contemporary Societies, Butterworths, Toronto, 1980 p. 293–298 and M. Geč-Korošec and S. Kraljić, 'The Influence of Validly Established Cohabitation on Legal Relations between Cohabitants in Slovene Law' in A. Bainham (ed.) *The International Survey of Family Law 2001 Edition*, Family Law, Bristol, 2001 p. 383–395.

29 For New Zealand, see the Property (Relationships) Act 1976 as amended in 2001 and B. Atkin, 'The legal World of Unmarried Couples: Reflections on 'De Facto Relationships' in Recent New Zealand Legislation', *Victoria University of Wellington Law Review*, Vol. 39, p. 793–812, Wellington 2008. For Australia, see the Northern Territory Family Provision Act 1970 s. 7(1) (a) and De Facto Relationships Act s. 3 A; New South Wales Family Provision Act 1982 s. 6(1) (paragraph (a)(ii) of the definition of 'eligible person) and Property (Relationships) Act 1984 s. 5 (definition of 'domestic relationship'); Queensland Succession Act 1981 s. 5 Aa (1) (definition of 'spouse' includes a 'de facto partner'); Southern Australia Inheritance (Family Provision) Act 1972 s. 4 (definition of 'domestic partner'); Tasmania Testator's Family Maintenance Act 1912 s. 2(1) (definition of 'spouse') and s. 3A; Western Australia Inheritance (Family and Dependants Provision) Act 1972 s. 7(1)(a) and Interpretation Act 1984 s, 13A. In Victoria, the legislation does not categorise particular persons who are eligible to apply for family provision, however the court must consider various matters submitted by an applicant before making any order. See also R. Graycar and J. Millbank, 'From Functional Family to Spinster Sisters: Australia's Distinctive Path to Relationship Recognition', *Journal of Law & Policy*, Vol. 24 p. 121–164.

of common law marriage and in the legislation in former Yugoslavia, New Zealand and Australia, is to equate cohabitants to married couples in relation to inheritance rights.

The right to inherit and keep an estate in '*uskifte*' is dependent on the cohabitants fulfilling the definition of cohabitants in the Inheritance Act section 28a. The law contains a general definition of the concept of cohabitation and cohabitants. In addition there are specific requirements that have to be met in order for a surviving cohabitant to obtain inheritance rights. The general definition is that cohabitants are 'two persons above 18 living together in a marriage-like relationship'. This means that in terms of the law a cohabitant relationship can only exist between two persons. It also means that a person cannot – according to the law – simultaneously be a cohabitant with several persons. It is required that the persons live together, which means they must permanently reside together. The requirement can be fulfilled even though the cohabitants live separately for short periods of time due to education, work, illness, living in an institution and similar circumstances. Further, both parties must be at least 18 years of age which is the Norwegian age of maturity, the age to decide marriage on one's own, and the age for obtaining rights under the Act relating to joint residence in a household community.[30] Both parties must be unmarried, not registered partners or cohabitant with another person. This condition was included in the Act to avoid collision of rights between several surviving persons connected to a decedent. Furthermore it is a requirement that the relationship is 'marriage-like'. Obviously this term is rather vague, but it includes both opposite-sex and same-sex cohabitants. If the persons are so closely related that according to section 3 of the Marriage Act they cannot be married,[31] then they cannot in law be cohabitants.

2.3. INHERITANCE WITH FREE RIGHT TO DISPOSE *INTER VIVOS* AND *MORTIS CAUSA*

The surviving spouse is entitled to inherit a share of the estate left by the decedent spouse. Chapter II in the Inheritance Act 1972 is titled 'Inheritance rights for the spouse.' The spouse's share of the deceased's estate is a quarter, half or the entire estate, depending on whether the closest relatives of the deceased were his children, parents and siblings or more distant relatives. If children or descendents

30 Act No. 45 of 4 July 1991 relating to the right to the joint residence and household goods when a household community ceases to exist.

31 Section 3 of the Marriage Act reads as follows: "(1) Marriage may not be contracted between relatives in direct line of ascent or descent or between brothers and sisters. (2)With regard to adopted children, the above prohibition applies to both the natural relatives and the adoptive parents and their relatives. If the adopted child has been adopted anew, the county governor may however consent to a marriage between the adopted child and one of the original adoptive parents or a relative of the latter."

of children survive the decedent, the surviving spouse inherits one-quarter of the decedent's estate. If the heirs belong to the second group, ie parents and first-line collaterals, the spouse inherits one-half of the estate. Finally, if the decedent only has heirs in the third group, ie grandparents and second-line collaterals, the surviving spouse inherits the entire estate. This share is at the free disposal of the surviving spouse *inter vivos* and *mortis causa*. The spouse's legal right to inherit a certain fraction of the estate is not a forced share (or legitimate portion); it may be reduced or eliminated by the will of the decedent. The validity of such a will is contingent upon the surviving spouse having received notification of the contents of the will. If the spouses' marital property regime was a (deferred) community property, the surviving spouse will of course receive half the net estate as his or her share.

Cohabitants with common children[32] have a legal right to inherit from each other. This right to inherit is limited to four times the basis amount in the national insurance system, currently about NOK 302.000 or around € 38.000. Payments from the national insurance system are calculated in terms of an amount determined by the Norwegian parliament ('*Stortinget*') each year.[33] The current basis amount this year is NOK 75.641, in other words approximately € 9.500. The cohabitant's right to inherit has priority over the protected right of children to inherit. A will is required if the cohabitants want the surviving cohabitant to inherit a larger share of the estate. This legal right to inherit applies to cohabitants who have, have had or expect a child together. In the first recommendation from the legal department of the Ministry of Justice, cohabitants who had lived together for five years were to be given the right to inherit, but this proposal was not adopted. The Ministry of Justice reasoned that cohabitants without children were a heterogeneous group and that, unlike in the case of cohabitants with children, it would be difficult to presume that cohabitants without children in general wanted to secure the surviving cohabitant. In addition, another argument was that it would be an advantage to operate with the same definition of cohabitants as far as inheritance and right to '*uskifte*' were concerned.[34] The right to inheritance may be restricted or expanded by writing a will.[35]

32 Cohabitants who previously have had common children and cohabitants who are expecting common children are also included.

33 The base rate is changed regularly on 1 May.

34 Ot.prp. nr. 73 (2007–2008) p. 25–27 (proposition to the Norwegian Parliament).

35 Inheritance Act s. 28(2).

2.4. MINIMUM INHERITANCE AND LEGITIMATE PORTION

Minimum inheritance and *legitimate portions* are examples of the third concept of securing the surviving spouse and descendants applied in Norwegian inheritance law.

Quite often a decedent spouse leaves a fairly modest net estate. In such cases the right to inherit one-quarter or one-half will result in a rather small inheritance: thus the surviving spouse will have difficulties maintaining his or her standard of living. We can use as an example a case where the decedent leaves children from a previous marriage and the estate amounts to NOK 500.000, which is roughly € 63.000. The surviving spouse's right to inherit one-quarter will amount to NOK 125.000 (about € 15.750) and the children will inherit the remaining three-quarters. In cases such as this it is impossible for the surviving spouse to settle the estate with the children and keep the common residence. For this reason the surviving spouse has been given what is called the right of *minimum inheritance*. The minimum inheritance is an alternative to the regular share-inheritance and its practical application is limited to estates of a small value.[36]

The amount of the minimum inheritance is connected to the basis amount used in rights under our National Insurance Act as mentioned above. If the decedent has children or direct descendents from children, the surviving spouse is entitled to a minimum inheritance of four times the basis amount or approx. NOK 302.000 (€ 38.000). Using the example above the surviving spouses' regular inheritance was NOK 125.000 but the minimum inheritance is NOK 302.000. The surviving spouse would therefore choose the minimum inheritance and inherit NOK 302.000 and the remaining estate is divided between the children. We can alter the example and use NOK 2 million as the value of the estate. The surviving spouse's right to inherit one-quarter will amount to NOK 500.000 (€ 63.000) and the minimum inheritance is irrelevant in this case. If the decedent spouse leaves no direct descendents the minimum inheritance is six times the basis amount, NOK 458.000 or roughly € 58.000. The minimum inheritance is a protected right to inherit and cannot be reduced or eliminated by a will.[37]

Spouses and cohabitants may of course write wills in favour of each other. As a matter of fact spouses or cohabitants without children quite often write reciprocal wills whereby the surviving spouse or cohabitant becomes the sole heir or beneficiary. Children under the Norwegian Inheritance Act have a protected

[36] The minimum inheritance came in to the Inheritance Act s. 6 first paragraph second and third sentence by an amendment (Act No. 40/1990). See Ot.prp. nr. 46 (1989–1990) (endringslov) Skifteloven m.m.

[37] Inheritance Act s. 7(3).

right of inheritance – a *legitimate portion* – consisting of two-thirds of the deceased parents' estate. There is, however, a limitation in this protected right of inheritance which has become increasingly important. The protected right of inheritance is limited to NOK 1 million for each child or each child's line (the forced sum). As far as every child is secured 1 million NOK, the forced share of two-thirds does not apply. Consequently, the forced sum is a limitation of the legitimate portion or an expansion of the freedom of testation for wealthy people. NOK 1 million is only € 125.000 which is hardly a substantial amount in Norway today.[38] If a person has two children the total protected inheritance would be € 250.000 for both together and the testator can bequeath the rest of his estate as he wishes. This means that rich or wealthy people, by writing a will, can to a large degree secure the surviving spouse financially regardless of their children's' protected right of inheritance.

The forced sum – the so called '*Lex Michelsen*' – is a specific Norwegian element in the regulation of the *legitimate portion*. It is called '*Lex Michelsen*' due to the initiator, the former Norwegian prime minister and ship-owner, *Christian Michelsen*, who used his freedom of testation to bequeath most of his huge fortune to the Chr. Michelsen Institute (CMI), an independent centre for research on international development and policy. Originally, from 1918, there was a condition that in order to apply *Lex Michelsen* the will should bequeath a non-profit institution. However, this condition was repealed in the 1930s. The forced sum is meant to be a compromise between freedom of testation and protection of family members. The new Danish Inheritance Act of 2007 introduces the forced sum according to the Norwegian model.[39]

As mentioned above, the forced sum is meant to be a compromise between freedom of testation and protection of family members. However, one may discuss how balanced the Norwegian legislation on imperative inheritance actually is. Due to a combination of the legitimate portion of the descendants and the minimum inheritance of the surviving spouse, many Norwegians have no freedom of testation at all. If the deceased is survived by his three children and his spouse, the spouse is entitled to four times the basis amount of the national insurance and the children are entitled to two-thirds of the estate, however with priority after their mother's (or stepmother's) minimum inheritance. This means that the deceased has no freedom of testation if the net estate is less than 12 times the base rate of the natural insurance (NOK 906.000 or €114.500). If the spouses had (deferred) community property and the deceased spouse owned all the assets during marriage, he would have to leave assets of more than 24 times the base

38 The sum has not been changed since 1985. Consequently inflation reduces the Norwegian legitimate portion each year.

39 Act No. 515 of June 6th 2007 section 5. The Danish sum will be adjusted to inflation.

rate of the national insurance (NOK 1.812.000 or €229.000) in order to make use of a will. Half of his fortune during marriage will be distributed to his spouse before the other half is divided between the surviving spouse and the children. If the deceased is survived by minor children and a spouse with almost no assets or income, this may be perfectly fair. However, if the widow is well-off and the children are high salary lawyers in their mid fifties, it is not obvious that these security provisions are necessary. However, the children may waive their right of inheritance or accept a will.

Cohabitants who do not have children together but have lived together for at least five years, may in a will give the surviving spouse the right to inherit an amount up to four times the basis amount.[40] This right contained in a will shall have priority over the protected right to inherit of the decedent's children from a previous relationship or marriage. A cohabitant without children may of course, as previously, in a will dispose of his or her entire estate in favour of the other cohabitant. Besides this, wills by cohabitants are subject to the regulations on the legitimate portion in the Norwegian Inheritance Act.

2.5. *USKIFTE*

By far the most important right of the surviving spouse is the right to keep the estate in '*uskifte*', which is an example of possession or ownership with limitations on disposal *mortis causa* and/or *inter vivos*. '*Skifte*' means to divide or settle and '*uskifte*' means '*not-dividing*'. '*Uskifte*' quite simply means that when one spouse dies, the settlement of the estate is postponed and the surviving spouse keeps the entire estate undivided. '*Uskifte*' is not an ordinary right to inherit, but a right to keep the whole (deferred) community property until the surviving spouse dies, remarries or decides to settle the estate with the other heirs. Obviously the surviving spouse usually prefers to keep the whole estate rather than immediately settling the estate and having to pay out their inheritance to the heirs. The purpose of the arrangement is for the surviving spouse to be able to maintain his or her standard of living and be able to keep the joint residence. The system is unique to Norway, Denmark and Iceland.[41]

One major advantage with '*uskifte*' is that the law stipulates that the surviving spouse may freely dispose of the *uskifte*-estate as an owner.[42] This means that the

40 Inheritance Act s. 28 b (1) second sentence.

41 However, similar systems are known both in Sweden and Finland and on the European continent (The Netherlands, Belgium, France etc.). See J. Asland, *Uskifte*, Gyldendal Akademisk, Oslo 2008 p. 26–27.

42 Inheritance Act s. 18(1). The legal status of '*uskifte*' is discussed in J. Asland, *Uskifte*, Gyldendal Akademisk, Oslo, 2008 p. 64–79.

surviving spouse can sell assets including the joint residence, spend the entire income of the *uskifte*-estate, increase his or her standard of living and reduce the capital of the *uskifte*-estate. The most important limitation in practice is that the surviving spouse is not allowed to give substantial gifts without the consent of the heirs.[43]

The default matrimonial property regime in Norway is a (deferred) community property. But spouses are free to depart from that by marriage contract or a pre-nuptial agreement.[44] If the spouses have (deferred) community property, the surviving spouse according to the Norwegian inheritance law has the right to keep the entire estate in '*uskifte*' regardless of its size. If the spouses have had separate property, '*uskifte*' has to be agreed upon in a marriage contract or the surviving spouse will need the consent of the heirs. If the decedent spouse has children from a previous marriage or relationship (separate offspring), these children may demand their inheritance paid out immediately when their mother or father dies. '*Uskifte*' can in such cases only be established with their consent. This limitation has become an important limitation in the right of '*uskifte*'.[45] The consent may be conditional,[46] eg given on the condition that the surviving spouse will not sell the family mansion.

Some conditions have to be met in order to keep the estate in '*uskifte*' even if the married couple had (deferred) community property and there are no separate offspring of the deceased.[47] A surviving spouse is not entitled to retain possession of the undivided estate if it is probable that the prospects of the decedent spouse's creditors obtaining payment or the prospects of the decedent spouse's heirs obtaining inheritance will be substantially reduced on account of the surviving spouse's obligations. The same rule applies if the surviving spouse, by improper conduct, has incurred or caused other persons to incur any considerable property loss and the court finds it unlikely that he or she will administer the estate in a proper manner.[48] A surviving spouse who has been declared to be without legal capacity is not entitled to retain possession of the undivided estate.[49] However,

---

43 Inheritance Act s. 19. The limitations are discussed by P. Lødrup, *Arverett*, Gyldendal Akademisk, Oslo, 2008 p. 375–383; P. Hambro, *Arveloven*, 4th ed., Universitetsforlaget, Oslo, 2007 p. 92–137, 140–152, 158–171 and 185–192 and J. Asland, *Uskifte*, Gyldendal Akademisk, Oslo, *Uskifte*, 2008 p. 164–305.

44 An exhaustive list of the alternative matrimonial property regimes recognized in Norwegian law is given in the Marriage Act chapter 9.

45 Uskifte established with consent of the heirs is discussed in P. Hambro, *Arveplanlegging og avtalt uskifte*, Universitetsforlaget, Oslo, 2006 and J. Asland, *Uskifte*, Gyldendal Akademisk, Oslo, 2008 p. 105–144, 175–296, 386–391 and 441–455.

46 Rt. 1992 p. 374 and Rt. 2004 p. 777 (decisions from the Norwegian Supreme Court).

47 For the details, see J. Asland, *Uskifte*, Gyldendal Akademisk, Oslo 2008 p. 80–147.

48 Inheritance Act s. 13(1).

49 Hardly nobody are declared without legal capacity in Norway today. See Nou 2004: 16 Vergemål [The Guardianship Commissions report] p. 116.

insofar as necessary to ensure proper subsistence of such a spouse and of children living in the same home and in order to maintain the home, the court may decide, subject to the consent of the board of guardianship, that the spouse shall take over all or part of the state for undivided possession.[50] A spouse who is a minor is only entitled to *'uskifte'* with the consent of the board of guardianship.[51]

A surviving spouse who has retained the estate in 'uskifte' is personally liable for the debts of the decedent spouse.[52]

The amendments of 2008 to the Norwegian Inheritance Act grant the surviving cohabitant the right to keep the estate in *'uskifte'* provided the cohabitants have, have had or expect a child together. This *uskifte*-right is limited to certain assets and includes the joint residence, household goods and a second home (holiday home) which have been used jointly by the cohabitants.[53] The decedent's assets that do not become part of the *'uskifte'* are divided immediately between the decedent's heirs according to the provisions in the Inheritance Act or provisions in the decedent's will.

The enacted law on cohabitants includes more assets than the original proposal. Household goods may have a substantial value and the *uskifte*-right is not limited to what may be termed *'average household goods'*. Certain assets are not included, such as items which merely have served for the personal use of one of the cohabitants, collections and investment objects which have been kept in the joint residence or second home. Automobiles mainly used for business purposes and a company second home are not included. Neither are financial assets such as stocks, bonds and bank accounts included. This may lead to unreasonable or random results that joint residence and automobiles are included in the uskifte-right whereas financial assets are not included. Some couples rent their joint residence and keep most of their savings in bank accounts or in stocks. Another quite common scenario is that a couple has sold their large joint residence and moved to a smaller flat in which they intend to spend their years after retirement. The net capital after the sale of their former joint residence is put into a bank account or is invested in the stock market. Upon the death of one of the cohabitants the surviving cohabitant will have to choose between *'uskifte'* with the small flat or inheriting four times the basis amount of the national insurance.

---

50 Inheritance Act s. 13(2).

51 Inheritance Act s.(3) Minor widows or widowers are (luckily) not very common. The Norwegian marriage age and the age of maturity are both 18 years. See the Marriage Act s. 1 a and the Guardianship Act s. 1.

52 Inheritance Act s. 20.

53 Inheritance Act s. 28 c (1)(a) and (b).

The surviving cohabitant using the *uskifte*-right thereby becomes personally liable for all of the decedent's debts.[54] This may lead to unreasonable results if most of the decedent's debts were connected to property that is not a part of the '*uskifte*' estate ie financial assets and business assets. In such cases the inheritance of four times the basis amount of the national insurance may be a more favourable solution to the surviving cohabitant than '*uskifte*'.

Either by a will or consent from the decedent's other heirs the *uskifte*-right can be expanded to include other items.[55] If such an expanded *uskifte*-right has been included in a will, this right of the surviving cohabitant has priority over the *legitimate portion* of common children. On the other hand, the inheritance rights of children from a previous marriage or relationship have priority over the *uskifte*-right of the surviving cohabitant. Such heirs may claim their inheritance immediately after the death of their parent.[56] However, the fact that one or more heirs may be entitled to take their inheritance immediately shall not entail the forfeiture of the surviving cohabitant's right to retain possession of the estate in '*uskifte*' in relation to other heirs.[57]

The new law has special rules for cases where either the deceased or the surviving cohabitant has an estate in '*uskifte*' from a previous spouse or cohabitant. The purpose of these rules is to avoid the situation where a surviving cohabitant can simultaneously have rights from several relationships. The law has included a new regulation for surviving spouses who already have an estate in '*uskifte*'. If the surviving spouse establishes a cohabitant relationship and this new relationship lasts more than two years, or the cohabitants have or expect a child together, the heirs of the decedent spouse may demand the '*uskifte*' estate be divided.[58]

Everything the surviving cohabitant acquires and which naturally belongs together with the assets in the '*uskifte*' estate, becomes part of the *uskifte*-estate.[59] In other words a new residence, car, second home or household goods automatically become part of the estate. If a joint residence or second home is sold and the surviving cohabitant reinvests in similar assets at a lower price, the excess amount becomes part of the *uskifte*-estate.

When the *uskifte*-estate is finally divided between the heirs, the division is based on the proportional value of each of the cohabitants assets included in the *uskifte*-

54 Inheritance Act s. 28d.
55 Inheritance Act s. 28 c (1) 2nd sentence.
56 Inheritance Act s. 28 c (2) 1st sentence.
57 Inheritance Act s. 28 f. compare s. 12.
58 Inheritance Act s. 24 (2) 2nd sentence.
59 Inheritance Act s. 28c (4).

estate at the time it was established.[60] The net-values are used as the basis for this calculation. If the division takes place during the lifetime of the surviving cohabitant he/she has the right to inherit four times the basis amount.

The regular rules concerning *'uskifte'* contained in chapter III of the Inheritance Act apply *mutatis mutandis* to *cohabitant-uskifte*. The regulation of *'uskifte'* contains specific provisions that apply if the spouses had separate property during marriage. For cohabitants, the terms separate and (deferred) community property of course do not apply. In Norway, the marital property regime is a consequence of the marriage, and the regime is not applicable to cohabitants, directly or through analogy.[61] In cases where there are special rules for *'uskifte'* with separate property, the rules for separate property shall apply to a cohabitant's *uskifte*-right. An example would be a case where the decedent owned property which is covered by the *uskifte*-right, but which according to a decision from a grantor or testator is to be separate property for the recipient. *'Uskifte'* with such property is only possible with the consent of the grantor/testator or heirs who benefit from this clause.

The surviving cohabitant's right to *'uskifte'* may by writing a will be restricted or expanded.[62]

2.6. DISTRIBUTION BASED ON NEEDS

There are also elements of distribution based on needs in Norwegian law of succession. Children whose fostering has not been completed at the time of the deceased's death are entitled to a lump sum of the estate as a prior share in order to secure their sustenance and education, wherever reasonable under the circumstances.[63] There is also an element of need based distribution in the Act Relating to Insurance Contracts section 15–6 regarding change of beneficiary at the request of dependants. Need-based distribution is also an element in the specific regulations of agricultural and forested land, the regulations on allodial rights or *retrait lignager* – the Norwegian *Odelsrett*.[64]

---

60 Inheritance Act s. 28e.

61 Unlike New Zealand, where the Property (Relationships) Act 1976 applies to de facto relationships.

62 Inheritance Act s. 28c (3).

63 The Inheritance Act s. 36.

64 The Act on Allodial rights of June 28th 1974 No. 58 ss. 34–39. See T. Falkanger, *Odelsrett og åsetesrett*, Universitetsforlaget, Oslo – Bergen – Tromsø – Stavanger, 1984; T. Falkanger, 'Forholdet mellom gjenlevende ektefelle og delsberettiget loddeier', *Lov og Rett*, 1974 p. 51–75 and T. Falkanger, 'Ektefelle eller samboer – og odelsrett', in K. S. Bull, V. Hagstrøm and T. Tjomsland (eds.) *Bonus Pater Familias. Festskrift til Peter Lødrup, 70 år*, Gyldendal Akademisk, Oslo 2002. p. 255–271.

3. CONCLUSIONS

It is clear that most jurisdictions have some form of protection of the surviving life partner and minor children, and that such protection limits the freedom of testation in varying degrees. This is also true for Norway. In my view it is right and natural to limit freedom of testation out of consideration for those persons with whom the decedent is closely related or with whom he shares his life. At least where there are minor children or a surviving spouse or cohabitant, the testator has a moral duty towards his children and life companion to care for them both during his life and thereafter. How far reaching this moral duty is – and to what extent the moral duty shall be expanded to a legal duty – is a question upon which there are differing opinions.

I have pointed out some concepts of protection for surviving spouses, cohabitants and other relatives or dependants of the deceased. These concepts are answers to how different legislators have struck the balance between the interests of (1) the surviving spouse (or cohabitant), (2) the interests of other family members and (3) the deceased's own preferences for the distribution of his property. I have also described how the balancing is performed in Norwegian law. However, I am not at all sure that the Norwegian legislators have struck the correct balance.

Of course it is impossible to find a solution to this different question that will please everyone. To choose is to lose.[65] We will probably never find a solution to the balancing of inheritance rights and the freedom of testation that is totally satisfactory to everybody. However, I think there are some shortcomings of the Norwegian system that ought to be improved.

Firstly, I find the minimum inheritance for the surviving spouse without any secondary heirship for the other heirs of the deceased – eg his children – problematic. Even if there is not much to inherit, for many people, there is a significant symbolic and emotional value in inheriting something from their parents. With the Norwegian minimum inheritance right for the surviving spouse, the children – typically separate offspring of the deceased – are totally disinherited. This could be a reasonable solution, had the minimum inheritance been needs-based. However, The Norwegian minimum inheritance is not needs-based. The wealthy widower, surviving his poor wife who has three young children from a previous relationship, will inherit the entire estate of his wife up to approx. NOK 302.000 (€ 38.000). The children may be entitled to a lump sum of the estate as a prior share in order to secure their sustenance and education, if

[65] C. Castelein, 'Introduction and objectives' in C. Castelein, R. Foqué and A. Verbeke (eds.) *Imperative Inheritance Law in a Late Modern Society*, Intersentia, Antwerp – Oxford – Portland, 2009.

their fostering was not completed at the time of the deceased's death.[66] However, it is not clear whether the claim for a lump sum has priority over the surviving spouse's minimum inheritance.[67] In my view, the solution chosen in Sweden and Denmark is better. The minimum inheritance is needs-based, and there is secondary heirship to the other heirs of the first deceased spouse.[68]

Secondly, and more important, there are some disturbing issues with the Norwegian forced sum, the so called *Lex Michelsen*. It is meant to be a compromise between freedom of testation and protection of family members. In many ways this institute is a useful tool in order to achieve flexible solutions eg in transferring a family business from one generation to the next generation without having to split up the enterprise. However, there is a lack of balance in the Norwegian legislation on imperative inheritance. Due to a combination of the legitimate portion of the descendants and the minimum inheritance of the surviving spouse, many Norwegians have no freedom of testation at all.[69] In my view, it is obviously unjust that some people have no freedom of testation at all whereas other very wealthy people may dispose of almost all their fortune by will. Again, if the entire estate of the deceased is needed to secure the sustenance of the surviving spouse and the children, it is perfectly fair that the deceased has no freedom of testation. But neither the minimum inheritance nor the legitimate portion of forced sum are needs-based. If the deceased was married and had children, and his estate amounted to less than 12 times the base rate of the national insurance, his widow and children – no matter how wealthy they are – may successfully protest against his will if he dared to donate anything to charity. Another unsatisfactory feature about the forced sum is that it is not adjusted to inflation. The sum has been the same since 1985. This implies that the true protection of the children of the deceased decreases every year. How much, depends on the inflation rate. I think it would be a better solution to link the forced sum to the retail prize index or the base rate of the national insurance in order to keep the same level of true protection over time and not only nominally the same level of protection.

Thirdly, I think the Norwegian solution on how to protect surviving cohabitants, is unsatisfactory. The Norwegian legislators have created a totally new system for cohabitants. It has some resemblance to inheritance rights and *'uskifte'* for surviving spouses, but the surviving spouse is protected to a lesser degree. It was the legislators intention to provide the surviving cohabitant a more

---

66 The Inheritance Act s. 36.

67 I. Unneberg, 'Ny minstearvm.v. for gjenlevende ektefelle', *Lov og Rett*, 1991 p. 274; P. Lødrup, *Arverett*, 5th ed., Gyldendal Akademisk, Oslo 2008, p. 64 and P. Hambro, *Arveloven*, 4th ed, Universitetsforlaget, Oslo, 2007 p. 37.

68 See above 2.1 and P. Lødrup, Nordisk arverett, *Nordisk arverett*, Nordisk Ministerråd, København 2002 p. 238–139 with further references.

69 See examples above 2.4.

limited protection than the surviving spouse.[70] In my view this is wrong both from a perspective of legal technicality and from a perspective of equal rights. The regulations on *'uskifte'* for cohabitants will raise many different questions about what belongs to the *'uskifte-estate'* and what is the surviving cohabitant's property outside the '*uskifte*-estate'.[71] The surviving cohabitants who are provided with the right to inheritance and *'uskifte'* are also functionally similar to spouses. The criteria 'common children' ensures that the cohabitants covered by the new regulations are usually closely connected and interdependent. If they are not as closely connected as the legislators presumed, they have the safety valve in the right to disinherit each other by testament – the opt out solution. I also find the inheritance right of four times the basis amount of the national insurance a bit odd. The surviving cohabitant will inherit the same share of the estate irrespective of the other heirs being the children of the deceased or his cousins – or the government.[72]

Fourthly, it is questionable whether children from different relations should be treated differently. Obviously, the prospects of the children obtaining the inheritance will be drastically reduced if, for example, their stepmother who is 20 years younger than the youngest of them, can retain the estate in *'uskifte'* compared to the situation where their mother is keeping the estate undivided. But the situations where there are separate offspring differ widely. Sometimes the separate offspring of the deceased and the common children of the deceased and the surviving spouse, have grown up together as a family. The separate offspring of the deceased may regard their stepparent as their mother or father. I think the legislators should consider if more flexible solutions are possible on this matter.[73]

These issues – and many more – will be discussed by a new Inheritance Act Commission that will be appointed in the near future.[74] The commission is free to design a completely new and future-oriented Inheritance Act. However, a complete break with the traditions is unlikely to happen. Inheritance law is a field of law with a remarkable continuity.[75] What seems modern and future-oriented today, may seem outdated and reactionary tomorrow. An illustrating example is from the Inheritance Commission's report from 1962. The commission anticipated

[70] Ot.prp. nr. 73 (2007–2008 p. 11–15.

[71] See J. Asland, *Uskifte*, Oslo, 2008 p. 502–504 and J. Asland, 'Samboernes arverettslige stilling om igjen', *Tidsskrift for familierett, arverett og barnevernrettslige spørsmål*, 2007 p- 251–255.

[72] 'If a decedent has no relatives or spouse to inherit form him, and he has not drawn up a testament, his inheritance devolves on the State' (inheritance Act s. 46),

[73] On this issue, see M. Brattström and A. Singer, *Rätt arv*, 3:a upplagan, Iustus förlag, Uppsala, 2011 p. 239–243.

[74] See A. Strandbakken, 'Ny arvelov?', Tidsskrift for familierett, arverett og barnvernrettslige spørsmål, 2010 p. 1–3.

[75] See D. Heirbaut, Perspective 2 Legal History' in C. Castelein, R. Foqué and A. Verbeke (eds.) *Imperative Inheritance Law in a Late Modern Society*, Intersentia, Antwerp – Oxford – Portland, 2009 p. 65–84.

that the number of separate offspring and children born out of wedlock would decrease in the future.[76] History has shown that they were wrong.[77] Whatever conclusions the commission reaches, it will be interesting to see how it strikes the balance between the decedent's freedom of testation and the survivor's interests. How much freedom of testation will there be?

[76] See Utkast til lov om arv [The Inheritance Act Commission], Oslo 1962 p. 56–57.

[77] By 1 January 2010 only 45,7% of children born in Norway had married parents. However, 41,2% of the parents were cohabitants. See www.ssb.no/emner/02/01/20/barn/tab-2010-04-29-01.html [Statistics Norway].

TESTAMENTARY FREEDOM AND CARING ADULT OFFSPRING IN ENGLAND & WALES AND IRELAND

Brian Sloan*

* The author is grateful to Professor Kevin Gray and Dr Jens M. Scherpe for their helpful comments on an earlier draft of this chapter. All errors are the responsibility of the author.

1. INTRODUCTION

The default rule in English succession law is that 'an Englishman still remains at liberty at his death to dispose of his own property in whatever way he pleases'.[1] Nevertheless, family provision legislation has made significant incursions into that principle in England and Wales, as well as its equivalent in other common law jurisdictions.[2] Under such family provision statutes, certain family members and dependants may apply for discretionary financial provision out of a deceased person's estate where the deceased's will and/or the default intestacy rules have failed to make suitable provision[3] for the applicant.

This chapter concerns family provision claims made in two European jurisdictions, namely England and Wales and the Republic of Ireland, by adult offspring who have provided care for their now-deceased parents. The ageing population in Europe[4] is highly relevant to this question in two respects. First, it may cast doubt on the purposes of family provision law and succession law in general,[5] since people are less likely to be in financial need by the time their parents die. Secondly, the fact that the population is ageing increases the long-term care needs present among the general population, and raises the question of whether and how the state should encourage informal care provided by family members, including offspring.

The chapter begins by discussing the purposes of succession law and considering the extent to which succession law can and should be used to reward, support or encourage informal care. After summarising succession law in England and Wales and the Republic of Ireland, the chapter then considers the relevance of care to family provision claims made by adult offspring in those jurisdictions. The chapter concludes by assessing the need for and likelihood of reform in those jurisdictions to increase the relevance of care to such claims.

---

1 *Re Coventry (deceased)* [1980] *Ch* 461, at 474.

2 For a brief historical overview covering England, Australia and New Zealand, see J.K. De Groot, and B.W. Nickel, *Family Provision in Australia*, LexisNexis Butterworths, Australia, 3rd ed 2007, ch 1.

3 The terminology used to describe the provision varies between jurisdictions.

4 See, *eg*, A. Börsch-Supan, K. Hank and H. Jürges, 'A New Comprehensive and International View on Ageing: Introducing the "Survey of Health, Ageing and Retirement in Europe"' in P.A. Kemp, K. Van den Bosch and L. Smith (eds) *Social Protection in an Ageing World*, Intersentia, Antwerp – Oxford – New York, 2008.

5 McGregor-Lowndes and Hannah have questioned whether family provision is justifiable at all in the twenty-first century (M. McGregor-Lowndes and F. Hannah 'Reforming Australian Inheritance Law: Tyrannical Testators vs Greying Heirs?' (2009) 17 *Australian Property Law Journal* 62, at 70), while Peart claims that as well as restricting testamentary freedom, claims against estates in New Zealand are 'unprincipled, uncertain in scope and unpredictable as to outcome' (N. Peart, 'New Zealand's Succession Law: Subverting Reasonable Expectations' (2008) 37 *Common Law World Review* 356, at 357).

2. THE PURPOSES OF SUCCESSION LAW

This section explores the purposes of succession law and assesses the extent to which it can and should be used to support, reward or encourage care provided by family members. Peart summarises the accepted purposes of succession law as:

> ... consider[ing] the wishes of the individual ... the preservation and security of the family, and ... [protecting] the welfare of society in general by promoting the equalization of fortunes.[6]

There is an inherent tension in these aims, and the relative importance attached to each of them varies between jurisdictions. Indeed, scholars such as Locke and Grotius regarded freedom of testation as inherent in Natural Law, while also accepting a child's natural right to succeed to his parent's estate.[7]

In the present context, a more fundamental problem is that, at first glance, recognition of care in itself is unlikely to satisfy any of these purposes. It may be that the rationale of succession law is in need of re-evaluation. Even if Peart's rationales are preferred, however, a relatively modest extension may be able to justify provision for a carer. The following sub-sections undertake this task.

2.1. GIVING EFFECT TO THE WISHES OF THE DECEASED

In some cases such provision for a carer may in fact reflect the wishes of the deceased. Since only 36% of English and Welsh respondents to a survey by the National Consumer Council had made a will,[8] it could be thought that family provision for a carer would give effect to the true wishes of the deceased in many cases. That said, where a will *is* made, it has been suggested that most testators bequeath property based on the formal 'positions' of each beneficiary in relation to the deceased,[9] *ie* the category of family member to which a beneficiary belongs. Often, it appears that little account is taken of the particular relationship between each individual and the deceased.[10] One study found that respondents

[6] N. Peart, 'The Direction of the Family Protection Act 1955' [1994] *New Zealand Recent Law Review* 193, at 210.

[7] A. Borkowski, *Textbook on Succession*, Oxford University Press, Oxford – New York – 2nd ed 2002, p 255.

[8] National Consumer Council, *Finding the Will: A Report on Will Writing Behaviour in England and Wales* (2007).

[9] J. Finch *et al*, *Wills, Inheritance and Families*, Clarendon Press, Oxford – New York, 1996, p 124.

[10] Izuhara contrasts this position with the tradition in Japan (now in decline), whereby the eldest son and his wife are placed under a duty to provide care to the parents, and the son inherits the house in return: M. Izuhara, *Housing, Care and Inheritance*, Abingdon, Routledge, 2008.

disapproved of linking inheritance with care,[11] although there is also at least some evidence to the contrary.[12]

The perceived importance of giving effect to the wishes of the deceased may lead to an argument that the law should provide for carers only when a promise has been made by the care recipient and relied upon by the carer. In many common law systems, the equitable doctrine of proprietary estoppel provides a mechanism for enforcing oral promises made by the deceased outside of succession law,[13] while in New Zealand there is a statute to perform this function.[14] The significance attached to promises in the context of family provision claims is considered below.

Nevertheless, it should be borne in mind that the intentions of the deceased are not always particularly relevant in relation to family provision claims, although they will often be taken into account.[15] If society is content to override the intention of the deceased for certain purposes, it could be argued that it should be willing to do so in order to recognise care provided.

2.2. THE PRESERVATION AND SECURITY OF THE FAMILY

Turning to the second of Peart's rationales, the preservation and security of the family is arguably furthered by care given to the deceased before death. It may therefore be legitimate to use family provision statutes to support or reward the carer.

It must be conceded, however, that a more plausible argument based on the preservation and security of the family is likely to be made in favour of those with an expectation of inheritance, whether they are spouses, offspring or others. In 1985, Ross Martyn argued that children of the deceased had a 'moral claim' on their parent's estate, irrespective of whether they were in need.[16] Frolik has gone as far as to claim that human beings are 'predisposed to leaving a legacy to our

---

11 K. Rowlingson, *Attitudes to Inheritance: Focus Group Report*, University of Bath, cited in Izuhara, *Housing, Care and Inheritance*, at 110.

12 See, *eg*, D.G. DRAKE and J.A. Lawrence, 'Equality and Distributions of Inheritance in Families' (2000) 13 *Social Justice Research* 271.

13 See, *eg*, S. Nield, 'Testamentary Promises: a Test Bed for Legal Frameworks of Unpaid Caregiving' (2007) 58 *Northern Ireland Legal Quarterly (NILQ)* 287.

14 Law Reform (Testamentary Promises) Act 1949 (NZ).

15 See R. Kerridge, *Parry and Kerridge: The Law of Succession*, Sweet & Maxwell, London, 12th ed 2009, at [8–31] for discussion. In the Irish Supreme Court case of *EB v SS*, for example, Keane J opined that 'the clearly expressed wish of the testatrix in this case to treat all her children equally, although not a decisive factor, is not entirely irrelevant' ([1998] 2 *ILRM* 141, at [29]).

16 J.G. Ross Martyn, *Family Provision: Law and Practice* Sweet & Maxwell, London, 2nd ed 1985, p 43.

children by our own genetic and cultural legacies'.[17] Moreover, a presumption that certain family members should inherit a deceased person's estate is arguably reflected in the intestacy rules[18] and in the practice of testators.[19]

Arguments about entitlement to inheritance would be particularly influential in those jurisdictions where certain relatives receive fixed portions of an estate.[20] That said, care is now recognised even in Germany, where a system of guaranteed rights to share in the estate is in operation.[21] Moreover, in Scotland, where children have the right to claim an amount of money representing a fixed proportion of a parent's estate irrespective of the provisions in the will, the Law Commission recently proposed two options for reform.[22] One of these would restrict any entitlement to dependent children.

Writing from a common law perspective, Peart and Borkowski claim that 'the great potential for harm resulting from the disinheritance of children is obvious'.[23] That may indeed be true in situations where there are dependent minor children to whom the deceased would owe a duty of support if she were still alive. But the fact that people are living longer may mean that parents expect their children to achieve financial independence rather than relying on inheritance.[24] Even historically, the potential for unearned distributions from estates has been invoked as a justification for limiting both testamentary freedom and rights of inheritance.[25] This is related to Blackstone's contention that wills were introduced as a result of the prevalence of 'disobedient and headstrong' heirs.[26] It is therefore possible to question the cogency of perceived rights of inheritance solely on the basis that a person is the son or daughter of the deceased, and the courts have done so when considering family provision claims by adult children.[27] Similar

17 L.A. Frolik, 'The Biological Roots of the Undue Influence Doctrine: What's Love Got to do with it?' (1996) 57 *University of Pittsburgh Law Review* 841, at 875.

18 Administration of Estates Act, s 46 (England & Wales); Succession Act 1965, Part VI (Ireland).

19 Finch *et al*, *Wills, Inheritance and Families.*

20 See, *eg*, M.J. De Waal, 'Comparative Succession Law' in M. Reimann, and R. Zimmermann (eds), *The Oxford Handbook of Comparative* Law, Oxford University Press, Oxford – New York, 2006; C. Castelein, R. Foqué and A. Verbeke (eds), *Imperative Succession Law in a Late-Modern Society: Five Perspectives*, Intersentia, Antwerp – Oxford – New York, 2009.

21 See, *eg*, G. Otte *'Bessere Honorierung von Pflegeleistungen – Plädoyer für eine Vermächtnislösung' Zeitschrift für Erbrecht und Vermögensnachfolge (ZEV)* 2008, 260.

22 Scottish Law Commission, *Report on Succession*, Scot Law Com No 215, The Stationery Office, Edinburgh, 2009.

23 N. Peart and A. Borkowski, 'Provision For Adult Children On Death – The Lesson From New Zealand' (2000) 12 *Child and Family Law Quarterly (CFLQ)* 333, at 343.

24 K. Rowlingson, '"Living Poor to Die Rich"? Or "Spending the Kids' Inheritance"? Attitudes to Assets and Inheritance in Later Life' (2006) 35 *Journal of Social Policy* 175.

25 Peart, 'The Direction of the Family Protection Act 1955', at 212.

26 W. Blackstone, *Commentaries on the Laws of England*, 1765–1769, Book II, 12.

27 See Section 3.2 below.

arguments could be made in the case of spouses, civil partners and unmarried cohabitants.

It is not necessarily the case, therefore, that succession law should give effect to expectations of inheritance based on familial relationships alone. Indeed, Rowlingson and McKay found that an expectation of inheritance was by no means universal among the cohort selected for their empirical study in the UK, although 90% of those who did expect to receive a bequest expected it to come from their parents.[28]

The diminishing significance of familial relationships in themselves in the context of property dealings may reduce the perceived moral entitlement of children to inherit their parents' property, and thereby benefit carers. While Reid sees the frequent assumption of responsibility for informal care as a potential justification for retaining fixed shares for family members in Scotland,[29] she also accepts that care responsibilities are often distributed among only a few family members.[30] This in turn suggests that entitlement to inherit could be confined to those who in fact provide care, or at least that it could be enhanced for such individuals. At the same time, the corresponding recognition of the potential for independence among adult children may work against those who have in fact provided care for the parent.

The corollary of doubt about provision for non-dependants on the basis of familial relationship alone is that provision for those who have earned it (including carers) may be a legitimate aim for succession law. In the context of proposed reforms to testamentary promises legislation, the New Zealand Law Commission have written that it is undesirable to confuse provision made in order to support family members and that made with the aim of 'rewarding valuable services for which the [deceased] should in fairness pay'.[31]

---

28 K. Rowlingson, and S. McKay, *Attitudes to Inheritance in Britain* (Joseph Rowntree Foundation, The Policy Press, Bristol, 2005.

29 D. Reid, 'From the Cradle to the Grave: Politics, Families and Inheritance Law' (2008) 12 *Edinburgh Law Review* 391. See also M. Oldham, 'Financial Obligations within the Family – Aspects of Intergenerational Maintenance and Succession in England and France' (2001) 60 *Cambridge Law Journal* 128 on the complementary nature of fixed succession rights and duties to support parents.

30 This point is made in Scottish Law Commission, *Report on Succession*, at [3.26].

31 New Zealand Law Commission, *Succession Law: Testamentary Claims*, New Zealand Law Commission Preliminary Paper No 24, Wellington, 1996, at [302].

2.3. THE WELFARE OF SOCIETY

Finally, the welfare of society is arguably protected if informal care is supported using succession law, although not specifically through 'the equalization of fortunes' as qualified by Peart. Scholars such as Fineman[32] argue that the support of informal care, and of the carers who provide it, is not a matter of empathy or altruism, but of the preservation of society itself. This analysis has been praised because it 'changes the basis of entitlement from need to desert',[33] but it does not of itself lead to a conclusion that succession law is the most appropriate mechanism through which to support carers.

Oldham, however, expresses concern about the heavy financial burden that would be imposed upon the state in the absence of private caring.[34] Indeed, while the outgoing UK Government recently announced a 'national care service' with the aim of providing formal care free of charge at the point of delivery,[35] it seems likely that the precise means of funding any similar service will remain unclear for some time. Oldham advocates a system of 'successional priority', which would give a person who takes care of a relative a prioritised right of compensation from that relative's estate.[36] She suggests that such a 'priority' concept could be combined with equity release and a state-sponsored loan system to provide a more instantaneous incentive for an informal carer. Oldham claims that private law measures such as those embodied in her proposal, with the idea of a *quid pro quo* for care, would foster the idea of interdependence rather than dependence. She goes as far as to argue that such measures could be necessary to support and encourage care.

Oldham accepts that some would reject her scheme on the basis that care should be provided on the basis of affection rather than mercenary considerations. While one recent report on care funding admitted that 'unpaid carers are by definition not 'in it for the money'',[37] Oldham claims that this sort of view can fail to take account of the 'modern, economy-driven world'.[38] Moreover, just as family members do not necessarily expect to receive a bequest on the death of a relative, there is evidence that most people legitimately expect to make a contribution

---

32 M.A. Fineman, *The Autonomy Myth: A Theory of Dependency*, New Press, New York, 2004.

33 M. Eichner, 'Dependency and the liberal polity: on Martha Fineman's *The Autonomy Myth*' (2005) 93 *California Law Review* 1285.

34 Oldham, 'Financial Obligations within the Family'.

35 HM Government, 'Building the National Care Service', Cm 7854, 2010.

36 Oldham, 'Financial Obligations within the Family', at 173.

37 Caring Choices, 'The future of care funding: Time for a change' (2008), at 26.

38 Oldham, 'Financial Obligations within the Family', at 177. For a discussion linking inheritance and care from a Law and Economics perspective, see B. Bouckaert, 'The Post Mortem Homo Economicus: What Does He Tell Us?' in C. Castelein, R. Foqué and A. Verbeke (eds), *Imperative Succession Law in a Late-Modern Society*, pp 96–98.

towards formal care (whether for themselves or someone else),[39] although many do resent the idea that they should sell their homes in order to pay for care.[40]

If it is assumed that support for carers using private law mechanisms can be justified at least partially, it could be argued that succession law is the ideal method by which to reward carers. The care recipient is no longer in need of her resources on her death, and there is less scope for the awkwardness that could prevail between carer and care recipient if the subject of reward is discussed during the care recipient's life.

It has been seen, however, that the use of family provision statutes to support or compensate the carer is likely to meet objections from those who emphasise either testamentary freedom or a perceived moral entitlement based on a blood or sexual relationship with the deceased.[41] At the other end of the spectrum, such usage of succession law is unlikely to satisfy feminist scholars on care. Given the high opportunity costs of caring, a reward given to a carer after he has finished caring may come too late. Indeed, some care recipients who participated in a qualitative study by Izuhara 'tried to compensate [their familial carers] on the spot rather than let them accumulate any advantage and pass it on to them at death'.[42]

Until large-scale structural changes to society are made in order to support carers more comprehensively, it could be said rewarding carers out of the estate of a care recipient is better than nothing. The argument to be pursued here is a modest compromise between public and private provision. It is suggested that if policy-makers are content to redistribute estates by statute to individuals with some connection to the deceased, care should be relevant when deciding upon any relief to be granted. Indeed, Deech has recently criticised the law of family provision in England and Wales for continuing to 'prefer the idle sexual partner over the deserving family member' who may provide care.[43]

Nevertheless, it is not the purpose of this chapter to argue that the level of reward can or should be commensurate with the commercial value of the services provided. Indeed, the precise basis for and measure of relief for an informal carer

---

39 Caring Choices, 'The future of care funding', at 14.

40 Rowlingson, '"Living Poor to Die Rich"? Or "Spending the Kids' Inheritance"?', at 177, and the references there cited. The proposed 'National Care Service' attempted to avoid this prospect.

41 *Perrins v Holland* [2009] *EWHC* 1945 (Ch) is a recent example of a case where a son of a testator sought provision under the English Inheritance (Provision for Family and Dependants) Act 1975 where the estate had been left to a woman whom the deceased described (perhaps misleadingly) as his 'carer' (at [1]). The trial, however, focussed on testamentary capacity.

42 M. Izuhara, 'Negotiating Family Support? The "Generational Contract" between Long-term Care and Inheritance' (2004) 33 *Journal of Social Policy* 649, at 660.

43 R. Deech, 'Sisters Sisters – and Other Family Members' [2010] Family Law 375, at 380.

would have to be a topic of further discussion. One possibility, based on the New Zealand Law Commission's proposal of a 'contribution claim', is discussed in the final section of the chapter. In addition, it is not suggested that a carer should necessarily trump the claims of others who expect a share in the care recipient's estate, or that the care recipient's wishes and intentions should be considered irrelevant.

Moreover, succession law can never be an all-encompassing solution to the conundrum of support for carers. Part of the reason for this is that some care recipients will not leave significant assets behind them, not least because many will have had to pay for formal care. What can be said is that, on the level of principle, succession law may be a useful tool in supporting informal carers in some circumstances.

2.4. SUMMARY

It has been argued thus far that the support of carers using succession law can be justified with reference to at least some of the accepted aims of that area of law, and that rights of inheritance on the basis of family relationship alone may no longer be justifiable. The remainder of this chapter considers the relevance of care to family provision claims in England and Wales and Ireland.

3. FAMILY PROVISION AND CARING OFFSPRING IN ENGLAND & IRELAND

This section begins by outlining the law of succession in the jurisdictions under consideration, before describing the general approach to family provision claims by adult offspring. As will become clear, it is highly significant that such claims are limited to providing for the offspring's 'maintenance' in England. The remainder of the section considers the relevance of care in adjudicating upon such claims. This is accomplished by assessing whether care is said to impose an obligation on the deceased to make provision, whether it constitutes pertinent conduct on the part of the applicant, and whether it is likely to be taken into account when combined with a promise of provision.

3.1. AN OUTLINE OF ENGLISH AND IRISH SUCCESSION LAW

As stated above, the predominant principle of English succession law is that of testamentary freedom. While Nield claims that the principle has existed since feudal times,[44] Borkowski argues that 'testamentary freedom was severely limited for much of English legal history' and testators were substantially unencumbered for only about a century.[45] Under the present law, nonetheless, it is perfectly possible for a care recipient to reward her carer by bequeathing property to him, and the converse is also true.

This possibility contrasts with the position in many civil law jurisdictions, where testamentary freedom is limited by compulsory portions of the estate being reserved for particular family members. The English Law Commission considered the introduction of compulsory portions for family members in 1971,[46] but subsequently rejected the idea.[47] Family provision, which originated in New Zealand,[48] is therefore an important exception to the general rule of testamentary freedom in England and Ireland, and on one view renders it 'not so far adrift' from the civil law approach.[49]

The scope of family provision law in England and Wales has widened considerably over the course of its history, as has that of its counterparts in Australia and New Zealand.[50] The English Inheritance (Provision for Family and Dependants) Act 1975 allows claims for financial provision[51] out of an estate by spouses and civil partners[52] of the deceased,[53] former spouses and civil partners who have not entered a subsequent marriage or civil partnership,[54] unmarried cohabitants who lived as if they were the deceased's spouse or civil partner for two years prior to the death,[55] all legal children of the deceased[56] and those whom she treated as a

44 S. Nield, '"If you look after me, I will leave you my estate": The enforcement of testamentary promises in England and New Zealand' (2000) 20 *Legal Studies* 85, at 86.

45 Borkowski, *Textbook on Succession*, p 258.

46 Law Commission, *Family Property Law*, Working Paper No 42, HMSO, London, 1971, part 4.

47 Law Commission, *First Report on Family Property: A New Approach*, Law Com No 52, HMSO, London, 1973.
Kerridge points out that fixed entitlements were effectively provided to children in the nineteenth century through the use of marriage settlements: Kerridge, *The Law of Succession*, at [8–80].

48 Testator's Family Maintenance Act 1900 (NZ).

49 P. Matthews, 'Perspective 5: Comparative Law – United Kingdom' in C. Castelein, R. Foqué and A. Verbeke (eds), *Imperative Succession Law in a Late-Modern Society*, at 151.

50 Peart and Borkowski, 'Provision For Adult Children On Death', at 333; de Groot and Nickel, *Family Provision in Australia*, at [1.6].

51 The court can make a wide range of orders, including for periodical payments, transfer of a lump sum or transfer of property: Inheritance (Provision for Family and Dependants) Act 1975, s 2.

52 Civil Partnership is the UK's legal near-equivalent of marriage, available exclusively to same-sex couples. See the Civil Partnership Act 2004.

53 Inheritance (Provision for Family and Dependants) Act 1975, s 1(1)(a).

54 Inheritance (Provision for Family and Dependants) Act 1975, s 1(1)(b).

55 Inheritance (Provision for Family and Dependants) Act 1975, s 1(1)(ba).

56 Inheritance (Provision for Family and Dependants) Act 1975, s 1(1)(c).

child of the family in relation to a marriage or civil partnership,[57] and those who were dependent on the deceased even in the absence of a familial relationship.[58] The English Act applies whether or not the deceased left a will. This contrasts with the position in Irish Law, under which claims by children are possible only where the deceased dies wholly or partially testate,[59] and not where the intestacy rules apply.[60] This state of affairs has been criticised.[61]

Further changes to English Law may materialise in the near future: the Law Commission is currently conducting a review of the 1975 Act alongside the rules of intestacy, and a report and draft Bill are expected in late 2011.[62]

Before proceeding with the discussion, it must be noted that despite its wide scope, the 1975 Act is a remedy for neither unfairness nor unjust enrichment.[63] The question to be asked by the court is not whether it would have been reasonable for the applicant to receive more out of the estate, but effectively whether it was *unreasonable* for him not to have done so. Similarly, it was emphasised in one Irish case that the court does not have 'a power to make a new will for the testator' and should not ask 'which of the alternative courses open to the testator the court itself would have adopted'.[64]

As Green puts it, when considering whether and how to exercise its discretion to make provision for an applicant, the court is given the difficult task of resolving:

> ... the claims of the testator to have her final wish enforced, the heir who may be deprived of her expectation ... and of the applicant who has some moral claim to the estate.[65]

---

57 Inheritance (Provision for Family and Dependants) Act 1975, s 1(1)(d). The Law Commission has recommended that the reference to a marriage or civil partnership be removed: Law Commission, *Intestacy and Family Provision Claims on Death*, Consultation Paper 191, HMSO, London, 2009, at [6.9].

58 Inheritance (Provision for Family and Dependants) Act 1975, s 1(1)(e).

59 Succession Act 1965, s 109.

60 However, the Act applies even where the will is rendered inoperative: *RG v PSG and Another* [1980] *ILRM* 225.

61 B. Spierin with P. Fallon, *The Succession Act 1965 and Related Legislation: A Commentary*, Tottel, Dublin, 2003, at [702].

62 Law Commission, *Intestacy and Family Provision Claims on Death*, Consultation Paper 191, HMSO, London, 2009. Changes to the relevant Irish Law have been made to accommodate formalised same-sex relationships and informal cohabiting relationships by the Civil Partnership and Certain Rights and Obligations of Cohabitants Act 2010. For commentary, see J. Mee, 'Succession and the Civil Partnership Bill 2009' (2009) 14 *Conveyancing and Property Law Journal (CPLJ)* 86.

63 J. Masson, R. Bailey-Harris and R. Probert, *Cretney's Principles of Family Law*, Sweet & Maxwell, London, 8th ed 2008, p 214.

64 *In the matter of the estate of ABC, deceased; XC v RT* [2003] 2 IR 250, at 264.

65 K. Green, 'The Englishwoman's Castle – Inheritance and Private Property Today' (1988) 51 *Modern Law Review* 187, at 187.

As such, it is perhaps unsurprising the emphasis in the English Act itself and in the case law remains upon providing maintenance for dependants unless the applicant is a spouse or civil partner. Therefore, even if care is seen as a relevant consideration in ascertaining the extent of the provision that he should receive, it is arguable that this does not give effect to the underlying purpose of the Act in its current form unless the carer needs to be maintained in the future.

Irish Law operates more of a fixed system than is in evidence in England and Wales, such that freedom of testation is less prominent, and it seems that this reflects a desire to replicate at least some of the principles found in civil law jurisdictions.[66] Under the Succession Act 1965, the surviving spouse has a 'legal right' to half of the estate where there are no children and one third of it where there are children.[67] This applies when the deceased left a will, and the spouse has a right to elect whether to take the portion allotted to her under the will (if any) or the 'legal right'.[68] Although former spouses do not possess the 'legal right', those who have not remarried can make a claim for provision out of their deceased former spouse's estate.[69] The Civil Partnership and Certain Rights and Obligations of Cohabitants Act 2010 largely extended the legal right to same-sex civil partners,[70] and 'qualified' unmarried cohabitants will be able to apply for discretionary provision out of their deceased partners' estates.[71]

Irish offspring, meanwhile, can make claims against an estate on the basis that the deceased 'failed in his moral duty to make proper provision for the child in accordance with his means'.[72] Such a claim cannot affect the legal right of the spouse, or indeed her share under the will or intestacy if that spouse is the parent of the applicant,[73] which will reduce the proportion of the estate available for redistribution in many cases. Relevant 'children' now include those born out of

66 J.C. Brady, *Succession Law in Ireland*, Butterworths, Ireland, 2nd ed 1995, at [7–01]-[7–04]. See also M. Cooney, 'Succession and Judicial Discretion in Ireland' (1980) 15 (NS) *Irish Jurist* 62 and C.H. Sherrin, 'Disinheritance of a Spouse: A Comparative Study of the Law in the United Kingdom and the Republic of Ireland' (1980) 31 *NILQ* 21.

67 Succession Act 1965, s 111.

68 Succession Act 1965, s 115. The 'legal right' can be renounced by pre-nuptial agreement, or in writing following the testator's death (s 113).

69 Family Law (Divorce) Act 1996, s 18.

70 See, generally, Civil Partnership and Certain Rights and Obligations of Cohabitants Act 2010, Part 8.

71 Civil Partnership and Certain Rights and Obligations of Cohabitants Act 2010, s 194.

72 Succession Act 1965, s 117(1).

73 Succession Act 1965, s 117(3). *Cf.* the English scepticism relating to the concept of 'moral duty', discussed in sub-section 3.3 below.

wedlock[74] and adopted children, but there does not appear to be any equivalent of the English 'child of the family'.[75]

In *Re GM; FM v TAM and others*, Kenny J emphasised that the Irish Act was not based on a duty to provide maintenance, and went as far as to say that authorities from New Zealand, New South Wales and England were of 'little assistance' when making decisions under the 1965 Act.[76] As discussed below, however, the needs of the applicant are often central to such determinations.

Having outlined the general scheme of family provision in England and Ireland, the next sub-section considers the approach to claims by adult offspring in more detail.

3.2. GENERAL APPROACH TO CLAIMS BY ADULT OFFSPRING

The position of the adult child who has cared for a parent is a complex one in the context of family provision law. The adjudication of a claim in both England and Ireland involves a two-stage process,[77] although similar considerations will be relevant at both stages.

Under the Inheritance (Provision for Family and Dependants) Act 1975, the court must ascertain, from an objective perspective, whether the will and/or the intestacy rules 'make reasonable financial provision'[78] for the applicant's maintenance.[79] The term 'maintenance', in turn, has been defined as encompassing 'payments which, directly or indirectly, enable the applicant in the future to discharge the cost of his daily living at whatever standard of living is appropriate to him.'[80] If the court concludes that reasonable financial provision has not been made, it must then decide which of its powers to exercise in order to remedy that insufficiency.[81]

Under the Irish 1965 Act, the first stage is to assess whether the testator 'has failed in his moral duty to make proper provision for the child in accordance with his

74 Status of Children Act 1987.

75 In *EB v SS* [1998] 2 *ILRM* 141, an attempt to argue that a moral duty was owed by the deceased to her grandchildren via her responsibility to the applicant was rejected by a majority of the Supreme Court.

76 (1972) 106 *ILTR* 82, at 86.

77 *Re Coventry* [1980] *Ch* 461, at 469; *L v L* [1978] *IR* 288, at 292.

78 Inheritance Act 1975, s 1(1).

79 Inheritance Act 1975, s 1(2)(b). Spouses and civil partners are not subject to this limitation: s 1(2)(a-aa).

80 *Re Dennis (Deceased)* [1981] 2 *All ER* 140, at 145.

81 Inheritance Act 1975, s 2.

means, whether by his will or otherwise'.[82] During the second stage, the court may 'order that such provision shall be made for the child out of the estate as the court thinks just'.[83]

The English Act contains a list of factors that to which the court should have regard in making its determinations, some of which apply to all applicants[84] and some of which are aimed specifically at claims by children of the deceased.[85] The Irish courts, on the other hand, are instructed to 'consider the application from the point of view of a prudent and just parent, taking into account the position of each of the children of the testator and any other circumstances which the court may consider of assistance in arriving at a decision that will be as fair as possible to the child to whom the application relates and to the other children'.[86] The extent of the deceased's moral duty is judged at the date of death with reference to the entitlement of the surviving spouse, the number, age and position in life of the testator's other children, the testator's means, the age, financial position and prospects of the applicant and any provision that the testator made during his life for the applicant.[87]

In England the focus of the award of relief is very much on the future needs of the applicant considered at the date of the hearing, due to the 'maintenance' limitation.[88] For example, the Act specifies 'the manner in which the applicant was being or in which he might expect to be educated or trained' as a relevant factor in applications by adult children, which is a distinctly forward-looking factor.[89] Indeed, although the award is not necessarily limited to providing 'bare necessities',[90] it has been suggested by Peart and Borkowski that the English judiciary have adopted a 'parsimonious' approach to claims by adult children.[91] This is encapsulated in Browne-Wilkinson J's remark that:

> A person who is physically capable of earning his own living faces a difficult task in getting provision made for him, because the court is inclined to ask: 'Why should anybody else make provision for you if you are capable of maintaining yourself?'[92]

---

82 Succession Act 1965, s 117(1).
83 Succession Act 1965, s 117(1).
84 Inheritance Act 1975, s 3(1).
85 Inheritance Act 1975, s 3(3).
86 Succession Act 1965 s 117(2).
87 *Re GM deceased; FM v. TAM* (1970) 106 *ILTR* 82, at 87.
88 See generally G. Miller, 'Provision for adult children under the Inheritance (Provision for Family and Dependants) Act 1975' [1995] *Conveyancer & Property Lawyer* 22.
89 Inheritance Act 1975, s 3(3).
90 N. Lowe and G. Douglas, *Bromley's Family Law*, Oxford University Press, Oxford - New York, 10th ed 2007, p 1113.
91 Peart and Borkowski, 'Provision For Adult Children On Death', at 333.
92 *Re Dennis*, at 145.

It seems that a claim by an adult child in employment and with future earning capacity is unlikely to succeed in England unless the applicant can show that the deceased owed a moral obligation to him, or that some other special circumstances justify the order,[93] although neither of these constitute a 'threshold requirement'[94] and the size of the estate is a pertinent consideration.[95] Moreover, Matthews claims that there has been a recent increase in successful claims by 'ostensibly able-bodied' adult children under the 1975 Act.[96]

Something of a focus on the future needs of the applicant is also prevalent in Ireland, although the courts are not formally constrained by a 'maintenance' limitation. As Kearns J explained in his much-quoted synthesis of the case law on s 117,[97] '[t]he social policy underlying s 117 is primarily directed to protecting those children who are still of an age and situation in life where they might reasonably expect support from their parents'.[98] Moreover, in the case of *in the Goods of JH, deceased*, Barron J expressed the view that:

> In general, [a failure to fulfil the moral duty] will arise where the child has a particular need which the means of the testator can satisfy in whole or in part. If no such need exists, even where no provision has been made by the testator by his will or otherwise, the Court has no power to intervene.[99]

The potential for education to provide long-term security and the importance of meeting needs caused by disability have also been recognised in Ireland.[100] Although the courts were initially generous to claimants who were adult children,[101] the onus of proof is 'relatively high'[102] and a positive failure to comply with the moral duty must be established.[103] This will be particularly true where the child is not dependent on the parent, although the application of the Act is not limited to such cases,[104] and some claims have succeeded where the applicant was in a relatively strong financial position.[105] Moreover, in contrast to the 'parsimonious' approach of English Law on Peart and Borkowski's account,

---

93 *Re Hancock (Deceased)* [1998] 2 *FLR* 346, 351.
94 *H v Mitson* [2009] *EWHC* 3114 (Fam), [49].
95 *Myers v Myers* [2004] *EWHC* 1944 (Fam).
96 Matthews, 'Perspective 5: Comparative Law – United Kingdom', p 145.
97 *In the matter of the estate of ABC, deceased; XC v RT* [2003] 2 *IR* 250.
98 [2003] 2 *IR* 250, at 262–263.
99 [1984] *IR* 599, at 608.
100 [2003] 2 *IR* 250, at 263–264.
101 Spierin with Fallon, *The Succession Act 1965 and Related Legislation: A Commentary*, at [698].
102 *CC and ChF v WC and TC* [1990] 2 *IR* 143, at 148.
103 [1990] 2 *IR* 143 at 148.
104 *Re GM; FM v TAM* (1972) 106 *ILTR* 82, at 86.
105 See Spierin with Fallon, *The Succession Act 1965 and Related Legislation: A Commentary*, at [719] for discussion.

Keane J described the provisions that can be invoked by children under the Irish legislation as 'extremely ample…even in the middle aged and elderly category'.[106]

In any case, the focus on needs is to some extent prevalent in both England and Ireland, and it may be problematic for the familial carer. Some carers may have needs caused by the opportunity costs of caring, not least because of the impact that care can have upon carers' earning capacity[107] and health,[108] and the desire to compensate and recognise the contribution of the carer will have a strong relationship with that fact. Indeed, the relationship between principles based on compensation and those based on need has been recognised by the UK House of Lords in the context of financial provision on divorce.[109] As Miles points out:

> Need and compensation will often be coterminous: the applicant's need is a symptom of the fact that … she forewent earning capacity in order to contribute to the welfare of the family through caring for home and children.[110]

This reasoning could apply to carers for adults. On the other hand, the very nature of the applicant's role as a carer means that he was addressing the needs of the deceased, and may not have any future needs of his own given that the care recipient has died.[111] Moreover, the courts have recently demonstrated more of an expectation that spouses who look after children will eventually return to work in some sense in the context of provision on divorce,[112] and a similar attitude could be taken to children who care for their parents.

Of course, the justification for providing for a carer may be greater when a carer has such needs, but it is questionable whether 'need' should be a necessary condition for a carer to receive something out of the care recipient's estate, since that would fail to recognise the value of care provided in the past. This issue is a recurring theme throughout this chapter.

Moreover, any difficulty in bringing a claim where earning capacity is retained is particularly problematic when compared to cases involving so-called 'lame

---

106 *EB v SS* [1998] 4 IR 527, at 560.

107 House of Commons Work and Pensions Committee *Valuing and Supporting Carers* HC 485, HMSO, London, 2008, at [102].

108 See the material cited in J. Herring, *Older People in Law and Society*, Oxford University Press, Oxford – New York, 2009, pp 99–100.

109 See, *eg*, *Miller v Miller*; *McFarlane v McFarlane* [2006] *UKHL* 24 at [155].

110 J. Miles, '*Charman v Charman (No 4)* – making sense of need, compensation and equal sharing after *Miller/McFarlane*' (2008) 20 *CFLQ* 378, at 389.

111 In *Graham v Murphy*, a case involving a carer who was applying for provision as a dependant of the deceased, Robert Walker J noted that the applicant was employed and 'no longer ha[d] to take time off to look after' the deceased ([1997] 1 *FLR* 860, at 867).

112 See, in particular, *Miller v Miller*; *McFarlane v McFarlane* [2006] *UKHL* 24.

ducks'[113] where the applicant has needs caused by his own failings. *Espinosa v Bourke*,[114] discussed in detail below, is arguably an example of such a case, since provision was made in spite of the fact that the applicant eventually neglected her father and found herself in necessitous circumstances due at least in part to a lifestyle of which the deceased clearly disapproved. Kerridge criticises the 'unfairness towards children...who, having led virtuous lives, are then treated less generously than their prodigal brothers and sisters'.[115]

In New Zealand, in contrast to England and Ireland, the relationship of parent and child was traditionally considered sufficient in itself to justify provision,[116] and a common reason for claims under the Family Protection Act 1955 was that the testator has failed to provide equally for each of her children.[117] The expansive interpretation of the Act undertaken by the courts led the New Zealand Law Commission to propose reforms that would restrict adult children from making support claims unless they are in genuine need or the claim relates to 'a memento or keepsake of modest value',[118] although they could make a 'contribution claim' if they had benefited the deceased in some way.[119] These proposals were never implemented, but as a result of the Law Commission's report, Peart and Borkowski claim that the New Zealand courts have recently adopted a more cautious approach, albeit still more liberal than in England.[120]

Before the more restrictive approach recently adopted, New Zealand was towards the other end of the scale from both English and Irish Law. There is a risk that a caring son or daughter will fall between these extremes. Such carers may fall outside the English or to a lesser extent the Irish Act through a lack of future need, and yet their care is given no recognition if they are provided for simply because of their legal relationships with their parents, as they may be under 'forced heirship' regimes. The next sub-section investigates whether these difficulties can be circumvented through the idea that the receipt of care generates an obligation on the part of the deceased such that it can be given specific recognition.

---

113 *Re Hatte* [1943] *St R Qd* 1 (Queensland), 26.

114 [1999] 1 *FLR* 747.

115 Kerridge, *The Law of Succession*, at [8–62].

116 Peart and Borkowski, 'Provision For Adult Children On Death'. *Cf, eg, In the matter of the estate of ABC, deceased; XC v RT* [2003] 2 IR 250, at 263, where Kearns J stated that '[t]he relationship of parent and child does not, itself and without regard to other circumstances, create a moral duty to leave anything by will to the child'.

117 Peart and Borkowski, 'Provision For Adult Children On Death'.

118 New Zealand Law Commission, *Succession Law: A Succession (Adjustment) Act*, NZLC R39, Wellington, 1997, at [77].

119 New Zealand Law Commission, *Succession Law: A Succession (Adjustment) Act*. See section 4 below for a discussion of the 'contribution claims' proposal.

120 Peart and Borkowski, 'Provision For Adult Children On Death', at 339–342.

3.3. CARE AND THE DECEASED'S OBLIGATIONS

There has been something of a tendency to emphasise a need to show moral obligations owed by the deceased in the English case law involving adult children,[121] and this has been criticised as a value-laden relic of earlier legislation.[122] In *Espinosa v Bourke*, Butler-Sloss LJ denied that the Court of Appeal had placed a 'gloss' on the language of the present legislation,[123] under which the court is directed to have regard, *inter alia*, to 'any obligations and responsibilities which the deceased had towards any applicant'.[124] All of the judges in that case expressed misgivings about the use of the word 'moral', emphasising that it was intended simply to avoid restricting relevant obligations to legal ones. In *Re Hancock*, moreover, it had previously been confirmed that a moral obligation was not a precondition of a successful application.[125] The concept of a moral obligation remains in evidence even in England, however, and Borkowski notes that the courts have often been reluctant to clarify its meaning.[126]

The English courts have said that care could generate a relevant 'moral obligation', even if it is not necessary to demonstrate one. In *Re Jennings*, Henry LJ considered a hypothetical scenario in which an adult child gave up a university place 'to nurse the deceased through his long last illness'.[127] Henry LJ suggested that there would be a 'clear' moral obligation on the deceased to enable the applicant to take up that place.[128] Inevitably, however, the focus would be on any need for maintenance generated by caring, even if the obligation could justify the success of a claim by a child in some form of employment or with earning capacity. That said, in the Northern Irish case of *Estate of McGarrell*,[129] applying legislation modelled on the English 1975 Act,[130] Hutton J found that the applicant had established a moral claim on her father's estate by doing housework for and looking after him. An order was made even though it is doubtful that the applicant's earning capacity was affected by the work she did.[131] Hutton J was content that the applicant was living in 'difficult financial circumstances', and for him it was sufficient that the

---

121 This has been caused mainly by the 'misinterpretation' of *Re Coventry*, which prevailed for some time: A. Borkowski, 'Moral Obligation and Family Provision: *Re Hancock (Deceased)* and *Espinosa v Bourke*' (1999) 11 *CFLQ* 305.

122 J. Wilson and R. Bailey-Harris, 'Family Provision: The Adult Child and Moral Obligation' (2005) 35 *Family Law* 555.

123 [1999] 1 *FLR* 747 at 755.

124 Inheritance Act 1975, s 3(1)(d).

125 [1998] 2 *FLR* 346.

126 Borkowski, 'Moral Obligation and Family Provision'.

127 [1994] *Ch* 286, at 300.

128 [1994] *Ch* 286, at 300.

129 [1983] 8 *NIJB*.

130 Inheritance (Provision for Family and Dependants) (Northern Ireland) Order 1979.

131 Miller, 'Provision for adult children under the Inheritance (Provision for Family and Dependants) Act 1975', at 29.

order would not 'constitute something in excess of maintenance'.[132] The case has been cited, albeit some time ago, as evidence that adult claimants are treated more generously in Northern Ireland than in England.[133]

In the English case of *Espinosa v Bourke*, it was accepted that the applicant was owed a moral obligation by her deceased father because of the care that she provided for him (as well as because of a promise that he would leave certain property to her).[134] The judge at first instance found that any obligation had been discharged by the deceased during his life through direct transfers and benefits in kind. Such countervailing benefits will be important considerations in any care scenario. On appeal, however, it was held that the judge had focused too heavily on the obligation question at the expense of considering the applicant's financial position. The Court of Appeal concentrated instead on the applicant's lack of earning capacity and the promise that the father had made in allowing the applicant's appeal and making an order. But Butler-Sloss LJ appeared to accept that the care in *Espinosa* could itself have generated an obligation if it had not been compensated for by the father's payment of the mortgage and other outgoings.[135]

Similarly, in *Re Coventry* it was suggested that a moral obligation may be generated by an applicant's forgoing of an adequate living to look after a disabled parent.[136] Nevertheless, neither the first instance judge nor the Court of Appeal could find sufficient evidence of such a sacrifice on the facts. It was noted that the applicant had the benefit of free accommodation provided by the deceased during the relevant period, and his claim failed in spite of the fact that his income was modest.

Re Callaghan demonstrates that care provided by a 'child of the family' may be relevant in determining whether reasonable financial provision has been made under the 1975 Act.[137] In that case, the deceased had treated a step-son as if he were a biological child of his own, and took responsibility for advising, supporting and disciplining him at various stages in the step-son's life. The applicant step-son and his wife undertook to provide care for the deceased during the last four months of his life, during which time he suffered from a 'painful and distressing illness' and was a 'bad patient' who discharged himself from hospital several times.[138] Booth J held that the deceased's obligations and responsibilities towards the applicant were 'very considerable indeed', effectively being those of a 'widowed parent to a

132 [1983] 8 *NIJB*.
133 S. Grattan, 'Of Lame Ducks, Black Sheep and Family Bonding' (2000) 51 *NILQ* 198, at 228.
134 [1999] 1 *FLR* 747.
135 [1999] 1 *FLR* 747, at 757.
136 [1980] 1 *Ch* 462, at 490 and 495.
137 [1985] *Fam* 1.
138 [1985] *Fam* 1, at 4.

dutiful and responsible only child'.[139] An award under the 1975 Act was therefore made, although the fact that the applicant was not the legal child of the deceased may have had a significant impact on the outcome in the case.

The English courts are therefore somewhat ambivalent on the question whether care is sufficient to generate a relevant obligation in any given case, as well as on the relevance of an obligation thereby generated when fashioning relief. Any obligation generated by care clearly interacts with the other statutory factors, and the 'maintenance' limitation is ever-present.

The English antipathy towards the concept of 'moral obligation' obviously contrasts sharply with the position in Ireland, where the language of 'moral duty' remains on the face of the legislation. There, the statute apparently assumes that such a moral duty to make proper provision for one's children originally exists and, although the duty is not absolute and its extent is variable, the first question for the court is generally whether the testator failed to discharge that duty in the particular case, whether by his will or otherwise, before death.[140]

In the case of *CW v LW*,[141] an order was made under the 1965 Act in favour of a daughter who had looked after both her parents, for a salary, and lived with them. However, the aim of the order was to provide greater security of income than would have resulted from the distribution of her parents' estate. The applicant's limited earning capacity, rather than the care itself, was the decisive factor, although Sullivan J explicitly rejected the suggestion that the applicant could embark upon a career as a carer as a result of her experience with her parents. The €600 per week paid to her by the Solicitor General by virtue of her mother being a ward of court was said to be 'a measure of her value to her mother rather than an estimate of her earning capacity in the open market'.[142]

Similarly, in *H v O'C and others*, provision was made for an applicant who cared for her mother, but on the basis that the daughter had 'no sufficient or reasonably secure income, or capacity to provide such an income because of her limited education and lack of any academic or vocational skills'.[143] Care provided by one child for another was taken into account in the case of *in the Goods of JH*,

139 [1985] *Fam* 1, at 7.

140 *Re J McD; P McD v MN* [1999] 4 *IR* 301, at 310. *Cf* the view of Hamilton J in *Re HD; W v Allied Irish Banks Ltd*, unreported, High Court, 2 March 1977, who said that the existence of a duty was a prior question.

141 [2005] *IEHC* 325, [2005] 4 *IR* 439. See also *Re AC; KC v CF* [2003] *IEHC* 109.

142 [2005] 4 *IR* 439, at [29].

143 [2007] *IEHC* 68.

deceased,[144] although of course care provided by a non-applicant may prejudice a claim.[145]

Care can apparently be a relevant consideration in both England and Ireland when assessing the extent of the deceased's obligation towards the applicant. But it seems that it will rarely be the sole, decisive factor, and that it will usually have to be combined with future need in order to justify provision. Admittedly, the case for relief is probably strongest where a carer does have needs generated by care undertaken in the past. Moreover, the approach of the courts is unsurprising. Even in New South Wales, for example, where carers are explicitly recognised among the categories of applicant for family provision,[146] need remains a highly significant factor.[147] Nevertheless, as argued above, the current approach in England and Ireland may not attach an appropriate value to the care itself, particularly if a shift towards 'desert' is considered appropriate. The present effect of care on the obligations of the deceased is unlikely to be sufficient to enable the encouragement of care through succession law.

3.4. CARE, CONDUCT AND NEGLECT

There is a possibility that care could be taken into account as conduct, which is specified as a relevant consideration in the English Act.[148] Nevertheless, in *Re Coventry* it was emphasised at first instance that '[i]t is not the purpose of the Act to provide legacies or rewards for meritorious conduct',[149] and conduct is more likely to be considered in a negative sense.

Negative conduct of the applicant directed towards the deceased is undoubtedly relevant in both England and Ireland, although it will not necessarily preclude a claim.[150] A related question is the effect of *neglect* on a moral obligation that would otherwise be present, and the courts have been surprisingly generous to neglectful claimants in some cases from England and Northern Ireland. Such generosity is inconsistent with the positive recognition of care.

---

144 [1984] *IR* 599.

145 See, *eg*, *Williams v Johns* [1988] 2 *FLR* 475.

146 Among the eligible applicants are parties to 'close personal relationships' (Succession Act 2006 (NSW), s 57(f)). These are defined as relationships 'between two adult persons, whether or not related by family, who are living together, one or each of whom provides the other with domestic support and personal care' (s 3(3)).

147 See, *eg*, *Jurd v Public Trustee* [2001] NSWSC 632.

148 Inheritance Act 1975, s 3(1)(g).

149 [1980] *Ch* 461, at 474.

150 *Re J McD; P McD v MN* [1999] 4 IR 301.

In *Espinosa*, the first instance judge was influenced by the fact that the applicant's commitment to her father dwindled, implying that a failure to care for a deceased parent may have a negative effect on a claim under the Act. Even though the Court of Appeal made an order on the basis of her need and the promise made to her, Butler-Sloss LJ admitted that the daughter's eventual neglect of her father could have counted against any obligation owed to her because of her care.[151]

A potentially inconsistent conclusion was drawn by Judge Norris QC in the extraordinary case of *in re Land*.[152] The applicant in that case had been so neglectful in the care of his mother that he had been convicted of her gross negligent manslaughter, and the forfeiture rule applied to his entitlement under her will.[153] Nevertheless, his application under the 1975 Act succeeded. To allow the forfeiture rule to govern the matter and preclude such a claim, in the view of Judge Norris QC, would:

> ... deprive [...] the one person who devoted himself to the deceased's care without significant outside support (albeit that he lapsed at the end) of the benefit she intended for him and confer [...] it upon remote relations most of whom did absolutely nothing for her.[154]

He was influenced by the fact that the applicant's situation had been one of 'inadequacy', a failure to recognise that inadequacy and a 'hesitancy' to ask for outside help, towards which Judge Norris QC appeared to be sympathetic.[155] Most importantly for present purposes, the judge accepted that the deceased recognised an obligation towards the applicant. He also refused to hold that that the applicant's conduct had a disentitling effect. While it was said to be correct that the applicant should be punished through criminal proceedings and by being deprived of the full legacy that his mother had left him, the judge was reluctant to impose a further penalty by denying reasonable financial provision.

A less extreme example of neglect was at issue in the Northern Irish case of *Re McKernan (deceased)*.[156] Deeny J recognised that 'the plaintiff daughter was not a dependable provider of care to the mother and was viewed by [the deceased]... as lazy'.[157] This was not considered to justify a total lack of provision for the daughter

---

151 [1999] 1 *FLR* 747, at 757.
152 [2006] *EWHC* 2069 (Ch).
153 According to section 1(1) of the Forfeiture Act 1982, this is 'the rule of public policy which in certain circumstances precludes a person who has unlawfully killed another from acquiring a benefit in consequence of the killing'. The equivalent rule in Ireland, which precludes an application for family provision, is contained in s 120 of the Succession Act 1965.
154 [2006] *EWHC* 2069 (Ch), at [24].
155 [2006] *EWHC* 2069 (Ch), at [27].
156 [2007] *NICh* 6.
157 [2007] *NICh*, at [37].

under the mother's will, although 'it could justify a distinction being drawn' between the applicant daughter and her siblings.[158]

The judicial sympathy bestowed on applicants in some 'neglect' cases is laudable. Nevertheless, it undermines the significance of care where it is in fact provided, and arguably results in injustice similar to that which can be caused by 'lame duck' cases.

3.5. THE SIGNIFICANCE OF A PROMISE OF PROVISION

As mentioned above, adult offspring may bring a claim based on the equitable doctrine of proprietary estoppel to enforce an oral, and otherwise generally unenforceable, promise of testamentary entitlement coupled with detriment such as care work. Indeed, in many cases, an estoppel claim would be more advantageous to the claimant because the remedy awarded will be affected by the value of what was promised and the extent of the applicant's detriment rather than the applicant's need for maintenance.[159] But such a promise can be significant in the context of family provision claims, and in England the two claims are often addressed in the same proceedings.[160]

As we have seen, in the particular circumstances of *Espinosa*, a promise made by the deceased father to leave to the applicant property that he originally inherited from his wife was a weighty consideration for the purposes of the 1975 Act, although it does not appear to have been related to the care provided by the daughter for the father. Express or implied promises to benefit the applicant are examples of situations where a moral obligation is likely to be found in England,[161] but it may be the promise rather than any care provided that is crucial.

That said, the significance of a combination of a promise and work has been recognised in several cases. A promise was said to generate a moral obligation in *Re Pearce*, which involved a son who was promised that he would inherit a farm on which he had worked for a number of years,[162] and in the 'child of the family'

158 [2007] *NICh*, at [37].

159 See S. Gardner, 'The remedial discretion in proprietary estoppel – again' (2006) 122 *Law Quarterly Review* 492 for a discussion of the remedy in estoppel cases.

160 M. Cardinal, 'In Practice – Inheritance Or Estoppel – How The Cohabitant Succeeded' (2004) 34 *Family Law* 362.

161 *Re Goodchild (Deceased) and Another* [1996] 1 *FLR* 591. For an account of the similarities between cases involving the 1965 Act and constructive trusts in Ireland, which have some features in common with proprietary estoppel, see A. Keating, 'The Moral Duty and "New Model" Constructive Trusts' (2007) 12 *CPLJ* 79.

162 [1998] 2 *FLR* 705.

case of *Re Leach*.[163] In *Re Abram*,[164] it was found that the 'case for moral obligation or special circumstances' remained 'overwhelming' because the applicant worked in the family business for a significant period for low pay in the belief that it would be his, even though he eventually left through 'force majeure'.[165]

Similar conclusions have been reached in several Irish cases, and in *XC v RT*, Breen J confirmed that:

> Special circumstances giving rise to a moral duty may arise if a child is induced to believe that by, for example, working on a farm, he will ultimately become the owner of it, thereby causing him to shape his upbringing, training and life accordingly.[166]

In *PG v RSG*,[167] the judge found that the applicant was encouraged to believe that the family farm on which he had worked since the age of 14 would be his, and discouraged from leaving home when he married. It was found that the deceased's equal treatment of the applicant as compared with his two siblings did not constitute proper provision.[168]

There is little to stop the reasoning in the farm cases from being applied to scenarios involving care work, and Keating contemplates this possibility in Ireland.[169] Indeed, identical principles have been applied to English cases involving farm labourers and carers in the context of proprietary estoppel.[170] Some would argue that the injustice is greatest where the deceased makes a promise of provision but fails to honour it. But if family provision law is to be used to support and encourage care, it seems likely that claims would have to be feasible even in the absence of a promise of provision made by the deceased.

163 [1996] 1 *Ch* 226.
164 [1996] 2 *FLR* 379.
165 [1996] 2 *FLR* 379, at 394.
166 [2003] 2 *IR* 250, at 263.
167 [1980] ILRM 225. See also *In the Goods of Breen (Deceased), Breen and Kennedy v Breen and others*, unreported, High Court, 5 May 1995.
168 The fact that a farm has been promised to someone other than the applicant is also relevant: *Re JH de B; J de B v HE de B and others* [1991] 2 *IR* 105.
169 Keating, 'The Moral Duty and "New Model" Constructive Trusts', at 79.
170 Compare, *eg*, *Jennings v Rice* [2002] *EWCA Civ* 159 and *Thorner v Major* [2009] *UKHL* 18.

4. CONCLUSIONS AND SCOPE FOR DEVELOPMENT IN THE LAW

It has been suggested in this chapter that family provision could legitimately be used to support, encourage or reward care provided by adult children to a now-deceased care recipient. But it has also been recognised that the approach of the relevant legislation in England and Ireland and the courts' interpretation of it is not entirely fit for that purpose at the present time.

Kerridge has pointed out that claims by adult children under the Inheritance (Provision for Family and Dependants) Act often occur in distinctive circumstances.[171] It can therefore be difficult to isolate the precise reasoning of the court in a given case. Care provided is often mentioned by judges, but it can be unclear what (if any) effect it has of itself on the result. This state of affairs is inevitable given the focus on maintenance that pervades the Act.

In its recent consultation paper on intestacy and family provision, the Law Commission of England and Wales invited consultees' views on whether and how adult children should be given a greater chance of success in claiming under an amended 1975 Act.[172] But the Commission expressed understandable concern that it would be 'difficult to find a justification for doing so that was both clear, and consistent with the rest of the law', particularly if the maintenance limitation were removed.[173] As a result, it provisionally recommended no change, but perhaps the provision of care would be a viable addition to the factors taken into account.

In Ireland, there is arguably greater scope for judicial innovation to recognise care in itself because of the lack of an express 'maintenance' limitation in the Succession Act 1965 and the seemingly more generous approach in general, but such innovation may not be forthcoming. Statutory reform, on the other hand, has tended to focus on claims by same-sex couples and unmarried cohabitants.[174]

Of course, if an award in favour of a caring adult son or daughter is to be recognised in itself and without a requirement to demonstrate loss or need, the basis and measure of relief would have to be addressed and that is unlikely to be a straightforward task. One example that may be of assistance is the New Zealand Law Commission's idea of a 'contribution claim' for children and others who are

[171] R. Kerridge, *The Law of Succession*, at [8–59] and [8–62].

[172] Law Commission, *Intestacy and Family Provision Claims on Death*, [5.19].

[173] Law Commission, *Intestacy and Family Provision Claims on Death*, [5.13].

[174] Civil Partnership and Certain Rights and Obligations of Cohabitants Act 2010 (Ireland). See, *eg*, B. Sloan and J.M. Scherpe, 'Vorschläge zur Regelung der Rechtsstellung nichtehelicher und gleichgeschlechtlicher Lebensgemeinschaften in Irland' *Zeitschrift für das gesamte Familienrecht (FamRZ)* 2008, 1697.

not in need but have contributed to the deceased in some way.[175] The proposal, made in the context of a discussion about the limitations of the 'promise' requirement in the New Zealand testamentary promises legislation,[176] would allow an applicant to claim 'an appropriate award in respect of their unremunerated services for the will-maker'[177] where, *inter alia*, 'it is unjust for the estate of the deceased to retain the benefit without provision being made for the contributor'.[178] The availability of a claim based on unjust retention would be subject to a number of specific limitations,[179] which were clearly influenced by principles of the law of unjust enrichment. The remedy would usually be to the 'value of the benefit' conferred in the absence of an express promise,[180] but the court would be given a discretion to consider other factors.[181] There is an inevitable degree of imprecision surrounding the practical operation of the New Zealand Law Commission's proposal. But it does demonstrate that it is at least possible to formulate provisions under which adult offspring who provide care could claim a share in a parent's estate by virtue of the benefit conferred.

Many of the issues raised in this chapter will cause disagreement, not least because of the varied philosophies governing succession law throughout Europe. But as welfare states face the challenge of an ageing population, perhaps both common law and civil law jurisdictions should consider the possibility of using succession law to recognise and encourage care.

---

175 New Zealand Law Commission, *Succession Law: A Succession (Adjustment) Act*, in particular Part IV of the Draft Succession (Adjustment) Act, which begins on p 92. See also New Zealand Law Commission, *Succession Law: Testamentary Claims*, ch 9.

176 Law Reform (Testamentary Promises) Act 1949.

177 New Zealand Law Commission, *Succession Law: A Succession (Adjustment) Act*, at [85].

178 Draft Succession (Adjustment) Act, s 31(1)(b).

179 Draft Succession (Adjustment) Act, s 35.

180 Draft Succession (Adjustment) Act, s 36(2).

181 Draft Succession (Adjustment) Act, s 36(3).

PART SIX
CHILD MAINTENANCE

THE LINK BETWEEN CHILD MAINTENANCE AND CONTACT

Branka Rešetar

1. INTRODUCTION

Child maintenance and contact concerning the child are the most important parts of the legal relationship between the child and the non-resident parent. However, these legal aspects of parentage are, in principle, regulated separately. The issue of maintenance as a child's right has been treated as an independent legal consequence of parentage, viewed from the fact that child maintenance should always be a duty of parents, regardless of whether parents perform their parental responsibilities or not. Thus, child maintenance tends to be regulated separately from the issue of parental responsibility in both national and international instruments.[1] On the other hand, the issue of the personal relationship between the non-resident parent and the child has been treated as a part of parental responsibilities. It is viewed in two distinct ways both as a parental right to contact and as a parental duty securing the child's right to maintain contact. If anyone has a duty, ironically it is the resident parent who has the responsibility to enable and support the non-resident parent's right to maintain contact with the child. Accordingly, international as well as national instruments regulate the issue of contact separately from child maintenance, without making any connection between the two.[2]

Frequently, the borderline between extended contact and alternative residence is not completely clear.[3] It is possible to decide that the child shall reside with one parent but shall have contact with the non-resident parent comprising up to 50% of its time. Alternatively the same arrangement can be viewed as one of shared or joint residence. In either case, in practice, the child lives equally with each parent but in the first case the arrangement is described as extended contact, while the second case is regarded as one of alternative residence. If a maintenance regime takes account of the amount of time a child lives with a parent, it implicitly makes a link between contact and maintenance. Whether one calls a 50/50 arrangement "residence" or "contact" obviously is a semantic game. Yet, it is a game with important consequences for maintenance, which is likely to be owed under one label but perhaps not under the other. The tension, it seems, is to preserve the

[1] Eg most recently: Hague Convention on the International Recovery of Child Support and Other Forms of Family Maintenance (2007) and Council Regulation (EC) No. 4/2009 of 18 December 2008 on Jurisdiction, Applicable Law, Recognition and Enforcement of Decision and Cooperation in Matters relating to Maintenance Obligations.

[2] Eg European Convention of 15 May 2003 on Contact concerning Children and Council Regulation (EC) No. 2201/2003 of 27 November 2003 concerning Jurisdiction and the Recognition and Enforcement of Judgments in Matrimonial Matters and the Matters of Parental Responsibility.

[3] A. Singer, „Active Parenting or Solomon's Justice?", in K. Boele-Woelki (ed.), *Debates in Family Law around the Globe at the Dawn of the 21st Century,* Intersentia, Antwerp-Oxford-Portland, 2009, p. 62.

theoretical separation of contact and maintenance, while acknowledging their linkage in practice (at least in some national legal systems).

The lack of a legal link between contact (or alternative residence) and maintenance might result from a lack of legislative intention to improve the personal relationship between the child and the non-resident parent (mostly fathers). If the level of contact or the costs of maintaining contact with the child do not affect child maintenance, this suggests that the role of fathers is viewed principally as that of financial provider, with less attention paid to nurturing a social, caring relationship between the father and child. That also suggests that the state is primarily interested in fathers' financial support of their children.[4]

However, most European systems have succeeded, on various bases, in establishing a connection between contact or alternative residence (including joint parental authority) and maintenance when calculating maintenance contributions. In such systems, the frequency of contact or alternative residence influences not only the amount due but sometimes whether there is a duty to pay maintenance at all.[5] This issue has lately evoked intensive discussions in some systems.[6]

The aim of this paper is to draw a comparison between some European legal systems according to the criterion of (non-)linking of child maintenance and contact between the child and the non-resident parent. After a brief glance at the regulation of contact concerning children and child maintenance, as well as at the links or lack of links between them in a chosen legal system, various similarities and differences will be identified. Then, consideration will be given to the latest comparative research in the areas of psychology and sociology aimed at providing evidence of a firm bond between fulfilling the duty of child maintenance and exercising contact between the child and the non-resident parent. In that regard, this chapter asks whether or not the bond between child maintenance and the exercise of contact when regulating contact, alternative residence or child maintenance should be neglected. The final answer will be based on the sociological research findings.

---

4 Compare: J. Fortin, *Children's Rights and the Developing Law*, Cambridge University Press, 2005, p. 292–293.

5 Sweden, Denmark, Norway, Belgium, Finland, France, Germany, Netherlands, Sweden. A. Saldeen, „Sweden“, in C. Hamilton and A. Perry, (eds.), *Family law in Europe*, Tottel Publishing Ltd, West Sussex, 2006, p. 655. and C. Skinner, J. Bradshaw and J. Davidson, *Child support policy: An international perspective, UK Department for Work and Pensions*, http://research.dwp.gor.uk/asd/asd5/rports2007-208/rrep405.pdf, p. 1–224. (last visited 01.12.2009.).

6 S. Gilmore, "ReB (Contact: Child Support) – horses and carts: contact and child support", *Child and Family Law Quarterly*, Vol. 19, No 3, 2007, p. 357- 373. and A. Singer, "Active Parenting or Solomon's Justice?", in K. Boele-Woelki (ed.), *Debates in Family Law around the Globe at the Dawn of the 21st Century*, Intersentia, Antwerp-Oxford-Portland, 2009, p. 66–68.

2. (NON-)LINKING BETWEEN CONTACT AND MAINTENANCE IN SOME EUROPEAN LEGAL SYSTEMS

National legal systems regulate the child's right to contact and his/her right to maintenance totally separately. However, there are some European legal systems where the legislation has indeed established a link between contact and child maintenance whereas, in others, there is no such bond. This paper will examine two legal systems which do not include a link between contact and maintenance: the German and the Croatian systems; and two systems which have, unlike the former two, created such a link on a legal level: the English and Swedish legal systems.

2.1. GERMAN LAW

Contact concerning children and child maintenance are regulated separately under German law.

According to the general provision, the child's right to contact with the mother and father is regulated under § 1626 para. 3. sent. 1. of the German Civil Code (Bürgerliches Gesetzbuch – BGB). This states that contact with both parents is in the interests of the child. The right and duties of contact exist irrespective of who actually holds parental custody. The child has a right of contact with each parent also according to § 1684 para. 1. BGB. Contact may become an issue in the case of sole parental custody, ie when the non-resident parent is restricted to contact, or in the case of joint parental custody. In the latter case the non-resident parent has the right and duty to contact with the child in addition to his continuing duties of parental custody.[7]

Child maintenance is regulated separately and special statutory provisions regulate maintenance claims of children against their parents. Child maintenance follows from being a (legal) parent. The duty to maintain minor children is independent of whether the parent has parental custody. However, there is an interdependence of parental care (by parent with whom the child is living) and the duty to maintain. That is reflected in the fact that – unlike any other obligees – by § 1606 III of the BGB, a parent with whom the child is living or who takes care of the child fulfils their obligation to contribute to the maintenance of the minor unmarried child by providing care and upbringing.[8] The parent who is not living

[7] D. Schwab, P. Gottwald and E. Nourney, "Germany" (September 2006), in W. Pintens (ed.), Family and Succession Law – Suppl. 32, *International Encyclopedia of Laws*, Kluwer Law International, The Hague/London/New York, 2002, p. 90.

[8] *Ibid.*, p. 102.

with the child is obliged to pay maintenance. This division of liabilities does not depend how parental custody is regulated. In such situations, the child has the right to contact with the non-resident parent according to § 1684 of the BGB.

The level of maintenance payable by the parent who is not living with the child is determined according to the general rule of § 1610 of the BGB. The minimum maintenance for the minor child is determined by § 1612a. The courts also use tables relating to the parent's income and child's age to harmonise judicial practice.[9] Neither regular contact with the child nor going on holiday with the non-resident parent influences the amount of child maintenance. On the contrary, it is derived from the monthly maintenance rates in the Düsseldorf Table which also sets out a framework for needs and assumes the ordinary right to contact.[10]

For a long time, the governing principle has been that the resident parent should provide care and the non-resident parent maintenance. However, in reality, more and more parents (married or unmarried) who exercise joint care after separation or divorce are taking care of their children in turns. The practical details of such care of children in turns are determined by the parents themselves, as they see fit, on a weekly or monthly basis or even on particular days in a week, share the children. That kind of provision of joint care is called *Wechselmodell.* Still, if both parents provide maintenance in kind by means of caring for children in turns, do they also have to provide financial maintenance? The BGB does not regulate this issue, so it has had to be dealt with by judicial practice.[11]

The Federal Court of Germany has, in two recent cases, determined whether certain contact arrangements amount to *Wechselmodell* or not, and what implications the model had on the child maintenance liability. In the first case, the mother took care of a minor child two-thirds of the time, and the father one third of the time. The mother argued that the father should pay the total amount of child maintenance. The court decided that the father, despite his share in the care of the child, had to provide 100% of maintenance in cash according to § 1606 para 3 of the BGB; the principle that one parent should provide maintenance in the form of care and upbringing refers only to the other parent. The amount of financial maintenance owed is determined simply according to the income and financial situation of the non-resident parent. In the view of the Federal Court of Germany, a different outcome is only possible in cases of "*reales Wechselmodell*",

9 *Ibid.*, p. 103.

10 H.J. Dose, P. Gerhard, W. Gutdeuch, O. Haußleiter, D. Pauling, H. Scholz, und W. Thalmann, *Das Unterhaltsrecht in der familienrichterlichen Praxis*, Verlag C.H. Beck, Munich, 2000, p. 228–229.

11 H. Luthin, BGH: Barunterhaltspflicht bei sog. "Wechelmodell", Zeitschrift für das gesamte Familienrecht, 14/2006, p. 1018. and www.anwalt.de/rechtstipps/kindesunterhalt (last visited 05.07.2010.).

ie when both parents provide the child with virtually the same level of care. This was the situation in the second case considered by the Federal Court. In that situation, irrespective of their personal financial situations, both parents have to provide comparable shares of financial maintenance. The maintenance in kind provided by both parents is taken into account to the same proportion of their income. The amount of financial maintenance is determined according to the parties' joint revenue and property. Therefore, if one parent's income is greater than the other's, the maintenance share of former should also be bigger. The exact amount of financial maintenance results from precise mathematical calculations of parents' income. The child's needs are also increased due to the shared care arrangement (*Wechselmodell*).[12]

One may draw the conclusion that the German legislation generally does not deem contact with the child and maintenance payment as mutually connected. Nevertheless, increasingly couples share the actual day-to-day care of the child, but unless the care is shared equally (*reales Wechselmodell*) this is not taken into account in the calculation of the child maintenance.

2.2. CROATIAN LAW

Under Croatian law, the term *'contact with children'* refers to the personal relationship between the child and the parent who lives in a different residence, including planned visits, the time spent together on particular days, weeks or even longer periods of time.[13] Decisions on contact are typically made after the parents' divorce or termination of their long-term relationship. Also, judicial decisions on contact with the child are made on occasions when the child is born in an extramarital relationship or when its parentage is determined in judicial proceedings. In those cases, whether or not the parents had ever lived together, or had any relationship before the child was born plays no role whatsoever. In such circumstances the non-resident parent must apply for a court decision on contact with the child, but the right to contact with the child arises from legal parentage. According to Article 87 para 3 of the Family Act, the child has the right to contact with the parent if they live separately.

Provisions on child maintenance are contained in a special part of the Family Act. Hence, child maintenance regulation is not connected with regulation of the child's right to contact in any way whatsoever. The basic principle for determining child maintenance has been copied from the German legal system: the principle

---

12 BGH 21.12.2005. NJW 2006, 2258; FamRZ 2006, 1015 and BGH 28.2.2007. NJW 2007; 1961, FamRZ 2007, 793. See H. Luthin, *FamRZ* 2006, 1018 and *FamRZ* 2007, 707–710.

13 D. Hrabar, "Obiteljskopravni odnosi roditelja i djece", in M. Alinčić, D. Hrabar, D. Jakovac-Lozić and A. Korać, *Obiteljsko pravo*, Narodne novine d.d., Zagreb, 2007, p. 270–271.

that equates the care of the resident parent with the maintenance or support of the non-resident parent. That means the legal equation of the care, protection and education of a minor child provided by the resident parent with the pecuniary maintenance from the non-resident parent (Article 233 of the Family Law Act).

Moreover, the Croatian legislation has determined guidelines for three age categories – children up to 6, children from 6 to 12 and children from 12 to 18, aimed at defining a minimum percentage of the average Croatian salary intended for child maintenance (17% for the first category, 20% for the second and 22% for the third). The court may additionally determine larger amounts of money for maintenance if the child's needs are greater, or where the parents are wealthy on the basis that the living standard of children should correspond to the living standard of the parent (Article 232 para 3 of the Family Act). If a maintenance debtor has more that one child who can claim maintenance (Article 232 para 5 of the Family Act) or a child has been receiving its own income[14] which contributes towards the child's maintenance (Article 211 of the Family Act), the court may order lower child maintenance, but not less than half the minimum support. This means that the amount of child maintenance can be reduced if the debtor has got more than one child or if the child has its own income and contributes towards its maintenance.[15]

Neither regular contact with the child nor going on holiday with the non-resident parent influences the amount of child maintenance. Moreover, repeated frequent contact with the child exceeding the period of time defined as regular contact (every second weekend and half of the school holidays) does not have an effect on child support liability. However, the principle equating the care of the resident parent with the maintenance or support of the non-resident parent should, according to academic commentaries, be seen as a rebuttable presumption.[16] According to that opinion, it is open to the non-resident parent , in any court proceedings, to try to prove the opposite, ie that he (or she) spends more time with the child than stipulated by regular contact, and thus provides the child with more care, protection and education. It further means that the non-resident parent, apart from meeting his (her) liability of maintenance, takes over part of the liabilities for which the resident parent is liable. In other words, on this view, child maintenance could be reduced if the contact between the child and the non-

---

14 According to Art. 259. of the Family Act: "A minor child can obtain property by inheritance, bestowal, based on its revenue or pursuant to some other legal basis. The minor's property is governed by its parents, except in cases a minor obtained its property based on its revenue after its 15th birthday." According to Art. 211. of the Family Act: "A child with its revenue is obliged to make contributions to its maintenance."

15 A. Korać, "Uzdržavanje", in M. Alinčić, D. Hrabar, D. Jakovac-Lozić and A. Korać, *Obiteljsko pravo*, Narodne novine 2006, p. 480–481.

16 B. Rešetar and S. Ledić, "Određivanje uzdržavanja za maloljetnu djecu prema Noveli Obiteljskog zakona iz 2007", *Hrvatska pravna revija*, 11/2009, p. 51.

resident parent goes beyond the regular framework – i.e. every second weekend, half of the winter and summer school holidays and every second holiday.[17] If the child, beside the regular contact, spends a further two days in a week with the non-resident parent, then the court should deem the time to be divided equally between the parents. On the other hand, logically, the amount of time the non-resident parent spends with the child indeed reduces the maintenance costs of the resident parent and, simultaneously, raises the maintenance costs of the non-resident parent. However, shared care or alternative residence is still very rare in practice and results only from mutual agreement of the parents. In such cases, parents must stipulate the level of maintenance, which can be zero.

Summing up, for the time being, Croatian legislation does not make any link between child maintenance and contact, regardless of the frequency of the latter. Consequently, Croatian judges, unlike their German colleagues, continue to refuse to deal with this issue, ie the existence of a bond between child maintenance and alternative residence or shared care. This has resulted in injustice in practice.

2.3. ENGLISH LAW

English law recognises no right to contact, as such, but contact with the child can be obtained by the non-resident parent or other person via a contact order made by the court, in accordance with the child's best interests.[18]

English law provides various mechanisms for facilitating child maintenance. Relevant parties can require support for the child from the liable person (usually a non-resident parent) within the child support scheme, by private agreements and finally via court orders.[19] The general rule is that the court plays a role inferior to that of the Child Support Agency. The competence of the courts is limited to making orders in exceptional cases (such as very high earning non-resident parents, or where extra costs are incurred in connection with the child's disability or education), where liability is imposed on a step-parent, and consent orders: private settlements for child maintenance subject to the court's approval. In all other cases, child maintenance is exclusively a matter for the Child Support Agency, now the Child Maintenance and Enforcement Commission.[20] I shall

---

17 *Ibid.*, p.

18 Provisions of Article 8 CA 1989 enlist orders available for the court for the purpose of exercising the content of parental care. These are *residence order, contact order, prohibited steps order* and *specific issue order*. S.M. Cretney *et al.*, *Principles of Family Law*, Sweet & Maxwell, London 2003, p. 589, and N. Lowe and G. Douglas, *Bromley's Family Law*, Oxford University Press, 2007, p. 521.

19 N. Lowe and G. Douglas, *Bromley's Family Law*, Oxford University Press, 2007, p. 914.

20 N. Wikeley, *Child Support – Law and Policy*, Hart Publishing, Oxford – Portland Oregon, 2006, p. 186, 190.

focus on provisions defining calculations of maintenance pursuant to the 1991 Child Support Act (CSA 1991, which has been amended in 1995, 2000 and 2008).

Either parent is entitled to apply for child maintenance calculation under CSA 1991.[21] In compliance with new rules, the method for calculating the amount of child maintenance which the non-resident parent has to pay for the benefit of the child is regulated under Schedule 1 CSA 1991 as amended in 2000 and 2008.[22] The rate of child maintenance is based on the non-resident parent's income. There are four possible rates which may be used in calculating a non-resident parent's child support liability: *a basic rate, a reduced rate, a flat rate and a nil rate.* In simple words, the basic rate is a normal rate which is used if none of the other three rates are applicable: usually, this simply means that the non-resident parent has income above £200 per week; the reduced rate is for a non-resident parent with a weekly revenue of between £100 and £200; the flat rate for a non-resident parent on benefits or with a weekly revenue of less than £100, and the nil rate refers to specific categories of non-resident parents against whom recovery of child support is regarded as unrealistic (eg prisoners).[23]

The new support scheme assures a direct reduction if the non-resident parent has contact with the child for at least on average one night a week. Maintenance payments calculated by applying the basic, reduced or flat rate can be affected by either or both of the sets of rules governing apportionment and shared care. Apportionment applies where the non-resident parent has more than one qualifying child and they are living with different persons with care, apportioning the maintenance due between those households; this is a purely arithmetical rule with minimal policy implications. However, shared care is much more often relevant and significant in terms of policy. These rules apply if the non-resident parent and the person with care are both involved in the care of the qualifying child, and the non-resident parent from time to time has care of the child *overnight*. Consequently, a non-resident parent who only shares *day-time* care of the child or day-time care together with less than one night a week of overnight care cannot benefit from a reduction for shared care. Once the decision on the extent of the overnight care provided by the non-resident parent is made, in basic rate cases[24] their child support liability is reduced by an appropriate fraction as follows:

21 *Ibid.*, p. 245, 246, 248, 249.

22 The latest amendments took place in 2008. – The Child Maintenance and Other Payments Act 2008, bearing in mind the fact that the new calculation method will come into operation in 2010 or 2011. www.oup.com/uk/orc/bin/9780199277162/resources/updates/ch06_1009.pdf, last visited 11.10.2010.

23 N. Wikeley, *Child Support – Law and Policy*, Hart Publishing, Oxford – Portland Oregon, 2006, p. 299.

24 Different rules apply to reduced and flat rate cases.

Effect of Shared Care on Basic and Reduced Rates

Number of nights	**Fraction to subtract**
52 to 103	one-seventh
104 to 155	two-sevenths
156 to 174	three-sevenths
175 or more	one-half

If the non-resident parent is ordered to pay the flat rate because of his benefit status, and they have shared care for at least 52 nights a year, then their liability for child support maintenance is simply reduced to nil.[25]

The non-resident parent may request reduction of the maintenance amount due to financial costs of contact. The regulations list in detail the types of contact-related costs which may qualify for this purpose. These might include purchase of travel tickets, fuel, taxi fares, car hire, overnight stays and minor incidental costs.[26]

The English legislation has thus established a clear link between child maintenance and contact as well as between shared care and child maintenance, where the key role is played by overnight care of the child by the non-resident parent. The link between maintenance and contact is also legally recognized in cases in which the maintenance amount is reduced in recognition of the special costs of maintaining contact between the non-resident parent and the child. However, English case law denies any connection between maintenance and contact in the opposite direction, i.e. it sees no link between the issues in contact cases, as shown by the recent case of *ReB (Contact: Child Support)*.[27] Pursuant to the Court of Appeal, it is inappropriate, when deciding on contact, to consider the consequences that the decision on contact will have on the potential maintenance liability. At the same time, this Court points out that such a connection regarding decisions on contact would be contrary to the child's welfare which is of paramount importance in making decisions about contact.[28]

25 *Ibid.*, p. 312–319.

26 *Ibid.*, p. 374–376.

27 [2006] EWCA Civ 1574.

28 S. Gilmore, "ReB (Contact: Child Support) – horses and carts: contact and child support", *Child and Family Law Quarterly*, Vol. 19, No 3, 2007, p. 357- 373.

2.4. SWEDISH LAW

In Swedish law, the child is granted the right to contact with the non-resident parent. The court may make a contact order within the framework of joint legal custody (The Children and Parent Code – CPC, Chapter 6, Section 15).[29]

If the parents live separately, the resident parent generally fulfils their maintenance obligation by taking care of the child and catering for the child's day to day needs, while the non-resident parent should pay an allowance for maintenance regardless of whether he or she has custody (CPC Chapter 7, Section 2).

There are two statutes regulating child maintenance in Sweden. Provisions on child maintenance are set out in Chapter 7 of the CPC and in the Maintenance Support Act (MSA). CPC lays down the general private legal principles of the parental obligation to maintain children. The maintenance is stipulated by the court in a private legal procedure or by agreement (CPC, Chapter 7, Section 2). According to the MSA, under certain conditions, the state will advance or supplement maintenance payments for children living with a sole parent. The public social insurance office then makes a decision on the amount of maintenance, disburses it to the child and demands a refund from the liable parent. There is a certain difference between these two statutes, promoting different principles for duration of maintenance as well as the amount and the formula for calculating it. In practice, the system outlined by the MSA tends to be used very often due to its advantages for parents with lower incomes and for its practicality, as well as for assuring the possibility of reduction of conflict since it is governed by the public social insurance office.[30]

The non-resident parent is required by the CPC to pay maintenance on a permanent basis and thus has a duty to pay maintenance if he/she a) neither has parental responsibility nor lives with the child on a permanent basis or b) has joint parental responsibility with the other parent, but the child resides only with the other parent (PCP Chapter 7, Section 5). Under the MSA, a child is entitled to maintenance payments if his/her parents do not live together and if the child permanently lives and is registered with one of the parents and that parent has parental responsibility (MSA, Section 3(1).[31]

Under the CPC, parents must provide the child with maintenance according to what is reasonable, bearing in mind the need of the child and their combined

29 M.K. Eriksson and J. Schiratzki, Sweden, in "Sweden" (October 2001), in W. Pintens (ed.), Family and Succession Law – Suppl. 15, *International Encyclopedia of Laws*, Kluwer Law International, The Hague/London/New York, 2002, p. 107.

30 *Ibid.*, p. 109.

31 *Ibid.*, p. 110.

resources (CPC, Chapter 7, Section 1). The child's need is in practice calculated schematically according to the non-binding guidelines issued by the National Board of Health and Welfare. Each parent should bear a share of the costs for the child, proportional to his or her economic ability, i.e. financial resources.[32] By contrast, under the MSA, no specific needs of the child are taken into account, nor is the age of the child. The parents' financial capacities are not judged on an individual basis when it comes to determination of child support. Hence, child support is payable irrespective of the financial situation of the resident parent. The non-resident parent shall reimburse the entire amount of payment support according to the MSA provisions.[33]

Swedish law identifies a clear link between contact and child maintenance in both the CPC and MSA. If the non-resident parent has had the child in his or her home for the whole of six days during a month, or for a consecutive period of five days, that parent may, according to both the CPC and MSA, deduct one fourteenth of the monthly maintenance payment for each 24 hour period of the child's stay (CPC, Chapter 7, Section 4 and MSA Section 23(2)).[34]

In order to make contact easier, the resident parent might have to pay part of the expenses for the child's travel in connection with contact. The resident parent should make contributions in accordance with what is reasonable having regard to the financial circumstances of the parents and the overall circumstances. Such an order should not be made if the distance between the child's residence and the residence of the non-resident parent is less then a 100 kilometres (CPC, Chapter 6, Section 15b).[35] This Swedish solution is similar to the English one which also recognizes the costs of maintaining contact with the child on occasions of deciding on maintenance. The difference between these two is that English law enables the non-resident parent to apply for reduction of maintenance owing to the special costs of maintaining their contact with the child.

When it comes to alternative residence or when the child permanently lives with both parents on an equal basis, there are no legal grounds for obliging a parent to pay maintenance for the child under Swedish law. Neither parent then is under a duty to contribute to the maintenance of the child.[36] If a child spends more than

---

32 A. Singer., "Time is money? – Support for children with alternating residence", in B. Verschraegen (ed.), *Family Finances,* Jan Sramek Verlag, Vienna, 2009, p. 596.

33 M.K. Eriksson and J. Schiratzki, Sweden, in "Sweden" (October 2001), in W. Pintens (ed.), Family and Succession Law – Suppl. 15, *International Encyclopedia of Laws*, Kluwer Law International, The Hague/London/New York, 2002, p. 112.

34 *Ibid.*, p. 113.

35 *Ibid.*, p. 108.

36 In theory, a parent can be obliged to pay special maintenance if they do not actually support or raise the child. However, this never happens in practice since a parent is automatically considered to support the child if they spend time with it. A. Singer., "Time is money? –

one third of his/her time with the non-resident parent, it might, according to the findings of the Supreme Court[37] be considered to live alternately with both of its parents.[38] Although alternative residence/contact and child maintenance are two different aspects of parenthood,[39] there is a clearly regulated link between them in the Swedish legal system. The number of days spent with the non-resident parent has an effect on child support liability while alternative residence implies child maintenance by both parents, irrespective of possible differences in their financial status.[40]

2.5. COMPARATIVE CONCLUSION

Contact with children and child maintenance are two different aspects of parenthood, generally seen as separate legal issues. The common principle of all the above systems is that the non-resident parent is liable to pay child maintenance unlike the parent with whom the child resides. Crucial discrepancies in this field relate to the effect of contact, alternative residence or shared care on determination of child support liability.

Among the jurisdictions described above, there seem to be two approaches to the link between contact and child maintenance. The first one, demonstrated by the German and Croatian legal systems, sees or at least identifies no link between contact and child maintenance rules. Regardless of the frequency and duration of contact between the child and the non-resident parent, they allow no reduction of child maintenance on their account. Still, it is vital to mention that, the German legal system does take account of contact costs which are derived from the monthly maintenance rates from the Düsseldorf Table, which sets out a

Support for children with alternating residence", in B. Verschraegen (ed.), *Family Finances*, Jan Sramek Verlag, Vienna, 2009, p. 596.

37 Supreme Court Decision NJA (Nytt Juridisk Arkiv) 1998 p. 267. See in M.K. Eriksson and J. Schiratzki, Sweden, in "Sweden" (October 2001), in W. Pintens (ed.), Family and Succession Law – Suppl. 15, *International Encyclopedia of Laws*, Kluwer Law International, The Hague/London/New York, 2002, p. 113 and in A. Singer, „Active Parenting or Solomon's Justice?", in K. Boele-Woelki (ed.), *Debates in Family Law around the Globe at the Dawn of the 21st Century*, Intersentia, Antwerp-Oxford-Portland, 2009, p. 62.

38 M.K. Eriksson and J. Schiratzki, Sweden, in "Sweden" (October 2001), in W. Pintens (ed.), Family and Succession Law – Suppl. 15, *International Encyclopedia of Laws*, Kluwer Law International, The Hague/London/New York, 2002, p. 113.

39 A. Singer., "Time is money? – Support for children with alternating residence", in B. Verschraegen (ed.), *Family Finances*, Jan Sramek Verlag, Vienna, 2009, p. 599.

40 For explicit criticism of the Swedish solution for the lack of maintenance payment see: A. Singer., "Time is money? – Support for children with alternating residence", in B. Verschraegen (ed.), *Family Finances*, Jan Sramek Verlag, Vienna, 2009, p. 591–601. and A. Singer, „Active Parenting or Solomon's Justice?", in K. Boele-Woelki (ed.), *Debates in Family Law around the Globe at the Dawn of the 21st Century*, Intersentia, Antwerp-Oxford-Portland, 2009, p. 66–71.

framework for needs and assumes the ordinary right to contact. Although the law does not regulate shared care or alternative residence, German judicial practice adjusts child support liability to the time spent with parents in cases where the care is provided in equal shares ("reales Wechselmodell"). Child support liability is then stipulated mathematically having regard to the financial status of both parents.

By contrast with the German and Croatian legal systems, England and Sweden clearly identify the link between contact and child maintenance. The latter systems go so far as to precisely specify the number of days or nights spent with the non-resident parent by the child, based on which maintenance payment is reduced or increased. If the child spends the same amount of time with both parents, maintenance payment in England is reduced by half whereas the Swedish legal system under the same circumstances, ie on the occasion of alternative residence, completely terminates maintenance payment.

It is obvious that there are differences regarding the existence of the link between contact, shared care or alternative residence and child maintenance amongst these legal systems. While some systems totally ignore the influence of contact on maintenance payment, others require strict legal regulation thereof. The time spent with both parents equally always affects child support liability somehow, but the solutions are rather different: termination in the Swedish law, staged reduction of maintenance in the English system, while in Germany, child maintenance is calculated by reference to the financial status of both parents. The Croatian law regulates neither the issue of alternative residence nor its link with maintenance.[41]

Despite the fact that German judicial practice is gradually closing the gap between the solutions of the systems which identify the link between child maintenance and shared care or alternative residence, different legislation may lead to completely different solutions. Let us imagine a case in which the child spends somewhat more than one third of the time with the non-resident parent. The German law would require the entire maintenance sum to be settled by that parent. If the same situation occurred in Sweden (pursuant to the viewpoint of the Supreme Court), the child might be considered to live alternately with both of its parents. That would lead to non-existence of child maintenance so neither parent would be obliged to pay anything to their ex-spouse. There is no doubt which legal system would be opted for by the non-resident parent! Also, it is obvious that the systems recognizing the link between contact and maintenance will encourage

---

41 This refers to a simplified comparison of different solutions. It is clear that in terms of a more thorough functional comparison, one would have to take into account everything what affects default maintenance payment in particular legal systems which is actually a ratio of child maintenance payment and financial status of one or both parents and reflects the living standard of the child in a particular legal system.

contact disputes: initiated by the non-resident parent in order to secure more frequent contact with the child, and so reduce the maintenance amount payable; by the resident parent in order to reduce the amount of contact and so increase the maintenance.

3. RESULTS OF INTERDISCIPLINARY RESEARCH

Although some legal systems deny the link between contact and child maintenance, this bond does exist in reality. There have been a number of international studies showing that fathers who pay child support maintain contact with their children to a greater extent.[42]

American research has shown that the percentage of non-resident fathers who maintain regular contact with their children has gone up in the USA since the 1990s when the law in some American states started to allow child support payments to be adjusted downward when father-child contact reaches a certain threshold.[43] A disadvantage of this trend of increasing frequency of fathers' contact with children is "bad" motivation – seeking more contact simply to reduce the maintenance payment.[44]

Other research in Anglo-Saxon jurisdictions has shown a firm bond between contact and child maintenance, but the bond was also connected with other circumstances: the fact that mothers are more willing to consent to contact with the child if fathers pay child support on a regular basis, and the feeling of equality of both parents under such circumstances. All these things together encourage cooperation between parents, which is undoubtedly for the child's benefit.[45]

A newer British survey on the views of parents concerning the issue has shown that contact was by far the most important factor expected to influence child maintenance. In the minds of parents it is difficult to distinguish between contact with the child and child maintenance. It is all due to the vast importance of the contact and its implications. According to the parents, emotional support to

---

42 See more in: B. Rešetar, "New Child Maintenance Obligations in Croatia", in B. Verschraegen (ed.), Family Finances, Jan Sramek Verlag, Vienna, p. 611–613.

43 J. Herring, "Contact in a Private Law Context" in A. Bainham, B. Lindley, M. Richards and L. Trinder (eds.), *Children and their Families: Contact, Rights and Welfare*, Hart Publishing, Oxford-Portland, Oregon, 2003., p. 107. and P.R. Amato, C.E. Meyers and R.E. Emery, "Changes in Non-Resident Father-Child Contact from 1976 to 2002", Family Relations – *Interdisciplinary Journal of Applied Family Studies*, 58 (February 2009), p. 43.

44 J. Herring, "Contact in a Private Law Context" in A. Bainham, B. Lindley, M. Richards and L. Trinder (eds.), *Children and their Families: Contact, Rights and Welfare*, Hart Publishing, Oxford-Portland, Oregon, 2003., p. 107–108.

45 *Ibid.*, p. 109.

the children mattered at least as much as financial support and many took the standpoint that both parents have equal rights to contact and equal responsibilities. A further possible link may be found in parents' attitudes; some parents thought that non-residents parents who were spending time with their children should pay less than those who did not facilitate the parent-child relationship. Following this research and prevailing opinion amongst parents, contact arrangements could undoubtedly alter obligations to pay.[46]

The latest American research has again confirmed the existence of a firm link between child maintenance payment and contact between non-resident fathers and children. Within the scope of this research, data from the 1970s to the 2000s have been analyzed. The results indicate that fathers who pay maintenance make frequent contact with their children. But the direction of causation is still unclear. The possible causes are multiple: non-resident fathers who often see their children have a better insight into the children's economic needs; on the one side, non-resident fathers who regularly make child maintenance payment have the feeling that they "have earned" the right to be with their children, while mothers, for their part, feel a sense of duty to support those contacts. However, it is still not possible to exclude the third external factor which has an effect on both maintenance payment and frequent contact with the child and that is "changing social norms that emphasize men's economic and social obligations to their children."[47]

As a rule, increasing the frequency of contact by non-resident parents and children is desirable both philosophically and for children's well-being. Still, judges are right to be sceptical that, in some cases, the non-resident parent's motivation for increased contact may be more to reduce maintenance than to preserve a close relationship with the child (a factor which judges should always consider in jurisdictions where maintenance and contact are linked). If this motivation ultimately leads to better non-resident parent-child relationships, perhaps the financial cost is worth the emotional gain. However, the reduced maintenance serves no one if the motivation is purely strategic. This would be evident if contact exercised in practice is notably less frequent than what was negotiated in order to lower maintenance. Since predicting the future is difficult, one solution to this last circumstance would be to increasing maintenance awards retroactively from the time of the original settlement.

---

46 A. Atkinson, S. McKay and N. Dominy, Future policy options for child support: The views of parents, Research Report No 380, Department for Work and Pensions, p. 24–29: http://campaigns.dwp.gov.uk/asd/asd5/report_abstracts/rr_abstracts/rra_380.asp last visited 11.10.2010.

47 P. R. Amato, C. E. Meyers and R. E. Emery, "Changes in Non-Resident Father-Child Contact from 1976 to 2002", Family Relations – *Interdisciplinary Journal of Applied Family Studies*, 58 (February 2009), p. 43.

4. CONCLUSION

While, on the one hand, the legal issues of contact and child maintenance are treated in national as well as in international legal systems as distinct, sociological research constantly confirms a relationship between these: ie the thesis that the non-resident parent who does pay maintenance also maintains regular and frequent contact with the child. As has been shown this link has been recognized by some legal systems, albeit with concerns about strategic bargaining for more contact to lower maintenance awards and with no legal consensus about how to address the link between contact and maintenance in the minds (and behaviour) of many parents. For instance, the English and Swedish legal systems regulate the relationship between contact and child maintenance in detail. In these systems the added expenses of the 'contact parent' are reflected in reduced payments even though certain expenses of the residential parent (particularly housing costs) are not reduced by the child's visits or stays elsewhere. Although not specifically regulated by the law, this bond is gradually emerging on the surface in Germany where – if only in cases of reales Wechselmodell – a special emphasis is put on how much time the child spends with both parents. In terms of Croatia, only academic commentaries mention this possibility. It is beyond any doubt that quality contact between the non-resident parent and the child represents an extremely important aspect for the child's long-term well-being. However, from the viewpoint of family law, the relationship between the non-resident parent and the child does not consist only of their contact, but also includes other legal issues such parental responsibility and payment of adequate child maintenance.

This aim of this paper was not to find a perfect solution for the regulation and recognition in child support law of a connection between that issue and contact. It has illustrated the varying degree of recognition of links between maintenance and contact in different legal systems. The issue is very complex and requires much more research and elaboration. The goals of this paper were, first, to call attention to the diversity of current legal systems in whether they link contact and maintenance in the hope that this might serve as an incentive for further discussion in the field. The second goal was also to emphasize the obvious difference between the legal and real status of the link between contact and child maintenance, which has been identified and explored in various studies. Although the nature and direction of the connection between financial support and emotional support through contact remains unclear it is absolutely certain that the separation of child maintenance and contact in the law and contrasting reality of their connection in practice will evoke new discussions in the future. I hope that this paper will contribute to that debate.

PARENTAL MAINTENANCE OBLIGATIONS TOWARDS CHILDREN IN CENTRAL EUROPE: THE HIGHWAY TO HELL OR A STAIRWAY TO HEAVEN?

Martin Kornel

SUMMARY

One of the major challenges that contemporary family law faces is how to ascertain proper maintenance for the child in the case of his or her parents' divorce or separation and how to ensure that this obligation will be carried out by the obliged parent. A variety of approaches to these problems are identifiable in Western countries. Although the shift towards maintenance based on obligatory or recommended mathematical formulas is discernible, there are still countries whose legislation contains only very vague rules in this field.

This article focuses on these questions in the light of the relevant laws in the Czech Republic, Slovakia and Poland. All the above-mentioned countries have much in common as far as contemporary family law is concerned. This is primarily the effect of previously similar family law legislation adopted in 1949 and 1950 and, secondly, the effect of the long-lasting socialist era. Thus, the legal regulation of the maintenance obligation by parents towards their children has remained almost unchanged since those times in Poland and the Czech Republic. The determination of maintenance is still based on very simple rules and wide discretion by the courts is preferred. In Slovakia, on the other hand, new and progressive legislation was adopted in 2005. Nowadays, a minimum amount of maintenance is laid down and if the non-residential parent does not fulfil his/her obligation the state guarantees maintenance for the child to some extent.

In this article, the development of legal regulation is explained and, furthermore, the practical impact of changes on the rights of parents and their children is explored. Such an exploration proves that contemporary vague and discretionary rules, which are effective in Poland and the Czech Republic, are problematical and are an inheritance from the socialist era. These kinds of rules could have possibly worked in times when the state was inclined to greatly interfere in the lives of families and children, and, furthermore, the divorce rate was then lower. However, nowadays such an approach impairs the best interests of the child and calls for change.

1. INTRODUCTION

One of the major challenges which contemporary family law faces is how to ascertain proper maintenance for a child in the case of his or her parents' divorce or separation and how to ensure that this obligation will be carried out by the obliged parent. A variety of approaches to these problems are identifiable in Western countries. Although the shift towards maintenance based on obligatory or recommended mathematical formulas is visible,[1] there are still countries whose legislation contains only very vague rules in this field.

This article focuses on the above questions in the light of the relevant laws in the Czech Republic, Slovakia and Poland. All these countries have much in common as far as contemporary family law is concerned. This is primarily the effect of previously similar family law legislation adopted in 1949 and 1950 and, secondly, the effect of the long-lasting socialist era. Therefore, the article explores the changes which have occurred since the unification of family law in the territory of Czechoslovakia and Poland since 1950.[2] Special attention is paid to the development of rules to determine the amount of child maintenance used by the courts.

2. SOVIET LAW AS THE NEW FAMILY LAW PARADIGM (1945–1963)

After the First World War, family law in Czechoslovakia and Poland reflected the fact that different civil laws were in force in the territory of both countries at once. The Austrian Civil Code (*Allgemeine Bürgerliche Gesetzbuch*) and Hungarian customary law were the primary sources of family law in Czechoslovakia. In Poland, the situation was complicated because the German Civil Code (*Deutsche Bürgerliche Gesetzbuch*), the Austrian Civil Code, the Code Napoleon and the civil law of Czarist Russia all applied.[3] Therefore legislators felt the necessity to adopt new legal rules on family relations in order to achieve more uniformity in the territory of their countries. Although some attempts to enact new rules were made, new legislation was not adopted until the Second World War had

1 B. Fehlberg, M. Maclean, 'Child Support Policy in Australia and the United Kingdom: Changing Priorities But a Similar Tough Deal for Children?,' (2009) 23 *Int J Law Pol Fam (International Journal of Law, Policy and the Family)*, pp. 1–4 or Ch. Skinner, J. Davidson, 'Recent Trends in Child Maintenance Schemes in 14 Countries ', (2009) 23 *Int J Law Pol Fam*, pp 38–40.

2 The names of both countries have changed many times during the relevant period. For clarity, 'Czechoslovakia' and 'Poland' are consistently used in this article in order to make it understandable. However, it is important to note that their official names were the Czechoslovak Republic in 1945–1960, the Czechoslovak Socialist Republic in 1960–1990, the Czech and Slovak Federal Republic in 1990–1992. In 1993, the Czech and Slovak Federal Republic dissolved and two independent countries have been established, the Czech Republic and Slovakia. The Polish Constitution of 22nd July 1952 used the name People's Republic of Poland. That name was changed by a new Constitution adopted in 1992 and the current official name is the Republic of Poland.

3 Z. Nagorski, 'Codification of Civil Law in Poland (1918–1939)' in W. Komarnicki and others, *Studies in Polish and Comparative Law*, Stevens & Sons Limited, London, 1945, p. 45 or K. Alexandrowitz, 'Marriage Law in Poland: A Problem of Comparative Law.' in W. Komarnicki and others, *Studies in Polish and Comparative Law*, Stevens & Sons Limited, London, 1945, p. 156–160. Available at http://ia351404.us.archive.org/0/items/studiesinpolishc00poliuoft/studiesinpolishc00poliuoft.pdf.

ended.[4] After the Second World War, political events resulted in the situation where the Communist parties of Poland and Czechoslovakia had taken control of the government and therefore the countries fell under the Soviet Union's sphere of influence. Thus, Soviet law became the example to be followed and Soviet legal doctrine introduced the new paradigm of the law.[5] For example, Rudzinski concludes that the new Communist regime did not trust the Polish family to support the new regime. Therefore, it had to be weakened and brought under the jurisdiction of the state courts which themselves became gradually more and more subject to political pressure and Communist direction from above.[6]

In 1948, the commissions for recodification were constituted and, in the field of family law, close collaboration between Czechoslovakia and Poland was established on the basis of the Polish/Czechoslovak Commission for Juridical Cooperation.[7] Soviet law was obviously the pattern to be followed during preparatory works on new legislation. Often proclaimed attributes of new laws were equality between men and women and equality between children born within marriage and out of wedlock.[8] Soviet legal doctrine was also of the opinion that family law does not form a part of the civil law because family relations in a socialist system are of a personal nature, not dominated as they allegedly are in capitalist societies by property and financial considerations.[9]

Soviet law would use simple rules for determining child maintenance and these rules were adopted on June 27, 1936, thereafter being constantly in use.[10] This law requires the payment by the obligor of one-quarter of his wages for the care of one child, one-third for the care of two children, and one-half for the care of three or more children. Proposals that an actual fixed sum be set as a minimum were not

4 P. Fiedorczyk, 'Czechosłovawacka droga do kodyfikacji prawa rodzinnego (1919–1949). Z dziejów współpracy z Polską,' in A. Litiński and others, *Państwo, prawo, społeczeństwo w dziejach Europy Środkowej*, Katowice – Kraków, 2009, pp 184–187.

5 J. Přibáň, 'Na stráži jednoty světa: marxismus a právní teorie' in M. Bobek, P. Molek, V. Šimíček, *Komunistické právo v Československu. Kapitoly z dějin bezpráví.* Masaryk University, Brno, 2009, p 39–59.

6 A. W. Rudzinski, 'Sovietization of Civil law in Poland,' (1956) 15 *American Slavic and East European Review*, pp 225–226.

7 P. Fiedorczyk, 'Czechosłovawacka droga do kodyfikacji prawa rodzinnego (1919–1949). Z dziejów współpracy z Polską.' in A. Litiński and others, *Państwo, prawo, społeczeństwo w dziejach Europy Środkowej*, Katowice – Kraków, 2009, p 191.

8 G. M. Sverdlov, *Sovietske rodinné právo*, Právnický ústav ministerstva spravedlivosti, Bratislava, 1953, pp 25–28.

9 A. W. Rudzinski, 'New Communist Civil Codes of Czechoslovakia and Poland: A General Appraisal,' (1965–1966) 33 *Ind L J (Indiana Law Journal)*, p 37.

10 J. Gorecki, 'Communist Family Pattern: Law as an Implement of Change,' (1972) *U Ill LF (University of Illinois Law Forum)*, pp 133–134.

adopted.[11] Therefore, the amount of the maintenance was decided regardless of the age or material situation of the child.[12]

Consequently, the civil section of the Polish/Czechoslovak Commission for Juridical Cooperation decided to coordinate the ideological principles of the civil codes of both countries and to introduce a "social reform of family obligations." As a result of the Commission's work, two parallel codes were enacted: the Czechoslovak Act on Family Law on December 7, 1949, No. 265 Coll. and the Polish Family Code on June 27, 1950.[13] The wording of these codes was almost identical and the rules concerning child maintenance were completely the same.

According to sec. 39 of the Czechoslovak Act on Family Law (hereinafter "CFL") and sec. 39 of the Polish Family Code (hereinafter "PFC"),[14] both parents were obliged to maintain and raise their children. Such a rule was evidently formulated on the basis of equality between both parents in their rights and duties and it departed from old rules which were generally based only on the father's duty to provide maintenance for his children. The maintenance duty towards children was therefore based on legal parenthood and was not part of parental authority or matrimonial duties.

Sec. 39 of CFL and sec. 39 of PFC also stipulated that the substantive resources for child maintenance and their upbringing could be substituted by personal care for children. Moreover, the maintenance obligation ceased when children were able to take care of themselves. Consequently, the law did not stipulate any exact age limit (eg the age of majority) as to when the parental maintenance obligation would cease. It follows that maintenance was primarily provided on a voluntary basis in the form of personal care or in kind. Only when parents were separated or divorced was maintenance usually paid in money on a monthly basis and was determined by a judicial decision.

The drafters of the new codes did not introduce any exact rules for determining the actual amount of money which should be paid by a parent obliged to pay maintenance. The codes included only a general rule legitimizing the needs of an obligee – in other words the actual requirements of the child – and taking into account the earning and property capacity of an obligor. Court practice provided some additional criteria, specifically to the effect that the actual requirements of

11 J. N. Hazard, 'Law and the Soviet Family,' (1939) *Wis. L. Rev. (Wisconsin Law Review)*, p 25.

12 G. M. Sverdlov, *Sovietske rodinné právo*, Právnický ústav ministerstva spravedlivosti, Bratislava, 1953, pp 157.

13 A. W. Rudzinski, 'Sovietization of Civil law in Poland,' (1956) 15 *American Slavic and East European Review*, p 235.

14 Ustawa z dnia 27 czerwca 1950 r. Kodeks rodzinny (*The Polish family code*). Dz. U. z 26.6.1950, Nr 034, poz. 308. Available at http://isap.sejm.gov.pl/DetailsServlet?id=WDU19500340308.

a child shall be defined by that child's age, physical and psychological maturity, state of health and the child's future career prospects.[15] Furthermore, earning and property capacity was explicated so that the obligor's potential earnings would be taken into account when it was obvious that the obligor had not been able to obtain higher earnings deliberately or by negligence.[16] The awarded maintenance had to respect a premise that the living standards of the parent and his or her children had to be equal. Even these rules were exploitable in the name of Communist ideology, which is observable from the Czechoslovakian court decision that stated the following: "A farming peasant has to pay maintenance for a child according to the potential earnings he can achieve as a member of a local agricultural association and not according to his actual lesser profit from individual farming".[17] The court decision clearly gave preference to the collectivization of agriculture as one of the country's paramount goals.

Another interesting example of an ideologically distorted decision is provided by the Polish Supreme Court when it stated that "... The court, whilst deciding the question of custody, is not bound by the interests of the parents or any other reason but solely by the well-understood interest of the child in accordance with the principles of the social system prevailing in People's Poland. In this sense the interest of the child requires that he be brought up and educated in conditions which ensure that he will grow up to be a citizen enjoying physical and moral health, conscious of his role and his duties, capable of working according to his predilection and abilities for the good of the State and society, sincerely devoted to progressive ideas and socialisation, which form the basis of the present social and political system of People's Poland. ...".[18]

Indeed, the above rule for determining maintenance was of its nature very discretionary and it caused problems in its application because judges did not have any exact formula to be used if needed. Therefore, the court practice in Czechoslovakia was not reluctant to use a mathematical formula which would be used before the CFL came into force. The formula was not based on any substantive law because it had been purely invented by the courts at a time when the Austrian Civil Code was in force; sometimes the formula is also known as "the Gerlich rule".[19] According to this rule, the earnings of an obligor should be

---

15 V. Knapp (ed), *Právo rodinné*, Univerzita Karlova v Praze, Prague, 1961, p 141.

16 J. Andrlík, J. Blažke, A. Kafka (eds), *Komentář k zákonu o právu rodinném*, Orbis, Prague, 1954, pp 177–204.

17 Sbírka rozhodnutí Československých soudů, č. 9/1952 (*Collection of decisions of Czechoslovak courts, No. 9/1952*). Quoted in V. Knapp (ed.), *Právo rodinné*, Charles University in Prague, Prague, 1961, pp 141.

18 Orzeczenie Sądu Najwyższego z dnia 7 czerwca 1950 r., Ł.C. 522/50 (*Polish Supreme Court Decision of June 7, 1950, No. C.522/50*). Quoted in D. Lasok, 'A Legal Concept of Marriage and Divorce: A Comparative Study in Polish and Western Family Law,' (1960) 9 *The International and Comparative Law Quarterly*, p 89–90.

19 K. Gerlich, *Rozvod, rozluka, alimenty*, Právnického knihkupectví a nakladatelství V. Linhart, Prague, 1934, pp 242–243.

divided, so that three parts remained for the obligor and one part was passed to each obligee.[20] Thus, in practice, when a father was supposed to pay maintenance for two children, three-fifths of his earnings were retained by him and one-fifth sent to each of his children.

The basics included in the new Polish and Czechoslovak family law obviously followed Soviet law.[21] Equality among children born within marriage and those born outside wedlock and equality between men and women when the fundamental rights and duties towards children are under consideration are clear examples.[22] However, the rules related to parental maintenance obligations toward children evidently slightly departed from the Soviet pattern as explained above.

3. CONTINUITY WITH VARIATIONS (1963–1989)

Society in both countries had undergone major transformations during the 1960s. According to the legislators it was necessary to express the changes accomplished in the development and function of the family and marriage by new legislation and subsequently to promote the further development of society towards the creation of socialism and communism.[23] Therefore, Act No. 94/1963 Coll. on the family (hereinafter "CAF") in Czechoslovakia and the Family and Guardianship Code of February 25, 1964 (hereinafter "PFGC") in Poland were adopted. Importantly, the CAF was more influenced by the socialist regime and doctrine than the PFGC. An example is sec. 30 of the CAF in which it is stated that "[p]arents, the state, and social organizations, particularly the Czechoslovak Association of Youth and its Young Pioneer Organization, together in inseparable unity, care about children's upbringing."

The rules concerning the maintenance obligations of parents remained almost untouched by the new legislation in Czechoslovakia. Legal experts in Czechoslovakia reached the conclusion that the legal regulation on determining

[20] K. Gerlich, *Rozvod, rozluka, alimenty*, Právnického knihkupectví a nakladatelství V. Linhart, Prague, 1934, pp 242–243.

[21] A. W. Rudzinski, 'Sovietization of Civil law in Poland,' (1956) 15 *American Slavic and East European Review*, pp 235–236.

[22] V. Knapp (ed.), *Právo rodinné*, Univerzita Karlova v Praze, Prague, 1961, pp. 9–12 or A. W. Rudzinski, 'Sovietization of Civil law in Poland,' (1956) 15 *American Slavic and East European Review*, p 238.

[23] Národní shromáždění Československé socialistické republiky, III. volební období, tisk č. 146, Vládní návrh zákona o rodině, Důvodová zpráva (*Explanatory report concerning governmental proposal of the act on family*). Available at http://www.psp.cz/eknih/1960ns/tisky/t0146_03.htm.

maintenance under the CAF had its weaknesses.[24] Unreasonable differences in awarding maintenance amounts and the lack of measures of assistance were the most significant problems.[25] Therefore, two surveys were carried out and they provided some proposals on how to improve the practice at that time.[26] An outcome of the surveys was not only one recommendation but several recommendatory formulas and tables which were published and were supposed to be used by the courts. All the recommendations took into account, as primary factors for determining maintenance, the age of the child, the earnings of the obligor and the number of children to be maintained by that obligor. In addition, some of the formulas took into account the earnings of the parent who had the child in his or her primary care. Nevertheless, these tables and formulas were not widely used in practice and some legal experts also criticized such mathematical methods for calculating maintenance.[27] Such criticism was based on the argument of the unique nature of each particular case and the improper simplification contained in the formulas.[28]

According to sec. 100 CAF, the People's Committee, as a state administrative body, was obliged to provide a maintenance allowance for children in need. When the allowance was provided to the child whose parent did not fulfil his maintenance obligation, the People's Committee had a claim for recourse against the obliged parent.[29] The maximum amount of the allowance was roughly the average amount of maintenance.

The PFGC also did not change much in the territory of Poland when parental maintenance obligations were considered. However, in sec. 144 the PFGC did introduce the maintenance obligations of step-parents towards their stepchildren. The obligation was limited to only those situations when an application for such payments was in compliance with the principle of social co-operation, in other words with socialist morality.[30] In the 1970s, an interesting shift in maintenance policy occurred. A special state-run Alimony Fund was created in 1974 to render financial assistance to persons who were entitled to maintenance, but were not

24 V. Másílko, S. Vaněček, *Výživné nezletilců v evropských právních řádech*, SEVT, Prague, 1971, p 36.

25 V. Másílko, S. Vaněček, *Výživné nezletilců v evropských právních řádech*, SEVT, Prague, 1971, p 36.

26 Právnický ústav ministerstva spravedlnosti v Praze a Ústav státu a práva ČSAV v Praze, *Zpráva o výzkumu výše výživného nezletilců (Research report on minor children maintenance)*, 1969, Spr 268/96.

27 O. Těžká, *Vyživovací povinnost*, Panorama, Prague, 1984, p 93.

28 O. Těžká, *Vyživovací povinnost*, Panorama, Prague, 1984, p 93.

29 T. Glos, *Rodinné právo*, Orbis, Prague, 1970, p 229–230.

30 D. Lasok, *Polish Family Law*, A.W. Sijthoff, Leyden, 1968, p 201.

receiving it. If these persons were in need because of the obligor's failure, they were to receive payments from the Fund, but monthly payments were limited.[31]

Interesting court practice concerning the determination of maintenance developed in Poland. The court decisions on maintenance generally stipulated the exact amount of money which the obliged parent was supposed to pay, but there were also some decisions containing the maintenance assessment as a percentage of the obliged parent's earnings.[32] The applicability of such a method for determining maintenance was obviously limited and had its weaknesses, but it is interesting that such a practice did not evolve in Czechoslovakia, notwithstanding the similarities in the substantive law of both countries.

4. FAMILY LAW AFTER THE TRANSITION (1990–2010)

In 1989, Czechoslovakia and Poland went through the turbulences of events when the socialistic regime was overthrown and a new regime, based on democratic elections, was established.[33] Moreover, shortly after the revolution Czechoslovakia ceased to exist and two independent states arose, the Czech Republic and Slovakia. Therefore, the need for a revision of family law arose shortly after the revolutionary changes. However, it took a long time to make any actual changes in substantive family law.

In the territory of the Czech Republic, a significant amendment of the CAF came into force as late as in 1998. Specifically, the hoarding of maintenance was introduced in sec. 97 CAF. Hence, the court may decide to order the obligor to pay in advance a lump sum of the maintenance payable in future according to sec. 97 CAF. Furthermore, the exclusively consumable nature of maintenance was rejected – as sec. 85a CAF states, the creation of savings can be considered as a legitimate need for children when this is justified by the earnings and property capacity of the obligor. The maintenance allowance provisions were repealed in 1998 and therefore the state has not provided any kind of guaranteed maintenance since that time. However, some proposals for a state-guaranteed maintenance were presented, but they were not accepted by Parliament.[34] The new economic order

31 S. Frankowski (ed.), *Introduction to Polish Law*, Kluwer Law International, The Hague, 2005, p 105.

32 Resolution of the Polish Supreme Court of 22nd September 1979, No. CZP 16/79. Published in Orzecznictwo Sądu Najwyższego Izba Cywilna, rok 1980, nr 7–8, pozycja 129, str. 1.

33 J. F. Haderka, 'Czechoslovakia: Decline and Fall of the Federation and Its Family Law,'(1993–1994) 32 *U Louisville J Fam L (University of Louisville Journal of Family Law)*, pp 281–283.

34 Parlament České republiky, Poslanecká sněmovna, 2005, IV. volební období, sněmovní tisk č. 964, Návrh na vydání zákona o náhradním výživném a o změně některých souvisejících zákonů (*Proposal of the Act on guaranteed maintenance*). Available at www.psp.cz/sqw/text/

brought about procedural problems when proving the earnings of an obligor who is not employed but conducts a self-employed business activity. Therefore, the obligor has the burden of proof when it comes to providing evidence of his or her earnings and when he or she fails to fulfil that burden a legal presumption on the extent of his or her earnings is applied according to sec. 85a CAF.

The substantive family law rules for determining maintenance included in the CAF have not changed since 1989. Some experts on Czech family law therefore criticize these vague contemporary rules for determining maintenance.[35] In answer to this criticism the Czech Ministry of Justice introduced a recommendatory table at the beginning of 2010, which should reflect the Austrian maintenance rules.[36] After further discussions on this topic, the table was slightly rearranged and published in May 2010. Nevertheless, judges are not obliged to follow these recommendations, but the Ministry hopes that the established recommendations will be used. It is still not clear how useful the table will be in practice, because it is necessary to postpone any evaluation until some years after its introduction. Obviously, the table cannot be used when the obliged parent has to provide maintenance for more than two children. The recommendatory table, as it should be distributed to the courts in the Czech Republic, is the following.

Child's age	**The percentage of the parent's earnings pertaining to maintenance**
0–5 years	11–15%
6–9 years	13–17%
10–14 years	15–19%
15–17 years	16–22%
18 years and older	19–25%

The CAF was adopted by Slovakia after its establishment. The Czech example was mainly followed with regard to changes in the family law, eg the rule that the creation of savings can be considered as a legitimate need for children and the legal presumption on the obligor's earnings were incorporated into the CAF in 2002. In addition, the maintenance allowance provisions were repealed in 1998;

tiskt.sqw?O=4&CT=964&CT1=0 or Parlament České republiky, Poslanecká sněmovna, 2007, V. volební období, sněmovní tisk č. 132, Návrh na vydání zákona o náhradním výživném a o změně některých souvisejících zákonů (*Proposal of the Act on guaranteed maintenance*). Available at www.psp.cz/sqw/text/tiskt.sqw?O=5&CT=132&CT1=0 or Parlament České republiky, Poslanecká sněmovna, 2009, V. volební období, sněmovní tisk č. 849, Návrh na vydání zákona o vyživovací povinnosti k nezaopatřeným dětem a o změně některých souvisejících zákonů (*Proposal of the Act on maintenance duty towards children in need*). Available at www.psp.cz/sqw/text/tiskt.sqw?O=5&CT=849&CT1=0.

35 M. Hrušáková, 'Family law in Czechoslovakia after the Revolution,' (1993) 7 *Int'l JL & Fam (International Journal of Law and the Family)*, p 132.

36 The table was published on the web pages of the Czech Ministry of Justice, Maintenance section. Available at http://portal.justice.cz/justice2/MS/ms.aspx?o=23&j=33&k=5224&d=310739.

however, a new compensatory maintenance law was enacted in 2002.[37] The Act was not bereft of some problematical issues, eg the narrow sphere of obligees; therefore the new act on compensatory maintenance was introduced in 2008.[38] Nowadays, the state is obliged to provide limited maintenance amounts for children whose parents do not fulfil their obligation voluntarily.

The major changes in the field of Slovakian family law occurred after the acceptance of the new Act No. 36/2005 Coll. on the Family (hereinafter "SAF") in 2005 which repealed the CAF. The new legislation did not bring much that was new as far as child maintenance is concerned and according to some family law experts it made the rules for determining maintenance even more unclear.[39] However, there was at least one achievement in that a minimum amount of maintenance for children was included in sec. 62 SAF. The minimum amount of maintenance is set at 30% of the minimum standard of living as defined by the Slovakian Ministry of Labour, Social Affairs and Family. The unresolved problem is that the minimum standard of living frequently changes and therefore the minimum maintenance should change accordingly. In this respect, it is not useful for the court to determine the amount of maintenance as a set amount of money because of the necessity to change this decision as frequently as the minimum standard of living changes.[40]

The regulation on child maintenance contained in the PFGC has remained almost untouched since 1989. However, the economic transition in Poland did not leave the Alimony Fund legislation untouched by the government cutbacks in state welfare services.[41] In 2004 the Alimony Fund ceased to exist and therefore a

37 Zákon č. 245/2002 Zz. z 10. apríla 2002 o náhradnom výživnom a Fonde náhradného výživného a ktorým sa mení a dopĺňa zákon č. 94/1963 Zb. Zákon o rodine v znení neskorších predpisov (*Act No. 245/2002 Coll., on compensatory maintenance*). The Act was amended on three occasions and in 2008 it was completely substituted by the new Act No. 201/2008 Coll.

38 Národná rada Slovenskej republiky, IV. Volebné obdobie, 558, Dôvodová správa (*Explanatory report concerning the governmental proposal for the Act on compensatory maintenance*). Available at http://www.nrsr.sk/.

39 N. Richterová, 'Vyživovacia povinnosť,' In D. Sehnálek, J. Valdhans, R. Dávid, L. Kyncl (eds), *Dny práva – 2009 – Days of Law: the Conference Proceedings*, Masaryk University, Brno, 2009. Available at http://www.law.muni.cz/sborniky/dny_prava_2009/files/prispevky/sblizovani/Richterova_Natalia__1131_.pdf.

40 N. Richterová, 'Vyživovacia povinnosť,' In D. Sehnálek, J. Valdhans, R. Dávid, L. Kyncl (eds), *Dny práva – 2009 – Days of Law: the Conference Proceedings*, Masaryk University, Brno, 2009.. Available at http://www.law.muni.cz/sborniky/dny_prava_2009/files/prispevky/sblizovani/Richterova_Natalia__1131_.pdf.

41 E. Fratczak, M. Kulik, M. Malinowski, E. Slotwinska-Roslanowska, 'Legal regulations related to demographic events and processes: Social policy pertaining to children and family – Poland, selected years 1945–2006,' (2007) *Section of Demographic Analyses working paper*, p 28. Available at http://www.ae.krakow.pl/~demograf/Publikacje/SAD17B.pdf.

huge social movement against the liquidation of the Fund emerged.[42] In 2008, as a result of strong social pressure, the Fund began functioning again with slight modifications.[43]

5. ARE WE GOING TO HELL OR TO HEAVEN?

Since the end of the socialist era, Czech, Polish and Slovakian legal experts have tended constantly to propose the embodiment of family law in the new civil codes. Such an approach clearly shows that legal doctrine rejects the old paradigm based on Soviet law and is returning to the Western civil law tradition. Therefore, new draft civil codes are pending. In the Czech Republic, a complete draft of the civil code was even approved by the government in 2009, but it has still not been passed by Parliament.[44] The drafters of the proposed code are clearly not in favour of any mathematical formulas for determining maintenance.[45] The rules on the determination of maintenance completely follow the old, vague and discretionary rules, based on the legitimate needs of a child who is in need of maintenance, the earning and property capacity of an obligor and the equality of the resulting living conditions of the obligor and oblige (ie the parent and the child).

In Slovakia the general objective of the new civil code was published in 2008 and nothing indicates that any significant changes to the determination of maintenance have been prepared.[46]

The preparation of the new civil code in Poland is also in its infancy and, up until now, only the Green Paper has been published and there is no indication that the rules on determining maintenance will become less unclear than in the Czech Republic or Slovakia.[47]

---

42 R. E. Hryciuk, 'Political Motherhood in Poland: The Emergence of Single-Mothers for the Alimony Fund Movement' (2005) *Women & Globalization* – conference paper. Available at http://www.globaljusticecenter.org/papers2005/hryciuk.htm.

43 Ustawa z dnia 22 kwietnia 2005 r. o postępowaniu wobec dłużników alimentacyjnych oraz zaliczce alimentacyjnej (*Act of 22nd April 2005*), Dz. U. z 17 maja 2005 r. Nr 86, poz. 732.

44 Parlament České republiky, Poslanecká sněmovna, 2009, V. volební období, sněmovní tisk č. 835, Vládní návrh na vydání Občanský zákoník (*Governmental proposal of the Czech civil code*). Available at http://www.psp.cz/sqw/text/tiskt.sqw?O=5&CT=835&CT1=0.

45 Důvodová zpráva k vládnímu návrhu občanského zákoníku (*Explanatory report to the Civil code proposal*), at 251. Available at http://obcanskyzakonik.justice.cz/tinymce-storage/files/Duvodova_zprava_OZ_LRV_090430_final.pdf

46 J. Lazar, *Návrh legislatívneho zámeru kodifikácie súkromného práva, Materiály z odbornej konferencie*, Ministerstvo spravodlivosti Slovenskej republiky, EUROKODEX, Bratislava, 2008.

47 Z. Radvański (ed.), *Zielona ksiega. Optymalna wizja Kodeksu cywilnego w Rzecpospolitej Polskiej*, Ministerstwo sprawiedliwości, Warszawa, 2006, p. 167–172.

Obviously, since the entry into force of similar family laws in Czechoslovakia and Poland at the beginning of 1950s, child maintenance laws have changed to some extent. Since the 1960s, legal experts in the countries under consideration have made attempts to explicate the rules for determining maintenance by mathematical formulas or recommended tables, but the tangible outcomes were very weak. Nowadays, we face another attempt of this kind in the Czech Republic, though no one can be certain as to the success of the recommended table. In Slovakia, the statutory minimum maintenance is laid down, while no such regulation is in force in Poland or the Czech Republic.

Some kind of state-guaranteed maintenance for children has been in force in all the countries under consideration during some period, but only Poland and Slovakia currently have such a regulation in force.

No one can say what 'heaven' in the case of child maintenance laws looks like, but we can assume how the 'stairway' appears. In this spirit, contemporary family law favours clear rules for determining maintenance because only such rules provide a sufficient level of legal certainty for the parties involved. This trend is also visible in the countries under consideration, but the Czech Republic with its recommended tables and Slovakia with its minimum amount of maintenance laid down in legislation are probably only on the first step, while Poland is within view of the 'stairway'.

THE PRE-HARMONIZATION AREA: A COMPARISON OF LITHUANIAN, LATVIAN AND ESTONIAN CHILD MAINTENANCE LAWS

Gediminas Sagatys

1. INTRODUCTION

Research shows that an ever-increasing number of child maintenance payments involve transnational elements.[1] The European Union has no right to ignore these trends in order to provide minimum guarantees for European citizens. In this regard Article 65 of the EC Treaty, which speaks of measures in the field of judicial cooperation in civil matters having cross-border implications, is of crucial importance. It provides a basis for two types of initiatives. First, the official efforts to establish simplified rules of procedure in relation to child maintenance obligations have been made.[2] Second, attempts to lay theoretical as well as practical foundations for harmonizing and unifying substantive family law are evident.[3]

Although child maintenance is still behind other fields of family law where practical harmonisation steps have already taken place,[4] it is rather a question of time when this will happen as the recent research in this field reveals great differences in EU Member States` legal systems.[5] Bearing in mind the substantial amount of scepticism towards the possibility of family law harmonisation,[6] a comparative look at the child maintenance laws of three EU countries – Estonia, Latvia and Lithuania – which were once already unified could be important. An overview and comparison of family legislation developed in each country after the re-establishment of independence might contribute to the search for an answer to the following question: are child maintenance laws suitable for harmonization at all?

1 I. Curry-Sumner, 'Transnational recovery of child maintenance in Europe: the future is bright, the future is central authorities' / www.law.muni.cz/edicni/Days-of-public-law/files/pdf/mep/Curry-Sumner.pdf.

2 See Regulation (EC) No. 44/2001 on jurisdiction and the recognition and enforcement of judgments in civil and commercial matters and the recent Regulation No. 4/2009 of 18 December, 2008 on jurisdiction, applicable law, recognition and decisions and cooperation in matters relating to maintenance obligations which came into force on 30 January, 2009.

3 The literature suggests that a broad interpretation of Article 65 EC Treaty on European Union may lead to a conclusion that the EU could even take measures in order to harmonize or unify *substantive* family law in Europe (see K. Boele-Woelki, ,'The principles of European family law: its aims and prospects' / www.utrechtlawreview.org/publish/articles/000012/article.pdf.

4 K. Boele-Woelki et al.,, *Principles of European Family Law Regarding Divorce and Maintenance Between Former Spouses*, Intersentia, Antwerp – Oxford – New York, 2004; K. Boele-Woelki, 'The CEFL principles regarding parental responsibilities: predominance of the common core' in K. Boele-Woelki and T. Sverdrup (eds.), *European challenges in contemporary family law*, Intersentia, Antwerp – Oxford – New York, 2008.

5 CH. Skinner, J. Bradshaw and J. Davidson, *Child support policy: an international perspective*, (2007) Department for Work and Pensions. Research Report No. 405 / www.york.ac.uk/inst/spru/pubs/pdf/rrep405.pdf.

6 D. Bradley, 'A Note on Comparative Family Law: Problems, Perspectives, Issues and Politics' (2005) Oxford University Comparative Law Forum 4 at ouclf.iuscomp.org.

2. HISTORICAL BACKGROUND

Often described as the 'Baltic states' and considered to be one region, in the 1940s Lithuania, Latvia and Estonia were included in the territory of the Soviet Union. During the period of Soviet rule all three countries experienced the impact of the unification of all legal spheres, including family law.

2.1. THE PERIOD OF SOVIET OCCUPATION

The developments in the three countries' family laws during the period of occupation encompass three main periods:

1. The period of Russian family law. The Soviet occupation of Lithuania, Latvia and Estonia in 1940 suspended the family legislation of the former independent states. A decree issued by the Presidium of the USSR Supreme Soviet on November 26, 1940 applied the civil legislation of the Russian Federation to the Baltic countries; in particular, the *Russian Federation's Code on Matrimony, Family and Wardship* adopted on November 19, 1926 came into force. Other laws and regulations regarding marriage and the family, ie civil registration, the institutions of wardship and trusteeship, were also adopted in a hurry.

2. The period of solely Soviet federal family law. In July 1944 all Soviet republics obtained a new law on the family: *'On increasing government support for pregnant women, mothers with many children, single mothers; on strengthening measures for the protection of motherhood and childhood; on the establishment of the honorary title 'Mother Heroine', the foundation on the institution of the order 'Motherhood Glory.' and the 'Motherhood Medal''.* The law was publicly presented as paternalistic state support for mothers and families. It was applied directly and was the ultimate source of family law in all Soviet republics until 1968.

3. The period of federal Soviet family law with some spheres attributed to national legal regulation. In 1968 the Supreme Council of the USSR passed a new family law: '*The Fundamentals of Legislation of the Soviet Union on Matrimony and the Family*' (hereinafter – 'the Fundamentals'). It established the main principles of the legal regulation of family relationships within the Soviet Union. Article 7 of the *Fundamentals* proclaimed: 'Matrimony and the family in the USSR and Soviet republics are regulated by these Fundamentals and other federal laws (...), matrimony and family codes and other laws of the Soviet republics. The laws of the Soviet republics regulate matters designated to them by these Fundamentals and matters which are not regulated by these Fundamentals.' Thus, a certain degree of liberalisation was introduced into Soviet family law. Technically, Soviet

republics were given, at least in theory, a right to legislate on family matters at least to some extent.[7]

The *Fundamentals* dealt with child maintenance issues in a fairly detailed way rather than merely establishing general principles. Thus, only a very limited scope or 'margin of appreciation' was left to each Soviet republic. The main principles of child maintenance established in the *Fundamentals* were the following:

1) Parents had equal rights and duties towards their children irrespective of whether the child was born to a married or unmarried couple, after divorce or a judicial nullity of marriage or separation;
2) Parents were obliged to maintain their underage children and disabled adult children who were in need of support;
3) If underage children had no parents, the maintenance obligation was transferred to other relatives – grandparents, siblings and step-parents. The family laws of the Soviet republics could envisage other maintenance rights and obligations between relatives and other persons;
4) Maintenance could be paid voluntarily either directly by the debtor or through his/her employer's (pension fund's or stipend payer's) administration;
5) If maintenance was not paid voluntarily or through his/her employer's (pension fund's or stipend payer's) administration or if a dispute over maintenance payments arose between the creditor and the debtor the court would make a formal determination of maintenance. Yet voluntary maintenance payments did not preclude the creditor's right to seek a formal court determination on the recovery of maintenance;
6) The amount of maintenance payable by a parent for his/her underage children was the following: ¼ of the parent's earnings (or other gains) for one child; ⅓ of the parent's earnings (or other gains) for two children; ½ of the parent's earnings (or other gains) for three or more children. In any case, maintenance for one child could not be lower than 20 roubles. The court could reduce the minimal amount of maintenance: 1) if, in case of maintenance recovery, other underage children of the debtor would then receive less material support than children for whom maintenance was being recovered; 2) if the debtor was disabled according to category I or II; 3) if children were in employment and their income was sufficient; 4) in other cases where

7 However, the imperial nature of the Soviet state did not presuppose the independence of the republics; on the contrary, it was implied that republics would copy the legislation of the Russian Soviet Federative Socialist Republic (RSFSR) – the "main" Soviet republic which was considered to be the first among equals. The result was that differences between the republican Family Codes (the Codes on Marriage and the Family), if any, were slight; and they all had the RSFSR Code on Marriage and the Family of 1969 as a common compulsory model (see more in O.A. Khazova, *'Family Law on Post-Soviet European Territory: A Comparative Overview of Some Recent Trends'* (2010) Electronic Journal of Comparative Law / www.ejcl.org/141/art141-3.pdf.

objective reasons required the maintenance to be reduced. The court was also entitled to reduce the amount of maintenance or release a debtor from his/her obligation if a child was being fully maintained by the State or a responsible organisation. If a child lived in a child-care institution, maintenance was paid to that institution. An increase in the amount of maintenance could have been ordered by the courts if there were additional expenses related to the care of the underage child (illness, the need for nursing or permanent attendance, etc.). The family laws of the Soviet republics could envisage a right for the courts to determine maintenance in the form of a set amount for underage children if the recovery of maintenance based on parts of the parent's earnings (or other gains) proved to be impossible or very difficult to implement;

7) The amount of maintenance payable by parents for disabled adult children who were in need of support was always established as a set amount depending on the family status and circumstances of both the creditor and the debtor.

It is obvious that the *Fundamentals* were drafted using the method of 'better law' rather than taking the trouble to find any kind of 'common core'. First, the socio-cultural diversity of 15 Soviet countries precluded any possibility to find some kind of 'common core'. Second, the principles of family law established in the *Fundamentals* reflected the goals of the communist state.

During 1969–1970 each Soviet republic adopted its 'own' family code based on the principles established in the *Fundamentals*. The codes were in force until the breakdown of the USSR and until they were changed by new national legislation of the independent countries.

2.2. FAMILY LEGISLATION AFTER THE RESTORATION OF INDEPENDENCE

After the restoration of independence in 1990–1991, Estonia, Latvia and Lithuania developed their own family laws separately. These developments differed in form and time.

In Estonia a separate 'Family Law Act' was adopted in 1995 and was in force until 2010. It was drafted taking into account the chapter on family law in the 1940 Draft Estonian Civil Code and by supplementing it with many innovations in compliance with modern family law in Western Europe.[8] A new edition of 'Family Law Act' was passed in 2009 and came into force in 2010.[9]

Latvia restored its principal source of private law – the 1937 Civil Code, including chapter I relating to family law – in 1992.[10] The chapter on family law was thoroughly revised in 1992–1993. Many rules, especially those regulating marriage and relations between parents and children, were fundamentally adapted in accordance with modern rules which are common to the family laws of the EU countries.[11]

Meanwhile, Lithuania modified and supplemented its 1969 Code of Matrimony and the Family, which was in force until 2001 when the new Civil Code of the Republic of Lithuania[12] with its Book III on 'Family Law' entered into force. When drafting Book III of the Civil Code, French Civil Code was taken as the main source of inspiration.[13]

3. CHILD MAINTENANCE LAW

The adoption of new family legislation in the three countries resulted *inter alia* in some differences in the substance of the law. The following section will try to explore the shifts which occurred in Estonia, Latvia and Lithuania during the last two decades in the legal regulation of child maintenance. In seeking to draw the best possible picture of the matter, a structuralized approach will be used, ie we will try to 'slice' the child maintenance obligation into pieces and deal with each piece separately. The following questions will be raised: Who is considered to be the creditor and the debtor in the child maintenance obligation? Do courts have discretionary powers to release the debtor from the maintenance obligation towards a minor child? What are the forms of child maintenance and what is the

---

8 J. Vebers 'Family law in Latvia: from establishment of independent state of Latvia to restoration of independence', in A.Bainham (ed.), *The international survey of family law*, Martinus Nijhof Publishers, The Hague – Boston – London, 1999.

9 The English version of the Estonian 'Family Law Act' may be found at: www.legaltext.ee/en/andmebaas/ava.asp?m=022.

10 The English version of the Latvian Civil Code may be found at: www.ebrd.com/downloads/legal/facts/latvia.pdf.

11 J. Vebers 'Family law in Latvia: from establishment of independent state of Latvia to restoration of independence', in A.Bainham (ed.), *The international survey of family law*, Martinus Nijhof Publishers, The Hague – Boston – London, 1999.

12 The English version of the Lithianian Civil Code may be found at: http://www3.lrs.lt/pls/inter3/dokpaieska.showdoc_l?p_id=379795.

13 S. Keserauskas, 'Moving in the Same Direction?' Presentation of Family Law Reforms in Lithuania in: The International Survey of Family Law, 2004 Edition, A. Bainham (ed.), Bristol: Jordan Publishing Limited, 2004, p. 316.

minimum amount thereof? These criteria have been selected as providing the best tools for identifying the similarities and differences in each jurisdiction.[14]

3.1. THE CREDITOR

In Soviet times, the issue of the creditor with respect to the child maintenance obligation was resolved on the federal level. Both the *Fundamentals* and the family laws of all three Baltic republics provided for the following order of priority in maintenance: first, underage children (under 18), second, disabled adult (over 18) children in need of support.

Table 1. The creditor

Period of Soviet law (1968–1991)[15]	**Legislation of the independent states**		
	Lithuania	Latvia	Estonia
1) underage (<18) child 2) disabled adult (>18) child in need of support	1) underage (<18) child (Article 3.192, paragraph 1 Civil Code of Lithuania) 2) (depending on the circumstances) adult child from 18 to 24 if he/she attends day classes at a secondary school, higher education institution or vocational college (Article 3.194, paragraph 3 Civil Code of Lithuania) 3) adult child who lacks capacity to work due to disability determined before the age of majority (Article 3.194, paragraph 3 Civil Code of Lithuania)	A child who is unable to provide for him/herself (Article 179, paragraph 1 Civil Code of Latvia)	1) underage (<18) child 2) a child who continues to acquire basic or secondary education in basic school, upper secondary school or vocational school as an adult but not more than until he or she attains 21 years of age 3) adult child who needs assistance and is unable to maintain himself or herself (§97 Family Law Act of Estonia)

[14] Obviously, there are much more criteria for identifying child maintenance systems used in different countries (see, for example, the method used by Skinner, Bradshaw and Davidson in CH. Skinner, J. Bradshaw and J. Davidson, *Child support policy: an international perspective*, (2007) Department for Work and Pensions. Research Report No. 405 / www.york.ac.uk/inst/spru/pubs/pdf/rrep405.pdf)

[15] Note that the 'period of Soviet law' in this context is considered only as the period from 1968 to 1991 – ie the last period of Soviet law, when the federal law '*The Fundamentals of Legislation of the Soviet Union on Matrimony and the Family*' was in force.

A similar legal regulation is established in the currently applicable family laws of Estonia, Latvia and Lithuania (see Table 1). However, each country's methods of legal regulation slightly differ. Lithuanian and Estonian laws explicitly distinguish minor age as a ground for the right to maintenance to arise, whereas the Civil Code of Latvia uses an abstract formulation – a child support duty lies upon the father and the mother 'until the time the child is able to provide for itself'. This, in turn, may be determined by objective factors (the child's minor age) and subjective individual circumstances (the child's disability or other factors established by the court).

It is interesting to point out that the right to maintenance by children who have reached the age of majority and who are still attending educational institutions is *expressis verbis* established in Lithuanian and Estonian laws. However, attitudes towards the absoluteness of this right differ. This right, though construed in a narrower way (it does not include students in higher education institutions), is absolute in Estonia, whereas in Lithuania a full-age studying child's right to maintenance is subject to a number of circumstances.[16] This is clearly reflected in Lithuanian case law. For instance, the Supreme Court of Lithuania has ruled that in deciding the issue regarding maintenance for a child who has reached the age of majority and who is studying in a daytime department of a secondary school and who needs support, 'the possibilities of parents, their duties towards other persons (*inter alia* underage children, other family members, dependants) may not be overlooked'.[17] The Court has also pointed out that a child claiming support 'must study honestly and with good evaluations' and that 'good evaluations at school would be evidenced by the promotion of the pupil to the next grade with

[16] The Lithuanian Constitutional Court ruled in 2007 that the legal regulation of the Civil Code obliging the parents to support their underage child to the extent that it establishes that the court must in all cases adjudge (that it does not have powers not to adjudge) the support from the parents (or one of them) to the person of full legal age, to whom the support is necessary, who has acquired secondary education and who is still studying at a daytime department of a higher education or vocational school, provided he is not older than 24 years of age, is in conflict with the Constitution of the Republic of Lithuania. The Court reasoned that the institution of support for underage children (parents have the duty to provide their underage children with material support) and the institution of support for the children of full legal age who are studying at daytime departments of secondary, higher education or vocational schools are not identical; they differ essentially, as the subjects of the corresponding legal relations are essentially different: in the first case, one of the subjects of the legal relations is always an underage child who has the right to receive material support from his parents, while the other subject is one of his parents or both his parents, thus, the legal relations appear between the underage person and the person(s) of full legal age (or emancipated persons); in the second case, one of the subjects of the legal relations is always a person of full legal age who is studying at the daytime department of a secondary, higher education or vocational school and to whom the support is necessary, and the other subject is also one of his parents or both his parents, thus, legal relations appear between persons of full legal age (see at www.lrkt.lt/dokumentai/2007/r070607.htm).

[17] Ruling of the Supreme Court of Lithuania of 25 May 2009 in the civil case No. 3K-7–204/2009.

satisfactory annual marks or admission to graduation examinations and the passing of such exams'.[18]

The legislative authorities of the three Baltic countries have slightly different views towards the right of adult disabled children to maintenance. In Lithuania, an adult disabled child's right to receive support from parents is construed very narrowly – the right to be maintained by parents may be enjoyed by only such disabled children whose disability was determined before they reached the age of majority. In other cases, the state social security mechanisms start working. In Estonia and Latvia, the time of determining disability does not limit a disabled child's right to claim maintenance from his/her parents. It is obvious that in this way the state dispenses with at least part of its burden of social support; therefore, we can assume that the main reason for differences in the legal regulation at issue is the choice of social policy by the particular state.

3.2. THE DEBTOR

Table 2 shows how the issue of the debtor, ie a person obliged to maintain a child, is dealt with in the Baltic States. The first post-Soviet change to catch our eye in the three countries is the ending of step-parents' duty to maintain stepchildren. This means that such a duty has lost its legal character and has become a moral issue, ie the step-parents' moral duty, the performance of which is ensured by good morals but not by legal means.

Other changes are not so drastic, except for, probably, a decision of the legislative authorities of Latvia and Estonia to release adult persons from a duty to maintain their underage siblings. Meanwhile Lithuania has 'inherited' from the Soviet period the adult persons' duty to maintain their underage siblings. An underage child may claim maintenance from an adult sibling not only when he/she is deprived of parents but also when the parents do not maintain him/her. However, the adult persons' duty to maintain their underage siblings has been made dependent upon certain circumstances rather than absolute.

It should also be pointed out that the parents' duty to maintain adult children (if such duty is established in law ie maintenance of children lacking capacity to work due to disability, maintenance of children, attending educational institutions) does not pass to other relatives on a subsidiary basis in Latvia and Lithuania; whereas in Estonia, an adult grandchild who is entitled to receive support has a right to claim support from his/her grandparents if it is not possible to file a claim

[18] Ibidem.

for provision of maintenance against parents or if it is too difficult to achieve ordering of provision of maintenance.

Table 2. The debtor

Period of Soviet law (1968–1991)	**Legislation of the independent states**		
	Lithuania	Latvia	Estonia
Both parents notwithstanding their marital status	Both parents notwithstanding their marital status (Article 3.156, paragraph 2 Civil Code of Lithuania)	Both parents notwithstanding their marital status (Article 179, paragraphs 1 and 2 Civil Code of Latvia)	Both parents notwithstanding their marital status (§96 Family Law Act of Estonia)
Adult brother (sister) must maintain his (her) minor sibling who is deprived of parents	Circumstances permitting, an adult brother (sister) must maintain his (her) minor sibling who is in need of support and deprived of parents or of their maintenance (Article 3.237, paragraph 1 Civil Code of Lithuania)	-	-
Grandparents must maintain their minor grandchildren who are deprived of parents	Circumstances permitting, grandparents shall maintain their minor grandchildren deprived of parents or adult siblings or of their maintenance (Article 3.237, paragraph 2 Civil Code of Lithuania)	Grandparents must maintain their minor grandchildren if the parents are absent or they are not able to maintain the child If the financial state of the grandparents is unequal, a court may specify for them the maintenance duty commensurate with the financial state of each (Article 179, paragraph 4 Civil Code of Latvia)	Grandparents must maintain their grandchildren if it is not possible to file a claim for provision of maintenance against the parents or if it is too difficult to achieve ordering of provision of maintenance (§106 Family Law Act of Estonia)
Step-parents must maintain their minor stepchildren who are deprived of parents	-	-	-

3.3. THE COURTS' DISCRETIONARY POWERS

Another issue distinguishing the child maintenance systems of the three countries is the nature of maintenance obligations. In the Soviet period, the parental obligation to maintain underage children was considered absolute – no institution, including the courts, had a right to release parents from the performance of such an obligation. Parents could only be released from their maintenance obligation if the child was fully maintained by the State or a responsible organisation (see Table 3). However, this release did not apply when the State took children on a compulsory basis and placed them in a child-care institution – in such cases maintenance by parents was awarded for the benefit of such an institution.

Today attitudes towards this matter are slightly different in the Baltic countries. Lithuanian law establishes, as stated earlier, that the obligation of the parents to maintain their underage children is absolute. Such a position is first of all related to the establishment of the parental obligation to maintain underage children in the Constitution of the Republic of Lithuania.[19] The courts shall in no case (even when parents have no income or property) have the right to release parents from their obligation to maintain their underage children. Furthermore, this rule has become a constituent part of public order in Lithuanian law. Therefore, in Lithuanian case law it is regarded as a circumstance which justifies a limitation to the application of foreign law. For instance, in 2009 the Vilnius Regional Court allowed a claim by a mother living together with her children in France and ordered the children's father living in Lithuania to pay maintenance for the benefit of his underage children until they reached the age of majority. The court was not deterred by the fact that French law had to be applied to the case (the children's permanent place of residence was in France) or even by the fact that an earlier decision by the Rennes Regional Court in France had released the father from the duty to financially support his children because of insufficient financial means. The court stated that 'French national law, based on which a release from the child maintenance obligation can be ordered due to a lack of financial means (which was confirmed by the said decision of the Rennes Regional Court) is demonstrably inconsistent with Article 38 of the Constitution of the Republic of Lithuania, which establishes a parental obligation to maintain children until the age of majority. (...) In this case all conditions to apply exceptions to the general rules regulating the application of foreign law have been determined (...); therefore, the national rules of law shall apply in the case at issue'.[20]

The situation in Estonia is quite similar. The general principle embedded in Estonian law also provides that the parents shall not be released from the obligation to provide maintenance to their minor child.

---

19 Article 38 paragraph 6 of the Constitution establishes: "The right and duty of parents is to bring up their children to be honest individuals and loyal citizens, as well as to support them until they come of age".

20 Ruling of the Vilnius District Court of 9 August, 2009 in the civil case No. 2A-156–464/2009.

The legal situation in Latvia as regards child maintenance can be considered the most complicated. On the one hand, the provision of child maintenance established in Article 179 of the Civil Code of Latvia stipulates that 'parents, commensurate to their financial situation, have a duty to maintain the child. Such duty lies upon the father and the mother until the time the child is able to provide for itself. The duty to provide for the maintenance of the child shall not terminate if the child does not live together with one of the parents or with both parents'. This constitutes grounds to assume that the courts have discretionary powers to decide when a child can be deprived of maintenance, ie the moment he/she is able to maintain him/herself (theoretically, it might be before the age of 18). On the other hand, there are no signs in Latvian case law to show that the courts could interpret this provision as permitting them to consider whether a child under 18 is able to maintain him/herself. Therefore, a conclusion can be made that Latvian law is also likely to resemble the Lithuanian and Estonian 'absolute' model.

Table 3. **The Courts' discretionary powers to release the parents from the maintenance obligation towards a minor child**

Period of Soviet law (1968–1991)	**Legislation of the independent states**		
	Lithuania	Latvia	Estonia
A court is entitled to release a parent from his/her obligation if a child is fully maintained by the State or a responsible organisation. However, if a child lives in a child-care institution, the maintenance shall be paid to such institution	Not specifically regulated by law. However in practice, courts never exercise a right to release the parents from the maintenance obligation towards a minor child Such attitude is also regarded as a part of 'public order' and 'good morals' in the case law	Not specifically regulated by law. However in practice, courts do not exercise a right to release the parents from the maintenance obligation towards a minor child	A court may not refuse to order support or terminate the payment of support (§102 subsection 2 Family Law Act of Estonia)

3.4. FORMS OF CHILD MAINTENANCE

It should be noted that disputes concerning a failure by parents to fulfil their maintenance obligations are subject to resolution by the courts in all three Baltic countries. Of great importance are the forms of awarding child maintenance. Table 4 compares different forms of child support used in three Baltic countries.

In the Soviet period, child maintenance was awarded exclusively in the form of a regular monthly support payment. Today, 'monthly support payment' serves as an exclusive form of child maintenance only in Latvia. The presumption of 'monthly support payment' is also embedded in Estonian law, with a slim exception based on a 'good reason', providing the obligated person a right to request that he or she be allowed to provide maintenance in another manner. Meanwhile Lithuanian law provides for a wider range of options. A court is entitled to decide that maintenance is to be paid not only as a 'monthly support payment' but also as a one-off lump-sum payment or through a transfer of assets. Yet, Lithuanian case law still considers regular monthly payments to be a preferable form of child maintenance.

Table 4. Forms of child maintenance

Period of Soviet law (1968–1991)	**Legislation of the independent states**		
	Lithuania	Latvia	Estonia
A court should award child maintenance in regular monthly payments: 1) as an appropriate percentage of income: ¼ of the parent's earnings (or other gains) for one child; ⅓ of the parent's earnings (or other gains) for two children; ½ of the parent's earnings (or other gains) for three or more children or 2) as a set amount of money or 3) as both	A court is entitled to decide how maintenance is to be paid in one of these three forms: 1) as a one-off lump-sum payment or 2) as regular monthly payments or 3) through a transfer of assets (Article 3.196, paragraph 1 Civil Code of Lithuania)	Not specifically regulated by law. In practice, courts usually grant maintenance for a child in certain periodically paid amounts of money, (eg salary deductions) or in other values (eg food, clothing, housing) or in both	Maintenance is generally provided by making periodic payments of money. With good reason, an obligated person may request that he or she be allowed to provide maintenance in another manner (§100 subsection 1 Family Law Act of Estonia)

However, even if the courts award 'monthly support payments' as child maintenance, the question arises how the amount of such payment is calculated. It this respect Latvia and Lithuania have abandoned a 'percentage of income' model (which was exclusively used by the courts during the Soviet period) and based their models on the balance between the child's needs and the financial situation of the parents (Article 3.192 paragraph 2 of Lithuanian Civil Code; Article 174 paragraph 1 of Latvian Civil Code). This is due to the changed economic and social conditions, which overturned the economic equality of all members of society, the equal quality of life, guaranteed pay, etc. Meanwhile Estonian legislator took a more flexible attitude allowing a court to order support as a 'fixed amount' or as a 'variable amount by determining in advance the bases for the calculation of the amount of support' (§101 subsection 2 of Estonian Family Law Act). The latter option in turn opens the door for the court to use 'percentage of income' model.

3.5. MINIMUM AMOUNT OF CHILD MAINTENANCE

Table 5 presents the variety in the legal regulations in relation to the minimum amount of child maintenance in the three Baltic countries. Whereas in the period of Soviet law the child maintenance obligation was considered to be absolute (see above), it was necessary to define the minimum amount of maintenance per child to be awarded by the courts. According to Article 22 of the *Fundamentals*, maintenance for one child must not have been lower than 20 roubles per month.[21] Parents who were unable or unwilling to pay this amount were subject to the deprivation of parental rights.

Currently, the problem of the minimum amount of child maintenance is resolved in different ways in Estonian, Latvian and Lithuanian laws. Lithuanian law does not establish a minimum amount of child maintenance or criteria for its calculation. Nevertheless, Lithuanian legal doctrine and case law customarily relate the minimum amount of child maintenance with the size of the *Basic Social Benefit* (earlier referred to as the *Minimum Standard of Living*) established by the Government. These issues are resolved in a rather analogous way (however, based on the law rather than on the case law or legal doctrine) in Latvia and Estonia. In Latvia, more criteria are established by law for the calculation of the minimum amount of child maintenance (besides the 'State specified cost of living' the child's age is always taken into account). The final decision is however taken by the Government. Meanwhile Estonian law provides that the monthly support payment for one child shall not be less than half of the minimum monthly wage established by the Government. With good reason, a court may, however, reduce the amount of support to less than the amount provided for by law.

It is difficult to explain the differences in the legal regulation between three countries. The decision by the Lithuanian legislator not to define the minimum amount of child maintenance or at least criteria for calculation thereof may seem quite strange in this respect, especially bearing in mind the absolute nature of the child maintenance obligation under Lithuanian law. The absolute discretional power of Latvian Government to determine the minimum amount of child maintenance is even more bizarre. It is obvious that it may raise constitutional problems as providing too much leverage to executive power in deciding on such sensitive issues. In this regard Estonian approach of balancing the legislative, executive and judicial powers seems to be the most appropriate one.

---

21 It constituted approximately 20% of the then average salary.

Table 5. **Minimum amount of child maintenance**

Period of Soviet law (1968–1991)	**Legislation of the independent states**		
	Lithuania	Latvia	Estonia
In any case maintenance for one child shall not be lower than 20 roubles per month	Not established in the law (only determined in the case law)	Determined by the Government taking into account the State specified cost of living and the child's age (Article 179, paragraph 5 Civil Code of Latvia)	The monthly support payment for one child shall not be less than half of the minimum monthly wage established by the Government of the Republic (§101subsection 1 Family Law Act of Estonia) With good reason, a court may, however, reduce the amount of support to less than the amount provided for by law (§102 subsection 2 Family Law Act of Estonia)

4. CONCLUSIONS

A historical comparative analysis of Estonian, Latvian and Lithuanian rules of law regulating child maintenance provides a sufficient reason to doubt the prospects of unifying this legal institution. Notwithstanding the common legal regulation for almost 50 years, three Baltic countries ran away from unification at the earliest possible opportunity. Today, all three countries organize their child maintenance regimes in different ways. Differences are due to a variety of reasons: a wish to base the legal system on 'transplants' of historical national sources of law and the social policy pursued by the state which conditions the scope of state social support to separate persons, and ultimately, different constitutional rules on child maintenance. It is interesting to note that even the similar socio-cultural background of all three countries cannot eliminate these differences. It is difficult to predict what possible benefits could force the legislative authorities of these countries to give up their wish to 'dictate fashion' in this area. Unfortunately, the main losers in this situation are persons who are faced with different interpretations of the child maintenance obligation in different jurisdictions.

It appears from the above that substantive child maintenance law is not the most suitable area of family law for seeking unanimity. It would be difficult to find indications showing that the situation could change. Reverse trends are more apparent.[22] Therefore, the thinkers of European law will have to think very hard about what 'carrots' could attract national legislative authorities (and sometimes entire populations) so that they would free this area of legal regulation from the hold of their exclusive national jurisdictions.

22 See, for example, the Ruling of the Federal Constitutional Court of Germany of 30 June, 2009 where the Court ruled *inter alia* that 'Elements which must be reserved to the State are fundamental rules of criminal law, the monopoly of the State to use force in the internal and external sphere, fundamental questions of the State financial system, the shape of the social security system, decisions of fundamental cultural relevance (family law, education, relation between State and religion).' (see at www.bundesverfassungsgericht.de/entscheidungen/es20090630_2bve000208en.html).

PART SEVEN

UNIFICATION OF PRIVATE INTERNATIONAL FAMILY LAW

THE UNIFICATION OF PRIVATE INTERNATIONAL LAW IN EUROPE: A SUCCESS STORY?

Cristina González Beilfuss

1. INTRODUCTION

If an outside observer were to look at the development of private international law in Europe during the last decade he or she would certainly be amazed at the amount of new Community legislation that has either already been passed or is currently being prepared. But not only would the sheer number of new rules catch his or her attention but also the speed of such development, which only started ten years ago when the Treaty of Amsterdam entered into force and the European Community gained competence to legislate in this area of the law.[1] The landscape of the unification of private international law in Europe has completely changed. Gone are the old days when after lengthy preparation the Hague Conference produced one instrument every four years and this instrument was carefully scrutinized and discussed before it eventually came into force! Instead there is hustle and bustle everywhere!

This is even the case in the area of family and succession law where Community involvement came somewhat as a surprise. The Brussels II bis Regulation on the dissolution of marriage and parental responsibility has been applicable since March 2005[2] and is already a substitute for Regulation 1347/2000.[3] It contains rules on jurisdiction, cooperation between authorities and the recognition and enforcement of decisions in the areas of divorce, separation and marriage annulment, as well as on parental responsibility. A new Maintenance Regulation was adopted in 2009.[4] When it comes into force it will replace the rules on jurisdiction, recognition and enforcement of the Brussels I Regulation,[5] and will also provide a new cooperation regime between the authorities of the different Member States. A Proposal for a new Regulation on Succession is currently

---

1 The *Treaty of Amsterdam amending the Treaty on the European Union, the Treaties establishing the European Communities and certain related acts* (OJ C 340 of 10.11.1997) entered into force on May 1st 1999. The introduction of a new Title IV in the Treaties establishing the European Communities produced the "communitarization" of Private international law. Among others see Boele Woelki, K. and R. van Oik: "The communitarization of Private international law", *Yearbook of Private International law*, vol. 4, 2002, 1–36.

2 COUNCIL REGULATION (EC) No. 2201/2003 of 27 November 2003 concerning jurisdiction and the recognition and enforcement of judgments in matrimonial matters and matters of parental responsibility, repealing Regulation (EC) No. 1347/2000 (OJ no. L 338 of 23 December 2003).

3 COUNCIL REGULATION (EC) No. 1347/2000 of 29 May 2000 on jurisdiction and the recognition and enforcement of judgments in matrimonial matters and in matters of parental responsibility for children of both spouses (OJ no. L 160 of 30 June 2000).

4 COUNCIL REGULATION (EC) No. 4/2009 of 18 December 2008 on jurisdiction, applicable law, recognition and enforcement of decisions and cooperation in matters relating to maintenance obligations (O J no. L 7 of 10 January 2009).

5 COUNCIL REGULATION (EC) No. 44/2001 of 22 December 2000 on jurisdiction and the recognition and enforcement of judgments in civil and commercial matters (OJ no. L 12 of 16 January 2000).

being discussed in Brussels.[6] Two new Proposals authorizing and implementing enhanced cooperation in the area of the law applicable to divorce and legal separation were made public at the end of March 2010.[7] The Council decision authorizing enhanced cooperation in this area was subsequently very quickly adopted on 12th July 2010.[8] On 20th December 2010 Council Regulation 1259/2010 was finally approved.[9] A working party is preparing a proposal for a Regulation on matrimonial property,[10] which should be ready during the second semester of 2010. The European Union can certainly not be blamed for not being productive.

There are, however, some important concerns as regards the added value of European family law. This is to my mind a crucial issue because the unification of private international law rules is not an end in itself, but is intended to make people's lives easier.

In this contribution, which closely corresponds to my intervention at the round-table held in Cambridge in April 2010 dealing with the unification of private international law, I will merely raise three issues. The first question which I will pose concerns the application of the new European rules. Due to a number of reasons that will be partly discussed below, European private international law is anything but easy to apply. It might therefore well be that, in practice, the new system is not as beneficial as intended.

The second issue that will be discussed concerns the connection between European rules and national legislation. Although the European legislator has demonstrated a preference for Regulations in the area of cooperation in civil matters, this should not be interpreted to mean that implementing legislation is not needed. Not only is there a need to adjust the application of the new European rules to the already existing national and international private international law sources, but quite often European private international law rules affect other areas of the law, especially procedural law, and require important changes. Unfortunately this is not always recognized in the Member States, which might cause further difficulties in practice.

---

6 Proposal for a REGULATION OF THE EUROPEAN PARLIAMENT AND OF THE COUNCIL on jurisdiction, applicable law, recognition and enforcement of decisions and authentic instruments in matters of succession and the creation of a European Certificate of Succession (COM(2009)154 final) See the contribution by A. Dutta in this book.

7 Proposal for a COUNCIL DECISION No .../2010/EU authorising enhanced cooperation in the area of the law applicable to divorce and legal separation {COM(2010) 105 final} and the Proposal for a COUNCIL REGULATION (EU) implementing enhanced cooperation in the area of the law applicable to divorce and legal separation {COM(2010) 104 final}.

8 OJ no. L 189 of 22 July 2010.

9 OJ no. L 343 of 29 December 2010.

10 A Green Paper was published in 2006. See Commission Green Paper of 17 July 2006 on conflict of laws in matters concerning matrimonial property regimes, including the question of jurisdiction and mutual recognition [COM (2006) 400].

In my last point I raise the issue of whether European private international rules will be able to bridge the gap between widely divergent substantive legal systems on a number of very controversial topics. The European legislator seems to assume that the unification of private international law is an alternative to the harmonization of substantive law for which it lacks competence. It is however questionable whether rules adopted under such a premise offer satisfactory outcomes.

2. IS COMPLEXITY THE PRICE THAT HAS TO BE PAID?

Private international law is a highly complex area of the law which has often caused perplexity and bewilderment among lawyers not trained in the subject. The technicalities of private international law rules are probably the main source of complexity. In many civil law countries a cause of further difficulty has been the fact that this area was judge-made and lacked the neat coherence of other sectors of private law that had been systematically developed and deployed in the Private Law Codes of the 19th century. The unsatisfactory nature of this situation is the main explanation for the comprehensive private international statutes or Codes that were enacted in the last decades of the 20th century in European countries such as Switzerland,[11] Italy[12] or Belgium.[13] Even in countries such as Germany or Spain which did not develop comprehensive statutes dealing with the core areas of jurisdiction, the applicable law and the recognition and enforcement of foreign decisions, these rules were also subject to at least some partial systematization that showed itself in the fact that the main choice of law rules were contained in the Preliminary title of the respective Civil Codes, whereas Procedural rules such as those on jurisdiction and the recognition and enforcement of judgments were contained in statutes dealing with civil procedure.

One source of difficulty for such national systematization was, however, the unification of private international law at the international level. There were certainly attempts to integrate treaties that had been ratified and formed an integral part of the private international law system of a given country into national private international law statutes. In legal systems that follow the so-called monist theory of treaty reception it is not strictly necessary to enact statutes on those treaties. However, there are examples of national statutes that

11 Switzerland's Federal Code on Private International Law of December 18, 1987.

12 The Italian Act on Private International Law of 31 May 1995.

13 The Belgian Private International Law Code of 16 July 2004.

either copy[14] or refer[15] to a treaty and thereby help practitioners not to overlook the existence of a relevant convention.

However, in spite of such endeavours it proved increasingly difficult to provide a clear picture of private international law sources because treaties tended to proliferate. One author stated that treaties emerged like mushrooms in a forest;[16] another referred to the jungle of international conventions.[17] In some cases different organizations dealt with the same topic and produced different treaties that competed with each other and attracted ratifications by different States.[18] More often than not, at least in the European context, the very same organization, the Hague Conference on Private International Law, produced different generations of treaties on the same or nearly the same topic.[19] Although the new treaty was meant to substitute the old, quite often this did not happen completely, because not all the States Parties to the old treaty ratified the new one and the scope of application of successive conventions differed. The relationship between treaties or the "conflicts between conventions"[20] became an ever more important topic not only for academics but also for practitioners.

Community legislation has added a further layer of complexity to the sources of private international law. Unfortunately the Community legislator has demonstrated a preference for topics that have been dealt with or even are being dealt with at the international level. In some cases there have been serious disputes between Member States as to whether Community legislation was really needed in the light of the fact that the unification of private international law rules had already been achieved or was being worked on internationally. Some authors even argued for "reverse subsidiarity", that is abstaining from Community

---

14 The best known example is to be found in the provisions of the Preliminary Title of the German Civil Code on contractual obligations (EGBGB) which copied the provisions o f the 1980 Rome Convention.

15 This method is used, for example, in Art. 83 of the Swiss private international law statute that refers to the Hague 1973 Convention on the law applicable to maintenance obligations.

16 Kegel, G., *Internationales Privatrecht*, 1960, Introduction.

17 de Boer, Th.M., "Jurisdiction and enforcement in International Family Law", *Netherlands international law review*, 2002, 307–351.

18 There are, for example, two Conventions dealing with international child abduction that were finalized in the same year by the Hague Conference on Private International Law and the Council of Europe respectively. Both have been ratified by Spain.

19 The Hague Conference has successively dealt with maintenance in the 1950s, 1970s and in 2007. There are four Conventions and one Protocol on the subject. All of them will apply in Spain.

20 See Briere, C. *Les Conflits de conventions internationales en droit privé*, Paris : Librairie Générale de Droit et de Jurisprudence, 2001.

intervention under the principle of subsidiarity when unification is being pursued or has already been attained at the international level.[21]

However, politically speaking it is hardly conceivable that the European legislator will retrench, because private international law is an integral part of a new Community policy – cooperation in civil matters – which is part and parcel of a more ambitious undertaking, namely the building up of a common area of justice. For this reason international and regional codifications have to be reconciled by integrating European and international rules. Let us provide just two examples. In the area of child abduction there was huge controversy as to whether the European legislator should intervene. Half of the Member States advocated abstention in order to preserve the 1980 Hague Child Abduction Convention which they considered to be working reasonably well in practice, while the other half argued that there was a need to draft European rules because the international ones had led to unsatisfactory results.[22] A compromise was eventually negotiated. On the one hand, Article 60 of the Brussels II bis Regulation establishes that the Regulation substitutes the 1980 Convention in relations between Member States; on the other hand, Article 11.1 of the same Regulation prescribes that the Convention is to be applied but supplemented with special rules contained in paragraphs 2 to 8 of Article 11 of the Regulation. The same pattern is repeated in a slightly more sophisticated form in the area of maintenance. Article 15 of the new Maintenance Regulation refers to the Hague Choice of Law Protocol instead of establishing Community rules on the law applicable to maintenance claims, but since not all Member States will ratify the new Hague Protocol there is a different regime for the recognition of decisions where the Protocol was applied and decisions that were taken without applying the Protocol (see Article 16). Technically, these solutions might be feasible; politically, they may be a nice way out of the difficulties of legislating under the unanimity rule since everybody's wishes are accommodated, but for the average non-expert lawyer such rules can very easily become a nightmare.

The need to reconcile international and regional unification is not the only source of the bewildering complexity of European private international family law. Another very important factor is the piecemeal approach which the European Community is taking, which produces the result that in order to solve one dispute European, national and international rules have to be applied together. Just take an ordinary divorce case. In some jurisdictions, like in Spain, there is a rule that establishes that a divorce may not be granted until all ancillary matters are

---

21 Beaumont, P., "International Family Law in Europe – the Maintenance Project, the Hague Conference and the EC: A Triumph of Reverse Subsidiarity"; *Rabels Zeitschrift für ausländisches und internationales Privatrecht* (2009), 509.

22 See Schulz, A.,"The New Brussels II Regulation ad the Hague Conventions of 1980 and 1996", *IFLJ*, 2004, p. 24 *sequitur.*

resolved.[23] In such jurisdictions there is a strong tradition of concentrating all issues in one competent authority. But this system is no longer workable under the Brussels II bis Regulation. The Regulation only deals with the matrimonial bond and parental responsibility and there are different rules on the international jurisdiction, recognition and enforcement of one issue or another. Maintenance between the spouses and as regards the children of the marriage is governed by the Brussels I Regulation which will be replaced in the near future by the new 2009 Regulation, while the division of matrimonial property and the attribution of the matrimonial home are not dealt with in Community legislation, at least not so far. That is not easy to deal with.[24]

It can be argued that complexity is a price that has to be paid if regional and international codifications of private international law are to live together and that the piecemeal approach is the only way forward under the Community's decision-making process. But it is indeed a high price to pay when, ironically, the initial purpose of Community intervention was to make people's lives easier. In the real world the more complex and difficult it becomes to discover which is the applicable rule and to understand what it actually establishes, the less time there is to devote to solving the real issue that is in dispute, the more likely it is that mistakes are made and the more expensive it is to obtain expert advice. International family law is no longer a minority subject, but a branch of the law that applies to quite a large number of people. These people are sometimes the wealthy who can afford complexity. But many third-country migrants to whom European rules also apply rely on legal aid that is supplied by ordinary family lawyers under unfavourable conditions. In the area of family law, applying private international law rules is very often the task of administrative authorities that are working under tremendous constraints. Whether the extent of the complexity demonstrated by European rules is workable under those conditions is indeed doubtful.

3. THE RELATIONSHIP BETWEEN EUROPEAN PRIVATE INTERNATIONAL LAW AND NATIONAL SUBSTANTIVE AND PROCEDURAL LAW

One of the important differences between the international unification of private international law and the unification of private international law at the European level is that the former mostly takes place by means of international treaties or

[23] For a brief overview of Spanish divorce law see Gonzalez Beilfuss, C.,"Gleichgeschlechtliche Ehe und Blitzscheidung im neuen spanischen Familienrecht", FamPra, 2006-4, 878-885.

[24] Gonzalez Beilfuss, C., " Jurisdiction rules in matrimonial matters under Regulation "Brussels II bis" en Fulchiron, H. and Nourissat, C. : *Le nouveau droit communautaire du divorce et de la responsabilité parentale* , Paris, Dalloz, 2005, 53-67.

conventions, whereas under the latter the sources are those of Community law, mainly Regulations and, to a much lesser extent, Directives. The advantages of Regulations over treaties are quite clear. Regulations do not require a long ratification process but apply directly and have supremacy over national law. Although the decision-making process at the European level is certainly complex and in the area of family law the unanimity rule still governs, it is altogether easier to reform a Regulation than to change a treaty.

From a certain point of view there are, however, also disadvantages in the use of Regulations. Unlike treaties, Regulations are not published in the national official journal but become known through the Official Journal of the European Union which is a relatively unfamiliar source for most family lawyers. But the most important side-effect of using Regulations is that national authorities might be inclined to think that there is not much that must be done after a Regulation has been finalized. While many States have come to understand that there is a need to implement legislation in order to ensure that international obligations can be effectively complied with, the need to implement legislation is less evident in the case of Regulations. Upon closer inspection, Regulations in the area of private international law habitually take quite a long time to enter into force and even longer to become applicable, which indicates that implementing measures should be considered. But in some Member States such signals are quite often overlooked with the result that some rules operate in a vacuum.

As pointed out above, Spanish divorce law departs from the basic assumption that no divorce should be granted until all ancillary matters have been decided upon. In the case of divorce based on mutual consent, the law prescribes that the parties have to reach agreement on all the issues listed in Article 90 of the Spanish Civil Code and such agreements have to be presented to the competent authority for scrutiny. In the case of divorce based on demand, the law requires the requesting spouse to make a proposal as to how ancillary matters should be dealt with and the final decision on such matters is taken by the competent authority before a divorce is granted. Unfortunately such a system does not match European international divorce law. The Brussels II bis Regulation is based on the idea that divorce and ancillary matters are independent from each other, that there might be an authority that can grant a divorce while this very same authority cannot determine ancillary matters or some of them. But if in such a case Spanish divorce law applies, it will need to be adjusted, which is not an easy task. Unfortunately this aspect was not considered when Spanish divorce law was reformed in 2005. This shows that European private international law is not sufficiently integrated into substantive domestic law.

The same holds true concerning the possibility to transfer cases outside of one's own jurisdiction where an authority of another Member State is more suitable.

The mechanism for this, which was taken over from the 1996 Hague Child Protection Convention, appears in Article 15 of the Brussels II bis Regulation and is also part of the Proposal for a Regulation on International Succession. It also seems to be under consideration in the context of the Regulation on matrimonial property that is currently being prepared.

Surprisingly, while the transfer of cases is becoming increasingly popular, little information seems to be available as to how the mechanism is working in practice in the different Member States. From the point of view of a Spanish lawyer the mechanism would seem to appear to create difficulties, especially in cases in which a Spanish authority has jurisdiction and transferring the case to another jurisdiction could be considered either at the authority's own motion or at the request of the authority in another Member State.[25] There are two main problematic aspects. The first is conceptual. In Spanish procedural law jurisdiction rules do not aim to identify the better court, but on the contrary are rather based on the idea of a minimal connection. A Spanish court has jurisdiction not because Spain is the most adequate forum, but because there is a sufficient connection with Spain and this connection justifies and, from a constitutional point of view, even requires that there is access to a Spanish court.[26] Spanish courts are therefore not in the habit of critically assessing whether their intervention is more or less adequate than the intervention of courts in other States. Courts can only decline to hear a case if they lack jurisdiction. Otherwise they are under an obligation to adjudicate the case. In so far as European rules introduce a more flexible approach, it would be necessary to reconceptualize this area of the law. Unfortunately it does not seem that specialists in procedural law have taken any notice of such a development.

From a more practical perspective what really makes the transfer rule difficult to apply is that the mechanism is not dealt with in domestic procedural law. There are simply no provisions clarifying at which stage of the procedure a transfer can be requested or considered, which should be the form of the decision, whether, as seems reasonable, the transfer decision can be appealed, etc. The transfer rule operates in a legal vacuum and is therefore difficult to apply.

The failure to integrate Community private international law rules into domestic substantive and procedural law is each Member State's responsibility. But the Community legislator should perhaps not lose sight of the fact that it is dealing with an area of the law in which the gap between the law in the books and the law in action was already very wide before Community intervention. As experience

---

25 The reverse possibility of a transfer to Spain can be accepted more easily because the prorogation of the Spanish courts is generally accepted.

26 See Otero Garcia-Castrillon, C.: "Problemas de aplicación de las normas de competencia judicial internacional en el Derecho español y comunitario: reflexiones en torno al forum non conveniens", *Revista de la Facultad de Derecho de la Universidad Complutense*, 1999, 99–128.

at the Hague Conference on Private International Law shows, it is very important to monitor and assist in the application of private international law. The Practice Guide on the application of the Brussels II bis Regulation[27] and the European judicial network in civil and commercial matters[28] are steps in the right direction.

4. PRIVATE INTERNATIONAL LAW UNIFICATION AND LEGAL DIVERSITY

European legal systems differ widely in the area of family and succession law. A superficial glance at an important area such as divorce shows an important contrast between Member States that still base divorce on fault, Member States that require the marriage to have irretrievably broken down and other Member States which allow divorce on the basis of mutual consent or at the unilateral request of one spouse (divorce on demand). In one European jurisdiction, namely in Malta, we find a system that does not even allow divorce.[29] Concerning controversial family law topics of today, like same-sex marriages, registered partnerships or surrogacy, there is an even wider discrepancy.

Community law is not supposed to interfere with such diversity. It is however questionable whether it is possible to draft private international rules that produce reasonable outcomes if there is no common ground. Such rules would necessarily have to be "neutral rules" that are not result-oriented. But when, as is often the case in family law, the issue at stake is connected to fundamental rights and principles, such rules may lead to results that are not acceptable.

Very recently a decision has authorized enhanced cooperation in the area of the law applicable to divorce. Fourteen Member States, namely Austria, Belgium, Bulgaria, France, Germany, Hungary, Italy, Latvia, Luxembourg, Malta, Portugal, Romania, Slovenia and Spain, wish to proceed further with a project from which the other Member States have distanced themselves. The main reason why this second group of countries does not want to go ahead is because they do not want to apply foreign law. Firstly, because they are generally opposed to the difficulties and the cost of such application and, secondly, because they have objections to what the content of such a foreign law may be, either because they do not wish

27 Practice Guide for the application of the new Brussels II Regulation (Council Regulation (EC) No. 2201/2003 of 27 November 2003 concerning jurisdiction and the recognition and enforcement of judgments in matrimonial matters and matters of parental responsibility, repealing Regulation (EC) No. 1347/2000) (ec.europa.eu/justice_home/doc.../parental_resp_ec_vdm_en.pdf).

28 http://ec.europa.eu/civiljustice/index_en.htm.

29 Boele-Woelki, K, et al.: (eds.), *European family law in action. vol. I Grounds for divorce*, Antwerp: Intersentia, 2003.

to impede divorce or make it more difficult or because they wish to uphold the institution of marriage and do not accept more liberal regimes than their own.

In certain areas of family law jurisdiction selection rules that are blind to the content of foreign law will certainly cause great difficulty. The Swedish delegation has consistently pointed out during the previous negotiations on the so-called Rome III Regulation that the decisional harmony that might be created by uniform European choice of law rules cannot prevail over the right of a spouse to obtain a divorce that is fundamental under Swedish law.[30] Other Member States that rather uncritically support enhanced cooperation might discover that the same conclusion applies to their systems. Spanish family law has undergone dramatic changes in recent years in order to make sure that the principles of equality, non-discrimination and self-determination prevail. Whether the application of foreign law is always compatible with upholding such principles is questionable. It should be noted that the choice of law rule on divorce was reformed upon the advice of the Spanish Ombudsman who reacted against the situation of Moroccan women who requested a divorce in Spain. In practice, the application of Moroccan law impeded the dissolution of such marriages. The new rules therefore promote the application of Spanish law.[31] After the opening up of marriage to same-sex couples and when the legal status of transgender individuals was reformed it was very soon discovered that private international law rules had to be changed if the principles of non-discrimination and self-determination that had motivated the substantive law changes were to be upheld in cross-border cases. In both cases the solution was found in an increased application of the *lex fori*.

The development of private international law rules would therefore seem to require at least a minimal degree of substantive law harmonization. The works of the Commission on European Family Law show that such harmonization is indeed possible. However, the harmonization of substantive law remains outside Community competence.

---

30 See further Jänterä-Jareborg, M.,"Jurisdiction and Applicable Law in Cross-Border Divorce Cases in Europe" in Jürgen Basedow, Hans Baum and Yuko Nishitani (eds) *Japanese and European Private International Law in Comparative Perspective* (Mohr Siebeck, Tübingen, 2008 317–343).

31 Arenas García, R.," La nueva redacción del artículo 107 del Código civil", *Revista española de derecho internacional,* vol. 56, 2004–1, pp. 205–224.

5. FINAL REMARKS

The communitarization of private international law has led to very important developments in the areas of family and succession law. It is not certain, however, that people's lives have been made easier . It might therefore be advisable to slow down the process and to proceed more cautiously.

THE EUROPEANISATION OF INTERNATIONAL SUCCESSION LAW

Anatol Dutta

1. THE EUROPEAN SUCCESSION PROJECT

When I told Adrian Briggs, Professor of private international law at Oxford, that the European Union was planning to tackle cross-border successions, he was not very impressed. He was rather surprised that, after the free movement of goods, persons, services and capital, the "free movement of the dead, previously only seen in cinema and by those who believe in zombies", had also become one of the policies of the European Union. Indeed at first sight it is surprising that the European Union has discovered succession law – an area of law which has been constantly neglected by the European legislator. Following the 1968 Brussels Convention on jurisdiction and enforcement in civil and commercial matters[1] most European private international law instruments expressly exclude "wills and succession" from their material scope.[2] However, since the Vienna Action Plan of 1998[3], the rules for international successions are officially on the European agenda. Based on a detailed comparative study by the German Notary Institute[4], in 2005 the Commission published a Green Paper on wills and succession identifying "a clear need for the adoption of harmonised European rules".[5] After further consultations and negotiations the Commission submitted, in October 2009, a formal Proposal for a Succession Regulation[6]. It is currently unclear whether and

1 Article 1(2) No. 1 of the Brussels Convention on jurisdiction and enforcement of judgments in civil and commercial matters of 27 September 1968, *Official Journal* 1998 C 27/1.

2 A recent example is Article 1(2)(c) of the Rome I Regulation (EC) No. 593/2008 of the European Parliament and of the Council of 17 June 2008 on the law applicable to contractual obligations, *Official Journal* 2008 L 177/6.

3 Action Plan of the Council and the Commission on how best to implement the provisions of the Treaty of Amsterdam on an area of freedom, security and justice of 3 December 1998, Text adopted by the Justice and Home Affairs Council, *Official Journal* 1999 C 19/1, para 41.

4 Rechtsvergleichende Studie der erbrechtlichen Regelungen des Internationalen Verfahrensrechtes und Internationalen Privatrechts der Mitgliedsstaaten der Europäischen Union, in: *Les successions internationales dans l'UE/Conflict of Law of Succession in the European Union/Internationales Erbrecht in der EU*, ed. by Deutsches Notarinstitut (2004) p 169–328.

5 Green Paper on succession and wills, COM(2005) 65 final of 1 March 2005, p 3.

6 Proposal for a Regulation of the European Parliament and of the Council on jurisdiction, applicable law, recognition and enforcement of decisions and authentic instruments in matters of succession and the creation of a European Certificate of Succession, COM(2009) 154 final of 14 October 2009, partly reproduced infra in section 6.3. See on the proposal eg the following contributions: Bonomi, "Choice-of-law Aspects of the Future EC Regulation in Matters of Succession – A First Glance at the Commission's Proposal", in: *Convergence and Divergence in Private International Law – Liber Amicorum Kurt Siehr*, ed. by Boele-Woelki, Einhorn, Girsberger and Symeonides (2010) p 157; Buschbaum/Kohler, "Vereinheitlichung des Erbkollisionsrechts in Europa", *Zeitschrift für Gemeinschaftsprivatrecht* 2010, p 106 (Part I) and p 162 (Part II); Dörner, "Der Entwurf einer europäischen Verordnung zum Internationalen Erb- und Erbverfahrensrecht – Überblick und ausgewählte Probleme", *Zeitschrift für Erbrecht und Vermögensnachfolge* 2010, p 221; Fötschl, "The Relationship of the European Certificate of Succession to National Certificates", *European Review of Private Law* 16 (2010) p 1259; Kindler, "Vom Staatsangehörigkeits- zum Domizilprinzip: das künftige internationale Erbrecht der Europäischen Union", *Praxis des internationalen Privat- und Verfahrensrechts* 2010, p 44; Kindler, "From Nationality to Habitual Residence: Some Brief Remarks on the Future EU Regulation on International Successions and Wills", in: *Convergence and Divergence in Private*

when the Succession Regulation will be adopted by the European Parliament and the Council; the only interesting news is that the United Kingdom and Ireland, which together with Denmark enjoy a special status in the European cooperation in the area of freedom, security and justice,[7] have so far not exercised their right to opt into the succession project.[8]

The Succession Proposal reveals ambitious legislative plans. The rules proposed by the European Commission go far beyond the classic areas of private international law, ie choice of law (Article 16 et seq of the Proposal), jurisdiction (Article 3 et seq of the Proposal) and recognition and enforcement of foreign decisions (Article 29 et seq of the Proposal). The Succession Proposal also aims to improve the cross-border administration and devolution of estates. For example, the Succession Proposal contains rules on the recognition of succession-

International Law – Liber Amicorum Kurt Siehr, ed. by Boele-Woelki, Einhorn, Girsberger and Symeonides (2010) p 251; M. Kohler/Buschbaum, "Die 'Anererkennung' öffentlicher Urkunden – Kritische Gedanken über einen zweifelhaften Ansatz in der EU-Kollisionsrec htsvereinheitlichung", *Praxis des internationalen Privat- und Verfahrensrechts* 2010, p 313; C. Kohler/Pintens, "Entwicklungen im europäischen Familien- und Erbrecht 2009–2010", *Zeitschrift für das Gesamte Familienrecht* 2010, p 1481, 1483 et seq; Lein, "A Further Step Towards a European Code of Private International Law – The Commission Proposal for a Regulation on Succession", *Yearbook of Private International Law* 11 (2009), p 106; Leipold, "Ist unser Erbrecht noch zeitgemäß?", *Juristenzeitung* 2010, p 802, 808 et seq; Max Planck Institute, "Comments on the European Commission's Proposal for a Regulation of the European Parliament and of the Council on jurisdiction, applicable law, recognition and enforcement of decisions and authentic instruments in matters of succession and the creation of a European Certificate of Succession", *Rabels Zeitschrift für ausländisches und internationals Privatrecht* 74 (2010) p 522; Pfundstein, *Pflichtteil und ordre public – Angehörigenschutz im internationalen Erbrecht* (2010) p 319 et seq; Rauscher, "Vorschlag vom 14. 10. 2009 für eine Verordnung des Europäischen Parlaments und des Rates über die Zuständigkeit, das anzuwendende Recht, die Anerkennung und Vollstreckung von Entscheidungen und öffentlichen Urkunden in Erbsachen sowie zur Einführung eines Europäischen Nachlasszeugnisses", in: *Europäisches Zivilprozess- und Kollisionsrecht: Brüssel IIa-VO, EG-UntVO, EG-ErbVO-E, HUntStProt 2007*, ed. by Rauscher (2010) p 813; Röthel, "Ist unser Erbrecht noch zeitgemäß?", *Gutachten A zum 68. Deutschen Juristentag* (2010) p A 97 et seq; Rudolf, "Vorschlag einer EU-Verordnung zum Internationalen Erb- und Erbverfahrensrecht", *Österreichische Notariats-Zeitung* 2010, p 353; Schurig, "Das internationale Erbrecht wird europäisch – Bemerkungen zur kommenden Europäischen Verordnung", in: *Festschrift für Ulrich Spellenberg* (2010) p 343; Süß, "Der Vorschlag der EG-Kommission zu einer Erbrechtsverordnung (Rom IV-Verordnung) vom 14. Oktober 2009", *Zeitschrift für die Steuer- und Erbrechtspraxis* 2009, p 342; R. Wagner, "Der Kommissionsvorschlag vom 14. 10. 2009 zum internationalen Erbrecht: Stand und Perspektiven des Gesetzgebungsverfahrens", *Deutsche Notar-Zeitschrift* 2010, p 506. See also the contributions collected in *Successions internationales – Réflexions autour du futur règlement européen et de son impact pour la Suisse*, ed. by Bonomi and Schmid (2010).

7 See Protocol No. 21 on the position of the United Kingdom and Ireland in respect of the area of freedom, security and justice, *Official Journal* 2010 C 83/295, and Protocol No. 22 on the position of Denmark, *Official Journal* 2010 C 83/299 – both protocols are annexed to the Treaty on European Union and the Treaty on the Functioning of the European Union.

8 See, as to the United Kingdom, the statement by the Secretary of State for Justice and Lord Chancellor of 16 December 2009, Column 140WS.

related authentic instruments, cf. Article 34 of the Proposal.[9] Furthermore, the Commission in Article 36 et seq introduces the idea of a European Certificate of Succession facilitating the evidence of status as an heir with uniform effects in all Member States.[10] Despite the ample scope of the Succession Project, I will restrict myself in the following text[11] to the choice of law issues, which will be, as already highlighted by the European Commission in the Green Paper, "the core aspect of any legislative initiative".[12] I will also not elaborate on problems of legislative competence.[13] I will rather assume that especially Article 81 of the new Treaty on the Functioning of the European Union – which has lowered competence hurdles compared to Articles 61(c) and 65 of the EC Treaty[14] – provide a sufficient basis for a European regulation on choice of law in successions, even with universal effect towards third States.[15]

But why harmonise the conflict rules for succession law in the first place? The idea of harmonising the conflict rules for successions in Europe is certainly not new. It was noted from the beginnings of European integration that divergent conflict rules for successions within the European Community, and now the European Union, would have, in the long term, disintegrative effects.[16] However, apart from some bilateral and regional instruments, attempts to harmonise conflict rules for successions were not very successful – despite constant activities by the Hague Conference on Private International Law. In particular, the comprehensive 1989 Hague Succession Convention[17] has not received much acceptance; indeed only the Netherlands has adopted the Convention unilaterally. In the area of the formal validity of testamentary dispositions the 1961 Hague Form Convention[18], which is in force at least for the majority of the old Member States, provides uniform conflict rules. The 1985 Hague Trust Convention[19], covering inter alia

[9] See also the criticism of that provision by the MAX PLANCK INSTITUTE (supra n. 6) para 255 et seq.

[10] See eg the comments by the MAX PLANCK INSTITUTE (supra n. 6) para 263 et seq on the Commission's plans to introduce such a certificate.

[11] Which is based on my earlier paper "Succession and Wills in the Conflict of Laws on the Eve of Europeanisation", *Rabels Zeitschrift für ausländisches und internationales Privatrecht* 73 (2009) p 547–606.

[12] Green Paper (supra n. 5) p 3.

[13] See for more details eg MAX PLANCK INSTITUTE (supra n. 6) para 11 et seq.

[14] Cf. also the opinion of Attorney General SHARPSTON delivered on 24 April 2008 in Case C-353/06 (*Grunkin-Paul*) [2008] *E.C.R.* I-7639, para 5 in n. 2.

[15] Cf. also Article 25 of the Proposal. Critically, however, KINDLER (supra n. 6) p 48.

[16] See eg ZWEIGERT, "Einige Auswirkungen des Gemeinsamen Marktes auf das Internationale Privatrecht der Mitgliedstaaten", in: *Probleme des europäischen Rechts, Festschrift Walter Hallstein* (1966) p 555, 558.

[17] Hague Convention of 1 August 1989 on the law applicable to succession to the estates of deceased persons, 28 *Int. Leg. Mat.* 150, partly reproduced infra in section 6.2.

[18] Hague Convention of 5 October 1961 on the conflicts of laws relating to the form of testamentary dispositions, 510 *UNTS* 175, partly reproduced infra in section 6.1.

[19] Convention of 1 July 1985 on the Law Applicable to Trusts and on their Recognition, 23 *Int. Leg. Mat.* 1389.

testamentary trusts,[20] also has some relevance for the choice of law in successions in some Member States.

However, the significance of choice of law in successions cannot be overestimated. Conflict rules in that area are not only crucial from a mere *quantitative* perspective. It is a truism that, in addition to globalisation, European integration has increased the number of cross-border successions in Europe. Choice of law in relation to successions is also highly relevant for *qualitative* reasons: the substantive succession laws of the Member States differ considerably, for example, concerning the succession rights of surviving family members, formal requirements of testamentary dispositions and the relationship between succession and the administration of the estate, to mention only a few issues. A direct harmonisation of substantive law is almost totally lacking, apart from the UNIDROIT Convention on the so-called International Will[21], offers an additional type of will and which has been adopted by some Member States. Also there has been, so far, only little indirect harmonisation. Although the European Court of Human Rights has recognised the impact of the Human Rights Convention[22], especially with regard to the discrimination of children born out of wedlock,[23] the Court has not, apart from abolishing these forms of discrimination, triggered any wider convergence of substantive succession laws.[24]

Against this background, the European Union's plans are readily comprehensible. The international harmony of decisions in Europe is, due to the differences in Member States' conflict rules, currently far off. This lack of harmony especially affects the interests of testators with regard to predictability and legal certainty – two concerns which are recognised as key objectives of European private international law in general.[25] At present, in cross-border successions a testator may possibly have to plan the succession to his or her estate in accordance with a number of substantive laws – a task which might turn out to be impossible if substantive laws cannot be reconciled. Also the heirs, legatees and other

---

20 See Article 2(1) of that Convention.

21 UNIDROIT Convention of 26 October 1973 providing a uniform law on the form of an international will, 12 *Int. Leg. Mat.* 1298.

22 European Convention of 4 November 1950 for the Protection of Human Rights and Fundamental Freedoms, 213 *UNTS* 222.

23 See eg ECHR 3 October 2000 (*Camp and Bourimi*) *ECHR* 2000-X, 119.

24 See Pintens, "Die Europäisierung des Erbrechts", *Zeitschrift für Europäisches Privatrecht* 2001, p 628, 646 et seq.

25 See eg Recital 11 of the Brussels I Regulation (EC) No. 44/2001 of 22 December 2000 on jurisdiction and the recognition and enforcement of judgments in civil and commercial matters, *Official Journal* 2001 L 12/1, consolidated version in *Official Journal* 2009 L 200/46; Recital 6 of the Rome I Regulation (supra n. 2) and of the Rome II Regulation (EC) No. 864/2007 of the European Parliament and of the Council of 11 July 2007 on the law applicable to non-contractual obligations, *Official Journal* 2007 L 199/40.

beneficiaries face considerable difficulties when winding up the estate according to different laws.

2. THREE GENERAL QUESTIONS

When drafting conflict rules for succession a legislator first has to decide three general questions.

2.1. A MONIST OR A DUALIST APPROACH?

As a first step, the legislator has to decide whether movables and immovables belonging to the estate shall be treated differently. Currently the majority of Member States and indeed the Hague Succession Convention (see Article 7(1) of that Convention) follow a *monist* approach. They use a *single* connecting factor – be it the nationality, the last habitual residence or the domicile of the deceased – for the succession as a whole wherever it is situated.[26] Other European countries adhere to a *dualist* conflict rule and differentiate between movables and immovables: succession to movables is governed by a law which is connected to the deceased, whereas succession to immovables is subject to the lex rei sitae, the law of the state where the immovables are situated.[27] Hence, for choice of law purposes the monists regard the estate as one unit, whereas the dualists split the estate into movables and immovables, which are regarded as independent estates potentially governed by different laws.

---

[26] See eg Sec. 28(1) of the Austrian Private International Law Act as interpreted by OGH 19 November 1986, *Praxis des internationalen Privat- und Verfahrensrechts* 1988, p 246; Sec. 17 of the Czechoslovakian Private International Law Act; Sec. 24 of the Estonian Private International Law Act; Book 26 Sec. 5 of the Finnish Succession Act; Article 25(1) of the German Introductory Act to the Civil Code; Article 28 of the Greek Civil Code; Sec. 36(1) sentence 1 of the Hungarian Legislative Decree on Private International Law; Article 46(1) of the Italian Private International Law Act; Article 34 of the Polish Private International Law Act; Article 62 of the Portuguese Civil Code; Article 32(1) of the Slovenian Private International Law Act; Article 9(8) sentence 1 of the Introductory Title to the Spanish Civil Code; Sec. 1 of chapter 1 of the Swedish International Successions Act.

[27] See eg Article 78 Sec. 1 and Sec. 2(1) of the Belgian Private International Law Act; Article 89(1) and (2) of the Bulgarian Private International Law Code; Article 1.62(1) of the Lithuanian Civil Code; Article 66 of the Romanian Private International Law Act. See for France Article 3(2) of the Civil Code and Cass. civ. 19 June 1939, *Revue critique de droit international privé* 34 (1939) p 480; Cass. civ. 14 March 1961, *Revue critique de droit international privé* 50 (1961) p 774, for Luxembourg Article 3(2) of the Civil Code and Trib. Lux. 11 June 1913, *Pas.* 9, p 478, for England and Wales Rules 141 and 146 of Dicey, Morris and Collins, *The Conflict of Laws*, vol. II (14th ed. 2006).

In principle, a European conflict rule for successions should stick to a monist approach and should perceive the estate as a unity,[28] as is now proposed by the European Commission, cf. Articles 16 and 19(1) of the Succession Proposal. Apart from resulting in additional legal costs, the scission of the estate by the dualists entails serious practical problems in coordinating the different applicable laws: nowadays not only a person planning his or her estate but also most substantive succession laws will regard the estate as one unit, even if it consists of movables and immovables; special regimes for succession to immovables have been abandoned in most legal systems, for example in England and Wales by the 1925 Administration of Estates Act. Hence, the substantive laws involved will assume their applicability to the whole of the estate – an assumption which can cause problems especially with regard to the distribution of the estate and forced heirship if more than one law applies to the same estate.[29] Therefore, the European Commission can only be supported in taking a monist view.

2.2. THE NATIONALITY OR RESIDENCE PRINCIPLE?

The second step which the European legislator has to take lies at the heart of every choice of law rule: the appropriate connecting factor. Which law shall govern successions? Almost all European conflict rules refer to a personal criterion of the deceased: the law of *his or her* nationality, *his or her* last habitual residence or *his or her* domicile will apply. The use of a personal criterion of the deceased complies especially with the lifetime interests of persons planning their succession. Succession law is traditionally conceived to be more deeply rooted in the legal culture of a country than other areas of the law. Indeed, at least some interrelationship between the culture of a country and its succession law cannot be denied. The German sociologist *Jens Beckert* has shown that the existing differences in succession laws are notably caused by different culturally formed perceptions of the political actors.[30] Therefore, a succession law to which the deceased was closely connected will probably be influenced, to a greater or lesser extent, by cultural and social values which the deceased might have shared. That law will therefore probably reflect the personal beliefs of a fair and just succession. Also a person planning his or her succession will normally *assume* the applicability of a succession law to whose country he or she is most closely linked. Meeting those expectations is especially important with regard to successions in order to secure that the freedom to testate is rightfully exercised – a freedom

---

28 For further details see eg Dutta (supra n. 11) p 554 et seq.

29 See eg the criticism in *In Re Collens* [1986] *Ch.* 505, 512 et seq.

30 Beckert, *Inherited Wealth* (2008) p 280 et seq.

which is constitutionally guaranteed not only in most national systems[31] but also on the European Union level by the Charter of Fundamental Rights[32].

Although the central role of the deceased in the choice of law process is recognised throughout Europe, there is disagreement on how to determine the law which is most closely connected to the deceased. Again two antagonist approaches face each other: the *nationality* principle and the *residence* principle. Some Member States[33] apply the law of the home country of the deceased to successions by using nationality as a *legal* connecting factor. Other Member States[34] refer to the last residence of the deceased by using habitual residence or domicile as more *factual* connecting factors. In its Article 3 the Hague Succession Convention tries to strike a balance between the nationality and the residence principle by eventually adhering to the nationality principle within the first five years of residence in a foreign country (paragraph 3), and afterwards changing to the residence principle (paragraph 2) – however, both attenuated by escape clauses.

The European legislator should – as proposed by the Commission in Article 16 of the Succession Proposal – follow the residence principle and should refer to the succession law of the country in which the deceased at the time of his or her death was habitually resident.[35] The struggle between the nationality and the residence principle is one of the classic disputes of private international law. It relates not only to successions but also to other areas of the law where a connecting factor shall determine a law to which a person is most closely connected. The pros and cons of both connecting factors have been exhaustively discussed for decades and are documented in nearly any pertinent textbook.[36] The issue will have to be generally decided for all future European instruments.

---

31 See eg Article 14(1) of the German Constitution and BVerfG 19 April 2005, *Entscheidungen des Bundesverfassungsgerichts* 112, p 332, para 63.

32 Article 17(1) sentence 1 of the Charter of Fundamental Rights of the European Union of 12 December 2007, *Official Journal* 2007 C 303/1.

33 See eg Sec. 28(1) in connection with Sec. 9(1) sentence 1 of the Austrian Private International Law Act; Sec. 17 of the Czechoslovakian Private International Law Act; Article 25(1) of the German Introductory Act to the Civil Code; Article 28 of the Greek Civil Code; Sec. 36(1) sentence 1 of the Hungarian Legislative Decree on Private International Law; Article 46(1) of the Italian Private International Law Act; Article 34 of the Polish Private International Law Act; Articles 62, 31(1) of the Portuguese Civil Code; Article 66(a) of the Romanian Private International Law Act; Article 32(1) of the Slovenian Private International Law Act; Article 9(1) and (8) sentence 1 of the Introductory Title to the Spanish Civil Code; Sec. 1(1) of chapter 1 of the Swedish International Successions Act.

34 See Article 78 Sec. 1 of the Belgian Private International Law Act; Article 89(1) of the Bulgarian Private International Law Code; Sec. 24 of the Estonian Private International Law Act; Article 1.62(1) sentence 1 of the Lithuanian Civil Code. See for France Cass. civ. 19 June 1939, *Revue de droit international privé* 34 (1939) p 480; Cass. civ. 22 December 1970, *Revue de droit international privé* 61 (1972) p 467, for Luxembourg Trib. Lux. 20 June 1931, *Pas.* 13, p 466, for English law Rule 140 of Dicey, Morris and Collins (supra n. 27).

35 See for further details eg Dutta (supra n. 11) p 560 et seq.

36 See, for instance, Briggs, *The Conflict of Laws* (2002) 27 et seq.

However, a *tendency* in favour of the residence principle has already appeared on the horizon. The use of habitual residence as a connecting factor does not only follow an international trend, especially set by the Hague Conventions. More importantly, habitual residence has, additionally, become a prominent connecting factor in *European* private international law.[37] A very recent example is the new Rome III Regulation on the law applicable to divorce.[38]

The general tendency in favour of habitual residence simplifies the decision on the appropriate connecting factor. The question whether the deceased was more closely connected to his or her home State or to the State of his or her last residence is not easy to answer if residence and nationality diverge. Notably a decision cannot be based on the lifetime interests of the deceased. To which of the States the deceased was most closely connected depends on his or her internal orientation, especially on whether the interests in *stability* with the home State or the interests in *integration* in the residence State have prevailed.[39] On a general level, it is impossible to establish whether the stability or the integration interests of the deceased were dominant. This would necessitate the collection of empirical data, which is, so far, at least as far as can I see, for the whole European Union currently lacking.[40] Nor can a choice of law rule for successions distinguish in

[37] See eg Article 5(2), Article 13(3) and Article 17(3) of the Brussels I Regulation (supra n. 25); Article 3(1)(a), Article 8(1), Article 9, Article 10 and Article 12(3)(a) of the Brussels IIbis Regulation (EC) No. 2201/2003 of 27 November 2003 concerning jurisdiction and the recognition and enforcement of judgments in matrimonial matters and matters of parental responsibility, *Official Journal* 2003 L 338/1; Article 4(2), Article 5(1)(a) and (1) subpara 2, Article 10(2), Article 11(2), Article 12(2)(b) of the Rome II Regulation (supra n. 25); Article 4(1)(a), (b), (d), (e) and (f), Article 5(1) and (2), Article 6(1), Article 7(2) subpara 2 and Article 11(2), (3) and (4) of the Rome I Regulation (supra n. 2); Article 3(a) and (b) and Article 4(1)(a) and (c)(ii) of the Maintenance Regulation No. 4/2009 of 18 December 2008 on jurisdiction, applicable law, recognition and enforcement of decisions and cooperation in matters relating to maintenance obligations, *Official Journal* 2009 L 7/1; Article 3 of the Hague Protocol of 23 November 2007 on the law applicable to maintenance obligations, which has been signed and adopted by the European Union, cf. Council Decision of 30 November 2009 on the conclusion by the European Community of the Hague Protocol of 23 November 2007 on the law applicable to maintenance obligations, *Official Journal* 2010 L 331/17.

[38] See Article 5(1)(a) and (b), Article 6(2), Article 7(2), (3) and (4), Article 8(a) and (b) and Article 14(b) of the Rome III Regulation (EU) No. 1259/2010 of 20 December 2010 implementing enhanced cooperation in the area of the law applicable to divorce and legal separation, *Official Journal* 2010 L 343/10. See also Article 20b of the Proposal for a Council Regulation amending Regulation (EC) No. 2201/2003 as regards jurisdiction and introducing rules concerning the applicable law in matrimonial matters, COM(2006) 399 final of 17 July 2006, and Article 4(a) and (b) of the Proposal for a Council Regulation (EU) implementing enhanced cooperation in the area of the law applicable to divorce and legal separation, COM(2010) 105 final of 30 March 2010.

[39] See eg Mansel, *Personalstatut, Staatsangehörigkeit und Effektivität* (1988) 73 et seq.

[40] See, however, the European Commission's Staff Working Document accompanying the proposal for a Regulation of the European Parliament and of the Council on jurisdiction, applicable law, recognition and enforcement of decisions and authentic instruments in matters of successions and on the introduction of a European Certificate of Succession – Summary of the impact assessment, SEC(2009) 411 final of 14 October 2009.

every individual case whether stability or integration interests prevailed. The compromise of the Hague Succession Convention shows the difficulty in drafting a kind of "individualistic" conflict rule which, for persons with a prevailing stability interest, points towards the law of their nationality and, for persons with a prevailing interest in integration, towards the law of their last habitual residence. It remains a mere fiction that having a residence in a State over a certain period of time demonstrates a predominant interest in integration; the deceased could still have had an interest in stability.

However, the stress placed on integration interests by the residence principle corresponds with an *integrative policy* of the European Union striving for an integration of persons residing outside their home states. One example where this policy becomes visible is Article 18 of the Treaty on the Functioning of the European Union, the former Article 12 of the EC Treaty, which prohibits discrimination on the grounds of nationality. Article 18 does not proscribe, in general, the use of nationality as a connecting factor in private international law. This has been expressly confirmed in the meantime by the European Court of Justice.[41] However, the prohibition of discrimination in Article 18 protects the interests of citizens in being integrated wherever they reside in the European Union, and can therefore speak for the residence principle. A similar integrative tendency can be traced in the common European immigration policy. The Recitals of the European instruments on immigration provide clear evidence that the Union aims to integrate third-state citizens.[42] The application of the succession law at the place of the last habitual residence could be regarded as a further step towards the legal integration of persons living outside their home countries, especially if one stresses the cultural conditionality of succession law.

2.3. FREEDOM TO CHOOSE THE APPLICABLE LAW?

Apart from those general decisions to be made by the European legislator – monist versus dualist approach and nationality versus residence principle – there is a third general issue to be decided, the question whether habitual residence as a connecting factor should be balanced by some degree of party autonomy. Most conflict laws in Europe do not grant any freedom to determine the governing succession law. A limited choice of law is only accepted by the Article 5 of the

41 ECJ 14 October 2008, Case C-353/06 (*Grunkin-Paul*) [2008] *E.C.R.* I-7639, para 19 et seq.

42 See, for instance, Recitals 3 and 4 of Council Directive 2003/86/EC on the right to family reunification of 22 September 2003, *Official Journal* 2003 L 251/12; Recitals 4 and 12 of Council Directive 2003/109/EC concerning the status of third-country nationals who are long-term residents of 25 November 2003, *Official Journal* 2004 L 16/44.

Hague Succession Convention and by a few Member States.[43] Article 17 of the Commission's Succession Proposal recognises only an express choice of law in favour of the law of nationality.

The future European instrument should at least allow a person to choose, to a limited extent, the law governing the succession to his or her estate.[44] Party autonomy would obviously best serve the interests of any person planning his or her estate. The reference by the objective choice of law rule to the law of the last habitual residence of the deceased has especially ignored, as already stressed, *stability* interests: The residence principle is based on the mere assumption, or the political goal, that an interest of the deceased in integration has prevailed.[45] This assumption is in particular flawed if the deceased had predominant stability interests to the home State or another State, for example, the State of his or her former residence. Stability interests *would* however be protected by a freedom to choose the law because a person could then determine the applicable succession law regardless of a future change of habitual residence.

In this context it should be noted that – apart from integration interests[46] – European Union law also and in particular strives to protect *stability interests* in the conflict of laws. The protection of stability interests is especially important for the realisation of the internal market. The basic freedoms can only be ensured if their exercise is not connected with the loss of legal positions already acquired. An early example of the protection of stability interests is the so-called country of origin principle, which safeguards stability interests – especially in the conflict of public laws.[47] Moreover and even more significantly, at least for conflict lawyers, the jurisprudence of the European Court of Justice in *Centros*[48], *Überseering*[49] and *Inspire Art*[50] has shown that the stability interests of a company validly established under the law of a Member State should not be affected by moving or acting within the internal market. Another example is the recent developments concerning the determination of surnames: In the *Grunkin-Paul* case the Court of Justice held that it would be incompatible with the freedom of movement and residence granted by Article 21 of the Treaty on the Functioning of the European

[43] See eg Article 79 of the Belgian Private International Law Act; Article 89(3) of the Bulgarian Private International Law Code; Article 25(2) of the German Introductory Act to the Civil Code; Book 26 Sec. 6(2) and (3) of the Finnish Succession Act; Sec. 25 of the Estonian Private International Law Act; Article 46(2) sentence 1 of the Italian Private International Law Act.

[44] See for further details eg Dutta (supra n. 11) p 569 et seq. On the freedom to choose the applicable succession law see, in general, the recent book by Fontanellas Morell, *La professio juris sucesoria* (2010).

[45] See supra in section 2.2.

[46] See supra in section 2.2.

[47] See notably ECJ 20 February 1979, Case 120/78 (*Cassis de Dijon*) [1979] *E.C.R.* 649, para 14.

[48] ECJ 9 March 1999, Case C-212/97 (*Centros*) [1999] *E.C.R.* I-1459.

[49] ECJ 5 November 2002, Case C-208/00 (*Überseering*) [2002] *E.C.R.* I-9919.

[50] ECJ 30 September 2003, Case C-167/01 (*Inspire Art*) [2003] *E.C.R.* I-10155.

Union, the former Article 18 of the EC Treaty, if, due to different choice of law rules, a name of a person validly registered in a Member State is not recognised in another Member State in which the person concerned will potentially move and reside.[51] Such stability interests are also endangered if a harmonised connecting factor, such as habitual residence, is used which points to a different law when exercising the freedom of movement and residence – setting aside, however, the very intricate question whether the fundamental freedoms can even require a mutual recognition of legal positions granted by succession law.

Additionally, a freedom to choose the applicable succession law would be part of a *libertarian trend* in private international law, and especially in European private international law – a trend which more and more frequently recognises that it is the *individual*, not the *State*, who can best weigh the relevant choice of law interests.[52] Is there any reason to deny party autonomy with regard to succession? I think not. In contrast to most areas of family law, where party autonomy is recognised at the European level,[53] with regard to succession even substantive law speaks for a liberal approach. The freedom to testate is widely accepted within Europe and is even constitutionally guaranteed.[54] This freedom should be continued at the choice of law level by a freedom of choice.

It cannot be denied, however, that the freedom to testate is *not unlimited*. The freedom of the testator is restricted in most substantive laws; on the one hand, by the private interests of third parties, especially of family members in the application of forced heirship or equivalent institutions, and, on the other hand, by State interests, especially in the enforcement of local public policy. Yet those interests are not *specifically* endangered by party autonomy. Already the use of a personal criterion of the deceased as the objective connecting factor – *his or her* residence or *his or her* nationality – is only suitable, to a very limited extent, to protect those interests internationally. This especially relates to the interests of family members: It is for family members a mere coincidence that under the

---

51 ECJ 14 October 2008, Case C-353/06 (*Grunkin-Paul*) [2008] *E.C.R.* I-7639, para 21 et seq. See also ECJ 30 March 1993, Case C-168/91 (*Konstantinidis*) [1993] *E.C.R.* I-1191, para 15 et seq; ECJ 2 October 2003, Case C-148/02 (*Garcia Avello*) [2003] *E.C.R.* I-11613, para 24 et seq; ECJ 22 December 2010, Case C-208/09 (*Sayn-Wittgenstein*), not yet published in *E.C.R*, para 52 et seq.

52 See eg Basedow, "The Recent Development of the Conflict of Laws", in: *Japanese and European Private International Law in Comparative Perspective*, ed. by Basedow/Baum/Nishitani (2008) p 4, 14 et seq.

53 See Article 7 et seq of the Hague Maintenance Protocol (supra n. 37) and Article 5 et seq of the Rome III Regulation (supra n. 38). See also Article 14 of the Proposal for a Council Regulation on jurisdiction, applicable law, recognition and enforcement of decisions and cooperation in matters relating to maintenance obligations, COM(2005) 649 final of 15 December 2005, Article 20a of the 2006 Rome III Proposal and Article 3 of the 2010 Rome III Proposal (both supra n. 38).

54 See supra note 31 et seq.

objective conflict rule a protective law might apply. Even under the objective conflict rule family members cannot avoid the situation where the deceased, just before his or her death, has altered the pertinent personal criterion by changing, for example, his or her habitual residence or nationality in order to evade a certain protective law. If the interests of family members should be effectively protected at all, a special conflict rule for the protection of family members would be necessary which, for example, subjects forced heirship to the law of the nationality or the habitual residence of the surviving family members. A mere limitation of the freedom of choice would not be sufficient. Moreover, most succession laws, especially within the European Union, provide at least minimum protection for family members. Even under English law – which is probably the most liberal in that respect – the 1975 Inheritance (Provision for Family and Dependants) Act allows the court to grant financial provision for family members (ie spouses, former spouses, cohabitants, children, and dependants of the deceased) if no reasonable financial provision is made by testate or intestate succession. Notably the surviving spouse is often well protected.[55]

Furthermore, apart from a change of the objective connecting factor, it should be noted that already under substantive law a testator is often not precluded from evading forced heirship or other mandatory inheritance rights of family members. Many legal systems offer tools which allow the estate to be shielded from claims by the family members. One only has to think of lifetime trusts in common law jurisdictions or foundations in civil law systems. Apart from tempting side-effects in tax law, all those instruments allow forced heirship provisions of the applicable succession law to be evaded – as long as the clawback periods under the applicable succession law (see for more details infra section 4. 1.) have not expired. But even if the clawback period has not expired, it will often be quite difficult to gain access to an estate held on trust or by a foundation. Often only the beneficiary – but not the family members – know that the foundation or trust exists at all. And even if the family members know of a foreign trust or foundation it will be quite difficult to enforce clawback claims before the foreign courts. For example, Liechtenstein has recently adopted legislation according to which, in effect, only Liechtenstein succession law will apply to clawback claims against Liechtenstein foundations.[56] To sum up that notion: If a testator is determined to evade forced heirship or other mandatory succession rights of close family members he or she will be able to do so irrespective of a freedom of choice. It should not be the task of a European

55 Especially as far as the "notional divorce" test of Sec. 3(2) of the 1975 Act is applied and the court considers what the surviving spouse would have received upon divorce, cf. eg *P. v. G.* [2004] EWHC 2944 (Fam.); *Cunliffe v. Fielden* [2005] EWCA Civ. 1508; *Baker v. Baker* [2008] EWHC 977 (Ch.).

56 Cf. the new Article 29(5) of the Liechtenstinian Private International Law Act. For details see Schauer, "Das neue liechtensteinische Stiftungsrecht", *Zeitschrift für Europäisches Privatrecht* 2010, p 338, 364 et seq.

conflict rule to restrain people from doing things which they can already do under substantive law (at the price of higher transaction costs).

The arguments in favour of a freedom of choice do not in fact justify any limits regarding the *eligible laws*. However, the reactions to the Green Paper and the Succession Proposal show that the time for a total freedom concerning a choice of law in successions has not yet arrived. Rather, it appears that only the possibility for the testator to choose a law which has a sufficient connection with the succession is politically acceptable. However, Article 17 of the Succession Proposal is far too narrow.[57] A person should not only be able to choose the law of his or her nationality. At least, a choice of the law of a former or present habitual residence, or a choice of the law governing the matrimonial property regime (in order to avoid any friction between succession law and matrimonial property law in legal systems where those areas overlap), and – as far as immovables are concerned – a choice of the lex rei sitae should be admissible. The freedom to choose the lex rei sitae for immovables would not – unlike one would think, at first sight – contradict the monist approach.[58] The monist approach is primarily aimed at protecting the interests of a person planning his or her estate. If a testator is not only aware of the fact that different laws apply but even produces this situation voluntarily, there is no reason not to accept that decision, especially as there may be in some cases, for example in connection with third states, good reasons for a dualist choice of law in order to facilitate the administration and winding up of the estate.

Finally, it is not entirely comprehensible why the choice of law by the testator must be express, as Article 17(2) of the Succession Proposal demands. First, it is already unclear what "express" exactly means. Also there might be good reasons to accept an implied choice of law, for example if a testator clearly testates against the background of a certain law by referring to a legal institution of that law.

3. THE SCOPE OF THE FUTURE EUROPEAN LEX HEREDITATIS

The general European conflict rule will cover all issues regarding testate and intestate "successions to the estates of deceased persons", cf. Articles 1(1), 2(1) and 19(1) of the Proposal. The Commission tries to define the edges of the future European lex hereditatis mainly by two lists: Article 1(3) of the Proposal – which not only describes the scope of the applicable law but the scope of the future Succession Regulation as a whole, including its jurisdictional rules, etc – *negatively* lists all issues which are *not* covered by the Proposal, including its conflict rules,

---

57 See also the criticism of that provision by the MAX PLANCK INSTITUTE (supra n. 6) para 134.

58 See supra section 2.1.

whereas Article 19(2) of the Proposal *positively* determines which issues *are* covered by the conflict rules of the Proposal.

Both lists are, however, by no means exhaustive. The point of departure for defining the scope of the applicable succession law is therefore the term "successions to the estates of deceased persons". In order to secure the uniform application of the European conflict rules, the concept of "successions to the estates of deceased persons" will have to be interpreted *autonomously*, as the European Court of Justice generally requires for European private international law.[59] Thus the term "successions to the estates of deceased persons" cannot be interpreted by mere reference to its meaning according to national law. As in other areas of European private international law the future instrument will have to be interpreted – as the European Court of Justice always states – in the light of its wording, its origins, its objectives and its scheme[60] as well as by reference to the general principles which stem from the corpus of the national legal systems.[61]

So far there is only a small amount of jurisprudence by the European Court of Justice which could be a point of departure when interpreting the term "successions to the estates of deceased persons", although – as already mentioned – the term "succession" has been used in European private international law very often, albeit only in a negative sense in order to state that "succession" is *not* covered by a certain instrument.[62] However, so far the Court of Justice has never defined – as far as I am aware – the succession law exception. There is only a mere obiter dictum in the recent case of *Vorarlberger Gebietskrankenkasse* from which we can infer little on the meaning of "succession". The court held that actions brought by the heirs of a deceased against a third party which are based on an inherited claim would fall within the scope of the Brussels I Regulation – and, therefore, are not matters of succession.[63] Given that lack of authority, the non-exhaustive lists of issues which – in the case of Article 19(2) – shall be covered by the European lex hereditatis or which – in the case of Article 1(3) – are excluded from the future Regulation are of the utmost importance.

---

59 See, in general, for all European instruments now based on Article 81 of the Treaty on the Functioning of the European Union, ECJ 8 November 2005, Case C-443/03 (*Leffler*) [2005] *E.C.R.* I-9611, para 45.

60 See eg ECJ 3 May 2007, Case C-386/05 (*Color Drack*) [2007] *E.C.R.* I-3699, para 17 et seq.

61 See eg ECJ 14 October 1976, Case 29/76 (*Eurocontrol*) [1976] *E.C.R.* 1541, para 3.

62 See supra section 1.

63 Cf. ECJ 17 September 2009, Case C-347/08 (*Vorarlberger Gebietskrankenkasse*) [2009] *E.C.R.* I-8661, para 44. See also Oberlandesgericht Stuttgart 9 June 2010, *Zeitschrift für die Steuer- und Erbrechtspraxis* 2010, p 336.

4. SOME SPECIAL ISSUES

Defining the scope of the applicable succession law is also rather challenging because here every answer gives rise to new questions: It is one thing to characterise an issue as a matter of succession law being subject to the general conflict rules on successions. Often the second question immediately arises whether a special conflict rule for that issue is needed. The general conflict rules in Articles 16 and 17 of the Commission Proposal – which provide that, failing a choice of law by the deceased in favour of his or her nationality, the succession is governed by the law of the last habitual residence of the deceased – might not be suitable for all issues of succession law. In the following, I would like to point very briefly to some special issues which could deserve special treatment – all of which could be, of course, the subject of a different conference paper.

4.1. PROTECTION OF FAMILY MEMBERS AND 'CLAWBACK' PROVISIONS

An issue which especially stirs emotions in the United Kingdom is the so-called clawback problem: Many succession laws provide that gifts by a person made within a certain period of time before his or her death can be reclaimed from the donee if the estate is not sufficient to satisfy the claims of family members of the donor under forced heirship (or equivalent) rules.[64] Clawback generally has to be characterised as a matter of succession law: clawback provisions are part and parcel of the protection of close family members by forced heirship; and the deceased shall not be able to devalue the rights of family members by diminishing the estate during his or her lifetime. It cannot be denied that such clawback provisions cause uncertainty for the donee. The donee, at least during a certain period of time, does not know whether the gift can eventually be reclaimed by family members. Notably English lawyers fear that applying foreign clawback provisions could endanger, for example, lifetime dispositions in the form of a trust which are common under English law.[65]

On the choice of law level the uncertainties are further increased by the fact that the donee does not know which law will finally apply to the succession of the donor as the donor, after having made the gift, can change his or her habitual residence or choose a different law. The Succession Proposal does not address those concerns but rather applies the lex hereditatis to the clawback issue.[66] One

64 See eg Sec. 2325, 2329 of the German Civil Code or Sec. 10 of the UK Inheritance (Provision for Family and Dependants) Act 1975.

65 Harris, "Understanding the English Response to the Europeanisation of Private International Law", (2008) 4 *Journal of Private International Law* p 347, 365.

66 See notably Article 19(2)(j) of the Succession Proposal.

viable solution could be a special rule stating that reclaiming a lifetime gift made by the deceased will only be possible if the gift is also reclaimable under the law which would have hypothetically governed the succession of the donor at the time the gift was made.[67]

4.2. TESTAMENTARY DISPOSITIONS: FORMAL VALIDITY

The formal validity of testamentary dispositions also calls for special attention. The Succession Proposal does not contain any provisions on the formal validity of testamentary dispositions, as especially Article 19(2)(k) clarifies. Rather the Commission is apparently of the opinion that the existence of the 1961 Hague Form Convention is sufficient. That view is not correct: Notably, the Hague Form Convention does not apply to all Member States. If I have counted correctly, eleven Member States are currently not parties to the Hague Form Convention. It would not be very convincing to address the conflict rules on successions in general but to neglect the practically important area of testamentary dispositions and their formal validity. Also a second consideration necessitates that the Succession Regulation should contain its own provisions on the law applicable to the formal validity of testamentary dispositions. Although the future Succession Regulation should, in general, adopt the favor negotii approach taken by the Hague Form Convention, some modifications to the Hague regime – which are not precluded by the Convention[68] – should be made. This relates especially to the extension of the model of the Hague Form Convention to succession agreements[69] which are so far not covered by the Convention.[70]

4.3. TESTAMENTARY DISPOSITIONS: EXISTENCE, MATERIAL VALIDITY, EFFECTS AND INTERPRETATION

The existence, material validity, effects and interpretation of testamentary dispositions also need a special conflict rule.[71] If the general conflict rules on successions were to be applied to those issues, the stability interests of the testator could be frustrated: The testator does not know at which place he or she will habitually reside at the time of his or her death and, hence, which law will

67 Dutta (supra n. 11) p 582 et seq; Max Planck Institute (supra n. 6) para 174 et seq.
68 Cf. Article 3 of the Convention.
69 For further possible amendments to the Hague Form Convention see eg Dutta (supra n. 11) p 584 et seq; Süß (supra n. 6) p 345; Max Planck Institute (supra n. 6) para 159 et seq.
70 Cf. Article 4 of the Convention.
71 See eg Dörner (supra n. 6) p 226; Dutta (supra n. 11) p 586 et seq. See also Buschbaum/Kohler (supra n. 6) p 112, 113, 163; Pfundstein (supra n. 6) p 324 et seq; R. Wagner (supra n. 6) p 515.

eventually govern the disposition. This lack of stability – which to a certain extent is compensated by a freedom to choose the applicable law – is best balanced by applying to the testamentary disposition the law which would *hypothetically* govern the succession at the time the disposition was made – an idea which can be found in Article 18(1) of the Succession Proposal, although astonishingly confined to succession agreements.[72]

4.4. TESTAMENTARY TRUSTS AND STATUTORY TRUSTS UPON INTESTACY

Much could be said about testamentary trusts and statutory trusts upon intestacy.[73] Without going into detail: succession-related trusts should be covered by the future Succession Regulation and the total exclusion of trusts in Article 1(3)(i) of the Succession Proposal should be reconsidered.[74] Such trusts are made for true succession purposes, just as is the case with comparable institutions in civil law countries, for instance the Vor- und Nacherbschaft or Testamentsvollstreckung in Germany;[75] they should therefore be subject to the same conflict rules.

4.5. RIGHTS OF THE STATE IN HEIRLESS ESTATES AND SIMULTANEOUS DEATHS

Special rules could also be discussed with regard to heirless estates and cases of simultaneous deaths. Articles 23 and 24 of the Succession Proposal are a good point of departure for discussion but deserve some fine-tuning.[76]

4.6. ADMINISTRATION OF THE ESTATE

I will only make a very brief remark on the administration of the estate: In general, the administration of the estate should also be covered by the general conflict rules for succession.[77] That is also the position of the Commission. Article 19(1) of the Succession Proposal states that the applicable succession law shall govern succession as a whole "from its opening to the final transfer of the inheritance to the

72 See the detailed special conflict rule proposed by the Max Planck Institute (supra n. 6) para 151 et seq.

73 See eg Harris, "The Proposed EU Regulation on Succession and Wills", *Trust Law International* 2008, p 181, 202 et seq; Dutta (supra n. 11) p 592 et seq.

74 See the proposed amendments by the Max Planck Institute (supra n. 6) para 44 et seq.

75 See Kötz, *Trust und Treuhand* (1963) p 97 et seq.

76 See eg Dutta (supra n. 11) p 595 et seq, 598 et seq; Max Planck Institute (supra n. 6) para 214 et seq, 224 et seq.

77 See for further details eg Dutta (supra n. 11) p 600 et seq.

beneficiaries" – a formulation which also covers the administration of the estate which occurs before the final transfer of the estate to the heirs. The fact that the lex hereditatis shall encompass the administration is also stressed by Article 19(3)(f) (which includes the devolution of the estate), Article 19(3)(g) (which refers to the powers of executors and other administrators), Article 19(3)(h) (which refers to the liability of the heirs) and Article 19(3)(l) (which includes the distribution of the estate). However, if under the lex rei sitae a special administration procedure is required, as is the case, for example, in Austria and England and Wales, the lex rei sitae should apply so as to allow those countries to retain their special procedures. Traces of that idea can also be found in Article 21(1) and (2)(a) of the Succession Proposal.[78]

5. INTERACTION WITH NEIGHBOURING CONFLICT RULES

I would like to conclude my brief overview with a look at the potential interaction of the future conflict rules on successions with neighbouring areas of the law. In most legal systems succession law is closely linked to other areas of the law, especially family law, property law, trust law, contract law and company law – areas which are subject to their own choice of law rules. On a very abstract level four different situations could be distinguished which flow from the possible hierarchies of conflict rules within the European Union.

Firstly, the future conflict rules for successions will have to be aligned with *overriding* conflict rules which are derived from primary European Union law. So far, this notably relates to the already mentioned jurisprudence of the European Court of Justice regarding the free movement of companies within Europe in areas where succession law and company law overlap – which is the case in many jurisdictions for certain private companies and partnerships.[79]

Secondly, a – general – problem of future European private international law will be the demarcation of neighbouring conflict rules contained in *secondary* European Union law. With regard to succession, it will be particularly essential to determine the boundary lines to the present and future European conflict rules on *contract* in the Rome I Regulation[80] (eg agreements and gifts inter vivos, the sale of the

---

78 For a different formulation of that idea see MAX PLANCK INSTITUTE (supra n. 6) para 187 et seq. See as to the administration of the estate also Article 20 of the Succession Proposal.

79 For details see DUTTA, "Die Abgrenzung von Gesellschaftsstatut und Erbstatut beim Tod des Gesellschafters", *Rabels Zeitschrift für ausländisches und internationales Privatrecht* 73 (2009) p 727, 736 et seq.

80 Supra n. 2.

estate), on *matrimonial property* in the future Matrimonial Property Regulation[81] (eg compensation by increasing the inheritance share of the surviving spouse), and on *maintenance* in the 2007 Hague Maintenance Protocol[82] (eg protection of the surviving children by maintenance rights). The pointillist technique employed by the European legislator will always entail frictions and gaps between the different instruments. A minor foretaste of the difficult questions which will arise when delimitating the future Succession Regulation with other European instruments can be obtained when looking at the increasing jurisprudence of the European Court of Justice[83] on the delimitation of the Insolvency Regulation[84] and the Brussels I Regulation[85].

Thirdly, the European conflict rules on succession will have to be coordinated with the conflict rules contained in the *conventions* of the Member States, especially in the Hague Trust Convention and the Hague Form Convention. As far as the Succession Proposal does not preserve the application of those rules (see Article 45 of the Succession Proposal), the European rules will prevail within the limits set by Article 351 of the Treaty on the Functioning of the European Union, the former Article 307 of the EC Treaty. However, the precedence of the European rules does not necessarily render those conventions meaningless. Notably if the European conflict rules have been inspired by, or adjusted to, those conventions – in the present case especially the Hague Succession Convention – the conventions will play an important role in the interpretation of European law, as can be shown by recent case law of the European Court of Justice where, for example, the "Hague roots" of the Brussels II bis Regulation[86] with regard to parental responsibility were considered.[87]

Fourthly and finally, the European conflict rules on succession will have to be coordinated with the remaining *national* conflict rules. Here especially the delineation of the conflict rules on successions, on the one side, and the conflict rules on property, on the other side, can be very problematic especially if the applicable succession law creates rights in rem which are not known to the lex

81 See the Green Paper on conflict of laws in matters concerning matrimonial property regimes, including the question of jurisdiction and mutual recognition, COM(2006) 400 final of 17 July 2006 – a formal Commission Proposal is still awaited.

82 Which is part of the European Union's private international law, see supra n. 37.

83 See eg ECJ 12 February 2009, Case C-339/07 (*Deko Marty Belgium*) [2009] *E.C.R.* I-767; ECJ 2 July 2009, Case C-111/08 (*SCT Industri*) [2009] *E.C.R.* I-5655; ECJ 10 September 2009, Case C-292/08 (*German Graphics*) [2009] *E.C.R.* I-8421.

84 Council Regulation (EC) No. 1346/2000 of 29 May 2000 on insolvency proceedings, *Official Journal* 2000 L 160/1.

85 Supra n. 25.

86 Supra n. 37.

87 See the opinions of Attorney General Kokott delivered on 20 September 2007 in Case C-435/06 (*C*) [2007] *E.C.R.* I-10141, para 48 et seq, and on 29 January 2009 in Case C-523/07 (*A*) [2009] *E.C.R.* I-2805, para 26.

rei sitae.[88] Again the process of characterisation will differ from the traditional methods: The focus will lie on the autonomous interpretation of the overriding European law and its effet utile.

6. ANNEX: SELECTED LEGAL MATERIALS

6.1. HAGUE CONVENTION ON THE CONFLICTS OF LAWS RELATING TO THE FORM OF TESTAMENTARY DISPOSITIONS OF 1961

Article 1 [General rule]

A testamentary disposition shall be valid as regards form if its form complies with the internal law:

(a) of the place where the testator made it, or
(b) of a nationality possessed by the testator, either at the time when he made the disposition, or at the time of his death, or
(c) of a place in which the testator had his domicile either at the time when he made the disposition, or at the time of his death, or
(d) of the place in which the testator had his habitual residence either at the time when he made the disposition, or at the time of his death, or
(e) so far as immovables are concerned, of the place where they are situated.

For the purposes of the present Convention, if a national law consists of a non-unified system, the law to be applied shall be determined by the rules in force in that system and, failing any such rules, by the most real connexion which the testator had with any one of the various laws within that system.

The determination of whether or not the testator had his domicile in a particular place shall be governed by the law of that place.

Article 2 [Revocation of earlier testamentary dispositions]

Article 1 shall apply to testamentary dispositions revoking an earlier testamentary disposition.

The revocation shall also be valid as regards form if it complies with any one of the laws according to the terms of which, under Article 1, the testamentary disposition that has been revoked was valid.

Article 3 [Relation with more favourable provisions]

The present Convention shall not affect any existing or future rules of law in Contracting States which recognise testamentary dispositions made in

---

88 See the proposal for a new Article 21(3) by the Max Planck Institute (supra n. 6) para 202 et seq.

compliance with the formal requirements of a law other than a law referred to in the preceding Articles.

Article 4 [Joint wills]
The present Convention shall also apply to the form of testamentary dispositions made by two or more persons in one document.

Article 5 [Scope of the applicable law]
For the purposes of the present Convention, any provision of law which limits the permitted forms of testamentary dispositions by reference to the age, nationality or other personal conditions of the testator, shall be deemed to pertain to matters of form. The same rule shall apply to the qualifications that must be possessed by witnesses required for the validity of a testamentary disposition.

6.2. HAGUE CONVENTION ON THE LAW APPLICABLE TO SUCCESSION TO THE ESTATES OF DECEASED PERSONS OF 1989

Article 3 [General rule]
(1) Succession is governed by the law of the State in which the deceased at the time of his death was habitually resident, if he was then a national of that State.
(2) Succession is also governed by the law of the State in which the deceased at the time of his death was habitually resident if he had been resident there for a period of no less than five years immediately preceding his death. However, in exceptional circumstances, if at the time of his death he was manifestly more closely connected with the State of which he was then a national, the law of that State applies.
(3) In other cases succession is governed by the law of the State of which at the time of his death the deceased was a national, unless at that time the deceased was more closely connected with another State, in which case the law of the latter State applies.

Article 5 [Freedom of choice]
(1) A person may designate the law of a particular State to govern the succession to the whole of his estate. The designation will be effective only if at the time of the designation or of his death such person was a national of that State or had his habitual residence there.
(2) This designation shall be expressed in a statement made in accordance with the formal requirements for dispositions of property upon death. The existence and material validity of the act of designation are governed by the

law designated. If under that law the designation is invalid, the law governing the succession is determined under Article 3.

(3) The revocation of such a designation by its maker shall comply with the rules as to form applicable to the revocation of dispositions of property upon death.

(4) For the purposes of this Article, a designation of the applicable law, in the absence of an express contrary provision by the deceased, is to be construed as governing succession to the whole of the estate of the deceased whether he died intestate or wholly or partially testate.

6.3. EUROPEAN COMMISSION'S PROPOSAL FOR A REGULATION OF THE EUROPEAN PARLIAMENT AND OF THE COUNCIL ON JURISDICTION, APPLICABLE LAW, RECOGNITION AND ENFORCEMENT OF DECISIONS AND AUTHENTIC INSTRUMENTS IN MATTERS OF SUCCESSION AND THE CREATION OF A EUROPEAN CERTIFICATE OF SUCCESSION, COM(2009) 154 FINAL

Article 1 – Scope

(1) This Regulation shall apply to successions to the estates of deceased persons. It shall not apply to revenue, customs or administrative matters.

(2) In this Regulation, "Member State" means all the Member States with the exception of Denmark, [the United Kingdom and Ireland].

(3) The following shall be excluded from the scope of this Regulation:
   (a) the status of natural persons, as well as family relationships and relationships which are similar in effect;
   (b) the legal capacity of natural persons, notwithstanding Article 19(2)(c) and (d);
   (c) the disappearance, absence and presumed death of a natural person;
   (d) questions regarding the matrimonial property regime and the property regime applicable to relationships which are deemed to have comparable effects to marriage;
   (e) maintenance obligations;
   (f) rights and assets created or transferred other than by succession to the estate of deceased persons, including gifts, such as in joint ownership with right of survival, pension plans, insurance contracts and or arrangements of a similar nature, notwithstanding Article 19(2)(j);
   (g) questions covered by company law, such as clauses contained in company memoranda of association and articles of association, associations and legal persons and determining what will happen to the shares upon the death of their partners;

(h) the dissolving, closure and merging of enterprises, associations and legal persons;
(i) the constitution, functioning and dissolving of trusts;
(j) the nature of rights in rem relating to property and publicising these rights.

Article 16 – General rule
Unless otherwise provided for in this Regulation, the law applicable to the succession as a whole shall be that of the State in which the deceased had their habitual residence at the time of their death.

Article 17 – Freedom of choice
(1) A person may choose as the law to govern the succession as a whole the law of the State whose nationality they possess.
(2) The law applicable to the succession must be expressly determined and included in a declaration in the form of a disposition of property upon death.
(3) The existence and the validity in substantive terms of the consent to this determination shall be governed by the determined law.
(4) Modification or revocation by its author of such a determination of applicable law must meet the conditions for the modification or revocation of a disposition of property upon death.

Article 18 – Agreements as to succession
(1) An agreement regarding a person's succession shall be governed by the law which, under this Regulation, would have been applicable to the succession of that person in the event of their death on the day on which the agreement was concluded. If, in accordance with this law, the agreement is not valid, its validity shall nevertheless be accepted if it is in accordance with the law which, at the time of death, is applicable to the succession under this Regulation. The agreement shall therefore be governed by this law.
(2) An agreement concerning the succession of several persons shall be valid in substantive terms only if this validity is accepted by the law which, pursuant to Article 16, would have applied to the succession of one of the persons whose succession is involved in the event of death on the day on which the agreement was concluded. If the contract is valid pursuant to the law applicable to the succession of only one of those persons, that law shall apply. Where the contract is valid pursuant to the law applicable to the succession of several of these persons, the agreement shall be governed by the law with which it has the closest links.
(3) The parties may determine as the law governing their agreement the law which the person or one of the persons whose succession is involved could have chosen in accordance with Article 17.

(4) The application of the law provided for in this Article shall not prejudice the rights of any person who is not party to the agreement and who, in accordance with the law determined in Article 16 or 17, has an indefeasible interest or another right of which it cannot be deprived by the person whose succession is involved.

Article 19 – Scope of applicable law

(1) The law determined in Chapter III shall govern the succession as a whole, from its opening to the final transfer of the inheritance to the beneficiaries.
(2) This law shall govern in particular:
  (a) the causes, time and place of the opening of succession;
  (b) the eligibility of the heirs and legatees, including the inheritance rights of the surviving spouse, determination of the respective shares of such persons, the responsibilities imposed on them by the deceased, and the other rights governing succession which have their source in the death;
  (c) the capacity to inherit;
  (d) the particular causes of the incapacity to dispose or receive;
  (e) disinheritance and debarment from succession;
  (f) the transfer of assets and rights making up the succession to the heirs and legatees, including the conditions and effects of accepting or waiving the succession or legacy;
  (g) the powers of the heirs, the executors of the wills and other administrators of the succession, in particular the sale of property and the payment of creditors;
  (h) responsibility for the debts under the succession;
  (i) the freely disposable portion, the reserved portions and the other restrictions on the freedom to dispose of property upon death, including the allocations deducted from the succession by a judicial authority or another authority for the benefit of the relatives of the deceased;
  (j) any obligation to restore or account for gifts and the taking of them into account when determining the shares of heirs;
  (k) the validity, interpretation, amendment and revocation of a disposition of property upon death, with the exception of its formal validity;
  (l) sharing the inheritance.

Article 20 – Validity of the form of the acceptance or waiver

Without prejudice to Article 19, acceptance or waiver of the succession or a legacy or a declaration made to limit the liability of the heir or legatee shall also be valid where it meets the conditions of the law of the State in which the heir or legatee has their place of habitual residence.

Article 21 – Application of the law of the State in the place in which the property is located

(1) The law applicable to the succession shall be no obstacle to the application of the law of the State in which the property is located where, for the purposes of acceptance or waiver of the succession or a legacy, it stipulates formalities subsequent to those laid down in the law applicable to the succession.

(2) The law applicable to the succession shall be no obstacle to the application of the law of the Member State in which the property is located where it:

(a) subjects the administration and liquidation of the succession to the appointment of an administrator or executor of the will via an authority located in this Member State. The law applicable to the succession shall govern the determination of the persons, such as the heirs, legatees, executors or administrators of the will, who are likely to be appointed to administer and liquidate the succession;

(b) subjects the final transfer of the inheritance to the beneficiaries to the prior payment of taxes relating to the succession.

Article 22 – Special succession regimes

The law applicable in accordance with this Regulation shall not prejudice the special succession regimes to which certain immovable property enterprises, enterprises or other special categories of property are subjected by the law of the Member State in which they are located on account of their economic, family or social purpose where, according to that law, this regime is applicable irrespective of the law governing the succession.

Article 23 – Simultaneous death

Where two or more persons whose successions are governed by different laws die in circumstances which do not allow the order of death to be determined and where the laws deal with the situation through provisions which are incompatible or which do not settle it at all, none of the persons shall have any rights regarding the succession of the other party or parties.

Article 24 – Estate without a claimant

Where, in accordance with the law applicable in accordance with this Regulation, there is neither an heir nor a legatee as determined by a disposition of property upon death and where no natural person is an heir by operation of law, the application of the law thereby determined shall not be an obstacle to the right of a Member State or a body appointed in accordance with the law of the Member State in question to seize the succession property located on its territory.

Article 25 – Universal nature

Any law specified by this Regulation shall apply even if it is not the law of a Member State.

Article 26 – Referral

Where this Regulation provides for the application of the law of a State, it means the rules of law in force in that State other than its rules of private international law.

Article 27 – Public policy

(1) The application of a rule of the law determined by this Regulation may be refused only if such application is incompatible with the public policy of the forum.

(2) In particular, the application of a rule of the law determined by this Regulation may not be considered to be contrary to the public policy of the forum on the sole ground that its clauses regarding the reserved portion of an estate differ from those in force in the forum.

Article 45 – Relations with existing international conventions

(1) This Regulation shall not affect the application of the bilateral or multilateral conventions to which one or more Member States are party at the time of adoption of this Regulation and which relate to the subjects covered by this Regulation, without prejudice to the obligations of the Member States pursuant to Article 307 of the Treaty.

(2) Notwithstanding paragraph 1, this Regulation shall take precedence as between Member States over conventions which relate to subjects governed by this Regulation and to which the Member States are party.

FREEDOM OF TESTATION AND THE PROTECTION OF THE FAMILY IN PRIVATE INTERNATIONAL LAW

Pia Lokin

1. INTRODUCTION

In this contribution the focus will be placed on rules which determine the law which is applicable to a cross-border succession. Currently, these rules are not unified because of the lack of binding international and European instruments in this area.[1] As a result, every state has its own national rules on the law which is applicable to succession. This situation can result in different outcomes to the question of which law is applicable to a cross-border succession. The following example may serve as an illustration:

> A Dutch person lives in the Netherlands and acquires a country house in France which he uses for holiday purposes. When he dies, he leaves movable and immovable property situated in the Netherlands as well as in France. According to Dutch conflict of law rules, the whole succession is governed by Dutch substantive inheritance law while, according to French conflict of law rules, the house situated in France is governed by French substantive inheritance law and the remainder of the estate is governed by Dutch substantive inheritance law.[2]

It goes without saying that the different approaches could have important consequences for the persons involved.

In a cross-border succession, when the deceased has made no choice as to the applicable law in a testamentary disposition, the applicable law is determined objectively at the moment of death. As the moment of one's death is uncertain, it can be difficult to plan one's estate during one's lifetime. A way to remove this uncertainty is to allow a testator to choose which law shall be applied. The chosen law, the subjective applicable law, replaces the objective applicable law including its mandatory provisions. This kind of choice is called a conflict of law designation, a '*kollisionsrechtliche Verweisung*'. A choice of law designation gives a testator the freedom to testate: the testator knows which law shall apply to his succession and, therefore, he can plan his estate during his lifetime.

---

1 Except for the Scandinavian Convention between Denmark, Finland, Sweden, Iceland and Norway of 1934: Konvention mellan Danmark, Finland, Island, Norge och Sverige om arv, testamente och boutredning (jämte slutprotokoll), Köpenhamn 19-11-1934 med ändringar 9-12-1975, and the Convention on the conflicts of laws relating to the form of testamentary dispositions, which was concluded on 5 October 1961 as well as the Convention on the law applicable to succession to the estates of deceased persons, concluded on August 1st, 1989. The first two instruments are not taken into account in this contribution.

2 Dutch rules: Article 1 Wet Conflictenrecht Erfopvolging (Succession (Conflict of Laws) Act) in conjunction with Article 3 of the Hague Convention on the law applicable to succession to the estates of deceased persons and Article 4 of the Wet Conflictenrecht Erfopvolging.
French rules: for the law which is applicable to movables see Labedan, Cour de Cassation, 19 June 1939, B. Ancel & Lequette, Les grands arrêts de la jurisprudence française de droit international privé, Paris : Dalloz, 2006, p. 157-163 and applicable law to immovables see Stewart, Cour de Cassation 14 March 1837, idem, p. 22-29.

Not only does the principle of freedom of testation play a role in private international law, the principle of family protection also gives rise to several important questions in this context. What if substantive inheritance rules which protect the family of a deceased are considered by a State to be overriding mandatory rules?[3] In general, the application of overriding mandatory rules of the forum shall not be restricted, even when, according to the conflict of law rules, the forum has to apply foreign law. Effect may be given to overriding mandatory provisions of a third state which is involved in the international legal relationship. In deciding whether to give effect to these provisions, their nature, their purpose and the consequences of their (non-)application are taken into consideration. When a forum has to apply foreign law, regardless of whether it is determined objectively or subjectively, the application of a provision of foreign law may be refused if such application is manifestly incompatible with the public policy of the forum. When rules on family protection in inheritance law are considered as fundamental principles of the legal system of the forum and are regarded as public policy rules, can the application of foreign law be refused when it is manifestly incompatible with the forum's inheritance rules on family protection? The principle of family protection can result in the following situation with regard to a choice of applicable law: a testator may choose the law which is applicable to his succession, but any such designation is without prejudice to the application of the mandatory rules of the objective applicable law. Such a choice is called a substantive law designation or '*materiellrechtliche Verweisung*'. In this way, the objective law's mandatory inheritance rules on family protection remain applicable.

Most Member States currently do not accept a choice of law designation in cross-border succession cases. Therefore, when a Member State allows a choice of law designation, the legal certainty that this choice creates is limited: although the testator knows during his lifetime which law shall apply to his succession according to that Member State's law, the choice of law designation is not recognized in other states and, as a result, the rights of his heirs or legatees are not guaranteed in every state. This legal uncertainty can be resolved when conflict of law rules, in particular rules on a choice of law designation, are uniformly applied. The Hague Convention on the law applicable to succession to the estates of deceased persons (hereinafter: the Hague Convention) contains uniform conflict of law rules on succession. In addition, a Regulation on jurisdiction, applicable law, recognition and enforcement of decisions and authentic instruments in matters of succession

3 Rome I gives a definition of these types of rules in Article 9 paragraph 1: "Overriding mandatory provisions are provisions the respect for which is regarded as crucial by a country for safeguarding its public interests, such as its political, social or economic organisation, to such an extent that they are applicable to any situation falling within their scope, irrespective of the law otherwise applicable (..) under this Regulation". Regulation (EC) No. 593/2008 of the European Parliament and the Council of 17 June 2008 on the law applicable to contractual obligations (Rome I), Official Journal of the EU, L 177/6.

and the creation of a European Certificate of Succession (hereinafter: the European Succession Proposal) is being prepared.[4] In this article, it will be examined how both the Hague Convention and the European Succession Proposal deal with the principle of freedom of testation and the protection of the family. In particular, it will be examined whether the instruments allow a choice of the applicable law which provides a testator with the freedom of testation by creating legal certainty and whether they contain provisions on overriding mandatory rules and public policy in order to protect the forum's or a third state's inheritance rules on the family of the deceased.[5] The focus will be placed on the European Succession Proposal.

2. THE HAGUE CONVENTION AND THE FUTURE EUROPEAN REGULATION ON SUCCESSION

2.1. THE HAGUE CONVENTION

Today, the Hague Convention has still not entered into force, because it needs three ratifications and, to date, only the Netherlands has ratified it and has incorporated the rules into its national law.[6] Nevertheless, the Hague Convention plays an important role. The Hague Convention and its explanatory report have been an inspiration for the European Commission in drafting the European Succession Proposal.[7] Besides, the Netherlands has incorporated the rules of the Hague Convention into its national law, and these rules are now applied by the Netherlands.[8]

---

4 Convention on the law applicable to succession to the estates of deceased persons, concluded on August 1st, 1989. COM (2009), 154 def., including an impact assessment, SEC (2009) 410 and SEC (2009) 411. The original text is the French version.

5 Provisions on the choice of the applicable law in agreements as to succession in this context are not taken into account in this contribution.

6 Tractatenblad 1994, 49 and 168. Switzerland, Luxembourg and Argentina have signed the Convention (situation as of July 2010) and the Wet van 4 september 1996, houdende regeling van het conflictenrecht inzake de erfopvolging alsmede de vereffening en de verdeling van de nalatenschappen, mede in verband met de bekrachtiging van het op 1 augustus 1989 te 's-Gravenhage tot stand gekomen Verdrag inzake het recht dat van toepassing is op de erfopvolging, Trb. 1994, 49.

7 Official Journal of the European Union C 19/10, Vienna Action Plan: to establish the European Regulation "work already undertaken within the framework of the Hague Conference of Private International Law should be taken into account".

8 Wet van 4 september 1996, houdende regeling van het conflictenrecht inzake de erfopvolging alsmede de vereffening en de verdeling van de nalatenschappen, mede in verband met de bekrachtiging van het op 1 augustus 1989 te 's-Gravenhage tot stand gekomen Verdrag inzake het recht dat van toepassing is op de erfopvolging, Trb. 1994, 49.

The Hague Convention allows a choice of law designation, although the choice is limited.[9] It provides a person with the choice of either the law of his nationality, at the time of the designation or at the time of his death, or the law of his habitual residence, at the time of the designation or at the time of his death.[10] The chosen substantive law in accordance with Article 5 replaces the objective applicable law and applies to the whole succession.[11] The objective applicable law is determined by Article 3 of the Hague Convention.

Another choice of applicable law provision is found in Article 6 of the Hague Convention. Article 6 provides for the option to choose the law of any state. There are two limitations to this choice. First, the choice has to be made with respect to certain assets. Secondly, it states that any such designation is without prejudice to the application of the mandatory rules of the law applicable according to Article 3 or Article 5 the Convention, the *lex causae*. As a result this choice of law provision only allows a '*materiellrechtliche Verweisung*'.

Article 15 states that the law applicable under the Convention does not affect the application of any rules of the law of the State where certain immovables, enterprises or other special categories of assets are situated and which institute a particular inheritance regime in respect of such assets because of economic, family or social considerations. According to the Waters Explanatory Report "the Convention is concerned with the protection of the family's indefeasible inheritance rights, with economic wealth that affects people when that wealth passes from generation to generation, such as in the form of small family businesses, and with social concerns such as the well-being of groups of people

---

9 Article 5: (1) A person may designate the law of a particular State to govern the succession to the whole of his estate. The designation will be effective only if at the time of the designation or of his death such person was a national of that State or had his habitual residence there. (2) This designation shall be expressed in a statement made in accordance with the formal requirements for dispositions of property upon death. The existence and material validity of the act of designation are governed by the law designated. If under that law the designation is invalid, the law governing the succession is determined under Article 3. (3) The revocation of such a designation by its maker shall comply with the rules as to form applicable to the revocation of dispositions of property upon death. (4) For the purposes of this Article, a designation of the applicable law, in the absence of an express contrary provision by the deceased, is to be construed as governing succession to the whole of the estate of the deceased whether he died intestate or wholly or partially testate.

10 It is irrelevant whether the chosen law is the law of a Contracting State or not. Article 2 of the Convention states that the Convention applies even if the applicable law is that of a non-Contracting State. When a choice of applicable law is made according to article 5 of the Convention, law means the law in force in a State other than its choice of law rules (see article 17 of the Convention).

11 According to the Waters Explanatory Report, a person with multiple nationalities may choose any of his nationalities. Hague Conference on private international law, Proceedings of the Sixteenth Session, Tome II, Successions to estates – applicable law, explanatory Report by Donovan W.M. Waters, p. 527–617 (available in French and English). Hereinafter: the Waters report, p. 554 (French) and p. 555 (English).

within society. Social concerns would also be reflected in the attempt of the estate to maintain the standards and values of society as those elements are reflected in laws concerning inheritance and the family".[12] Article 15 does not explicitly speak of (overriding) mandatory rules. The Waters report explains this as follows: "Mandatory rules of the situs inevitably result in a setting aside of main provisions of the Convention, and it was felt that State authorities should not be encouraged to discern mandatory rules more than where it is absolutely essential".[13]

Finally, it should be noted that the Hague Convention contains a special provision on public policy. Article 18 states that the application of any of the laws determined by the Convention may be refused only where such application would be manifestly incompatible with public policy.

2.2. THE FUTURE EUROPEAN REGULATION ON SUCCESSION

For the European Union important changes are foreseen in the field of cross-border succession. The preparatory work for a European Regulation started more than ten years ago. The European Council called on the Council of the EU and the European Commission to present, at its meeting in Vienna, an Action Plan concerning the implementation of the provisions of the Treaty of Amsterdam on an area of freedom and security and justice.[14] The Action Plan was presented in December 1998 and it announced an examination, within five years, of the possibility of drawing up a legal instrument on international jurisdiction, applicable law, recognition and enforcement of judgments relating to matrimonial property regimes and those relating to succession.[15] In October 1999 in Tampere a special meeting of the European Council was held on the creation of an area of freedom, security and justice. The Vienna Action Plan was taken as a starting point.[16] The European Commission gave orders to undertake a preparatory study on succession in the European Union, which was published in 2002.[17] At that time the European Union consisted of only 15 Member States. The comparative study did not take into account the judicial systems of the Member

---

12 Waters Report, p. 588 (French) and p. 589 (English).

13 Waters Report, p. 590 (French) and p. 591 (English).

14 Presidency Conclusions – Cardiff, 15 and 16 June 1998: www.consilium.europa.eu/ueDocs/cms_Data/docs/pressData/en/ec/54315.pdf, number 48.

15 Official Journal of the European Union C 19/10.

16 Presidency Conclusions – Tampere, 16 and 16 October 1999, www.europarl.europa.eu/summits/tam_en.htm.

17 "Étude de droit comparé sur les règles de conflits de juridictions et de conflits de lois relatives aux testaments et successions dans les Etats membres de l'Union Européenne, Rapport Final: Synthèse et Conclusions, 18 septembre/8 novembre 2002, délivré par Deutsches Notarinstitut en coopération avec professeur Heinrich Dörner (Münster) et Professeur Paul Lagarde (Paris) comme coordinateurs scientifiques". From now on GNotI report.

States which subsequently joined the European Union in May 2004 and January 2007. In November 2004 the European Council approved the Hague Programme on strengthening freedom, security and justice in the European Union.[18] The European Commission was requested to submit a Green Paper on succession which was realised in March 2005.[19] More then 50 comments on the Green Paper were received from Member States and several scientific institutions, as well as from legal practice. The European Commission also requested the opinion of the European Economic and Social Committee (EESC) on the Green Paper on succession which was received in October 2005.[20] The EESC considered that "the testator should also be allowed, subject to certain limits, to choose which law should be applicable to his estate, for example that of his nationality (or one of his nationalities), or that of his usual place of residence".[21] In November 2006 the European Parliament established a resolution with twelve recommendations for the European Commission on succession.[22] A group of experts advised the European Commission in preparing the Succession Proposal, which was finally published in October 2009.[23]

Two institutions made concrete propositions to the European Commission on rules for the Regulation of Succession: the German Notary Institute and the European Parliament. Briefly these suggestions, in particular on the choice of the applicable law, will be mentioned before the actual European Succession Proposal is discussed.

2.2.1. Report by the German Notary Institute

First, for cross-border succession, the study of the German Notary Institute suggests using the 'last habitual residence' as the objective connecting factor. Second, a future deceased should be entitled to choose the applicable law according to the study, because such a choice creates legal certainty. The choice of law should be limited to the following options: the law of the nationality of a deceased at the moment of his death, the law of the nationality of the future deceased at the moment of designation and the law of his habitual residence at the moment of designation. To prevent a future deceased from avoiding his obligations towards

18 Official Journal of the EU 2005, C 53/1.

19 COM (2005), 65 def. See in more detail about the Green Paper on succession among others: C. Stumpf, Europäisierung des Erbrechts: Das Grünbuch zum Erb- und Testamentsrecht, EuZW, Heft 19, 2006, p. 587–592, K. Boele-Woelki, Internationaal privaatrecht, Europese regelgeving, Ars Aequi Katern 95, 2005, p. 5245–5246 and P. Terner, Perspectives of a European Law of Succession, Maastricht Journal of European and Comparative Law, 2007, p. 147–178.

20 Official Journal of the EU 2006, C 28/1.

21 Official Journal of the EU 2006, C 28/5.

22 2005/2148 (INI), A6-0359/2006.

23 COM (2009), 154 def. See the list of the group of experts on the property consequences of marriage and other forms of union and on succession and wills in the European Union ('PRM-III/IV') Official Journal of the EU 2006, C 51/3.

family members, the study recommends the following: the validity of a choice of law designation can only be contested when the law of the last habitual residence of a deceased and the law of his nationality at the moment of death coincide and this law provides for provisions to protect family members. The following example might be illustrative: a Dutch resident moves to England where he establishes his habitual residence. There he makes a choice for English law which allows him to disinherit his children. He later returns to the Netherlands where he re-establishes his habitual residence. When he dies the chosen law may be set aside when it affects the protective family provisions of the objective applicable law, in this case Dutch inheritance law.[24] In other words: if the law of the last habitual residence of the deceased is also the law of his nationality at the time of his death, the applicability of the objective law's inheritance rules on family protection cannot be set aside by the chosen law; in this case the objective applicable law's rules on family protection are considered to be overriding mandatory rules.

2.2.2. *European Parliament*

As already mentioned above, the European Parliament made a resolution with recommendations for the European Regulation on Succession in November 2006. The European Parliament also recommended using the last habitual residence as an objective connecting factor. Therefore, the law of the last habitual residence should be applied to an international succession.[25] In respect of the subjective conflict of law rule the following proposal was submitted:

> "The European Parliament considers that the legislative act to be adopted should allow a degree of freedom of choice, in particular by permitting the testator to choose which law should govern the succession, the law of the country of which he is a national or the law of the country of his habitual residence at the time the choice is made; this choice should be indicated in a statement taking the form of a testamentary clause."[26]

2.2.3. *The European Succession Proposal*

In October 2009 the European Commission launched the European Succession Proposal.[27] The main objective of the Proposal is "to enable people living in the European Union to organize their succession in advance and effectively

[24] Gnotl Report, p. 68–72 (French) and p. 265–270 (German).

[25] 2005/2148 (INI), A6–0359/2006, recommendation two (on the criteria for establishing jurisdiction and the objective connecting factor).

[26] The reference date for determining the law of the nationality of a deceased remains unclear.

[27] COM (2009), 154 def, SEC (2009) 410 and SEC (2009) 411. For this contribution the original French text is taken as a starting point as errors occur in the other language version. The UK and Ireland have stated that at this moment in time they do not intend to opt in.

to guarantee the rights of heirs and/or legatees and of other persons linked to the deceased, as well as creditors of the succession."[28] The European Succession Proposal consists of seven chapters containing 51 articles. In the third chapter the conflict of law rules are laid down.

Article 16 of the Proposal determines the objective applicable law: the whole succession is governed by the law of the State of the last habitual residence of the deceased.[29] According to Article 17 of the Proposal, however, a person may choose the law of the State of his nationality.[30] This choice of law provision makes no distinction between movables and immovables, wherever they may be situated.[31] Unlike in Article 6 of the Hague Convention, the Proposal does not provide for a '*materiellrechtliche Verweisung*'. Consequently, the testator's party autonomy granted in Article 17 of the Proposal encompasses a conflict of law designation. However, a reference date on the possession of a certain nationality is now lacking in the provision. To create legal certainty for a testator during his lifetime, the moment of designation should be decisive. If the testator has multiple nationalities, it remains unclear whether he is allowed to designate the law of his most effective nationality or whether any one of these laws may be chosen. Furthermore, it should be noted that the Proposal does not provide any choice for the situation where the testator has no nationality. The Explanatory Memorandum to the European Succession Proposal explains why the choice of the applicable law should be restricted to the law of the testator's nationality:

> "En permettant au testateur un choix de loi, il fallait trouver un compromis entre les avantages d'un tel choix, comme la sécurité juridique et la plus grande facilité à planifier sa succession, et la protection des intérêts légitimes des proches du défunt, notamment du conjoint et des enfants survivants. C'est pourquoi le

---

28 COM (2009), 154 def., p. 2. In French: "La présente proposition vise à permettre aux personnes résidant dans l'Union Européenne d'organiser à l'avance leur succession et de garantir d'une manière efficace les droits des héritiers et/ou légataires, et des autres personnes liées au défunt ainsi que des créanciers de la succession."

29 Article 16 (Règle générale) : Sauf disposition contraire du présent règlement, la loi applicable à l'ensemble de la succession est celle de l'État dans lequel le défunt avait sa résidence habituelle au moment de son décès.

30 Article 17 (Liberté de choix) : 1. Une personne peut choisir comme loi régissant l'ensemble de sa succession la loi de l'État dont elle possède la nationalité. 2. La désignation de la loi applicable à la succession doit être expresse et contenue dans une déclaration revêtant la forme d'une disposition à cause de mort. 3. L'existence et la validité au fond du consentement quant à cette désignation sont régies par la loi désignée. 4. La modification ou la révocation par son auteur d'une telle désignation de la loi applicable doit remplir en la forme les conditions de la modification ou de la révocation d'une disposition à cause de mort.

31 This choice is not limited to the law of a Member State. Next to the fact that articles 16 and 17 speak of 'État' in stead of 'État membre', article 25 of the Proposal determines that any law specified by the Regulation shall apply, even if it is not the law of a Member State. Article 25 (Caractère universel): La loi désignée par le présent règlement s'applique même si cette loi n'est pas celle d'un État membre.

règlement ne permet au testateur que de choisir la loi de sa nationalité et cela doit être apprécié en rapport avec la règle générale qui conduit à l'application de la loi de la résidence."[32]

According to this explanation, a compromise is attempted between creating legal certainty and protecting legitimate expectations of persons close to the deceased, in particular the surviving spouse and children.[33] This consideration illustrates that a careful balance is sought between both principles: on the one side, freedom of testation and, on the other, the protection of the family.

A note should be made concerning one of the main objectives of the European Succession Proposal, namely to enable people living in the European Union to organise their succession in advance.[34] The European Regulation shall apply to the successions of persons whose demise takes place after the Regulation's date of application. The transitional provision of the Proposal, laid down in Article 50, determines that if a deceased has designated an applicable law to his succession prior to the date of the Regulation's application, the designation shall be considered to be valid provided that it meets the conditions listed in Article 17 of the Proposal.[35] It is undesirable that choices of applicable law which are now considered to be valid in a Member State will be considered invalid once the Regulation will become applicable, e.g. choices for the law of one's habitual residence. As described by the Max Planck Institute in its reply to the Proposal: "it would be unjust and undermine legal certainty to subject a testator and his or her will to conditions not in existence at the time of the testamentary disposition."[36]

---

32 Com (2009), 154 def., p. 6. According to the Explanatory Memorandum the European Parliament has also advocated this solution. As we have seen under section 2.2.2 the European Parliament indeed proposes a choice of law, but its proposition is a less limited choice.

33 The Explanatory Memorandum states explicitly that the possibility to choose the law which is applicable to matrimonial property as the law which is applicable to succession has been removed, because it would introduce multiple choices for spouses and therefore greater flexibility. This would be against the objectives of the Proposal. COM (2009), 154 def., p. 7.

34 If we look at the reasons why the rules of the Hague Convention of 1989 were incorporated into national Dutch law, it appears that one of the main reasons was the fact that the rules create legal certainty for a future deceased during his lifetime concerning the law which will govern his succession, see TK II 1993–1994, 23 863 (R 1510) Memorie van Toelichting op Goedkeuring van het op 1 augustus 1989 te 's-Gravenhage tot stand gekomen Verdrag inzake het recht dat van toepassing is op de erfopvolging (Tractatenblad 1994, 49), p. 4–9.

35 Article 50 (Dispositions transitoires) 1. Le présent règlement s'applique aux successions des personnes décédées après sa date d'application. 2. Lorsque le défunt avait, avant la date d'application du présent règlement, désigné la loi applicable à sa succession, cette désignation est considérée comme valide pour autant qu'elle remplisse les conditions énoncées à l'article 17. 3. Lorsque les parties à un pacte successoral avaient, avant la date d'application du présent règlement, désigné la loi applicable à ce pacte, cette désignation est considérée comme valide pour autant qu'elle remplisse les conditions énoncées à l'article 18.

36 See the Comments of the Max Planck Institute of 26 March 2010, www.mpipriv.de/shared/data/pdf/mpi_comments_succession_proposal.pdf, p. 154: 'If the choice of law was valid under the regime in the place when the choice was made, that choice should remain valid even if it is in conflict with the requirements of the new Art. 17.'

The Member States concerned should still be able to consider current valid choices of applicable law to be valid after the Regulation applies, even though these choices of applicable law are not made in accordance with the provisions of the Regulation.

It is worth noticing that Article 22 of the European Succession Proposal seems to be inspired by Article 15 of the Hague Convention. Article 22 states that the applicable law in accordance with this Regulation shall not prejudice the special succession regimes to which certain immovable property enterprises, enterprises or other special categories of property are subjected by the law of the Member State in which they are located on account of their economic, family or social purpose where, according to that law, this regime is applicable irrespective of the law governing the succession. The Explanatory Memorandum explains that "this exception requires strict interpretation in order to remain compatible with the general objective of this Regulation. In particular, it does not apply to the system of scission or to the reserved portion of an estate."[37]

Article 27 of the European Succession Proposal contains a public policy exception. Section 2 of this article underlines that the applicable law according to the Regulation should not be considered to be contrary to the public policy of the law of the forum on the sole ground that its rules regarding the reserved portion differ from those of the forum.[38] According to this provision, the rules on family protection of the *lex fori* cannot restrict the applicability of the *lex causae* on the sole ground that its rules on the reserved portion differ from the *lex causae*.

The question arises as to how the courts of the Member States will apply foreign law when its mandatory inheritance rules regarding family protection differ from those of the foreign law once the Regulation has entered into force. In Germany, for example, Article 14 paragraph 1 of the Constitution (*Grundgesetz*) protects the right of succession and the right of ownership, whereas Article 6 of the Constitution specifically protects the family. As a result, the Constitution reserves a compulsory portion of the estate for certain relatives.[39] Which consequences will this have when a German court is competent according to the Regulation and has to apply, for instance, English law, a law that does not contain mandatory provisions on a

---

37 Com (2009), 154 def., p. 7.

38 Article 27 (Ordre public): 1. L'application d'une disposition de la loi désignée par le présent règlement ne peut être écartée que si cette application est incompatible avec l'ordre public du for. 2. En particulier, l'application d'une disposition de la loi désignée par le présent règlement ne peut être considérée comme contraire à l'ordre public du for au seul motif que ses modalités concernant la réserve héréditaire sont différentes de celles en vigueur dans le for. Noteworthy is that the word 'manifestement' is lacking in this provision.

39 See W. Pintens and S. Seyns in: Imperative Inheritance Law in a Late-Modern Society, five perspectives, C. Castelein, R. Foqué and A. Verbeke (eds), Intersentia 2009, p. 169.

fixed share of the estate for certain relatives?[40] Another example relates to French law. Article 2 of the Code of July 14th 1819, which has obtained the character of a conflict of law rule, because of a broad interpretation by the courts, provides a '*droit de prélèvement*': every French heir of an estate which is (partly) governed by foreign law, and as a consequence does not receive his share of the estate which he would receive according to French intestacy rules, can claim his loss from the property of the estate situated in France.[41] Will this provision still be enforceable once the Regulation enters into force? When according to the Regulation a foreign law is applicable, can application be restricted by giving effect to the forum's or a third state's overriding mandatory inheritance rules on family protection or can application of foreign law be refused when it is manifestly incompatible with the forum's mandatory inheritance rules on family protection which are considered to be public policy? Should national inheritance rules on family protection be qualified as non-mandatory, "ordinarily" mandatory, overridingly mandatory or public policy rules? Then, although the Regulation contains uniform conflict of law rules, the different qualification per State of its inheritance rules on family protection will result in unexpected outcomes for persons involved in a cross-border succession.

3. CONCLUSIONS

Inheritance law is an area of the law which is strongly defined by culture and tradition. The main reason to allow persons to designate the applicable law in a cross-border succession is to ensure that people are able to organise their succession in advance. As the objective applicable law is determined at the moment of death, it does not provide such final legal certainty. Connecting factors used in choice of law rules are carefully selected to achieve legitimate and effective outcomes. A balance must be drawn between, on the one side, the freedom of the testator to choose, which creates legal certainty, and, on the other side, the protection of the legitimate expectations of third parties, including the protection of the family. The Hague Convention deals with this balancing of interests by allowing for a conflict of law designation and at the same time limiting this choice to several options for

[40] In England & Wales, a person domiciled there is permitted to bring a claim under the Inheritance Act of 1975 if the claimant was financially dependent on the deceased and no reasonable financial provisions were made in his favour or if the claimant is not entitled to reasonable financial support on the basis of intestacy rules.
Possible claimants may be relatives or other dependents. The allowance of a share in the estate is more for maintenance purposes and is by no means a fixed proportion. See P. Matthews in: Imperative Inheritance Law in a Late-Modern Society, five perspectives, C. Castelein, R. Foqué and A. Verbeke (eds), Intersentia 2009, p. 137–142.

[41] Art. 2 "Dans le cas de partage d'une même succession entre des cohéritiers étrangers et français, ceux-ci prélèveront sur les biens situés en France une portion égale à la valeur des biens situés en pays étrangers dont ils seraient exclus à quelque titre que ce soit, en vertu des lois et coutumes locales".

law systems that can be chosen with the use of subjective connecting factors. The European Succession Proposal provides for a limited choice of law designation for a testator in that he can choose the law of his nationality as laid down in Article 17. For a clear understanding of Article 17, a reference date for possessing a certain nationality, which is now lacking, is required. To create legal certainty during one's lifetime, at least the moment of designation should be decisive. It should also become clear exactly which options a testator with multiple nationalities has. Moreover, the transitional provisions of the European Succession Proposal create uncertainty towards choice of law designations which are currently considered as valid, but which are not in conformity with Article 17 of the Proposal. Such a provision damages the trust created by a Member State towards people who have made a testamentary disposition in accordance with the conditions existing at the time of making the disposition. Therefore, current valid choices of applicable law according to the conflict rules of the Member States should also remain valid after the Regulation applies. Special attention should be given to the following questions. Are the inheritance rules on family protection of the *lex fori* or of the law of a third state to be considered as overriding mandatory rules and if so, considering their nature, their purpose and the consequences of their (non-) application, can effect be given to these provisions? Finally, can the application of the *lex causae* be refused when the forum's inheritance rules on family protection are considered to be public policy rules? The answers to these questions should be provided before the final version of this new private international law instrument will be adopted.

EU SUCCESSION REGULATION: CHOICE OF APPLICABLE LAW AND PROTECTION OF FAMILY MEMBERS

Anna Wysocka

1. INTRODUCTION

On 14 October 2009, the European Commission published the eagerly awaited proposal for a European Union Regulation on jurisdiction, applicable law, recognition and enforcement of decisions and authentic instruments in matters of succession and the creation of a European Certificate of Succession[1] (hereinafter referred to as the "proposal" or "Succession Regulation").

The preparation of this proposal was preceded by a comparative research into the international succession laws of the Member States conducted by German Notarial Institute located in Würzburg (*Deutsches Notarinstitut*). In 2002, on the basis of national reports submitted by experts from 15 old Member States, the German Notarial Institute prepared a summary report which contained a synthesis of the private international laws of succession in the European Union, as well as recommendations as to the future unification of international succession within the European Union (hereinafter referred to as the "DNotI report").[2] The results of the comparative study and recommendations as to the future unification of rules on jurisdiction, applicable law and the recognition of judgments in succession matters were discussed during the conference held in Brussels on May 10–11, 2004.[3] Additionally, it was proposed that the future EU

1 COM (2009) 154 final of 14.10.2009. For a comprehensive commentary on the Succession Regulation see: J. Basedow, A. Dutta, *Comments on the European Commission's Proposal for a Regulation of the European Parliament and of the Council on jurisdiction, applicable law, recognition and enforcement of decisions and authentic instruments in matters of succession and the creation of a European Certificate of Succession* fothcoming in (2010) 3 *RabelsZ (Rabels Zeitschrift für ausländisches und internationales Privatrecht)*. Available at: http://www.mpipriv.de/shared/data/pdf/mpi_comments_succession_proposal.pdf. E. Lein, A Further Step Towards a European Code of Private International Law. The Commission Proposal for a Regulation on Succession, (2009) 11 *Yearbook of Private International Law*, p. 107-141.

2 P. Lagarde, H. Dörner, *Étude de droit comparé sur les règles de conflits de juridictions et de conflits de lois relative aux testaments et successions dans les États membres de l'Union Européenne. Étude pour la Commission des Communautés Européennes - Direction Général Justice et Affaires intérieures. Rapport Final: Synthèse et Conclusion* in: *Les Successions Internationales dans l'UE Perspectives pour une Harmonisation/ Conflict of Law of Succession in the European Union Perspectives for a Harmonisation/ Internationales Erbrecht in der EU Perspektiven einer Harmonisierung*, Deutsches Notarinstitut, Würzburg 2002.

3 During the conference the following papers were discussed: D. Hayton, *Determination of the objectively applicable law governing succession to deceaseds' estates*; T. Pajor, *Rapport sur le rattachement objectif en droit successoral*; A. Davi, *L'autonomie de la volonté en droit international privé de successions dans la perspective d'une future réglementation européenne*; F. Bouckaert, *Professio juris dans le code de droit international privé belge*; E. Bajson, *Zur Interdependenz von IPR und IZVR bei der Schaffung eines europäischen Justizraums für grenzüberschreitende Nachlassangelegenheiten*; H. Gaudamet-Tallon, *Quelques réflexions sur les propositions concernant la compétence judiciare, la reconnaissance et l'exécution des décisions en matiére successorale dans l'Union Européenne*; M. ten Wolde, *Will professionals in other countries be able to rely on a European Certificate of Inheritance for all purposes?* M. Revillard, *L'introduction d'un certificat international d'héritier et la pratique du droit international privé des successions*. All papers were published in: *Les Successions Internationales dans l'UE Perspectives pour une Harmonisation/ Conflict of Law of Succession in the European*

instrument could influence the creation of a European certificate of succession and a European register of wills.

The next milestone on the road towards a unified European private international law of succession was the EU Council's summit held in Brussels on November 4–5, 2004, during which the document entitled "The Hague Programme: Strengthening freedom, security and justice in the European Union" (hereinafter: "the Hague Programme")[4] was adopted. The Hague Programme assumed that until 2011 the law applicable to contractual obligations, non-contractual obligations, maintenance, matrimonial property regimes, divorces and succession will be regulated at the EU level. As underlined in the Hague Programme, EU instruments should cover only matters of private international law and should not be based on harmonized concepts of the family or marriage. In the Hague Programme the EU Council invited the European Commission to submit, in 2005, "a green paper on the conflict of laws in matters of succession, including the question of jurisdiction, mutual recognition and enforcement of decisions in this area, a European certificate of inheritance and a mechanism allowing precise knowledge of the existence of last wills and testaments of residents of the European Union". In response to this invitation, on March 1, 2005 the EU Commission presented a document called the "Green Paper: Successions and wills" (hereinafter: "Green Paper").[5]

As the Green Paper was supposed to open a broad-based consultation process with respect to the future instrument on the private international law of succession in the European Union it contained thirty-nine questions addressed to all the interested parties, which were asked to send responses and other useful contributions. The Commission received more than sixty responses coming from governments of Member States, supreme courts, corporations, academics, associations and individuals.[6] Relying on these responses the work on the future regulation commenced. On November 30, 2006 a public hearing on the law applicable to succession and wills in the European Union took place.[7] On March 1, 2006 the Commission set up the group of experts known as "PRM III/IV".[8] The group met for discussions on several occasions in 2006–2008.

Union Perspectives for a Harmonisation/ Internationales Erbrecht in der EU Perspektiven einer Harmonisierung, Deutsches Notarinstitut, Würzburg 2002.

4 OJ C 53, 3.3.2003, p. 1.

5 COM (2005) 65 final of 1.3.2005.

6 The responses are published on the website of the European Commission: http://ec.europa. eu/ justice_home/news/consulting_public/successions/news_contributions_successions_en.htm.

7 A summary of the debate is presented in the document called 'Audition publique: Successions et testaments – 30 Novembre 2006. Résumé des réponses au Livre Vert'. Document is available at: http://ec.europa.eu/justice_home/news/consulting_public/successions/contributions/sum mary_contributions_successions_fr.pdf

8 OJ C 51, 1.3.2006, p. 3.

In the Resolution with recommendations to the Commission on succession and wills[9] issued on October 16, 2006 the European Parliament underlined once again that "it would be advisable to draw up a Community legal instrument relating to private international law on successions and wills." A national experts meeting took place on June 30, 2008, during which a working paper was presented revealing the proposed wording of the future regulation[10] (hereinafter: "Working paper").[11] The final proposal was presented by the Commission more than a year later on October 14, 2009.

Comparing the Succession Regulation to the Brussels and Rome regulations, as well as the regulation with respect to maintenance,[12] it becomes obvious that it is a new type of EU instrument with respect to private international law which in the legal literature has been somewhat wittingly referred to as an "all inclusive regulation".[13] This is because in one act the Commission has gathered rules on jurisdiction, applicable law and the recognition and enforcement of foreign judgments as in a so-called *convention triple.* In accordance with the proposal the courts of the Member State in which the deceased had his habitual residence will have jurisdiction over matters of succession. The law which is applicable to succession will also be designated by the connecting factor of the last habitual residence of the deceased, unless the deceased has benefited from the possibility to designate the applicable law in accordance with the Succession Regulation. The rules on the recognition and enforcement of judgments issued by the courts of the Member States are almost identical to the Brussels I Regulation. The proposal also provides for the establishment of a European succession certificate.

---

9 The Resolution is available at: www.europarl.europa.eu/sides/getDoc.do?pubRef=-//EP//TEXT+TA+P6-TA-2006-0496+0+DOC+XML+V0//EN.

10 The working paper entitled 'Succession upon death. Discussion paper. Meeting of national experts. 30.6.2008' may be found on the website of the Austrian Federal Chamber of Commerce: http://wko.at/ooe/Branchen/ Industrie/Zusendungen/EU-VO_Erbrecht_1.pdf.

11 For comments on the solution included in the Working Paper see: J. Harris, 'The proposed EU Regulation on Succession and Wills: Prospectus and Challenges,' 2008 (22) *Trolley's Trust Law International,* p 181 and A. Dutta, 'Succession and wills in the conflict of laws on the eve of Europeanization', (2009) 73 *RabelsZ,* p 574.

12 Council Regulation No. 44/2001 of 22 December 2000 on jurisdiction and the recognition and enforcement of judgments in civil and commercial matters, OJ L 12, 16.1.2001, p. 1–23.; Council Regulation 2201/2003 of 27 November 2003 concerning jurisdiction and the recognition and enforcement of judgments in matrimonial matters and in matters of parental responsibility, repealing Regulation 1347/2000. OJ L 338, 23.12.2003, p. 1; Regulation No. 593/2008 of the European Parliament and of the Council of 17 June 2008 on the law applicable to contractual obligations (Rome I), OJ L 177, 4.7.2008, p. 6; Regulation No. 864/2007 of the European Parliament and of the Council of 11 July 2007 on the law applicable to non-contractual obligations (Rome II), OJ L 7, 10.1.2009, p. 1; and Council Regulation No. 4/2009 of 18 December 2008 on jurisdiction, applicable law, recognition and enforcement of decisions and cooperation in matters relating to maintenance obligations, OJ L7, 10.1.2009, p. 1–79.

13 J. Harris, [note. 11] at 188.

The analysis of the proposal suggests that in numerous places it was strongly inspired by the Convention of 1 August 1989 on the law applicable to succession to the estates of deceased persons (hereinafter: "Hague Convention") adopted in October 1988 during the XVIth session of the Hague Conference on Private International Law.[14] This convention has never entered into force as it was only signed by four countries (Argentina, Luxembourg, the Netherlands and Switzerland[15]) and only ratified by the Netherlands, which unilaterally incorporated the convention in its domestic private international law.[16]

2. APPLICABLE LAW – GENERAL RULE

The EU Commission, while creating conflict rules aimed at designating the law which is applicable to succession, could decide – just as national legislators do – that the applicable law will be designated by connecting factors, being circumstances relating to the deceased. In such a case, one single connecting factor from among nationality, domicile or habitual residence may be used (a unitary system). However, being inspired by such jurisdictions as France, Belgium or the UK the Commission could decide that with respect to succession to certain categories of assets, in particular immovables, the designation of the applicable law should be done with reference to circumstances relating to these assets and not the deceased him/herself. In such a case the applicable law would be

14 It should be reiterated that the Hague Conference on Private International Law has been working on conventions with respect to the law applicable to succession since the beginning of its existence, i.e., since its first diplomatic session held in 1893. The need for a multilateral convention on the law applicable to succession was once raised up during the XIVth session. In 1984 work on the new convention was officially included in the working plan of the XVIthe session. The Permanent Bureau of the Hague Conference established a special commission in that respect. A draft convention, after minor changes, was adopted by the national delegates. Works on the convention were supervised by M. Alfred Overbeck from Switzerland and the explanatory report was written by M. Donovan Waters from Canada. See: M. D. Waters, 'Explanatory Report on the Convention on the Law Applicable to Succession to the Estates of Deceased Persons', in: *Conference de la Haye de droit international privé/Hague Conference on private international law, Actes et Documents de la Seizième session 3 au 20 octobre 1988/ Proceedings of the Sixteenth Session 2 to 20 October 1988, Tome II: Successions – loi applicable*, La Haye/The Hague 1991. See also: L. Frankel, 'Ratification of the Hague Convention on the law applicable to the estates of deceased persons: toward uniformity in United States estate planning', (1991) 12 *New York Law School Journal on the International and Comparative Law*, p 177–201, P. Lagarde, 'La nouvelle Convention de la Haye sur la loi applicable aux successions', (1989) 78 *Revue critique du droit international privé*, p 249–275, E. Scoles, 'The Hague Convention on Succession", (1994) 42 *American Journal of Comparative Law*, p 85–123 and J. Schoenblum, 'Choice of Law and Succession to Wealth: A Critical Analysis of the Ramifications of the Hague Convention on Succession to Decedents' Estates', (1991–1992) 32 *Virginia Journal of International Law*, p. 83–155.

15 See the status table at: www.hcch.net/index_en.p hp?act=conventions.status&cid=62.

16 I. Sumner and H. Warendorf, *Inheritance law legislation of the Netherlands: a translation of Book 4 of the Dutch Civil Code, procedural provisions and private international law legislation*, Antwerp, 2005.

designated by the connecting factor of the place where the assets are located (*lex rei sitae*). Once the legislator decides that the connecting factor of the place where the assets are located should be used it becomes necessary also to use a personal connecting factor to designate the law applicable to succession to assets which are not so closely connected with the place where they happen to be located – in accordance with the rule that *mobilia personam sequuntur*. The designation of the applicable law with the use of two connecting factors depending on the nature of an asset at hand may lead to scission; this is a situation in which the estate is divided into separate parts for the purpose of succession in accordance with different succession laws.[17]

It should be underlined that, currently, only in some Member States has the unitary system been adopted (in Austria, Bulgaria, Spain, Greece, Hungary, Poland, Portugal, Slovakia, Sweden, the Czech Republic and, as a rule, in Germany[18]), whereas Belgium, France, Ireland, Luxembourg, Cyprus and Malta[19] allow for scission. In the DNotI Report its authors recommended that the law applicable to succession should be designated by one single connecting factor.[20] The report listed numerous inconveniences caused by the scission system. In the conflict of laws literature it has also been underlined that scholars and experts coming from jurisdictions with a scission system could see more benefits in the unitary system than vice versa.[21] Hence, due to incorporating the unitary system into the Succession Regulation, together with the exclusion of *renvoi* in Article 26 of the proposal, one estate will be governed by one legal system. As underlined in the explanatory memorandum to the Succession Regulation this solution will allow the deceased to plan the sharing of assets among heirs in an equitable manner, irrespective the place where these assets are located.

Once the Commission decided that the unitary system will be incorporated into Succession Regulation, the next crucial choice was to decide which connecting factor should designate the law applicable to succession. Currently, in Member States the law applicable to succession is designated with the use of the following personal connecting factors: nationality (in Austria, Spain, Greece, Hungary,

---

17 A. Grahl-Madsen, 'Conflict between the principle of unitary succession and the system of scission', (1979) 28 *International and Comparative Law Quarterly*, p 589, F. Boulanger, *Droit international des successions. Nouvelles approches comparatives et jurisprudentielles*, Paris 2004, p 31.

18 M. Revillard, *Droit international privé et communautaire. Pratique notariale*, Paris, 2006 p 302.

19 *Ibid* at 304.

20 DNotI report at 65.

21 A. Bonomi, 'Successions internationales: l'unification des règles de droit international prive dans l'Union européenne', in: *La planification du patrimoine. Journée de droit civil 2008. En L'honneur du Professeur Andreas Bucher*, Geneva 2009, p. 149.

Poland, Portugal, Slovakia, Sweden, the Czech Republic and Germany[22]), domicile (in Denmark and Finland[23]), nationality for succession to movables (in Romania[24]) or domicile for succession to movables (in Belgium, France, Ireland, Luxembourg, the UK, Cyprus and Malta).[25]

According to the authors of the DNotI Report, succession should be governed by the law of the deceased's last domicile.[26] This connecting factor was found to be the most appropriate, taking into account the *principe de proximité*.[27] The DNotI Report includes a discussion on whether there should be any additional requirement as to the duration of domicile as in the Hague Convention· In accordance with Article 3(2) of the Hague Convention, succession is governed by the law of the State in which the deceased at the time of his/her death was habitually resident if he had been resident there for a period of no less than five years immediately preceding his death. However, it was concluded that adding this duration of habitual residence as a requirement is always too arbitrary. Instead, it was suggested that the general rule may be subject to certain exceptions, for example due to the operation of the closer connection clause. When it comes to nationality this connecting factor was perceived to be impossible to reconcile with the prohibition of discrimination based on nationality and was therefore inappropriate for an EU instrument.[28]

As a result, in accordance with Article 16 of the proposal the law applicable to succession shall be that of the State in which the deceased had his/her habitual residence at the time of his/her death. The use of habitual residence as a connecting factor was justified by the Commission in the explanatory memorandum as follows: "the regulation retains this law, instead of the law of nationality, as it coincides with the centre of interest of the deceased and often with the place where most of their property is located. Such a connection is more favourable to integration into the Member State of habitual residence and avoids any discrimination regarding persons who are resident there without possessing the relevant nationality. Habitual residence has also been retained in the conflict-of-law rules of several Member States and in all modern legal instruments, in particular in the Convention [i.e. the Hague Convention]."

---

22 M. Revillard, [note 18] at 302. See also: R. Züß, 'Rattachement de la loi applicable en matière successorale – un aperçu sur différents pays', (2001) 3–4 *Notarius International*, p 239 and 'World Map: Conflicts of Laws in Successions', (2005) 3–4 *Notarius International.*

23 *Ibid.*

24 M. Revillard, [note 18] at 305.

25 *Ibid.*

26 DNotI Report at 66.

27 Compare: P. Lagarde, 'Le principe de proximité dans le droit international privé contemporain; cours général de droit international privé', 1986 (196) *Recueil des Cours* (*Recueil des Cours de l'Académie de droit international de la Haye*) p 9.

28 A. Bonomi, [note 21] at 152.

It is quite interesting that the DNotI Report speaks of the connecting factor of *domicile*, whereas the proposal uses the connecting factor of habitual residence. Probably due to different meanings of the notion of domicile in the domestic laws of the Member States, in particular divergences between the understanding of the concept of domicile in continental Europe and common law countries, the Commission wanted to use a concept which was free from the influences of the domestic laws of the Member States. The use of a neutral connecting factor which is not influenced by the understanding of similar concepts in domestic laws will undoubtedly foster the harmonized interpretation of habitual residence once the proposal enters into force. Additionally, in Recital 32 of the Preamble it is underlined that in every case where the proposal speaks of nationality with respect to common law countries this notion should be understood as domicile. As a result the Commission could not use the connecting factor of domicile as the English word domicile would have two different meanings in the same regulation.

It should be mentioned that Article 25 of the proposal states that any law specified by the Regulation shall apply even if it is not the law of a Member State. This means that rules contained in chapter 3 of the Succession Regulation have a universal nature. Hence, Article 25 obliges the courts of the Member States to apply these conflict of law rules to any succession cases regardless of whether they have any connection with the European Union. This means that once the Succession Regulation enters into force any domestic conflict of law rules now present in the Member States which regulate the law which is applicable to succession would become useless.[29]

3. CHOICE OF THE APPLICABLE LAW

Currently any discussion with respect to the law applicable to succession is accompanied by the question whether the choice of applicable law by the deceased should be admitted. Such a discussion was also present during the work on the proposal. The main argument used by the opponents of the choice of the applicable law in succession is that party autonomy in this respect might be used for the purpose of depriving forced heirs of their indefeasible rights in the estate of the deceased.[30] As the need to protect family members is perceived as being

29 *Ibid.*

30 B. Audit, *Droit international privé*, Paris 2000 at 717, P. Mayer, V. Heuze, *Droit international privé*, Paris 2007 at 603, B. Chappuis, 'L'utilisation de véhicules successoraux dans un contexte international et la lésion de la réserve successorale. Considération de droit civil et de procédure', (2005) 2 *Semaine Judiciaire* 2005, p. 37. Another agrument against the choice of the applicable law in successions may be found in: M. Goré, 'De la mode'... dans les successions internationales: contre les prétentions de la professio iuris, in: *L'Internationalisation du droit. Mélanges en l'honneur de Yvon Loussouarn*, Paris 1994, p 193. Criticisms of arguments against the choice of the applicable law in successions may be found in: , L. Haopei, 'Some

preponderant to the autonomy of the deceased several mechanisms exist in private international law to ensure that the rights of family members are protected. Such mechanisms will be discussed below, starting from simply excluding any choice of the applicable law in successions.

3.1. PROTECTION OF FAMILY MEMBERS BY EXCLUDING THE POSSIBILITY TO CHOOSE THE APPLICABLE LAW

According to the opponents of the choice of the applicable law in successions, it is possible that a future deceased could designate as being applicable, in order to damage the interests of forced heirs, a law that provides for weaker protection for forced heirs' rights.[31] This argument is not really convincing, however. First of all, it should be underlined that in practice every substantive succession law provides for some kind of protection for forced heirs – at least those in need – including English law, which is often given as an example of a jurisdiction with unlimited freedom of testation.[32] As a result, there are no succession laws that may be perceived as being generally better or worse; there are simply different ones.[33] Also the practice in countries already allowing for the choice of the applicable law in successions reveals that this argument is erroneous. In fact it never occurs that a future deceased chooses the applicable law for the sole purpose of depriving the members of his/her family of their indefeasible rights in the estate.[34]

Additionally, according to some authors, in the modern world (due to increasing life expectancy, the position of females in society etc.) substantive rules on the reserved portion and forced heirship have ceased to serve the purpose for which they were adopted and there are significant arguments supporting a limitation to

recent developments in the conflict of laws of successions', (1990) 224, *Recueil des Cours*, p 6, S. Billarant, *Le caractère substantiel de la réglementation française des successions internationales. Réflexions sir la méthode conflictuelle*, Paris 2004 at 330.

31 Comparative the analysis of different measures for protecting family members: A. Bonomi, *La vocation successorale volontaire dans certains droits européens* in: *Le droit des successions en Europe. Actes du colloque de Lausanne du 21 février 2003*, Geneva 2003, p 31 and the UK Ministry of Justice, *European Commission proposal on succession and wills – a public consultation* published on the website: www.justice.gov.uk/consultations/docs/ec-succession-wills.pdf.

32 On the protection of certain family members by means other than the reserved portion: B. Hanotiau, *Rapport sur la réserve en droit anglais et en droit americain* and M. Calier, *A propos du droit québécois*, in: *Examen critique de la réserve successorale*, Fédération royale des notaires de Belgique, Comité d'études et de législation, congrès notarial, v. I, Brussels 1997.

33 G. Droz, *La codification du droit international prive des successions. Perspectives nouvelles*, "Travaux du Comité français de droit international privé" 1966–1969, s. 326.

34 Ibid at 326, L. Haopei, [note 30] at 85, A. Davi, 'L'autonomie de la volonté en droit international privé des successions dans la perspective d'une future réglementation européenne', (2004) 2 *Rivista di diritto internazionale privato et processuale*, p 475.

their extent or even their abolition.[35] Hence, referring to substantive rules on forced heirship as an argument against being able to choose the law which is applicable to succession is not very convincing. Another counterargument is that family members are not protected when a change in the habitual residence of the future deceased results in a change in the applicable law designated by the objective connecting factor – as would be possible under the Succession Regulation.[36] As a result, there is no justification for such protection by not allowing a choice of law at all.

On the other hand, supporters of the choice of the applicable law in successions often refer to freedom of testation which exists in substantive succession laws stating that a choice of the applicable law is nothing more than its reflection in private international law.[37] Just as contractual freedom in civil law justifies the possibility to choose the law which is applicable to contractual obligations, freedom of testation justifies a choice of the applicable law in successions.[38] However, it seems that it was not the above argument that convinced the EU Commission to include the choice of the applicable law in the Succession Regulation.

It is quite obvious that the main argument that convinced the EU Commission to include the choice of the applicable law in the proposal was the fact that the objective connecting factors used by domestic legislators in international successions are nationality, domicile or habitual residence. The use of each of them may be justified and it is not entirely possible to prove which one is the most suitable and acceptable for all Member States. As a result, allowing a choice between at least nationality and habitual residence would allow the future deceased to decide which law is more appropriate in a given case.[39] Hence, allowing a choice of the applicable law in the Succession Regulation is nothing more than a mere compromise between various conflict of law rules currently in force in the Member States.

---

35 A. Davi, *L'autonomie de la volonté en droit international privé des successions dans la perspective d'une future réglementation européenne*, "Rivista di diritto internazionale privato et processuale" 2004, t. 2, s. 473. On the history and evolution of rules on the reserved portion in the comparative context, as well as on the raison d'être of the reserved portion in the modern world see: *Examen critique de la réserve successorale*, Fédération royale des notaires de Belgique, Comité d'études et de législation, congrès notarial, t. I, II i III, Brussels 1997–2000.

36 A. Dutta [note 11] at 574. DNotI report at 71.

37 H. Dölle, *Die Rechtswahl im internationalen Erbrecht*, (1966) 30 RabelsZ at 265.

38 Ibid.

39 A. Overbeck, 'La professio iuris comme moyen de rapprocher les principes du domicile et de la nationalité en droit international privé', in: *Liber Amicorum Baron Louis Fredericq*, Ghent 1965 at 1085.

3.2. PROTECTION OF FAMILY MEMBERS BY PROVIDING AN EXHAUSTIVE LIST OF LAWS THAT MAY BE CHOSEN BY THE FUTURE DECEASED

Once the EU Commission decided that a choice of the applicable law should be admissible under the Succession Regulation, another dilemma that needed to be resolved was providing limits to that choice. The question that had to be answered by the Commission was whether any law could be designated by the testator, or maybe whether this autonomy should be limited to the possibility of choosing only certain laws with which the future deceased was somehow connected. Some voices in the legal literature have suggested that the protection of family members should not be ensured by not allowing a choice of law, but instead by providing an exhaustive list of laws that may in fact be chosen.[40] According to the responses to the Green Paper in general, a choice of the applicable law in succession has been favourably received. However, these responses have underlined the need to limit such a choice by indicating that the only laws that may be chosen are those of the deceased's nationality or habitual residence at the time of making the designation or at the time of death.

In accordance with Article 3.2 of the Working Paper the testator was allowed to designate as the law which is applicable to the succession to his/her estate in its entirety the law of his/her nationality at the time of his/her death, the law of his/her nationality at the time of designation or the law of his/her habitual residence at the time of the designation. Theoretically, the testator could choose between three different laws. However, the extent of this autonomy was restricted during further work on the proposal. In accordance with Article 17 of the Succession Regulation the testator may only choose the law of his/her nationality. To discern the limited nature of this choice one must compare Article 17 of the proposal with the tendencies in other private international law instruments.

Currently, a choice of the law which will apply to succession is available in the following Member States: Germany, Italy, Belgium, the Netherlands, Denmark and Finland. When it comes to European countries which are not EU Members it is crucial to point out that Switzerland is a pioneer in the choice of the law which is applicable to successions. The Canadian province of Quebec may serve as an example of non-European jurisdictions allowing for a choice of the law which is applicable to successions.

The most restricted choice of the applicable law in succession is provided by German private international law. In accordance with Article 25 of the German statute of 18 August 1986 introducing the civil code, succession is governed by

40 A. Davi [note 35] at 475.

the law of the deceased's nationality at the time of death. However, a testator may choose German law to govern succession to immovables which are located on German territory.[41]This provision indicates that the choice of the applicable law may only be made by foreigners. In the case of German nationals the law which is applicable to successions will generally be German law. This rule has a unilateral character as it does not allow for a choice of the applicable law concerning immovables which are located outside Germany. Hence, the testator may only designate German law as the law which is applicable. Such a choice may be partial and may only concern some of the testator's immovables located in Germany.[42]

In accordance with Article 90 of the Swiss Federal Law of 18 December 1987 on private international law[43] succession to the estate of a person with his/her last habitual residence in Switzerland is governed by Swiss law; however, by means of a will or a succession agreement a foreign national may subject succession to his/her estate to the law of one of his/her nationalities.[44] Such a designation will not be valid if at the time of death the deceased was no longer a national of that country or had already obtained Swiss nationality. In accordance with Article 91 of this law, succession to the estate of a person having his/her last habitual residence abroad is governed by the law designated by the private international law rules of this country. However, if the Swiss authorities have jurisdiction, then succession to the estate of a Swiss national having his/her last habitual residence abroad is governed by Swiss law unless this person has expressly chosen in a will or succession agreement for the law of his/her last habitual residence. Hence, in comparison to German private international law Swiss law also allows its own nationals to choose the law which is applicable to succession provided that the testator had his/her last habitual residence outside Switzerland.[45]

Ukrainian and Estonian private international law provide for a choice of the law which is applicable to succession to an extent which is similar to the Succession Regulation. In accordance with Article 70 of the Ukrainian statute

---

41 F. Sturm, *Personnes, famille et successions dans la Loi du 25 juillet 1986 portant reforme du droit international prive allemand*, (1987) 1 *RCDIP* (*Revue critique du droit international privé*) p 33–76; H. Bauer, W. Bauman, P. Limmer, 'Allemagne' in: M. Verwilghen (ed) *Régimes matrimoniaux, successions et libéralités dans les relations internationales et internes*, Brussels 2003, p 574.

42 H. Bauer, W. Bauman, P. Limmer [note 41] at 574.

43 Amtliche Sammlung des Bundesrechts 1988, no. 41, s. 1776.

44 A. von Overbeck, 'Le droit des personnes, de la famille, des régimes matrimoniaux et des successions dans la nouvelle loi fédérale suisse sur le droit international prive', (1988) 2 *RCDIP* at 237; A. Bonomi, 'Autonomie des parties en droit patrimonial de la famille et intérêt des entrepreneur: aspects de droit matériel et de droit international privé', (2004) 4 *SZIER* (*Schweizerische Zeitschrift fur internationales und europaisches Recht*) at 459; A. Bonomi, J. Betholet, 'La professio iuris en droit international privé suisse et comparé' in: *Mélanges publié par l'Association des notaires vaudois a l'occasion de son centenaire*, Geneva 2005, p 359.

45 B. Dutoit, *Droit international prive suisse. Commentaire de la loi fédérale du 18 décembre 1987*, Geneva 2001, p 275.

of 1 September 2005 on private international law succession is governed by the law of the deceased's last habitual residence unless he/she has chosen his/her national law to be applicable.[46] Ukrainian law directly states that the choice of the applicable law will be void if the testator has changed his/her nationality after the designation. This provision indicates that the testator may only choose the law of his/her nationality at the time of his/her death. Similar provisions are included in Estonian private international law.[47]

As opposed to Ukrainian and Estonian law, the Succession Regulation does not contain any provision indicating that if the testator, at the time of his/her death, is no longer a national of the country whose law he/she has chosen to govern succession, then the choice is invalid. Hence, in accordance with the Succession Regulation, only the time of designation is taken into account when assessing the validity of a choice of law. If, after making the designation, the testator changes his/her nationality, the choice of the applicable law will remain valid.

In this context the question arises whether under the Succession Regulation the testator has the possibility to choose the law of the country whose nationality he/she plans to acquire in the future (i.e. nationality at the time of death). Even though the Succession Regulation does not state this directly, it does seem that such a solution is not in fact possible. The wording of Article 17 of the proposal (i.e. "*whose nationality they possess*") suggests that it is possible to choose the law of the country whose nationality the testator possesses at the time of making the designation. As a result, a choice designating the law of one's nationality at the time of death will not be valid if the testator did not possess this nationality at the time of designation.

In such a case this solution is somewhat too strict. As a choice of the applicable law was supposed to be the outcome of a compromise between the laws of those Member States in which the law of one's nationality, domicile or habitual residence at the time of death currently governs succession, then it is not really understandable why a choice of the law of one's nationality at the time of death should not be valid. The possibility of choosing this law was recommended in the DNotI Report[48] and by private international law experts.[49] It should also be added that the proposal is not clear as to whether persons with multiple nationalities may designate any of their national laws or only the law of their so-called effective

[46] L. Pavlova, 'Ukraine' in: M. Verwilghen (ed) *Régimes matrimoniaux, successions et libéralités dans les relations internationales et internes. Mise a jour 2007 de la 3e édition parue en 2003*, Brussels 2007, p 284.

[47] K. Sein, 'The development of private international law in Estonia', (2008) 10 *Yearbook of private international law* p 459.

[48] DNotI Report at 69.

[49] A. Davi [note 35] at 481.

nationality. The need for a rule which would unambiguously decide this issue has been underlined in the legal literature.[50]

When it comes to Italy, a choice of the law which is applicable to successions was introduced by the statute of 31 March 1995 on private international law.[51] As a rule, succession is governed by the law of the deceased's nationality at the time of his/her death. In accordance with Article 46(2) of the Italian statute on private international law the testator may explicitly designate the law of his/her habitual residence as the law which is applicable to succession to his/her estate in its entirety. Italian law directly states that the choice of the applicable law is invalid if at the time of death the deceased no longer had his/her habitual residence in that country. As in the Succession Regulation the law which is applicable by default will be the law of the deceased's last habitual residence, allowing for the possibility to choose this law, as in the Italian statute, would obviously make no sense.[52]

It should be mentioned that the Hague Convention also allowed for a choice of the applicable law. The Hague Convention was unilaterally adopted by the Netherlands by incorporating it into its domestic law. In accordance with Article 5(1) of the Hague Convention a person may designate the law of a particular State to govern succession to the whole of his/her estate. This designation will only be effective if at the time of designation or of his/her death this person was a national of that State or had his/her habitual residence there. The possibility to choose the law of the deceased's habitual residence at the time of making the designation was recommended by the DNotI Report,[53] but this does not appear in the Succession Regulation.

The Belgian statute of 16 July 2004 introducing the code of private international law[54] states, in its Article 78, that succession to movables is governed by the law of the state in which the deceased had his/her habitual residence at the time of death, whereas succession to immovables is governed by the law of the state in which the immovables are located. If that foreign law designates the law of the deceased's habitual residence to be applicable, the Belgian courts will apply the law of the deceased's last habitual residence to succession to both movables and immovables. In accordance with Article 79 of the Code the testator may designate the law which is applicable to the whole estate. Similar to the Hague Convention, Belgian law states that a choice of law is only valid if the deceased was a national

50 *Ibid.*

51 F. Cardillo, D. Damascelli, 'Italie' in : M. Verwilghen (ed.), *Régimes matrimoniaux, successions et libéralités dans les relations internationales et internes,* Brussels 2003, p 1571.

52 A. Davi [note 35] at 481.

53 DNotI Report at 70.

54 P. de Page, 'Les règles de conflit de lois du nouveau Code de droit international prive relatives aux régimes matrimoniaux et aux successions', (2005) 3 *Revue trimestrielle de droit familial* p 647.

of or had his/her habitual residence in that country at the time of his/her death or at the time of making the designation.[55]

The extent of the choice of law is even broader in the private international law of the Canadian province of Quebec as contained in the tenth book of its Civil Code.[56] In accordance with Article 3098 of the Code succession to movables is governed by the law of the deceased's last habitual residence whereas succession to immovables is governed by the law of the country where the property is located. The Code provides that the testator may designate, by means of a will, the law which is applicable to succession subject to the condition that the chosen law is that of the deceased's nationality or his/her habitual residence at the time of his/her death or designation, as well as the law where the property is located when this concerns succession to immovable property. This last option is not provided for in the Succession Regulation in accordance with recommendations included in the DNotI Report.[57] Allowing one to choose the law where the property is located as being applicable to succession to certain assets – in particular immovables – would lead to scission, which was perceived as unwelcome from the very beginning.

The most liberal approach to a choice of the law which is applicable to succession is to be fund in Finnish law. In accordance with Article 26(6) of the Finnish statute on succession law,[58] as amended on 1 March 2002, the testator may designate the law of his/her nationality at the time of his/her death or at the time of designation or the law of his/her habitual residence at the time of his/her death or at the time of designation, as well as the law of his/her habitual residence at any time during his/her life. Additionally, if at the time of making the designation the testator was married, it is possible to choose the law which is applicable to the matrimonial property regime as being applicable to succession.[59] Moreover, as underlined by Finnish authors, if at the time of making the designation the future deceased has multiple nationalities, it is possible to choose the law of any of these nationalities irrespective of whether it amounts to the so-called effective nationality.[60] The

55 F. Rigaux, M. Fallon, *Droit international privé*, Brussels 2005, s. 743.

56 J. Talpis, J. Castel, *Interpreting the rules of private international law* w: *Reform of the Civil Code. Texts written for the Barreau du Quebec and the Chambre des notaires du Québec, Volume 5B: Private International Law*, Montreal 1994 (English translation: S. Altschul), p 29. C. Emanuelli, *Droit international privé québécois*, Montreal 2006, p 297, E. Groffier, *La réforme du droit international prive québécois. Supplément au Précis de droit international prive québécoise*, Cownswille 1990, p 88.

57 DNotI report at 70.

58 English translation available at: http://www.finlex.fi/en/laki/kaannokset/1965/en19650040.pdf.

59 U. Kangas, 'Finland' in: *Les Successions Internationales dans l'UE Perspectives pour une Harmonisation/ Conflict of Law of Succession in the European Union Perspectives for a Harmonisation/ Internationales Erbrecht in der EU Perspektiven einer Harmonisierung, Deutsches Notarinstitut*, Würzburg 2002, s. 350.

60 DNotI Report at 70.

possibility to choose the law of any previous habitual residence was criticized in the DNotI Report.[61] According to its authors the connection between the testator and the country that he/she had already left is so weak that it should not justify the possibility to designate that law as being applicable.

When it comes to choosing the law which is applicable to matrimonial property regimes the authors of the DNotI Report suggested that such a solution could be taken into account. However, as underlined in the explanatory memorandum to the proposal "*the Regulation has removed the possibility of choosing as the law applicable to succession the law applicable to matrimonial property scheme of the testator. Such a provision would have allowed multiple choices where, for the matrimonial property schemes, the spouses benefit from greater flexibility in their choice of applicable law. This would have run counter to the above objectives* [i.e. *the protection of the legitimate interests of the relatives of the deceased, in particular the surviving spouse and children* – N/A]".

A solution provided under Danish law should also be mentioned. In this jurisdiction the law which is applicable to the liquidation in a succession may be chosen by the heirs. The liquidation of an estate is generally governed by the law which is applicable to the succession; however, the heirs may decide unanimously that the liquidation should be governed by the law where the proceedings take place or where one or more assets are located.[62] The authors of the DNotI Report did not recommend such a solution and they stated that in the case of consensus between the heirs it is possible to liquidate the estate in accordance with their will. When there is a lack of such a consensus as to the liquidation it is difficult to imagine that they could agree on the applicable law.[63]

Finally, the solution to be found in the Romanian statute of 22 September 1992 on private international law should be mentioned.[64] In accordance with Article 66 of this statute succession as movables is governed by the law of the deceased's nationality, whereas succession to immovables is governed by the law of the place where they are located. Article 68 states that the testator may choose any other law to be applicable; however, such a designation is without prejudice to the application of the mandatory rules of the law which is applicable according to Article 66.[65] As succession law generally contains mandatory rules it seems that

---

61 DNotI Report at 70.

62 DNotI Report at 70.

63 *Ibid.*

64 English and French translation in: *Le Parlament de la Roumanie/The Parlament of Romania: Législation roumaine/Romanian Legislation* 1993, t. 11. The statute on private international law will be replaced by the new civil code adopted in July 2009.

65 I. Filipescu, A. Filipescu, *Tratat de drept internațional privat*, Bucharest 2007, s. 413.

Romanian law does not provide for a choice of the applicable law but only the so-called material law reference (*materialrechtliche Verweisung*).[66]

Having examined all the possibilities that the EU Commission had at its disposal while deciding which laws may be chosen by testators under the Succession Regulation it should be noted that the choice provided in the regulation is very limited; in fact it only consists of a right to waive a default habitual residence rule and to designate the law of the country of which the testator has nationality.

3.3. PROTECTION OF FAMILY MEMBERS BY LIMITING THE IMPLICATIONS OF THE CHOICE OF THE APPLICABLE LAW BY THE DECEASED

Another mechanism for the protection of the deceased's family members is to limit the implications of any choice of applicable law. Such mechanisms are provided for in Italian and Belgian private international law, as well as in the private international law of the Canadian province of Quebec.

As mentioned above, Article 46(2) of the Italian statute on private international law states that the testator may designate the law of his/her habitual residence as being applicable to succession to the whole of his/her estate. If the deceased had chosen the applicable law then Italian law provides for a specific mechanism to protect certain forced heirs. If the succession concerns the estate of an Italian national the choice of law is without prejudice to the rights accorded by Italian law to forced heirs residing in Italy at the time of the testator's death.[67] In practice this provision obliges the Italian courts to compare the outcome of the application of the chosen law and the law that would be applicable without this choice (i.e. Italian law). In the case of any differences Italian law will be applied in place of the chosen law, but only to the extent that the latter deprives the forced heirs residing in Italy of the rights that they would have under Italian law.[68] With respect to other issues concerning succession the chosen law remains applicable. Hence, this institution leads to scission, i.e. the application of different succession laws to one succession case. It should be underlined that this provision is of a unilateral nature as it is relates only to succession to the estate of an Italian national, therefore the law that may be applied in place of the chosen law will only be Italian law. Hence this provision clearly favours Italian law. Due to its unilateral character

---

66 Compare: A. Dutta [note 11] at 569.

67 A. Bonomi, 'The influence of Swiss private international law on the Italian codification', (2002) 30 *IJLI* (*International Journal of Legal Information*) p. 252 and 'The Italian statute on private international law', (1999) 27 *IJLI* p 247.

68 A. Bonomi, 'La loi applicable aux successions dans le nouveau droit international prive italien et ses implications and les relations italo-suisses', (1996) 4 *SZIER* p 479.

this provision does not grant any protection to the forced heirs of foreigners even if they are Italian nationals or have their domicile or habitual residence in Italy.[69] Additionally, the said provision only provides protection to forced heirs who are habitually resident in Italy at the time of the testator's death. As a result, forced heirs with Italian nationality having their habitual residence abroad could not benefit from such protection. In practice this provision is criticized as leading to unjustified inequalities between heirs. According to some authors it is also irreconcilable with Article 3 of the Italian Constitution which lays down the principle of non-discrimination.

The Belgian statute on private international law states that succession may be governed by the chosen law. The choice of law will be valid as long as this would be the law of the deceased's nationality at the time of his/her death or at the time of designation.[70] At the same time the law states that the choice of the applicable law may not result in depriving the heir of his/her right to a reserved portion to which he/she would be entitled according to the law which would be applicable when there has been no choice of law.[71] As Belgian succession law provides for the reserved portion system, Article 79 of the Belgian Act on private international law refers directly to "réserve", therefore the question arises whether Article 79 provides an obligation to apply the rules on the reserved portion of the otherwise applicable law or whether it is possible to apply the chosen law if it provides for other mechanisms similar to the reserved portion, such as monetary claims.[72] It seems that this Article only provides for the minimum protection standard. If the chosen law is more favourable to forced heirs than the law which would be applicable without a choice of the applicable law, the former will be applied. As opposed to Italian law, Article 79 is of a universal nature.

A similar mechanism exists in Quebec private international law. Article 3099 of the Civil Code limits the implications of a choice of the applicable law in successions by stating that the designation of a law which is applicable to the succession is without effect to the extent that the designated law deprives the married or civil union spouse or a child of the deceased, to a large degree, of a right of succession to which, but for such designation, he or she would have been entitled. This provision has been criticized for being ambiguous as the legislator has not defined what it means for someone to be deprived of a right of succession "to a large degree".[73] In order to apply this mechanism the courts would have to

69 *Ibid* at 500.

70 P. de Page, 'Les règles de conflit de lois du nouveau Code de droit international prive relatives aux régimes matrimoniaux et aux successions', (2005) 3 *Revue trimestrielle de droit familial*, p 647, F. Rigaux, M. Fallon, *Droit international privé*, Brussels 2005, p 743.

71 F. Rigaux, M. Fallon [note 70] at 743.

72 P. Wautelet, 'Le nouveau régime des successions internationales', (2005) 7 *Revue général de droit civil belge* p 380.

73 C. Emanuelli, *Droit international prive québécois*, Montreal 2006, s. 298.

compare the level of protection provided under the chosen law and the law that would be applicable without any choice of law. Taking into account the different mechanisms which exist in different states, this might be a great challenge.

Another problem caused by this mechanism in Quebec and Belgian law – jurisdictions which provide for scission as a default rule – has been explained in the literature by using the following example:[74] A Belgian who is habitually resident in the Netherlands prepares a will. According to the will 9/10 of the estate should be inherited by his son, whereas immovable property located in Belgium, which amounts to 1/10 of the estate, should be inherited by the testator's friend. The testator has designated Dutch law as being applicable to succession. A few months later the testator moves to Spain.

Bearing in mind that Belgian law, in the absence of any choice of applicable law, provides for scission, the question arises as to how the necessary comparison required by Article 79 of Belgian Act on private international law can be made. It seems that concerning succession to immovable property the comparison should be between Dutch law as the chosen law and Belgian law as the law of the country where the immovable property is situated. Simultaneously, concerning succession to movables the court should make a comparison between Dutch and Spanish laws. With respect to the immovable property situated in Belgium the court will be obliged to verify whether the protection granted to a forced heir – here the son – by the Dutch law is similar to that granted by Belgian law.

If it transpires that Dutch law grants protection to forced heirs on a level which is lower than Belgian law two possible solutions may be imagined. According to the first one, the deceased's son could claim his reserved portion from the immovable property located in Belgium; irrespective of taking into account the estate as a whole, his reserved portion is already satisfied in accordance with both laws which are applicable in the absence of a choice of law. According to the second solution, which seems far more reasonable, the son's rights to the reserved portion should be assessed taking into account the estate as a whole without differentiating between movables and immovables.

The above mechanism seems to be reminiscent of Article 24(1)(d) of the Hague Convention, which states that a contracting state may make a reservation to the effect that it will not recognize a designation made under Article 5 if the law of that state would have been the applicable law if there had been no valid designation, and the application of the designated law would totally or very substantially deprive the spouse or a child of the deceased of an inheritance or family provision, to which the spouse or child would have been entitled under the mandatory rules

[74] Example used in: P. Wautelet [note 72] at 381.

of the law of the State making this reservation. An additional requirement is that the spouse or child is habitually resident in or is a national of that state. It should be underlined, however, that Article 24(1)(d) allowing for such a reservation was perceived from the very beginning as contradicting the possibility of choosing the applicable law and it has been criticized as being "essentially destructive" to the compromises reached by the Hague Convention.[75]

After publication of the Regulation of Succession by the Commission, the French National Assembly, while providing its opinion on the compatibility of the proposal with the principle of subsidiary,[76] suggested that a similar solution should be included in the Succession Regulation. Such a suggestion should not be welcomed. If the EU legislator decides to allow a choice of the applicable law in successions and that choice – as proved above – is already very limited, then the legislator should not introduce a mechanism that would make the possibility of choosing the applicable law almost completely useless. Why allow a choice of the applicable law if mandatory rules of another law would still be applicable?

3.4. PROTECTION OF FAMILY MEMBERS BY REFERRING TO PUBLIC POLICY

In the legal literature it has been underlined that the possibility to choose the applicable law which may turn out to have consequences which are manifestly contrary to the law of the forum is not an argument against the possibility of choosing the law which is applicable to succession in general. Just as the fact that the application of foreign law may lead to consequences which are incompatible with fundamental principles of the forum is not an argument against the application of foreign law in general, the potential consequences of allowing for a choice of the applicable law is not an argument against the choice of the applicable law in general. If the applicable law has been chosen the operation of the public policy clause is admissible just as in the case of the designation of a foreign law by a conflict of law rule.[77]

The operation of the public policy clause should be the same irrespective of whether the applicable law is designated by the objective connecting factor of habitual residence or by a choice of law clause contained in a will. For example, Article 18 of Hague Convention states that the application of any of the laws determined by the Convention may only be refused where such application would

75 M. D. Waters [note 14] at 613.

76 *Assemble National, Compte Rendu. Commission des affaires européennes. Mardi 17 novembre 2009* available at: http://www.assemblee-nationale.fr/13/pdf/europe/c-rendus/c0126.pdf.

77 L. Haopei [note 30] at 89, H. Yntema, "Autonomy' in choice of law', (1952) 1 *The American Journal of Comparative Law* at 353.

be manifestly incompatible with public policy (*ordre public*). As underlined in the explanatory report to the Hague Convention the expression "laws determined by the convention" was expressly used. The construction of Article 18 was supposed to make it obvious that the public policy clause may also be used against the application of the law designated by the testator.[78]

Similarly, in the DNotI Report it was mentioned that minor differences between succession laws in EU Member States do not require any special intervention by the EU legislator. According to the DNotI Report, inserting a classical public policy clause into the Succession Regulation would be enough. However, the public policy clause in the Succession Regulation is far from classical. Article 27 of the proposal states that: the application of a rule of the law determined by this Regulation may be refused only if such application is incompatible with the public policy of the forum. At the same time the next paragraph states that: in particular, the application of a rule of the law determined by this Regulation may not be considered to be contrary to the public policy of the forum on the sole ground that its clauses regarding the reserved portion of an estate differ from those in force in the forum.

As the explanatory memorandum explains, any recourse to public policy must occur in exceptional circumstances only. Differences between the laws relating to the protection of the legitimate interests of the relatives of the deceased must not be used to justify its use, as this would be incompatible with the objective of ensuring the application of a single law to all of the property which is subject to succession. The explanatory memorandum underlines that in every EU Member State succession laws provide for mechanisms aimed at ensuring support to close relatives from the deceased's estate.

Due to the ambiguous wording of Article 27 of the proposal, doubts as to the real intention of the drafters may arise. The second sentence of Article 27 may be interpreted as stating that the sole fact that the succession law of the forum provides for the reserved portion system, whereas the law chosen provides for other mechanisms like monetary claims instead of the reserved portion should not result in resorting to the public policy clause.[79] This provision may however be interpreted as stating that the public policy clause may not be used when it comes to the protection of forced heirs, even against the succession law which would not provide for any protection to close family members.[80]

---

78 M. D. Waters [note 14] at 265.

79 A. Bonomi, *Le choix de la loi applicable à la succession dans la proposition de règlement européen* in: A. Bonomi, C. Schmid (eds.) *Successions internationales. Réflexions autour du futur règlement européen et de son impact pour la Suisse.* Actes de la 22e journée de droit international privé du 19 mars 2010 à Lausanne, Zürich 2010 at 35.

80 *Ibid*, at 35–36.

If the first interpretation is correct, there is no need for the second sentence of Article 27. The DNotI Report reveals that in this case in general the courts of the Member States would never refer to the public policy clause.[81] If, on the other hand, the second interpretation is correct the limitation provided in the second sentence of Article 27 goes too far. It should be underlined that due to the universal nature of the conflict of law rules in the Succession Regulation a succession may be governed by the law of a country from outside the European Union. As the level of integration between Member States may justify such faith in each other's succession laws, it has no justification when it comes to other succession laws emanating from any part of the world. For example, in the Belgian legal literature it has been stated that if the chosen law does not provide any protection for forced heirs, it is possible to resort to the public policy clause.[82] Similar views are to be found in French and German literature.[83] Hence, the second paragraph of the public policy clause should be deleted.

3.5. PROTECTION OF FAMILY MEMBERS BY FOLLOWING SPECIAL RULES PROVIDED IN THE MEMBER STATES' PRIVATE INTERNATIONAL LAW

While commenting on the mechanism for protecting the family members of the deceased in the private international law of the Member States it is necessary to mention the French institution called *droit de prélèvement*. The beginnings of this institution go back to the statute of 14 July 1819 which states that heirs and legatees with French nationality may claim as much of the whole value of assets situated in France as to provide them with what they would receive under French inheritance law from all French assets and foreign movables.[84] Based on that provision, French heirs may claim from an estate situated in France as much as they would inherit in accordance with French succession law, irrespective of the foreign law designated as being applicable by a French conflict of law rule. For almost two centuries this institution has been subject to vigorous criticism as being contrary to the very idea of private international law. It is also contrary to European Union law, in particular the principle of non-discrimination.[85]

In accordance with Article 25 of the proposal, the rules on the applicable law contained in the Succession Regulation have to be applied by Member States'

---

81 DNotI Report at 59.

82 P. Wautelet [note 72] at 382.

83 Compare: S. Othenin-Girard, *La réserve d'ordre public en droit international prive suisse. Personne-Famille-Successions*, Zurich 1999 at 587.

84 E. Rabel, *The Conflict of Laws. A comparative study. Volume IV: Property, Bills and Notes, Inheritance, Trusts, Application of foreign law, Intertemporal relations*, Ann Arbor 1958, p. 262.

85 S. Billarant, *Le caractère substantiel de la réglementation française des successions internationales. Réflexions sur la méthode conflictuelle*, Paris 2004, s. 164.

courts, on a mandatory basis, to all succession cases irrespective of their connection with the European Union. Hence, once the proposal enters into force, the rules on the applicable law to succession which currently exist in the domestic laws of the Member States will cease to be applicable.[86] Fortunately, this will also be true of the droit de prélèvement.[87]

4. CONCLUSION

Once the Succession Regulation enters into force it will unify the private international law on succession in all EU Member States (excluding Denmark and maybe the UK, due to their special status with respect to EU instruments in this field of law). As this regulation contains rules which have a universal nature it will almost entirely replace the international succession rules which are currently in force in the Member States. The proposal introduces a choice of the applicable law in successions – a complete novelty for the majority of Member States, but also a retrograde step for others. The admission of the choice of the applicable law in the EU regulation is the outcome of a compromise between the principle of nationality and the principle of domicile, rather than a solution aimed at respecting the testator's "autonomy". Generally, the most important argument raised against this admission is that it could serve as a vehicle for the testator to circumvent forced heirs' rights which exist under the law that would otherwise be applicable. It should be noted that these rights are already protected by limiting the testator's autonomy which in fact consists of a right to waive a default habitual residence rule and to designate the law of the testator's nationality. No additional measures that would limit the effects of a choice of law should be allowed regardless of whether the measures are provided for in the Succession Regulation or in the domestic laws of the Member States. The only protection of family members against outcomes which are manifestly contrary to fundamental principles of the forum that should be admitted is the operation of the public policy clause.

---

86 A. Bonomi [note 21].

87 *Compte Rendu. Commission des affaires européennes. Mardi 17 novembre 2009.* Published at http://www.assemblee-nationale.fr/13/pdf/europe/c-rendus/c0126.pdf.

INTERNATIONAL CHILD MAINTENANCE IN EUROPE

PHILIP BREMNER*

* The author wishes to thank Professor Paul Beaumont and Dr Christa Roodt for their comments on earlier drafts.

INTRODUCTION[1]

In the past few years, there has been considerable reform within Europe of how child maintenance claims are handled both at the regional[2] and international level.[3] Until 2007, the recovery of international child maintenance was regulated by dated and largely ineffective international conventions.[4] This all changed when the Hague Conference on Private International Law adopted a Convention on the International Recovery of Child Support and Other Forms of Family Maintenance and an additional Protocol on the Law Applicable to Maintenance Obligations. The main objective of this new Convention is to facilitate the enforcement of international child maintenance claims. This is achieved by building on the strengths of supranational measures previously adopted in other areas to establish a strong system of administrative cooperation in dealing with international child maintenance claims. At the same time as the Child Maintenance Convention was being developed in The Hague, parallel negotiations were being conducted within the EU on the Maintenance Regulation. This sought to achieve similar goals as the Convention but also to go a step further and take advantage of closer regional integration to abolish exequatur, or the requirement for formal recognition of foreign maintenance decisions, within the EU.

Somewhat unusually, however, it was action at the international level that prompted closer cooperation at the regional level. This is illustrated by the key innovation achieved in The Hague, namely free legal assistance for child maintenance claims, which was later mirrored in the EU. This demonstrates the advantages of coordination between developments at the international and regional level

1 This conference paper presents a necessarily cursory overview of international child maintenance in Europe, focussing on more recent developments. For an in-depth analysis of the background and detail of the transnational instruments discussed in this paper, see I Curry-Sumner, Transnational recovery of child maintenance in Europe: The future is bright, the future is central authorities, in: Masaryk University, Days of Public Law. Collection of Articles, Brno 2007.

2 Council Regulation (EC) 4/2009 of 18 December 2008 on jurisdiction, applicable law, recognition and enforcement of decisions and cooperation in matters relating to maintenance obligations (the Maintenance Regulation) [2009] OJ L 7/1.

3 Convention of 23 November 2007 on the international recovery of child support and other forms of family maintenance (the Child Maintenance Convention) www.hcch.net/index_en.php?act=conventions.text&cid =131, accessed 13 July 2010.

4 Convention on the law applicable to maintenance obligations towards children (adopted 24 October 1956, entered into force 1 January 1962) 510 UNTS 161; Convention on the law applicable to maintenance obligations (adopted 2 October 1972, entered into force 1 October 1977) 1056 UNTS 199; Convention of 15 April 1958 concerning the recognition and enforcement of decisions relating to maintenance obligations towards children (adopted 15 April 1958, entered into force 1 January 1962) 539 UNTS 27; Convention on the recognition and enforcement of decisions relating to maintenance obligations (adopted 2 October 1972, entered into force 1 August 1976) 1021 UNTS 209; Convention of 20 June 1956 on the recovery abroad of maintenance (adopted 20 June 1956, entered into force 25 May 1957) 268 UNTS 3 (New York Maintenance Convention).

because without such progress being made in The Hague, it is unlikely that there would have been such extensive legal aid provisions within the EU.

From a British perspective, it was most welcome that negotiations with the EU were able to take account of developments in The Hague, which resulted in reference to the Hague Protocol on Applicable Law[5] in the EU's Maintenance Regulation.[6] Initially, the European Commission had envisaged a mandatory, autonomous applicable law regime,[7] which would have been unpalatable for the United Kingdom, which does not apply foreign law in child maintenance cases, given the disproportionate costs involved. Therefore, it was integral to the success of the EU's Maintenance Regulation that it adopted the optional applicable law regime that had been developed in The Hague.

This article attempts to explore the interaction between these two instruments both in terms of the negotiations leading up to their adoption and as they exist now. Although the EU has internal legislation of its own, there is still considerable benefit in it ratifying the Hague Convention. The paper argues that the Regulation and Convention are not only important instruments in facilitating child maintenance but are also important for European and international family law generally because they evidence an internationalist approach in Europe that has been somewhat lacking in the past.

The article will begin by discussing the framework created by the Child Maintenance Convention, which was concluded in The Hague in 2007. Although this Convention has only received two signatures so far, the European Union and various other countries have reported that preparations for ratification are well underway. The European Union has already ratified the Hague Protocol on Maintenance, which will come into force when it has been ratified by at least one other state.

The article will then go on to discuss the progress that was made during the Special Commission on the Child Maintenance Convention that was held in The Hague in November 2009. Feedback from states during this was encouraging and progress was made towards adopting measures that will improve the

---

5 Protocol on the law applicable to maintenance obligations (Hague Protocol on Applicable law) (adopted 23 November 2007).

6 'The law applicable to maintenance obligations shall be determined in accordance with the Hague Protocol of 23 November 2007 on the law applicable to maintenance obligations (hereinafter referred to as the 2007 Hague Protocol) in the Member States bound by that instrument' Maintenance Regulation (n 2) art 15.

7 Commission of the European Communities, 'Proposal for a Council Regulation on jurisdiction, applicable law, recognition and enforcement of decisions and cooperation in matters relating to maintenance obligations' Com (2005) 649 final article 25 <http://eur-lex.europa.eu/ LexUriServ/LexUriServ.do?uri=COM:2005:0649:FIN:EN:PDF> accessed 13 July 2010.

implementation of the Convention. Although strong, directly effective enforcement measures were proposed for the Maintenance Regulation, they did not appear in the final text and this article will discuss the reasons for that before exploring, in some detail, the relationship between the EU Maintenance Regulation and the Hague Child Maintenance Convention.

This article will also discuss certain issues related to the recognition and enforcement of child maintenance orders within Europe following the adoption of the Regulation. Finally, the article will situate developments in international child maintenance within a broader European family law context, and attempt to highlight how lessons learned in the former regard can be applied to the latter.

1. THE NEW HAGUE CHILD MAINTENANCE CONVENTION

The objective of the Child Maintenance Convention is 'to ensure the effective international recovery of child maintenance and other forms of family maintenance.'[8] It does this through the establishment of a system of administrative cooperation, such as that seen in other Hague Conventions like the Child Abduction Convention,[9] coupled with an expedited procedure for the recognition and enforcement of maintenance orders. Although the scope of the Convention is not limited to child maintenance, it is only to these claims and any associated spousal maintenance claims that the whole of the Convention applies on a mandatory basis, leaving the possibility for states to extend the Convention to other family relationships.[10]

The Convention's focus on establishing a system of administrative cooperation rather than on the traditional aspects of private international law makes it rather procedural in nature. This is partly a reaction to procedural delays experienced under the existing Conventions, such as the New York Convention,[11] and partly in recognition of the fact that many of the most widely ratified and successful Hague Conventions have focussed on procedural matters such as the Taking of Evidence[12] and Service[13] Conventions.

---

8 Child Maintenance Convention (n 3) art 1.

9 Convention of 25 October 1980 on the Civil Aspects of International Child Abduction (Child Abduction Convention).

10 Child Maintenance Convention (n 3) art 2(3).

11 Convention of 20 June 1956 on the recovery abroad of maintenance (adopted 20 June 1956, entered into force 25 May 1957) 268 UNTS 3 (New York Convention).

12 Convention of 18 March 1970 on the Taking of Evidence Abroad in Civil or Commercial Matters.

13 Convention of 15 November 1965 on the Service Abroad of Judicial and Extrajudicial Documents in Civil or Commercial Matters.

The Convention achieves this administrative cooperation by utilising a system of Central Authorities. Each Contracting State is required to designate a Central Authority, which will be the administrative point of contact that handles all maintenance claims. In this way, a maintenance creditor in possession of a maintenance order from a court can go to the Central Authority in their own state, who will then be responsible for transmitting an application for recognition and enforcement of that decision to the central authority in the requested state. The duties of Central Authorities extend beyond the mere transmission of decisions and applications to include helping to locate the maintenance debtor and creditor, obtaining and communicating relevant information and facilitating the enforcement of maintenance orders and the collection of payments.[14]

As regards recognition and enforcement, cumbersome national procedures for reviewing maintenance orders can lead to considerable delays. The 1973 Hague Convention on Recognition and Enforcement of Decisions Relating to Maintenance Obligations did little to address this, leaving it to be regulated by the law of the receiving state. The 2007 Convention prescribes a more streamlined procedure for recognising decisions emanating from a potentially large number of states but most significantly in practice, from the creditor or debtor's habitual residence.[15] In a similar way as Brussels I,[16] the Convention creates a presumption in favour of recognition and enforcement of decisions with the burden lying with the respondent to object based on a limited number of well-defined grounds for refusing recognition and enforcement (such as it being contrary to public policy[17] or the decision was made in default of appearance without proper notice of the proceedings being given).[18]

This was taken a step further in the EU Maintenance Regulation, which sought to abolish *exequatur* between EU Member States as regards maintenance decisions. The current regime for the enforcement of decisions relating to maintenance obligations is governed by Article 38(1) of Brussels I, which requires a declaration of enforceability. This requirement is abolished, for the vast majority of Member States, by Article 17(2) of the Maintenance Regulation.

Initially, the Commission envisaged that exequatur would be abolished between all the Member States of the EU. In its proposal, the Commission highlighted

[14] Child Maintenance Convention (n 3) art 6.

[15] Maintenance Convention (n 3) art 20.

[16] Council Regulation (EC) 44/2001 of 22 December 2000 on jurisdiction and the recognition and enforcement of judgments in civil and commercial matters (Brussels I) [2001] OJ L 12/1.

[17] For more on the role of public policy in Brussels I see P Beaumont and E Johnston, Can *Exequatur* Be Abolished in Brussels I Whilst Retaining a Public Policy Defence? (2010) 6 *Journal of Private International Law* 249.

[18] Maintenance Convention (n 3) art 22.

the intrinsic link between the abolition of exequatur and the harmonisation of applicable law:

... the conflict-of-law rules accompany and facilitate the elimination of 'intermediate measures' at the stage of recognition: the decision is less problematic to accept if it is given in accordance with a law designated according to harmonised rules.[19]

In light of this, the Commission's proposal contained detailed provisions on applicable law, which did not appear in the final regulation. The reason for this was that by the time negotiations on the Maintenance Regulation had begun in earnest, a protocol on applicable law had already been concluded in The Hague. Therefore, it was decided to simply adopt those rules wholesale and refer to the protocol in the regulation.

This was a compromise solution to the divisive issue of the harmonisation of the applicable law. The compromise in the regulation reflects the optional nature of the protocol. Only those Member States which will become a party to the protocol will have harmonised conflict-of-law rules. In practice, this will be the majority of states. By contrast, those Member States which will not be party to the protocol, notably the United Kingdom, will not have harmonised applicable law rules. Given that the automatic recognition and enforcement of judgments relating to maintenance obligations is only palatable if they are made on the basis of harmonised applicable law rules, the abolition of exequatur is only possible between those Member States who are contracting parties to the Hague Protocol. Therefore, decisions emanating from Member States who are party to the Hague Protocol will not be subject to a declaration of enforceability; whereas, decisions from Member States that are not party to the protocol will be.

In the United Kingdom, this means that a decision given in another Member State will be enforceable without the need for a declaration from a UK court. However, decisions given by UK courts will still require a declaration of enforceability from the court in the Member State of enforcement. This may not seem fair but it is the necessary corollary of the UK's rejection of the harmonisation of applicable law rules. Essentially the Brussels I regime, with stricter time limits, will apply to UK decisions.

Although the abolition of exequatur was a specific aim within the EU, it is not self-evident that the regime that will apply to decisions emanating from the majority of Member States is more advantageous and expeditious than that which applies to UK decisions. Whilst the abolition of exequatur seems desirable in uncontested cases, those are not the cases where the most problems are encountered. Indeed,

[19] Commission of the European Communities, 'Proposal for a Council Regulation on jurisdiction, applicable law, recognition and enforcement of decisions and cooperation in matters relating to maintenance obligations' Com (2005) 649 final [1.2.2]. http://eur-lex.europa.eu/ LexUriServ/LexUriServ.do?uri=COM:2005:0649:FIN:EN:PDF, accessed 13 July 2010.

in uncontested cases it should be relatively unproblematic to acquire a declaration of enforceability under Brussels I. Therefore, the potential benefit of the abolition of exequatur in these cases seems rather limited.

However, it is in the heavily contested cases that the Maintenance Regulation could cause more problems than it solves because it allows for greater delays than Brussels I did if pernicious litigants want to drag out proceedings. This is due to the complicated relationship between the court in the Member State of origin and the court of the requested Member State. The Maintenance Regulation creates a limited right to apply for a review of a maintenance decision (for example, where the defendant was prevented from appearing in court) in the court of the Member State of origin. If this occurs, this provides a ground for suspending the enforcement of the decision in the requested Member State. Therefore, this creates additional delays as proceedings in the requested Member State are suspended pending the outcome of the proceedings in the Member State of origin. This was not the case under Brussels I because the matter could be definitively decided by the court of the requested Member State without waiting for further proceedings in the Member State of origin. The main improvement that the abolition of exequatur brings is the removal of the possibility of challenging recognition and enforcement on the basis of public policy, but the role of this ground for the refusal of recognition seems limited in respect to maintenance claims.

2. THE 2009 SPECIAL COMMISSION

In November 2009, there was a Special Commission on the Child Maintenance Convention at the Hague Conference on Private International Law. The various reports on the progress of preparation for ratification from a number of countries as well as the European Commission were encouraging. In addition to this, significant progress was made towards facilitating the smooth operation of the Convention once it comes into force and several documents were produced to this end. The Explanatory Report had been finalised by the time of the Special Commission, which was a welcome development. Given the complexity of implementing the Convention and the problems states have had in the past with enforcing decisions under other Hague Conventions, some additional research and explanation will, however, be required in order that states apply and understand the Convention correctly thus ensuring the most effective recovery of child maintenance.

Significant progress was made in this regard at the Special Commission, which discussed in some detail the draft Practical Handbook for Caseworkers. A considerable amount of effort on the part of the drafters went into its creation and it was subject to quite intense scrutiny during the Special Commission. Now the Permanent Bureau is putting the finishing touches to the handbook. Once it is finalised, it should prove a useful aid to central authorities when applying the Convention. The intention seems to be to continually update the Practical Handbook on the basis of states' experience in implementing the Convention. In this way, it should remain a relevant and valuable resource for states.

In addition to this, several other useful advances were made at the Special Commission that ought to promote the implementation of the convention. The implementation checklist, which is designed as a means through which the permanent bureau can continue to support states in their implementation of the Convention, was amended and eventually adopted by the Special Commission, as were the Recommended Country Profile Form and other Recommended Forms. The Country Profile is intended to provide as much information as possible on how maintenance claims will be handled in a given country. This is a novel feature of the Convention and should greatly facilitate the enforcement of cross-border maintenance claims.

There were two major initiatives proposed at the Special Commission that have the potential to greatly improve the recovery of international child maintenance and so deserve to be mentioned. One is the iSupport system, which seeks to make use of information technology, as specifically envisaged in the preamble to the convention, to create an electronic case management and communication system for the international recovery of maintenance, in order to bridge the gap between states both where such a system already exists and where one does not. During the Special Commission, the Permanent Bureau presented a draft business plan for the development of iSupport based on their discussions with IT consultants. Although the Special Commission gave its support in principle for the continuing development of iSupport, it would be a costly and resource-intensive project and, therefore, would require significant voluntary contributions. Fortunately, several states expressed willingness at the Special Commission to share their expertise during the development of this useful electronic resource.

The final advancement made at the Special Commission that is worth mentioning here is the proposal for the establishment of a standing central authority co-operation committee. This was prompted by the success of the Administrative Co-operation Working Group during the development of the Convention as 'a prototype for the kind of continuing international co-operation and networking which will be needed if the Convention is to be a success.'[20] Initially, the working group was intended to exist only for a limited period. In 2007, however, the Twenty-First Session recommended that it continue on an interim basis whilst the Council of General Affairs and Policy considers the establishment of a standing Central

[20] Final Act of the Twenty-First Session of the Hague Conference on Private International Law, The Hague, 23 November 2007, Part C.

Authority Co-operation Committee. This recommendation was strengthened by the recent Special Commission which recommended to 'the Council on General Affairs and Policy that it give serious consideration to the merits of establishing a Central Authority Co-operation Working Group as well as the relevant issues, including its potential impact upon the Hague Conference and other Hague Conventions, subject to available resources and overall consideration of the work priority of the Hague Conference'.[21]

The wording of this recommendation may not seem to be much, if any, advance on the recommendation made at the Twenty-First Session in 2007. However, it does represent the consensus at the 2009 Special Commission that the establishment of such a committee would be a useful undertaking in promoting the Convention and assisting with its implementation. It also reflects the concerns expressed by some over the impact of this project on the budget and institutional structure of the Hague Conference. The final decision rests with the Council on General Affairs and Policy, which met in April. However, the Council decided to defer the decision as to the establishment of such a committee until 'the time when there is a sufficient number of Central Authorities designated under the 2007 Child Maintenance Convention'.[22] In the meantime, the Permanent Bureau has recommended that the Administrative Co-operation Working Group be able to continue its work as a 'forum for discussion of issues of administrative co-operation' as was recommended by the twenty-first session of the Hague Conference in 2007.[23]

Whilst the establishment of a standing central authority cooperation committee would seem to be a positive development in the context of the Hague Conference generally, it is questionable whether it would be especially effective in remedying the particular problems raised in the context of maintenance claims. Such a committee may not go far enough in answering the criticisms of those who felt that the nature of the administrative cooperation in the context of the Maintenance Regulation had not been fully fleshed out and were looking to The Hague to resolve this.[24] It is hard to see, for example, how a standing administrative cooperation

---

21 See Conclusions and Recommendations of the Special Commission on the Implementation of the 2007 Child Support Convention and of the 2007 Protocol on the Law Applicable to Maintenance Obligations (10–17 November 2009) Conclusion 12 www.hcch.net/upload/wop/maint2009concl_e.pdf, accessed 13 July 2010.

22 Conclusions and Recommendations adopted by the Council on General Affairs and Policy of the Conference (7–9 April 2010) www.hcch.net/upload/wop/genaff2010concl_e.pdf, accessed 13 July 2010.

23 Prel. Doc. No 3B of February 2010 – Establishment of a Standing Central Authority Co-operation Committee under the 2007 Child Support Convention [9] <http://www.hcch.net/upload/wop/genaff2010pd03be.pdf> accessed 13 July 2010.

24 I Curry-Sumner (n 1) 14. For a critical comment on the administrative cooperation provisions of the EU Maintenance Regulation and the Hague Convention see I Curry-Sumner, Administrative co-operation and free legal aid in international child maintenance recovery.

committee could address one of the main problems involved in the international recovery of child maintenance, namely locating the debtor.[25] The committee may be useful in identifying ways in which central authorities could work more efficiently but could do little to facilitate the recovery of child maintenance in individual cases.

3. ENFORCEMENT UNDER THE EU MAINTENANCE REGULATION

In order to ensure effective and rapid access to local justice, the Commission, in its proposal, set out a number of hard-hitting enforcement measures that could be instigated from the country of origin rather than the country of enforcement. These were by way of derogation to the principle that enforcement is carried out by the competent authorities in the Member State of enforcement. These measures included the garnishment of wages and the freezing of bank accounts. The former allowed the court of the Member State of origin to give a direct order for monthly payments in the Member State of enforcement. Whilst this measure is available in some Member States, this provision would ensure that it is available in all. Furthermore, it would mean that payment was rapid and not subject to the delays that enforcement by the authorities in the Member State of enforcement entails. The latter measure was meant only as a temporary step in order to prevent debtors from avoiding the claim by moving their assets. Given how time-sensitive this measure is, the ability of the court of origin to issue it would have been desirable in eliminating delay.

Although these proposals were well intentioned, and reflect two of the main means of enforcement available in national law that are suggested by the Hague Child Maintenance Convention,[26] it is hard to imagine them being implemented in reality. As regards wage garnishment, this involves courts directly in actual enforcement which might not be an established practice in every Member State and therefore the court may not have the necessary expertise. In addition, there is a risk of causing the debtor to pay twice. This is something that the central authorities in the country of enforcement are in the best position to prevent.

What is the added value of the European Maintenance Regulation? (2010) 4 *Netherlands Internationaal Privaatrecht* 611–621.

25 This is the subject of the research project entitled 'Transnational recovery of child maintenance in Europe: a multidisciplinary approach' being carried out at the Molengraaff Institute for Private Law. For more details see www.onderzoekinformatie.nl/en/oi/nod/onderzoek/OND1327012/, accessed 13 July 2010. See also I. Curry-Sumner, The future of international child maintenance recovery in Europe, in: I. Curry-Sumner and C. Skinner (eds.), Child Maintenance in The Netherlands and the United Kingdom. Persistent Problems, Finding Solutions, Nijmegen: Wolf 2009, pp. 151–168.

26 (N 3) Art. 34(2).

As far as the freezing of bank accounts is concerned, this provision may go further than is necessary. The EESC suggest that it would be better to allow for the freezing of only part of the money so as to avoid a situation where the debtor does not have money to meet living expenses.[27] The problem is perhaps more fundamental than that because it could be seen as an intolerable intrusion into the sovereignty of the Member States. Given that this measure should not be commonly used with regard to maintenance obligations, perhaps it is best dealt with in another context, eg, in the context of the Commission's Green Paper on the attachment of bank accounts, as some commentators have suggested.[28]

Whilst such immediate enforcement measures seem desirable in theory, they are not very feasible in reality. It is probably for this reason that they were not included in the final maintenance regulation. Instead, the central authority in the state of origin can request its counterpart in the state of enforcement to take specific measures and the latter will have discretion over which enforcement mechanism to employ. This seems a more acceptable solution because it removes the judicial element, which may not normally be involved in enforcement and instead places the responsibility on the authorities that are best placed to discharge it effectively.

4. RELATIONSHIP BETWEEN THE EU REGULATION AND THE HAGUE CONVENTION

The Maintenance Regulation has replaced the preexisting rules on jurisdiction, applicable law, recognition and enforcement of decisions and cooperation in matters relating to maintenance obligations in the EU. In addition to this, all the Member States of the EU are set to become contracting parties of the Hague Child Maintenance Convention; in fact, given the EU's rules on external competence, the EU will probably be exclusively competent to ratify the Convention and it has already done so with the Protocol on Applicable Law. Despite this, the EU Maintenance Regulation cannot be said to be superfluous because it achieves things that were not possible in The Hague. This is the advantage of closer regional integration over the more global Hague Conference. The Maintenance Regulation in fact builds on the foundations that were laid down in the Hague Convention. Therefore, many of the key features of the Maintenance Regulation owe their existence to negotiations at The Hague.

---

27 European Economic and Social Committee, Opinion of the European Economic and Social Committee on the Proposal for a Council Regulation on jurisdiction, applicable law, recognition and enforcement of decisions and cooperation in matters relating to maintenance obligations *COM(2005) 649 final - 2005/0259 (CNS)* [2006] OJ C 185/35.

28 See M Hellner, 'The Maintenance Regulation: A Critical Assessment of the Commission's proposal' in K Boele-Woelki and T Sverdrup (eds), *European Challenges in Contemporary Family Law* (European Family Law, Intersentia, Antwerp 2008) 266.

The aims of the Maintenance Regulation and the Child Maintenance Convention are broadly similar. Both aim to speed up the collection of international maintenance obligations and both do this through an enhanced system of administrative cooperation. However, the main area where the Maintenance Regulation was able to go further is the abolition of exequatur, which could not have been achieved in The Hague. This, however, was only possible because of the conclusion of the additional protocol on applicable law at The Hague.

Although the Commission initially proposed its own set of applicable law rules, the Council decided that the final regulation should state that the Hague Protocol on Applicable Law should determine the law that applies within the Community. Ironically, although the rest of the regulation builds on and is inspired by work at The Hague, the Hague Protocol seems to take its inspiration from the Commission proposal. This is understandable given that the majority of the contracting states to the earlier conventions on applicable law were EU Member States. Many of the non-EU Member States at The Hague are less interested in creating harmonised applicable law rules especially considering that the common law countries do not usually apply foreign law in maintenance disputes.

In addition to laying down foundations, which the EU was able to build on, the negotiations in The Hague also acted as a spur for developments that might not have otherwise occurred within the EU. An example of this is the provisions on legal aid. The Commission's initial proposal, which contained extensive provisions on legal aid, met with resistance from certain Member States. This would have resulted in much more limited legal aid provisions than had originally been envisaged and eventually appeared in the final regulation. The reason for their inclusion in the final regulation is most likely that more extensive provisions were agreed upon in The Hague and the EU wanted to match them. Such agreement would not have been reached within the EU itself because of the Member States' mixed feelings on legal aid. The impetus for this was provided by the US in The Hague negotiations which insisted on the inclusion of such wide provisions.

This analysis highlights the importance of reverse subsidiarity.[29] Measures dealing with international child maintenance obligations cannot be adequately dealt with at the national level because of the strong transnational element involved. Therefore, the conditions of subsidiarity are met. However, the EU must consider whether the matter could be more adequately addressed at the global rather than regional level. The above comparison between the Hague Child Maintenance Convention and the EU Maintenance Regulation suggests that international family law and child maintenance obligations in particular are best addressed,

---

29 See on this P Beaumont, 'International Family Law in Europe – the Maintenance Project, the Hague Conference and the EC: A Triumph of Reverse Subsidiarity' (2009) 73 *Rabels Zeitschrift für ausländisches und internationales Privatrecht* 509–546.

at least in the first instance, at the more global Hague Conference. After this has occurred, the advantage of closer regional integration means that the EU can build on the strengths of the work at The Hague and go even further.

CONCLUSION

Overall, therefore, the EU Maintenance Regulation and the Hague Child Maintenance Convention represent a necessary reform of the current regime for the enforcement of child maintenance obligations both within Europe and internationally. Both create a strong system of transnational administrative cooperation designed to facilitate the recovery of cross-border child maintenance claims. This system is strengthened by measures proposed at the 2009 Special Commission on the Hague Child Maintenance Convention, particularly the recommendation to establish a standing central authority administrative cooperation committee. However, various problems still remain, which the current and proposed measures do not address, such as the problem of locating a debtor who is in default of his child maintenance obligations. These problems require more comprehensive, and potentially invasive, solutions than those currently on the table.

However, the importance of these private international law instruments for European Family Law goes beyond the achievements they have made in facilitating the speedy recovery of child maintenance claims. The way in which they were adopted has wider significance for the conclusion of future private international law instruments in the area of European Family Law. It is necessary to acknowledge that regional reform within the European Union is not limited, in its effect, to Europe, but rather has a more global impact due to the interconnected nature of communities dealing with international family law. On this basis, it is commendable that the European Union adopted an internationalist perspective in the adoption of the Maintenance Regulation by coordinating closely with the work being done in The Hague.

The Maintenance Regulation and the Child Maintenance Convention represent a significant improvement in the recovery of international child maintenance claims and will have a real impact on the citizens of Europe and beyond. More than this, though, they are significant because of the internationalist and collaborative approach the EU adopted in relation to parallel developments in The Hague. This is a hopeful sign that the EU is moving away from an introspective approach when it comes to private international law and European Family Law and is realising its potential to be a responsible international actor in this field. Now, as progress continues towards the widespread ratification of the Hague Child Maintenance Convention, the EU can continue this role by facilitating the process of ratification and the operation of the Convention and sharing its experience with third states of how its system operates internally within the EU.

PART EIGHT
CLOSING REMARKS

THE FUTURE OF FAMILY PROPERTY IN EUROPE

Jo Miles and Jens M. Scherpe

1. COMMON LAW MEETS CIVIL LAW...

Once upon a time, a German heiress met a French merchant banker in London. They decided to marry. But in order that she could be sure that he was marrying for love and prompted by her father, they concluded in Germany a pre-nuptial agreement the effect of which would be to preclude any provision for the husband in the event of their divorce. That agreement was concluded with the assistance of a notary in circumstances such that it would be binding as a matter of both French and German law. They married and set up home in England. When divorce sadly came some years and two children later, the proceedings were heard in London. This meant that English law would be applied, the English family courts invariably applying the *lex fori* to such matrimonial disputes. What standing would the pre-nuptial agreement have in these circumstances, given the substantial foreign aspects of the case? What relevance, if any, would be attached to the fact that the agreement would have been binding before a German or French court?

When we met in Cambridge in April 2010, the Supreme Court had just weeks before heard the appeal in the international pre-nuptial agreement case, *Radmacher v Granatino*. The Court's decision was handed down during the latter stages of the preparation of this volume in October 2010.[1] Our conference proceedings and book editing could not have been framed by a more apt case: *Radmacher v Granatino* is a microcosm of so many of the debates pertinent to the future of family property law in Europe: about the jurisdiction in which matrimonial disputes and associated property and maintenance proceedings should be heard; about the law which should be applied by whichever court decides the case; about the force which parties' own agreements – whether about the disposition of their property, or about choice of forum or law – should have; most basically, about how any domestic law ought to allocate property and award maintenance on divorce. And how apt too that the case should involve citizens of civil law jurisdictions being confronted by the rather different traditions of the common law world in which they had come to live, just as we at Cambridge were delighted to welcome so many of our civil law friends, and some common law cousins, to England for three days!

The contrast between common law and civil law ways of thinking about these issues is not unfamiliar to the authors of this chapter. Teaching together on a postgraduate paper on Comparative Family Law & Policy, we regularly evaluate the different traditions and legal regimes with which we are each familiar and, not uncommonly, discover that what appear to be differences nevertheless share a common core. We may have different starting points, but we often – though not always – meet somewhere in between them. So what do we have in common, and

1 [2010] UKSC 42.

what separates us, in the broad area of family property regulation? What are the next challenges going to be?

2. SHARED SOCIAL AND LEGAL POLICY CHALLENGES

We are all increasingly experiencing broadly similar demographic trends and the social – and legal – policy challenges that accompany them. As was discussed in many of the conference's plenary sessions, the increase in international mobility and multi-jurisdiction couples poses both increased pressure to provide private international law solutions, and also propels us towards the idea of substantive harmonisation, at least for cross-border couples. The increasing divorce rate in many jurisdictions means that matrimonial property and maintenance issues are becoming ever pressing for a greater proportion of spouses. Other social changes, such as increased female, including maternal, labour market attachment may prompt us to reconsider the appropriate basis for financial relief between spouses should their relationship end. All jurisdictions are also seeing a growing population of couples living together and having children outside marriage.[2] In many jurisdictions, the question of how to respond in law to this social change is intensely politicised, as 'defenders of marriage' raise concerns that legal recognition of cohabitants will erode the standing of that venerated institution. With the increased proportion of births taking place outside marriage, and absent remedies between the parents themselves, the remedy of child maintenance becomes supremely important.[3] Meanwhile, fertility rates are overall in decline and our populations are ageing, with increasing numbers of very elderly people requiring costly personal and medical care. The combined effect of these trends raises pressing and, again, highly politicised questions, for example about how to pay for their care.[4] Moreover, family structures are becoming more complex: by the time we die, we may have experienced divorce, cohabitation, step-parenthood, the arrival of a second or third set of children from a later relationship. And so we pose further problems for succession law which needs to determine the

---

[2] See M. GARRISON's chapter in Part 3 of this volume. There is a vast literature in this area, including: A. BARLOW, S. DUNCAN, G. JAMES and A. PARK, *Cohabitation, Marriage and the Law*, Hart Publishing, Oxford, 2005; J.M. SCHERPE and N YASSARI (eds), *Rechtsstellung nichtehelicher Lebensgemeinschaften – The Legal Status of Cohabitants*, Mohr Siebeck, Tübingen 2005; I KROPPENBERG, D SCHWAB, D HENRICH, P GOTTWALD and A SPICKHOFF (eds), *Rechtsregeln für nichteheliches Zusammenleben, Beiträge zum europäischen Familienrecht*, vol. 12, Gieseking, Bielefeld 2009; LAW COMMISSION OF ENGLAND AND WALES, *Cohabitation: The Financial Consequences of Relationship Breakdown*, (Consultation Paper no. 179 and Report No 307, both available at www.lawcom.gov.uk/cohabitation.htm; K KIERNAN, 'The Rise of Cohabiting and Childbearing Outside Marriage in Western Europe', (2001) 15 *International Journal of Law, Policy and the Family* 1.

[3] See Part 6 of this volume.

[4] See Parts 4 and 5 of this volume.

appropriate priority amongst the survivors.[5] Of course, we may have further complicated matters by having crossed borders, bought a holiday home abroad, acquired a spouse from another jurisdiction, moved away from our country of birth, and have children from a past relationship living in yet another jurisdiction. And so the private international family law issues become significant as well.

3. MATRIMONIAL PROPERTY AND MAINTENANCE: JOINT OR SEVERAL ISSUES?

So, we all face broadly similar problems, but we reach our own solutions, creating an impression – at least – that how we resolve family property and financial disputes is very different. As we have seen,[6] there is huge variety within continental Europe to the resolution of these disputes, and so we must beware of simplistic comparisons. However, there is perhaps one large structural issue where we can see a particular contrast between many civil law jurisdictions and common law systems, and that is the separate or combined treatment of matrimonial property and maintenance, one of the issues that has posed particular problems for the UK and Ireland in the EU private international family law schema.[7]

At first sight, what might very crudely be dubbed the "(continental) European" approach looks alien to English eyes. Where England and Wales adopts a holistic approach, using all forms of asset and available income streams to address both needs-based relief and a partnership-based distribution of assets in order to approach an overall package of financial remedies on divorce, "Europeans" commonly *appear* to draw rigid distinctions between maintenance and property, the latter (or some sub-set of it, such as acquests) very usually divided equally. English lawyers look at this from across *la Manche* and are concerned, rightly or wrongly, about where this leaves the homemaker and primary carer of the children, a point discussed further below. This European maintenance/property distinction is reflected in the European instruments in the private international law field, where the regulation of jurisdiction and (now, for most jurisdictions) applicable law on maintenance[8] is dealt with entirely separately from matrimonial property, which is not yet – but perhaps one day soon will be – subject to a separate Regulation. This difference of conceptual approach to economic disputes

5 Part 5 of this volume.

6 See W. Pintens' chapter in Part 2 of this volume.

7 See M Ni Shúilleabháin, 'Ten Years of European Family Law: Retrospective Reflections from a Common Law Perspective', (2010) 59 *International and Comparative Law Quarterly* 1021.

8 Now in Council Regulation (EC) No 4/2009 of 18 December 2008 on jurisdiction, applicable law, recognition and enforcement of decisions and cooperation in matters relating to maintenance obligations.

on divorce is one of the factors which has contributed to the UK's difficulty in engaging in this European venture.

It is first worth acknowledging that the distance between the English position and the European approach is somewhat reduced as a result of English judicial developments.[9] The House of Lords' decisions in *White*[10] and *Miller&McFarlane*[11] and the Court of Appeal decision in *Charman*[12] have instantiated a principle of equal sharing (arguably) as a permissible starting point for deciding financial relief on an English divorce. Moreover, the Supreme Court decision in *Radmacher v Granatino* makes it easier for couples to displace the operation of this principle than relief for "real need",[13] to some extent mirroring the European position whereby contracting out of maintenance obligations is commonly more difficult than agreement to disapply the default matrimonial property regime. As Dr Cretney (perhaps prematurely) observed in 2003,[14] England is closer to having some sort of deferred community of property. But it is important not to overstate this position: the "community" created by the equal sharing principle is of uncertain scope and weight owing to the judicial discretion on which its operation depends in any case; and in a large majority of cases the dominant basis for both the division of existing property and future income provision is the parties' respective needs.

Whether similar to the European model or not, the English model has had to be tested against this European demarcation. The *Van den Boogaard v Laumen*[15] decision on the scope of "maintenance" under the Brussels I Regulation accommodates to some extent the fact that English family lawyers may distribute capital, in particular the owner-occupied family home, as a form of maintenance provision. But it is clear that the European concept of maintenance and the English concept of need are not coterminous: the latter seems to be broader, or is certainly taken to be so by some continental lawyers called upon to determine the matter, particularly where capital assets are transferred outright.[16]

---

9 See E. Cooke's chapter in Part 3 of this volume.

10 [2001] AC 596.

11 [2006] UKHL 24.

12 [2007] EWCA Civ 503.

13 [2010] UKSC 42.

14 S Cretney, 'Community of Property Imposed by Judicial Decision', (2003) 119 *Law Quarterly Review* 349.

15 Case C-220/95, [1997] ECR I-1147.

16 See the Bundesgerichthof case (12.8.2009, XII ZB 12/05, *FamRZ (Zeitschrift für das gesamte Familienrecht)* 2009, 1659) discussed by J.M. Scherpe and A. Dutta, 'Cross-Border Enforcement of English Ancillary Relief Orders: Fog in the Channel – Europe Cut Off?', (2010) 40 *Family Law* 385.

4. A SPECIAL DOMESTIC PROBLEM: THE FAMILY HOME

This brings us on to the fraught question of the family home. English family lawyers are very accustomed to using the former matrimonial home flexibly on divorce. All manner of orders are available: from outright transfer to own spouse, to affording one spouse (commonly the primary carer with dependent children) the right to occupy the property until the children reach majority, at which point (which may be several years away) the primary carer might be allowed to stay on, or the property might be sold and the proceeds divided, leaving the primary carer with funds to help acquire new, smaller accommodation. The "European" model of asset division, rightly or wrongly, generates anxiety amongst many common lawyers about its ability to protect the economically weaker party's housing situation, particularly in a jurisdiction where owner-occupation is the norm, but very expensive, and rental accommodation regarded as disadvantageous, and again, in some sectors, very costly and/or difficult to obtain. The flexibility afforded by the holistic English model to fashion the settlement around ensuring housing security for the primary carer and children is regarded as an indispensable feature of the English, predominantly needs-based system of resource allocation on divorce.

However, English concerns about the apparent inability of European systems to achieve similar outcomes may be – to some extent – misplaced. European lawyers do not have the benefit of trusts law to help fashion similar outcomes. But it might nevertheless be possible to use other more familiar juristic tools to do so: occupation orders, deferred distribution of assets, and associated ancillary orders governing the management of the home in the meantime, perhaps also releasing the respondent from his maintenance obligation to the extent that it corresponds with the value conferred (in terms of a notional occupation rent) by permitting the primary carer to remain in the home. This sort of approach, effectively capitalising the maintenance obligation and trading it for the house, also has the potential to produce a clean break. That is perhaps not very different from an English outcome, where payment of spousal maintenance – as opposed to child maintenance – is not common.

It is through dialogue on these sorts of practical questions that we can reach better, more sophisticated understandings about what it is that we are all doing in our own legal systems, ostensibly in pursuit of the same broad objectives. But it is of course also vitally important to bear in mind the profound non-legal differences that jurisdictions may have, for example in relation to the nature of their housing and labour markets, extent of social security provision, state-funded pensions, and so on. All of these wider features necessarily impact on the sorts of settlements which are regarded as feasible and necessary in a given jurisdiction. And that in turn affects the shape which any proposals for harmonisation of domestic law can have:[17] too "tight" a model is likely to leave insufficient scope to accommodate different socio-economic conditions and cultures.

5. THE SCOPE FOR AUTONOMY

Another recurring theme in many parts of the conference[18] was the question of how much autonomy the parties should have to regulate their own affairs. In many jurisdictions, including England & Wales[19] and Germany,[20] the highest courts have had to deal with these issues very recently, and overturned long-established precedents and/or statutory interpretations.[21] The difficulty in all jurisdictions seems to lie in striking the right balance in protecting a person's (or a couple's) autonomy and protecting them from the consequences that may flow from the exercise of his or her own (or their) autonomy. It is therefore necessary to analyse the mechanisms employed to strike this balance, distinguishing (on the one hand) those that are designed to ensure that the individual is actually in a position to make an autonomous decision when the agreement is made from (on the other hand) those that prevent or at least impede the enforcement of an apparently autonomous decision, while making clear what the policy reasons for those latter restrictions are.

The discussions at this conference unsurprisingly also demonstrated that one's understanding of the function and the nature of marital agreements greatly depends on the rules applicable in the absence of such agreements.[22] Exercising one's autonomy in this sphere essentially means contracting out of the default regime or, where there is no comprehensive regime (as is the case for cohabitants in many jurisdictions), creating a legal framework for one's relationship. Importantly, common lawyers must also concede that marital agreements on the continent often perform a function *during* the marriage – by altering the way property is distributed during the marriage, namely whether it becomes part of the community of property or not – and on death. Taking this into account is essential when dealing with the recognition of foreign marital agreements on

---

17 See chapter by K. Boele-Woelki and M. Jänterä-Jareborg in Part 2 of this volume.

18 See especially the contributions by N. Dethloff, E. Cooke and M. Garrison in Part 3 above, but also the contributions in Parts 4, 5 and 6.

19 *Radmacher v Granatino* [2010] UKSC 42.

20 Bundesverfassungsgericht (Constitutional Court) 6.2.2001, *FamRZ* 2001, 343 and 29.3.2001, *FamRZ* 2001, 985, and especially Bundesgerichtshof (Federal Court of Justice) 11.2.2004, *FamRZ* 2004, 601.

21 For a comparative overview see the contributions in S. Hofer, D. Schwab and D. Henrich (eds.), *From Status to Contract? – Die Bedeutung des Vertrages im Familienrecht*, Beiträge zum europäischen Familienrecht, vol. 9, Gieseking, Bielefeld, 2005 and J.M. Scherpe (ed), *Marital Agreements in Comparative Perspective*, Hart Publishing, Oxford, forthcoming in 2011.

22 See sections 3. and 4. above, and Part 2 of this volume.

divorce, because the parties' arrangement may well have had significant legal effect for a long period of time and the couple (and even third parties) may have relied on the agreement and acted accordingly. This cannot be ignored: it might be critical to what the agreement was intended for in the first place, for example protecting one spouse from the other's creditors.[23]

The approaches of the common law and civil jurisdictions to marital agreements at first glance appear to be diametrically opposed: in civil law jurisdictions, such agreements are in principle binding and enforceable, and are even regulated in various civil codes; whereas in the European common law jurisdictions, notably England & Wales and Ireland, the status of such agreements is much more uncertain and the court's jurisdiction to decide on the financial relief to be granted on divorce cannot be ousted.[24] However, when one takes a 'broad brush' (and somewhat crude) comparative approach, the differences can seem less marked: civil law courts will set aside marital agreements if they are judged to be unfair, and the English common law courts will 'give effect' to such agreements 'unless in the circumstances prevailing it would not be fair to hold the parties to their agreement'.[25] While this of course technically means that the onus of proof and persuasion falls on different parties, the crucial question in all jurisdictions seems to be to ask 'what is fair?'.

A common aspect of fairness in this context seems to be that the parties cannot contract out of covering the basic needs of the other spouse and the children in case of divorce or separation. As explained above,[26] in the continental systems maintenance plays a much greater role in this respect, and contracting out of maintenance obligations in full or in part often is therefore made difficult or impossible. The common law jurisdictions take a more holistic approach, and essentially ancillary relief is a 'package deal', comprising both property and maintenance. This makes it more difficult for common law jurisdictions to accept marital agreements concerning assets as binding, since all assets in principle can be used to cover the needs of the spouses. However, as noted above, one of the most striking features of the recent Supreme Court decision in *Radmacher* is the conclusion that parties may more readily contract out of the 'equal sharing' principle, under which assets may prima facie be divided equally between the spouses (provided needs will be met), than they can avoid liability to meet needs (or 'real need', as the Supreme Court in *Radmacher* describes it) arising on divorce. The result is not far from reflecting the continental European approach.

---

23 See J.M. Scherpe, 'Foreign Marital Agreements: the Approach of the English Courts', [2010] *Private Client Business* 190–195.

24 *Hyman v Hyman* [1929] AC 601, HL.

25 *Radmacher v Granatino* [2010] UKSC 42, para 75. See also *Edgar v Edgar* [1980] 3 All ER 887.

26 See section 3. above, and Parts 2 and 3 of this volume.

Despite the marked differences in the underlying matrimonial property and maintenance regimes, a comparative analysis therefore reveals that the approaches of the civil and the common law jurisdictions to marital agreements are not as different as they seem at first glance.

6. PRIVATE INTERNATIONAL LAW

Common private international law rules might provide one answer (but certainly not *the* answer) to some of the international, cross-border family law issues.[27] However, here the differences between the common law and the civil law jurisdictions, somewhat surprisingly, seem to be more entrenched and insurmountable than those that exist in substantive law. The common law position (roughly speaking) is that it is always the *lex fori* that should be applied to issues arising on divorce, and that where the dispute should better be heard in another jurisdiction the court will declare itself to be a *forum non conveniens*. In the common law world, foreign law is a matter of fact and to be proved by the parties, often at great cost. Civil law courts, on the other hand, will often apply foreign law when they have jurisdiction according to their private international law rules. This has its own difficulties, particularly since the court will hardly ever be in a position to decide the matter in the same way as the appropriate national court would have done. This, too, requires the consultation of experts, if not courts, in another country and might be equally burdensome. Increased judicial co-operation might be the way forward here, and perhaps the possibility for a court to transfer cases outside where a forum in another Member State appears better placed to hear the case.[28]

To date, the instruments on private international law issued by the European Union have adopted the civil law model, depriving common law courts of their power to stay proceedings on *forum non conveniens* grounds.[29] Unwilling thus far to opt in to instruments that contain rules of applicable law, the common law jurisdictions find themselves in an awkward position within the Brussels regime. It will be interesting therefore to see how this area develops, not least with the anticipated publication in 2011 of a draft regulation in the field of private international matrimonial property law.

---

27 See Part 7 of this volume.

28 See Parts 1 and 7 of this volume, especially the chapters by M. Thorpe and C. González Beilfuss. Article 15 of the Brussels II bis Regulation (Council Regulation (EC) No. 2201/2003 of November 2003, concerning jurisdiction and the recognition and enforcement of judgments in matrimonial matters and the matters of parental responsibility, repealing Regulation (EC) No 1347/2000) provides for the possibility of such a transfer. On this see A. Dutta, 'Europäische Zuständigkeiten und Kindeswohlvorbehalt', in J. von Hein, D. Baetge and M. von Hinden (eds.), *Die richtige Ordnung, Festschrift für Jan Kropholler zum 70. Geburtstag*, Mohr Siebeck, Tübingen, 2008, pp 281 ff.

29 But cf Article 15 of Brussels II bis (n. 28.).

7. CONCLUSIONS – AND THE ROAD AHEAD

And so we look to the future and all its uncertainties. Will we see increasing convergence in the substantive domestic laws of European jurisdictions concerning family property issues? From a parochial perspective in Cambridge, we shall be particularly interested to see how the law of marital property agreements in England & Wales will be developed following the decision of the Supreme Court in *Radmacher* and the work of the Law Commission for England and Wales in this area – a Report with recommendations for law reform, including a draft Bill, is due to be published in 2012.[30] On the international plane, we eagerly await the draft regulation on private international matrimonial property law. How will it be framed? Will it continue with the standard Brussels 'first seized' model, or will a facility for transferring cases be included? Will the UK and Ireland opt in? What will be the impact of the newly adopted Rome III Regulation enhancing cooperation in the area of the law applicable to divorce and legal separation?[31] Last but by no means least, we look forward to the publication of the next set of Principles of the Commission on European Family Law in its ambitious project on property relations between spouses and to the next CEFL conference.

---

30 Law Commission of England and Wales, *Marital Property Agreements: a consultation paper*, Law Com CP 198 (2011), available at www.lawcom.gov.uk/marital_property.htm.

31 Council Regulation (EU) No 1259/2010 of 20 December 2010 implementing enhanced cooperation in the area of the law applicable to divorce and legal separation.

European Family Law Series

1. *Legal Recognition of Same-Sex Couples in Europe*, K. Boele-Woelki and A. Fuchs (eds.)
2. *European Family Law in Action Volume I: Grounds for divorce*, K. Boele-Woelki, B. Braat and I. Sumner (eds.)
3. *European Family Law in Action Volume II: Maintenance Between Former Spouses*, K. Boele-Woelki, B. Braat and I. Sumner (eds.)
4. *Perspectives for the Unification and Harmonisation of Family Law in Europe*, K. Boele-Woelki (ed.)
5. *Family Law Legislation of the Netherlands*, I. Sumner and H. Warendorf
6. *Indépendance et interdépendance patrimoniales des époux dans le régime matrimonial légal des droits néerlandais, français et suisse*, B. Braat
7. *Principles of European Family Law Regarding Divorce and Maintenance Between Former Spouses*, K. Boele-Woelki, F. Ferrand, C. González Beilfuss, M. Jänterä-Jareborg, N. Lowe, D. Martiny and W. Pintens
8. *Inheritance Law Legislation of the Netherlands*, I. Sumner and H. Warendorf
9. *European Family Law in Action Volume III: Parental Responsibilities*, K. Boele-Woelki, B. Braat and I. Curry Sumner (eds.)
10. *Common Core and Better Law in European Family Law*, K. Boele-Woelki (ed.)
11. *All's well that ends registered?*, I. Curry-Sumner
12. *Model Family Code – From a global perspective*, I. Schwenzer and M. Dimsey
13. *Harmonisation of Family Law in Europe. A Historical Perspective*, M. Antokolskaia
14. *Brussels II bis: Its Impact and Application in the Member States*, K. Boele-Woelki and C. González Beilfuss (eds.)
15. *Tensions between Legal, Biological and Social Conceptions of Parentage*, I. Schwenzer (ed.)
16. *Principles of European Family Law Regarding Parental Responsibilities*, K. Boele-Woelki, F. Ferrand, C. González Beilfuss, M. Jänterä-Jareborg, N. Lowe, D. Martiny and W. Pintens (eds.)
17. *Juxtaposing Legal Systems and the Principles of European Family Law on Divorce and Maintenance*, E. Örücü and J. Mair (eds.)
18. *Convergence and Divergence of Family Law in Europe*, M. Antokolskaia (ed.)
19. *European Challenges in Contemporary Family Law*, K. Boele-Woelki and K. Sverdrup (eds.)
20. *Children and their parents*, M. Vonk
21. *La capacité de l'enfant dans les droits français, anglais et écossais*, L. Francoz-Terminal
22. *Joint Parental Authority*, C.G. Jeppesen de Boer
23. *Debates in Family Law around the Globe at the Dawn of the 21st Century*, K. Boele-Woelki (ed.)

24. *European Family Law in Action Volume IV: Property Relations between Spouses*, K. Boele-Woelki, B. Braat and I. Curry-Sumner (eds.)
25. *Foundational Facts, Relative Truths. A Comparative Law Study on Children's Right to Know Their Genetic Origins*, J. Blauwhoff
26. *Imperative Inheritance Law in a Late-Modern Society. Five Perspectives*, Christoph Castelein, René Foqué and Alain Verbeke (eds.)
27. *Juxtaposing Legal Systems and the Principles of European Family Law on Parental Responsibilities*, Esin Örücü and Jane Mair (eds.)
28. *La justice des mineurs en Europe*, Yann Favier and Frédérique Ferrand (eds.)

www.ingramcontent.com/pod-product-compliance
Ingram Content Group UK Ltd.
Pitfield, Milton Keynes, MK11 3LW, UK
UKHW051925100926
8556IPUK00022B/1371

9 789400 000544